U. Banerjee   D. Gelernter   A. Nicolau
D. Padua (Eds.)

Languages and Compilers for Parallel Computing

Fourth International Workshop
Santa Clara, California, USA, August 7-9, 1991
Proceedings

Springer-Verlag

Berlin Heidelberg New York
London Paris Tokyo
Hong Kong Barcelona
Budapest

Series Editors

Gerhard Goos
Universität Karlsruhe
Postfach 69 80
Vincenz-Priessnitz-Straße 1
W-7500 Karlsruhe, FRG

Juris Hartmanis
Department of Computer Science
Cornell University
5148 Upson Hall
Ithaca, NY 14853, USA

Volume Editors

Utpal Banerjee
Intel Corporation
2801 Northwestern Parkway
Santa Clara, CA 95052-8122, USA

David Gelernter
Dept. of Computer Science, Yale University
51 Prospect St., New Haven, CT 06520, USA

Alex Nicolau
Dept. of Information & Computer Science
University of California
444 Computer Science Bldg., Irvine, CA 92717, USA

David Padua
Center for Supercomputing Research and Development
University of Illinois
104 S. Wright St., Urbana, IL 61801, USA

CR Subject Classification (1991): F.1.2, D.1.3, D.3.1, B.2.1, I.3.1

ISBN 3-540-55422-X Springer-Verlag Berlin Heidelberg New York
ISBN 0-387-55422-X Springer-Verlag New York Berlin Heidelberg

Typesetting: Camera ready by author
Printing and binding: Druckhaus Beltz, Hemsbach/Bergstr.
45/3140-543210 - Printed on acid-free paper

Lecture Notes in Computer Science 589

Edited by G. Goos and J. Hartmanis

Advisory Board: W. Brauer   D. Gries   J. Stoer

Foreword

This book contains the papers presented at the Fourth Workshop on Languages and Compilers for Parallel Computing held during August 7-9, 1991 in Santa Clara, California. The workshop was sponsored this year by the Intel Corporation. The previous workshops in this series were held in Irvine, California (1990), Urbana, Illinois (1989), and Ithaca, New York (1988).

The papers in this book cover several important topics including: (1) languages and structures to represent programs internally in the compiler, (2) techniques to analyze and manipulate sequential loops in order to generate a parallel version, (3) techniques to detect and extract fine-grain parallelism, (4) scheduling and memory-management issues in automatically-generated parallel programs, (5) Parallel programming language designs, and (6) compilation of explicitly parallel programs.

We are very pleased with the breadth and depth of the work presented in these papers. Taken together, these papers are an accurate reflection of the state of research in languages and compilers for parallel computing in 1991. We hope this book will be as interesting to the reader as it was for us to compile.

January 1992

Utpal Banerjee
David Gelernter
Alex Nicolau
David Padua

Contents

I. EXPLICITLY PARALLEL LANGUAGES

Distributed Execution of Actor Programs 1
    G. Agha, C.Houck, and R. Panwar
    University of Illinois at Urbana-Champaign

An Overview of the Fortran D Programming System. 18
    S. Hiranandani, K. Kennedy, C. Koelbel, U. Kremer, and C.-W. Tseng
    Rice University, Houston, Texas

The Interaction of the Formal and the Practical in Parallel Programming . . . 35
Environment Development: CODE
    J. Werth, J. Browne, S. Sobek, T. Lee, P. Newton, and R. Jain
    University of Texas at Austin

Hierarchical Concurrency in Jade 50
    D. Scales, M. Rinard, M. Lam, and J. Anderson
    Stanford University, Stanford, California

II. EXPERIMENTATION WITH PARALLEL PROGRAMMING

Experience in the Automatic Parallelization of Four Perfect-Benchmark . . . 65
Programs
    R. Eigenmann, J. Hoeflinger, Z. Li, and D. Padua
    University of Illinois at Urbana-Champaign

Programming SIMPLE for Parallel Portability 84
    J. Lee, C. Lin, and L. Snyder
    University of Washington at Seattle

III. INTERNAL REPRESENTATION

Compilation of Id 99
    Z. Ariola, *Harvard University, Cambridge, Massachusetts*
    Arvind, *Massachusetts Institute of Technology, Cambridge, Massachusetts*

An Executable Representation of Distance and Direction 122
    R. Johnson, W. Li, and K. Pingali
    Cornell Unversity, Ithaca, New York

Integrating Scalar Optimization and Parallelization 137
    S. Tjiang, M. Wolf, M. Lam, K. Pieper, and J. Hennessy
    Stanford Univesity, Stanford, California

Optimization of Data/Control Conditions in Task Graphs 152
    M. Girkar and C. Polychronopoulos
    University of Illinois at Urbana-Champaign

IV. LOOP PARALLELISM

Recognizing and Parallelizing Bounded Recurrences 169
    D. Callahan
    Tera Computer Company, Seattle, Washington

Communication-Free Hyperplane Partitioning of Nested Loops 186
    C.-H. Huang and P. Sadayappan
    The Ohio State University, Columbus, Ohio

Parallelizing Loops with Indirect Array References or Pointers. 201
    L.-C. Lu and M. Chen
    Yale University, New Haven, Connecticut

V. FINE GRAIN PARALLELISM

Register Allocation, Renaming and Their Impact on Fine-Grain Parallelism . . 218
    A. Nicolau, R. Potasman, and H. Wang
    University of California at Irvine

Data Flow and Dependence Analysis for Instruction Level Parallelism 236
    B.R. Rau
    Hewlett-Packard Laboratories, Palo Alto, California

VI. ANALYSIS TECHNIQUES

Extending Conventional Flow Analysis to Deal with Array References 251
    A. Kallis and D. Klappholz
    Stevens Institute of Technology, Hoboken, New Jersey

VII. COMPILERS & SCHEDULING

Run-Time Management of Lisp Parallelism and the Hierarchical Task 266
Graph Program Representation
    M. Furnari, *Institute of Cybernetics, Arco Felice (Na), Italy*
    C. Polychronopoulos, *University of Illinois at Urbana-Champaign*

A Multi-Grain Parallelizing Compilation Scheme for OSCAR 283
(Optimally Scheduled Advanced Multiprocessor)
  H. Kasahara, H. Honda, A. Mogi, A. Ogura, K. Fujiwara, and S. Narita
  Waseda University, Tokyo, Japan

Balanced Loop Partitioning Using GTS 298
  J. Labarta, E. Ayguade, J. Torres, M. Valero, and J.M. Llaberia
  Polytechnic University of Catalonia, Barcelona, Spain

VIII. CACHE MEMORY ISSUES

An Iteration Partition Approach for Cache or Local Memory Thrashing 313
on Parallel Processing
  J. Fang, *Hewlett-Packard Laboratories, Palo Alto, Calfornia*
  M. Lu, *Texas A&M University, College Station, Texas*

On Estimating and Enhancing Cache Effectiveness 328
  J. Ferrante, *IBM T.J. Watson Research Center, Yorktown Heights, New York*
  V. Sarkar, *IBM Palo Alto Scientific Center, Palo Alto, California*
  W. Thrash, *University of Washington at Seattle*

Reduction of Cache Coherence Overhead by CompilerData Layout 344
and Loop Transformation
  Y.-J. Ju and H. Dietz
  Purdue University, Lafayette, Indiana

IX.   COMPILERS FOR DATAFLOW MACHINES

Loop Storage Optimization for Dataflow Machines 359
  G. Gao and Q. Ning
  McGill University, Montreal, Quebec, Canada

Optimal Partitioning of Programs for Data Flow Machines 374
  R. Hardon and S. Pinter
  Technion - Israel Institute of Technology, Technion City, Haifa

X.   ANALYSIS OF EXPLICITLY PARALLEL PROGRAMS

A Foundation for Advanced Compile-time Analysis of Linda Programs 389
  N. Carriero and D. Gelernter
  Yale University, New Haven, Connecticut

Analyzing Programs with Explicit Parallelism 405
  H. Srinivasan and M. Wolfe
  Oregon Graduate Institute, Beaverton, Oregon

1   Distributed Execution of Actor Programs

G. Agha, C. Houck, and R. Panwar

University of Illinois at Urbana-Champaign

Abstract

A number of programming language models, including actors, provide inherent concurrency. We are developing high-level language constructs using actors and studying their implementation on multiprocessor architectures. This report describes our experience with programming in actors by means of a specific example of scientific computation. We also discuss work in progress on compilation technology for efficient program execution on multiprocessors.

1   Introduction

Concurrent language models, such as concurrent logic programming, functional programming and actors, provide inherent concurrency in the evaluation of expressions. However, unlike other models, actors allow state to be directly expressed and manipulated. Our experience suggests that this enables us to write programs which not only avoid unnecessary

---

*This work has been made possible by support provided by a Young Investigator Award from the Office of Naval Research (ONR contract number N00014-90-J-1899), by an Incentives for Excellence Award from the Digital Equipment Corporation Faculty Program, and by joint support from the Defense Advanced Research Projects Agency and the National Science Foundation (NSF CCR 90-07195).

We would like to thank Professor Reed at the University of Illinois at Urbana-Champaign for the use of his Intel iPSC/2. In addition, we thank the anonymous referees for their careful reading of this paper.

sequencing of actions but which are also easily understandable. We discuss the structure of actor languages and issues related to their implementation on distributed memory architectures.

Inherently concurrent languages often suffer from an embarrassing amount of concurrency. Current compiler technology is not sufficiently developed to optimize placement and migration of objects in order to provide sufficient execution efficiency on distributed memory architectures. Furthermore, in some cases, the structure of a problem is *crystalline* and well-understood by the programmer. In these cases, the use of annotations for specifying processor locations for expression evaluation to guide the runtime system has been suggested (e.g. [11]). However, in the context of actors, explicit message passing primitives imply that a separate syntax to specify such annotations is superfluous.

The organization of this paper is as follows. In Section 2 we give a brief overview of the actor model. Section 3 outlines multi-send constructs to increase concurrency. Section 4 illustrates concurrency in actors by an algorithm namely the Cholesky Decomposition of an SPD matrix. In Section 5 we discuss the representation of actors on multiprocessors. The final section presents some conclusions.

2 The Actor Model

Actors are self-contained, interactive, independent components of a computing system that communicate by asynchronous message passing. Each actor has a conceptual location, its *mail address*, and a *behavior*. An actor's *acquaintances* are all of the actors whose mail addresses it knows. In order to abstract over processor speeds and allow adaptive routing, preservation of message order is not guaranteed. However, messages sent are guaranteed to be received with an unbounded but finite delay.

State change in actors is specified using replacement behaviors. Each time an actor processes a communication, it also computes its behavior in response to the next communication it may process. The replacement behavior for a purely functional actor is identical to the original behavior; in general it may change. The change in the behavior of an actor may represent a simple change of state variables, such as change in the balance of an account, or it may represent changes in the operations (methods) which are carried out in response to messages. For example, suppose a bank account actor accepts a withdrawal request. In response, it will compute a new balance which will be used to process the next message.

Replacement is a serialization mechanism which supports a trivial pipelining of the replacement actions: the aggregation of changes allows an easy determination of when we have finished computing the state of an actor and are ready to take the next action [3]. For example, as soon as the bank account actor has computed the new balance in the account, it is free to process the next request – even if other actions implied by the withdrawal request are still being carried out. This allows concurrent execution of actions specified within the body of the actor.

The concept of actors was originally proposed by Hewitt [10]. The actor model has been formally characterized by means of power domain semantics [7], by a transition system [1], and by Colored Petri Nets [13]. Complexity measures for actor programs have been defined [5]. The model has been proposed as a basis for multiparadigm programming [2] and has been used as a programming model for multicomputers [4] and [8].

Rosette

Our work uses Rosette, an actor language developed at MCC in collaboration with one of the authors [14]. The following code-fragment gives a flavor of the Rosette language. It defines a behavior template for actors, Add-Counter, which accept two kinds of messages and has an acquaintance (cf. local variable) called count, initially set to zero. Upon receipt of an add message with parameters x and y an actor of this type returns the sum of x and y and specifies its replacement behavior using the same behavior definition and local count incremented. If the actor receives a [die bookkeeper] message it sends a message [total count] to bookkeeper and becomes a sink, an actor which ignores all future messages that it receives.

```
(define-Actor Add-Counter (acquaintance count 0)
   (method (add x y)
      (become Add-Counter (+ count 1))
      (+ x y))
   (method (die bookkeeper)
      (total bookkeeper count)
      (become sink)))
```

Notice that the (become Add-Counter (+ count 1)) and the (+ x y)) statements do not affect each other and can therefore be executed concurrently.

Actor programs have a fine-grained concurrent structure which is quite similar to that in functional and concurrent logic languages. Actors can be used to represent purely functional programs as well as programs that require objects with history sensitive behavior. There are two sources of concurrency in actor programs. First, actions on different actors can be executed in parallel, allowing us to write parallel programs which require expression of state changes in history sensitive behaviors in objects. Second, actions carried out within an actor are executed concurrently. The efficiency of an actor program on a distributed memory architecture depends on where different actors are placed and the communication traffic between them. Thus the placement and migration of actors can drastically affect the overall efficiency.

Execution of actor programs on parallel architectures requires a translator which takes an actor program as input and generates executable code for a given parallel machine. In general, the compiler should be able to efficiently decide where to place actors and when to migrate them. However, it may be necessary for a programmer to specify the topological structure in a way that promotes efficient locality and distribution. We provide some simple schemes for avoiding hot-spots and ensuring optimum parallelism. The next section discusses in greater detail how the execution efficiency of actor programs on parallel machines can be ensured by using these constructs.

3 Actor Multicast Constructs

Suppose we have a vector v which we want to multiply by a matrix M as in Figure 1. According to actor semantics, commands such as (matrix-* v M) result in the matrix M being sent to the actor v where the computation takes place. Assume, v to be of size p and M to be of size $p \times q$. Also assume that to allow concurrency of access, the matrix M is distributed column-wise between several processors. The vector v is assumed to be in one processor (P0 in Figure 1). If the command (matrix-* v M) is executed by sending the matrix M to the actor v, all the computation has to be carried out by processor P0 and the potential parallelism is lost. Furthermore, the processor P0 may not have enough memory to store all the columns of matrix M and this may clog the network around P0. Besides, communicating matrix M to processor P0 can require more data communication than multicasting the vector v to the processors containing columns of matrix M. This problem can be analyzed as follows.

- If several columns of M are mapped to a processor, then more data communication occurs if M is sent to P0 instead of multicasting vector v.

- If only one column of M is mapped per processor, then we need to compare the data communication for multicasting p elements vs. collecting $p * q$ elements to one processor. On most architectures it is possible to optimize a multicast so that the processor P0 does not become a communication bottle-neck and parallelism is exploited in multicasting the data. On the other hand, collecting elements to one processor is a sequential operation since all the $p*q$ elements are distinct and processor P0 itself takes $\Omega(pq)$ time inputting the elements.

Thus sending the vector to the processors containing M avoids contention for a processor and its communication links. We have defined a command, `trojan-multisend`, with the following syntax.

```
(trojan-multisend argument-bindings [ locations ] actor  message)
```

Locations specifies a set of actor mail addresses. Actors of kind `actor` are mailed to these addresses and sent along a message which they will process when they get there. The different values of *locations* and *actor* are specified using certain parameters. The values taken by these parameters are specified in the *argument-bindings* using the `forall` construct. The syntax for `forall` construct is,

```
(forall  variable in [  list  ])
```

When the processor containing *location* receives the message, it creates a new actor at the node with *message* as the first message in the new actor's queue. Assuming the matrix is stored column-wise, we can distribute instances of the Vector object to the locations of the matrix with the following code:

```
(trojan-multisend (forall j in [1..q]) [ M[·,j] ] Vector (scalar-* M[·,j] join-continuation))
```

The above code generates results in a non-deterministic order; it is necessary to tag the results of different invocations. The tags are passed on to the join-continuation which

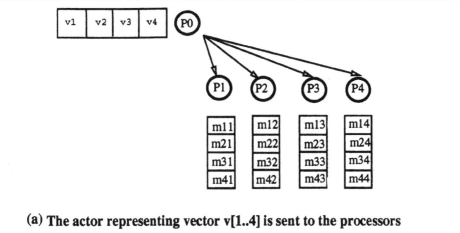

(a) The actor representing vector v[1..4] is sent to the processors containing columns of matrix M

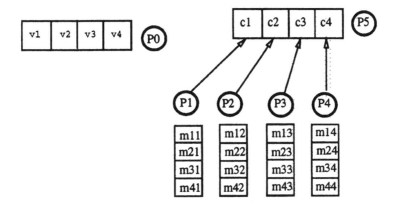

(b) The scalar product of vector v and column M[. , j] is sent with tag j to the join-continuation actor

Figure 1: Illustrating the execution of vector-matrix multiplication

collects all the results. An actor sent in the trojan-multisend operation does not have to be an unserialized actor. The multisend operation is atomic and copies of the same actor and message may be sent to different destinations. Also note that if the join-continuation is located on a single node, we may have another serializing bottleneck. To address this problem, a distributed form of join-continuation is needed (specifically the join-continuation may be a *Concurrent Aggregate* [6]).

Figure 1 shows how a vector-matrix multiplication is carried out using the `trojan-multisend` operation described above. The vector `v` is sent to the processors containing the columns of matrix `M`. If a column of the matrix is distributed between several processors, the vector `v` is sent to the processor containing the first element of the column: an inefficient, but semantically correct execution occurs. When processor `Pj` receives a copy of the vector `v`, the scalar product of column `M[·,j]` and `v` is computed and the resulting scalar sent to the join-continuation `c`.

4   Cholesky Decomposition of an SPD Matrix

We now discuss an example, the Cholesky Decomposition (CD) of a Symmetric Positive Definite (SPD) matrix, to illustrate how the actor model enables us to represent different ways of solving a problem in parallel. Assume A is a symmetric positive definite matrix of size $n \times n$. The following algorithm computes a lower triangular matrix G, of size $n \times n$ such that $A = GG^T$ [9]. Since A is a symmetric matrix, it can be stored as a lower triangular matrix. The elements of G overwrite the corresponding elements of A.

```
for k := 1 : n
   if(k > 1) A[k:n, k] = A[k:n, k] - A[k:n, 1:k-1] * A[k, 1:k-1]ᵀ
   A[k:n, k] = A[k:n, k] / sqrt(A[k, k])
end
```

The above algorithm is suitable for solving dense systems of SPD equations. Most of the problems involving large systems of equations have very few non-zero elements in the matrices and require methods for solving sparse linear systems. But some of the methods used for solving sparse systems of equations (e.g. [16]) require solution of a dense block of equations as an intermediate step. Depending on the size and structure of the original systems of equations, this dense block may be huge and sequential solution of such a block may reduce the overall performance significantly. We discuss ways of computing the CD of dense matrices in parallel.

Figure 2 illustrates the maximal parallelism available in the CD. Note that the communication requirements are language independent — they are characteristics of the algorithm at hand. With a two dimensional mesh of n^2 processors [9], the algorithm takes $O(n^2)$ time if all the steps of one iteration are completed before starting the next one. Pipelining the

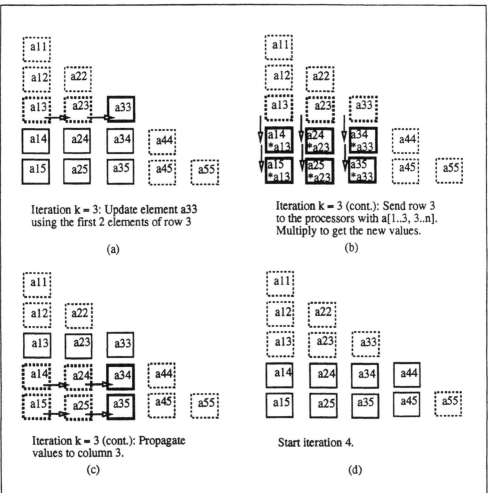

Iteration k = 3: Update element a33
using the first 2 elements of row 3

(a)

Iteration k = 3 (cont.): Send row 3
to the processors with a[1..3, 3..n].
Multiply to get the new values.

(b)

Iteration k = 3 (cont.): Propagate
values to column 3.

(c)

Start iteration 4.

(d)

Figure 2: Parallelism available in CD algorithm *Bold elements are written to. Dashed elements are read from and dotted elements are not involved with the current iteration.*

execution of different iterations gives an $O(n)$ time parallel implementation. In general the number of processors available is fewer than the number of elements in the matrix and several elements are assigned to each processor. For example, if n processors are available, one row can be assigned per processor to get an $O(n^2)$ time parallel implementation. We now show details of two representations of the CD algorithm using actors. The first representation is purely functional whereas the second uses destructive updates and pipelines the execution of different iterations.

A Functional Implementation of CD

We define an actor Mat-ops with a method cholesky. A message cholesky can be sent to Mat-ops to compute the CD of a given matrix. The arguments sent with the message cholesky are the matrix itself (which is essentially the location of the first element of the matrix) and the size of the matrix. The matrix is represented as a tuple of rows, where each row itself is a tuple of floating point numbers. The matrix is stored as a lower triangular matrix and the tuple representing the ith row is of size i.

```
(define-Actor Mat-ops
  (method (cholesky Matrix num-rows)
          ((iteration 1 Matrix num-rows))))
```

The function *iteration* organizes the execution of the n iterations of the algorithm. The function (compute-row Row) returns a new row obtained by updating the diagonal element of row k for starting the kth iteration as shown in Figure 2. Similarly, (compute-matrix Row Matrix) returns a matrix obtained by updating its elements as required in iteration k.

```
(define-Proc (iteration iter Matrix n)
    (if (> k n)
      []
      (let [[ X ((compute-row (head Matrix)))]]
        (concat X (iteration (inc iter) ((compute-matrix X (tail Matrix))))))))
```

The input matrix is distributed between different processors, and the execution of function compute-matrix can result in large data movements if not done carefully. In this case, the system checks on the size of a predefined large data structures such as matrices before deciding whether to move it.

```
(define-Proc (compute-matrix Row Matrix k)
    (if (= (size Mat) 1)
      ((compute-row Row (head Matrix)))
      (concat
        ((compute-matrix Row (first-half Matrix) k)
        ((compute-matrix Row (second-half Matrix) k)))))
```

We have implemented code using this style of programming on an Intel iPSC/2 hypercube. The results are summarized in Table 1.

nodes	32×32	64×64	128×128	256×256
1	131	873	6450	49656
2	127	788	5757	44186
4	103	581	3937	29886
8	101	445	2536	17598
16	133	451	1882	10773
32	222	645	1984	8091

Table 1: Results from a functional (synchronous) implementation of the Cholesky algorithm on an Intel iPSC/2 with an equal number of matrix rows per processor. *Times are in milliseconds.*

A More Concurrent Implementation of CD

The program illustrated above is written in a purely functional style with a call-by-value semantics. This results in two problems. First, it sequentializes the execution of different iterations by forcing completion of one iteration before starting the next one, and second, its straight-forward implementation is inefficient in space utilization. The first issue can be handled by observing the fact that iteration $(k + 1)$ can be started as soon as row $(k + 1)$ has been updated for the kth iteration. A call-by-name semantics with implicit futures would be one way to address this problem. By allowing destructive updates in the implementation, the space utilization problem can be addressed without changing the functional specification. However, a concurrent implementation of lazy functional languages with implicit futures and side-effects in the implementation has to address the effects of the asynchrony of components and the indeterminacy in message order. Interestingly, because the implementation itself involves a nondeterministic merge, it cannot be expressed functionally. For this reason, we believe that it is better to provide a more powerful linguistic model. We find actors a suitable alternate for two reasons. First, the use of actors with local states makes the structure of the algorithm more perspicuous. Second, it allows us to write efficient programs whose execution has not been optimized by the compiler.

As before, assume that the matrix is available as an acquaintance of a given master actor. This actor creates several Row-act actors, one for each row. Each Row-act actor has three acquaintances, the row of the matrix associated with the Row-act , the next Row-act actor (nextRow-act) and the number of its row Row-num. Since messages corresponding to several iterations exist in the system at the same time and messages can be delivered out of order, it is necessary for Row-act to impose some order on the messages it processes. For example, an actor on processor P1 can send a message to Row-act R_m to update its row for the iteration k and P2 can send a similar message to R_m for iteration $(k+1)$. Even if the message from P2 is sent after the message from P1 the two messages may follow different paths and reach R_m in an unpredictable order. Since processing messages for two different iterations in a wrong order leads to incorrect results, R_m needs some mechanism to decide which message should be picked from the mailbox for processing next. We use a mechanism called *enabled sets* in Rosette for imposing order on the processing of messages [15]. The following code uses the block construct which packages a set of expressions which are evaluated concurrently. The **next** construct specifies the next enabled-set of message that the actor will accept.

```
(method (update-mat iter nextRow-act inpRow)
   (block
      (update-row iter diag-value)
      (if (present nextRow-act)
         (update-mat iter nextRow-act  inpRow)))
      (cond (< iter (dec Row-num))
            (next [[update-mat (inc iter)]])
         (= iter (dec Row-num))
            (next [[start-iter]]))))
(method (start-iter)
   (let [[x (new-diagonal (head Matrix))]]
      (block
         (update-diagonal x)
         (if (present  nextRow-act)
            (block
               (update-mat Row-num nextRow-act x)))
            (start-iter nextRow-act)))
         (next [[return-ans]]))))
```

When Row-act R_m receives an update-mat message with value of iter equal to k, it updates its row and enables the next set of messages which is a singleton set containing messages of type update-mat with value of iter equal to one more than the current value of iter. Thus only the update corresponding to $(k+1)^{th}$ iteration will be carried out after iteration k. Once the value of iter reaches $m-1$ i.e. is one less than the row number of R_m, the next set of messages enabled is the singleton set containing the message

nodes	32×32	64×64	128×128	256×256
1	123	857	6415	49583
2	111	760	5680	43957
4	80	518	3760	29349
8	48	308	2182	16603
16	29	173	1204	8981
32	19	99	931	5613

Table 2: Results from an actor-like implementation of the Cholesky algorithm on an Intel iPSC/2 with an equal number of matrix rows per processor. *Times are in milliseconds.*

of type `start-iter`. Finally, an actor can receive the resulting matrix by sending the `return-ans` message to the first `Row-act` actor. The complete result is returned when the last `Row-act` finishes processing. Performance data for executing this algorithm on an Intel iPSC/2 hypercube are given in Table 2. Both the functional an actor-style programs were actually written in C. In addition, both algorithms utilize a simple, static data allocation scheme, initial estimates suggest only the actor implementation would further benefit from an optimized placement strategy. Currently, our actor compiler (Section 5) is not powerful enough to process this algorithm.

Figure 3 is a plot of the performance times of the actor-like implementation as a function of the input size and the number of nodes. Figure 4 gives a comparison the functional implementation with our more concurrent implementation on matrices of size 32×32 and 64×64.

5 Representation of Actors

Sequential processes with sends and receives form a low level language support available on many distributed memory architectures. We are currently developing a translator to transform the Rosette specification of an actor language to code for a dialect of C requiring explicit sends and receives. There are a number of design issues which result from the static nature of C. We discuss one of these issues, namely the internal representation of an actor.

An actor's *behavior* specifies new tasks to create and communications to send as a function of its local state and the message being processed. As stated in Section 2, upon

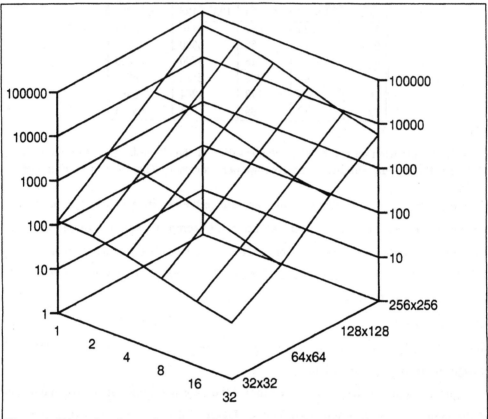

Figure 3: Execution times of an actor-like implementation of the Cholesky Decomposition as a function of hypercube and matrix sizes.

receipt of a message an actor may replace its current behavior with a new behavior that is used to process all subsequent messages. The replacement behavior may involve a change of functionality, not just a state change.

In a statically specified language, such as C, behavior replacement is a troublesome feature to represent; an actor may choose its future behavior definition completely dynamically. One possibility is to use static analysis to determine the set of behavior definitions that an actor may use and encode them into a single behavior. While this technique will work for many actor programs, it is insufficient in general. For example, a behavior definition may be specified in a message. Furthermore, this technique may create source code on the order of the product of the number of possible actor classes by the number of actor definitions in the user's program.

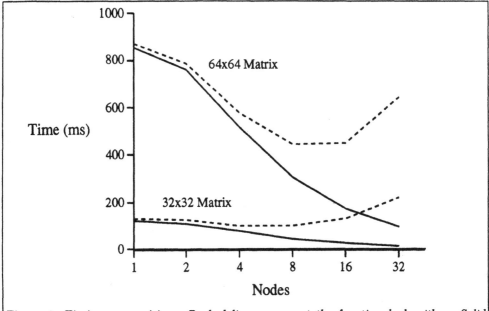

Figure 4: Timing comparision. *Dashed lines represent the functional algorithm. Solid lines represent the more concurrent implementation.*

Forwarding Pointers. An attractive, and fairly simple idea, is to represent each actor with a separate process which executes its behavior. When an actor changes its behavior definition, we simply create a new process which executes all future messages that get sent to the original actor. We should first note that it will be necessary to keep the original actor around, since its acquaintances may only know of it by the original mail address. So when messages get delivered to the original mail address, the actor simply forwards them to the new process that it created. While there are typically few behavior redefinitions in practice, this method can entail a significant performance loss if the network gets filled with messages getting forwarded from previous behaviors to new ones. Furthermore, it is not clear how to implement enabled-sets [15] and inheritance under such a scheme.

Actors as Processes. The representation that we are implementing models actors as light-weight processes and requires the presence of a *kernel* run-time system on each node. Each actor that gets created is represented as a unique process. The process has a local `Current-Behavior` variable which specifies the type of actor it is currently representing. Method definitions are stored in the kernel. When an actor receives a message it hands

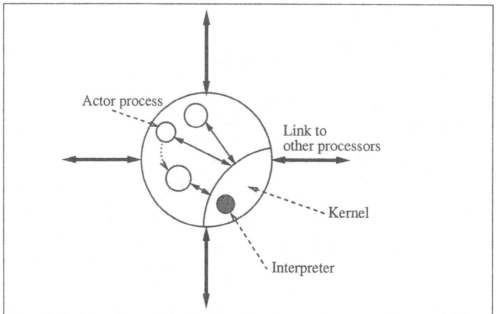

Figure 5: Conceptual view of a node: *Dotted lines are messages sent between actors. Solid lines are function invocations*

control to an interface routine in the kernel which takes the actor's state and the new message and calls the appropriate function to execute the actor's behavior. A message sent to an actor goes directly to that actor's process and doesn't have to go through a driver or any intermediate processes. Figure 5 is a conceptual view how a node is organized, the section labeled *Interpreter* is necessary for reflection and will be explained later.

Since behavior definitions are stored in the local kernel, it keeps the amount of code that has to be placed on each node at a minimum. The kernel code size is linear in the number of methods defined in a user's program. Actor processes require storage linear in the size of an actor's acquaintance list. Furthermore, the actors are self-contained and can thus be dynamically load balanced without having to worry that storage will be configured differently on the node to which it is moved.

By placing all of the user code in a kernel we are able to easily modularize the system. For example, enabled-sets are not currently in the multiprocessor implementation; however, adding them will entail a simple modification of the code for the actor/kernel interface routine.

Reflection requires that Figure 5 contain a section labeled *Interpreter*. If the runtime system can change dynamically, we no longer have a static specification and have to interpret the user's code in real-time. In practice, it would be very inefficient to locate an actor interpreter on each node. More realistically, interpreters will be placed on a few nodes and actors which require the power of reflection are dynamically transported to those nodes. The migration cost will be subsumed within the larger cost of running an actor through the interpreter.

6 Conclusions

The language support currently provided on a number of distributed memory architectures consists of sequential procedures which can send and receive data across processors. The intel iPSC also provides the ability to choose specific (tagged) messages out of the mail box [12], thus allowing a user to handle arrival order non-determinism efficiently. However, programmers have to specify explicit processor addresses with every message that is sent across nodes. In particular, this means that they have to keep track of the precise mapping of the original data on the processors and compute the processor number where certain data that is needed may be available or where the next message to start some computation should be sent. Although the CD algorithm discussed above allows a fully static mapping of data to processors, more generally optimal execution may require that objects be moved dynamically to different processors. It then becomes increasingly difficult for the programmer to keep track of the object to processor mapping. We feel that the actor model enables a programmer to have a logical view of the locality and communication of an algorithm, thereby hiding some architecture dependent details. Our work also suggests that it is possible to easily represent algorithms using actors and that such representations can be efficiently executed on distributed memory architectures.

References

[1] G. Agha. *Actors: A Model of Concurrent Computation in Distributed Systems.* MIT Press, 1986.

[2] G. Agha. Supporting multiparadigm programming on actor architectures. In *Proceedings of Parallel Architectures and Languages Europe, Vol. II: Parallel Languages (PARLE '89)*, pages 1–19. Espirit, Springer-Verlag, 1989. LNCS 366.

[3] G. Agha. Concurrent object-oriented programming. *Communications of the ACM*, 33(9):125–141, September 1990.

[4] W. Athas and C. Seitz. Multicomputers: Message-passing concurrent computers. *IEEE Computer*, pages 9–23, August 1988.

[5] F. Baude and G. Vidal-Naquet. Actors as a parallel programming model. In *Proceedings of 8th Symposium on Theoretical Aspects of Computer Science*, 1991. LNCS 480.

[6] A. Chien. *Concurrent Aggregates: An Object-Oriented Language for Fine-Grained Message-Passing Machines*. PhD thesis, MIT, 1990.

[7] W. Clinger. Foundations of actor semantics. AI-TR- 633, MIT Artificial Intelligence Laboratory, May 1981.

[8] W. Dally. *A VLSI Architecture for Concurrent Data Structures*. Kluwer Academic Press, 1986.

[9] G. Golub and C. Van Loan. *Matrix Computations*. The Johns Hopkins University Press, 1983.

[10] C. Hewitt. Viewing control structures as patterns of passing messages. *Journal of Artificial Intelligence*, 8(3):323–364, 1977.

[11] P. Hudak. Para-functional programming. *IEEE Computer*, pages 60–70, August 1986.

[12] Intel Corporation, Beaverton, Oregon. *iPSC/2 C Programmers reference manual*, 1988. Order Number: 311017-002.

[13] Y. Sami and G. Vidal-Naquet. Formalisation of the behaviour of actors by colored petri nets and some applications. In *Proceedings of Parallel Architectures and Languages Europe, (PARLE '91)*, 1991.

[14] C. Tomlinson, W. Kim, M. Schevel, V. Singh, B. Will, and G. Agha. Rosette: An object oriented concurrent system architecture. *Sigplan Notices*, 24(4):91–93, 1989.

[15] C. Tomlinson and V. Singh. Inheritance and synchronization with enabled-sets. In *OOPSLA Proceedings*, 1989.

[16] P. Vaidya. Solving linear equations with symmetric diagonally dominant matrices by constructing good preconditioners. Technical report, University of Illinois Department of Computer Science, In Preparation.

2 An Overview of the Fortran D Programming System

S. Hiranandani, K. Kennedy, C. Koelbel,
U. Kremer, and C.-W. Tseng
Rice University

Abstract

The success of large-scale parallel architectures is limited by the difficulty of developing machine-independent parallel programs. We have developed Fortran D, a version of Fortran extended with data decomposition specifications, to provide a portable data-parallel programming model. This paper presents the design of two key components of the Fortran D programming system: a prototype compiler and an environment to assist automatic data decomposition. The Fortran D compiler addresses program partitioning, communication generation and optimization, data decomposition analysis, run-time support for unstructured computations, and storage management. The Fortran D programming environment provides a static performance estimator and an automatic data partitioner. We believe that the Fortran D programming system will significantly ease the task of writing machine-independent data-parallel programs.

1 Introduction

It is widely recognized that parallel computing represents the only plausible way to continue to increase the computational power available to computational scientists and engineers. However, it is not likely to be widely successful until parallel computers are as easy to use as today's vector supercomputers. A major component of the success of vector supercomputers is the ability to write machine-independent vectorizable programs. Automatic vectorization and other compiler technologies have made it possible for the scientist to structure Fortran loops according the well-understood rules of "vectorizable style" and expect the resulting program to be compiled to efficient code on any vector machine [6, 32].

Compare this with the current situation for parallel machines. Scientists wishing to use such a machine must rewrite their programs in an extension of Fortran that explicitly reflects the architecture of the underlying machine, such as a message-passing dialect for MIMD distributed-memory machines, vector syntax for SIMD machines, or an explicitly parallel dialect with synchronization for MIMD shared-memory machines. This conversion is difficult, and the resulting parallel programs are machine-specific. Scientists are thus discouraged from porting programs to parallel machines because they risk losing their investment whenever the program changes or a new architecture arrives.

One way to overcome this problem would be to identify a "data-parallel programming style" that allows the efficient compilation of Fortran programs on a variety of parallel machines. Researchers working in the area, including ourselves, have concluded that such a programming style is useful but not sufficient in general. The reason for this is that not enough information can be included in the program text for the compiler to accurately evaluate alternative translations. Similar reasoning argues against cross-compilations between the current parallel extensions of Fortran.

For these reasons, we have chosen a different approach. We believe that selecting a data decomposition is one of the most important intellectual step in developing data-parallel scientific codes. However, current parallel programming languages provide little support for data decomposition [26]. We have therefore developed an enhanced version of Fortran that introduces data decomposition specifications. We call the extended language Fortran D, where "D" suggests data, decomposition, or distribution. When reasonable data decompositions are provided for a Fortran D program written in a data-parallel programming style, we believe that advanced compiler technology can implement it efficiently on a variety of parallel architectures.

We are developing a prototype Fortran D compiler to generate node programs for the iPSC/860, a MIMD distributed-memory machine. If successful, the result of this project will go far towards establishing the feasibility of machine-independent parallel programming, since a MIMD shared-memory compiler could be based directly on the MIMD distributed-memory implementation. The only additional step would be the construction of an effective Fortran D compiler for SIMD distributed-memory machines. We have initiated at Rice a project to build such a compiler based on existing vectorization technology.

The Fortran D compiler automates the time consuming task of deriving node programs based on the data decomposition. The remaining components of the Fortran D programming system, the static performance estimator and automatic data partitioner, support another important step in developing a data-parallel program—selecting a data decomposition. The rest of this paper presents the data decomposition specifications in Fortran D, the structure of a prototype Fortran D compiler, and the design of the Fortran D programming environment. We conclude with a discussion of our validation strategy.

2 Fortran D

The data decomposition problem can be approached by considering the two levels of parallelism in data-parallel applications. First, there is the question of how arrays should be *aligned* with respect to one another, both within and across array dimensions. We call this the *problem mapping* induced by the structure of the underlying computation. It represents the minimal requirements for reducing data movement for the program, and is largely independent of any machine considerations. The alignment of arrays in the program depends on the natural fine-grain parallelism defined by individual members of data arrays.

Second, there is the question of how arrays should be *distributed* onto the actual parallel machine. We call this the *machine mapping* caused by translating the problem onto the finite resources of the machine. It is affected by the topology, communication mechanisms, size of local memory, and number of processors in the underlying machine. The distribution of arrays in the program depends on the coarse-grain parallelism defined by the physical parallel machine.

Fortran D is a version of Fortran that provides data decomposition specifications for these two levels of parallelism using DECOMPOSITION, ALIGN, and DISTRIBUTE statements. A decomposition is an abstract problem or index domain; it does not require any storage. Each element of a decomposition represents a unit of computation. The DECOMPOSITION statement declares the name, dimensionality, and size of a decomposition for later use.

The ALIGN statement is used to map arrays onto decompositions. Arrays mapped to the same decomposition are automatically aligned with each other. Alignment can take place either within or across dimensions. The alignment of arrays to decompositions is specified by placeholders in the subscript expressions of both the array and decomposition. In the example below,

```
REAL X(N,N)
DECOMPOSITION A(N,N)
ALIGN X(I,J) with A(J-2,I+3)
```

A is declared to be a two dimensional decomposition of size $N \times N$. Array X is then aligned with respect to A with the dimensions permuted and offsets within each dimension.

After arrays have been aligned with a decomposition, the DISTRIBUTE statement maps the decomposition to the finite resources of the physical machine. Distributions are specified by assigning an independent *attribute* to each dimension of a decomposition. Predefined attributes are BLOCK, CYCLIC, and BLOCK_CYCLIC. The symbol ":" marks

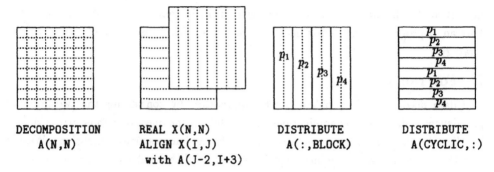

Figure 1: Fortran D Data Decomposition Specifications

dimensions that are not distributed. Choosing the distribution for a decomposition maps all arrays aligned with the decomposition to the machine. In the following example,

```
DECOMPOSITION A(N,N)
DISTRIBUTE A(:, BLOCK)
DISTRIBUTE A(CYCLIC,:)
```

distributing decomposition A by (:,BLOCK) results in a column partition of arrays aligned with A. Distributing A by (CYCLIC,:) partitions the rows of A in a round-robin fashion among processors. These sample data alignment and distributions are shown in Figure 1.

Predefined regular data distributions can effectively exploit regular data-parallelism. However, irregular distributions and run-time processing is required to manage the irregular data parallelism found in many unstructured computations. In Fortran D, irregular distributions may be specified through an explicit user-defined function or data array. In the example below,

```
INTEGER MAP(N)
DECOMPOSITION IRREG(N)
DISTRIBUTE IRREG(MAP)
```

elements of the decomposition IRREG(i) will be mapped to the processor indicated by the array MAP(i). Fortran D also supports dynamic data decomposition; *i.e.*, changing the alignment or distribution of a decomposition at any point in the program.

We should note that our goal in designing Fortran D is not to support the most general data decompositions possible. Instead, our intent is to provide decompositions that are both powerful enough to express data parallelism in scientific programs, and simple enough to permit the compiler to produce efficient programs. Fortran D is a language with semantics very similar to sequential Fortran. As a result, it should be quite usable by computational scientists. In addition, we believe that our two-phase strategy for specifying data decomposition is natural and conducive to writing modular and portable code. Fortran D bears similarities to both CM Fortran [31] and KALI [22]. The complete language is described in detail elsewhere [8].

3 Fortran D Compiler

As we have stated previously, two major steps in writing a data-parallel program are selecting a data decomposition, and then using it to derive node programs with explicit communications to access nonlocal data. Manually inserting communications is unquestionably the most time-consuming, tedious, non-portable, and error-prone step in parallel programming. Significant increases in source code size are not only common but expected. A major advantage of programming in Fortran D will be the ability to utilize advanced compiler techniques to automatically generate node programs with explicit communication, based on the data decompositions specified in the program. The prototype compiler is being developed in the context of the ParaScope parallel programming environment [4], and will take advantage of the analysis and transformation capabilities of the ParaScope Editor [19, 20].

The main goal of the Fortran D compiler is to derive from the data decomposition a parallel node program that minimizes load imbalance and communication costs. Our approach is to convert Fortran D programs into *single-program, multiple-data* (SPMD) form with explicit message-passing that executes directly on the nodes of the distributed-memory machine. Our basic strategy is to partition the program using the *owner computes* rule, where every processor only performs computation on data it owns [5, 29, 34]. However, we will relax the rule where it prevents the compiler from achieving good load balance or reducing communication costs.

The Fortran D compiler bears similarities to ARF [33], ASPAR [18], ID NOUVEAU [29], KALI [22], MIMDIZER [13], and SUPERB [34]. The current prototype generates code for a subset of the decompositions allowed in Fortran D, namely those with BLOCK distributions. Figure 2 depicts the output of a Livermore loop kernel generated by the Fortran D compiler.

3.1 Program Partitioning

The first phase of the compiler partitions the program onto processors based on the data decomposition. We define the *iteration set* of a reference R on the local processor t_p to be the set of loop iterations that cause R to access data owned by t_p. The iteration set is calculated based on the alignment and distribution specified in the Fortran D program. According to the *owner computes rule*, the set of loop iterations that t_p must execute is the union of the iteration sets for the left-hand sides (*lhs*) of all the individual assignment statements within the loop.

To partition the computation among processors, we first reduce the loop bounds so that each processor only executes iterations in its own set. With multiple statements in the loop, the iteration set of an individual statement may be a subset of the iteration set

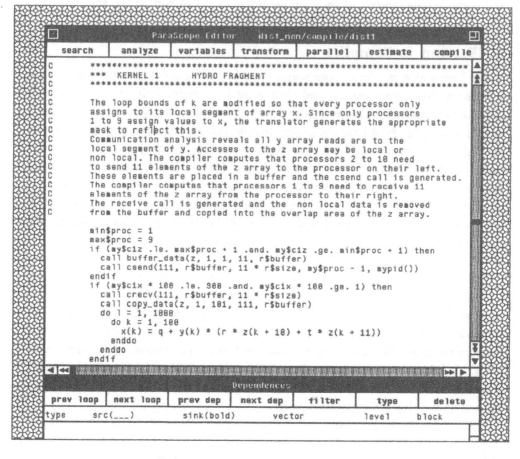

Figure 2: Fortran D Compiler Output

for that loop. For these statements we also add guards based on membership tests for the iteration set of the *lhs* to ensure that all assignments are to local array elements.

3.2 Communication Introduction

Once the computation has been partitioned, the Fortran D compiler must introduce communications for nonlocal data accesses to preserve the semantics of the original program. This requires calculating the data that must be sent or received by each processor. We can calculate the *send iteration set* for each right-hand side (*rhs*) reference as its iteration set minus the iteration set of its *lhs*. Similarly, the *receive iteration set* for each *rhs* is the iteration set of its *lhs* minus its own iteration set. These sets represent the iterations for which data must be sent or received by t_p. The Fortran D compiler summarizes the array locations accessed on the send or receive iterations using rectangular or triangular regions known as *regular sections* [12]; they are used to generate calls to communication primitives.

3.3 Communication Optimization

A naive approach for introducing communication is to insert send and receive operations directly preceding each reference causing a nonlocal data access. This generates many small messages that may prove inefficient due to communication overhead. The Fortran D compiler will use *data dependence* information to determine whether communication may be inserted at some outer loop, *vectorizing* messages by combining many small messages. The algorithm to calculate the appropriate loop level for each message is described by Balasundaram *et al.* and Gerndt [2, 10].

A major goal of the Fortran D compiler is to aggressively optimize communications. We intend to apply techniques proposed by Li and Chen to recognize regular computation patterns that can utilize collective communications primitives [24]. It will be especially important to recognize reduction operations. For regular communication patterns, we plan to employ the collective communications routines found in EXPRESS [27]. For unstructured computations with irregular communications, we will incorporate the PARTI primitives of Saltz *et al.* [33].

The Fortran D compiler may utilize data decomposition and dependence information to guide program transformations that improve communication patterns. We are considering the usefulness of several transformations, particularly loop interchanging, strip mining, loop distribution, and loop alignment. Replicating computations and processor-specific dead code elimination will also be applied to eliminate communication.

Communications may be further optimized by considering interactions between all the loop nests in the program. Intra- and interprocedural dataflow analysis of array sections can show that an assignment to a variable is *live* at a point in the program if there are no intervening assignments to that variable. This information may be used to eliminate redundant messages. For instance, assume that messages in previous loop nests have already retrieved nonlocal elements for a given array. If those values are *live*, messages to fetch those values in succeeding loop nests may be eliminated. Data from different arrays being sent to the same processor may also be buffered together in one message to reduce communication overhead.

The *owner computes* rule provides the basic strategy of the Fortran D compiler. We may also relax this rule, allowing processors to compute values for data they do not own. For instance, suppose that multiple *rhs* of an assignment statement are owned by a processor that is not the owner of the *lhs*. Computing the result on the processor owning the *rhs* and then sending the result to the owner of the *lhs* could reduce the amount of data communicated. This optimization is a simple case of the *owner stores* rule proposed by Balasundaram [1].

In particular, it may be desirable for the Fortran D compiler to partition loops amongst processors so that each loop iteration is executed on a single processor, such as in KALI [22] and PARTI [33]. This technique may improve communication and provide greater control over load balance, especially for irregular computations. It also eliminates the need for individual statement guards and simplifies handling of control flow within the loop body.

3.4 Data Decomposition Analysis

Fortran D provides dynamic data decomposition by permitting ALIGN and DISTRIBUTE statements to be inserted at any point in a program. This complicates the job of the Fortran D compiler, since it must know the decomposition of each array in order to generate the proper guards and communication. We define *reaching decompositions* to be the set of decomposition specifications that may reach an array reference aligned with the decomposition; it may be calculated in a manner similar to *reaching definitions*. The Fortran D compiler will apply both intra- and interprocedural analysis to calculate reaching decompositions for each reference to a distributed array. If multiple decompositions reach a procedure, node splitting or run-time techniques may be required to generate the proper code for the program.

To permit a modular programming style, the effects of data decomposition specifications are limited to the scope of the enclosing procedure. However, procedures do inherit the decompositions of their callers. These semantics require the compiler to insert calls to run-time data decomposition routines to restore the original data decomposition upon every procedure return. Since changing the data decomposition may be expensive, these calls should be eliminated where possible.

We define *live decompositions* to be the set of decomposition specifications that may reach some array reference aligned with the decomposition; it may be calculated in a manner similar to *live variables*. As with reaching decompositions, the Fortran D compiler needs both intra- and interprocedural analysis to calculate live decompositions for each decomposition specification. Any data decompositions determined not to be *live* may be safely eliminated. Similar analysis may also hoist dynamic data decompositions out of loops.

3.5 Run-time Support for Irregular Computations

Many advanced algorithms for scientific applications are not amenable to the techniques described in the previous section. Adaptive meshes, for example, often have poor load balance or high communication cost if static regular data distributions are used. These algorithms require dynamic irregular data distributions. Other algorithms, such as fast multipole algorithms, make heavy use of index arrays that the compiler cannot analyze. In these cases, the communications analysis must be performed at run-time.

The Fortran D project supports dynamic irregular distributions. The *inspector/executor* strategy to generate efficient communications has been adapted from KALI

[22] and PARTI [25]. The inspector is a transformation of the original Fortran D loop that builds a list of nonlocal elements, known as the IN set, that will be received during the execution of the loop. A global transpose operation is performed using collective communications to calculate the set of data elements that must be sent by a processor, known as the OUT set. The executor uses the computed sets to control the actual communication. Performance results using the PARTI primitives indicate that the inspector can be implemented with acceptable overhead, particularly if the results are saved for future executions of the original loop [33].

3.6 Storage Management

Once guards and communication have been calculated, the Fortran D compiler must select and manage storage for all nonlocal array references received from other processors. There are several different storage schemes, described below:

- *Overlaps*, developed by Gerndt, are expansions of local array sections to accommodate neighboring nonlocal elements [10]. They are useful for programs with high locality of reference, but may waste storage when nonlocal accesses are distant.

- *Buffers* are designed to overcome the contiguous nature of overlaps. They are useful when the nonlocal area is bounded in size, but not near the local array section.

- *Hash tables* are used when the set of accessed nonlocal elements is sparse. This is the case in many irregular computations. Hash tables provide a quick lookup mechanism for arbitrary sets of nonlocal values [16].

Once the storage type for all nonlocal data is determined, the compiler needs to analyze the space required by the various storage structures and generate code so that nonlocal data is accessed from its correct location. Storage management and other parts of the Fortran D compiler are described in more detail elsewhere [14, 15].

4 Fortran D Programming Environment

Choosing a decomposition for the fundamental data structures used in the program is a pivotal step in developing data-parallel applications. Once selected, the data decomposition usually completely determines the parallelism and data movement in the resulting program. Unfortunately, there are no existing tools to advise the programmer in making this important decision. To evaluate a decomposition, the programmer must first insert the decomposition in the program text, then compile and run the resulting program to determine its effectiveness. Comparing two data decompositions thus requires implementing and running both versions of the program, a tedious task at best. The process is prohibitively difficult without the assistance of a compiler to automatically generate node programs based on the data decomposition.

Several researchers have proposed techniques to automatically derive data decompositions based on simple machine models [17, 28, 30]. However, these techniques are

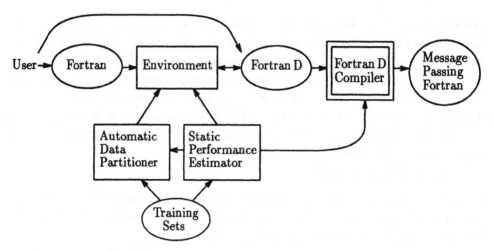

Figure 3: Fortran D Parallel Programming System

insufficient because the efficiency of a given data decomposition is highly dependent on both the actual node program generated by the compiler and its performance on the parallel machine. "Optimal" data decompositions may prove inferior because the compiler generates node programs with suboptimal communications or poor load balance. Similarly, marginal data decompositions may perform well because the compiler is able to utilize collective communication primitives to exploit special hardware on the parallel machine.

What we need is a programming environment that helps the user to understand the effect of a given data decomposition and program structure on the efficiency of the *compiler-generated* code running on a given target machine. The Fortran D programming system, shown in Figure 3, provides such an environment. The main components of the environment are a static performance estimator and an automatic data partitioner [2, 3].

Since the Fortran D programming system is built on top of ParaScope, it also provides program analysis, transformation, and editing capabilities that allow users to restructure their programs according to a data-parallel programming style. Zima and others at Vienna are working on a similar tool to support data decomposition decisions using automatic techniques [7]. Gupta and Banerjee propose automatic data decomposition techniques based on assumptions about a proposed Parafrase-2 distributed-memory compiler [11].

4.1 Static Performance Estimator

It is clearly impractical to use dynamic performance information to choose between data decompositions in our programming environment. Instead, a *static* performance estimator is needed that can accurately predict the performance of a Fortran D program on the target machine. Also required is a scheme that allows the compiler to assess the costs of communication routines and computations. The static performance estimator in the Fortran D programming system caters to both needs.

The performance estimator is not based on a general theoretical model of distributed-memory computers. Instead, it employs the notion of a *training set* of kernel routines that measures the cost of various computation and communication patterns on the target machine. The results of executing the training set on a parallel machine are summarized and used to train the performance estimator for that machine. By utilizing training sets, the performance estimator achieves both accuracy and portability across different machine architectures. The resulting information may also be used by the Fortran D compiler to guide communication optimizations.

The static performance estimator is divided into two parts, a machine module and a compiler module. The *machine module* predicts the performance of a node program containing explicit communications. It uses a *machine-level* training set written in message-passing Fortran. The training set contains individual computation and communication patterns that are timed on the target machine for different numbers of processors and data sizes. To estimate the performance of a node program, the machine module can simply look up results for each computation and communication pattern encountered.

The *compiler module* forms the second part of the static performance estimator. It assists the user in selecting data decompositions by statically predicting the performance of a program for a set of data decompositions. The compiler module employs a *compiler-level* training set written in Fortran D that consists of program kernels such as stencil computations and matrix multiplication. The training set is converted into message-passing Fortran using the Fortran D compiler and executed on the target machine for different data decompositions, numbers of processors, and array sizes. Estimating the performance of a Fortran D program then requires matching computations in the program with kernels from the training set.

The compiler-level training set also provides a natural way to respond to changes in the Fortran D compiler as well as the machine. We simply recompile the training set with the new compiler and execute the resulting programs to reinitialize the compiler module for the performance estimator.

Since it is not possible to incorporate all possible computation patterns in the compiler-level training set, the performance estimator will encounter code fragments that cannot be matched with existing kernels. To estimate the performance of these codes, the compiler module must rely on the machine-level training set. We plan to incorporate elements of the Fortran D compiler in the performance estimator so that it can mimic the compilation process. The compiler module can thus convert any unrecognized Fortran D program fragment into an equivalent node program, and invoke the machine module to estimate

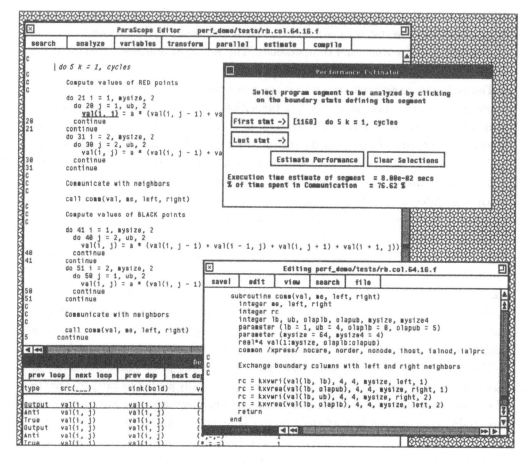

Figure 4: Static Performance Estimator

its performance.

Note that even though it is desirable, to assist automatic data decomposition the static performance estimator does not need to predict the *absolute* performance of a given data decomposition. Instead, the it only needs to accurately predict the performance *relative* to other data decompositions. A prototype of the machine module has been implemented for a common class of *loosely synchronous* scientific problems[9]. It predicts the performance of a node program using EXPRESS communication routines for different numbers of processors and data sizes [27]. The prototype performance estimator has proved quite precise, especially in predicting the relative performances of different data decompositions [3].

A screen snapshot during a typical performance estimation session is shown in Figure 4. The user can select a program segment such as a do loop and invoke the performance estimator by clicking on the Estimate Performance button. The prototype responds with an execution time estimate of the selected segment on the target machine, as well as an estimate of the communication time represented as a percentage of the total execution time. This allows the effectiveness of a data partitioning strategy to be evaluated on any part of the node program.

4.2 Automatic Data Partitioner

The goal of the automatic data partitioner is to assist the user in choosing a good data decomposition. It utilizes training sets and the static performance estimator to select data partitions that are efficient for both the compiler and parallel machine.

The automatic data partitioner may be applied to an entire program or on specific program fragments. When invoked on an entire program, it automatically selects data decompositions without further user interaction. We believe that for regular loosely synchronous problems written in a data-parallel programming style, the automatic data partitioner can determine an efficient partitioning scheme without user interaction.

Alternatively, the automatic data partitioner may be used as a starting point for choosing a good data decomposition. When invoked interactively for specific program segments, it responds with a list of the best decomposition schemes, together with their static performance estimates. If the user is not satisfied with the predicted overall performance, he or she can use the performance estimator to locate communication and computation intensive program segments. The Fortran D environment can then advise the user about the effects of program changes on the choice of a good data decomposition.

The analysis performed by the automatic data partitioner divides the program into separate *computation phases*. The *intra-phase* decomposition problem consists of determining a set of good data decompositions and their performance for each individual phase. The data partitioner first tries to match the phase or parts of the phase with computation patterns in the compiler training set. If a match is found, it returns the set of decompositions with the best measured performance as recorded in the compiler training set. If no match is found, the data partitioner must perform alignment and distribution analysis on the phase. The resulting solution may be less accurate since the effects of the Fortran D compiler and target machine can only be estimated.

Alignment analysis is used to prune the search space of possible arrays alignments by selecting only those alignments that minimize data movement. Alignment analysis is largely machine-independent; it is performed by analyzing the array access patterns of computations in the phase. We intend to build on the inter-dimensional and intra-dimensional alignment techniques of Li and Chen [23] and Knobe *et al.* [21].

Distribution analysis follows alignment analysis. It applies heuristics to prune unprofitable choices in the search space of possible distributions. The efficiency of a data distribution is determined by machine-dependent aspects such as topology, number of processors, and communication costs. The automatic data partitioner uses the final set of alignments and distributions to generate a set of reasonable data decomposition schemes. In the worst case, the set of decompositions is the cross product of the alignment and distribution sets. Finally, the static performance estimator is invoked to select the set of data decompositions with the best predicted performance.

After computing data decompositions for each phase, the automatic data partitioner must solve the *inter-phase* decomposition problem of merging individual data decompositions. It also determines the profitability of realigning or redistributing arrays between computational phases. Interprocedural analysis will be used to merge the decomposition schemes of computation phases across procedure boundaries. The resulting decompositions for the entire program and their performance are then presented to the user.

5 Validation Strategy

We plan to establish whether our compilation and automatic data partitioning schemes for Fortran D can achieve acceptable performance on a variety of parallel architectures. We will use a benchmark suite being developed by Geoffrey Fox at Syracuse that consists of a collection of Fortran programs. Each program in the suite will have five versions:

(v1) the original Fortran 77 program,

(v2) the best hand-coded message-passing version of the Fortran program,

(v3) a "nearby" Fortran 77 program,

(v4) a Fortran D version of the nearby program, and

(v5) a Fortran 90 version of the program.

The "nearby" version of the program will utilize the same basic algorithm as the message-passing program, except that all explicit message-passing and blocking of loops in the program are removed. The Fortran D version of the program consists of the nearby version plus appropriate data decomposition specifications.

To validate the Fortran D compiler, we will compare the running time of the best hand-coded message-passing version of the program (v2) with the output of the Fortran D compiler for the Fortran D version of the nearby program (v4). To validate the automatic data partitioner, we will use it to generate a Fortran D program from the nearby Fortran program (v3). The result will be compiled by the Fortran D compiler and its running time compared with that of the compiled version of the hand-generated Fortran D program (v4).

The purpose of the validation program suite is to provide a fair test of the prototype compiler and data partitioner. We do not expect these tools to perform high-level algorithm changes. However, we will test their ability to analyze and optimize whole programs based on both machine-independent issues such as the structure of the computation, as well as machine-dependent issues such as the number and interconnection of processors in the parallel machine. Our validation strategy will test three key parts of the Fortran D programming system: the limits of our machine-independent Fortran D programming model, the efficiency and ability of our compiler technology, and the effectiveness of our automatic data partitioning and performance estimation techniques.

6 Conclusions

Scientific programmers need a simple, machine-independent programming model that can be efficiently mapped to large-scale parallel machines. We believe that Fortran D, a version of Fortran enhanced with data decompositions, provides such a portable data-parallel programming model. Its success will depend on the compiler and environment support provided by the Fortran D programming system.

The Fortran D compiler includes sophisticated intraprocedural and interprocedural analyses, dynamic data decomposition, program transformation, communication optimization, and support for both regular and irregular problems. Though significant work remains to implement the optimizations presented in this paper, based on preliminary experiments we expect the Fortran D compiler to generate efficient code for a large class of data-parallel programs with only minimal user effort.

The Fortran D environment is distinguished by its ability to accurately estimate the performance of programs using collective communication on real parallel machines, as well automatically choose data partitions that account for the characteristics of both the compiler-generated code and underlying machine. It will assist the user in developing efficient Fortran D programs. Overall, we believe that the Fortran D programming system is a powerful and useful tool that will significantly ease the task of writing portable data-parallel programs.

7 Acknowledgements

The authors wish to thank Vasanth Bala, Geoffrey Fox, and Marina Kalem for inspiring many of the ideas in this work. We are also grateful to the ParaScope research group for providing the underlying software infrastructure for the Fortran D programming system.

References

[1] V. Balasundaram. Translating control parallelism to data parallelism. In *Proceedings of the Fifth SIAM Conference on Parallel Processing for Scientific Computing*, Houston, TX, March 1991.

[2] V. Balasundaram, G. Fox, K. Kennedy, and U. Kremer. An interactive environment for data partitioning and distribution. In *Proceedings of the 5th Distributed Memory Computing Conference*, Charleston, SC, April 1990.

[3] V. Balasundaram, G. Fox, K. Kennedy, and U. Kremer. A static performance estimator to guide data partitioning decisions. In *Proceedings of the Third ACM SIGPLAN Symposium on Principles and Practice of Parallel Programming*, Williamsburg, VA, April 1991.

[4] D. Callahan, K. Cooper, R. Hood, K. Kennedy, and L. Torczon. ParaScope: A parallel programming environment. *The International Journal of Supercomputer Applications*, 2(4):84–99, Winter 1988.

[5] D. Callahan and K. Kennedy. Compiling programs for distributed-memory multiprocessors. *Journal of Supercomputing*, 2:151–169, October 1988.

[6] D. Callahan, K. Kennedy, and U. Kremer. A dynamic study of vectorization in PFC. Technical Report TR89-97, Dept. of Computer Science, Rice University, July 1989.

[7] B. Chapman, H. Herbeck, and H. Zima. Automatic support for data distribution. In *Proceedings of the 6th Distributed Memory Computing Conference*, Portland, OR, April 1991.

[8] G. Fox, S. Hiranandani, K. Kennedy, C. Koelbel, U. Kremer, C. Tseng, and M. Wu. Fortran D language specification. Technical Report TR90-141, Dept. of Computer Science, Rice University, December 1990.

[9] G. Fox, M. Johnson, G. Lyzenga, S. Otto, J. Salmon, and D. Walker. *Solving Problems on Concurrent Processors*, volume 1. Prentice-Hall, Englewood Cliffs, NJ, 1988.

[10] M. Gerndt. Updating distributed variables in local computations. *Concurrency—Practice & Experience*, 2(3):171–193, September 1990.

[11] M. Gupta and P. Banerjee. Automatic data partitioning on distributed memory multiprocessors. In *Proceedings of the 6th Distributed Memory Computing Conference*, Portland, OR, April 1991.

[12] P. Havlak and K. Kennedy. An implementation of interprocedural bounded regular section analysis. *IEEE Transactions on Parallel and Distributed Systems*, 2(3):350–360, July 1991.

[13] R. Hill. MIMDizer: A new tool for parallelization. *Supercomputing Review*, 3(4):26–28, April 1990.

[14] S. Hiranandani, K. Kennedy, and C. Tseng. Compiler optimizations for Fortran D on MIMD distributed-memory machines. In *Proceedings of Supercomputing '91*, Albuquerque, NM, November 1991.

[15] S. Hiranandani, K. Kennedy, and C. Tseng. Compiler support for machine-independent parallel programming in Fortran D. Technical Report TR90-149, Dept. of Computer Science, Rice University, January 1991. To appear in J. Saltz and P. Mehrotra, editors, *Compilers and Runtime Software for Scalable Multiprocessors*, Elsevier, 1991.

[16] S. Hiranandani, J. Saltz, P. Mehrotra, and H. Berryman. Performance of hashed cache data migration schemes on multicomputers. *Journal of Parallel and Distributed Computing*, 12(4), August 1991.

[17] D. Hudak and S. Abraham. Compiler techniques for data partitioning of sequentially iterated parallel loops. In *Proceedings of the 1990 ACM International Conference on Supercomputing*, Amsterdam, The Netherlands, June 1990.

[18] K. Ikudome, G. Fox, A. Kolawa, and J. Flower. An automatic and symbolic parallelization system for distributed memory parallel computers. In *Proceedings of the 5th Distributed Memory Computing Conference*, Charleston, SC, April 1990.

[19] K. Kennedy, K. S. McKinley, and C. Tseng. Analysis and transformation in the ParaScope Editor. In *Proceedings of the 1991 ACM International Conference on Supercomputing*, Cologne, Germany, June 1991.

[20] K. Kennedy, K. S. McKinley, and C. Tseng. Interactive parallel programming using the

ParaScope Editor. *IEEE Transactions on Parallel and Distributed Systems*, 2(3):329–341, July 1991.

[21] K. Knobe, J. Lukas, and G. Steele, Jr. Data optimization: Allocation of arrays to reduce communication on SIMD machines. *Journal of Parallel and Distributed Computing*, 8(2):102–118, February 1990.

[22] C. Koelbel and P. Mehrotra. Compiling global name-space parallel loops for distributed execution. *IEEE Transactions on Parallel and Distributed Systems*, 2(4), October 1991.

[23] J. Li and M. Chen. Index domain alignment: Minimizing cost of cross-referencing between distributed arrays. In *Frontiers90: The 3rd Symposium on the Frontiers of Massively Parallel Computation*, College Park, MD, October 1990.

[24] J. Li and M. Chen. Compiling communication-efficient programs for massively parallel machines. *IEEE Transactions on Parallel and Distributed Systems*, 2(3):361–376, July 1991.

[25] R. Mirchandaney, J. Saltz, R. Smith, D. Nicol, and K. Crowley. Principles of runtime support for parallel processors. In *Proceedings of the Second International Conference on Supercomputing*, St. Malo, France, July 1988.

[26] C. Pancake and D. Bergmark. Do parallel languages respond to the needs of scientific programmers? *IEEE Computer*, 23(12):13–23, December 1990.

[27] Parasoft Corporation. *Express User's Manual*, 1989.

[28] J. Ramanujam and P. Sadayappan. A methodology for parallelizing programs for multicomputers and complex memory multiprocessors. In *Proceedings of Supercomputing '89*, Reno, NV, November 1989.

[29] A. Rogers and K. Pingali. Process decomposition through locality of reference. In *Proceedings of the SIGPLAN '89 Conference on Program Language Design and Implementation*, Portland, OR, June 1989.

[30] L. Snyder and D. Socha. An algorithm producing balanced partitionings of data arrays. In *Proceedings of the 5th Distributed Memory Computing Conference*, Charleston, SC, April 1990.

[31] Thinking Machines Corporation, Cambridge, MA. *CM Fortran Reference Manual*, version 5.2-0.6 edition, September 1989.

[32] M. J. Wolfe. Semi-automatic domain decomposition. In *Proceedings of the 4th Conference on Hypercube Concurrent Computers and Applications*, Monterey, CA, March 1989.

[33] J. Wu, J. Saltz, S. Hiranandani, and H. Berryman. Runtime compilation methods for multicomputers. In *Proceedings of the 1991 International Conference on Parallel Processing*, St. Charles, IL, August 1991.

[34] H. Zima, H.-J. Bast, and M. Gerndt. SUPERB: A tool for semi-automatic MIMD/SIMD parallelization. *Parallel Computing*, 6:1–18, 1988.

3 The Interaction of the Formal and the Practical in Parallel Programming Environment Development: CODE

J. Werth, J. Browne, S. Sobek, T. Lee, P. Newton, and R. Jain
University of Texas at Austin

Abstract
The most visible facet of the Computationally-Oriented Display Environment (CODE) is its graphical interface. However, the most important fact about CODE is that it is a programming system based on a formal unified computation graph model of parallel computation which was intended for actual program development. Most previous programming systems based on formal models of computation have been intended primarily to serve as specification systems. This paper focuses on the interaction between the development of the formal model of parallel computation and the development of a practical programming environment. Basing CODE on a formal model of parallel computation was integral to attainment of the initial project goals of an increase in level of abstraction of representation for parallel program structure and architectural independence. It also led to other significant research directions, such as a calculus of composition for parallel programs, and has suggested other directions of research in parallel programming that we have not yet had the opportunity to pursue. We hope this experience with the interaction of the theoretical and the practical may be of interest and benefit to other designers and developers of parallel programming systems.

I Introduction

I.1 Parallel program development: The CODE/ROPE design environment

The initial version of CODE (the Computationally-Oriented Display Environment) [4] was based upon a unified model of parallel computation defined by Browne [2, 3] and extended to have a proper formal basis by Sobek [13]. The original motivations for basing the CODE programming system on a formal model of computation were to be able to raise the level of abstraction at which parallel programs are expressed and to provide a solid foundation for the difficult problem of compiling to multiple parallel architectures. As is frequently the case in research, unplanned results arose. CODE requires, because of the level of granularity of its typical unit of computation, a component library. ROPE (the Reuseability-Oriented Parallel Environment), which implements a library capability for CODE was a response to this requirement. ROPE stores and retrieves subgraphs for insertion in CODE graphical representations of parallel programs. Observation and analysis of the process of inserting subgraphs into existing program graphs led to the observation that there was a well-defined calculus of composition for composing subgraphs representing parallel computation structures defined in the CODE representation into "larger" graphs also representing parallel computation structures. Continuation of this line of reasoning revealed that there is a full calculus (or algebra for that matter as well) of composition for parallel program structures based on the definition of program elements in CODE and ROPE [5]. Characterization of the family of program graphs has also suggested some algorithms for identification of parallelism in existing programs.

It was actually the case that the first implementation of CODE preceded the formalization of the model of parallel computation. The initial implementation has also undergone substantial revision as a result of deficiencies revealed by use. The implementation and the formal model were brought back into closer harmony in the current version of CODE, Version 1.2.

This paper first defines and illustrates the formal model of parallel computation underlying Version 1.2 of CODE. There are few if any parallel programming languages intended for production use of executable programs for which a precise formal model can be written down. The formally based parallel programming systems such as CSP [9] and UNITY [6] have not typically not been given full implementations although there are exceptions such as Linda [7]. Consistency between CODE and its model of parallel computation is possible because CODE expresses only the parallel structure of a program and because of the high level of declarative abstraction at which CODE expresses parallel structure.

Use of the formal model of parallel structure as the basis for CODE has strongly influenced its evolution. Extensions to provide greater convenience in expressing programs has been constrained to constructs which can be straightforwardly incorporated in the model of parallel computation. This has enabled us to avoid introducing inconsistent or incompletely thought-through constructs on several occasions, notably in the representation of exclusion relations. There are possibilities for analysis of safety, liveness and performance properties of executable parallel programs based on this formal model which have not yet been exploited.

I.2 An Informal Introduction to CODE/ROPE

CODE is a program development system for parallel programs. In CODE, programs are organized as graphs with three possible types of nodes and two possible types of arcs. The nodes are associated with computations, and the arcs are associated with data.

1. **Directed arcs** (denoted by arrows, also called data dependencies) indicate data being generated by the source node, and then flowing to the sink node.

2. **Hyperarcs** (undirected arcs potentially joining more than two nodes, denoted by dotted lines and also called exclusion dependencies) indicate data which is shared by the computations represented by the nodes joined by the hyperarc. The hyperarcs have associated constraints that control access to the data; this is the basic mechanism for preventing race conditions.

3. **Schedulable Units of Computation (SUC)** nodes (denoted by circles) are associated with some computation. They are distinguished by only being able to execute when data is present on all incoming directed arcs. They place data on all of their outgoing directed arcs at the end of their execution.

4. **Switch nodes** (denoted by diamonds) perform specialized computations associated with making choices as well as merging and distributing data. They are enabled for execution if data is present on any input arc. These nodes may also place data on any subset of their outgoing directed arcs after execution.

5. **Subgraph nodes** (denoted by boxes) encapsulate computations performed by entire graphs.

Program development with CODE requires first specifying the graph (which represents the overall organization of the computation) and then providing details about each graph element:

• For SUC nodes, the user supplies a computation in the form of a subprogram which may come from a library or be written from scratch.

• For switch nodes, the user supplies a condition on each input arc which describes the conditions under which data on that arc are to be passed through the node and on to the destination node(s) to which it is routed.

• For directed arcs, the user supplies a data name and data type.

• For hyperarcs, the user supplies a data name, a data type and a data sharing constraint to be preserved by the system among the nodes sharing the data. (We will see later that this condition is actually specified by annotating the nodes)

Once program development is complete, the user is able to request translation of the program to any of several executable forms. Each executable form is targeted to the specific hardware and software environment in which the program will be executed. By analogy with the compilation process, the system specific portion of CODE which creates these executables is called a backend. The current version of the software supports backends for Ada and Fortran on a variety of architectures.

ROPE[11] is a software reuse system integrated with CODE. The user model is essentially one of selecting a subgraph from a library and then connecting that subgraph to the CODE graph under construction by using data dependencies and exclusion dependencies. The user may also create new modules and insert them in the library.

The implementation of CODE/ROPE is distinguished by the software engineering features which have been incorporated to facilitate its practical use. These features encompass the user interface, provisions for reuse of program fragments, and facilities for structuring programs. The system has been through several versions and has had substantial use by graduate and undergraduate students in classes.

II A Formal Definition of the Unified Computation Graph Model

The purpose of this section is to give a formal notation for the model of computation used in the definition of Versions 1.0 and 1.2 of the CODE/ROPE systems developed at the University of Texas at Austin. Though these definitions differ to some degree from those of [13], closely related material may be found there. The approach taken here is fairly general and in some cases contains ideas not actually implemented in CODE 1.2. Notes are supplied to indicate limitations of the existing CODE/ROPE system. A new version, CODE/ROPE 2.0, is currently under development; it is based on a further enriched model of parallel computation with complete realization of the model of computation [12].

The formal definition is organized as follows.

1.   The elements of the unified model of parallel computation are defined in set notation in terms of a graph model, the **Unified Computation Graph (UCG)** model (Section II).

2.   The semantics of each element of the model are specified as they are realized in CODE 1.2 (Section III).

3.   The graph model is shown to lead naturally to a formal definition of a reuseable component as any full closed subgraph of a **UCG** (Section IV).

Sections II and IV are necessarily quite formal. While the formality is essential to completeness, the concepts are simple and what is essential for extracting the content of the rest of the paper can be obtained by reading the definitions and the explanatory notes, the italicized intuitive notes and Section III.

Definition II.1. Type System

Given a countably infinite set of values U, a type system is a family of subsets of U called types. There are n distinguished subsets B1,. ., Bn of U called **basic types.** There is also a set of strings called identifiers or names. These subsets and strings together constitute a type system, T. We write n:t if identifier n has type t. A **type, t,** is either

1. A basic type
2. U
3. (Records) The union of the sets {Namej} X tj where Namej is an identifier and tj is a type, given a fixed set of names and types, Name1,. ., Namem and t1,. ., tm.
4. (Arrays) If I1,. ., Im are finite totally ordered sets and t is a type then the set of functions f: I1 X I2 X...X Im -> t is a type.

Definition II.2.

A **Unified Computation Graph (UCG),** G, is a tuple (S, D, E, T)

S is the set of **nodes,** s, of G.

D is the set of **data dependencies,** d, of G.

E is the set of **exclusion dependencies,** e, of G.

T is some **type system**

Definition II.3. A Data dependency d has an associated pair of nodes, s1 = Source(d), s2 = Sink(d), a type t = T(d), and a name N(d).

There are unique start (sI) and end (sO) nodes in S(G) and G has the property that for every node s there is a directed path from sI to sO passing through s. There is a unique data dependency du from sI to sO. The trivial UCG for type system T is ({sI,sO}, {du}, {},T). We assume there are no dependencies with sink sO and source sI except du.

An **Input data dependency** d is one with source(d) = sI; that is. d= ((sI, s), n:t)

An **Output data dependency** d is one with sink(d) = sO; that is. d= ((s, sO), n:t)

Intuitively a data dependency is a buffer which carries a sequence of typed values from source to sink.

Notation II.1.

We use an operator style notation; for example, if G is a UCG then S(G) is the set of nodes, D(G) is the set of data dependencies of G.

a. If d is a data dependency then

S(d) = {Source(d), Sink(d)}, the node set of the dependency

b. If s is a node then

In(s) = {d | Sink(d) = s)}, Out(s) = {d | Source(d) = s)}

D(s) = In(s) union Out(s), E(s) = {e | s ∈ S(e) }

c. If G is a UCG then

ID(G) is the set of input dependencies contained in D(G)

OD(G) is the set of output dependencies contained in D(G)

IOD(G) = ID(G) ∪ OD(G) is called the **I/O dependencies** of G

IND(G) = D(G) - IOD(G) is called the **internal dependencies** of G

CODE 1.2 Implementation Notes

1. The only types, t, which may appear are integer, character, boolean, real, and arrays of these of dimension less than or equal 2.

2. Nodes sI and sO are not explicitly mentioned for main graphs; in subgraphs they are called To-Node (sO) and From-Node (sI).

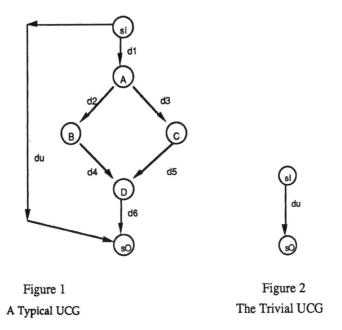

Figure 1	Figure 2
A Typical UCG	The Trivial UCG

Figure 1 might be a program which generates a vector of integers in A, while B and C sort the list into sublists of even and odd integers and D prints the two lists. d2, d3, d4 and d5 are data dependencies each of which carries a vector of integers. sI, sO, d1, d6 and du, while they are not essential to the specification of a computation are necessary to the definition of reuseable components for the UCG model.

Definition II.4. Exclusion Constraint

An exclusion constraint, ec, on a set S, is a function on the power set P of S to {true, false} such that

    i. $ec(\{\}) = true$,   ii. $ec(\{s\}) = true$ for every $s \in S$ and

    iii. if V is a subset of P, $ec(V) = true$, and R is a subset of V, then $ec(R) = true$.

Definition II.5.

Let ec be an exclusion constraint on S and let M be a subset of S. M is a **max-run set** if $ec(M) = true$ and $ec(N) = false$ for any superset N of M.

Intuitively an exclusion constraint is a predicate which evaluates to true or false when acting on subsets of nodes of a UCG.

Lemma II.1.   Let ec be an exclusion constraint for S, then clearly

    a. If V is any set for which $ec(V) = true$ then there exists a max-run set containing V.

    b. If {Mi} is the set of all max-run sets for the constraint ec, then $\cup$ Mi $= S$.

    c. The set of max-run sets uniquely determines ec

Definition II.6.   Let {Mi} be the set of all max-run sets for the constraint ec.

    a. **Share(ec)** $= \cap$ Mi

    b. If the Mi are pairwise disjoint then ec is said to be **mutex**. If they are singleton sets ec is said to be **strong mutex**

    c. An exclusion constraint ec' for S' is **weaker than** exclusion constraint ec for S (or ec is **stronger than** ec'), if $S \supseteq S'$ and for every subset V of S', $ec(V) = true$ implies $ec'(V) = true$. We write $ec' < ec$.

Intuitively, the sets of nodes for which the exclusion constraint evaluates to true can execute in parallel with conformance to the specifications of the computation.

Definition II.7.

An **Exclusion Dependency**, e, has an associated set of nodes S(e), a type $t = T(e)$, a name $n = N(e)$, and an exclusion constraint $ec = EC(e)$ on S(e). EC(G) is the set of exclusion constraints, ec, of the UCG, G

Intuitively, an exclusion dependency synchronizes the execution of a set of nodes to conform to the semantics of the computation as expressed in an exclusion constraint.

Definition II.8.

A node, **n**, is a two-tuple, **n(firing rule**, relation).

Definition II.9.

A **firing rule, fr**, is a predicate over the state of the input dependencies, In(s), of a node. *Intuitively the relation is executed in finite time after the predicate of the firing rule evaluates to true.*

Two UCGs are **equivalent** if they differ at most in the names associated with their nodes and data and exclusion dependencies

CODE 1.2 Implementation Notes

1.   A node may take part in at most one exclusion dependency.

2.   CODE 1.2 allows only two types of exclusion dependencies, those in which S(e)=Share(EC(e)) and those in which EC(e) is strong mutex.

III. Semantics

Roughly, one can picture the CODE 1.2 execution model as a dataflow graph which allows more flexible execution rules for some node types and which allows data sharing among the nodes. However, there are many other features which are further discussed below. The nodes are "black boxes" with their properties reflected only by their behavior at their interfaces.

III.1. Data Dependencies

Data dependencies are like pipes, with a buffering capacity, that connect nodes. If there are items in the buffer then the dependency is said to be bound, otherwise it is unbound. The capacity of the buffers is an implementation issue that effects the semantics of the model. In CODE 1.2 the capacity is nominally infinite.

III.2. Nodes

During execution, a node n of a UCG, G, may be in one of the states: idle, ready, or running. Legal transitions are from idle to ready to running to idle. There are two types of node:

1. A **SUC**, s, is a unit of computation with the properties that

a.   When the computation changes state from running to not-running then data is placed on every output data dependency.

b. When the computation changes state from ready to running one data item is removed from each member of In(s).

2. A **Switch** s a unit of computation with the properties that

a. Data is consumed from one non-deterministically selected element of In(s) (which must be bound) when the state changes from ready-to-run to running.

b. Data are placed in a subset of Out(s) when state changes from running to not-running

In CODE 1.2, switches are limited in the computations they may perform. They may test data on a single input arc only, and based on that data alone, they may distribute the data, unchanged to a subset of the output data dependencies. They may not participate in exclusion dependencies.

A node, n, is eligible to be promoted **from idle to ready** if sufficient data is available on its input dependency arcs. For SUCs this means that data is available on all input dependencies; that is, the state of d is bound for all d in In(s) {see below}. For switches it means that at least one element of In(d) is bound.

A node is eligible to be promoted from **ready to running** if doing so leaves the exclusion constraints in which it participates satisfied {see below}. On such a transition, one item is removed form each of the elements of In(n) for SUCs and from a single non-deterministically chosen element of In(n) for switches.

A node is always eligible to be promoted from **running to idle**. On such a transition, one item is placed in each element of Out(n) for SUCs and in some data-dependent subset of Out(n) in the case of switches.

III.3 Exclusion Dependencies

If e is an exclusion dependency then there is assumed to be some object of type t which is shared by the elements of S(e) according to the discipline described by ec = EC(e). Consequently if V is a subset of S(e), ec(V) = true is the statement that it is permissible to have every node in V running, and every node of S - V not-running. This expresses a constraint on the ability of the computations associated with nodes in S(e) to access the shared data item whose type is t. Recalling the definition of exclusion constraint Definition II.4:

Condition i. means that the constraint is automatically satisfied if no node is running,

Condition ii. means that the constraint is automatically satisfied if a single node is running,

Condition iii. means that if the constraint is satisfied then if a running node changes state to idle then the constraint is still satisfied.

An interesting issue is whether i, ii and iii. are reasonable. For example, iii. does not allow the case that a set of nodes may only run if some other node is running {as in a monitor construct}.

We say exclusion dependency e1 is weaker than e2, if EC(e1) is weaker than EC(e2). This means that any set of nodes which e2 will allow to run together may run together under e1.

III.4 Subgraphs
Subgraphs are strictly a program-creation-time structuring device and have no other semantics.

III.5 State of a UCG
A **state**, s, of a CODE graph is defined by two functions

f_s: S(G) -> {idle, ready, running}

g_s: D(G) -> {bound, unbound} X N

The **initial state** is

F(n)= idle for all n in S(G) - sI

F(sI) = ready

G(d)= (unbound, 0) for all d in D(G)

The **terminated state** has F(n) = idle for all n.

III.6 Firing rules {UCG state transitions}
In execution it is the responsibility of the runtime system to maintain the truth of all exclusion constraints. The way this has been done in CODE 1.2 is to use the following technique for starting computations:

From the nodes that are ready, a single node is chosen and started. This node must have the property that if it is started, then no exclusion dependency will be invalidated. This is then repeated until no ready nodes exist.

IV Composition and Decomposition of Dependencies
To reach our goal of describing the composition of UCGs we must first describe how to compose and decompose dependencies. Ultimately these dependencies couple the interfaces of the components into parallel computation structures.

Definition IV.1. Compose two data dependencies
If G is a graph with data dependencies d1 and d2 with d1 = ((s1, sO), n1:t1) and d2 = ((sI, s2), n2:t2), s1 <> sI and s2 <> sO, and if t = t1 = t2 then the graph G' obtained by

composing d1 and d2 is created by deleting d1 and d2 from G and adding the dependency d = ((s1, s2), n':t).

The intuition is that if an output data dependency of one node and an input dependency of another node match in type then the two dependencies can be joined to establish a data dependency between the node pair.

Definition IV.2. Decompose a data dependency

If G is a graph with data dependency d and d = ((s1,s2), n:t) where s1 <> sI and s2 <> sO, then the graph G' obtained by decomposing d is created by removing the dependency d from G and adding the pair of dependencies d1 = ((s1, sO), n:t) and d2 = ((sI, s2), n:t).

The intuition is that decomposition of a data dependency creates an input dependency/output dependency pair to be matched when the nodes are composed into a larger graph.

Definition IV.3. Projection of an exclusion dependency.

Let e be an exclusion dependency. Let S' be any subset of S(e). The projection of e on S', written e proj S', is an exclusion dependency e' defined as follows:

    1. S(e') = S'

    2. ec' = EC(e') is defined as follows: If V is a subset of S(e') then ec'(V) = true iff ec(V) = true. ec' is also referred to as a projection of EC(e).

    3. T(e') = T(e)

    4. N(e') = N(e)

A projection of an exclusion dependency maintains for subsets of nodes from the exclusion dependency the synchronization conditions for those subsets in the original exclusion constraint.

Definition IV.4. Consistent exclusion dependencies

If e1 and e2 are exclusion dependencies then they are consistent if

    e1 proj (S(e1) ∩ S(e2)) = e2 proj (S(e1) ∩ S(e2))

    Note that if S(e1) ∩ S(e2) = { }, then e1 and e2 are consistent.

Two exclusion dependencies can be composed into a single exclusion dependency if the projections of each with their intersection are equal.

Definition IV.5. Composing two consistent exclusion dependencies

If G is a UCG and e1 and e2 are two consistent exclusion dependencies in G where t = T(e1) = T(e2) and if ec is an exclusion constraint such that EC(e1) = ec proj S(e1), and EC(e2) = ec proj S(e2) then the graph G' is obtained by **composing e1 and e2** as follows: e1 and e2 are removed from G and the exclusion dependency e is added where $T(e) = t$, $N(e) = n'$, $S(e)=S(e1) \cup S(e2)$, and $EC(e) = ec$. If the max-run sets of e are exactly the max-run sets of e1 together with those of e2 then we say e is the **strongest** composition of e1 and e2, denoted e_{st}. If the max-run sets of e are all possible pairwise unions of a max-run set of e1 together with a max-run set of e2 then e is the **weakest** composition of e1 and e2, denoted e_{wk}. We say e is the composition of e1 and e2.

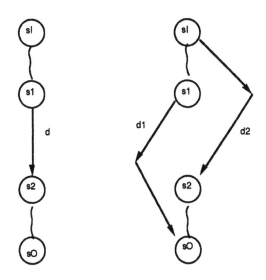

Figure 3

d is the composition of d1 and d2. d1 and d2 are the decomposition of d.

The following lemma assures us that the projections of a composition of two consistent exclusion dependencies are the original dependencies. Also, if e is any composition of e1 and e2 then e will be weaker than the strongest composition and stronger than the weakest composition of e1 and e2.

Lemma IV.1 If e is a composition of e1 and e2 then

  i. $e1 = e \text{ proj } S(e1)$
  ii. $e2 = e \text{ proj } S(e2)$
  iii. $e_{wk} < e < e_{st}$

The exclusion constraint ec associated with an exclusion dependency e obtained by composition of two exclusion constraints e1 and e2 is is the range of constraints defined by the relations EC(e1) = ec proj S(e1) and EC(e2) = ec proj S(e2).

CODE 1.2 Implementation Note

In the case of share constraints Code 1.2 assigns ec to be e_{wk}. In the case of strong mutex constraints Code 1.2 assigns ec to be e_{st}.

V Subgraphs

Definition V.1. A **subgraph**, G', of a UCG, G, is a UCG such that

1. Nodes. $S(G) \supseteq S(G')$

2. Data Dependencies

   a. $d \in IND(G') \Rightarrow S(G') \supseteq S(d) \wedge d \in IND(G)$

      {An internal data dependency of G' is an internal data dependency of G with both its nodes in G'}

   b. $d' \in IOD(G') \Rightarrow$

      i. $d' \in IOD(G)$ or

      ii. there is a $d \in IND(G)$ and some d" such that $d = d' \mid d"$

      {Input and output dependencies come from those of G or they are created by decomposing dependencies of G}

3. Exclusion Dependencies

$e' \in E' \Rightarrow$ there exists $e \in E$ such that $e' = e$ proj S'

{Every exclusion dependency of G' is derived from one of G}

Definition V.2.

A **full subgraph**, G', of a UCG, G, is a subgraph such that each of the '⇒'s in 2 and 3 is replaced by '⇔'.

The intuition is that a subgraph is a subset of nodes and a set of data dependencies which are either from the original graph or arise from decomposing data dependencies whose sinks and sources are not both in the subset.. The subgraph is full if all possible dependencies are included. Exclusion dependencies of the subgraph must be projections of those in the original graph. Note that we allow single node exclusion dependencies. This is so they may be rejoined on a composition.

Code 1.2 Implementation Notes

1. The CODE/ROPE system allows any full subgraph of a UCG to be identified and stored in the library of reusable modules.

2. The CODE/ROPE system allows any full subgraph of a UCG to be identified and replaced with a single symbol. This allows hierarchical structuring of the graph under development.

VI Applicability of Model of Computation

The applicability of a programming system is based not only on its representational power but also its representational efficiency. The underlying model of computation is complete as has been shown by Brock [1]. The interesting question to be answered is, "What is the class of parallel programs which can be readily expressed in the CODE/ROPE programming system?" "Readily" is a concept such as beauty which is measurable only in terms of individual reactions. CODE/ROPE has been fairly widely used in classes and in experimental studies with very positive results [11]. There have been reports in the literature on several significant programs written in CODE/ROPE [10]. An informal opinion is that the current CODE/ROPE 1.2 is effectively restricted to algorithms which result in static or at most parameterized graphs such as result from the unrolling of loops. In fact, the approach we have taken in the CODE/ROPE project is: design, implement,use, evaluation and redesign. CODE/ROPE 2 utilizes a much more dynamic model of programming and should relieve this limitation.

VII Conclusion

The development of CODE and ROPE has been focused and directed by interaction with the formal model of parallel computation upon which they are founded. The role of CODE and ROPE has been to identify the requirements for a practical parallel programming environment while the formal model has first enabled a consistent evolution of the programming environment and then supplied directions for extending the programming environment to include significant capabilities not in view when the system was first being developed.

VIII Acknowledgements

This research was supported by the IBM Corporation through grant 61653 and by the State of Texas through TATP Project 003658-237.

References

1. Brock, J., and Ackerman, W., Scenarios: A Model of Non-determinate Computation, In *Lecture Notes in Computer Science #107*, Springer-Verlag, New York, 1981.

2. Browne, J., Formulation and Programming of Parallel Computations: A Unified Approach, *Proceedings IEEE International Conference of Parallel Programming*, 1985.

3. Browne, J., Framework for Formulation and Analysis of Parallel Computation Structures, *Parallel Computing 3*, 1986, 1-9.

4. Browne, J., Azam, M. and Sobek, S. CODE: A Unified Approach to Parallel Programming, *IEEE Software 6*, July 1989, 10-19.

5. Browne, J., Werth, J. and Lee, T.J. Intersection of Parallel Structuring and Reuse of Software Components: A Calculus of Composition of Components for Parallel Programs, *Proceedings of the 1989 International Conference on Parallel Processing*, August 1989.

6. Chandy, K. M. and Misra, J. *Parallel Program Design*, Addison-Wesley, New York, 1988.

7. Gelenter, D., Parallel Programming in Linda, *Proceedings IEEE International Conference of Parallel Programming*, 1985, 281-291.

8 Goguen, J., Reusing and Interconnecting Software Components, *IEEE Computer*, Feb. 1986.

9. Hoare, C. A. R., Communicating Sequential Processes, *CACM 21*, August 1978.

10. Jain, R., Werth, J. and Browne, J. C. An Experimental Study of the Effectiveness of High Level Parallel Programming, *Proceedings of the 1991 SIAM Meeting on Parallel Computation*.

11. Lee, T. J., Werth, J. and Browne, J. C. Experimental Evaluation of a Reusability-Oriented Parallel Programming Environment, *IEEE Transactions on Software Engineering*, Vol. 16, No. 2, February 1990.

12. Newton, P. CODE 2.0 Prototype, unpublished manuscript, Department of Computer Science, University of Texas at Austin, July 1991.

13. Sobek, S.A Constructive Unified Model of Parallel Computation, Ph.D. Dissertation, Department of Computer Science, University of Texas at Austin, December 1990.

4   Hierarchical Concurrency in Jade

D. Scales, M. Rinard, M. Lam, and J. Anderson
Stanford University

Abstract

Jade is a data-oriented language for exploiting coarse-grain parallelism. A Jade programmer simply augments a serial program with assertions specifying how the program accesses data. The Jade implementation dynamically interprets these assertions, using them to execute the program concurrently while enforcing the program's data dependence constraints. Jade has been implemented as extensions to C, FORTRAN, and C++, and currently runs on the Encore Multimax, Silicon Graphics IRIS 4D/240S, and the Stanford DASH multiprocessors. In this paper, we show how Jade programmers can naturally express hierarchical concurrency patterns by specifying how a program uses hierarchically structured data.

1   Introduction

Jade is a data-oriented language for expressing coarse-grain concurrency. Instead of using explicit control constructs to express the concurrency available in a program, a Jade programmer augments a serial program with Jade constructs that declare how the various sections of the program access data. The Jade implementation uses this information to execute the program concurrently while enforcing the program's underlying data dependence constraints. Jade programmers therefore create coarse-grain parallel programs that preserve the semantics of the original serial programs.

A Jade programmer first divides a sequential program up into tasks. Tasks interact

This research was supported in part by DARPA contract N00014-87-K-0828.

through accesses to *shared objects*. The programmer summarizes each task's accesses by specifying which shared objects the task will read or write. The Jade implementation uses this information to relax the program's serial execution order; for example, tasks which access distinct shared objects can execute concurrently. Because each task's access specification is determined dynamically, Jade programs can exploit data-dependent concurrency available only at run time.

We may contrast Jade's data-oriented approach to concurrency with the control-oriented approach provided by many parallel programming languages [1, 2, 3, 5]. Control-oriented languages typically provide low-level constructs for creating and synchronizing parallel tasks. These constructs provide precise control over the concurrent behavior of a program. However, it can be difficult to create and maintain parallel programs which contain such a low-level specification of the concurrency structure. Programmers using these low-level constructs must often establish explicit synchronization connections between logically unrelated modules which access the same data. These connections violate the modular structure of the original serial program, making the parallel program harder to understand and modify.

Jade, with its data-oriented constructs, provides a less familiar but conceptually higher-level approach to concurrency. Jade programs only contain local information about the pieces of data that tasks read and write. The Jade implementation, not the programmer, extracts and enforces the global concurrency pattern implicit in the program's data dependence constraints. By requiring only local data usage information, Jade promotes modularity in parallel programs.

Data-oriented expression of parallelism is not limited to simple concurrency patterns. Simple data structures can be used for simple concurrency patterns such as dynamic task graphs and pipelining [4]. This paper shows that more complicated patterns such as nested levels of parallelism can be achieved via hierarchically structured data. For example, the Jade implementation can generate a parallel tree traversal from a specification of how a program accesses nodes and subtrees. Similarly, a Jade program that accesses a matrix hierarchically as a collection of columns may create a task to perform a matrix operation, which in turn creates tasks to perform the operation on each of the columns in the matrix.

The organization of this paper is as follows. We first briefly review the basic concepts of Jade: the shared objects and the language constructs. We then demonstrate how the use of hierarchical data structures in Jade programs leads to hierarchical concurrency patterns. We also illustrate how the structure of the data hierarchy can be used to refine incrementally the specified accesses of tasks. Finally, we show that hierarchical concurrency makes the generation of concurrency in a Jade program more efficient.

2 Shared Objects

Each Jade task contains a section of code declaring which shared objects the task will read or write. The programmer uses a synchronization abstraction called *tokens* to express how the task will access data. The programmer first decides on the granularity at which tasks will access each piece of data, then associates a token with each piece of data at that level of granularity. To declare that a task will access a given piece of data, the programmer uses an *access specification operation* applied to the corresponding token.

Each token has rd and wr access specification operations, specifying, respectively, a read access and a write access. Two access specifications *conflict* if they refer to the same token and at least one of them specifies a write access. Tasks with conflicting access specifications must execute in the original serial execution order to maintain the serial semantics of a program.

Jade programmers usually encapsulate data and the tokens which represent the data as an object. (We use the C++ class notation below to make this encapsulation more apparent.) Each such object provides its own access specification interface, implementing its access specification operations internally using its private tokens. In the simplest such use of tokens, the programmer associates one token with each object and augments the object's interface with the appropriate access specification operations. The following SharedMatrix class illustrates such a use. This class directly translates its access specification operations into operations on its private token. (We describe the df_rd, df_wr, no_rd and no_wr access operations in sections 3.2.2 and 3.2.1.)

```
class SharedMatrix {
     token _token;
     double elements[N][N];
  public:
     void read_matrix() { _token.rd(); };
     void write_matrix() { _token.wr(); };
     void df_read_matrix() { _token.df_rd(); };
     void df_write_matrix() { _token.df_wr(); };
     void no_read_matrix() { _token.no_rd(); };
     void no_write_matrix() { _token.no_wr(); };
     . . .
}
```

This practice of associating one token with each object works well for data that is created and accessed as a unit. In section 4 we will show how a Jade programmer can create token hierarchies that correspond to the hierarchical structure of the data. These token hierarchies allow the programmer to specify naturally how tasks manipulate hierarchically structured shared objects.

3 Jade Constructs

Jade is a language for declaratively expressing data usage information; the names of the Jade constructs reflect this declarative perspective. The Jade implementation assigns an operational meaning to Jade programs by using this data usage information to create concurrency and synchronization. In this section we present the Jade constructs, giving both the declarative and operational meanings.

3.1 Basic Constructs

Jade programmers use the `withonly` construct to declare how a section of code will access shared objects:

```
withonly { access specification } do ( parameters ) {
    task body
}
```

The Jade implementation creates a task when it executes a `withonly` construct. The `task body` contains the serial code to be executed when the task runs. The `parameters` section contains a list of variables from the enclosing environment. The values of these parameters are copied into the task's context when it is created. In this way, the new task can reference shared objects that are only locally visible in the enclosing scope.

The `access specification` section declares how the task will access shared objects. This section is an arbitrary piece of code containing access specification operations. The implementation executes this piece of code when the task is created to determine which shared objects the task will read and/or write. This section may contain dynamically resolved variable references and control flow constructs such as conditionals, loops and function calls. The programmer may therefore use information available only at run time when declaring how a task will access data.

The `withonly` construct indicates that the task body will execute *with only* the accesses declared in the access specification section. The Jade implementation uses the access specification to determine when two tasks can execute concurrently. Tasks whose access specifications do not conflict are free to execute concurrently. Conversely, tasks with conflicting access specifications must execute in the original serial execution order. To enforce this restriction, the Jade implementation does not allow a task to execute until all earlier tasks (in the underlying sequential execution order) with conflicting access specifications have completed.

We illustrate the use of the `withonly` construct with a simple example. The following Update routine creates a task to update a `SharedMatrix`:

```
void Update(SharedMatrix *M) {
   withonly { M->read_matrix(); M->write_matrix(); } do (M) {
      /* code to update the matrix */
   }
}
```

The created task can run concurrently with tasks accessing other shared objects, but must execute serially with respect to other tasks which access M. For example, the following code fragment takes pointers to two SharedMatrices A and B, and either updates A twice or updates both A and B:

```
Update(A);
if (flag > 0)
   Update(B);
else
   Update(A);
```

If flag is not positive, then both Updates operate on the matrix A. The Jade implementation will therefore serialize the tasks because their access specifications conflict. However, when flag is positive, the two Update tasks can execute concurrently because they modify different matrices.

This example demonstrates how a Jade program can exploit dynamically available concurrency. Because the access specification of the withonly construct is executed when a task is created, a Jade program can build up a dynamic task graph and exploit concurrency between tasks that is dependent on input data.

3.2 Advanced Constructs

It is the programmer's responsibility to ensure that the Jade program accurately declares how each task will access data. Given accurate access specifications, the Jade implementation can exploit concurrency available in the program while still preserving the semantics of the original serial program. However, the amount of concurrency that the Jade implementation can exploit depends on the precision with which the accesses are specified.

We have demonstrated how the execution of the access specification of the withonly at run-time allows the programmer to be precise about the accesses of a task that vary in a data-dependent manner. However, the withonly construct only allows accesses to be specified at the granularity of a task. More complicated concurrency patterns can be expressed by providing more detailed information about accesses during the execution of a task.

Consider the following code fragment, which operates on three SharedMatrices A, B, and C:

```
Update(A);
withonly {
    A->read_matrix(); B->read_matrix();
    C->write_matrix();
} do (A, B, C) {
    Matrix *Tmp = f(B);
    g(Tmp, A, C); /* modify C as a function of Tmp and A */
}
Update(B);
```

Based on the definition of Update above, the two Update calls create tasks to modify A and B respectively; the withonly between the two Update calls creates another task which reads A and B and modifies C. The first two tasks conflict in their declared accesses to A and the second and third tasks conflict in their specified accesses to B; hence, based on the above code, the three tasks execute serially. However, there is some available concurrency between the tasks which is not exploited. The second task does not read matrix A immediately, so the call to f in the second task can run concurrently with the first task. Similarly, the second task completes it access to B early, so the call to g in the second task can run concurrently with the third task.

To allow accesses to be specified with more precision, Jade provides the with construct, which allows a task's access specification to be updated dynamically during the execution of the task:

```
with { access specification } cont;
```

As in the withonly construct, the access specification section is an arbitrary piece of code containing access specification operations. The changes to the access specification indicated by the with construct apply to the remainder (continuation) of the current task, as suggested by the cont keyword. Using the with construct and the variants of the basic access specification operations described in the next two sections, the Jade programmer can incrementally update a task's access specification to keep it as precise as possible.

3.2.1 Deferred Accesses

We can describe a task's accesses with more precision by indicating that some of the declared accesses of a task will occur sometime after the task begins execution, rather than immediately. For example, the second task above does not access matrix A until after the call to f. In this case, we say that the task's access to A is *deferred*. The programmer can express such deferred accesses at task creation time using the df_rd (deferred read) and df_wr (deferred write) access specification operations. The programmer indicates when the task will actually access the shared object using the with construct. We say that such a with construct converts the deferred access to an *immediate* access.

In our example, we modify the second task to declare a deferred access to matrix A and convert it to an immediate access just before A is used as in the call to g:

```
Update(A);
withonly {
    A->df_read_matrix(); B->read_matrix();
    C->write_matrix();
} do (A, B, C) {
    Matrix *Tmp = f(B);
    with { A->read_matrix(); } cont;
    g(Tmp, A, C);
}
Update(B);
```

A task with a deferred access to a shared object can run even if previous tasks have not yet completed conflicting accesses to that object. The task will wait for the previous tasks to complete their accesses only when it executes a `with` statement which converts the deferred access to an immediate access. Deferred accesses allow the Jade implementation to execute concurrently the non-conflicting parts of tasks with access conflicts. In the example, deferred accesses allow the call to f in the second task to execute concurrently with the `Update(A)` task.

3.2.2 Completed Accesses

A task's accesses can also be specified with more precision by indicating when a task has finished accessing a piece of data. For example, the second task above does not access B after the call to f has finished. We say that the task has *completed* its access to B. Programmers express completed accesses during the execution of a task by using the `with` construct in conjunction with the no_rd (no future read) and no_wr (no future write) access operations. Hence, in our example, we augment the existing `with` to also specify a completed access to B after the call to f:

```
Update(A);
withonly {
    A->df_read_matrix(); B->read_matrix();
    C->write_matrix();
} do (A, B, C) {
    Matrix *Tmp = f(B);
    with { A->read_matrix(); B->no_read_matrix(); } cont;
    g(Tmp, A, C);
}
Update(B);
```

The combination of a with construct and no_rd and/or no_wr access operations allows the programmer to reduce a task's access specification dynamically during the execution of the task. This reduction may eliminate conflicts between the task executing the with and other tasks occurring later in the sequential execution order. The later tasks may therefore be able to execute as soon as the with completes. In the absence of the with, these tasks would have had to wait until the first task finished. In our example, the with construct allows the Update(B) task to execute concurrently with the call to g.

In this section, we have described the constructs used by the Jade programmer to declare how a program accesses shared objects. The basic Jade construct, withonly, allows the Jade programmer to specify the accesses of a task via a dynamically executed access specification. The with construct provides more precision by allowing the access specification of a task to be updated while the task is executing. The with construct can be used for converting deferred accesses, declared using df_rd and df_wr access operations, to immediate accesses; it can also be used for declaring completed accesses via the no_rd and no_wr access operations. By using with to update a task's access specification incrementally, a Jade program can exploit concurrency that requires synchronization during the execution of tasks.

4 Hierarchical Shared Objects

Programmers frequently organize the data of an object in a hierarchical fashion, as a method of hiding complexity, structuring access to the data, and promoting modularity. Different parts of the program may access the data at different levels of the hierarchy. Because Jade adopts a data-oriented approach to concurrency, it is natural for the concurrency pattern of a Jade program to assume the same hierarchical structure as the data on which it operates. A Jade program may therefore preserve the complexity hiding and modularity advantages of the original serial program. In this section we show how the programmer uses hierarchical access specifications to create concurrency patterns that match the hierarchical structure of the data.

Let us reconsider the matrix update routine described above. Suppose that the programmer can decompose the matrix update into a set of independent column updates. To exploit the concurrency available between column updates, the programmer must be able to express the Update operation's column-oriented data usage pattern. The programmer therefore creates a token for each column and defines access specification operations on the columns, in addition to those on the whole matrix:

```
class SharedColumnMatrix {
    token _token;
    token _column_token[N];
    double elements[N][N];
  public:
    SharedColumnMatrix();
    void read_column(int i) { _column_token[i].rd(); };
    void write_column(int i) { _column_token[i].wr(); };
    . . .
}
```

Because the column tokens' data are part of matrix token's data, there is a hierarchical relationship between the column tokens and the matrix token. The programmer declares this hierarchical relationship when the matrix is created using the token's sub_token operation:

```
SharedColumnMatrix :: SharedColumnMatrix() {
  /* Other matrix initialization code */

  for (int i = 0; i < N; i++) {
    _column_token[i].sub_token(_token);
  }
}
```

We say that the column tokens are *sub-tokens* of the matrix token, and the matrix token is their *super-token*. Any token that is part of a token hierarchy is called a *hierarchical token*.

The matrix is now expressed as a hierarchical shared object which may be viewed either as a single shared object (the matrix), or as a collection of lower-level shared objects (the columns). Because the matrix has been decomposed in this way, the programmer can implement an update operation which exploits concurrency between column operations on the same matrix. The new update task can perform the column updates concurrently:

```
void Update(SharedColumnMatrix *M) {
  withonly { M->df_write_matrix(); } do (M) {
    for (int i = 0; i < N; i++) {
      withonly { M->write_column(i); } do (M, i) {
        /* code to update column i */
      }
    }
  }
}
```

This example contains three hierarchies: a data hierarchy (i.e., the matrix is decomposed into columns), a token hierarchy (which is an abstraction of the data hierarchy), and a task hierarchy (i.e., the Update task is hierarchically decomposed into column update tasks). The match between the data and token hierarchies allows the programmer to express naturally the available concurrency of the Update operation. In addition, the use of the token hierarchy is a natural data hiding technique: it allows a high-level task to specify its accesses at a high level. The task's access specification need not change if the lower-level decomposition of the data changes.

The Jade implementation correctly synchronizes accesses at different levels of the hierarchy. For example, the Jade implementation will serialize two tasks if one declares a column access and the other declares a conflicting matrix access. Also, as the preceding example demonstrates, programmers can specify a deferred access at one level of the hierarchy and then specify an immediate access at a lower level.

We have shown how Jade programmers exploit concurrency within a shared object's operation. Jade's data-oriented approach to hierarchical concurrency, however, also allows the programmer to express the concurrency available across operations. The following example, which applies several Update operations to SharedColumnMatrices, exploits concurrency between matrix operations (the Update operations on A and B run completely in parallel) and concurrency within a matrix operation (operations on different columns of the same matrix run in parallel).

```
UpdateABA(SharedMatrix *A, SharedMatrix *B) {
    Update(A);
    Update(B);
    Update(A);
}
```

This example contains yet another form of concurrency – concurrency between the two Updates of A. As each column task of the first update of A completes, the corresponding column task of the second update of A can execute. The second column update task does not depend on the progress of any other column update task.

The synchronization between the individual column update tasks necessary to exploit this concurrency is difficult to express in control-oriented parallel languages. A programmer using such a language would typically not attempt to exploit all of the concurrency available between separate matrix updates. Instead, the programmer would ensure that successive column updates occur serially by using a full barrier between successive matrix updates. This barrier would waste available concurrency by unnecessarily serializing updates to different columns. In contrast, the Jade implementation only enforces the serializations required to correctly preserve the serial semantics. Figure 1 illustrates the concurrency pattern of the preceding matrix update example.

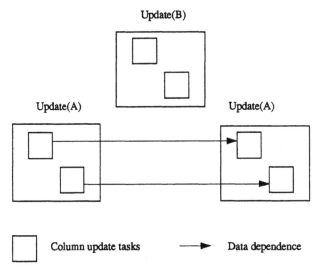

Figure 1: Concurrency Structure of `UpdateABA`

5 Refining Access Specifications

The preceding `SharedColumnMatrix` example demonstrates how programmers use token hierarchies to create task hierarchies. Jade programmers can also use hierarchical tokens to refine incrementally a single task's access specification. It is sometimes impossible to determine the exact set of shared objects that a task will access at the start of the task. A token hierarchy allows a task to refine its access specification as more information becomes available. When it is created, the task declares a deferred access to a hierarchical token representing all the possible objects that the task might access. As the task runs, the set of potentially accessed objects becomes smaller. The task can then refine its access specification by specifying an access to a token lower in the hierarchy and cancelling the access to the higher-level token. This refinement of an access specification is most useful if a large amount of computation is required to determine exactly which shared objects the task will access.

As an example, suppose a program manipulates a `SharedColumnMatrix`, and the `ProcessUpdates` operation on the matrix executes a sequence of updates to individual columns of the matrix. `ProcessUpdates` is passed an array that provides information on the updates to be processed, but it still requires a lengthy computation (represented below by the function `ComputeWhichColumn`) to determine the exact column to update.

The simplest implementation of `ProcessUpdates` creates a task to do a column update only after determining the exact column to update. Such an implementation reduces the potential concurrency by serializing all of the calls to `ComputeWhichColumn`. On the other hand, if the programmer includes the `ComputeWhichColumn` computation in each task, then it is impossible to determine exactly which column the task will update at task creation time. The programmer therefore uses the hierarchical relationship between the matrix token and the column tokens to refine the access specification of the task in two stages. The task first declares a deferred write access to the entire matrix using the matrix token. When the task determines the exact column to update, it refines the task's access specification to indicate the exact column that it will update:

```
void ProcessUpdates(SharedColumnMatrix *M,
        UpdateInfo UpdateList[], int UpdateLength)
{
   for (int i = 0; i < UpdateLength; i++) {
      UpdateInfo update;

      update = UpdateList[i];
      withonly { M->df_write_matrix(); } do (M, update) {
         int column;
         column = ComputeWhichColumn(update);
         with { M->write_column(column);
               M->no_write_matrix(); } cont;
         M->UpdateColumn(column, update);
      }
   }
}
```

Refining a task's access specification as information becomes available is useful for creating concurrent tasks as early as possible. In this case each task's initial access specification is highly imprecise, but still provides the information that the task will only touch columns in the indicated matrix. Therefore, later tasks that do not access the matrix can execute concurrently with the update task. However, a subsequent task which modifies a column of the same matrix will be held up. This task can execute only after the first task declares the column access and cancels its access to the entire matrix. If the tasks modify different columns, they can then execute concurrently. If the tasks modify the same column, they must execute serially.

6 Efficient Generation of Concurrency

In the preceding sections, we have described how programmers use hierarchical tokens to express the concurrency within and across operations on hierarchical data structures. In this section, we describe how Jade extracts the concurrency pattern dynamically during the program execution. In particular, we will show how hierarchical concurrency makes the parallelization more efficient.

As described above, the `access specification` sections of Jade constructs are executable pieces of code which dynamically compute how tasks will access shared objects. Because the access specifications are computed at run-time, the Jade implementation must dynamically determine the inter-task dependences as the program executes. The execution of a Jade program may therefore be viewed as a process of dynamically creating and executing a task graph, whose edges result from conflicting accesses to shared objects by tasks. A task cannot run until all of its predecessors in the task graph have completed. In addition, a task cannot possibly execute until it has been created and added to the task graph. Therefore, the speed with which the implementation builds the graph may limit the amount of exploitable concurrency.

Let us illustrate the issues related to Jade's dynamic generation of concurrency with an example. Below we give a "flat" version of the `Update` operation which creates the column update tasks directly, rather than creating a task which in turn creates the column tasks:

```
void Update(SharedColumnMatrix *M;) {
    for (int i = 0; i < N; i++) {
        withonly { M->write_column(i); } do (M, i) {
            /* code to update column i */
        }
    }
}
```

In this flat version, the thread of control that calls the `Update` operation creates all the tasks before returning from the function. Thus, the use of the flat `Update` may delay the generation and exploitation of concurrency available in code following the call to `Update`.

Suppose the programmer wishes to `Update` two distinct matrices. First, all of the tasks are created serially in the main thread of control that calls the `Update` operations. Even if all the tasks can be executed in parallel, Amdahl's Law indicates that the serial task creation bottleneck could significantly limit the exploitable concurrency in the program. Second, the tasks which update the first matrix are all created before the tasks which update the second matrix. Thus, the concurrency available between operations on the two matrices cannot be exploited until the implementation creates all of the tasks which update the first matrix.

Hierarchical concurrency provides a natural solution to reduce the serial task creation overhead. Consider the update of two distinct matrices using the hierarchical version of `Update` given in Section 4. Because the `Update` of the first matrix immediately creates a task to create the individual column update tasks, the main thread of control proceeds directly to the `Update` of the second task. This enables the concurrent creation of the column update tasks from *both* `Update` operations. In fact, the column update tasks from the second `Update` operation can execute before the implementation creates all of the tasks from the first `Update` operation. This is possible because the access specification of each parent Update task accurately summarizes the access specifications of its column update tasks. Thus, hierarchical concurrency parallelizes the task creation overhead and relaxes the task creation order to expose concurrency early.

Let us now consider the case where the parent tasks operate on the same data, as in the function UpdateABA defined in Section 4. Figure 2 displays the process of generating the concurrency in UpdateABA. The shaded area within each task box indicates the work performed by the parent task to create that task. The shaded lines indicate serial execution within a task. For example, the main thread of control follows a path through the shaded areas of the three main Update tasks, indicating that its only work is to create these three tasks. Each of the main Update tasks, in turn, serially creates the column update tasks for that invocation of Update. The sub-task creation threads can all execute concurrently.

However, unlike the updates to B, the column tasks of the second update to A cannot execute immediately after being created. Since the top-level task of the first update to A has declared a deferred access to the entire matrix A and may potentially access A, tasks of the second update to A must at least wait until the first parent task has completed. (We depict this dependence with edges between the top-level task of the first update of A and the sub-tasks of the second update of A.) The parent task completes when it has created all the sub-tasks; it need not wait for its children to complete. In this way, parallelism between sub-tasks of the first and second updates to A is exposed as soon as all the sub-tasks of the first update are created. This process may be thought of again in terms of refinement. While the sub-tasks have not yet all been created, the withonly task declares a deferred access that includes all the possible accesses of sub-tasks. As the sub-tasks are created, they refine the access specification by indicating which task accesses which data. When all the sub-tasks have been created and the access specifications have been fully refined, the deferred access to the entire matrix declared by the withonly is no longer needed, and naturally goes away when the withonly task completes.

7 Conclusion

Jade is a language for exploiting coarse-grain concurrency in programs written in imperative programming languages. The key insight behind Jade is that concurrency is best expressed indirectly with data usage information. Because the Jade constructs express only local information about how tasks use data, Jade promotes the development of modular parallel programs. Also, large programs often manipulate complex hierarchical data structures. In this paper we have demonstrated how Jade allows programmers to express naturally the complex concurrency patterns generated by programs that operate on these data structures.

Jade programmers can create token hierarchies which match the hierarchical structure of the data. Such hierarchies allow the programmer to express tasks' accesses at different levels,

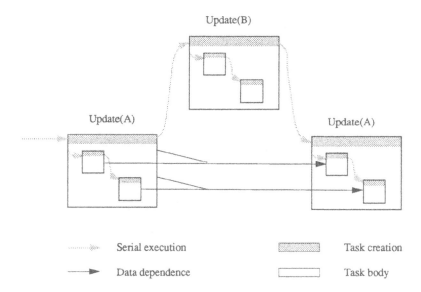

Figure 2: Dynamic Generation of Concurrency in UpdateABA

corresponding to how the tasks access the data. In this way, the programmer can express a task's accesses at the most appropriate level for that task. Expressing accesses hierarchically can also be useful for refining the access specification of a task which incrementally narrows down the set of data it can potentially access. When a programmer expresses how tasks access data in this hierarchical manner, the Jade implementation can fully exploit the natural concurrency available within and among operations on hierarchically structured data. The resulting hierarchical concurrency patterns also naturally speed up the generation of the dynamic task graph in a Jade program.

References

[1] Carriero, N., and Gelernter, D. How to Write Parallel Programs: A Guide to the Perplexed. *ACM Computing Surveys*, 21,3 (September 1989), 323–357

[2] Dongarra, J. J. and Sorenson, D. C. A portable environment for developing parallel FORTRAN programs. *Parallel Computing*, 5, 1 & 2 (1987), 175–186.

[3] Inmos Ltd. *Occam Programming Manual*. Prentice-Hall, Englewood Cliffs, N.J., 1984.

[4] M. S. Lam and M. C. Rinard. Coarse-grain parallel programming in Jade. In *Proceedings of the Third ACM/SIGPLAN Symposium on Principles and Practice of Parallel Programming* (April 1991).

[5] United States Department of Defense. *Reference Manual for the Ada programming language*. DoD, Washington, D.C., January 1983. ANSI/MIL-STD-1815A.

5 Experience in the Automatic Parallelization of Four Perfect-Benchmark Programs

R. Eigenmann, J. Hoeflinger, Z. Li, and D. Padua

University of Illinois at Urbana-Champaign

Abstract.

This paper discusses the techniques used to hand–parallelize, for the Alliant FX/80, four Fortran programs from the Perfect–Benchmark suite. The paper also includes the execution times of the programs before and after the transformations. The four programs considered here were not effectively parallelized by the automatic translators available to the authors. However, most of the techniques used for hand parallelization, and perhaps all of them, have wide applicability and can be incorporated into existing translators.

1. Introduction

It is by now widely accepted that in many real–life applications, supercomputers have been unable to deliver a reasonable fraction of their peak performance. An illustration of this is provided by the Perfect Benchmark programs [3], many of which effectively use less than 1% of the computational resources available in the most powerful supercomputers. While it is apparent that the reason for this dismal behavior is sometimes the result of the machine organization and the algorithms used, we believe that much better performance could be achieved by using more powerful compilers than those available today. In this paper we present some evidence to back this claim.

This work was supported by the U.S. Department of Energy under grant no. DOE DE–FG02–85ER25001

During the last couple of years, our group at CSRD has developed a modified version of the KAP parallelizer with optimizations for the Cedar machine [4]. We ran several simple kernels through our parallelizer and the results were satisfactory. However, when we ran the Perfect Benchmark programs, we obtained limited success or just complete failures in several of the codes for reasons that have nothing to do with the Cedar architecture or with Cedar–specific transformations, but are instead related to the general capability of the existing technology to detect and exploit parallelism. This raised questions on the effectiveness of the restructuring compiler approach in general and on the compiler framework we and many others have been using for many years. To determine the cause of the difficulties and to try to design strategies to overcome them, we decided to do hand–analyses of some of the Perfect Benchmark programs and of their restructured versions produced by the two restructuring compilers available to us: the Alliant Fortran compiler and a 1988 version of KAP.

We proceeded on a loop–by–loop basis and in each loop we tried to determine why the parallelizer had failed and then hand–manipulated the loop to exploit implicit parallelism. This manipulation was done using new transformations, most of which we believe can be easily incorporated in the parallelizers of today. The transformations we used are relatively simple extensions of well known techniques. We concentrated our work on loop parallelism because most of the existing compiler methodology is aimed at loop parallelization.

Because hand parallelization is cumbersome, we decided in this first experiment not to use Cedar [6] as our target machine but rather to use the Alliant FX/80 which is the main building block of Cedar and therefore has a simpler organization than the complete system. The Alliant FX/80 is an eight–processor shared–memory multiprocessor which includes pipelined units to process vector instructions. A speedup greater than eight is possible in this machine because of its two levels of parallelism.

In this paper we report the results of the manual analysis and transformation of four of the Perfect Benchmarks programs. The names and some of the characteristics of these are shown in Table 1. Table 2 shows the rather low speedups obtained from the parallelization option of the Alliant Fortran compiler. Similar speedups were obtained with a 1988 version of the KAP parallelizer.

We obtained a speedup about five times larger after manually transforming the programs, as shown in Table 3. These speedups can probably be improved by using better techniques or by a more careful analysis. However, we believe that the most important contribution of this paper is not the specific speedup values obtained but presenting examples for which meaningful speedup improvements can be achieved by using techniques that could be added to existing parallelizers.

2. Compiler Techniques

In this section we describe the techniques we used to parallelize those loops that the automatic parallelizers were unable to transform. Table 4 indicates which transformation we applied to the most important loops of the programs in Table 1 to obtain the speedups in Table 3.

In the discussion below, we assume that the reader is familiar with basic parallelizing compiler concepts including the notion of dependence, dependence analysis techniques and some basic transformations. Introductory material on parallelizing compilers can be found in [8], [9], and [11]. Also, all the parallel programs presented in the examples below use extensions similar to those described in the preliminary draft of the X3H5 ANSI committee that is developing parallel constructs for high level programming languages.

2.1. Run–Time Dependence Analysis

Many of the dependence analysis techniques used in today's compilers need the values of the coefficients in the subscript expressions. Most often, the precise set of values of these coefficients is needed, even though in some cases a range of values is sufficient. When some of the coefficient values are not available at compile–time, parallelizing compilers have to compute the dependence assuming that these coefficients may take on any value.

Because of this conservative assumption it is possible that compile–time dependence analysis may lead to unnecessary serialization. This happened in several multiply–nested loops of the OCEAN program, including the main loop. In these loops, the arrays causing the serializing dependences are one–dimensional and their subscripts are linear combinations of the indices of surrounding loops.

We attempted to expose this parallelism by doing the dependence test at run–time, when all coefficients are known. The test takes the form of a conditional statement which chooses between versions of the loop. If a dependence exists in the loop, the serial version of the loop is executed. Otherwise, the parallel version of the loop is executed.

The idea is to test whether the singly–dimensioned array is being used as a linearization of a multi–dimensional array. The terms of the subscripting expression are checked in order, from least significant to most significant, to determine whether or not they meet the criteria for being such a linearization. If the array is being used in this linearized fashion, then all subscript values are unique within the nest, and the loops may be parallelized.

Suppose the following expression is the subscripting expression:

$$I_1 \times K_1 + I_2 \times K_2 + \cdots + I_n \times K_n$$

in which I_i is the index of the ith (normalized) loop in the nest and K_i is the coefficient of that index in the subscripting expression. Assume that $I_1 \times K_1$ is the least significant term in the expression, $I_2 \times K_2$ is the next most significant term, and so on. Or, stated in another way,

$$\left|K_1\right| < \left|K_2\right| < \cdots < \left|K_n\right|.$$

The values for each index run from 0 up to some maximum:

$$I_i = \left[0..N_i\right].$$

The tests which we need to make are simply:

$$\text{For all } j<n, \sum_{i=1}^{j} \left| N_i \times K_i \right| < \left| K_{j+1} \right|.$$

In other words, the sum of the maximum values which each term can take on, up to a given term, must be less than the coefficient of the next–most significant term.

To illustrate the technique, we present a simple two–dimensional loop with its translation. The translation includes a test for the linearization condition.

```
do i=1,N
    do j=1,M
         a(K*i+L*j)=b(i)
    end do
end do
```

The following shows the translation of the loop:

```
loop_is = serial
if (abs(K).lt.abs(L)) then
        if (abs(K*(N-1)).lt.abs(L))loop_is=parallel
else
        if (abs(L*(M-1)).lt.abs(K))loop_is=parallel
endif

if (loop_is.eq.parallel) then
    parallel do i=1,N
        parallel do j=1,M
            a(K*i+L*j)=b(i)
        end parallel do
    end parallel do
else
    do i=1,N
        do j=1,M
            a(K*i + L*j) = b(i)
        end do
    end do
endif
```

This test is not an exact test in that it will not always find parallelism where it exists for all possible combinations of K, L, M, and N. It is only exact when a one–dimensional array is a proper linearization of a higher–dimensioned array.

Other run-time dependence tests have also proven useful in the past. A very simple such test has been used in commercially-available parallelizers for loops containing statements of the form

```
v(k*i+m) = ...
```

where i is the loop index and the value of k is unknown. The test in this case checks whether k is zero or not to determine whether or not there is a self output dependence. Also, we have found one case in the Perfect codes (not included in Table 4) where a run-time version of the GCD test [2] allowed the parallel execution of the loop.

One difficulty presented by run-time test is that, depending on the program and the target machine, they may severely increase the execution time of the transformed program. Therefore, these tests should only be used when it is likely that they will succeed. This likelihood is difficult to determine. Querying the user or gathering information from actual runs of the program are possible approaches in this case.

2.2. Array Privatization

Many of the recently-developed parallel Fortran extensions such as Cedar Fortran[5], the IBM parallel Fortran, and the Parallel Computing Forum (PCF) Fortran include parallel loop constructs with private declarations. A copy of each private item is allocated for each processor cooperating in the execution of the loop. For example, the loop

```
        do i=1,n
S1:             a=b(i)+c(i)
S2:             d(i)=a**2
        end do
```

can be transformed into parallel form by declaring a private

```
        parallel do i=1,n
                private a
S1:                     a=b(i)+c(i)
S2:                     d(i)=a**2
        end parallel do
```

Privatization makes parallelization possible by replicating a, and in this way avoiding the two cycles, caused by memory–related dependences (i.e. anti– and output dependences), in the dependence graph of the original loop. An alternative to scalar privatization is scalar expansion which achieves the same effect as privatization by replacing all occurrences of a scalar variable with an array element whose subscript is the loop index. However, expansion may consume an unnecessary amount of memory, since all that is needed when parallelizing a loop is a copy of each expandable scalar for each processor cooperating in the parallel execution of the loop.

In the previous example we tacitly assumed that the value of a when the loop completes is not used anywhere else in the program. If a is used after the loop, a last–value assignment has to be performed. A way to do this for the previous loop is as follows:

```
        parallel do i=1,n
                private a'
                if (i.lt.n) then
S1':                    a'=b(i)+c(i)
S2':                    d(i)=a'**2
                else
S1:                     a=b(i)+c(i)
S2:                     d(i)=a**2
                end if
        end parallel do
```

The private variable a' is used in all the iterations of the parallel loop except for the last one where a is used instead. In this way, a will have the expected value just after the loop completes.

Even though the previous discussion dealt with scalars, all that was said applies also to arrays. However, the parallelizers we used were only capable of doing scalar privatization, not array privatization. For this reason they failed to parallelize several loops in the programs we analyzed. Table 4 lists the loops that could be parallelized thanks to array privatization.

Despite its apparent importance, very little has been published on array privatization even though scalar expansion is frequently mentioned and sometimes carefully described. The criterion for privatizing a scalar is that all accesses to the scalar be either an assignment or be preceded (in the control–flow sense) by an assignment inside the loop body. The equivalent criterion for array privatization is that each element of the array be assigned before it is used in the loop body.

Clearly, there will be some cases where the compiler will be unable to determine whether privatization is or is not possible, and last value assignment could present difficulties if not all loop iterations assign to the same set of array elements. However, all cases we found when transforming the programs in Table 1, were relatively straightforward, and there is no doubt that a parallelizing compiler can perform the same array privatizations we did by hand.

Interprocedural analysis is an important complementing technique to detect arrays that can be privatized. Many of the loops we parallelized contain subroutine calls. As a result, definitions and uses of the candidate arrays had to be searched across procedure bounds.

2.3. Generalized Induction Variables

The sequence of values that an induction variable receives throughout the execution of a loop form an arithmetic progression [1]. Most often, a new value is assigned to an induction variable, say V, in statements of the form

$$V = V + K$$

where K is a value that remains constant throughout the execution of the loop. To eliminate the loop–carried dependences generated by this statement, parallelizing compilers replace the occurrences of the induction variable with a linear function of K and the loop index (or indices). For example, variable j in statement S2 of the loop

```
        j=0
        do i=1,n
S1:             j=j+m
S2:             b(i)=j+d(i)
        end do
```

can be replaced by m*i. Formally, this means that the cycle in the dependence graph caused by the use of j in S2 will no longer exist, and the assignment to b(i) can execute in parallel. Statement S1 can then be eliminated if j is never used again after the loop completes. Otherwise it should be replaced by a new assignment j=n*m to be placed immediately after the transformed loop.

Another important class of variables, which we will call here *generalized induction variables*, are those that assume a sequence of values which do not necessarily constitute an arithmetic progression but for which a closed–form expression can be computed at compile–time. In our work we found only two types of GIVs. The first type is updated using multiplication instead of the addition typical of the regular induction variable. The sequence of values generated in this way forms a geometric progression and clearly the same machinery used for regular induction variables can be used to process this type of GIV. As can be seen in Table 4, one loop in the program OCEAN could be parallelized thanks to the recognition of this type of GIV.

The second type of GIV consists of those variables whose sequence of values do not form an arithmetic progression even though they are updated using constant increments. For example, in the following loop

```
              j = 0
              do i=1,n
                  . . .
S1:               j=j+1
                  . . .
              do k=1,i
                      . . .
S2:                   j=j+1
                      . . .
                  end do
              . . .
          end do
```

the occurrences of j after S1 and before the inner loop could be replaced by

$$1+\sum_{q=1}^{i-1}1+\sum_{q=1}^{i-1}\sum_{r=1}^{q}1 = i+i*(i-1)/2.$$

The occurrences between S2 and the end of the inner loop could be replaced by

$$i+i*(i-1)/2+k.$$

As shown in Table 4, we found some generalized induction variables of this second type in the program TRFD. Because the existing parallelizers can only handle regular induction variables we had to find the closed–form expression by hand. The methodology used was to compute the contribution of each assignment statement by symbolically evaluating a nested summation. The expressions were then formed as the sum of the contributions of all the assignment statements in the loop body. A symbolic algebra package, Maple, was used to help our hand calculations, and clearly, some form of symbolic algebra algorithms will be needed to implement powerful GIV transformation algorithms.

One important limitation of today's symbolic algebra packages arises when an inner loop containing an increment to a GIV is not executed in all the iterations of the outer loop because in some cases its upper limit is less than its lower limit. In this case, the contribution of the increment operation has the form of a nested summation where one of the inner summations have an upper bound less than the lower bound. The value of this inner sum has to be defined as zero in order to obtain the right answer to our problem. However, the symbolic algebra packages we tried make other assumptions, and therefore they produced incorrect results in these cases.

An important observation is that when the GIVs are used as subscripts it is necessary to detect the monotonicity of the sequence of values for the purpose of dependence analysis. This has to be done before the GIV is replaced by a closed form expression because these could be non–linear on the loop indices, and current dependence analysis techniques do not work on non–linear subscript expressions. In the programs discussed in this paper, detecting the monotonicity of the sequence of values was necessary to perform an accurate dependence analysis. This was accomplished by analyzing the original assignment statements. In our case, monotonicity could be guaranteed because the GIVs were always incremented by values of the same sign.

2.4. Doacross transformations

A doacross is a parallel loop, automatically generated from a sequential version, where synchronization takes place in the form of a cascade. In other words, a wait in iteration i can only be triggered by an event in an iteration j which precedes i in the sequential version of the loop. For example, one way in which the loop

```
            do i=1,n
S1:             a(i) = b(i) + a(i-1)
S2:             c(i) = b(i) + e(i-1)
S3:             e(i) = c(i) + 1
S4:             d(i) = e(i) ** 2
            end do
```

can be executed in parallel is by executing the π–blocks with cross–iteration dependences ($\{S1\}$ and $\{S2, S3\}$) sequentially across the iteration space. It is usually said that each such π–block is enclosed in an *ordered critical section*. In this type of translation, parallelism is achieved by overlapping the execution of the different π–blocks as illustrated in the following translation of the previous loop.

```
            post (s1(O))
            post (s2(O))
            parallel do (ordered) i=1,n
                    wait (s1(i-1))
S1:                 a(i) = b(i) + a(i-1)
                    post (s1(i))
                    wait (s2(i-1))
S2:                 c(i) = b(i) + e(i-1)
S3:                 e(i) = c(i) + 1
                    post (s2(i))
S4:                 d(i) = e(i) ** 2
            end parallel do
```

In doacross loops, when only assignment statements are considered, the translator only has to consider issues related to synchronization and statement reordering. However, the presence of conditional statements introduce other difficulties. In this section, we discuss two transformations that we found useful when dealing with conditional statements in the loop body.

The first transformation operates on do loops which could potentially terminate by executing conditional goto statements targeted outside the loop body. Several strategies can be used to parallelize these loops. The technique we used in TRACK consists in letting all the iterations of the loop run in parallel and storing all the results only in temporary locations. A boolean vector is used to keep a record of which iterations execute the exit goto statement.

After the loop containing the exit goto, we generated a second parallel loop which stores the values computed in the first loop in their definitive locations. For example:

```
do i=1,n
        a(i) = b(i) ** 2
        if a(i) < 5 then go to 5

    end do
    ...
5   ...
    ...
```

can be transformed into

```
parallel do i=1,n
        a'(i) = b(i) ** 2
        if a'(i) < 5 then bool_vector(i) = .true.

end parallel do
parallel do i=1,first_true(bool_vector(1:n))
        a(i) = a'(i)
end parallel do
```

where first_true computes the location of the first true value in a boolean vector.

The second doacross transformation to be discussed in this section operates on loops of the form

```
do i=1,n
        if a(b(i)) < k then to to L
        ...
        a(b(i)) = a(b(i)) - 1
        ...
    L:  ...
        ...
    end do
```

where there is an if statement whose boolean expression is persistent, i.e. if it is true in iteration k, then it is also true in all iterations $j>k$. In a parallel execution of the loop, such an if statement will have to wait for the values used in the boolean expression to be computed on previous iterations only if at the time of evaluating it, its boolean expression is found to be false. However, if its boolean expression is true, there is no need to wait and the processor may proceed immediately to the `else` branch.

For example, the previous loop can be transformed into the parallel loop

```
parallel do (ordered) i=1,n
        if a(b(i)) < k then go to L
        wait(ev(i-1))
        if a(b(i)) < k then go to L
        ...
        a(b(i)) = a(b(i)) - 1
        post (ev(i))
        ...
L:      if posted(ev(i-1)) then post (ev(i))
        ...
        ...
        wait(ev(i-1))
        post (ev(i))
    end parallel do
```

where a wait at the top is only necessary when the boolean expression $a(i) < k$ is false. This transformation was applied to a loop of the program TRACK. A related transformation strategy is described in [7].

2.5. Unordered Critical Sections and Parallel Reductions

The techniques described in this section allow the transformation of do loops into parallel form by exploiting the fact that we can reorder the execution of certain operations even though they are involved in data dependences.

The first case is illustrated by the increment operation to $a(k)$ in the following loop.

```
do i=1,n
        do j=1,m
        S1:      k=funct(i,j)
                 . . .
        S2:      a(k) = a(k) + <expression>
        end do
end do
```

We will assume that S2 is the only statement accessing an element of array a in the loop. This assumption is not necessary to apply the technique, but it helps in the discussion. Depending on the function funct(i,j) it may be possible to transform the outer do loop into a doacross. For example, if funct(i,j) is just j then different iterations of the outer loop could proceed in parallel and synchronization will only take place between assignments to the same array element as shown next.

```
parallel do j=1,m
   post (e(0,j))
end parallel do
parallel do (ordered) i=1,n
        do j=1,m
                 . . .
                 wait (e(i-1,j))
                 a(j) = a(j) + <expression>
                 post(e(i,j))
        end do
end parallel do
```

However, if we are willing to allow the order of the additions to change, we can apply a more general transformation that will work for any form of the function funct and will not require enforcing a particular order to the different assignments to a(j) for a given j. This transformation consists of surrounding the assignment statement with a critical section which guarantees that, at any time, only one processor updates each element a(k).

This transformation is called in this paper *unordered reduction*, and its main advantage over the doacross transformation is that it does not require total serialization of the assignment statement even when the subscripts are non–linear or include unknown terms. Unordered reduction only requires that the modification to each array element proceed serially. In the traditional doacross transformation, if the subscripts are not analyzable at compile–time, the statement will have to be executed serially across all loop iterations. In some cases, the transformation may also produce a faster parallel loop than the doacross transformation because it allows total flexibility in the scheduling of the iterations and their critical sections.

In our work, instead of synchronizing the update of variable a(k), we accumulated the values on each processor separately and summed up the partial results after the loop. In this approach, there is no need to synchronize on every iteration to guarantee mutual exclusion. However, if the array elements incremented are very sparsely distributed throughout the array (which was not the case in the loops we transformed), the summation at the end of the loop could significantly hurt performance.

The second type of transformation which we call *unordered assignment* is illustrated by the assignment to x(k) in the loop

```
do i=1,n1
        do j=1,n2
                k=funct(i,j)
                ...
                x(k) = <expression>
        end do
end do
```

This is very similar to the previous case, except that instead of accumulating on an array element, successive iterations may rewrite the array element. As in the previous case we assume that there are no other references to the array x in the loop. As can be inferred from the discussion that follows it is not difficult to extend this transformation if x appears in other statements but only on the left–hand side. The technique, however, will not work if x also appears on the right–hand side (see [10] for a discussion of this case).

As in the previous case, a doacross transformation could be used. However, the resulting loop may not be efficient if funct cannot be analyzed at compile–time. However, because x(k) is not read in the loop body an assignment to x will not affect the correctness as long as each element of x has, at the end of the loop, the value assigned in the last iteration accessing the element. A parallel version of the loop is shown next:

```
order = 0
parallel do i=1,n1
        private k
        do j=1,n2
                k = funct(i,j)
                ...
                critical section c(k)
                        if order(k) <= i then
                                x(k) = <expression>
                                order(k)=i
                        end if
                end critical section
        end do
end parallel do
```

In this loop, the assignment to x(k) is surrounded by a critical section controlled by a lock variable, c indexed by k. An integer array, order, is also introduced in such a way that order(k) at any point during the execution of the loop will contain the value of the last iteration where x(k) was assigned or zero if x(k) has not been assigned. Inside the critical section, the value of order(k) is compared against the current iteration. If it is lower, it means that either x(k) has not been assigned yet or was assigned in an iteration that precedes the current one in the sequential version of the loop. In this case, x(k) should be assigned a new value. On the contrary, if order(k) is greater than the current iteration, then x(k) should not be assigned in this iteration because an iteration with a higher value has already been assigned to it. In the sequential program, a later iteration would have rewritten the variable.

2.6. Assignment Compaction

In this technique, used in TRACK, we assume the subscript values cannot be computed independently in each iteration, but are conditionally incremented in each iteration under the control of an if statement. A typical situation is shown in the next loop:

```
do i=1,n1
        do j=1,n2
            ...
            k=m+1
            ...
            a(k) = <expression-1>
            ...
            if <expression-2> then m=k
        end do
end do
```

To allow the loop to execute in parallel, `<expression-1>` could be stored in a temporary two–dimensional array, say `ta`, and a two dimensional boolean array, say `ma`, can be used to keep track of the iteration in which `k` is assigned to `m`.

```
parallel do i=1,n1
        do j=1,n2
            ...
            ta(i,j)=<expression-1>
            ...
            if <expression-2> then ma(i,j)=.true.
                               else ma(i,j)=.false.
        end do
end parallel do
```

After the loop completes, `ma` can be used to gather `ta` into array `a`. This can be expressed in Fortran 90 using the `pack` intrinsic function:

```
a(m+1:):=pack(ta(1:n1,1:n2), mask=ma)
```

3. Conclusions

The study reported in this paper deals with a small sample of programs. Some of the transformations we present here were useful in only one of the programs. Nevertheless, the resulting speedup of those programs demonstrates that there is much room for improvement in the existing parallelizing compiler methodology. Our strategy to demonstrate this was to hand–analyze the output of existing parallelizers, study the reasons for their failures, and then develop strategies to overcome some of these limitations. We believe that this is a good approach to advance compiler technology.

Even though this is an obvious strategy, a careful reading of the compiler literature reveals surprisingly few experimental compiler studies. Much of the literature focuses on improving the efficiency of existing compiler algorithms or on the development of techniques with very few experimental results to demonstrate their effectiveness. Much more experimental work is needed. We believe that only through the analysis of a large collection of programs will it be possible to develop successful techniques applicable across a wide spectrum of programs.

References

[1]   Alfred Aho and Jeffrey Ullman. *The Theory of Parsing, Translation, and Compiling, Vol. 2*. Prentice–Hall, Inc., Englewood Cliffs, NJ, 1973.

[2]   Utpal Banerjee. *Dependence Analysis for Supercomputing*. Kluwer. Boston, MA. 1988.

[3]   George Cybenko, Lyle Kipp, Lynn Pointer and David Kuck. Supercomputer Performance Evaluation and the Perfect Benchmarks[TM]. *Proceedings of ICS, Amsterdam, Netherlands*, March 1990.

[4]   Rudolf Eigenmann, Jay Hoeflinger, Greg Jaxon, Zhiyuan Li and David Padua. Restructuring Fortran Programs for Cedar. *Proc. of the Int. Conf. on Parallel Processing*, pp. I 57–66, August 1991.

[5]   Mark D. Guzzi, David A. Padua, Jay P. Hoeflinger and Duncan H. Lawrie. Cedar Fortran and Other Vector and Parallel Fortran Dialects. *Jour. of Supercomputing*, Vol. 4, No. 1, pp. 37–62, March 1990.

[6]   David Kuck, Edward Davidson, Duncan Lawrie and Ahmed Sameh. Parallel Supercomputing Today and the Cedar Approach. In: *Experimental Parallel Computing Architectures*, J. J. Dongarra, ed. Elsevier Science Publishers B.V. (North–Holland), New York, NY, pp. 1–20, 1987.

[7]   Zhiyuan Li. Compiler Algorithms for Event Variable Synchronization. *Proceedings of ICS 91*, pp. 85–95, June 1991.

[8]   David Padua and Michael Wolfe. Advanced Compiler Optimizations for Supercomputers. *Communications of the ACM*, Vol. 29, No. 12, pp. 1184–1201. December 1986.

[9]   Michael Wolfe. *Optimizing Supercompilers for Supercomputers*. The MIT Press. Boston, MA. 1989.

[10]   Chuan–Qi Zhu and Pen–Chung Yew. A Scheme to Enforce Data Dependence on Large Multiprocessor Systems. *IEEE Trans. on Software Eng.*, Vol. SE–13, No. 6, pp. 726–739, June 1987.

[11]   Hans Zima. *Supercompilers for Parallel and Vector Computers*. ACM Press. New York, NY. 1991.

Table 1. The names of four of the codes in the Perfect Benchmarks, their application areas, the dominant algorithms in the codes, and the number of lines of Fortran source code.

Code	Application Area	Dominant Algorithm(s)	Lines of Fortran source
MDG	Chemical & Physical Model	ODE Solvers	1238
OCEAN	Fluid Dynamics	FFTs	4343
TRACK	Signal Processing	Convolution	3784
TRFD	Chemical and Physical Model	Integral Transforms	435

Table 2. Speedups produced by the Alliant FX/80 Fortran compiler.

Code	Speedup
MDG	1.1
OCEAN	1.42
TRACK	0.90
TRFD	2.36

Table 3. Speedups on the Alliant FX/80 after our hand transformations.

Code	Speedup
MDG	5.5
OCEAN	8.3
TRACK	5.1
TRFD	13.2

Prog	Label	Routine	Loop Spdup	% of Seq	Array Privatization	GIV (additive)	GIV (multiplicative)	Unordered Reduction	Unordered Assignment	DOACROSS Conditional	DOACROSS Exit	DOACROSS Stmts	Runtime Dependence Test	Multi-version Loops	Assignment Compaction	Interprocedural Analysis
TRACK	300	nlfilt	5.2	40%	x					x						
	300	fptrack	6.0	9%							x		x			
	400	extend	7.0	34%						x	x		x			
MDG	1000	interf	6.0	90%	x				x							
	2000	poten	5.2	8%	x											
TRFD	100	olda	16.4	69%	x	x										
	300	olda	12.3	29%	x	x										
	140	intgrl	5.5	1%							x					
OCEAN	109	ftrvmt	8.1	40%					x					x	x	
	20	csr	6.6	4%										x	x	
	30	acac	3.8	3%										x	x	
	40	acac	6.1	2%										x	x	
	30	scsc	9.6	2%										x	x	
	20	rcs	6.6	1%										x	x	
	116	ftrvmt	5.0	4%										x	x	
	270	ocean	8.0	3%	x											
	480	ocean	6.1	4%	x											
	500	ocean	6.5	3%	x											
	340	ocean	5.5	4%												x
	360	ocean	6.3	2%												x
	400	ocean	6.0	2%												x
	420	ocean	5.8	3%												x
	440	ocean	7.4	3%												x
	460	ocean	5.1	3%												x

Table 4. Summary of transformations used.

6 Programming SIMPLE for Parallel Portability

J. Lee, C. Lin, and L. Snyder
University of Washington

Abstract

The Phase Abstractions formulation of Livermore's SIMPLE computation is described in detail. This new program is of interest for three reasons. First, it enables the Phase Abstractions approach to be easily compared with the many other programming styles illustrated by SIMPLE in the past. Secondly, this program has recently been reported to execute on five diverse MIMD computers, in all cases achieving speedups in excess of 50% of linear. Thirdly, the Phase Abstractions permit easy revisions of the program that enable performance experimentation. Specifically, "array blocks" are compared to "column strips" as a means of array decomposition. Results comparing the two approaches are presented for the Sequent Symmetry, BBN Butterfly, Intel iPSC/2 and NCUBE/7. The results confirm the intuition that blocks are superior.

1 Introduction

The SIMPLE program, a "simple" computational fluid dynamics code, was released by Lawrence Livermore National Laboratory in 1978 [6] as a benchmark program to evaluate new computers and Fortran compilers. Since that time the program has frequently been used to illustrate new computational approaches [8, 9, 10, 18] and to estimate machine performance [4, 7, 10, 12, 13]. This paper follows both themes by presenting a version of SIMPLE written using the Phase Abstractions [2, 3, 22] as well as certain performance data.

The Phase Abstraction version of SIMPLE is notable because it has recently been shown to be portable across a wide variety of MIMD parallel computers [16]. Figure 1 shows the speedups achieved for the BBN Butterfly, the Intel iPSC/2, the NCUBE/7, the Sequent Symmetry, and a detailed simulator for a Transputer-based multicomputer. Though the machines differ substantially, e.g. in memory structure, the speedups fall roughly within the same range.

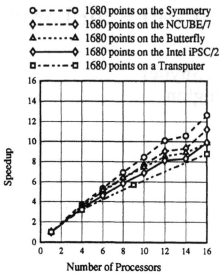

Figure 1: SIMPLE on Various Machines

```
data := Load();
while (error > δ)
{
    Delta(data);
    Hydro(data);
    Heat(data);
    Energy1(data);
    error := Energy2(data);
}
Output (data);
```

Figure 2: Z Level for SIMPLE

The Phase Abstractions – the XYZ programming levels and the ensemble structures – provide critical information about a program that can be used by a compiler to generate efficient code for the target machine. These include locality, scalable concurrency, granularity and communication patterns. It is the goal of this paper to present SIMPLE and to illustrate how these features are described and controlled to achieve portability

To illustrate how abstractions can structure a program to improve portability, consider the grain size of SIMPLE.

The program presented here is the latest in a series of improvements beginning with the work of Gannon and Panetta [9], who developed a version of SIMPLE suitable for the CHiP architecture and programmed it using early Poker software. Their emphasis [10] was on extracting the essence of the computation from the original Fortran version and reformulating it using highly parallel algorithms suitable for the nonshared memory model of computation. Their code used a one-point-per-process approach, i.e. each process retains the values describing a single point of the state space, rather than, say, a region of points. A similar approach was taken by Gates [11] in his later Poker version of SIMPLE. Such fine grain solutions achieve a very high degree of concurrency and are conceptually easy to program, but they have a serious drawback: They can be too concurrent!

Since problems tend to have many more data points than physical processors, the parallel execution of a one-point-per-process program requires many logical processes to be executed on each physical processor. This generally requires that processes be multiplexed, though compilation techniques are now being developed that can in some cases "aggregate" fine grain processes into coarser grain processes to avoid multiplexing [23]. Multiplexing, whether done in hardware [24] or software [5], incurs overhead because at the very least there is context switching overhead, and in the usual case many instructions are executed that are superfluous in the absence of physical concurrency.

But if the finest granularity is not ideal, neither is any specific choice of coarse granularity. Clearly, the problem size and number of processors available will change. Moreover, though multiple processes are useful for hiding communication latency, machines differ greatly on their ability to benefit from them.

The Phase Abstractions approach supports the definition of variable grain size programs. The processes are parameterized so that grain size can be customized based on the problem size, number of processors, operating characteristics of the target architecture, etc. The customization is performed by the compiler, loader, or runtime system depending on when sufficient information is known to define the granularity. The Phase Abstraction mechanisms that support this control of granularity are the ensembles and the X programming level. Both are described in the next section.

2 Phase Abstractions

The Phase Abstractions [2, 3, 22] are a non-shared memory programming model that encompasses both the XYZ programming levels and the ensemble structures.

The XYZ programming levels are an abstraction that recognizes that the instructions of a parallel program serve different purposes. Beginning at the lowest level, instructions are combined to form *processes* (X level), which are the basic building blocks of a computation. Processes are then composed to form concurrent *phases* (Y level). Phases correspond to our informal notion of a parallel algorithm (e.g. matrix multiply, Fast Fourier Transform, global maximum). Finally, the *problem level* (Z level) controls the overall phase invocation to solve the user's problem.

The XYZ decomposition of the SIMPLE computation is (partially) illustrated in Figure 2. The computation begins by invoking a phase that reads in the problem state and initializes program variables. Then a series of five phases – *Delta, Hydro, Heat, Energy1,* and *Energy2* – is iteratively invoked to implement the state changes required in one logical iteration of the algorithm. When convergence is achieved, an output phase is invoked. Each phase is a parallel algorithm composed of processes, as explained below.

Phases are defined using ensembles. An *ensemble* is a set with a partitioning. The set is generally composed of names having additional structure and the partitioning describes how it is decomposed into constituent parts. A partition is called a *section.*

Three kinds of ensembles are used to define a phase: A *data ensemble* is a data structure with a partitioning, a *code ensemble* is a set of process instances with a partitioning, and a *port ensemble* is a set of adjacency names with a partitioning. Ensembles will be discussed extensively in subsequent sections, but illustrations of a data ensemble can be seen in Figure 4, a code ensemble in Figure 5, and a port ensemble in Figure 7.

To define a phase, the partitionings of the data, code and port ensembles must be isomorphic. This requirement permits the process(es) of each section of a code ensemble to be associated with the data of the corresponding section of the data ensemble and with the ports of the corresponding section of the port ensemble. Each section will be allocated to a processor for execution: The process executes on that processor, the data can be stored in memory local to that processor, and ports support interprocessor communication.

The data ensemble provides a (logically) global view of the problem state as represented by its data structures, but it does so in a way that permits data to be allocated to separate address spaces if necessary. The code ensemble gives a (logically) global view of the processes performing the parallel computation; when the process instances differ the model is MIMD, but it can be SPMD if they are all identical. Finally, the port ensemble gives the overall communication structure of the phase, which is extremely useful in cases where interprocessor communication can be optimized.

To complete the illustration begun earlier, the "size" of a section, that is, the amount of data allocated to the section in the data ensemble and the amount of computation required to execute the process in that section, defines the granularity of the parallel computation. Changes to the data ensemble – in the total number of partitions or in the amount of data allocated to a section – are the means of changing the granularity of the computation. Notice that the section also captures the important notion of locality.

The ensembles provide flexibility via modularity and encapsulation. The above example shows some of the power of data ensembles. Furthermore, programs can scale in the number of processors or in problem size by changing the ensemble definition without changing the X level code. In addition, the logical communication graphs can be adapted to suit the underlying architecture by modifying only the port ensembles. Even in cases where the logical communication graphs don't change, the port ensembles provide information that can be useful in finding the best mapping from processes to processors.

3 The SIMPLE Computation

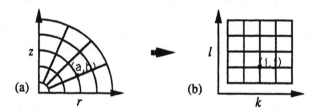

Figure 3: Mapping of Physical Domain to Computation Domain

The SIMPLE computation simulates the hydrodynamics of a pressurized fluid inside a spherical shell. The state of the simulation is maintained by recording the values of various physical quantities at various points inside the shell. As simulated time progresses, these values – representing such things as pressure, density, viscosity and temperature – are updated. Due to the spherical nature of the problem, it is natural to discretize the sphere using polar coordinates. Because of the symmetry of the shell, the simulation involves just the 2D projection of one quadrant of the sphere. See Figure 3 (a). For the purposes of computer simulation, this 2D projection can be transformed into cartesian coordinates as shown in Figure 3 (b). Finally, note the 3 types of boundary conditions: there is the outer surface of the shell, there is the inner surface of the shell, and there are the two sides of the shell that lie on the border of the quadrant.

The algorithm is based on Lagrangian hydrodynamics, which gives the following set of equations [15]:

$$\frac{d}{dt}(\rho V) = 0 \qquad (1)$$

$$\rho\frac{d\vec{u}}{dt} + \vec{\nabla}(p + q) = 0 \qquad (2)$$

$$\frac{d\epsilon}{dt} + (p + q)\frac{d\tau}{dt} = 0 \qquad (3)$$

$$\frac{d\vec{x}}{dt} - \vec{u} = 0 \qquad (4)$$

$$q = q(\rho, \delta u) \qquad (5)$$

$$p = p(\rho, \epsilon) \qquad (6)$$

$$\frac{\partial\epsilon}{\partial t} = \left(\frac{\partial\epsilon}{\partial\theta}\right)\frac{d\theta}{dt} + \left(\frac{\partial\epsilon}{\partial\tau}\right)\frac{d\tau}{dt} \qquad (7)$$

where
$\vec{x}$ is position vector,
$\vec{u}$ is velocity vector,
ρ is mass density,
τ is specific volume,
ϵ is specific internal energy,
q is artificial viscosity,
p is pressure,
θ is temperature,
κ is heat conductivity and
t is time.

In the following, the notation $V_{i,j}$ is used to denote the physical variable of node (i, j) in the computation grid (Figure 3 (b)). It is assumed that the values of pressure, density, etc. are constants inside any square surrounded by nodes (i, j), $(i, j+1)$, $(i+1, j+1)$ and $(i+1, j)$ and that they are represented as values in the node at the upper right corner of the square, node $(i+1, j+1)$.

What follows is the basic algorithm to solve the above equations. For clarity the equations to deal with boundary conditions are omitted. More detailed descriptions, including the treatment of boundary conditions, can be found in the literature[6, 10]. In the following r and z denote the r and z components of the coordinate, u and w denote the r and z component of the velocity and a^r and a^z denote the r and z component of the acceleration.

The SIMPLE algorithm:

First compute the initial coordinates of all nodes and initialize the variables of every node, then iteratively carry out the following sequence of steps until the error is sufficiently small:

1. Compute the next time step (δt).

$$\delta t := \min_{i,j}\left[\frac{0.5 J_{ij}}{C_A\left[\Delta r_{ij}^2 + \delta r_{ij}^2\right]^{1/2}}\right]$$

Here, the following notation is used:

$$2\Delta f_{ij} = f_{i,j} + f_{i-1,j} - f_{i,j-1} - f_{i-1,j-1}$$
$$2\delta f_{ij} = f_{i,j} + f_{i,j-1} - f_{i-1,j-1} - f_{i-1,j}$$

where f stands for any point quantity such as r, z, u, w. C_A is the local speed of sound and can be computed as follows, where γ is the specific heat ($\gamma = 1.4$ for air):

$$C_A := \sqrt{\gamma\frac{p_{ij}}{\rho_{ij}}}.$$

2. Compute the new acceleration (a). Let f denote $p + q$.

$$a_{ij}^r := \frac{f_{i,j}\left(z_{i-1,j} - z_{i,j-1}\right) + f_{i,j+1}\left(z_{i,j+1} - z_{i-1,j}\right) + f_{i+1,j+1}\left(z_{i+1,j} - z_{i,j+1}\right) + f_{i+1,j}\left(z_{i,j-1} - z_{i+1,j}\right)}{0.5\left(\rho_{i,j}J_{i,j} + \rho_{i,j+1}J_{i,j+1} + \rho_{i+1,j+1}J_{i+1,j+1} + \rho_{i+1,j}J_{i+1,j}\right)}$$

$$a_{ij}^z := \frac{f_{i,j}\left(r_{i-1,j} - r_{i,j-1}\right) + f_{i,j+1}\left(r_{i,j+1} - r_{i-1,j}\right) + f_{i+1,j+1}\left(r_{i+1,j} - r_{i,j+1}\right) + f_{i+1,j}\left(r_{i,j-1} - r_{i+1,j}\right)}{0.5\left(\rho_{i,j}J_{i,j} + \rho_{i,j+1}J_{i,j+1} + \rho_{i+1,j+1}J_{i+1,j+1} + \rho_{i+1,j}J_{i+1,j}\right)}$$

3. Compute the new velocity ($\vec{u}$) and new coordinates ($\vec{x}$).

$$\vec{u}_{i,j} := \vec{u}_{i,j} + \delta t \, \vec{a}_{i,j}$$
$$\vec{x}_{i,j} := \vec{x}_{i,j} + \delta t \, \vec{u}_{i,j}$$

4. Compute the new Jacobian (J) and volume of revolution (new_S).

$$tmp\_J1_{i,j} := \frac{1}{2}\left[r_{i,j}\,(z_{i,j-1} - z_{i-1,j}) + r_{i,j-1}\,(z_{i-1,j} - z_{i,j}) + r_{i-1,j}\,(z_{i,j} - z_{i,j-1})\right]$$

$$tmp\_J2_{i,j} := \frac{1}{2}\left[r_{i,j-1}\,(z_{i-1,j-1} - z_{i-1,j}) + r_{i-1,j-1}\,(z_{i-1,j} - z_{i,j-1}) + r_{i-1,j}\,(z_{i,j-1} - z_{i-1,j-1})\right]$$

$$J_{i,j} := tmp\_J1_{i,j} + tmp\_J2_{i,j}$$

$$old\_S_{i,j} := new\_S_{i,j}$$

$$new\_S_{i,j} := \frac{1}{3}\left[(r_{i,j} + r_{i,j-1} + r_{i-1,j})\,tmp\_J1_{i,j} + (r_{i,j-1} + r_{i-1,j-1} + r_{i-1,j})\,tmp\_J2_{i,j}\right]$$

5. Compute the new density (ρ) and artificial viscosity (q).

$$\rho_{i,j} := \rho_{i,j}\,\frac{old\_S_{i,j}}{new\_S_{i,j}}$$

$$tmp1 := \begin{cases} \frac{[\Delta r \delta w - \Delta z \delta u]^2}{\Delta r^2 + \Delta z^2} & \text{if } [\,] < 0 \\ 0 & \text{otherwise} \end{cases}$$

$$tmp2 := \begin{cases} \frac{[\Delta u \delta z - \Delta w \delta r]^2}{\delta r^2 + \delta z^2} & \text{if } [\,] < 0 \\ 0 & \text{otherwise} \end{cases}$$

$$q_{i,j} := 1.5\rho_{i,j}\,(tmp1 + tmp2) + 0.5\rho_{i,j}C_A\sqrt{tmp1 + tmp2}$$

6. Compute the new energy (ϵ) and pressure (p).

$$\epsilon_{i,j} := \epsilon_{i,j} - (p_{i,j} + q_{i,j})\,delta\_\tau_{i,j}$$
$$tmp_{i,j} := (\gamma - 1)\,\epsilon_{i,j}\rho_{i,j}$$
$$\epsilon_{i,j} := \epsilon_{i,j} - \left(\frac{1}{2}\,(tmp_{i,j} + p_{i,j}) + q_{i,j}\right) delta\_\tau_{i,j}$$
$$p_{i,j} := (\gamma - 1)\,\epsilon_{i,j}\rho_{i,j}$$

where $delta\_\tau$ is the difference between the new τ (specific volume) and the τ in the previous iteration. $\tau = 1/\rho$.

7. Compute the new temperature (θ) and heat ($heat$).

for each pair (i,j) **do**

$$\sigma_{i,j} := 0.1\rho_{i,j}r_{i,j}J_{i,j}/\delta t \tag{8}$$

$$CC_{i,j} := 0.0001\theta_{i,j}^{5/2}/J_{i,j} \tag{9}$$

$$KJ_{i,j} := \frac{CC_{i,j}CC_{i,j+1}}{CC_{i,j} + CC_{i,j+1}} \tag{10}$$

$$R_{i,j} := (r_{i,j} + r_{i,j-1})\left((r_{i,j} - r_{i,j-1})^2(z_{i,j} - z_{i,j-1})^2\right)KJ_{i,j} \tag{11}$$

end for

for j := 0 to max$\_$K **do**
  for each i **do**

$$D_{i,j} := \sigma_{i,j} + R_{i,j} + R_{i,j-1}(1 - \alpha_{i,j-1}) \tag{12}$$

$$\alpha_{i,j} := R_{i,j}/D_{i,j} \tag{13}$$

$$\beta_{i,j} := \frac{R_{i,j-1}\beta_{i,j-1} + \sigma_{i,j}\theta_{i,j}}{D_{i,j}} \tag{14}$$

        end for
      end for
     for j = max_K **to** 0 **do**
      for each i **do**

$$\theta_{i,j} := \alpha_{i,j}\theta_{i,j+1} + \beta_{i,j} \tag{15}$$

        end for
     end for
     for i := 0 **to** max_L **do**

$$heat_{i,0} = (\theta_{i,0} - \theta_{i,1})\, R_{i,0}\, \delta t \tag{16}$$

    end for
Repeat the calculations of statements 13 – 16 in the l direction.

8. Compute the energy (*energy*) and work (*work*). Compute the error.
  for each pair (i,j) **do**

$m_{i,j} := \rho_{i,j} S_{i,j}$

$energy_{i,j} := \epsilon_{i,j} m_{i,j} + \dfrac{1}{8}(m_{i,j} + m_{i,j+1} + m_{i+1,j+1} + m_{i+1,j})\left(u_{i,j}^2 + w_{i,j}^2\right)$

$tmp_{i,j} := \dfrac{1}{4}\delta t\,(p_{i,j} - p_{i,j+1})(r_{i,j-1} - r_{i,j})\,[(r_{i,j} - r_{i,j-1})(u_{i,j} + u_{i,j-1}) - (z_{i,j} - z_{i,j-1})(u_{i,j} + u_{i,j-1}$

$work_{i,j} := \begin{cases} -tmp_{i,j} & \text{if (i,j) is on the west boundary of the computation grid} \\ 0 & \text{otherwise} \end{cases}$

  end for

$$total\_energy := \sum_{i,j} energy_{i,j}$$

$$total\_work := \sum_{i,j=0} work_{i,j}$$

$$total\_heat := \sum_{i,j=0} heat_{i,j}$$

$$error := total\_energy - total\_work + total\_heat$$

The Parallel Algorithm

Logically, each of the above steps is a phase of a Z level program. However, closer inspection reveals that this problem is naturally composed of just 5 phases. To create the parallel algorithm, note that the above equations only involve local neighbor values. For example, the first step computes a global minimum; this computation can be affected using only communication with neighboring data points. In the second step, the acceleration at point (i, j) is based on the (i, j) value and six neighbors: $(i + 1, j), (i + 1, j + 1), (i, j + 1), (i - 1, j), (i - 1, j - 1)$ and $(i, j - 1)$, which we refer to as its North, NorthEast, East, South, SouthWest and West neighbors, respectively. Similarly, step 4 requires the same six neighbors to compute the value of the Jacobian, while step 7 requires only four neighbors and differs from the others in that it has a series of loops with data dependencies between loops. Finally, step 9 computes a series of summations over the entire data space.

When this algorithm is parallelized, each type of data dependency induces a different communication pattern (since we assume a distributed memory model). Since steps 2 and 4 share the same data dependencies, and since steps 3, 5, and 6 have no dependencies, these steps can all be combined into a single phase, yielding the following phases, where each phase is characterized by a single data dependency pattern:

Delta Phase:	step 1
Hydro Phase:	steps 2, 3, 4, 5 and 6.
Heat Phase:	step 7
Energy1 Phase:	step 8
Energy2 Phase:	step 9

4 The SIMPLE Program

Having presented the SIMPLE algorithm in high level terms, the Z level program follows naturally (see Figure 2). In addition to the five phases described above, phases are added to load the initial problem state and output the result of the simulation. Since we presume that input and output are handled by phases provided by the system, it remains to define the five computational phases as Y level programs.[1] To do so, we define ensembles, which in turn require that we define data structures, processes, and communication graphs. Each type of ensemble will be discussed in its own subsection.

Data Ensembles. Most programs will require many data ensembles for each phase. Since all of the ensembles will require the same partitioning in order to be part of the phase, it is convenient to define all of the data structures first, then define a single partitioning, and finally apply the partitioning to all data structures to form ensembles.

In a sequential implementation, 18 2D arrays are used to represent the state of the SIMPLE computation. For example, *pressure* and *acceleration* are represented as follows:

```
double   p[rows][cols];        /* fluid pressure */
Vector   a[rows][cols];        /* acceleration vector */
```

The elements of the *a* array are two element double precision vectors representing the r and z components in the physical domain. In addition to these arrays, three global scalar values are used to keep track of *time*, the iteration number, and the pressure at the inner shell.

Our parallel implementation will partition the arrays into contiguous two dimensional subarrays (blocks). This choice reflects the assumptions that contiguous blocks give the greatest locality of reference, and that because data dependencies are local in nature blocks will minimize the amount of communication among sections. It is not immediately obvious that this is true and we return to this issue in Section 5. The block partitioning of the *pressure* array is specified below:

$$rows := \bar{r} \cdot s$$
$$cols := \bar{c} \cdot t$$
$$\forall i \ni 0 \leq i < \bar{r}, \quad \forall j \ni 0 \leq j < \bar{c}$$
$$section[i][j] := \{ \ p[x][y] \ | \ i \cdot s \leq x < (i+1) \cdot s, \quad j \cdot t \leq y < (j+1) \cdot t \ \}$$

which states that a *rows · cols* array (p) is to be partitioned into a collection of $\bar{r} \cdot \bar{c}$ blocks each of size $s \cdot t$. This partitioning is applied to each of the arrays. For example, we indicate that the pressure array, p, is converted into an ensemble by specifying $block(p)$. This has

---

[1] At this time no language implementation of the Phase Abstractions exists (a compiler is under construction) so the program text given in this paper is all expressed in pseudocode. To achieve the results presented in Figure 1, this pseudocode was hand translated into C code.

the effect of associating $p[i \cdot s + x][j \cdot t + y]$ with element x, y of section i, j. Figure 4 illustrates the *pressure* array converted into an ensemble.

P00	P01	P02	P03	P04	P05
P10	P11	P12	P13	P14	P15
P20	P21	P22	P23	P24	P25
P30	P31	P32	P33	P34	P35
P40	P41	P42	P43	P44	P45
P50	P51	P52	P53	P54	P55

Data Structure

P00	P01	P02	P03	P04	P05
P10	P11	P12	P13	P14	P15
P20	P21	P22	P23	P24	P25
P30	P31	P32	P33	P34	P35
P40	P41	P42	P43	P44	P45
P50	P51	P52	P53	P54	P55

Data Ensemble

Figure 4: The *Pressure* Array and Ensemble, where $rows = cols = 6$, $\bar{r} = \bar{c} = 3$, $s = t = 2$.

In addition to converting the data structures into data ensembles, it is useful to assign a copy of the global scalars to each section for use in local computations.

Code Ensembles. Having defined the data partitioning, the next task is to provide processes to operate on each region. This is the role of the code ensemble.

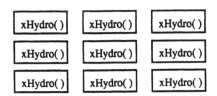

Figure 5: The Code Ensemble for the Hydro Phase.

In SIMPLE, the processes forming each phase are instances of a single process. For example, the *Hydro* phase uses instances of the *xHydro()* process (an X level program). Thus, SIMPLE appears not to require the full MIMD capability of code ensembles – where the instances can be instances of different processes – but requires only the SPMD capability. This apparent uniformity derives largely from mechanisms provided by the Phase Abstractions. Specifically, it has been necessary in the past [11] to provide nine different process types to handle the nine combinations of boundary conditions, e.g. North edge, NorthEast corner, etc. But with Phase Abstractions only a single code defining the activity on interior nodes is required. Boundary computations are specified using "port bindings," as explained in the next subsection.

The specification of a code ensemble for a phase, say the *Hydro* phase, is accomplished by declaring the process instance that is assigned to each section:

$$\text{Hydro[i][j].code} := \text{xHydro();} \qquad 0 \le i < \bar{r}, \quad 0 \le j < \bar{c}$$

Each of the $\bar{r} \cdot \bar{c}$ sections will be assigned an instance of the *xHydro()* code. More complex code ensembles are possible, e.g. with multithreading, but they are not needed in SIMPLE.

The *xHydro()* code is too large to be given in complete detail. Figure 6 shows a schematic of the process code. Several features are noteworthy:

- *parameters* – The arguments to the process are formals that establish a correspondence between local variables and the sections of the ensembles. For example, the local *pressure* array will be bound to a block of ensemble *p*.

- *local declarations* – The size of the local array is based on the size of the data ensemble and is thus logically an input to the process. Furthermore, the local array may be larger than its corresponding ensemble section, as shown by the local declaration *pressure*[0:s+1][0:t+1] and the formal declaration *p*[1:s][1:t]. Thus the local *pressure* array contains extra rows and columns to hold values from neighboring sections.

- *sends/receives* – The port declarations define the port names used by this process. Communication is implemented with the transmit operator ($<-$) for which a port name on the left specifies a send of the righthand side, and a port on the right indicates a receive into the variable on the lefthand side. The semantics are that sends transmit immediately, with data buffered at the destination, and receives remove data from the buffer in order of arrival, blocking on empty.

- *local computation* – The logic of the process is essentially the sequential computation of the original program, a characteristic that allows the number of partitions in the ensembles to go to one, yielding serial computation.

The syntax in this paper is intended to illustrate the full flexibility of the ensembles. In practice the ensembles may be specified in some higher level manner so the programmer will not have to specify these bindings and ensembles in such detail. For example, there may be a *Block* ensemble which defines a 2D array of square sections. Similarly, we envision a *Strips* ensemble which defines an array of long narrow sections. Also, the neighbor communication might be specified implicitly, freeing the programmer from the details of message passing.

Port Ensembles. The process instances of the code ensembles must communicate with one another as determined by the data partitioning and the data dependencies of each phase. The communication structures for the five phases are illustrated in Figure 7, where the boxes represent processes and edges indicate pairs of processes that must transmit information. The port ensemble is used to specify this association.

The *Hydro* phase, for example, uses a hex mesh where each section has six ports specified in the port ensemble:

$$Hydro.portnames \qquad \leftrightarrow \qquad N, NE, E, S, SW, W$$

which binds the section's ports to the (possibly different) names used in the process' port declaration. The pairing of port names to define a communication channel is specified as follows:

```
xHydro(p[1:s][1:t], rho[1:s][1:t], J[1:s][1:t] ... bound_p)
    double    pressure[0:s+1][0:t+1];
    double    rho[0:s+1][0:t+1];
    double    J[0:s+1][0:t+1];
      . . .
    double    bound_p;
    port      North, NorthEast, East, South, SouthWest, West;
{
    int       i, j;
    double    denom;

    /* Receive from the East a column of the rho array */
    /* and place it in the rightmost column of rho. */
    rho[0:s][t+1] < - East;

    /* other communication . . . */

    /* Compute acceleration */
    for (i=0; i<s; i++)
    {
        for (j=0; i<t; i++)
        {
            denom = (rho[i][j]     * J[i][j]     + rho[i][j+1] * J[i][j+1] +
                    rho[i+1][j+1] * J[i+1][j+1] + rho[i+1][j] * J[i+1][j]) / 2;
              . . .
        }
    }
    /* other computation . . . */
}
```

Figure 6: X Level Code for the Hydro Phase

$Hydro[i\text{-}1][j].port.S$	$\leftrightarrow$ $Hydro[i][j].N$	$1 \le i < \bar{r},\quad 0 \le j < \bar{c}$
$Hydro[i][j\text{-}1].port.E$	$\leftrightarrow$ $Hydro[i][j].W$	$0 \le i < \bar{r},\quad 1 \le j < \bar{c}$
$Hydro[i][j\text{-}1].port.NE$	$\leftrightarrow$ $Hydro[i\text{-}1][j].SW$	$1 \le i < \bar{r},\quad 1 \le j < \bar{c}$

This specification associates only a subset of all ports, namely, those that are connected as in Figure 7. The remaining ports, those on the boundary of the problem space, can be bound to functions that compute the boundary conditions using data local to the section. For example, the specification

$$Hydro[i][t].port.E \text{ receive} \quad \leftrightarrow \quad Eboundary(); \qquad 0 \le i < \bar{r}$$

states that for sections along the East boundary, a "receive" from the E port will return the value computed by the function $Eboundary()$. Figure 8 shows the definition of this boundary condition.

Other boundaries can be defined similarly. For example,

$$Hydro[i][t].port.E \text{ send} \quad \leftrightarrow \quad No\text{-}op(); \qquad 0 \le i < \bar{r}$$

states that sending data to an unbound East port results in a no-op (this is the default). Once these functions have been defined, boundary values can be accessed through ports in

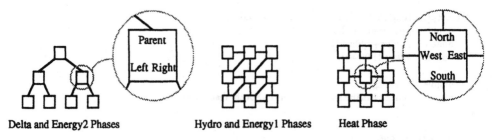

Figure 7: Communication Graphs and Port Ensembles for SIMPLE

```
Eboundary(x, u)
    Vector   x[s+1][t+1];
    Vector   u[s+1][t+1];
{
    double   alpha, beta, omega;
    int      i, j;

    for (i=1; i<s+1; i++)
    {
        x[i][t+1].r = x[i][t].r + (x[i][t].r − x[i][t−1].r);
        x[i][t+1].z = x[i][t].z + (x[i][t].z − x[i][t−1].z);
        u[i][t+1].r = u[i][t−1].r;
        u[i][t+1].z = u[i][t−1].z;
    }
}
```

Figure 8: Function to Handle East Boundary Condition in *xHydro()*

the same manner that interior processes access values in neighboring sections. Thus, all processes can execute the same source level code.

Phase Definition. A phase is the composition of data ensembles, a code ensemble and a port ensemble. For the *Hydro* phase, for example, the latter two bindings have already been made explicitly. To incorporate the necessary data ensembles we specify

Hydro.data   ↔   *x, u, a, rho, p, q, delta_tau, e, J, S, bound_p*

which conceptually declares the actual parameters that correspond to the formals in the process preamble. Any or all of these could have been specified at the call site if they varied from call to call in the problem level (Z level) program.

5   Experiments

For a given application and a given machine, the best partitioning strategy is not always known [21]. Two obvious choices are to partition the data into squares or into strips. For applications with nearest neighbor communication, square sections result in less data transmission but in more messages, since each interior section has up to six neighbors.

With strips, each section has at most two neighbors, but more data is transmitted because each section has a larger perimeter to area ratio.

Pingali and Rogers [20] pose the question of whether squares are better than strips for SIMPLE. Data ensembles ease the task of changing data partitions and provide a mechanism for studying this question. The *Block* partitioning is the data ensemble described in the previous section. This will be compared against the *Strip* partitioning in which each section contains a vertical strip of the data arrays.

Recall that the data ensembles discussed earlier create $\bar{r} \times \bar{c}$ arrays of blocks. With the Phase Abstractions, the *Strip* partitioning is easily derived from the *Block* partitioning by setting $\bar{r} = 1$ and $\bar{c} = Number\text{-}of\text{-}Processors$. In addition, *Strips* require that each process have only East-West neighbors instead of the six neighbors used in *Block*. By using the port ensembles to bind functions to unused ports – in this case the North, South, NorthEast and SouthWest ports – the program can easily accommodate this change in the number of neighbors. *No other source level changes are required.*

Before presenting the results, we first explain our experimental methodology and hardware environment.

Methodology. Since the Phase Abstractions version of SIMPLE is portable, it can execute on several different machines and serve as a tool for studying the effects of various program characteristics. Using a single portable program has the advantage of controlling one important variable, namely, the application under study.

Because no Phase Abstractions compiler currently exists we hand ported our program to run on the various machines. Our X level language was C, and we used machine specific routines (also written in C) to implement the other Phase Abstractions entities. In porting this program, only rudimentary source level changes dealing with the differences in message passing and process/node management were necessary.[2]

Hardware. We used four multiprocessors in our experiments. The first is a Sequent Symmetry Model A, which has 20 Intel 80386 processors connected by a shared bus to a 32 MB memory module. Each processor has a unified 64K cache and an 80387 floating point accelerator [17].

A second machine is a 24 node BBN Butterfly GP1000. Each node has a Motorola 68020 processor, 4 MB of local memory, and a processor node controller (PNC) which interacts with an omega network to make remote references when needed. Together, the memory modules, the PNC's, and the network form a single shared memory that all processors can access. Local memory access is about 12 times faster than remote access [1].

The remaining machines are hypercubes. On the 32 node Intel iPSC/2 each node contains an 80386 processor, an iPSC SX floating point accelerator, and 8 MB of memory. All interprocessor communication is through message passing [14]. On the 64 node NCUBE/7 each node has a custom main processor and 512 KB of memory. Like the iPSC/2, the NCUBE/7 is a nonshared memory machine [19].

Results. Figure 9 shows our results for problem sizes of 1K and 2K points. The *Block* partitioning performed better in every case, and the difference between the two strategies generally increases as the number of processors grows. This means that the overhead of

---

[2]For the shared memory machines, message passing routines were implemented using shared memory.

sending more messages in *Blocks* is offset by the fact that *Block* transmits less overall data than *Strips*. Thus, we expect *Block's* performance advantage to increase with the problem size since such changes do not alter the number of messages sent, but only increase the size of these messages. Our results appear to confirm this intuition. We conclude that for SIMPLE, partitioning by blocks is superior to partitioning by strips.

6 Conclusion

We have presented the Phase Abstractions and shown how they can be used to write a parallel version of SIMPLE. Furthermore, we have demonstrated how the port and data ensembles facilitate the creation of alternate program implementations, and we have used this flexibility to study the issue of choosing the best data partitioning for SIMPLE.

Acknowledgments We wish to thank our colleagues on the Orca Project; Hans Mandt and the Advanced Systems Laboratory of Boeing Computing Services for providing access to a Butterfly multiprocessor; and Walter Rudd and others at the Oregon Advanced Computing Institute for providing access to their iPSC/2 and NCUBE/7. This research was supported in part by Office of Naval Research Contract N00014-89-J-1368.

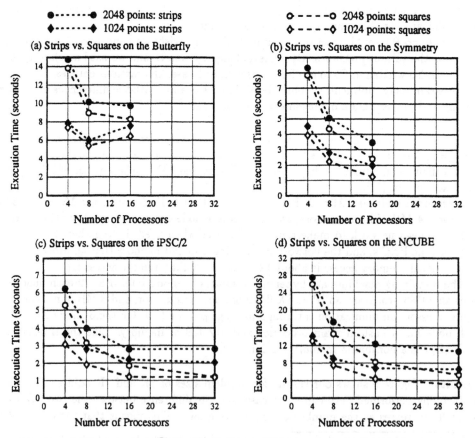

Figure 9: Strips vs. Squares.

References

[1] G. Alverson. *Abstractions for Effectively Portable Shared Memory Parallel Programs*. PhD thesis, University of Washington, Department of Computer Science and Engineering, 1990.

[2] G. Alverson, W. Griswold, D. Notkin, and L. Snyder. A flexible communication abstraction for nonshared memory parallel computing. In *Proceedings of Supercomputing '90*, November 1990.

[3] G. Alverson, W. Griswold, D. Notkin, and L. Snyder. Scalable abstractions for parallel programming. In *Proceedings of the Fifth Distributed Memory Computing Conference*, 1990. Charleston, South Carolina.

[4] T. S. Axelrod, P. F. Dubois, and P. G. Eltgroth. A simulator for MIMD performance prediction - application to the S-1 MkIIa multiprocessor. In *Proceedings of the International Conference on Parallel Processing*, pages 350–358, 1983.

[5] F. Berman, M. Goodrich, C. Koelbel, W. R. III, and K. Showell. Prep-P: A mapping preprocessor for CHiP computers. In *Proceedings of the International Conference on Parallel Processing*, pages 731–733, August 1985.

[6] W. Crowley, C. P. Hendrickson, and T. I. Luby. The Simple code. Technical Report UCID-17715, Lawrence Livermore Laboratory, 1978.

[7] D. E. Culler and Arvind. Resource requirements of dataflow programs. In *Proceedings of the International Symposium on Computer Architecture*, pages 141–150, 1988.

[8] K. Ekanadham and Arvind. SIMPLE: Part I, an exercise in future scientific programming. Technical Report CSG Technical Report 273, MIT, 1987.

[9] D. Gannon and J. Panetta. SIMPLE on the CHiP. Technical Report 469, Computer Science Department, Purdue University, 1984.

[10] D. Gannon and J. Panetta. Restructuring Simple for the CHiP architecture. In *Parallel Computing*, pages 3:305–326, 1986.

[11] K. Gates. Simple: An exercise in programming in Poker. Technical report, Applied Mathematics Department, University of Washington, 1989.

[12] R. E. Hiromoto, O. M. Lubeck, and J. Moore. Experiences with the Denelcor HEP. In *Parallel Computing*, pages 1:197–206, 1984.

[13] T. J. Holman. *Processor Element Architecture for Non-Shared Memory Parallel Computers*. PhD thesis, University of Washington, Department of Computer Science, 1988.

[14] Intel Corporation. *iPSC/2 User's Guide*. October 1989.

[15] J. Lee. Extending the SIMPLE program in Poker. Technical Report 89–11–07, Department of Computer Science and Engineering, University of Washington, 1989.

[16] C. Lin and L. Snyder. Portable parallel programming: Cross machine comparisons for SIMPLE. In *Fifth SIAM Conference on Parallel Processing*, 1991.

[17] T. Lovett and S. Thakkar. The Symmetry multiprocessor system. In *Proceedings of the International Conference on Parallel Processing*, pages 303–310, 1988.

[18] J. M. Meyers. Analysis of the SIMPLE code for dataflow computation. Technical Report MIT/LCS/TR-216, MIT, 1979.

[19] NCUBE Corporation. *NCUBE Product Report*. 1986. Beaverton OR.

[20] K. Pingali and A. Rogers. Compiler parallelization of SIMPLE for a distributed memory machine. Technical Report 90–1084, Cornell University, 1990.

[21] J. Saltz, V. Naik, and D. Nicol. Reduction of the effects of the communication delays in scientific algorithms on message passing MIMD architectures. *SIAM Journal of Statistical Computing*, 8(1):s118–134, January 1987.

[22] L. Snyder. Applications of the "Phase Abstractions" for portable and scalable parallel programming. In *Proceedings of the ICASE Workshop on Programming Distributed Memory Machines*.

[23] D. Socha. An approach to compiling single-point iterative programs for distributed memory computers. In *Proceedings of the Fifth Distributed Memory Computing Conference*, 1990.

[24] M. R. Thistle and B. J. Smith. A processor architecture for Horizon. In *Proceedings of Supercomputing '88*, pages 35–41, 1988.

7   Compilation of Id

Z. Ariola
Harvard University
Arvind
Massachusetts Institute of Technology

Abstract

In this paper we illustrate, using the Id language, that both the operational semantics of a language and its compilation process can be formalized together. Id is a higher-order non-strict functional language augmented with I-structures and M-structures. The operational semantics of Id is given in terms of a smaller *kernel* language, called Kid. Kid is also the intermediate form used by the compiler to perform type checking and optimizations. Optimizations are described as extensions of Kid operational semantics. A criteria for correctness of optimizations is presented. P-TAC, a lower-level language, is introduced to capture some efficiency issues related to code generation. The salient features of translating Kid into P-TAC are presented.

1   Introduction

Modern (functional) languages are too complex to be given direct operational semantics. It is usually better to translate the source language into a simpler and smaller *kernel* language in order to explain its meaning precisely [11]. A program is said to be *well-formed* if it can be translated into the kernel language, and if it satisfies certain other constraints such as type correctness. Operational or dynamic semantics is concerned only with well-formed programs.

All compilers do a similar translation into an intermediate form in the process of generating code for a machine. A compiler performs type checking and optimizations on this intermediate form before generating machine code. In this paper we will show that the intermediate form can actually be the kernel language. In fact, we may translate the kernel language into still lower-level language(s), where more machine oriented or efficiency related concerns can be expressed directly. Furthermore, compiler optimizations may be expressed as source-to-source transformations on an intermediate language. The semantics of well-formed programs in these intermediate languages is important if we want to show the correctness of these optimizations or the translation process. Thus, each module of the compiler does one of the following three things:

- translate a language L_i into language L_{i+1}; or
- optimize, *i.e.*, source-to-source transformation in language L_i; or
- annotate a program in language L_i with some properties, such as types, scopes or source line numbers.

An advantage of formalizing the compiler modules in these terms is that it gives flexibility to the compiler writer in choosing data structures for various modules. For example, our presentation does not take a position regarding the representation of terms in our kernel language. The compiler may choose different data structures, such as, parse trees or graphs, for terms in different modules. The idea of viewing intermediate forms as languages is not new in the functional language community [6, 9, 14], but it is still rare in the Fortran community (Pingali's work being a notable exception [15]).

In this paper we will show certain aspects of the process of compiling Id, an implicit parallel language [13]. Id is a higher-order functional language augmented with I-structures [5] and M-structures [7]. I-structures add a flavor of logic variables, while M-structures add side-effects and non-determinism to Id. Id, like most modern functional languages, has a Hindley-Milner type system and non-strict semantics. Id has been in use at MIT as the language for programming dataflow machines. In the last few years interest has grown in compiling Id for workstations and stock parallel machines [16, 17]. We have recently started a project to write the Id compiler in Id, which will embody the strategy outlined in this paper.

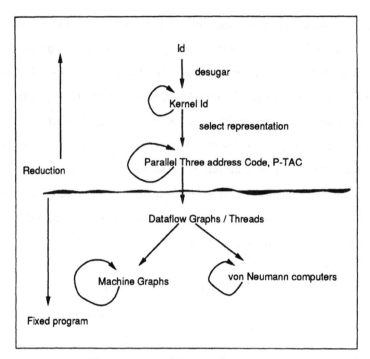

Figure 1: Compilation scheme of Id

Figure 1 shows the high-level Id compilation process, while Figure 2 shows some of the steps in going from Id to Kid, the kernel Id language. The circular arrows in Figure 1 refer to optimizations. The steps in Figure 2 together with the operational semantics of Kid are needed to formalize the operational semantics of Id. The compiler needs to do parsing and scope analysis in order to actually carry out the steps shown in Figure 2; we have not shown these phases explicitly.

As an example of the desugaring process, consider the following function which maps f to each element of a list.

```
Def map f Nil = Nil
  | map f x:xs = (f x) : map f xs;
```

The multi-clause definition gets turned into a case expression and the function definition into a λ-expression as follows:

```
map = { Fun t1 t2 = { Case (t1, t2)  of
                    | (f,  Nil) = Nil
                    | (f,  x:xs) = (f x) : map f xs } }
```

where t1 and t2 are new variables. The pattern matching module simplifies the case-expression into the following simple case expression:

```
map = { Fun t1 t2 = { Case t2   of
                    |  Nil  = Nil
                    |  x:xs = (t1 x) : map t1 xs } }.
```

In Section 2 we will describe Kid, some aspects of translating desugared Id into Kid, and some optimizations on Kid programs. The Kid to P-TAC translation, which involves choosing representations for data structures and higher-order functions, is discussed in Section 3. The tone of the paper is informal throughout; for a more comprehensive description of the compiler the reader may refer to [3]. However, even in [3], M-structures are not discussed.

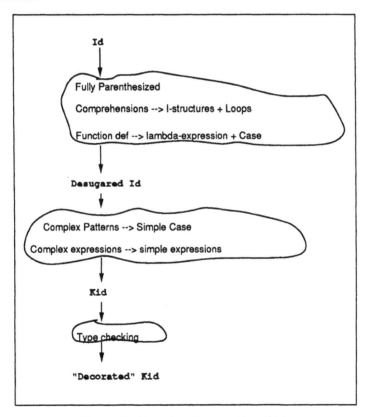

Figure 2: Operational semantics of Id

2   Kid: The Kernel Id language

In Kid every expression, except a block, a case or a λ-expression, is of the form

$$PF_n(SE_1, \cdots, SE_n)$$

where PF_n is the name of a *primitive function* of arity n, and SE stands for *simple expression* which is either a constant or a variable. Some examples of primitive functions are the $+$ operator, the application operator Apply, and the array constructor I_array. A simplified description of the language is given in Figure 3; for a complete understanding of Kid the reader may refer to [4]. As a strongly typed language, Kid needs a different case-expression and a set of selector and constructor operators for each algebraic type. Since a discussion of user defined types will complicate our presentation without necessarily providing additional insight, we have only included the operators for the list type.   Kid can

$$
\begin{array}{lll}
SE & ::= & Variable \mid Constant \\
E & ::= & SE \mid PF_n(SE, \cdots, SE) \\
  &   & \mid \text{Bool\_Case}(SE, E, E) \\
  &   & \mid \text{List\_Case}(SE, E, E) \\
  &   & \mid Block \\
  &   & \mid \lambda(x_1, \cdots, x_n).E \\
Block & ::= & \{[Statement;]^* \text{ In } SE\} \\
Statement & ::= & Binding \mid Command \\
Binding & ::= & Variable = E \\
Command & ::= & \text{P\_store}\,(SE,\ SE,\ SE) \\
  &   & \text{Store\_error} \mid \top,
\end{array}
$$

Figure 3: Grammar of Kid

be seen as the λ-calculus with constants and let-blocks. However, unlike other functional languages [14], let-blocks play a fundamental role in the operational semantics of Kid. Our let-block semantics precisely defines how arguments are shared; an essential feature for Id extended with I-structures and M-structures. Sharing is expressed by giving a name to each subexpression and by allowing substitution of values and variables only. This idea can be formalized in a *Contextual Rewriting Systems* (CRS) [2, 4] by the following *Substitution rules*:

$$\frac{X = V}{X \longrightarrow V} \qquad \frac{X = Y}{X \longrightarrow Y}$$

where V is either an Integer or a Boolean or an **Error**. Intuitively, the above rule should be read as follows: occurrences of X in a program M can be rewritten to V, only if the binding X = V appears in the context of X in M. A context represents a term with "holes", that is, a term with some unspecified subexpressions or bindings. If we substitute V for X, or Y for X, everywhere then the corresponding binding can be deleted from the term.

The following *Block Flattening rule* is essential in all CRS's.

$$
\begin{array}{ccc}
\{_{m} \vec{X}_n = \{_{n} SS_1;\ SS_2;\ \cdots & & \{_{m} \vec{X}_n = \vec{Y}_n; \\
\quad\quad \text{In}\ \ \vec{Y}_n\} & \longrightarrow & SS_1;\ SS_2;\ \cdots \\
S_1;\ \cdots\ S_n & & S_1;\ \cdots\ S_n \\
\quad \text{In}\ \vec{Z}_m\} & & \text{In}\ \vec{Z}_m\}
\end{array}
$$

where $\vec{X}_n$ represents *multiple variables*. Multiple variables allow expressions in Kid to return multiple values without the necessity of packaging them into a data structure. A reader familiar with dataflow graphs may think of multiple values as a graph with multiple input or output arcs. Multiple values require the following CRS rule:

$$
\vec{X}_n = \vec{Y}_n \longrightarrow (X_1 = Y_1; \cdots X_n = Y_n).
$$

2.1 Translating Id into Kid

We will use **foldl**, the Id definition of the fold-from-left function to demonstrate the translation from an Id program to a Kid program. The pictorial description of **foldl** is given in Figure 4.

```
Def foldl f s A = { (l,u) = Bounds A;
                    In
                    { for i<- 1 to u do
                          next s = f A[i] s;
                      finally s }}
```

Some of the uses of the **foldl** are:

```
foldl (+) 0;    % sums elements of an array
foldl (≤) ∞;    % computes the minimum element in an array
foldl (:) Nil;  % converts an array into a list
```

The translation into Kid introduces explicit **Apply** operators and converts the loop into a λ-expression and **FLoop** combinator:

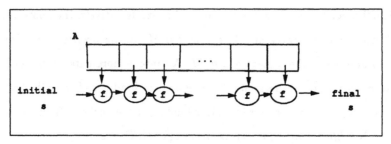

Figure 4: An application of the foldl function to array A

```
foldl = λ(f,s,A).{ t1 = Bounds A;
                   l = P-select(t1,1);
                   u = P-select(t1,2);
                   tf1 = { b = λ(i,s).{ t1 = Select A i;
                                        t2 = Apply(f,t1);
                                        next-s = Apply(t2,s);
                                          In next-s };
                          tp = ≤(1,u);
                          tf = FLoop(u,1,b,1,s,tp);
                            In tf}
                     In tf1}
```

Now we discuss some salient aspects of this translation process.

Array selection

In Id there are only two operations defined on arrays. *Selection, i.e.* A[i], which returns the value of the ith slot of array A assuming that i is within the bounds, and (Bounds A), which returns the tuple containing the bounds. The selection A[i] is translated into the Kid expression (Select A i). However, Select is not a primitive operator in Kid, due to the complexity of bound checking. Kid uses P_select as a primitive selection operator whose semantics does not require bounds checking. Thus, Select may be expressed in terms of P_select as follows:

```
Select = λ(x,i).{ (1,u) = Bounds x;
                  In If (i > u Or i < 1)  then
                     Error
                     else
                     P_select(x,i) }
```

Notice that the translation of the tuple pattern in the foldl program is given using the primitive select operator because type checking guarantees that the indices will be within bounds.

The definition of array elements in Id are given either by array comprehension expressions or by using I-structure assignment rules. In either case, the definition of an array element translates into a `P_store` command. The behavior of `P_select` can be explained using the following rule:

$$\frac{\text{P\_store}(X, Y, Z)}{\text{P\_select}(X, Y) \ \longrightarrow \ Z}$$

The above CRS rule says that the expression `P_select(X, Y)` in a program M, can be rewritten to Z, if `P_store(X, Y, Z)` appears in its context in M. Notationally a context is represented by $C[\Box]$. $C[\text{P\_store}(X, Y, Z)]$ then represents the program obtained by filling the hole with `P_store(X, Y, Z)`. Thus, we can say that if M is the program $C[\text{P\_store}(X, Y, Z), \text{P\_select}(X, Y)]$, then we can *rewrite* M to the program $C[\text{P\_store}(X, Y, Z), Z]$. Notice that the precondition is not affected by the rewriting; it only enables the rewriting. Furthermore, the precondition does not imply any semantic check; it involves only syntactic pattern matching.

The rule for the Bounds operator is as follows:

$$\frac{X = \text{I\_array}(X_b)}{\text{Bounds}(X) \ \longrightarrow \ X_b}$$

I-structure semantics prohibits multiple definitions for an array element. This condition can not be checked statically at compile time. Thus, we need the following rules for generating and propagating inconsistent state represented by $\top$ or $\top_s$. These rules are needed to guarantee the confluence of Id.

$$\frac{\text{P\_store}(X, i, V)}{\text{P\_store}(X, i, V') \ \longrightarrow \ \top_s}$$

$$\{_m X = \top; \ S_1; \cdots S_n \ \text{In} \ \overrightarrow{Z_m} \} \ \longrightarrow \ \top$$
$$\{_m \top_s; \ S_1; \cdots S_n \ \text{In} \ \overrightarrow{Z_m} \} \ \longrightarrow \ \top$$

Higher-order functions

Another part of the translation deals with higher-order functions. All functions in Id have an associated *arity*. For example, the arity of `foldl` is 3. When all the three arguments for a **fold** application are available the **Apply** rewrites to an Ap_n operator, and then the following *full application* rule is used:

$$\frac{F = \lambda_{n,m}\,(\vec{Z_n})\,.\,E}{Ap_{n,m}(F,\,\vec{X_n}) \;\longrightarrow\; (\mathcal{RB}[\![E]\!])\,[\vec{X_n}\,/\,\vec{Z_n}]}$$

where $\mathcal{RB}$ is a function which renames the bound variables of E to avoid name conflicts. $\mathcal{RB}$ corresponds to the allocation of a *frame* in a stack-based implementation. The notation $[\vec{X_n}\,/\,\vec{Z_n}]$ stands for the substitution of $X_1 \cdots X_n$ for each occurrence of $Z_1 \cdots Z_n$.

Exactly how does an **Apply** become an **Ap** operator? Since the function being applied is not necessarily known at compile time, we need to compile applications for all contingencies. Notice that the Id expression (**f A[i] s**) is a legal expression even if the arity of **f** is greater than 2 or less than 2. We compile each application as a function of one argument. Thus, the Id expression (**f A[i] s**) is translated into the following Kid expression:

```
{ t1 = Select A i;
  t2 = Apply(f,t1);
  t3 = Apply(t2,s);
  In t3 }
```

The **Apply** operator can now be described as follows:

$$\begin{array}{rcl}
F & = & \lambda_n(\vec{Z_n})\,.\,E \qquad | \\
F_1 & = & \text{Apply}(F,\,X_1) \qquad | \\
F_2 & = & \text{Apply}(F_1,\,X_2) \qquad | \\
& \vdots & \\
\hline
F_{n-1} & = & \text{Apply}(F_{n-2},X_{n-1}) \\
\hline
\end{array}$$
$$\text{Apply}(F_{n-1},X_n) \;\longrightarrow\; Ap_n(F,\vec{X_n})$$

The above rule says that in order to fire a function **f** of arity n, we need to collect n arguments. Thus, for example, the expression **Apply(f,x)** will not get subjected to any rewriting. An alternative and easier way of expressing the above rule is:

$$\frac{F = \lambda_n(\vec{Z_n})\,.\,E}{\text{Apply}(F,X) \;\longrightarrow\; \text{Apply}_1(F,\underline{n},X)}$$

$$\frac{F' = \text{Apply}_i(F,\underline{n},\vec{X_i}) \quad i < (n-1)}{\text{Apply}(F',X_{i+1}) \;\longrightarrow\; \text{Apply}_{i+1}(F,\underline{n},\vec{X_{i+1}})}$$

$$\frac{F' = \text{Apply}_i(F,\underline{n},\vec{X_i}) \quad i = (n-1)}{\text{Apply}(F',X_{i+1}) \;\longrightarrow\; Ap_n(F,\vec{X_n})}$$

where each operator **Apply$_i$** remembers the i arguments collected so far.

Loops

The left-hand-side variable of a binding in a loop gets a new value in each iteration of the loop. When a variable in a loop binding is preceded by the keyword next, (for example, next x = ...), x and next x are two distinct variables which can exist simultaneously. One should not think of variable x as being updated in a loop as one does in an imperative language. A natural way of expressing this flow of information is by translating the loop body into a function. For example, the body of the following loop in the foldl definition:

```
{ for i<- 1 to u do
    next s = f A[i]  s;
    finally s }}
```

is translated into the following function:

```
λ(i,s).{ t1 = Select A i;
         t2 = Apply(f,t1);
         next-s = Apply(t2,s);
         In next-s};
```

which returns the nextified variable. The FLoop operator invokes this function under the appropriate conditions. The paramenters of the FLoop operator correspond to the upper bound, the step (1 in our example), the loop-body function, the nextified variables (including the index variable), and finally, the predicate. The rule for the FLoop operator is as follows:

$$
\begin{aligned}
\text{FLoop}_n(U, D, B, \vec{X_n}, \text{True}) \quad &\longrightarrow \quad \{_n \; \overrightarrow{t_{2,n}} \; = \; \text{Ap}_{n,n-1}(B, \vec{X_n}); \\
& \qquad\qquad\quad t_1 \; = \; +(X_1, D); \\
& \qquad\qquad\quad t_p \; = \; <(t_1, U); \\
& \qquad\qquad\quad \vec{t_n'} \; = \; \text{FLoop}_n(U, D, B, \vec{t_n}, t_p) \\
& \qquad\qquad\quad \text{In} \; \vec{t_n'} \} \\
\text{FLoop}_n(U, D, B, \vec{X_n}, \text{False}) \quad &\longrightarrow \quad \vec{X_n}
\end{aligned}
$$

If the index variable is within the loop bounds, that is, the value of the last argument of FLoop is True, then function b is invoked, index X_1 is incremented and checked to see if X_1 is still less than the upper bound, U, and finally, a new instance of the loop is generated. In case the index variable is outside the loop bounds, that is, the value of the last argument of FLoop is False, the values of the nextified variables are returned.

The reason for introducing special combinators for for-loops and while-loops is to facilitate loop optimizations that a compiler may perform.

Lists

For the sake of completeness, we also give the rules for the algebraic type list.

$$\frac{Z = \text{Cons}(X, Y)}{\text{Cons\_1}(Z) \ \longrightarrow \ X}$$

$$\frac{Z = \text{Cons}(X, Y)}{\text{Cons\_2}(Z) \ \longrightarrow \ Y}$$

$$\text{List\_case}_m(\text{Nil}, E_1, E_2) \ \longrightarrow \ E_1$$

$$\frac{Z = \text{Cons}(X, Y)}{\text{List\_case}_m(Z, E_1, E_2) \ \longrightarrow \ E_2}$$

2.2 Optimizations on Kid

There are many situations where a Kid rewrite rule can be applied at compile time. Take for example, the following Kid program:

```
Def f x = { i = +(2,3); P-store(x,i,v); ... a = P-select(x,5); ... }
```

The compiler could clearly replace the expression $+(2, 3)$ by 5 and substitute 5 for i everywhere. These optimizations are often referred to as *constant folding* and *constant propagation* [1]. Moreover, knowing that the 5th element of array x is v, the compiler can rewrite the P_select(x, i) to v. This optimization is called *fetch-elimination*, and is performed in hardware by many supercomputers! The Id compiler also does many optimizations which are not directly derived from the rewrite rules used for giving the operational semantics of Id. A partial list of these other optimizations is:

- inline substitution;
- partial evaluation;
- algebraic rules;
- eliminating circulating variables and constants;
- loop peeling and unrolling;
- common subexpression elimination;
- lift free expressions (loop invariants);
- loop variable induction analysis;
- dead code elimination.

A very interesting fact is that all the above optimizations, except the last two, can be expressed as Kid rewrite rules. For example, *common subexpression elimination* (cse) and the *algebraic rules* may be specified in terms of the following rules:

Cse rule:
$$\frac{Z_1 = +(X, Y)}{Z_2 = +(X, Y) \longrightarrow Z_2 = Z_1}$$

Algebraic rules:
$$*(X, 0) \longrightarrow 0$$
$$\text{Equal}(X, X) \longrightarrow \text{True}$$
$$\frac{X = +(Y, 3)}{< (Y, X) \longrightarrow \text{True}}$$

Reduction Strategy for Optimizations

The example at the beginning of this section shows that an optimization can trigger another one. Furthermore, optimizations can be applied in many different orders. Thus, interesting questions arise regarding the uniqueness of the final program, and regarding the termination of the optimization process. Since we have expressed the optimizations as rewrite rules, the problem of termination and the effect of reduction strategies can be stated in terms of *strongly normalizing* rules and *confluence*, respectively [10].

Most optimization rules are indeed *confluent*. A few that do destroy confluence do so only in programs with deadlocks. The confluence of optimization rules gives us some flexibility in choosing the order in which rules are to be applied. A powerful and efficient strategy is to apply the first five rules along with all the normal Kid rules in an *outside-in* manner. After that, common subexpression elimination and the lifting of free expressions can be done in an *inside-out* manner. Unfortunately, inside-out rules can trigger more outside-in optimizations, and thus, the whole process needs to be repeated until the expression stops changing.

The only optimization rules that can cause non-termination are the partial evaluation and the inline substitution rules. This problem of termination has been studied extensively in the partial evaluation literature which an interested reader may refer [19]. The deadcode elimination can be done at any stage but must be done once more in the end to pick up maximum dead code. Though we are not sure, we think that the loop variable induction analysis should be done as late as possible, so that maximum information about array subscripts and loop index variables can be used.

The Correctness of Optimizations

Optimizations extend the operational semantics of Kid, and therefore, it is interesting to study if they preserve the *meaning* of a term. Questions about meanings are usually addressed in denotational semantics. However, we think that a great deal of knowledge can be drawn from just the syntactic structure of terms, and thus, we prefer to formulate the correctness problem from a more syntactic or operational point of view. We define several different notions of equality for Kid terms. The first and the least troublesome equality is based on the notion of *convertibility*, which is induced by replacing the arrow in the rules by the equality sign. For example, constant folding and inline substitution can easily be shown to preserve convertibility and thus, correctness.

Suppose we consider a slightly more complicated optimization, like the common subexpression elimination, it is easy to see that convertibility will not suffice for correctness. Consider the following example:

```
M = { x = +(a,b);   cse      M1 = { x = +(a,b);
      y = +(a,b);   --->            y = x;
      z = +(x,y);                   z = +(x,y);
      In z }                        In z}
```

M is not convertible to M1. It is, however, easy to see that the *unravelled* version of M, +(+(a,b),+(a,b)), is equal to the unravelled version of M1. In fact, M and M1 are said to be *tree equivalent*. It is possible to show that the tree equivalence preserves semantics, that is, no context will be able to distinguish between two terms that are tree equivalent. Thus, we can conclude that the cse rule is correct.

Convertibility and tree equivalence are still very syntactic notions to show the equivalence of the following terms related by an algebraic rule:

```
M = { y = *(x,0);   --->      M1 = 0
      In y }
```

A still harder question arises when we consider "infinite terms" (such as the infinite list of 1's shown below), that can be found in any non-strict functional language.

```
M = { x = 1:x;                M1 = { Def f x = x:(f x);
      In x}                          In f 1}
```

At this point we need to ask exactly what external behavior of a program we want to preserve. In defining the concept of observable behavior or *answer*, we first introduce the notion of a *printable value* associated with a term. Intuitively, the printable value of a term corresponds to the stable or fixed part of the term, that is, the part which will not be subjected to further reduction. For example, we could say that the printable value of { x = +(2,3); In x} is Ω, which means no useful information is printable. Only after we reduce +(2,3) to 5, we can say that the printable value of the term is 5. This concept of printable value is related to the notion of *instant semantics* introduced by Welch [18]. The answer is then defined in terms of the maximum information that can be extracted by reducing that term. Levy [12] and Ariola [2] have shown that by picking a suitable definition of print, the domain of answers becomes a term model for the language. Suppose $\mathcal{A}(M)$ denotes the answer associated with M. Then we will say that a rule r is correct if it preserves the answer, that is, for all programs M, we have:

$$M \xrightarrow{r} M1 \Longrightarrow \mathcal{A}(M) = \mathcal{A}(M1)$$

This notion is strong enough to show the correctness of all optimizations.

3 P-TAC: Parallel Three Address Code

If we were only interested in giving operational semantics to Kid then we could stop at the Kid level; however, we want to generate code for a specific machine. Rather than trying to generate code for a specific machine directly, we introduce a level of detail in the translation process that will be relevant to (almost) all machines. We call this next lower level language P-TAC. In P-TAC we have only one data structure called an I-structure array. I-structures have the following rules associated with them:

$$\text{Allocate}(\underline{n}) \longrightarrow \text{L}$$

where L is a brand new label. Labels are treated like other scalar values such as integers and booleans, and can be freely substituted and stored. The rest of the rules for I-structures are very similar to Kid rules and are as follows:

$$\frac{\text{P\_store}(\text{L},\underline{i},\text{V})}{\text{P\_select}(\text{L},\underline{i}) \longrightarrow \text{V}}$$

$$\frac{\text{P\_store}(\text{L},\underline{i},\text{V})}{\text{P\_store}(\text{L},\underline{i},\text{V}') \longrightarrow \top_s}$$

where V is either an Integer or a Boolean or a Label or Error.

$$\{_m \text{X} = \top\ S_1; \cdots S_n \text{ In } \vec{Z_m} \} \quad \longrightarrow \quad \top$$

$$\{_m \top_s;\ S_1; \cdots S_n \text{ In } \vec{Z_m} \} \quad \longrightarrow \quad \top$$

All composite objects, that is, tuples, arrays, higher-dimension arrays, all algebraic types, and closures are represented using I-structure arrays. There are usually several reasonable ways to represent each data structure in terms of I-structures. For each type we give one representation, though not necessarily the most efficient one. We have included a "type" tag field for all composite objects, even though it is not needed by the P-TAC interpreter since Id is a statically typed language. However, we might need type information for other reasons, such as garbage collection, and for printing values in a partially executed program.

The grammar of P-TAC is given in Figure 5. Notice that in P-TAC, case expressions for all algebraic types are translated into a single untyped dispatch operator.

$$\text{Dispatch}_{n,m}(\mathbf{i}, E_1, \cdots, E_i, \cdots E_n) \quad \longrightarrow \quad E_i$$

Prior to translating Kid into P-TAC, all nested λ-expressions are lifted to the top level by a

SE	::=	*Variable* | *Constant*
*PF*₁	::=	Allocate
*PF*₂	::=	P_select
E	::=	*SE* | *PF*ₙ(*SE*, ⋯ , *SE*)
		| Dispatchₙ(*SE*, *E*₁, ⋯ , *Eₙ*)
		| FLoop(*SE*, *SE*, *SE*, *SE*, *SE*)
		| *Block*
Block	::=	{[*Statement*;]* In *SE*}
Statement	::=	*Binding* | *Command*
Binding	::=	*Variable* = *E*
Command	::=	P_store (*SE*, *SE*, *SE*)
		Store_error | ⊤,

Figure 5: Grammar of P-TAC

process known as λ-lifting [8]. A Kid program after λ-lifting only contains closed λ-expressions. The translator, given a Kid program, produces the corresponding P-TAC program and a set,"D", of definitions. The set D is initialized with constants that are introduced by the translator.

3.1 Translation from Kid into P-TAC

In the following we will only discuss how arrays, lists and functions are represented in P-TAC; the interested reader may refer [3] for more details.

Arrays

The representation of Array(l, u) is given in Figure 6. The constant definitions for Headersize, Upper, Lower, *etc.* should be included in D.

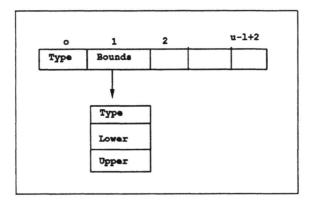

Figure 6: Representation of 1D-array

$$\text{TE}[\![\text{Bounds}(X)]\!] \quad = \quad \text{P\_select}(X, \text{Bounds})$$

$$\text{TE}[\![I\_\text{array}(X)]\!] \quad = \quad \{ \begin{array}{lll} 1 & = & \text{P\_select}(X, \text{Lower}); \\ u & = & \text{P\_select}(X, \text{Upper}); \\ s & = & -(u, 1); \\ \text{size} & = & +(s, 3); \\ t & = & \text{Allocate}(\text{size}); \\ \multicolumn{3}{l}{\text{P\_store}(t, \text{Type}, \text{``Array''});} \\ \multicolumn{3}{l}{\text{P\_store}(t, \text{Bounds}, X);} \\ \multicolumn{3}{l}{\text{In } t\}} \end{array}$$

$$\text{TE}[\![\text{P\_select}(X_1, X_2)]\!] \quad = \quad \{ \begin{array}{lll} t_b & = & \text{P\_select}(X_1, \text{Bounds}); \\ 1 & = & \text{P\_select}(t_b, \text{Lower}); \\ t_1 & = & -(X_2, 1); \\ t_2 & = & +(t_1, \text{Headersize}); \\ t & = & \text{P\_select}(X_1, t_2) \\ \multicolumn{3}{l}{\text{In } t\}} \end{array}$$

$$TE[\![\text{P\_store}(X_1, X_2, X_3)]\!] \;=\; \{ \begin{aligned}[t] t_b &= \text{P\_select}(X_1, \text{Bounds}); \\ 1 &= \text{P\_select}(t_b, \text{Lower}); \\ t_1 &= -(X_2, 1); \\ t_2 &= +(t_1, \text{Headersize}); \\ t &= \text{P\_store}(X_1, t_2, X_3) \\ &\text{In } t\} \end{aligned}$$

A representation that may be more efficient for computing slot addresses would store l and u values redundantly in two additional fields in the array.

Lists

The representation of the list data type is shown in Figure 7. The constant definitions for Cons_size, Hd, Tl, *etc.* should be included in D.

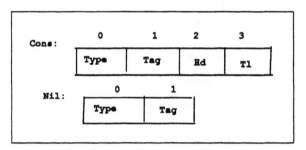

Figure 7: Representation of lists

$$TE[\![\text{Cons\_1}(X)]\!] \;=\; \text{P\_select}(X, \text{Hd})$$

$$TE[\![\text{Cons\_2}(X)]\!] \;=\; \text{P\_select}(X, \text{Tl})$$

$$TE[\![\text{Cons}(X_1, X_2)]\!] \;=\; \{ \begin{aligned}[t] t &= \text{Allocate}(\text{Cons\_size}); \\ &\text{P\_store}(t, \text{Type}, \text{"List"}); \\ &\text{P\_store}(t, \text{Tag}, \text{Cons\_Tag}); \\ &\text{P\_store}(t, \text{Hd}, X_1); \\ &\text{P\_store}(t, \text{Tl}, X_2); \\ &\text{In } t\} \end{aligned}$$

$$TE[\![\text{List\_case}_m(X, E_1, E_2)]\!] \;=\; \{ m \; \begin{aligned}[t] \vec{t} &= \text{P\_select}(X, \text{Tag}); \\ \vec{t_m} &= \text{Dispatch2}_m(t, E_1, E_2); \\ &\text{In } \vec{t_m}\} \end{aligned}$$

Function Calls and Closures

At the machine level, the apply operator checks if the arity of the function has been satisfied. If the arity has not been satisfied, it stores the argument in a data structure called a *closure*. There is a wide range of representations of closures and associated function calling conventions. In fact, it is possible for a function to be compiled using several different calling conventions; the compiler can pick the most appropriate one for a given application. A representation for the closure data type is shown in Figure 8. The constant definitions for Closure_size, *etc.* should be included in D.

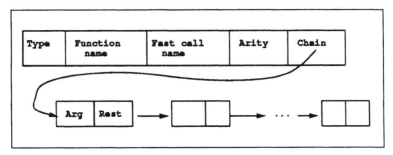

Figure 8: Representation of a closure

We begin by describing a procedure that builds a new closure given an old closure and an argument.

$$
\begin{aligned}
\text{Make\_closure} = \lambda\,(\text{cl},\text{X})\,.\,\{\ \ &\text{f} &=&\ \ \text{P\_select}(\text{cl},\text{Funcname}); \\
&\text{f}_{\text{fc}} &=&\ \ \text{P\_select}(\text{cl},\text{Fastcallname}); \\
&\text{n} &=&\ \ \text{P\_select}(\text{cl},\text{Arity}); \\
&\text{ch} &=&\ \ \text{P\_select}(\text{cl},\text{Chain}); \\
&\text{cl}' &=&\ \ \text{Allocate}(\text{Closure\_size}); \\
&\multicolumn{3}{l}{\text{P\_store}(\text{cl}',\text{Type},\text{``Closure''});} \\
&\multicolumn{3}{l}{\text{P\_store}(\text{cl}',\text{Functionname},\text{f});} \\
&\multicolumn{3}{l}{\text{P\_store}(\text{cl}',\text{Fastcallname},\text{f}_{\text{fc}});} \\
&\multicolumn{3}{l}{\text{P\_store}(\text{cl}',\text{Arity},\text{n}');} \\
&\multicolumn{3}{l}{\text{P\_store}(\text{cl}',\text{Chain},\text{ch}');} \\
&\text{n}' &=&\ \ -(\text{n},1); \\
&\text{ch}' &=&\ \ \text{Ap}_2(\text{Arg\_chain},\text{X},\text{ch}); \\
&\multicolumn{3}{l}{\text{In cl}'\}}
\end{aligned}
$$

where the function to build argument chains is defined as follows:

$$
\begin{aligned}
\text{Arg\_chain} = \lambda\,(\text{X},\text{Xs})\,.\ \ \{&\text{xs}' = \text{Allocate}(2); \\
&\text{P\_store}(\text{xs}',\text{Arg},\text{X}); \\
&\text{P\_store}(\text{xs}',\text{Rest},\text{Xs}); \\
&\text{In xs}'\}
\end{aligned}
$$

The argument chain can be destructured using the following function:

$$\text{Args}_n = \lambda\,(X)\,.\,\{_n \quad \begin{aligned}
t_1 &= \text{P\_select}(X, \text{Chain}); \\
a_n &= \text{P\_select}(t_1, \text{Arg}); \\
t_2 &= \text{P\_select}(t_1, \text{Rest}); \\
a_{n-1} &= \text{P\_select}(t_2, \text{Arg}); \\
t_3 &= \text{P\_select}(t_2, \text{Rest}); \\
&\vdots \\
a_1 &= \text{P\_select}(t_{n-1}, \text{Arg}); \\
\text{In } &\vec{a_n}\}
\end{aligned}$$

These three definitions must be included in D.

Now we can give the translation for the apply operator. As stated earlier, the apply basically checks to see if the arity is satisfied and either makes a new closure or calls Ap.

$$\text{TE}[\![\text{Apply}(F, X)]\!] = \{\, \begin{aligned}
n &= \text{P\_select}(F, \text{Arity}); \\
\text{fire}_b &= \text{Equal?}(n, 1); \\
\text{fire}_i &= \text{BooltoInt}(\text{fire}_b); \\
\text{res} &= \text{Dispatch}_{2,2}(\text{fire}_i, \\
&\qquad \{\, \begin{aligned}
\text{fun} &= \text{P\_select}(F, \text{Functionname}); \\
\text{as} &= \text{P\_select}(F, \text{Chain}); \\
\text{as}' &= \text{Ap}_2(\text{Arg\_chain}, X, \text{as}); \\
\text{res}' &= \text{Ap}(\text{fun}, \text{as}'); \\
\text{In } &\text{res}'\}, \\
&\text{Ap}_2(\text{Make\_closure}, F, X)) \\
\text{In } &\text{res}\}
\end{aligned} \end{aligned}$$

Notice that the building of closures corresponds to the Apply$_i$ combinators. The first closure for a function, which corresponds to the Apply$_1$ combinator, is processed during the translation of λ-expressions, as follows:

$$\text{TE}[\![\lambda_n\,(\vec{X_n})\,.\,E]\!] = \{\, \begin{aligned}
\text{cl} &= \text{Allocate}(\text{Closure\_size}); \\
&\text{P\_store}(\text{cl}, \text{Type}, \text{``Closure''}); \\
&\text{P\_store}(\text{cl}, \text{Functioname}, \text{`}T_c\text{`}); \\
&\text{P\_store}(\text{cl}, \text{Fastcallname}, \text{`}T_{fc}\text{`}); \\
&\text{P\_store}(\text{cl}, \text{Arity}, \underline{n}); \\
&\text{P\_store}(\text{cl}, \text{Chain}, \text{``End''}); \\
\text{In } &\text{cl}\}
\end{aligned}$$

The following two function definitions are included in D.

$$T_c = \lambda_1\,(Xs)\,.\,\{\, \begin{aligned}
\vec{X_n} &= \text{Ap}_{1,n}(\text{Args}_n, Xs); \\
t &= \text{TE}[\![E]\!]; \\
\text{In } &t\}
\end{aligned}$$

$$T_{fc} = \lambda_n\,(\vec{X_n})\,.\,\text{TE}[\![E]\!]$$

'T_c indicates the name T_c and not the value associated with T_c. Note that $\text{TE}[\![E]\!]$ can be computed once and shared between the curried and the fastcall version of the function.

3.2 Signals generation

In P-TAC we can express some more low-level machine concerns, such as the generation of a signal to indicate that a function call has terminated. Signals are needed, for example, for deallocating frame storage. Signals are also needed to express sequencing in the presence of M-structures in Id. Before introducing signals, the P-TAC program is canonicalized, that is, all blocks are flattened and variables and values are substituted. Furthermore, dead code should be eliminated. We add signals only to non-strict combinators, and to combinators that produce side-effects, such as P_store. The output of a strict operator can be interpreted as a signal that the instruction has indeed fired. We give the signal transformation using the translation functions S, SE and SC. The transformation is also applied to each constant definition in D.

$$
\begin{aligned}
S[\![\lambda_{n,m}(\vec{X_n}).\{_m\ Y_1 &= Se_1 = \lambda_{n,m+1}(\vec{X_n}). \\
&\qquad (\{_{m+1}\ Y_1 = Se_1 \\
\vdots & \qquad\qquad \vdots \\
Y_n &= Se_n \qquad\qquad Y_n = Se_n \\
Y_{n+1} &= Nse_1 \qquad\quad Y_{n+1}, S_1 = SE[\![Nse_1]\!] \\
\vdots & \qquad\qquad\qquad \vdots \\
Y_{n+m} &= Nse_m \qquad\quad Y_{n+m}, S_m = SE[\![Nse_m]\!] \\
C_1 &\qquad\qquad\qquad S_{m+1} = SC[\![C_1]\!]; \\
\vdots & \qquad\qquad\qquad \vdots \\
C_k & \\
In\ \vec{R_m}\}]\!] &\qquad\quad S_{m+k} = SC[\![C_k]\!]; \\
&\qquad\quad S' = Sync_{m+k+i}(Deadvar, \vec{S_{m+k}}) \\
&\qquad\qquad In\ \vec{R_m}, S'\})
\end{aligned}
$$

Where Se_i stands for an expression involving strict operators, and Nse_i stands for either an applicative or a loop expression. Deadvar are the parameters that are not being used in the body of the function.

$$SE[\![WLoop_n(P, B, \vec{Y_n}, Y)]\!] = WLoop'_n(P, B, \vec{Y_n}, S_p, Y)$$

where S_p is the signal associated with the invocation of the loop predicate.

$$SE[\![Ap_{n,m}(F, \vec{X_n})]\!] = Ap_{n,m+1}(F, \vec{X_n})$$
$$SC[\![P\_store(X, I, Z)]\!] = Ack\_store(X, I, Z)$$

where **Ack_store** is a new P-TAC function symbol of arity 3, which generates a **Signal** when the store actually takes place, that is, when X, I and Z all become values.

The new rewrite rules are:

$$
\begin{aligned}
\text{WLoop}'_n(P, B, \vec{X_n}, S, \text{True}) \quad &\longrightarrow \quad \{_{n+1} \; \vec{t_n}, S_b \; = \; Ap_{n,n+1}(B, \vec{X_n}); \\
&\qquad\qquad\quad t_p, S_p \; = \; Ap_{n,2}(P, \vec{t_n}); \\
&\qquad\qquad\quad S' \; = \; \text{Sync}_3(S, S_b, S_p); \\
&\qquad\qquad\quad \vec{t'_n}, S_1 \; = \; \text{WLoop}'_n(P, B, \vec{t_n}, S', t_p) \\
&\qquad\qquad\qquad \text{In } \vec{t'_n}, \; S_1 \} \\[4pt]
\text{WLoop}'_n(P, B, \vec{X_n}, S, \text{False}) \quad &\longrightarrow \quad \vec{X_n}, S \\[4pt]
\text{Ack\_store}(L, \underline{i}, V) \quad &\longrightarrow \quad \{ t = \text{Signal}; \\
&\qquad\qquad\quad \text{P\_store}(L, \underline{i}, V); \\
&\qquad\qquad\quad \text{In } t \} \\[4pt]
\text{Sync}_n(\vec{V_n}) \quad &\longrightarrow \quad ()
\end{aligned}
$$

Sync produces a void value when all the signals are received.

4 Conclusions

This paper has informally described the compilation process of Id. Following these lines a project "Id-in-Id compiler" led by Shail Aditya and Yuli Zhou is under progress. Besides easing the portability of Id, the Id compiler in Id will allow us to study the implicit parallelism in the Id compiler.

We have not discussed the operational semantics of M-structures, even though we think it is quite straightforward. However, the definition of a *term model* in the presence of non-determinism is a difficult issue, and has not been investigated yet.

We also plan to formalize the compilation process beyond P-TAC, for both parallel and sequential machines. For example, the notion of a *frame* to hold the temporary variables for a function application or loop iteration, can be abstracted in a useful way for most machines. We think this will facilitate the study of issues related to reuse of frames, storing of loop constants, and pre-allocation of multiple frames for parallel execution. Similarly, the analysis required for detecting sequential threads can also be performed in a machine independent manner.

Acknowledgments

This paper describes research done at the Laboratory for Computer Science of the Massachusetts Institute of Technology. Funding for this work has been provided in part by the Advanced Research Projects Agency of the Department of Defense under the Office of Naval Research contract N00014-89-J-1988 (MIT) and N00039-88-C-0163 (Harvard). This paper has benefitted by informal discussions with the members of Computation Structures Group. In particular, we would like to thank Id compiler gurus Jamey Hicks and Shail Aditya Gupta. Thanks to Paul Barth, Steve Glim, Derek Chiou and Boon Ang for proof reading the final draft of this paper.

References

[1] A. Aho, J. Ullman, and R. Sethi. *Compilers: Principles, Techniques, Tools.* London, Addison-Wesley, 1986.

[2] Z. M. Ariola. Orthogonal Graph Rewriting Systems. Technical Report CSG Memo 323, MIT Laboratory for Computer Science, 1991.

[3] Z. M. Ariola and Arvind. Compilation of Id$^-$: a Subset of Id. Technical Report CSG Memo 315, MIT Laboratory for Computer Science, November 1990.

[4] Z. M. Ariola and Arvind. A Syntactic Approach to Program Transformations. In *Proc. ACM SIGPLAN Symposium on Partial Evaluation and Semantics Based Program Manipulation, Yale University,* 1991.

[5] Arvind, R. Nikhil, and K. Pingali. I-Structures: Data Structures for Parallel Computing. In *Proceedings of the Workshop on Graph Reduction, Santa Fe, New Mexico, Springer-Verlag LNCS 279,* pages 336–369, September/October 1987.

[6] L. Augustsson. *Compiling Lazy Functional Languages, Part II.* PhD thesis, Chalmers University of Technology, Department of Computer Science, 1987.

[7] P. Barth, R. Nikhil, and Arvind. M-structures: Extending a Parallel, Non-strict, Functional Language with state. In *Proc. ACM Conference on Functional Programming Languages and Computer Architecture, Cambridge,* 1991.

[8] T. Johnsson. Lambda Lifting: Transforming Programs to Recursive Equations. In *Proc. Conf. on Functional Programming Languages and Computer Architecture, Nancy, France,* September 1985.

[9] T. Johnsson. *Compiling Lazy Functional Languages.* PhD thesis, Chalmers University of Technology, Department of Computer Science, 1987.

[10] J. Klop. Term Rewriting Systems. Course Notes, Summer course organized by Corrado Boehm, Ustica, Italy, September 1985.

[11] P. Landin. A Correspondence between Algol60 and Church's Lambda notation. *Communications ACM,* 8, 1965.

[12] J.-J. Lévy. *Réductions Correctes et Optimales dans le Lambda-Calcul.* Ph.D. thesis, Université Paris VII, October 1978.

[13] R. S. Nikhil. Id (Version 90.0) Reference Manual. Technical Report CSG Memo 284-a, MIT Laboratory for Computer Science, 545 Technology Square, Cambridge, MA 02139, USA, July 1990.

[14] S. L. Peyton Jones. *The implementation of Functional Programming Languages.* Prentice-Hall International, Englewood Cliffs, N.J., 1987.

[15] K. Píngali, M. Beck, R. Johnson, M. Moudgill, and P. Stodghill. Dependence Flow Graphs: An Algebraic Approach to Program Dependencies. In *Proceedings of the 18th ACM Symposium on Principle of programming Languages*, pages 67–78, January 1991.

[16] K. Schauser, D. Culler, and T. von Eicken. Compiler-Controlled Multithreading for Lenient Parallel Languages. In *Proc. ACM Conference on Functional Programming Languages and Computer Architecture, Cambridge*, 1991.

[17] K. Traub. Compilation as Partitioning: A New Approach to Compiling Non-strict Functional Languages. In *Proc. ACM Conference on Functional Programming Languages and Computer Architecture, Cambridge*, 1991.

[18] P. Welch. Continuous Semantics and Inside-out Reductions. In *λ-Calculus and Computer Schience Theory, Italy (Springer-Verlag Lecture Notes in Computer Science 37)*, March 1975.

[19] *Proc. ACM SIGPLAN Symposium on Partial Evaluation and Semantics Based Program Manipulation, Yale University, New Haven, CN.* June 1991.

8 An Executable Representation of Distance and Direction

R. Johnson, W. Li, and K. Pingali
Cornell University

Abstract

The dependence flow graph is a novel intermediate representation for optimizing and parallelizing compilers that can be viewed as an executable representation of program dependences. The execution model, called dependence-driven execution, is a generalization of the tagged-token dataflow model that permits imperative updates to memory. The dependence flow graph subsumes other representations such as continuation-passing style [12], data dependence graphs [13], and static single assignment form [8]. In this paper, we show how dependence distance and direction information can be represented in this model using *dependence operators*. From a functional perspective, these operators can be viewed as functions on streams [4].

1 Introduction

The growing complexity of optimizing and parallelizing compilers has led the compiler community to re-examine the design of intermediate program representations. Traditionally, compilers have used the control-flow graph augmented with dependence information such as def-use chains [1], data dependences [13] and control dependences [10]. The control-flow graph represents the execution semantics of the program (how the program can be executed), while dependences are viewed as precedence constraints between statements that

---

[1]This research was supported by an NSF Presidential Young Investigator award (NSF grant #CCR-8958543), NSF grant CCR-9008526, and grants from IBM and HP.

must be maintained for correct execution.

The separation of execution semantics from dependence information results in a number of problems.

When a program is transformed, dependence information may need to be modified, but it is usually difficult to do this incrementally; for example, it is hard to update def-use chains after eliminating unreachable code [15]. Therefore, the full benefit of program optimization must be obtained in one of two ways. One way is to perform repeated passes of program analysis and transformation. Alternatively, the problem can be circumvented through the use of complex algorithms such as the global constant propagation algorithm of Wegman and Zadeck, which combines constant propagation with unreachable code elimination. This algorithm requires simultaneous traversals of both the control-flow graph and def-use chains [17]. Neither approach is satisfactory; the first is expensive and the second does not solve the problem of out-of-date dependence information.

The separation of execution semantics and dependence information has also inhibited the development of an adequate semantic account of dependences. Such a semantic account is useful for two reasons. First, it would enable us to prove correctness of transformations. Second, like all semantic descriptions, it has prescriptive value in identifying and fixing weaknesses since constructs that are difficult to model semantically are usually difficult to use in practice — for example, consider the unstructured goto in high-level programming languages [9]. A first step towards a semantic account of dependences has been taken by Selke [16] and Cartwright and Felleison [5], who give a λ-calculus based execution model for the special case of program dependence graphs arising from a structured programming language without aliasing or arrays. Their approach is limited by the simple execution model that underlies it. For example, loops are represented as tail-recursive procedures and loop execution is modeled in terms of infinite unfoldings of tail-recursive procedures. It is unclear how one should view transformations such as loop interchange in such a model. In the absence of an updatable store, assignments to possibly aliased variables involve code that checks whether variables are indeed aliased, which results in significant code expansion[2]. Nevertheless, we note that difficulties in modeling conditional assignments in program dependence graphs has led to the proposal of the program representation graph which has turned out to be better suited than the program dependence graph for problems such as integration of program versions [11]; this illustrates the prescriptive power of giving semantics to dependence information.

In a previous paper [14], we showed that all these problems can be avoided by using an executable representation of dependences called the *dependence flow graph*. The

---

[2]A similar problem is encountered in using the static single assignment form [8].

dependence flow graph can be viewed either as a data structure incorporating dependence information or as a program that can be executed. Our execution model is called *dependence-driven execution* and is a generalization of the tagged-token dataflow model of computation; the generalization permits imperative updates to memory locations. Dependence flow graphs have the following advantages:

1. Since the representation is executable, we can use abstract interpretation to design optimization algorithms, facilitating systematic algorithm development and proof of correctness [7]. From a software engineering perspective, this is advantageous because algorithms based on abstract interpretation have the same structure, which permits code sharing.

2. Algorithms based on abstract interpretation of dependence flow graphs are efficient. Abstract interpretation fell out of favor when the compiler community realized that optimization algorithms based on dependences were more efficient than abstract interpretation algorithms for the same problem, since abstract interpretation had to be done on the control-flow graph. The dependence flow graph is an executable representation of dependence information, and abstract interpretation algorithms that use the dependence flow graph do not suffer from this problem. We have used this idea to design a simple global constant propagation algorithm that is as powerful as the complex one of Wegman and Zadeck that uses both the control-flow graph and def-use chains [14].

3. The dependence flow graph is compact — it is asymptotically smaller than the data dependence graph.

Interestingly, dependence flow graphs incorporate all the advantages of recently proposed representations such as the program dependence graph and web [10, 3], program representation graph [5], static single assignment form [8] and continuation-passing style [12].

In our earlier presentation, we considered only scalars, and arrays were handled by treating them as scalars (that is, an assignment to an array element was treated as an assignment to the entire array). However, over the last fifteen years, a number of subscript analysis tests, such as the GCD test and Banerjee test [18], have been developed, which provide finer-grain dependence information. These tests not only yield information about the existence of dependences, but they also give semantic information such as dependence *directions* and *distances* needed to parallelize programs more effectively. The contribution of this paper is to show how this information can be incorporated into dependence flow graphs, and to demonstrate the ability of our execution model to exploit the parallelism that this exposes. We also show how our approach handles reductions, imperfectly nested loops, and non-nested loops [18]. For readers familiar with the concept of streams in functional languages, our results can be interpreted as a generalization of the ideas of Landin who first used streams to model functionally the execution of loops in imperative languages [4][3]. To simplify our presentation we only consider rectangular iteration spaces; a generalization of our methods to non-rectangular iteration spaces will appear in a forthcoming technical report.

The rest of the paper is organized as follows. In Section 2, we introduce dependence flow graphs and their execution model. In Section 3, we include distance and direction vector information in our execution model. In Section 4, we show how reduction operators and producer-consumer parallelism fit naturally in our framework.

2   The Dependence Flow Graph

In this section, we give a brief introduction to the dependence flow graph and its execution model. The reader who is interested in a more detailed account is referred to our earlier paper [14]. We assume that the reader is familiar with the program dependence graph and with the tagged-token dataflow model. Hereafter, we abbreviate dependence flow graph as DFG and program dependence graph as PDG.

Figure 1 shows a small program for computing partial sums, along with its PDG and DFG representations. The PDG consists of control and data dependences. In Figure 1b, there are flow dependences from S_1 to S_3, from S_2 to S_3 (the value of I), from S_2 to itself, and from S_3 to S_4. The control dependence of S_3 on the for statement is represented by a dashed line. Note that control and data dependences are represented by distinct edges.

In the DFG, control information is threaded into data dependences through the use of dependence operators, and data dependences between statements having different control dependences pass through these operators. For example, the flow dependence from S_1 to S_3 in the PDG is from a statement outside a loop to one that is inside the loop; in the DFG, this dependence edge becomes a path punctuated by the loop$_1$ operator. The flow dependence from S_3 to itself also passes through this operator. Similarly, the dependence from S_3 inside the loop to S_4 outside the loop passes through a sync operator. Thus, traditional data dependence edges become dependence paths in our representation; perhaps surprisingly, this results in an asymptotically smaller representation, since these paths may share vertices [14].

---

[3]No knowledge of streams is needed to read this paper, since we have tried to avoid such 'cultural' references.

$$S_1: \quad \texttt{A[1] := 1}$$
$$S_2: \quad \texttt{for I := 1,N-1}$$
$$S_3: \quad\quad\quad \texttt{A[I+1] := A[I]+1}$$
$$S_4: \quad \texttt{P := A[Q]}$$

(a) Source Program

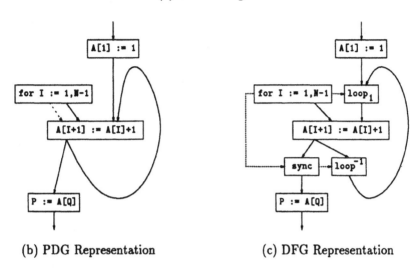

(b) PDG Representation   (c) DFG Representation

Figure 1: Summation Example

The integration of control and data dependences enables us to give a parallel, compositional execution semantics to dependence flow graphs. To introduce this parallel semantics, we first consider the sequential execution of statements in a control-flow graph modeled in a dataflow style as follows. The program counter is represented by a token whose arrival at the input of a statement signifies that the statement may execute. Execution begins by passing the token to the first statement in the control-flow graph. On receiving the token, a statement executes by reading its operands from a global store, performing the specified computation, writing the result into the store, and then passing the token along the control-flow edge to its successor. Conditional statements pass the token down the control-flow edge indicated by the computed predicate.

In this simple sequential model, the arrival of the token at the input of a statement signifies that all prior statements have executed; therefore, all dependences of the statement are satisfied and the statement may execute. Since a statement does not usually depend on all statements preceding it, we can introduce parallelism into the execution by notifying a statement as soon as all its dependences are satisfied, even if not all prior statements have executed. In the dependence flow graph, tokens flow down dependence paths and represent satisfied dependences; a statement executes once tokens have arrived on all incoming edges, and tokens are produced on its outedges and enable subsequent statements to execute. To distinguish between statement instances in different iterations, we tag each token with an iteration number, and require that a statement in iteration i must receive a token with tag i on each input before executing in that iteration. Once the statement has executed, it produces tokens with tag i at its outputs.

Consider the graph in Figure 1c. The instance of statement S_3 in the first iteration depends on a flow dependence from S_1 and the value $I = 1$ from the for statement. When S_1 executes it produces a token δ which flows to the loop$_1$ operator. The loop$_1$ operator tags this token, producing $\delta.1$, effectively notifying S_3 that the flow dependence in the first iteration is satisfied. Tokens may also carry values. The for statement produces tokens carrying the appropriate value of I for each iteration; in the first iteration, S_3 receives the token $\langle 1 \rangle.1$ representing the value $I = 1$ with tag 1. When both tokens, $\delta.1$ and $\langle 1 \rangle.1$ have arrived at S_3, the statement executes and produces a token $\delta.1$ on its outedge. The loop$_1$ operator increments the tag on this token by 1 and sends it to S_3; this token satisfies the flow dependence for the instance of S_3 in the second iteration.

In general, an instance of S_3 in iteration $i+1$ depends on an instance of itself in iteration i. When S_3 in iteration i executes, it produces a token $\delta.i$ which flows to the loop$_1$ operator[4]. The loop$_1$ operator increments the token's tag by 1, producing the token $\delta.i+1$ which flows to S_3 in iteration $i+1$. (The reader familiar with the tagged-token dataflow model will recognize that the loop$_1$ operator implements the function of the D operator in that model [2].)

Since we do not know which element of array A is read by statement S_4, we conservatively say S_4 depends on all instances of S_3. The sync operator implements this 'barrier' synchronization for this dependence from all iterations of the loop by waiting until a token from every iteration has arrived on its input edge before producing a token δ on its output.

A detailed account of the semantics of dependence operators is given in Section 3. For the reader familiar with the static single assignment form (SSA), we point out some important differences between that representation and ours. In SSA, variables are single assignment as in functional languages: if X and Y are two possibly aliased variables, an assignment to either variable must be followed by statements that test whether the other variable is actually an alias, and if so, perform a redefinition of that variable. These tests and redefinitions can significantly increase code size [6]. Note that in our model, we retain an imperative, updatable store using dependences to disambiguate which 'version' of the

---

[4]Ignore the loop^{-1} operator for now; its function is described in Section 3.

variable is needed by a statement; therefore, modeling possibly aliased variables does not result in code explosion. Another major difference is illustrated by the loop_1 operator. At join points in the control-flow graph, such as at the bottom of conditionals and at the top of loops, the SSA representation introduces ϕ-functions that serve to combine dependences on the same variable; thus, the SSA would have a ϕ-function where we have introduced the loop_1 operator. In DFG's, we have a variety of operators that combine dependences together in many ways. In Section 3, we use this flexibility to incorporate distance and direction information into DFG's.

3 Representing Distance and Direction

In the previous section, we showed how a simple loop-carried dependence could be represented within the dependence-driven execution model by augmenting tokens with iteration tags that are manipulated by the loop_1 operator. In this section we present the full method for representing distance and direction information operationally. Since this information is relative to an n-dimensional iteration space, one challenge is to retain compositionality; that is, the representation of a loop nested at level k should depend only on the kth elements of distance or direction vectors of dependences within the nested loops, and not on surrounding loops or even the particular value of k. A main difficulty in accomplishing this is correctly generating dependences for initially satisfied iterations. We first show the normal behavior of operators representing distance and direction information and then discuss their initialization behavior.

3.1 Distance Operators

In Figure 1, the loop-carried dependence has a distance of 1 and this fact is reflected operationally in the loop_1 node: when a statement instance in iteration i completes, a token $\delta.i$ is generated and passed to the statement instance in iteration $i+1$ by the loop_1 node. In general, a dependence between some statements S and S' may have an associated n-dimensional distance vector, $(d_1, \ldots, d_n)$. When statement S executes in iteration $(i_1, \ldots, i_n)$, it generates a token $\delta.i_1 \ldots i_n$ which must be passed to statement S' in iteration $(i_1+d_1, \ldots, i_n+d_n)$. To do this, we must transform $\delta.i_1 \ldots i_n$ into $\delta.i_1+d_1 \ldots i_n+d_n$.

Our approach is to represent the dependence $S \; \delta_{(d_1,\ldots,d_n)} \; S'$ with a path from S to S' passing through special operators that manipulate iteration tags, effectively passing tokens between points in iteration space. The first special operator, loop_k, is a generalization of the loop_1 operator; it increments a tag element by the constant integer k. We insert a special pointer symbol ($_\wedge$) in the tag to indicate which tag element should be incremented.

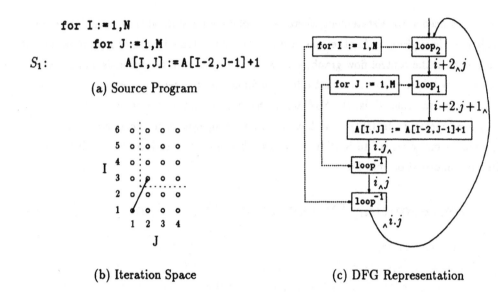

(a) Source Program

(b) Iteration Space

(c) DFG Representation

Figure 2: Distance Vector Example

After incrementing an element, loop_k moves the pointer right one position, so a subsequent loop_k will modify the next element; when all elements have been modified, the pointer is to the right of all tag elements and the token is ready to be consumed. The second operator, loop^{-1}, simply moves the pointer left one position.

We construct a path from S to S' which passes out through one loop^{-1} node for each of the n nested loops surrounding both S and S', and then passes in through loop_k nodes, where $k = d_i$ for the ith-nested loop. For example, consider the program in Figure 2a. The dependence from S_1 to itself has distance $(2, 1)$. When S_1 executes in iteration (i, j), it produces a token $\delta.i.j_\wedge$ intended to satisfy the dependence in iteration $(i+2, j+1)$. After passing through the first loop^{-1} (associated with the J loop), the token become $\delta.i.j$; after passing through the second loop^{-1}, it is $\delta_\wedge i.j$. Note that the pointer is immediately left of the tag element associated with the outer loop. loop_2 consumes the token and produces $\delta.i+2_\wedge j$; loop_1 consumes this token and produces $\delta.i+2.j+1_\wedge$, allowing S_1 to execute in iteration $(i+2, j+1)$ as required.

Using the $_\wedge$-pointer to encode nesting level allows the operators to be compositional: the function of loop_k nodes does not depend on their position in the graph. We will show in section 4 how our choice of operators also leads to natural extensions of distance and direction vectors such as representing reductions and producer-consumer parallelism.

Several additional points should be noted. First, the distance vector for any dependence can be read directly from the loop$_k$ nodes along the path representing the dependence. Also, dependences can be accessed by dimension; transformations such as loop interchange can easily access a particular distance vector element of all loop-carried dependences.

Although we have described the behavior of dependence operators using the $_\wedge$-pointer, readers familiar with the concept of streams in non-strict functional languages such as Id [2] should note the correspondence with streams and stream operators. The tokens flowing down a dependence arc can viewed as elements of a non-strict data structure called a stream whose elements can be used before the entire data structure is produced. On a token, the integer(s) to the right of the $_\wedge$-pointer constitute the position of that token in the stream. The dependence operators we have discussed can be interpreted as stream operators. A full discussion of this connection is beyond the scope of this paper.

3.2 Initially Satisfied Dependences

In the partial sums example (Figure 1), the first iteration received a token representing its satisfied flow dependence from a statement outside the loop, while subsequent iterations received tokens from the previous iteration. In the second example (Figure 2), multiple iterations depend on statements outside the loops; we say these statements are in *initial iterations*. In Figure 2b, the initial iterations are below and left of the dotted line. Statements in iterations above and right of the dotted line receive tokens representing satisfied flow dependence from previous iterations. In this section we describe how a single token representing access to the entire array is expanded into tokens satisfying dependences in the initial iterations. In section 4 we take a different approach to dependences in initial iterations based on producer-consumer parallelism.

Let $I_1, \ldots, I_n$ be the loop indices and $N_1, \ldots, N_n$ be the number of iterations for n nested loops. Let $(d_1, \ldots, d_n)$ be the distance vector associated with some dependence between statements within the nested loops. To simplify the discussion, assume all distances are non-negative. For any dimension l, all iterations $(i_1, \ldots, i_l, \ldots, i_n)$ are initial provided $1 \leq i_l \leq d_l$. In other words, the set of initial iterations may be decomposed by dimension into the union of subregions:

$$\bigcup_{l=1,\ldots,n} \{(i_1,\ldots,i_n) \mid 1 \leq i_l \leq d_l\}$$

In Figure 2b, this L-shaped region is decomposed by dimension as:

$$I = 1: \quad L = \{(1,1),(1,2),(1,3),\ldots,(1,M)\} \ \cup$$
$$I = 2: \qquad \{(2,1),(2,2),(2,3),\ldots,(2,M)\} \ \cup$$
$$J = 1: \qquad \{(1,1),(1,2),(1,3),\ldots,(1,N)\}$$

Since each loop_{d_i} node knows d_i, it should be able to generate tokens for the appropriate subregion of the initial iterations. The main difficulty is suppressing the generation of multiple tokens for iterations in the intersection of the above subregions[5]. We accomplish this by adding a new pointer symbol ($_+$) which may take the place of $_\wedge$ in the right-most position of a partially expanded tag. When a single token, δ_+, is consumed by loop_{d_1} at the outermost loop, the node generates $\delta.1_\wedge, \ldots, \delta.(d_1)_\wedge$ and $\delta.(d_1+1)_+, \ldots, \delta.(N_1)_+$. The $_\wedge$-pointer with nothing to its right indicates that all innermost loop_k nodes should expand their dimension's range completely; the $_+$-pointer with nothing to its right indicates that the next nested loop should expand its range just as this one did, generating tokens with added suffix $.i_\wedge$ for $1 \leq i \leq d_2$, and added suffix $.i_+$ for $d_2 < i \leq N_2$. At the inner loop, the tokens produced ending with $_\wedge$ exactly cover the initial iterations, and the tokens ending with $_+$ cover the remaining iterations and are simply ignored (consumed without action) by statements.

Thus, in Figure 2(c), loop_2 consumes δ_+ and generates $\delta.1_\wedge, \delta.2_\wedge, \delta.3_+, \delta.4_+, \ldots, \delta.N_+$. Each of these tokens is consumed by loop_1 and generates:

$$\delta.1_\wedge \ \rightarrow \ \delta.1.1_\wedge, \quad \delta.1.2_\wedge, \quad \delta.1.3_\wedge, \quad \ldots, \quad \delta.1.M_\wedge$$
$$\delta.2_\wedge \ \rightarrow \ \delta.2.1_\wedge, \quad \delta.2.2_\wedge, \quad \delta.2.3_\wedge, \quad \ldots, \quad \delta.2.M_\wedge$$
$$\delta.3_+ \ \rightarrow \ \delta.3.1_\wedge, \quad \delta.3.2_+, \quad \delta.3.3_+, \quad \ldots, \quad \delta.3.M_+$$
$$\vdots \qquad \qquad \vdots$$
$$\delta.N_+ \ \rightarrow \ \delta.N.1_\wedge, \quad \delta.N.2_+, \quad \delta.N.3_+, \quad \ldots, \quad \delta.N.M_+$$

Tokens ending with $_\wedge$ satisfy the initial iterations, whereas tokens ending with $_+$ are ignored (consumed without action) by statement S_1. As instances of S_1 execute in initial iterations, tokens are produced which flow through the loop operators and satisfy instances of S_1 in subsequent iterations. The loop operators are shown in Figure 3.

3.3 Direction Operators

Direction information is a conservative approximation to distance information. Thus, it is not surprising that the operators for encoding direction information are closely related to the loop operators. Rather than consuming a single token and then generating a token

---

[5]It is possible to define an operational semantics based on environment bindings rather than token passing in which satisfying a dependence multiple times is allowed, but we want to show that this can be done within the dataflow context as well.

Node	Input	Output	
loopC	$\delta.I_+$ or $\delta.I_\wedge$	$\delta.I.i_\wedge$	for $1 \leq i \leq N$
loop$_k$	$\delta.I_\wedge$	$\delta.I.i_\wedge$	for $1 \leq i \leq N$
if $k \geq 0$:	$\delta.I_+$	$\delta.I.i_\wedge$	for $1 \leq i \leq k$
		$\delta.I.i_+$	for $k < i \leq N$
	$\delta.I_\wedge i.J$	$\delta.I.i+k_\wedge J$	for $1 \leq i \leq N - k$
if $k < 0$:	$\delta.I_+$	$\delta.I.i_\wedge$	for $N - |k| \leq i \leq N$
		$\delta.I.i_+$	for $1 \leq i < N - |k|$
	$\delta.I_\wedge i.J$	$\delta.I.i+k_\wedge J$	for $|k| < i \leq N$
loop^{-1}	$\delta.I.i_\wedge J$	$\delta.I_\wedge i.J$	
sync	$\delta.I.i_\wedge$ or $\delta.I.i_+$	$\delta.I_+$	when inputs consumed for $1 \leq i \leq N$

Figure 3: Loop Nodes

k iterations away, the loop$_<$ operator waits until it has consumed all tokens of the form $\delta.I_\wedge j.J$ for $1 \leq j < i$ before generating a token for iteration $\delta.I.i_\wedge J$. Here, I, J are any constant index strings. Similarly, the other direction operators wait until consuming tokens from the appropriate subrange before generating the ith token. The direction operators are shown in Figure 4.

4 Extensions to Distance and Direction Vectors

Although distance and direction vectors provide dependence information needed in many loop transformation, not all dependence information needed by transformations is expressible within this framework. In this section we show how important extensions to distance and direction vector information fit naturally into our framework.

4.1 Representing Reductions

A reduction is a statement which accumulates into a single variable the result of applying an associative operator to values from each iteration of a loop. For example, statement S_1 in Figure 5a is a reduction statement; there are output and flow dependences from S_1 to itself, each having distance 1. Recognizing reductions is essential to generating good vector and concurrent code [18]. Many vector machines support vectorization of reductions; without special recognition, reductions appear unvectorizable. Recognizing commutative reduction operators allows more flexible scheduling of iterations on multiprocessors and transformations such as loop interchange which appear illegal otherwise. Thus, reductions may often be handled specially, allowing their loop-carried dependences to be ignored. For

Node	Input	Output	
$loop_<$	$\delta.I_\wedge j.J$	$\delta.I.i_\wedge J$	when $\delta.I_\wedge j.J$ defined for $1 \leq j < i$
	$\delta.I_\wedge$	$\delta.I.i_\wedge$	for $1 \leq i \leq N$
	$\delta.I_+$	$\delta.I.1_\wedge$	and
		$\delta.I.i_+$	for $1 < i \leq N$
$loop_>$	$\delta.I_\wedge j.J$	$\delta.I.i_\wedge J$	when $\delta.I_\wedge j.J$ defined for $i < j \leq N$
	$\delta.I_\wedge$	$\delta.I.i_\wedge$	for $1 \leq i \leq N$
	$\delta.I_+$	$\delta.I.N_\wedge$	and
		$\delta.I.i_+$	for $1 \leq i < N$
$loop_=$	$\delta.I_\wedge j.J$	$\delta.I.i_\wedge J$	when $\delta.I_\wedge j.J$ defined for $j = i$
	$\delta.I_\wedge$	$\delta.I.i_\wedge$	for $1 \leq i \leq N$
	$\delta.I_+$	$\delta.I.i_+$	for $1 \leq i \leq N$
$loop_{\neq}$	$\delta.I_\wedge j.J$	$\delta.I.i_\wedge J$	when $\delta.I_\wedge j.J$ defined for all $j \neq i$
	$\delta.I_\wedge$	$\delta.I.i_\wedge$	for $1 \leq i \leq N$
	$\delta.I_+$	$\delta.I.i_+$	for $1 \leq i \leq N$
$loop_*$	$\delta.I_\wedge j.J$	$\delta.I.i_\wedge J$	for $1 \leq i \leq N$
			when $\delta.I_\wedge j.J$ defined for $1 \leq j \leq N$
	$\delta.I_\wedge$	$\delta.I.i_\wedge$	for $1 \leq i \leq N$
	$\delta.I_+$	$\delta.I.i_+$	for $1 \leq i \leq N$

Figure 4: Direction-Vector Operators

```
          sum := 0
          for I := 1,N
S₁ :          sum := sum + A[I]
```

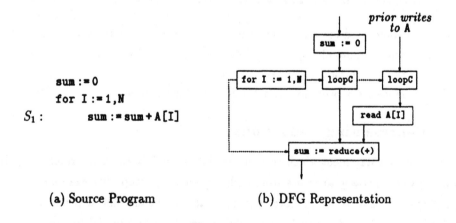

(a) Source Program   (b) DFG Representation

Figure 5: Reduction Example

this reason, we represent reductions as an operator having no loop-carried dependences.

Recall the sync operator described in Section 3.1. This operator accumulates a dependence from each iteration and produces a single token representing the boolean AND of these dependences; we could relabel this operator as a reduce(AND) to indicate that it is a reduction. We generalize this operator to allow any associative operation in place of AND. In Figure 5b, statement S_1 is represented as a reduction operator. Reduction operators are located at the bottom of loops since they take tokens from every iteration whereas statements are associated with individual iterations.

4.2 Representing Producer-Consumer Parallelism

Another important extension to dependence vectors is the representation of producer-consumer parallelism. For example, information about dependences between non-nested loops is used in generating pipelined code for multiprocessors.

Consider the example in Figure 6. Values written in iteration i of the I loop are used in iteration $i+1$ of the J loop. Figure 6b shows a conservative representation of this flow dependence from S_1 to S_2; all iterations of the I loop must terminate before any iteration of the J loop begins. In Figure 6c, we represent more detailed information about the flow dependence; in particular, the producer-consumer relationship between iteration i of the I loop and iteration $i+1$ of the J loop is indicated explicitly. Note that S_2 executing in the first iteration ($J = 2$) uses A[1] which is not written by any instance of S_1, and thus depends on some prior write to A. Thus, some prior barrier synchronization provides token δ_+ to the loop$_1$ node, thereby initializing S_2 in iteration 1. Instances of S_2 in subsequent iterations receive tokens from instances of S_1 in a producer-consumer manner.

5 Conclusions

Traditionally, dataflow has been viewed as a way of organizing hardware to exploit fine-grain parallelism in functional language programs. We have chosen to use it for a radically different purpose — to organize information in (imperative language) compilers! At a fundamental level, both these uses rely on the ability of dataflow graphs to generate names for all the concurrent activities in the program through mechanisms like tagging. We have described the dependence flow graph which is an executable representation of program dependences; the underlying execution model, called dependence-driven execution, is a generalization of the tagged-token dataflow model that permits imperative memory operations. In this paper, we have shown that dependence distance and direction information can be incorporated into this model through the use of dependence operators, and that the execution model is capable of exploiting the additional parallelism that is exposed through the use of such information. A fundamental question that is preoccupying the field is the determination of how good parallelizing compilers are in exposing parallelism in programs.

for I := 2,N
S_1:   A[I] := I

for J := 2,N
S_2:   B[J] := J * A[J-1]

(a) Source Program

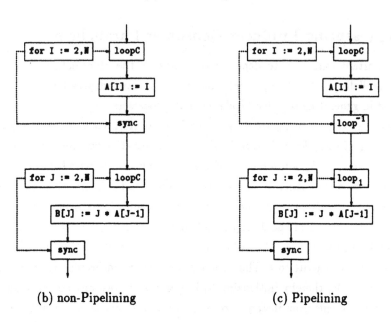

(b) non-Pipelining   (c) Pipelining

Figure 6: Producer-Consumer Example

We believe that the dependence flow graph is the right representation on which to perform such studies. The results of these experiments will be discussed elsewhere.

References

[1] A. V. Aho, R. Sethi, and J. D. Ullman. *Compilers: Principles, Techniques, and Tools.* Addison-Wesley, Reading, MA, 1986.

[2] Arvind, K. P. Gostelow, and W. Plouffe. An asynchronous programming language and computing machine. Technical Report 114a, Univ. of Calif., Irvine, Dec. 1978.

[3] R. A. Ballance, A. B. Maccabe, and K. J. Ottenstein. The Program Dependence Web: A representation supporting control-, data-, and demand-driven interpretation of imperative languages. In *Proc. of the 1990 SIGPLAN Conference on Programming Language Design and Implementation*, pages 257–271, June 1990.

[4] W. H. Burge. *Recursive Programming Techniques*. Addison-Wesley, Reading, MA, 1975.

[5] R. Cartwright and M. Felleisen. The semantics of program dependence. In *Proc. of the 1989 SIGPLAN Conference on Programming Language Design and Implementation*, pages 13–27, June 1989.

[6] J.-D. Choi. personal communication, 1991.

[7] P. Cousout and R. Cousout. Abstract Interpretation: A unified lattice model for static analysis of programs by construction of approximations of fixpoints. *Proc. of the 4th ACM Symposium on Principles of Programming Languages*, pages 238–252, Jan. 1977.

[8] R. Cytron, J. Ferrante, B. K. Rosen, M. N. Wegman, and F. K. Zadeck. An efficient method of computing static single assignment form. In *Proc. of the 16th ACM Symposium on Principles of Programming Languages*, pages 25–35, Jan. 1989.

[9] E. W. Dijkstra. *A Discipline of Programming*. Prentice-Hall, Englewood Cliffs, NJ, 1976.

[10] J. Ferrante, K. J. Ottenstein, and J. D. Warren. The program dependency graph and its uses in optimization. *ACM Transactions on Programming Languages and Systems*, 9(3):319–349, June 1987.

[11] S. Horwitz. Identifying the semantic and textual differences between two versions of a program. In *Proc. of the 1990 SIGPLAN Conference on Programming Language Design and Implementation*, pages 234–245, 1990.

[12] G. L. S. Jr. and G. J. Sussman. Scheme: An interpreter for extended lambda calculus. Technical Report Memo 349, M.I.T. Artificial Intellegence Laboratory, 1975.

[13] D. J. Kuck. *The Structure of Computers and Computations*, volume 1. John Wiley and Sons, New York, 1978.

[14] K. Pingali, M. Beck, R. Johnson, M. Moudgill, and P. Stodghill. Dependence Flow Graphs: An algebraic approach to program dependencies. In *Proc. of the 18th ACM Symposium on Principles of Programming Languages*, pages 67–78, Jan. 1991.

[15] B. Rosen. Linear time is sometimes quadratic. In *Proc. of the 8th ACM Symposium on Principles of Programming Languages*, Jan. 1981.

[16] R. P. Selke. A rewriting semantics for program dependence graphs. In *Proc. of the 16th ACM Symposium on Principles of Programming Languages*, pages 12–24, 1989.

[17] M. N. Wegman and F. K. Zadeck. Constant propagation with conditional branches. In *Proc. of the 11th ACM Symposium on Principles of Programming Languages*, pages 291–299, 1984.

[18] M. Wolfe. *Optimizing Supercompilers for Supercomputers*. Pitman Publishing, London, 1989.

9   Integrating Scalar Optimization and Parallelization

S. Tjiang, M. Wolf, M. Lam, K. Pieper,
and J. Hennessy
Stanford University

Abstract

Compiling programs to use parallelism and memory hierarchy efficiently requires both parallelizing (high-level) transformations and traditional scalar (low-level) optimizations. Our compiler has only one intermediate language — SUIF (Stanford University Intermediate Form) — for both parallelization and scalar optimizations. Having only one intermediate language offers two advantages: no duplication of functions between the two levels, and availability of high-level information at the low-level. This paper shows how SUIF integrates the two levels of abstraction, and how the SUIF compiler is organized to take advantage of this integration.

1   Introduction

Two trends are clear in computer architecture: the use of parallelism both within processors (instruction-level) and among processors (multiprocessing), and the use of memory hierarchies to match high speed CPUs to low-speed memories. In the future, the performance of a compiled program will be largely determined by how well it can use the parallelism inherent in a machine and whether the program is well-behaved in its use of the memory hierarchy.

Compiling programs to use parallelism and memory hierarchy efficiently requires both parallelizing transformations and traditional scalar optimizations, which interact in many ways. Scalar transformations and analyses are often required as a prelude to a parallel transformation. Likewise, information gathered in parallelism analyses can be used to improve

---

This research was supported in part by DARPA contract N00014-87-K-0828.

scalar optimizations. For machines with instruction-level parallelism, scalar and parallelizing transformations are intimately linked. The key challenge in integrating these transformations is that they require different kinds of knowledge and manipulate the code differently. This paper describes the architecture of a compiler system that integrates both scalar and parallelizing optimizations in one system.

Existing parallelizing FORTRAN compilers typically use two different program representations, a high-level one for parallelization and a low-level one for scalar optimizations. Many of these compilers compile in two stages. In the first stage the compilers, using source or abstract syntax trees as its high-level representation, parallelize a program via a source-to-source translation. In the second, the parallelized source is compiled and optimized by a traditional scalar compiler.

Our compiler has only one program representation, integrating both high and low levels in one intermediate language: SUIF (Stanford University Intermediate Format). Both parallelizing and scalar phases read and write programs in the same intermediate language (IL). This integration offers two key advantages over existing compilers.

No duplication of effort. Because they use two different representations, traditional compilers require two versions of many transformations and analyses, one in the first stage when high-level representation is used and another in the second stage when low-level representation is used. Instead, our compiler has only one version.

Availability of high-level information at the low level. Having two representations hinders the communication of high-level information to low-level transformations. Consider a low-level transformation like instruction scheduling. For it to use high-level information such as data-dependence and aliasing information, the information must be attached to individual loads and stores. Doing this at the source level, which is not sufficiently fine grained to identify individual memory references, requires auxiliary files or ad hoc commenting conventions. Our compiler provides a simple mechanism called annotations to attach information to individual instructions.

The SUIF intermediate language supports a wide range of both high- and low-level transformations. SUIF has as a core a small set of simple instructions that manipulate an infinite number of virtual registers. Although this core is commonly considered to be suitable only for low-level scalar optimizations, this paper shows how, with a register naming convention, the core is also suitable for high-level transformations. To support parallelization, SUIF has explicit representations for high-level control structures (for-loops, if-then-else) and an array indexing instruction; both are features necessary for data-dependence testing.

Our compiler is a set of scalar and parallelizing phases that can be reordered. The scalar phases are implemented with Sharlit[12], a tool for writing data-flow analyzers as sets of independent rules. By adding new rules, we extend these phases to recognize high-level control flow and indexing instructions. Once extended, the scalar phases can be used at both the high- and low-levels, before and after parallelization.

In this paper, we first discuss how the scalar optimizing and parallelizing transformations interact. Then we describe how SUIF integrates the features required by both kinds of transformations. Finally, we give an overview of the compiler.

In the following, the acronym SUIF can refer to either the IL or the compiler system depending on the context. Where the context does not help, we will use SUIF system to refer to the compiler system.

2 Interactions between Scalar Optimization and Parallelization

In traditional compilers, we can separate the transformations and analyses into two categories by the kind of information they use. There are low-level ones that optimize scalar code; they rely on information gathered by traditional data-flow analysis. There are high-level ones that parallelize and transform loops; they rely on data-dependence information, information that tells us whether two array references can refer to the same location, and if so, the relationships between them.

Many compilers strictly separate the two categories by using two representations: a low-level one such as Ucode[5] and a high-level one such as abstract syntax trees. When there are two representations, many of the functions provided by scalar phases must be re-implemented for each representation, and high-level analyses can no longer directly communicate with low-level transformations.

Scalar phases are indispensable for preparing the code for data-dependence testing. Testing works best when array indexes are affine functions of the loop index variables, and when the bounds of the arrays are constants. Consider the code shown in Figure 1. Before testing, we apply *induction variable expansion*[1] and constant propagation, two scalar optimizations. Induction variable expansion translates k into 2i, an affine function. Second, by propagating the constant to the variable n, the data-dependence tester can tell that A[k] cannot refer to A[200] and the loop is therefore parallelizable.

Scalar phases simplify many transformations by cleaning up after them. Constant propagation, for example, can potentially create dead code, which must be eliminated before scalar privatization. Not only does this reduce the work for scalar privatization, but privatizing dead code has a large performance penalty. However, eliminating dead code is also necessary to remove code made redundant by scalar optimizations. In both instances, the SUIF compiler eliminate dead code with the same phase.

---

[1] *Induction variable expansion* detects induction variables within for-loops, and expresses them in terms of the loop index.

```
1   n = 49;
2   k = 0;
3   for(i = 0;i<=n;i++){
4       A[k] = A[200];
5       k += 2;
6   }
```

Figure 1: A small example

In the examples above, if we had used another totally different representation for high-level transformations, then we would have to write, as in source-to-source compilers, two different sets of optimizations.

When one IL can support the two categories of transformations, the scalar phases and parallelizing phases can be freely intermixed. This freedom permits us to take a tool-based approach to building the SUIF compiler. Each phase is like a tool. A tool can prepare the code for other tools, just as constant propagation and induction variable expansion does for data dependence analysis. By cleaning up after other phases, a tool allows them to concentrate on generating simple, correct code.

Integrating the two levels has another advantage, the ease with which information can flow from high-level to low-level phases. In superscalar instruction scheduling, for example, it is not sufficient just for the high-level analyzer to label a loop as a DOALL loop. Even non-DOALL loops, those with loop-carried data dependences, contain useful parallelism. In general, high-level data-dependence information must be available to a superscalar scheduler, so that it has maximum flexibility in reordering loads and stores within loops.

3   Overview of the SUIF IL

It is difficult to support scalar optimization and parallelization in one IL because each desires program representations at different levels of abstraction. Effective scalar optimization prefers a low-level IL, to expose as many operations as possible. Array indexing, for instance, should be expressed as address calculations to expose common subexpressions and strength reduction candidates. Loops should be expressed in terms of labels and jumps, with landing pads where an optimizer can insert code and still preserve control dependences. Parallelizing transformations, however, prefer the loop structure to have a unique induction variable, and an explicit representation of loop bounds. Some dependence tests (for example, *extended GCD*[4]) require that each index expression in a multidimensional array reference be identifiable. Linearizing these array references by combining the index expressions into one lengthy computation would limit our choice of dependence tests.

SUIF has a core of small set of simple instructions with register operands. This set is called low-SUIF, and is similar to quad-based ILs used in traditional scalar optimizers.

To support parallelization, SUIF uses a register-naming convention that helps to extract expression trees from the SUIF instructions, and SUIF has explicit representation for high-level control flow and array indexing. When these features are present in a SUIF program, we say that the program is represented in high-SUIF.

Having high-SUIF is not the same as having a separate high-level IL. Except for high-level control flow and array-indexing operators, all other instructions, in both high- and low-SUIF, are identical. Thus low-SUIF is a proper subset of high-SUIF. High-SUIF features do not exclude low-SUIF features: branches and labels (low-level control-flow), address arithmetic, high-level control-flow and array-indexing operators can all coexist together.

Low-SUIF instructions are chosen to minimize case analysis during optimization and code generation. We reduce the number of cases by having a small set of operations and by not hiding operations[2]. All computational instructions require a type argument. All but one instruction[3] require their operands be in virtual registers, even branch targets and memory addresses, and all results are returned in registers. Load and store instructions are the only way to move values between registers and memory. Load constant instructions or ldcs (lines 16–18 in Figure 2) are the only way to put constants into registers. There is only one natural way to express a computation.

The SUIF type system is similar to the Ucode type system[11]. SUIF types represent data types and sizes that are naturally representable on the target machine. In Figure 2, the types (s.32) and (a.32) stand for a 32-bit signed integer and a 32-bit address respectively. Even though SUIF types are machine dependent, past experiences[5, 11] have shown that we can easily control this dependency by parameterizing the compiler.

3.1 Registers

Normally, registers and low-level instructions like SUIF's are good for scalar optimizations, but undesirable for high-level transformations. The latter transformations prefer expression trees to be represented explicitly. Using expression trees reduces the work for high-level transformations because the large number of instructions are grouped into a smaller number of trees. Trees bound the computation and use of intermediate values, reducing the number of variables to be considered. On the other hand, scalar optimizations treat all values, intermediate and otherwise, equally. These optimizations want to find redundant computations and strength reduction candidates regardless of whether they compute intermediate values or not.

---

[2]Our call instruction cal does hide operations, those that load argument registers or stack and those that copy the returned result. These operations, however, depend on the target machines. We hide this machine dependence, to simplify our inliner.

[3]In the case of the multi-way branch mbr which occurs rarely, we opted to have a format for easy code generation, with a list of branch targets.

```
 1 ldc (s.32) nr#0,49; // n = 49;
 2 cpy (s.32) pr#0,nr#0; // k = 0;
 3 ldc (s.32) nr#1,0;
 4 cpy (s.32) pr#2,nr#1;
 5 *["for" "begin" pr#1 pr#3 pr#4 pr#5 "slte"
 6         <function.f.label.L14>
 7         <function.f.label.L15>];
 8   ldc (s.32) nr#2,0;
 9   cpy (s.32) pr#3,nr#2;
10 *["for" "ub"];
11   cpy (s.32) pr#4,pr#0;
12 *["for" "step"];
13   ldc (s.32) nr#3,1;
14   cpy (s.32) pr#5,nr#3;
15 *["for" "body"]; // for(i = 0;i<=n;i++){
16   ldc (s.32) nr#5,300;
17   ldc (s.32) nr#6,200;
18   ldc (a.32) nr#7,<global.A>;
19   array (a.32) nr#7,nr#8,32,(nr#6),(nr#5);
20   lod (s.32) nr#9,nr#8;
21   ldc (s.32) nr#10,300;
22   ldc (a.32) nr#11,<global.A>;
23   array (a.32) nr#11,nr#12,32,(pr#2),(nr#10); // A[k] = A[200];
24   str (s.32) nr#12,nr#9;
25   ldc (s.32) nr#13,2;
26   add (s.32) pr#2,pr#2,nr#13; // k += 2;
27 *["for" "end"];
```

Figure 2: SUIF code for Figure 1

SUIF resolves this conflict by providing two different views of its instructions: expression trees and lists of quads. This is done by using a register naming convention. SUIF has three kinds of registers:

Hard Registers: SUIF uses hard registers to refer to real machine registers.

Node Registers: Intermediate values — data with only one point of definition and one point of use, and both points are limited to a basic block — are held in *node registers*. These values are *single-def-single-use* and correspond to values generated and used inside an expression tree. In Figure 2, node registers are those instruction operands with nr# prefixes.

Node registers make it easy to reconstruct expression trees. To build trees, make a tree node out of each SUIF instruction and connect the instruction defining a node register to the instruction using the node register with a tree edge.

Besides being easy to build trees, bounding the lifetimes of node registers is useful to those parts of the compiler that don't use trees. For example, node registers provide clues to interpretive code generators[7]. These generators associate information, machine resources, and machine instructions with each encountered node register as it scans through a SUIF program. When the last and only use of a node register is encountered, they can forget the associations.

Although node registers are distinguished from other registers, the form of instruction is the same and independent of the kind of registers it uses. Therefore, even when the internal representation is an instruction list, the lifetime information provided by node registers are still present. Reaching definitions analysis takes advantage of this situation. Since it knows definitions of node registers are limited in extent, it ignores them, thus reducing the number of cases it must consider.

Pseudo Registers: Pseudo registers hold values that are not single-def-single-use and values that flow between basic blocks. In Figure 2, register names with the prefix pr# denote pseudo registers. The compiler, in Figure 1, has assigned pr#0, pr#1, and pr#2 to n, i, and k respectively.

Pseudo registers (pregs) form an infinite register file with which we can allocate user and temporary variables.

The SUIF compiler identifies, in a procedure, those local variables with no aliases, and assigns each permanently to a preg for the duration of the procedure. To find these local variables, the front-end scans a procedure and makes a list of those locals whose addresses are never taken. These variables are not the only candidates for permanent residence in pregs. If a variable — including global and compiler-generated temporary variables — has no aliases in a region of a procedure, we can promote that variable, throughout the region, to a preg. Finding such candidates is more difficult, requiring the tracking of pointer values.

Splitting up register allocation into two phases — first allocating to pregs, then allocating pregs to machine registers — has several benefits. Because they are unaliased, pregs are ideal candidates for allocation to machine registers. In addition, assigning preg to a machine register involves only substituting the preg with the assigned hard (physical) register.

Global data-flow analysis, in SUIF, concentrates on pseudo registers. Because pregs are not aliased, gen/kill [1] information for them becomes very simple. When the analysis encounters an assignment of a preg, only the data-flow information about that register has to be changed. The assignment cannot affect information collected about other registers. Similarly, this assurance of nonaliasing simplifies other passes by restricting what is changed by an assignment to a pseudo register.

SUIF's virtual registers cannot mediate all data-flow. Memory is required for arrays and those variables that are referenced indirectly. To hide addressing details, SUIF organizes memory with *paths*.

3.2 Paths

Addressing details and relationships are expressed using paths. Paths hide many addressing details from the high-level phases, details such as accesses to a function's activation record, accesses within a record, and up-level accesses. Paths encode aliasing relationships in a language-independent way, making it easy to pass aliasing information to the low-level phases.

The path system organizes the names of program variables (including temporary ones) and labels into a tree structure. At the leaves are the variables, temporary variables, or fields of aggregates, all of which we will refer to as storage areas. An internal node groups a set of children nodes — related, for example, by scope or by being components of the same aggregate — to form a larger storage area. Each node is labeled with an identifier that is not necessarily unique. Its unique name is derived by concatenating all the identifiers along the path from the root to the node itself. For example, in the following code

```
int f ()
{   int a;
    struct { int a;
             int b;
           } c;
}
```

all variables declared in function f can be specified by the path ⟨function.f⟩. Individually, their names are ⟨function.f.a⟩ and ⟨function.f.c⟩. The two fields of the variable ⟨function.f.c⟩ are ⟨function.f.c.a⟩ and ⟨function.f.c.b⟩. In Figure 2, the path ⟨function.f.label.L14⟩ is a label and the path ⟨global.A⟩ refers to the array A in Figure 1.

A path serves not only as a unique identifier, but also succinctly encodes how the address for the variable is generated. Stored in the symbol table is the addressing relationship between an internal node of a path and each child of the node, and the code to be generated that derives the child's address from the parent's. For high-level phases that are not concerned with address computations, the address is represented by a path, which is treated as a constant. When necessary, the path can be expanded into a series of instructions by looking up the code corresponding to each edge in the path. This technique can be used for accesses into data structures, variables off the stack, or even up-level accesses in nested functions.

More importantly, SUIF's hierarchical name-space design simplifies many optimizations. One example is inlining. Suppose function g is to be inlined at a call site in function h. To get the new name space, we duplicate the subtree rooted at ⟨function.g⟩, give the root of the new subtree a unique name, and place the copy as a new subtree under ⟨function.h⟩. Name clashes are automatically avoided and we do not have to give all the variables of inlined g obscure names. Contrast this to Ucode, which provides one level of grouping with memory blocks. Each function can only have one memory block; thus a variable would be represented as a region within such a block. Ucode instructions would reference the variables using an index and a length. For inlining, Ucode must merge the variables of the callee and the caller into one flat area, thus losing high level information.

Paths simplify alias analysis. Our approach with alias analysis is modeled after the resource IDs of Coutant[6]. Alias analysis[1] tracks each variable's *reference set*, the set of addresses it can point to. A variable is aliased if its address is in a reference set of a pointer used as a memory address of a load or store. Computing these sets exactly is undecidable, so the reference sets will be conservative.

Reference sets can be succinctly represented as sets of paths in SUIF. If a register, for example, points to a record $\langle$global.r$\rangle$, then it is not necessary to enumerate all the fields of the record in r. The reference set is simply $\{\langle$global.r$\rangle\}$. Paths are particularly convenient for large reference sets: The set of all global variables is $\{\langle$global$\rangle\}$. Enumerating all the global variables can be very inefficient. An example of a need to describe all the global variables is the reference set of a procedure call. When no interprocedural analysis is performed, the conservative reference set for a function is often all the globals.

3.3 High-SUIF

The previous sections described low-SUIF, a set of features for both the high- and low-level phases of the SUIF compiler. High-SUIF is SUIF when it has the following high-level constructs:

- An ARRAY instruction explicitly indicates each index expressions of array reference. Line 19 in Figure 2 is an example of an array instruction. The ldc instruction on line 18 loads into node register nr#7 the base address of the array. Node register nr#6 holds the index value, the constant 200; nr#5 holds the upper bound 300; and nr#8 holds the computed address of the indexed element.

- A FOR construct represents a FORTRAN DO-loop. In Figure 2, the lines beginning with the character * are the parts of the FOR construct. The begin line tells us that pr#1, pr#3, pr#4 and pr#5 are the loop variable, lower bound, upper bound, and step respectively. The bounds and step registers are compiler generated, hence invisible to the programmer of the source program and cannot be modified within the loop body, as required under FORTRAN DO-loop semantics. The string slte indicates the loop test is pr#1≤pr#4. The two labels are the *break* and *continue* labels. Break and continue statements inside the loop would be translated by the front-end into jumps to these labels. The lower bound computation follows the loop begin marker; The ub marker precedes the upper bound calculation; and the step maker precedes the step initialization code. Finally, the body and end lines mark the boundaries of the loop body.

- An IF construct has three lists of instructions corresponding to the test, the *then* part and the optional *else* part.

- A LOOP construct contains two lists of instructions, one representing the body and one representing the test; the test implicitly occurs at the bottom of the loop body.

We represent C for-loops not matching FORTRAN DO-loop semantics with LOOP construct surrounded by an IF construct. The outer IF decides whether the loop should execute at least once, while the test at the end of the LOOP construct decides whether to execute the loop again.

Not all control-flow within high-SUIF is represented by our constructs; unstructured control-flow are represented with the usual low-level jumps, branchs and labels.

Our front end translates source programs to high-SUIF directly. (We also use a preprocessor that restructures Fortran into structured code). We have found that our high-SUIF constructs, array-indexing and loop structures, are convenient and sufficient for data-dependence analysis and loop transformations, without sacrificing any functionality. The fields of the ARRAY instruction provide the arguments for dependence testing. The control-flow constructs delimit the code regions of interest to loop transformations. Loops can be permuted by updating the fields of the FOR constructs; loops can be distributed by surrounding new loop bodies with FOR constructs.

After analysis and optimizations on high-level constructs, the *expander* phase lowers the high-level constructs to low-level SUIF. Following the approach of Harrison[2, 9] and of Auslander[3], our expander macro substitutes the high-level constructs into lower level code with a code template. Each construct can be lowered independently. The expander makes no attempt to generate tight, fast code. Instead, later optimizations tune and customize the result to fit the surrounding code. For example, when expanding an array instruction representing $a[3][4]$, the expander does not fold any constants; it is done later by a generic constant-folding phase.

Because high-SUIF includes low-SUIF as a subset, we have built many compiler passes that accept high-SUIF by extending passes that accepts low-SUIF. Most of our scalar optimizations fit this model and will accept high-SUIF. For instance, we obtained a high-SUIF reaching-definitions analyzer by including, in the data flow analyzer, knowledge about how the FOR construct generates and uses definitions. Except for those operations hidden by the high-level constructs, our scalar phases are equally effective on both high-SUIF and low-SUIF.

3.4 Annotations

Annotations in SUIF offer a flexible way of transmitting information (e.g. data dependence results) between phases of the compiler. Analyzers attach annotations to instructions, procedures, data declarations or control constructs; and program transformers look for and interpret specific annotations, leaving other annotations intact for subsequent passes. A parallelizing pass, for example, can annotate a FOR loop as a DOALL, indicating the loops that need to be implemented with parallel multiprocessor code. Likewise, an interprocedural analysis tool can annotate a procedure and call sites with summary information. Currently, the phases of the SUIF compiler tell each other a wide variety of information — such as ud-chains, symbol table information, and data dependences — with annotations.

An annotation consists of a name, a string, followed by a list of fields. Each field can be a string, register, integer, SUIF type or path. Any specific annotation has a known format agreed upon by the compiler phases producing and consuming the annotations. For example, if an alias analysis phase determines that a store instruction could write any global or the function f's local variable r, it might attach the following annotation to the store instruction:

```
["alias set" <global> <function.f.r>]
```

Subsequent passes look for the `"alias set"` annotation on loads and stores and use this information. In general, the annotation format is simple and flexible. Thus it is easy to add new information into SUIF, an important property for a research compiler.

Annotations allow us to separate analysis phases of the compiler from transformation phases, improving the modularity of the compiler. The separation permits the substitution of analysis phases, a capability that is invaluable for experimental purposes.

4 Overview and Status of the SUIF compiler system

In this section, we show how our compiler has been organized to take advantage of the integration of optimizations and parallelizations. The SUIF compiler separates its functions into distinct phases which communicate only through a SUIF file. Because SUIF has only one representation, we are free in ordering the phases with respect to each other. We have found this structure to be invaluable for experimentation, permitting several implementation projects to coexist.

Let us follow the progress of a typical FORTRAN program as it flows through the SUIF compiler. Figure 3 is a flow chart of our compiler. The first phase f2c, a FORTRAN-to-C converter [8] translates the program to an equivalent C program. Then the program FE, a front-end based on the portable C compiler, translates the C program to a high-SUIF program.

During parallelization, the program representations have the features of high-SUIF. The high-SUIF program is passed through a sequence of phases. This sequence includes not only parallelizing phases, but also includes scalar optimizations, each providing information or preparing the program for later phases in the sequence. Which phases are present and how they are ordered in the sequence will depend on the goal of the compilation — compiling for multiprocessors and compiling for superscalar machines require different sequences. They will also depend on the information requirements of the phases — some phases (dependence analysis) work better if others (constant propagation, induction variable expansion) precede them in the sequence. The output of the sequence is another program in high-SUIF that has been parallelized and improved by scalar optimizations.

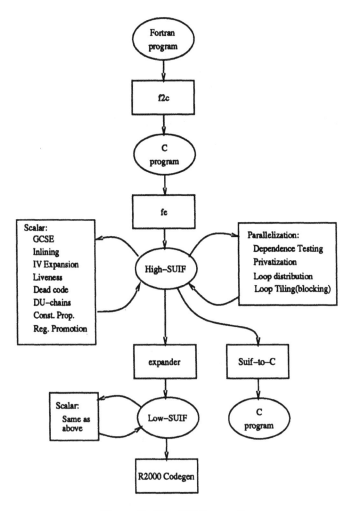

Figure 3: The SUIF compiler

To further optimize the program a special phase, the expander, translates the high-level constructs of the high-SUIF program into low-SUIF (See Section 3.3) The low-SUIF program is optimized and customized by scalar phases, many the same as those previously applied to high-SUIF.

Eventually, low-SUIF is translated into target code. As operators in SUIF correspond closely to RISC instructions, it is easy to build code generators for various RISC machines. We have developed code generators for the Mips R2000 and the VAX.

Our compiler has a comprehensive repertoire of transformations and analyses, which we now discuss in more detail.

4.1 Scalar Optimizations

Scalar phases improve the code directly through traditional optimizations[1], and they prepare the code so that parallelization phases are more effective. So far, we have implemented a set of optimizations organized into the following groups.

- Strength reduction, global common subexpression elimination, loop invariant removal — based on elimination of partial redundancy[5].

- Constant propagation, constant folding, copy propagation,

- Dead-code elimination, dead-store elimination, live-range determination — based on liveness analysis.

- Def-use and use-def chains

- Register allocation using priority-based coloring.

- Induction variable expansion — using symbolic analysis.

All the above phases have a common structure: a sequence of data-flow analyzers, each solving a data-flow problem over a single procedure. Exploiting this common structure, we have created *Sharlit*[12], a tool for building control-flow and data-flow analyzers that are extensible.

To write a data-flow solver, we write a sharlit program that describes the types of nodes and regions in the graph, the values flowing through the graph, and how each node and region type computes an out-flowing value from its in-flowing values. All these descriptions are rule-based, so they can be easily extended. To extend control-flow analysis, we add rules describing new control structures. To extend data-flow analysis, we add new node types describing how new instructions change the data-flow values.

Because they are written with Sharlit, our scalar phases are extended to understand the high-level control structures (for-loops, if-then-else) and the indexing instruction.

4.2 High-level Transformations and Analysis

Array- and loop-level analyses and transformations require data-dependence information. By arranging dependence tests in increasing strengths and costs, and using memoization, our compiler can generate exact dependence information efficiently[10]. This dependence information can be used in low-level passes such as a superscalar/VLIW instruction scheduler, and in high-level passes that privatize scalars, distribute and transform loops.

We have unified unimodular transformations — interchange, reversal, skewing — with a new transformation theory[14, 13]. Our theory shows how these transformations, together with tiling (or blocking), can expose parallelism and improve data locality, without introducing excessive communication or over-committing caches. Our theory simplifies implementation, finding directly the optimal loop transformations and computing directly the loop bounds without searching exhaustively through the transformation space.

In addition to unimodular transformations, we have implemented several well-known transformations: loop distribution, scalar privatization and scalar expansion. Scalar privatization is important because it allows loops which define scalars for every iteration to be parallelized. Loop distribution and scalar expansion work in concert to allow sequential portions of the loop to be split from parallel computations in a loop.

4.3 Status and Experience

Over the last three years, our efforts have created an effective research compiler, a compiler that can be extended to run new experiments, a compiler capable of generating good optimized and parallelized code. We can compile and validate nine of the Perfect club benchmarks with full scalar optimizations. The high-level phases are functioning. Data-dependence tests will run on all the Perfect club[10]. Linear loop transformations can automatically block matrix algorithms such as QR decomposition and LU decomposition without pivoting, whose performance we have measured on an SGI multiprocessor[13]. We continue to build upon SUIF, with eight projects adding new transformations to the SUIF compiler.

5 Conclusions

Optimizing compilers for modern high-performance computers must implement not just traditional scalar optimizations, but also array level analyses and loop transformations. Such an optimizing compiler is a very large system. Moreover, to keep up with the rapid pace of processor architecture advances, the compiler system must be able to incorporate new optimizations developed for specific architectures. Thus, it is even more important that the system be modular and well-engineered to support growth and experimentation.

Our project at Stanford is building such a system. Central to the project is our SUIF intermediate format. It is designed so that tools of vastly different nature can work together, while allowing each tool to operate in different internal representations. Moreover, the annotation system makes the system easily adaptable to new changes.

Based on this intermediate format, we have built an interesting set of tools, ranging from scalar data flow optimizations to compound loop transformations. Our experience suggests that our design does provide a useful platform for multiple simultaneous projects on a variety of compiler research topics. We have been able to leverage off the code sharing ability of the system and have, in a reasonable time frame obtained interesting results in individual topics such as data flow optimizations, data dependence analysis and loop transformations. There are still many subjects to be explored with the SUIF platform.

Our goal is to use this comprehensive optimizing system as a tool to gather meaningful statistics on complete programs, experiment with new architectural designs, and evaluate new compilation techniques.

6 Acknowledgements

We thank Saman Amarasinghe, Jennifer Anderson, Robert French, Dror Maydan, Michael Smith, Malcolm Wing and others who helped in the building of the SUIF system. Also, we thank Peter Schnorf and Mahadevan Ganapathi for their comments on this paper.

References

[1] Alfred V. Aho, Ravi Sethi, and Jeffrey D. Ullman. *Compilers: principles techniques, and tools*. Addison-Wesley, 1988.

[2] F. E. Allen, J. L. Carter, J. Fabri, J. Ferrante, W. H. Harrison, P. G. Loewner, and L. H. Trevillyan. The experimental compiling system. *IBM Journal of Research and Development*, 24(6), November 1980.

[3] M. Auslander and M. Hopkins. An overview of the PL.8 compiler. In *SIGPLAN Conference on Compiler Construction*, 1982.

[4] U. Banerjee. *Dependence Analysis for Supercomputing*. Kluwer Academic, 1988.

[5] F. C. Chow. *A Portable Machine-Independent Global Optimizer — Design and Measurement*. PhD thesis, Stanford University, 1983.

[6] D. S. Coutant. Retargetable high-level alias analysis. In *Proceedings of the 13th ACM Symposium on Principles of Programming Languages*, 1986.

[7] M. Ganapathi, C. N. Fischer, and J. L. Hennessy. Retargetable compiler code generation. *ACM Computing Surveys*, 14(4):573–592, 1982.

[8] D. Gay. Private communication. ATT Software, 1988.

[9] W. Harrison. A new strategy for code generation — the general purpose optimizing compiler. In *ACM Fourth Symposium on Principles of Programming Languages*, pages 29–37, 1977.

[10] D. E. Maydan, J. L. Hennessy, and M. S. Lam. Efficient andb exact data dependence testing. In *SIGPLAN Conference on Programming Language Design and Implementation*, June 1991.

[11] D. L. Perkins and R. L. Sites. Machine-independent pascal code optimization. In *Proceedings of the SIGPLAN Symposium on Compiler Construction*, pages 201–207, 1979.

[12] S. W. K. Tjiang. Sharlit: A tool for scalar optimizers. Expected, 1991.

[13] M. E. Wolf and M. S. Lam. A data locality optimizing algorithm. In *SIGPLAN Conference on Programming Language Design and Implementation*, 1991.

[14] M. E. Wolf and M. S. Lam. A loop transformation theory and an algorithm to maximize parallelism. *IEEE Transactions on Parallel and Distributed Systems*, Oct 1991.

10 Optimization of Data/Control Conditions in Task Graphs

M. Girkar and C. Polychronopoulos
University of Illinois at Urbana-Champaign

Abstract

Thus far, parallelism at the loop level (or data-parallelism) has been almost exclusively the main target of parallelizing compilers. The variety of new parallel architectures and recent progress in interprocedural dependence analysis suggest new directions for the exploitation of parallelism across loop and procedure boundaries (or functional-parallelism). This paper presents an intermediate parallel program representation which encapsulates minimal data and control dependences, and which can be used for the extraction and exploitation of functional, or task-level parallelism. We focus on the derivation of the execution conditions of tasks which maximizes task-level parallelism, and the optimization of these conditions which results in reducing synchronization overhead imposed by data and control dependences.

1 Introduction

The familiar task graph, a directed acyclic graph, has become synonymous with a parallel program. Task graphs have been used as a convenient abstraction of parallel computations and programs in virtually all areas of parallel processing. Task graphs take the form of a partial ordering imposed on a set of nodes representing computations. The partial ordering is normally described by data dependences. These models, however, ignore dependences arising due to the flow of control in a program. Control dependences change the nature of the task graph because not all tasks are guaranteed to execute in such a model.

In this paper we model the program as a set of tasks in an acyclic control flow graph. Programs with loops can be transformed into such a structure by recursively collapsing nodes in the loop into a single node. This leaves the control flow graph of the body of any loop acyclic [8]. We tackle the problem of automatic extraction of task-level parallelism in such a graph. At present, only a handful of parallelizing compilers employ similar mechanisms for task-level parallelism [2, 5, 11].

Section 2 gives basic definitions and states some useful properties related to the control dependence graph (CDG). Section 3 proposes a parallel execution model of such a graph. The augmentation of the CDG with data dependences is considered in Section 4. Section 5 develops a platform for the computation of the execution conditions of tasks based on data and control dependences. Section 6 presents a technique for the optimization of control conditions in detail. Finally, Section 7 covers parallel source code generation issues.

2 The Control Dependence Graph (CDG)

A *control flow graph* is a directed graph $CFG = (V, E)$ with unique nodes $START$, $STOP \in V$ such that there exists a path from $START$ to every node in V and a path from every node to $STOP$; $START$ has no incoming arcs, and $STOP$ has no outgoing arcs. We will use an acyclic CFG to model the task graph of a program. Although we shall be dealing mainly with acyclic control flow graphs, we relax this restriction in this section to state more general properties of the control dependence graph, explicitly mentioning CFG to be acyclic whenever needed.

Node x *dominates* node y, denoted by $x\Delta_d y$, iff every path from $START$ to y contains x [1]. A node always dominates itself. We use $x\cancel{\Delta}_d y$ to denote x does not dominate y.

Node y *post-dominates* node x, denoted by $y\Delta_p x$, iff every path from x to $STOP$ (not including x) contains y [6]. A node never post-dominates itself. We use $y\cancel{\Delta}_p x$ to denote y does not post-dominate x. The *reflexive closure* of the post-dominance relation will be denoted by $\bar{\Delta}_p$, $y\bar{\Delta}_p x$ iff $y\Delta_p x$ or $y = x$. The following is well known [6].

Lemma 1 *Let y and z be distinct nodes. For any x, if $y\bar{\Delta}_p x$ and $z\bar{\Delta}_p x$ then either $y\Delta_p z$ or $z\Delta_p y$.*

Lemma 1 suffices to show that the set of post-dominators of a node x form a chain. The least element in the chain is called the *immediate post-dominator* of x. The set of post-dominators of a node x is non-empty (except when x is the $STOP$ node) as $STOP\ \Delta_p x$. Hence, all nodes except $STOP$ have a unique immediate post-dominator. If we draw an arc from x to y whenever x is an immediate post-dominator of y, the resulting graph is a tree rooted at $STOP$ and called the *post-dominator tree*.

Node y is *control dependent* on node x with *label* $x - a$ ((x, a) is an arc in CFG), denoted by $x\delta_c y$, iff

1. $y \not\Delta_p x$, and

2. $\exists$ a non-null path $P = <x, a, \ldots, y>$, such that for any $z \in P$ (excluding x and y) $y \Delta_p z$.

Our definition of control dependence differs only slightly from [6] where nodes were restricted to have at most two outgoing arcs; we relax this restriction. An immediate consequence of the definition is that if $x \delta_c y$ with label $x - a$, then $y \bar{\Delta}_p a$.

The *control dependence graph* CDG, of a control flow graph CFG, is defined as the directed graph with labeled arcs, $CDG = (CV, CE)$ such that

1. $CV = V$ and

2. $(x, y) \in CE$ with label $x - a$ iff $x \delta_c y$ with label $x - a$.

CDG can be built from CFG using the post-dominance tree [6] as follows. If (x, y) is any branch in CFG, then it can be shown that

1. Let z be the immediate ancestor of x in the post-dominator tree. Then the least common ancestor of x and y in the post-dominator tree, $LCA(x, y)$, is either x or z.

2. All nodes on the path from y to z (not including z) in the post-dominator tree are control dependent on x with label $x - y$.

The *transitive closure* of δ_c will be denoted by δ_c^*, $x \delta_c^* y$ iff there exists a non-null path from x to y in CDG. This corresponds to the notion of the range of a branch given in [12]. The reflexive closure of δ_c^* will be denoted by $\bar{\delta}_c^*$, $x \bar{\delta}_c^* y$ iff $x \delta_c^* y$ or $x = y$. We now state some important properties of the CDG which are directly or indirectly used in later optimization phases. Proofs are omitted for brevity and can be found in [8]. The acyclicity of CFG is carried over to the CDG by Theorem 1; a related result for forward control dependence graphs is proved in [5].

Theorem 1 *CDG is cyclic iff CFG is cyclic.*

Lemma 2 is useful in the optimization phase in Section 6.

Lemma 2 *Let CFG be acyclic. If there is a path from x to y in CFG, then there exists a unique node z such that $z \bar{\Delta}_p x$ and $z \bar{\delta}_c^* y$.*

3 Parallel execution of acyclic CFG

In the absence of data dependences, the parallel execution of CFG is based on CDG [5] where identically control dependent nodes are executed in parallel:

1. Initially, only nodes that do not have any incoming arcs in the CDG begin execution in parallel.

2. After executing a node, say x, if label $x - a$ is true (i.e., the branch $x - a$ would have been taken in the sequential execution of CFG), then all nodes y such that $x\delta_c y$ with label $x - a$ start execution in parallel.

The execution terminates when all nodes finish execution. By Theorem 1, CDG is acyclic and hence it is obvious that the parallel execution will terminate.

Let S and P denote the *sequential* and *parallel* execution of CFG respectively. S specifies a single path, P, in CFG from $START$ to $STOP$. The parallel execution of CFG specifies a tree in the forward control dependence graph [5].

A node is executed in S if it lies on P. A label $x - y$ will be *true* in P if the arc $x - y$ lies on P. According to the above model, a node x is executed in P when there is a path in the CDG, $< a_0, a_1, \ldots, a_n = x >$ such that a_0 is a node with no incoming arcs and $a_j\delta_c a_{j+1}$ $(0 \leq j < n)$ with some true label $a_j - b_j$.

The following theorem states the correctness of the parallel execution.

Theorem 2 *Let CFG be acyclic. The parallel execution of CFG executes the same nodes as the sequential execution.* (A proof is given in [8].)

4 The data dependence graph (DDG)

Node y *conflicts* with node x if either x or y share access to a common memory location, at least one of which is a "write" operation. Conflicts induce a data dependence [3, 4, 10, 13] relation among nodes. Exactly one of the following can occur between two distinct nodes x and y.

1. y is reachable from x.

2. x is reachable from y.

3. x is not reachable from y, and y is not reachable from x.

If x and y conflict with each other, then we say that y is *data dependent* on x in Case 1, (denoted by $x\delta_d y$), and x is data dependent on y in Case 2 ($y\delta_d x$). In Case 3 the conflict does not matter as x and y will not be executed together in any execution instance of CFG and can be ignored.

The *data dependence graph* $DDG = (DV, DE)$ is defined as the directed graph with labeled arcs such that

1. $DV = V$ and

2. $(x, y) \in DE$ if $x\delta_d y$.

Note that since $x\delta_d y$ implies a path from x to y in CFG, the graph containing the arcs of both CFG and DDG is also acyclic owing to the acyclicity of CFG. Similarly, the graph containing the arcs of both CDG and DDG is also acyclic.

5 Conditions for execution of task nodes

With the addition of data dependences, when a node is to be executed, it must be verified whether the nodes on which it is data dependent have completed execution or are not going to be executed; in both cases the data dependences are satisfied. This can be done by defining conditions for each node so that the condition evaluates to true only when the node is ready; i.e., it must be executed and the data dependences, if any, be satisfied. Our approach proceeds by formalizing the notion of execution conditions based on data and control dependences (similar to [9]), and by tackling the problem of optimizing such conditions.

Conditions contain *literals* representing nodes (x) or arcs $(x-y)$ in CFG. The condition (x) will be true when node x has finished execution. The condition $(x - y)$ will be true when node x finishes execution and in addition control follows the arc $x - y$ in CFG. A node, x, will be ready to execute when:

1. The control conditions which force the execution of x are true.

2. If $y\delta_d x$, then either y has finished execution or it is known that y will not be executed.

An example will make this clear. Consider the control flow graph shown in Figure 1(a). Its post dominator tree and control dependence graph are shown in Figure 1(b) and Figure 1(c). Let the data dependence graph be as shown in Figure 1(d). Since we will be dealing with acyclic graphs, we will assume from now on that the nodes are numbered in such a way that if there is an arc (x, y) in the CFG, $x < y$.

The conditions for node 5 to be executed are that the branch from node 3 to node 4 is taken (the necessary control condition), and either node 4 has finished execution or it is determined that it will not be executed at all (the necessary data dependence condition). Node 4 will not be executed when the branch $3 - 9$ or $1 - 8$ is taken. Thus the condition for the execution of node 5 can be compactly represented by $3-4 \land (4 \lor 3-9 \lor 1-8)$. When nodes 3 and 4 finish execution, they will try to update the condition of node 5 (provided it has not been executed yet), and if the update causes the condition to be true, node 5 can be executed. We now formally define the procedure for deriving the conditions for a node.

5.1 Control dependence conditions

The control conditions for a node x are easily derived from the CDG. Let x in the CDG be control dependent on a_1, a_2, ..., a_n with labels $a_1 - b_1$, $a_2 - b_2$, ..., $a_n - b_n$ respectively. Then the control condition for x is

$$a_1 - b_1 \lor a_2 - b_2 \lor \ldots \lor a_n - b_n.$$

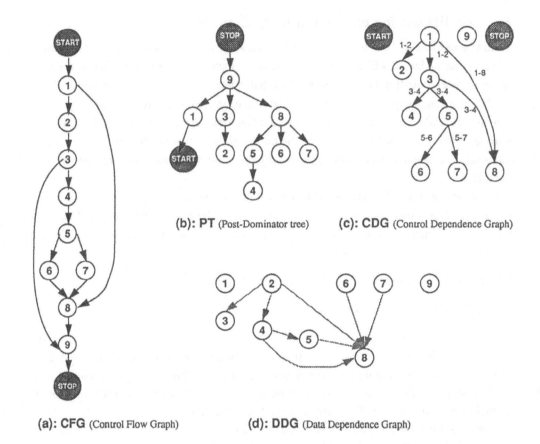

(b): PT (Post-Dominator tree)   **(c): CDG** (Control Dependence Graph)

(a): CFG (Control Flow Graph)   **(d): DDG** (Data Dependence Graph)

Figure 1: An example.

5.2 Data dependence conditions

For data dependence conditions we need to know when a node will not be executed. It is easier to do the reverse computation, namely, to find the nodes that will not be executed if a branch is taken in the flow graph. We first define $REAC(x)$ to be the set of nodes reachable from a node x in the CDG.

$$REAC(x) = \{y \mid x\delta_c^* y\}.$$

This can be done by a simple depth-first traversal of the CDG. The sets $REAC(x)$[1]

---
[1] In [5] $REAC(x)$ included x also.

were also defined and used in [5]. Thus, for the example control dependence graph shown in Figure 1(c), we have $REAC(3) = \{4,5,6,7,8\}$, $REAC(1) = \{2,3,4,5,6,7,8\}$, $REAC(5) = \{6,7\}$ and for all other nodes, x, $REAC(x) = \emptyset$. Similarly, we define the set of nodes reachable from a branch in the CDG, denoted by $REAC(x - y)$.

$$REAC(x - y) \;=\; \{a \mid \exists z \text{ such that } x\delta_c z \text{ with label } x - y \text{ and } z\bar{\delta}_c^* a\}.$$

Obviously, $REAC(x - y) \subseteq REAC(x), \forall x$. In our example we get $REAC(1 - 2) = \{2,3,4,5,6,7,8\}$, $REAC(1-8) = \{8\}$, $REAC(3-4) = \{4,5,6,7,8\}$, $REAC(3-9) = \emptyset$, $REAC(5 - 6) = \{6\}$ and $REAC(5 - 7) = \{7\}$. Based on these definitions we can define $BranNeg(x - y)$ for a branch $x - y$ in the CFG.

$$BranNeg(x - y) \;=\; REAC(x) \;-\; REAC(x - y).$$

In the process we also define the set $Neg(x)$ for each node x. $Neg(x)$ is the set of all branches in CFG whose traversal bypasses the execution of x (a formal statement is given in Lemma 3 and Lemma 4).

$$Neg(x) \;=\; \{y - z \mid x \in BranNeg(y - z)\}.$$

or equivalently,

$$Neg(x) \;=\; \{y - z \mid x \in REAC(y) \text{ and } x \notin REAC(y - z)\}.$$

In the example we have $BranNeg(1 - 2) = BranNeg(3 - 4) = \emptyset$, $BranNeg(1 - 8) = \{2,3,4,5,6,7\}$, $BranNeg(3 - 9) = \{4,5,6,7,8\}$, $BranNeg(5 - 6) = \{7\}$ and $BranNeg(5 - 7) = \{6\}$. From these we can compute $Neg(START) = Neg(1) = Neg(9) = Neg(STOP) = \emptyset$, $Neg(2) = Neg(3) = \{1 - 8\}$, $Neg(4) = Neg(5) = \{1 - 8, \ 3 - 9\}$, $Neg(6) = \{1 - 8, \ 3 - 9, \ 5 - 7\}$, $Neg(7) = \{1 - 8, \ 3 - 9, \ 5 - 6\}$ and $Neg(8) = \{3 - 9\}$.

We now state some of the properties of the Neg sets. Proofs can be found in [8].

Lemma 3 *Let $p - q \in Neg(r)$. If label $p - q$ is true then r will not be executed.*

Lemma 4 *If r is not executed then exactly one of the labels in $Neg(r)$ will be true.*

We can now define the data dependence condition for a node x when it is dependent on another node y. Let $Neg(y)$ be $\{a_1 - b_1, a_2 - b_2, \ldots, a_n - b_n\}$. Then the data dependence condition is

$$y \ \vee \ a_1 - b_1 \ \vee \ a_2 - b_2 \ \vee \ \ldots \ \vee \ a_n - b_n.$$

If x is data dependent on other nodes, then we take a conjunction of all conditions. The conditions for all the nodes in the example flow graph of Figure 1 are shown in Table 1. A blank entry indicates that the condition is always true.

Node	Condition
START	$-$
1	$-$
2	$1 - 2$
3	$1 - 2 \wedge (2 \vee 1 - 8)$
4	$3 - 4 \wedge (2 \vee 1 - 8)$
5	$3 - 4 \wedge (4 \vee 1 - 8 \vee 3 - 9)$
6	$5 - 6$
7	$5 - 7$
8	$(1 - 8 \vee 3 - 4) \wedge (2 \vee 1 - 8) \wedge (4 \vee 1 - 8 \vee 3 - 9) \wedge$ $(5 \vee 1 - 8 \vee 3 - 9) \wedge (6 \vee 5 - 7 \vee 1 - 8 \vee 3 - 9) \wedge$ $(7 \vee 5 - 6 \vee 1 - 8 \vee 3 - 9)$
9	$-$
STOP	$-$

Table 1: Unoptimized conditions for all nodes in Figure 1.

6 Optimization of data and control dependences

Since the conditions for a node will be repeatedly updated and evaluated for satisfaction, it is important that they be as simple as possible. For example, some of the data dependences need not be synchronized by way of execution conditions because they are always satisfied by other control and data dependences which have been enforced. In such cases the data dependence term in the condition can be omitted. In this section we show how optimizations can be performed to simplify the conditions. Optimizations are done in two phases:

Phase I Elimination of redundant dependences.

Phase II Simplification of execution conditions.

6.1 Elimination of redundant dependences

Let $x \prec y$ (x *precedes* y) denote that x finishes before y in all parallel executions of the CFG in which both x and y execute. The following lemma will be useful in the optimization phase.

Lemma 5 *If* $x\delta_c^* y$ *then* $x \prec y$. *(A proof is given in [8].)*

It is clear that if we can determine that $x \prec y$ then the data dependence $x\delta_d y$ (if present) is satisfied and does not need explicit synchronization. A general outline of our algorithm is given in Figure 2. At any stage, we have information (the set S) for a subset of nodes determining which nodes precede other nodes, due to data dependences which

Data Dependence Optimization Algorithm

1. Number the nodes of CFG such that if there is an arc (x, y) then $x < y$.

2. Construct set S to consist of pairs (x, y) such that $x \prec y$. Initially, if $x \delta_c^* y$ then $(x, y) \in S$ (see Lemma 5).

3. **for** each node x in increasing order **do**

   (a) **for** each node y from $x - 1$ **downto** 1 **do** /* check if (y, x) can be added to S */

      i. Find unique z such that $z \bar{\Delta}_p y$ and $z \bar{\delta}_c^* x$ (see Lemma 2).

      ii. Let A be the set of nodes, a, such that $a \delta_c x$ and $z \bar{\delta}_c^* a$.

      iii. If $(y, a) \in S$ for each a in A, add (y, x) to S.

   (b) **for** each data dependence $y \delta_d x$ in decreasing order of y **do** /* Now consider dependences into x and check which are redundant */

      i. if $(y, x) \in S$ then $y \delta_d x$ is redundant.

      ii. Otherwise, $y \delta_d x$ needs to be enforced. Add (y, x) to S. Enforcing $y \delta_d x$ may cause additional pairs to be added to S. This update of S is done by repeatedly executing the following two steps till no further updates can be done:

         A. If $(a, x) \in S$ then add (z, x) to S for all z such that $z \delta_c^* a$.

         B. For a node z if $z \delta_d a$, $(a, x) \in S$, and either $a \Delta_p z$ or $a \Delta_d z$, then add (z, x) to S.

Figure 2: Algorithm to eliminate redundant dependences.

have been enforced and control dependences. Whenever a new node (x) is added, this information is updated (step 3(a)) by checking if (y, x) can be added to S for all $y < x$. When we consider the data dependences incident on the new node (step 3(b)), we check if they are implied by previous data and control dependences or are really necessary. In the former case, we can ignore the dependence (step 3(b)i). In the latter case, we must enforce the dependence (by synchronization), which may result in determining the execution order of other nodes, and hence may lead to an update in our information (step 3(b)ii).

We illustrate the method on the example control flow graph in Figure 1. The working of the algorithm at various stages is shown in Figure 3. The information available in set S is shown in Figure 3 by two sets associated with each node, x, shown by square (where x is the first component) and round brackets (where x is the second component). Looking at the sets associated with node 3 in Figure 3(a), one can see that the pairs

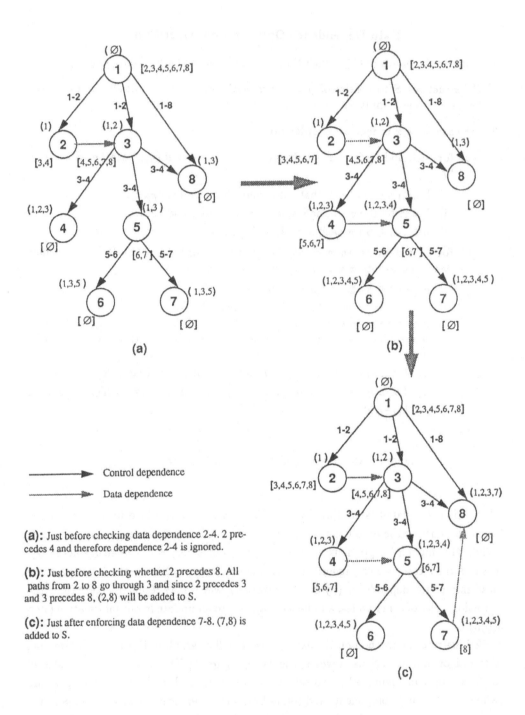

Control dependence

Data dependence

(a): Just before checking data dependence 2-4. 2 precedes 4 and therefore dependence 2-4 is ignored.

(b): Just before checking whether 2 precedes 8. All paths from 2 to 8 go through 3 and since 2 precedes 3 and 3 precedes 8, (2,8) will be added to S.

(c): Just after enforcing data dependence 7-8. (7,8) is added to S.

Figure 3: Removing redundant data dependences.

$(1,3)$, $(2,3)$, $(3,4)$, $(3,5)$, $(3,6)$, $(3,7)$, $(3,8)$ belong to S. Initially, S consists of pairs (x,y) where $x\delta_c^* y$. The **for** loops in Steps 3 and 3(b) imply that data dependence (a,b) will be considered before (c,d) if $b < d$ or if $b = d$ and $a > c$. For our example graph in Figure 1(d), this order is $(2,3)$, $(2,4)$, $(2,5)$, $(7,8)$, $(6,8)$, $(5,8)$, $(4,8)$, $(2,8)$.

When dependence $2\delta_d 3$ is considered in step 3(b) it will have to be synchronized as $2 \not\prec 3$. However, after that is done, $(2,3)$ will be added to S (step 3(b)ii). When determining whether $2 \prec 4$ in step 3(a)($y = 2, x = 4$), the set A will evaluate to $\{3\}$ and since $(2,3) \in S$, $(2,4)$ will also be added to S (step 3(a)iii). This causes the data dependence $2\delta_d 4$ to be considered redundant in step 3(b)i (see Figure 3(a)).

The status of the algorithm when considering the question whether $(2,8) \in S$ (step 3(a), $y = 2, x = 8$) is shown in Figure 3(b). The unique z is found to be 3 and hence A will again evaluate to $\{3\}$. Note that the set A does not consist of the predecessors of 8 in the control dependence graph (e.g. $1 \notin A$); instead it is the set of predecessors of 8 which can lie on a path from 2 to 8. Thus, $(2,8)$ will be added to S. Subsequently, this information will be used to eliminate the dependence $2\delta_d 8$.

Figure 3(c) shows the status when it has been determined that $7\delta_d 8$ needs to be enforced (step 3(b)ii). Enforcing new dependences may cause updates in current information. In this case because the dependence $7\delta_d 8$ was enforced, the pair $(5,8)$ will be added to S (step 3(b)iiA). This in turn will cause $(4,8)$ to be added to S because of the data dependence $4\delta_d 5$ (step 3(b)iiB). This propagation of information is shown in Figure 4. This information will be used later to show that the dependences $5\delta_d 8$ and $4\delta_d 8$ are redundant and need not be enforced.

For our example graph of Figure 1 the algorithm will determine that the dependences $2\delta_d 4$, $5\delta_d 8$, $4\delta_d 8$ and $2\delta_d 8$ are redundant.

6.2 Further simplification (Control dependence "elimination")

The algorithm in Section 6.1 will inform us of the essential dependences which need to be satisfied before a node can commence execution. It may still be possible to simplify the condition further. For example, in a term due to dependence $y\delta_d x$, some of the literals in $Neg(y)$ can be omitted if they also belong to $Neg(x)$ as they will not result in the execution of x. Under certain conditions the simplification process can be very powerful yielding consistently "better" conditions as is illustrated by the following proposition which allows for the simultaneous removal of terms from the control/data conditions of x.

Proposition 1 *Let $y\delta_d x$ and let x be control dependent on c_1, ..., c_m with labels $c_1 - d_1$, ..., $c_m - d_m$ respectively. Let $Neg(y) = \{a_1 - b_1, ..., a_n - b_n\}$. Then the condition for x is $(c_1 - d_1 \lor ... \lor c_m - d_m) \land (y \lor a_1 - b_1 \lor ... \lor a_n - b_n)$. Whenever $x\Delta_p y$, this condition can be replaced by the simpler condition $y \lor e_1 - f_1 ... \lor e_p - f_p$, where each $e_j - f_j$ is added as a result of some $a_k - b_k$ as follows:*

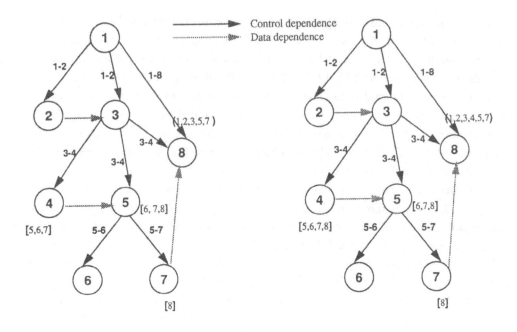

(a): First step - propagation up to **5**   **(b):** Second step - propagation up to **4**

Figure 4: Propagating information.

1. $e_j - f_j = a_k - b_k$ when $x\Delta_p a_k$.

2. $e_j - f_j = a_k - b_k$ when $a_k\delta_c x$ with label $a_k - b_k$.

3. $e_j - f_j = c_i - d_i$ for some $i \in 0 \dots m$ when $a_k\delta_c^* x$ and $c_i \in REAC(a_k - b_k)$.

(A proof is given in [8].)

Although the proof of Proposition 1 is intricate, the actual computation can be done easily, as all that needs to be done is to find the immediate predecessors of x in CFG which are also in $REAC(a-b)$ for each $a-b \in Neg(y) - Neg(x)$. Consider the example control flow graph shown in Figure 5. $Neg(5)$ is $\{1 - 7, 3 - 8, 4 - 8\}$ and $Neg(6)$ is $\{7-8, 3-8, 4-8\}$. The condition for 6 is $(7-6 \vee 3-5\vee 4-5) \wedge (5 \vee 1-7 \vee 3-8 \vee 4-8)$. Since $6\Delta_p 5$ we can use the above proposition to simplify the condition. The branch $1-7$ falls under Case 3. It is now sufficient to look at predecessors of 6 which are descendants of $1-7$. Thus, due to the arc $1-7$ we include only $7-6$ in the condition. Branch $3-8$ also falls under Case 3; however, 6 has no predecessors which are also descendants

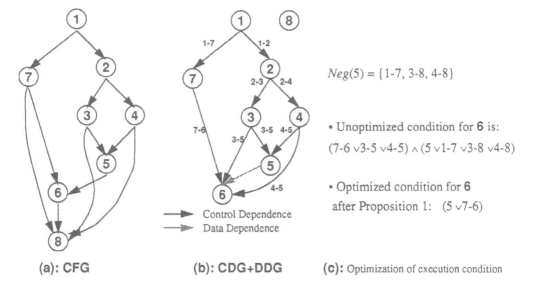

$Neg(5) = \{1\text{-}7, 3\text{-}8, 4\text{-}8\}$

• Unoptimized condition for **6** is:

$(7\text{-}6 \lor 3\text{-}5 \lor 4\text{-}5) \land (5 \lor 1\text{-}7 \lor 3\text{-}8 \lor 4\text{-}8)$

• Optimized condition for **6**
after Proposition 1: $(5 \lor 7\text{-}6)$

(a): CFG   (b): CDG+DDG   (c): Optimization of execution condition

Figure 5: Further optimization of execution condition.

of $3 - 8$ and hence no literals are added to the condition for 6. This can also be seen from $3 - 8$ being in $Neg(6)$. Similarly, no new terms are added due to $4 - 8$, and the final condition for 6 is evaluated to $(5 \lor 7 - 6)$.

The conditions for our example flow graph of Figure 1 after elimination of redundant dependences and simplification are shown in Table 2. The condition for 8 can be further simplified to $(6 \lor 7 \lor 1 - 8)$, however, Proposition 1 can be applied to only a single data dependence at a time and hence this is not done. The complexity issues of the optimization algorithms are considered in [8].

7   Parallel source code generation

Let us consider the problem of parallel source code generation based on the execution conditions derived and optimized as discussed in the previous sections. We use the **cobegin ... coend** parallel construct with its ordinary semantics, and the synchronization primitives **wait, post, clear**. The synchronization primitives operate on *events*. The **wait**(a) statement induces a wait on the event "a" until a corresponding **post**(a) is done by some other task. A **clear**(a) clears all prior posts. Multiple posts with no wait or clear operations in between are equivalent to a single post. Figure 6 shows the parallel code

Node	Condition
START	—
1	—
2	$1 - 2$
3	2
4	$3 - 4$
5	4
6	$5 - 6$
7	$5 - 7$
8	$(6 \lor 5 - 7 \lor 1 - 8) \land (7 \lor 5 - 6 \lor 1 - 8)$
9	—
STOP	—

Table 2: Optimized conditions for all nodes in Figure 1.

for our example. Curly brackets are used to group one or more program statements separated by semicolons. Such statements execute sequentially in the obvious lexicographic order.

Assuming all events have been cleared initially, code for any node has the following appearance.

1. **wait**(own event).

2. Do own work.

3. Update the conditions which are dependent on it and if any evaluate to true, then do the corresponding posts.

We assume that the updates to the condition for any node are done through a critical section as different nodes could be updating the condition for a node simultaneously.

The starting point for code generation is the CDG, and identically control dependent nodes are executed in parallel barring data dependences. There are two kinds of optimizations which can be done immediately.

1. If it is known at compile time that an update is going to change a condition to evaluate to true, one can replace Step 3 above by just the corresponding **post**. For instance, in our example, as the condition for 3 is just 2, node 2 instead of updating the condition for 3 proceeds directly with **post**($sem(3)$).

2. While generating code, the placement of a node in the program will cause certain conditions to be true at that point in the program, and hence the condition for a node can be further simplified. For example, when 8 is executed under the branch

$1-8$, $1-8$ is true at that point in the program and hence the condition for 8 is true (both clauses of the conjunction will be true, see Table 2) and hence 8 need not wait for any event. However, when 8 is placed under the $3-4$ branch, no such inference can be made and there must be a synchronization instruction for 8.

It will be observed that the code for node 8 has been duplicated. Duplication of code is a known problem while generating code from the control dependence graph and can be avoided, sometimes at the expense of parallelism [5].

Another optimization which can be done is to note that since 2 is the only node updating the condition for 3, and 3 and 2 are identically control dependent, the synchronization can be removed by executing 2 and 3 in sequence. The same applies for nodes 4 and 5. For more details on parallel source generation the reader is referred to [7].

8 Conclusion

The capacity of a compiler to encapsulate task-level parallelism from a sequential or parallel program is critically dependent on accurate estimation of data and control dependences, and more importantly on the derivation of minimal execution constraints for each task in a program. In this paper we presented a framework for the construction of a program's task graph based on data and control dependences, the derivation of execution conditions for each task node, and the optimization of these conditions.

Brute-force derivation of control and data constraints would result in little or no parallelism in the resulting code. Finding the minimal set of such constraints necessary to preserve program correctness during parallel execution is therefore instrumental in extracting and exploiting parallelism from sequential and parallel programs.

Note: An extended version of this paper is to appear in IEEE Transactions on Parallel and Distributed Systems.

References

[1] A. V. Aho, R. Sethi, and J. D. Ullman. *Compilers : Principles, Techniques and Tools.* Addison Wesley, March 1986.

[2] F. E. Allen, M. Burke, P. Charles, R. Cytron, and J. Ferrante. An overview of the PTRAN analysis system for multiprocessing. *The Journal of Parallel and Distributed Computing*, 5(5):617–640, October 1988.

[3] R. Allen and K. Kennedy. Automatic translation of FORTRAN programs to vector form. *ACM Transactions on Programming Languages and Systems*, 9(4), October 1987.

[4] U. Banerjee. *Dependence Analysis for Supercomputing.* Kluwer Academic Publishers, 1988.

```
for all task_semaphore do
  clear(sem(task_semaphore))
endfor;
cobegin
 ▶{ 1;
    if 1-2 then
      cobegin
     ▶{ 2; post(sem(3)) }
     ▶{ wait(sem(3)); 3;
        if 3-4 then
          cobegin
         ▶{ 4; post(sem(5)) }
         ▶{ wait(sem(5)); 5;
            if 5-6 then
              update condition for 8;
              if condition for 8 is true then
              post(sem(8)) endif;
              6;
              update condition for 8;
              if condition for 8 is true then
              post(sem(8)) endif;
            else
              update condition for 8;
              if condition for 8 is true then
              post(sem(8)) endif;
              7;
              update condition for 8;
              if condition for 8 is true then
              post(sem(8)) endif;
            ▶ endif }
         ▶{ wait(sem(8)); 8 }
              coend
        ▶ endif }
        coend
    else
        { 8 }
  ▶ endif }
 ▶{ 9 }
coend
```

● The statements of a block {stmt_1; stmt_2;...; stmt_n} execute in sequential order.

Figure 6: Parallel code for our example flow graph.

[5] R. Cytron, M. Hind, and W. Hsieh. Automatic generation of DAG parallelism. In *Proceedings of the 1989 SIGPLAN Conference on Programming Language Design and Implementation*, pages 54–68, July 1989.

[6] J. Ferrante, K. J. Ottenstein, and J. D. Warren. The program dependence graph and its use in optimization. *ACM Trans. on Programming Languages and Systems*, 9(3):319–349, July 1987.

[7] M. Girkar. *Automatic Detection and Management of Parallelism in Programs.* PhD thesis, Center for Supercomputing Research and Development, University of Illinois at Urbana-Champaign, August 1991. In preparation.

[8] M. Girkar and C. D. Polychronopoulos. An intermediate representation for programs based on control and data dependences. Technical Report 1046, Center for Supercomputing Research and Development, University of Illinois at Urbana-Champaign, 1990.

[9] H. Kasahara, H. Honda, M. Iwata, and M. Hirota. A compilation scheme for macro-dataflow compuatation on hierarchical multiprocessor systems. unpublished manuscript, 1989.

[10] D. J. Kuck, R. H. Kuhn, D. A. Padua, B. Leasure, and M. J. Wolfe. Dependence graphs and compiler optimizations. In *Proceedings of the 8th Annual ACM Symposium on Principles of Programming Languages*, pages 207–218. ACM, January 1981.

[11] C. D. Polychronopoulos, M. Girkar, M. R. Haghighat, C. L. Lee, B. Leung, and D. Schouten. Parafrase-2: An environment for parallelizing, partitioning, synchronizing, and scheduling programs on multiprocessors. In *Proceedings of the 1989 International Conference on Parallel Processing*, St. Charles, IL, August 1989.

[12] M. Weiser. Programmers use slices when debugging. *Communications of the ACM*, 25(7):446–452, July 1982.

[13] M. J. Wolfe. *Optimizing Supercompilers for Supercomputers.* The MIT Press, Cambridge, Massachusetts, 1989.

11   Recognizing and Parallelizing Bounded Recurrences

D. Callahan
Tera Computer Company

Abstract[1] This paper examines the problem of recognizing and optimizing a class of recurrences called *bounded recurrences* which are a generalization of the *parallel prefix problem*. I show how these recurrences can be executed concurrently and examine the problem of detecting them automatically. The contribution of this paper is a framework for representing information about recurrences and examination of some structural aspects of bounded recurrences. I also examine linear recurrences in some detail showing how to generate efficient code directly from source expressions.

1   Introduction

The historic goal of parallelizing compilers was to recognize so called "implicit" parallelism in sequential programs and to transform those programs so that that parallelism can be exploited by parallel architectures. The core research has been on recognizing when the separate iterations of a FORTRAN DO loop can be executed concurrently and how to transform the loop so that concurrent execution is possible. The primary issue is whether there is an interaction between these iterations which must be respected and hence induces a total or partial order on the execution of the iterations.

A *recurrence* is a computation of the general form:[2]

[1]This research sponsored by Defense Advanced Research Projects Agency Information Science and Technology Office ARPA Order No. 6512/2-4; Program Code No. 0T10 issued by DARPA/CMO under Contract MDA972-90-C-0075.

The views and conclusions contained in this document are those of Tera Computer Company and should not be interpreted as representing the official policies, either expressed or implied, of the Defense Advanced Research Projects Agency or the Uniter States Government.

[2]Notation: I will use typewriter font for Fortran or similar lower level language, *italics* and mathematical notation for meta-language constructs and abstractions, and the syntax $[A_1, \ldots, A_n]$ to indicate a vector of values. Generally,

```
DO I = 1, N
    A_i = f_i(A_{i-1})
ENDDO
```

where the values A_i may be a k-tuple of separate values. This is a classic example of a loop where the iterations interact and hence does not fit the basic model of a "parallel loop". Recurrences of this form are very common in numerical algorithms and considerable effort has been expended in parallelizing special cases (for examples, see Rodrigue[15]). A quarter of the 24 Livermore Loops[12] are recurrences which can not be parallelized without applying special techniques.

This paper explores a class of recurrences called *bounded recurrences* for which compositions of the functions f_i can be computed efficiently. This ability allows the above recurrence to be solved using the techniques developed for solving the *parallel prefix* problem. The parallel prefix problem is the special class of recurrences of the form:

```
DO I = 1, N
    A_i = A_{i-1} ⊕ X_i
ENDDO
```

where $\oplus$ is an arbitrary associative binary operator. There are known methods[11] for executing this loop in $O(log_2(N))$ time on an unbounded number processors and $O(N/P)$ time on P processors.

The general recurrence case can be parallelized if we are able to compute compositions of the operations f_i. For example, we can rewrite the basic loop into:

```
DO I = 1, N
    g_i = g_{i-1} ∘ f_i
ENDDO
DO I = 1, N
    A_i = g_i(A_0)
ENDDO
```

where g_0 is the identify function. The second loop is trivially parallel and the first is an instance of parallel prefix.[3]

The potential speedup of this transformation depends on the cost of computing compositions and finally applying the composite functions, as well as the number of processors p applied to the problem. In the simple case of a parallel prefix problem, the cost of composing the functions is equal to the application cost and speedup is limited to $p/2$. For more complex recurrences this limit will be lower. The extra work which limits speedup is referred to as *redundant* work.

In the following sections, I will define bounded recurrences and discuss some structural properties which shows how complex bounded recurrences can be recognized based on simpler component recurrences. I will examine in depth the special case of linear recurrences of bounded order giving algorithms to generate code to compute compositions based on input expression trees. I also show how to estimate the amount of redundant work in the parallel code which in turn allows cost-benefit decisions to be made. I will give some examples based on hand-compiled loops running on an instruction level simulator for one Tera processor[4] and discuss related work.

---

variable names may refer to either scalar or vector values depending on context. The operator "∘" denotes function composition.

[3] We see that "reductions" are special cases in which only the final A_N is required and so the second "application" loop can be eliminated.

2   Structure of Bounded Recurrences

Consider again the general recurrence:

```
DO I = 1, N
    A_i = f_i(A_{i-1})
ENDDO
```

where the functions f_i are elements of a class O of *operators* which is closed under composition. The functions f_i are actually instances of some base function f applied to a set of values C_i which are defined before the loop begins execution: $f_i(A) = f(A, C_i)$. This function is assumed to have no side-effects other than the definition of A_i. The operator class O will not usually be mentioned explicitly and it should be assumed that it is simply the smallest set closed under composition which includes all f_i for $1 \leq i \leq N$.

We say elements of the set O are *bounded operators* if there exist functions $\hat{f}$, g and $\hat{g}$ such that for all f and f' in O and A in the domain of elements of O:

$$\hat{f}(g(f), A) = f(A)$$

and:

$$\hat{g}(g(f), g(f')) = g(f \circ f')$$

We further require that both g and $\hat{g}$ to have $O(1)$ time-complexity and $\hat{f}$ to have $O(f)$ complexity. Here we will call a recurrence involving bounded operators a *bounded recurrence* and these two equations the *bounded operator requirements*. Intuitively, the function g maps the operator into a concrete representation. The function $\hat{g}$ simulates function composition within the space of representations. The function $\hat{f}$ emulates application of a function given its representation.

Example. As an example, I will use the following simple recurrence loop which is a common step in solving tri-diagonal systems of equations:

```
DO I = 1,N
    X(I) = Z(I)*(Y(I)-X(I-1))
ENDDO
```

here the set of operators is the space of affine functions from reals to reals.[4] Each operator f can be expressed as $f(x) = ax + b$ and this set is closed under composition: $(f_1 \circ f_2)(x) = a_1(a_2 x + b_2) + b_1 = a_1 a_2 x + (a_1 b_2 + b_1)$ and we can define: $g(f) = [a, b]$, $\hat{g}([a_1, b_1], [a_2, b_2]) = [a_1 a_2, a_1 b_2 + b_1]$, and $\hat{f}([a, b], x) = ax + b$ which satisfy the bounded operator requirements. In this example, $g(f_i) = [-Z_i, Z_i \cdot Y_i]$.

The major contribution of this paper is the observation that the functions g, $\hat{g}$, and $\hat{f}$ provide a useful basis for automatically parallelizing source programs which implement these recurrences. In particular we can separate the algorithm for solving the recurrence from the details of the particular problem. The rest of this section discusses how a compiler can use this framework.

We need a few standard definitions from the literature on automatic program parallelization.[5] We are concerned with inner loops which I assume are represented by an expression-level dependence graph where loop independent true dependences connect operands to operators, stores are

---

[4]Of course computers approximate real numbers with values of bounded precision. For this reason, primitive arithmetic operations do not form a field and the usual duality between $R^{n \times n}$ and linear functions from R^n to itself does not hold. The effect of parallelizing such recurrences on the numerical stability of an algorithm depends on the degree of parallelism and the amount of redundant work and is discussed by Sameh and Brent[16]. Explicit disabling of this transformation should therefore be an option to the programmer if it turns out to be numerically unstable.

[5]For example, Kuck et al.[10], Allen and Kennedy[2], or Ferrante, Ottenstien, and Warren[6].

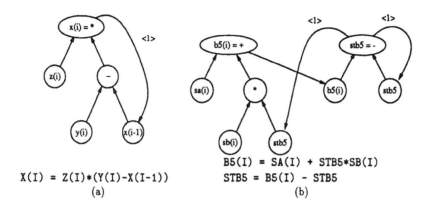

$$X(I) = Z(I)*(Y(I)-X(I-1))$$
(a)

B5(I) = SA(I) + STB5*SB(I)
STB5 = B5(I) - STB5
(b)

Figure 1: Example dependence graphs for two simple loops whose bodies are shown. The curved edges are loop carried and in this case both have a distance of 1.

represented by labels on the nodes and loop carried dependences are annotated with distances. Figure 1(a) shows the graph for the example loop. Note that for nodes with loop-carried input arcs with distance d, these nodes implicitly represent initial values on the first d iterations. I will use D to denote this graph with nodes N and edges E. Each edge $e = (n, m)$ has source node n and sink node m and distance δ_e. Each node has an operator op_n and may have an output label which is either a scalar or an array reference. The set of nodes with output labels will be called the *outputs* of the loop.

Given this representation, we can locate strongly connected regions of the graph. Each such region that includes a loop carried dependence forms a recurrence. Distinct regions can be separated via loop distribution into distinct loops and so we can say a particular region is a bounded recurrence if the post-distribution loop that implements that region would be a bounded recurrence.

When a loop can be distributed into a set of simpler loops and each is a bounded recurrence, then we can clearly parallelize the code by simply parallelizing each separate loop. Thus data dependence graphs provide a powerful mechanism for isolating the structure of recurrences so that pattern matching can be applied effectively. The goal of this research however is to allow the original loop to be parallelized as a single loop; this is an important alternative since a single parallel loop is likely to be much more efficient then a collection of individual loops.

Assume we have a loop which can be distributed into two component loops, each of which is known to be a bounded recurrence. Thus we might have two loops:

```
DO I = 1, N
    A_i = f_i^A(A_{i-1})
ENDDO
DO I = 1, N
    B_i = f_i^B(B_{i-1})
ENDDO
```

The operators f_i^B may be parameterized by elements of A_i. To combine these two loops into a single recurrence we first must make these values explicit. This involves two steps: altering f_i^A so that earlier results are retained for subsequent use and abstracting parameters to f_i^B.

The first step involves a transformation I call *n-fold dragalong* which transforms the first loop into:

$$C_0 = [A_0, 0, \ldots, 0]$$
$$\text{DO I = 1, N}$$
$$\quad C_i = f_i^C(C_{i-1})$$
$$\text{ENDDO}$$

where C_i is a vector of length n and $f_i^C([x_1, \ldots, x_n])$ is defined to be $[f_i(x_1), x_1, \ldots, x_{n-1}]$. A proof that an n-fold dragalong of a bounded recurrence is also a bounded recurrence can be found in the appendix.

The second step, abstraction, involves altering the operators so that a formly implicit parameter is made explicit. For example, if we consider the earlier example of the linear recurrence $x_i = z_i(y_i - x_{i-1})$, operator $f_i(x)$ is equal to $z_i(y_i - x)$. We can abstract y in this example to get a new set of operators $f_i'(x, y)$ defined by the expression $[z_i(y - x), y]$. Here we see that abstracting y may preserve boundedness; however if we were to abstact z: $f''(x, z) = z(y_i - x)$ then the resulting recurrence is no longer bounded. Thus an abstraction of a bounded recurrence may not necessarily be a bounded recurrence. Which parameters may be abstracted without affecting boundedness will be part of the compiler's knowledge base about core recurrences.

We can now consider two loops which implement bounded recurrences:

$$\text{DO I = 1, N}$$
$$\quad A_i = f_i^a(A_{i-1})$$
$$\text{ENDDO}$$
$$\text{DO I = 1, N}$$
$$\quad [B_i, A_i] = f_i^b([B_{i-1}, A_i])$$
$$\text{ENDDO}$$

where dragalong and abstraction have been applied to make all parameters explicit. For each pair of operators $f_a \in O_a$ and $f_b \in O_b$ we can construct an operator h defined by:

$$h(X, Y) = [f_b(X, Z)] \text{ where } Z = f_a(Y)$$

We can now generate the combined loop:

$$\text{DO I = 1, N}$$
$$\quad [B_i, A_i] = h_i([B_{i-1}, A_{i-1}])$$
$$\text{ENDDO}$$

where each h_i is constructed from f_i^a and f_i^b as above.

Under what circumstances is the second loop a bounded recurrence?

1. When either component loop is a "parallel operation" — a loop which does not carry data dependences. For example, if the first loop is parallel and therefore no information is passed from iteration to iteration, then we can simply evaluate the portions of A_i needed in the second loop and therefore the functions g_b, $\hat{g}_b$, and $\hat{f}_b$ which satisfy the bounded operator requirements for the second loop (prior to abstraction) can be used for the combined loop

as well.[6] When the second loop is parallel, we simply delay evaluation of f_b until we are ready to apply the composite functions for the first loop. So given functions which satisfy the bounded operator requirements for the original component loops, we get:

$$g_h(f_a, f_b) = [g_b(f_b(A)), A] \qquad\qquad g_h = g_a$$
$$\text{where } A = f_a()$$
$$\hat{g}_h([a, A], [b, B]) = [\hat{g}_b(a, b), A] \qquad\qquad \hat{g}_h = \hat{g}_a$$
$$\hat{f}_h(x, [G, A]) = [\hat{f}_b(x, A), A] \qquad\qquad \hat{f}_h(x, G) = [f_b(), \hat{f}_a(G)]$$

where the left-hand set covers the case where the first loop is parallel and the right-hand set covers the case where the second loop is parallel.

2. When the source loop is a *finite state transducer* — a recurrence in which the inputs and the output are elements of a finite set and each operator has complexity $O(1)$ (such as a lexical scanner). The most common case will be boolean recurrences from boolean variables in the program or which represent control dependences[3, 6]. The appendix includes a construction that shows that if the definition of a value is a finite state transducer, then that value can always be abstracted from a second bounded recurrence and the two recurrences combined to form a bounded recurrence, even though the abstracted second recurrence may not be a bounded recurrence.

3. When both recurrences are linear recurrences over the same ring. Linear recurrences are discussed in depth in the next section.

4. When the composition of functions h_i are separable. We define a function ϕ which maps a $\phi(f_a, f_b) = h$ as above. When ϕ satisfies the relation:

$$\phi(f_a \circ f_a', f_b \circ f_b') = \phi(f_a, f_b) \circ \phi(f_a', f_b')$$

then we can construct functions which satisfy the bounded operator requirements for the combined loop from those of the component loops. This construction is given in the appendix. This case is a generalization of the case where the two recurrences are unrelated and its simply better to have one parallel loop than two.

It is not expected that different sorts of inter-dependent recurrences will be often parallelized collectively since, for the common core recurrences, few parameters can be abstracted. However when vectorizable operations appear with recurrences — which will be very common — it is important to avoid loop distribution and the introduction of vector temporaries and associated memory traffic whenever possible.

Thus a compiler will have a set of recurrences which it can recognize and for which it knows how to implement suitable functions which satisfy the bounded operator requirements. It can then apply the above properties to combine recurrences in order to reduce the overheads associated with separate parallel loops. Finally, it will select a parallelization strategy to implement the recurrence. The choice of parallelization strategy is independent of the particular recurrence being solved and is influenced most by the granularity of various operations. One possible choice is shown in Figure 2.

For the schema shown in Figure 2, iteration i of the outer loop computes $A_{i+1}..A_{i+C}$. I will refer to the first inner loop as the *composition* loop and the second as the *application* loop. The composition loop is executed for all iterations except the first and the last.

---

[6]In this case, dragalong is similar to code replication discussed by Allen *et al.*[1] and can be avoided with loop alignment as described in that paper.

```
        DOALL I = 0, N , C
            IF(I.GT.0 .AND. I+C.LE. N) THEN
    C composition loop
                DO K = 1, C
```
$$g_{i+1}^k = \hat{g}(g(f_{i+k}), g_{i+1}^{k-1})$$
```
                ENDDO
                IF(I .GT. 1) wait for A_i
```
$$A_{i+C} = \hat{f}(g_{i+1}^C, A_i)$$
```
                signal A_{i+C} available
            ELSE IF(I.GT.0) THEN
                wait for A_i
            ENDIF
    C application loop
                DO K = 1, C-1
```
$$A_{i+k} = f_{i+k}(A_{i+k-1})$$
```
                ENDDO
                IF(I.EQ.0) THEN
```
$$A_{i+C} = f_{i+C}(A_{i+C-1})$$
```
                    IF(I+C .LE. N) signal A_{i+C} available
                ENDIF
            ENDDO
```

Figure 2: A schema for parallel execution of bounded recurrences using a *doacross* style.

From a compiler's perspective, this scheme has advantages over alternatives (such as a $log_2(N)$-deep fan in tree). First, aside from the selection of C, the schema does not depend on the value N or the number of available processors. Second, the amount of additional storage required is proportional to the number of processors and not to the problem size. Further, since f_i is used twice, any parameters that are expressions can be evaluated once and stored in temporary storage local to a particular processor. The amount of such storage depends only on C and the number of processors. Finally, it is not necessary to actually compose arbitrary images using $\hat{g}$, rather only operations of the form $\hat{g}(g(f), G)$ are evaluated. This allows us to exploit special characteristics of $g(f)$. The downside of this schema is that it is only efficient when the number of processors is much less than N.

3 Linear Recurrences

A linear recurrence is a loop in which the set of output values of each iteration is an affine function of the input values. Here is an example of a linear recurrence (Livermore loop number 19):

```
        DO I = 1, N
            B5(I) = SA(I) + STB5*SB(I)
            STB5 = B5(I) - STB5
        ENDDO
```

This section examines linear recurrences in depth, showing how they are recognized and how code

```
select
    when   region(n) < k
        form(n) := invariant
    when   n = load A[s]
        form(n) := variable  ;  var(n) := A
    when   n = store A[s]   := m
        form(n) := form(m)
    when   n = p + q,  form(p) = variable,
                form(q) = variable,  var(p) = var(q)
        form(n) := variable  ;  var(n) := var(p)
    when   n = p + q,  form(p) ≠ other,  form(q) ≠ other
        form(n) := combination
    when   n = p * q,  form(p) = invariant,  form(q) ≠ other
        form(n) := form(q)
        var(n) := var(q)
    when   n = p * q,  form(q) = invariant,  form(p) ≠ other
        form(n) := form(p)
        var(n) := var(p)
    otherwise
        form(n) := other
```

Figure 3: Rules for synthesizing attributes *form* and *var* over expression trees. The first rule which matches a node in this list is the rule that applies. The value k is the number associated with the strongly connected region being examined.

can be generated to implement functions g, $\hat{g}$ and $\hat{f}$ in the context of the parallelization schema shown in Figure 2.

Recognition   Recognition of linear recurrences is a simple data flow problem. When the loop is separated in to strongly connected components, each node can be assigned a region number such that for all nodes n:

$$(m, n) \in E \;\; \Rightarrow \;\; region(m) \leq region(n)$$
$$region(m) = region(n) \;\; \Rightarrow \;\; (m, n) \in E^*$$

Now we can test whether each region is a linear recurrence by synthesizing two attributes for each node, called *form* and *var* based on the type of operations and their attributes using the equations in Figure 3. A node is an affine combination of the input terms if its form is not *other*; an entire region is a linear recurrences if no node in the region is marked *other*. These equations simply confirm that every operator in the region is either addition or multiplication and that at most one input variable contributes to a multiplication.

   When a parameter is abstracted, the effect is to change the *form* associated with some **load** operators from *invariant* to *variable*. This change will propagate up the expression tree, perhaps "lowering" some node to *other*. Thus it is a simple matter to test if a particular set of variables can be abstracted. However, given two variables each of which can be abstracted independently, it may not be possible to abstract them both and so it may be difficult to select a "maximal" set of such variables. Thus from $z \cdot (y - x)$ we can abstract either both x and y or only z.

Each arithmetic operator in an expression tree which is marked *invariant* is a candidate for common subexpression elimination between the composition and application loops in Figure 2. Each input parameter defined by a vector operator is treated similarly: the vector operator can be performed in the composition loop and its result stored to memory for later use in the application loop.

Composition The images $g(f)$ are $r \times r$ matrices of real values, the function $\hat{g}$ is simply multiplication of these matrices, and the application $\hat{f}(A, x)$ is simply $A \cdot x$. The top row of these matrices is always the vector $[1, 0, \ldots, 0]$ due to the fact that $g(f)$ is really affine in $r - 1$ variables. Historically, the value $r - 1$ is called the *order* of the recurrence and is related to the number of values transmitted from one iteration to the next. For each variable A, let r_A be the largest distance associated with any *true* dependence carried by A. The value r is equal to 1 more than $\sum r_v$, where v ranges over variables defined in the recurrence.

The matrix $g(f_i)$ will not be explicitly constructed. Rather, the source expression trees will be used directly to compute $\hat{g}(g(f_i), G)$. Each row of the matrix can be thought of as a linear function mapping initial values to final values. The following paragraphs prove that if we simply re-interpret the source expression trees as manipulating rows of the matrix G — so addition is elementwise and multiplication is scaling — we get expressions for computing a row of the matrix $\hat{g}(g(f_i), G)$.

Let V be the set of variables defined in the recurrence and $v(i)$ denote the value of variable v defined on iteration i. Let $V(i)$ denote the vector of values $[1, v_1(i), \ldots, v_n(i)]$ over all variables in V. For each $v \in V$, define I_v to be vector which is zero every where except in the position corresponding to v in $V(i)$ where it is one. For each variable $v \in V$ we define a vector-valued array $\bar{v}(k, i)$ where the elements satisfy the invariant: $\bar{v}(k, i) \cdot V(i)^t = v(i + k)$. For this purpose it is convenient to assume that $v(i - k)$ is defined for all k even though the actual values will not be needed. Note that we have $\bar{v}(k, i) = I_v$ for $k = 0$.

By hypothesis, each value $v(i)$ is defined by an expression $\mathcal{E}_v[i]$ with input values $v_l(i - 1)$. By replacing each such occurrence in the expression with a reference to $\bar{v}_l(k - 1, i)$ and each input parameter $p(i)$ with $p(i + k)$ we get expressions which define $\bar{v}_l(k, i)$ in terms of "previous" values. Each multiplication by an invariant is interpreted as element-wise multiplication of a vector by a scalar and each addition of an invariant c is treated as addition of the vector $[c, 0 \ldots, 0]^t$. This transformation is illustrated in parts (a) and (b) of Figure 4. With this substitution we have:

$$
\begin{aligned}
\mathcal{E}_v[i + k](\bar{v}_1(k - 1, i), \ldots, \bar{v}_n(k - 1, i)) \cdot V(i) & \\
&= \mathcal{E}_v[i + k](\bar{v}_1(k - 1, i) \cdot V(i), \ldots, \bar{v}_n(k - 1, i) \cdot V(i)) \\
&= \mathcal{E}_v[i + k](v_1(i + k - 1), \ldots, v_n(i + k - 1)) \\
&= v(i + k) \\
&= \bar{v}(k, i) \cdot V(i)
\end{aligned}
$$

where the first rewrite depends on $\mathcal{E}_v$ being linear over a vector space.[7]

This relationship provides a mechanism for computing $\bar{v}$ which is illustrated in parts (c) and (d) of Figure 4. An outer loop is added which constructs $\bar{v}(k, *)$ from $\bar{v}(k - 1, *)$. Elements of the base case $\bar{v}(0, i)$ are simply the basis vectors I_v. It is simple to see that the loop nest part (c) can be interchanged to get the parallel loop in the outer position. The resulting inner loop is the

---

[7]This is where the non-associativity of fixed-precision arithmetic separates the mathematics from the implementation

```
DO I = 1 ,N
   b5(i) = sa(i) + stb5 * sb(i)
   stb5 = b5(i) - stb5
ENDDO
```

(a)

```
DO I = 1 ,N
   stb5(0,i) = [0,1]
ENDO
DO I = 0 ,N-K
   b5(k,i) = [sa(i + k),0]+
             stb5(k - 1,i) * sb(i + k)
   stb5(k,i) = b5(k,i) - stb5(k,i)
ENDDO
```

(b)

```
DO I = 1 ,N
   stb5(0,i) = [0,1]
ENDO
DO K = 1 ,C
   DO I = 0 ,N-K
      b5(k,i) = [sa(i + k),0]+
                stb5(k - 1,i) * sb(i + k)
      stb5(k,i) = b5(k,i) - stb5(k,i)
   ENDDO
ENDDO
```

(c)

```
DOALL I = 0, N
   stb5(0,i) = [0,1]
   DO K = 1,MIN(C, N-(I+C))
      b5(k,i) = [sa(i + k),0]+
                stb5(k - 1,i) * sb(i + k)
      stb5(k,i) = b5(k,i) - stb5(k,i)
   ENDDO
ENDDO
```

(d)

Figure 4: Example of generating the composition loop for a linear recurrence.

"composition" loop for this recurrence. Since we only need $\bar{v}(C,i)$ for $i \equiv 0$ modulo C, a stride is added to the outer loop and intermediate results can be discarded to get the final code needed for Figure 2.

Note that there is an assumption that only values from the previous iteration are referenced. This assumption is enforced by applying a variant of drag-along in which each variable v with $r_v > 0$ is replaced with r_v variables labeled v_j for $0 \le j < r_v$, where $v_j(i)$ is defined to be equal to $v_{j-1}(i-1)$ for $j > 0$ and v_0 is defined by $\mathcal{E}_v$ where each reference to $v(i-k)$ is replaced with $v_{k-1}(i-1)$.

Given the construction above, the function $\hat{f}$ is reduced to the computation $\bar{v}(k,i) \cdot V(i)$ for each i.

Redundancy We would expect that the time to compute $\hat{g}$ would be proportional to $(r-1)r$ multiply-adds.[8] However we see from the construction of the composition loop that composition

---
[8]Recall that the top row is invariant so need not be computed.

takes roughly r times as many primitive operations as the application loop.[9] This can be more than $(r-1)r$ when the expressions are complex with much interaction between terms. However, we expect that the expressions are fairly simply yielding rather sparse matrices. In any case, the ratio of redundant work to the original computation is roughly r (ignoring parallelism overheads) rather than r^2. This reduction in complexity is due to the implicit use of sparsity in the matrices $g(f_i)$: when variable x does not appear in the expression defining y, then the corresponding element of each $g(f_i)$ is zero which is reflected in the fact that the meta-variable $\bar{x}$ does not appear in the expression defining $\bar{y}$.

An estimate of the amount of redundancy is important when the available parallel resources are limited. In the above example, the amount of redundant work is roughly twice the amount of original work and so we need more than a factor of two in hardware parallelism before we can expect any speedup.[10] Redundancy further influences whether two linear recurrences which are in separate strongly connected regions should be executed as one loop or two. Consider the recurrences defined by:

$$x_i = a_i x_{i-1} + b_i$$
$$y_i = c_i x_i + d_i y_{i-1} + e_i$$

where we have a choice of evaluating the first recurrence completely and then evaluating the second or of evaluating them together as a single recurrence. In the first case, the redundancy of the first recurrence is 2 and the second is less than 2 (because of the vector operation). In the second case, the redundancy would be 3. In the absence of compensating factors (such as common subexpressions) the first case is preferable unless the target machine has excess of arithmetic power compared to data transfer power in which case the excess arithmetic power would be idle.

4   Examples

Table 1 shows results of simulated execution of a simple loop. In this case, we use a hand-compiled version of the subroutine:

```
c
C*** KERNEL 5
C TRI-DIAGONAL ELIMINATION, BELOW DIAGONAL (NO VECTORS)
c
        subroutine k5(loop,n, x,y,z)
        integer n, loop
        real x(n), y(n), z(n)
        do 20 l = 1, loop
          do 10 i = 2, n
              x(i) = z(i)*(y(i)-x(i-1))
10        continue
20      continue
        return
        end
```

---

[9]This is an overestimate since adding an "invariant" to a "non-invariant" expression translates to adding a vector of the form $[a, 0, \ldots, 0]$ to another vector which takes only one addition, not r additions.

[10]For simple loops such as this one, executed on processors capable of exploiting fine-grain concurrency, the number of arithmetic operations is often not as important as the number of memory operations in determining the execution rate. We observe that for small values of r — where the meta-variables $\bar{v}$ could be kept completely in registers — the amount of memory traffic in the composition loop is actually less than the original loop and so the amount of redundant work may be effectively much less than r .

Loop	Length	Loop	Memory Latency	Kcycles 1 Stream	Kcycles 16 Streams	Speedup
k5	101	4	44	18.9	12.7	1.5
k5	101	40	44	187.4	108.3	1.7
k5	101	4	62	18.9	13.7	1.4
k5	101	40	62	187.4	114.7	1.6
k5	1001	4	44	180.9	32.8	5.5
k5	1001	40	44	1807.4	309.1	5.8
k5	1001	4	62	180.9	33.8	5.3
k5	1001	40	62	1807.4	316.7	5.7

Table 1: Simulation results for a simple linear recurrence.

The phrase "hand-compiled" means that the implementation used no technique which could not be mechanized and added to a compiler. The outer timing loop is preserved as a sequential loop and no overlap between its iterations occurs. Parallel resources are acquired once when the routine is entered and barrier points occur after each inner loop. The results for 1 stream are from a "best-sequential" implementation and therefore do not have any parallelism-related overheads. The multi-stream numbers use the algorithm shown in Figure 2.

The machine simulated is a single Tera processor as described by Alverson *et al.*[4] This is a multi-threaded processor in which the hardware supports up to 128 independent execution streams which share a single arithmetic pipeline and path to memory. The motivation for this architecture is to allow parallelism in the form of independent streams to hide the latency of the floating point pipeline and the latency to memory. The instructions are "slightly" wide, allowing three operations to be issued each cycle. For these codes a typical mix is a memory operation, a floating-point add-multiply, and an operation to support address generation or loop control.

This architecture allows up to eight memory operations from a single stream be in concurrent execution. Two key parameters to the simulation are therefore the average memory latency — which depends on system configuration — and the arithmetic pipeline latency. Both of these latencies are implementation dependent. In this table, the single processor configuration has an average memory latency of 44 cycles and the 16 processor configuration has an average latency of 62 cycles. In both machines, the arithmetic pipeline latency is set to 15 cycles which means that a single stream can issue every fifteenth cycle and at least 15 streams are required to saturate the pipelines. We observe from the data in the table that the running time is largely insensitive to memory latency. This is not surprising since its is possible to always have 8 memory operations in execution for this loop so the effective latency is always less than 15.

For loop k5 running on a single processor, the asymptotic maximum speedup is 7.5 — since there is a redundancy of 2 for this kernel — assuming that a single stream is not delayed due to memory latency. For vector lengths of 101, the reduction in time barely balances the overhead of startup and the barriers but for lengths of 1001 we see speedups of around 5.5. The execution time is quite insensitive to memory latency.

5 Related Work

Related work falls into two categories: algorithms for parallel evaluation of recurrences and methods for automatically recognizing parallelism. In the following I will use the term *schedule* to refer to a specification of which composite functions are computed and where they are applied.

The technique of *recursive doubling* to solve linear recurrences is described by Kogge and Stone[8]. This technique amounts to a particular schedule for composing functions and applying the composites to get the results. A different schedule for this problem is *cyclic reduction* described by Heller[7]. Ladner and Fisher[11] describe families of schedules for the parallel prefix problem which together with this work generalize these techniques. There has also been work examining schedules for bounded parallelism. This includes the work by Kruskal, Rudolph, and Snir[9] and Snir[17] and the more recent results of Nicolau and Wang[13]. Any of these methods can be applied to bounded recurrences.

The literature on automatic parallelization is extensive much of which has focused on the problems of recognizing when separate iterations of a loop can execute concurrently, how to transform loop nests to enhance available parallelism, and how to map that parallelism onto different target architectures. Banerjee *et al.*[5] show how the data dependence graph common to this literature can be used to isolate recurrences so that pattern matching techniques can be applied. Here, I improve on this work by showing how arbitrary bounded recurrences can be combined and provide engineering improvements on the generation of parallel code. This also generalizes the algorithm of Tanaka *et al.*[18] for vectorizing first-order linear recurrences.

More recently, Pinter and Pinter[14] provide a graph-rewriting technique for recognizing recurrences for which special case solvers are available. Their technique is essentially syntactic (over the dependence graph) while the approach described here is provides an algebra for combining recurrences. The algebraic approach is superior in that it allows the structural properties of section 2 to be stated and general recurrences solvers to be constructed from special cases automatically. Further, this approach uses the standard form of data dependence graph of parallelizing compilers and does not require the cumbersome "unfolding" Pinter and Pinter perform to construct the "computation graph". It is not clear whether the general case of linear recurrences can be described in a graph-rewriting framework which has a bounded set of rules nor how to generate efficient code based on that information. The techniques described in this paper however are limited to bounded recurrences and still rely on some mechanism to recognize the core recurrences.

6 Summary

This paper has provided a framework in which bounded recurrences expressed via serial algorithms can be transformed into parallel algorithms. This framework allows core recurrences to be combined with other computation from the program context thus allowing efficient parallel code to be generated. The special case of linear recurrences has been examined and it was shown how for a given parallelization schema, we can exploit sparsity in the problem thus reducing the amount of redundant work.

A Proofs

Dragalong Here I prove that an n-fold dragalong of a bounded recurence is a bounded recurrence. Let O, f, g, $\hat{g}$, and $\hat{f}$ refer to the original recurrence and O_n, f_n, g_n, $\hat{g}_n$, and $\hat{f}_n$ be the correspondng entities for the transformed recurrence.

We define the function d_n which maps each operator in O to its dragalong. The set O_n is the closure under composition of the image of O under d_n and so each operator h in O_n can be expressed as $d_n(f_1) \circ \cdots \circ d_n(f_k)$ for some set of operators f_i from O. Given this sequence, we know that $h([A_1, \ldots, A_n]) = [B_1, \ldots, B_n]$ where:

$$B_i = \begin{cases} (f_i \circ \cdots \circ f_k)(A_1) & \text{if } i \leq k \\ A_{i-k} & \text{otherwise} \end{cases}$$

This relation gives rise to the definition, $g_n(h) = [k, a_1, \ldots, a_n]$ where:

$$a_i = \begin{cases} g(f_i \circ \cdots \circ f_k) & \text{if } i \leq k \\ \bot & \text{otherwise} \end{cases}$$

and we define:

$$\hat{g}_n([k_a, a_1, \ldots, a_n], [k_b, b_1, \ldots, b_n]) = [k_a + k_b, c_1, \ldots, c_n]$$

where:

$$c_i = \begin{cases} \hat{g}(a_i, b_1) & \text{if } i \leq k_a \\ b_{i-k_a} & \text{otherwise} \end{cases}$$

Finally we define:

$$\hat{f}_n([k, a_1, \ldots, a_n], [A_1, \ldots, A_n]) = [B_1, \ldots, B_n]$$

where:

$$B_i = \begin{cases} \hat{f}(a_i, B_1) & \text{if } i \leq k \\ B_{i-k} & \text{otherwise} \end{cases}$$

Let h and h' be elements of O_n and assume h is the composition $d_n(f_1) \circ \cdots \circ d_n(f_k)$ and h' is the composition $d_n(f_1') \circ \cdots \circ d_n(f_{k'}')$. Now let:

$$\begin{aligned} [k, a_1, \ldots, a_n] &= g_n(h) \\ [k', b_1, \ldots, b_n] &= g_n(h') \\ [k + k', c_1, \ldots, c_n] &= g_n(h \circ h') \\ [k + k', d_1, \ldots, d_n] &= \hat{g}_n(g_n(h), g_n(h')) \end{aligned}$$

and let $f' = f_1' \circ \cdots \circ f_{k'}'$. From the definitions above, we know that:

$$c_i = \begin{cases} g(f_i \circ \cdots \circ f_k \circ f') &= \hat{g}(a_i, b_1) &= d_i & \text{if } i \leq k \\ g(f_{i-k}' \circ \cdots \circ f_k') &= b_{i-k} &= d_i & \text{if } i \leq k + k' \\ \bot &= b_{i-k} &= d_i & \text{otherwise} \end{cases}$$

and we conclude that $\hat{g}_n(g_n(h), g_n(h')) = g_n(h \circ h')$.

Now let h be an element of O and assume h is the composition $d_n(f_1) \circ \cdots \circ d_n(f_k)$. Let:

$$\begin{aligned} [k, a_1, \ldots, a_n] &= g_n(h) \\ [B_1, \ldots, B_n] &= h([A_1, \ldots, A_n]) \\ [C_1, \ldots, C_n] &= \hat{f}(g_n(h), [A_1, \ldots, A_n]) \end{aligned}$$

For $i > k$, we have $B_i = A_{i-1} = C_i$ trivially. For $i \leq k$,

$$\begin{aligned} C_i &= \hat{f}(a_i, A_1) \\ &= \hat{f}(g(f_i \circ \cdots \circ f_k), A_1) \\ &= (f_i \circ \cdots \circ f_k)(A_1) \\ &= B_i \end{aligned}$$

and we conclude that $\hat{f}(g_n(h), [A_1, \ldots, A_n]) = h([A_1, \ldots, A_n])$ for all h and $[A_1, \ldots, A_n]$.

Finite State Transducers Next we show that if a parameter of a bounded recurrence is defined by a finite state transducer then we can abstract that parameter and combine the bounded recurrence with the definition of the parameter and the result will be a bounded recurrence. Assume we have a bounded recurrence defined by functions f_i, g_f, $\hat{g}_f$, and $\hat{f}$ and we have a parameter x_i defined by a finite state transducer: $x_i = m_i(x_{i-1})$ with corresponding functions g_m, $\hat{g}_m$ and $\hat{m}$. Assume the values of x_i are elements of the set $V = \{v_1, \ldots, v_n\}$.

As in the general case, we identify the combined functions h with pairs of functions $[m, f']$ where $f'(x, a)$ is the abstraction of some f with respect to x. We represent this latter function by $f'(x)$. The basic strategy for constructing g_h and $\hat{g}_h$ will be to construct a table indexed by elements in V:

$$g_h([m, f']) = [g_f(f'(v_1)), \ldots, g_f(f'(v_n)), g_m(m)]$$

where the ith element corresponds to the input value x being v_i. Tables are combined as follows:

$$\hat{g}_h([a_1, \ldots, a_n, b], [c_1, \ldots c_n, d]) = [\hat{g}_f(b_{i_1}, c_1), \ldots, \hat{g}_f(b_{i_n}, c_n), \hat{g}_m(b, d)]$$

where i_j is defined by $\hat{m}(d, c_j) = v_{i_j}$. Here, if the input element is v_j, then we can compute the input to the second function as $\hat{m}(d, c_j)$, which in turn identifies which elements of the table to compose.

The function $\hat{h}$ is simply:

$$\hat{h}([a_1, \ldots, a_n, b], x) = \hat{g}_f(a_j, \hat{m}(b, x))$$

where $\hat{m}(b, x) = v_j$.

The functions g_h, $\hat{g}_h$, and $\hat{h}$ satisfy the bounded operator conditions and hence show that the combined loop is a bounded recurrence.

Separable Composites Recall from Section 2 we have constructed a composite loop:

```
DO I = 1, N
    [B_i, A_i] = h_i([B_{i-1}, A_{i-1}])
ENDDO
```

where

$$\phi(f_a, f_b)(X, Y) = h(X, Y) = [f_b(X, Z)] \text{ where } Z = f_a(Y)$$

and we know that f_b and f_a are bounded recurrences and the functions h_i are separable:

$$\phi(f_a \circ f'_a, f_b \circ f'_b) = \phi(f_a, f_b) \circ \phi(f'_a, f'_b)$$

Here I show how to construct functions which satisfy the bounded recurrence conditions for the combined loop from those of the component loops.

By hypothesis there exist functions g_a, $\hat{g}_a$, and $\hat{f}_a$ which satisfy the bounded operator requirements for a class of operators O_a containing all f_i^a, and there exist functions g_b, $\hat{g}_b$, and $\hat{f}_b$ which satisfy the bounded operator requirements for a class of operators O_b containing all f_i^b.

We now define:

$$g(h) = [g_b(f_b), g_a(f_a)] \text{ where } h = \phi(f_a, f_b)$$
$$\hat{g}([b_1, a_1], [b_2, a_2]) = [\hat{g}_b(b_1, b_2), \hat{g}_a(a_1, a_2)]$$
$$\hat{f}([b, a], [B, A]) = [\hat{f}_b(b, [B, X]), X] \text{ where } X = \hat{f}_a(a, A)$$

and we have:

$$
\begin{aligned}
\hat{g}(g(f), g(f)) &= \hat{g}([g_b(f_b), g_a(f_a)], [g_a(f'_a), g_b(f'_b)]) \\
&\qquad \text{where } f = \phi(f_a, f_b) \text{ and } f' = \phi(f'_a, f'_b) \\
&= [\hat{g}_b(g_b(f_b), g_a(f'_b)), \hat{g}_a(g_a(f_a), g_a(f'_a))] \\
&= [g_b(f_b \circ f'_b), g_a(f_a \circ f'_a)] \\
&= g(f \circ f') \text{ since } f \circ f' = \phi(f_a \circ f'_a, f_b \circ f'_b) \\
\hat{f}(g(f), [B, A]) &= \hat{f}([g_b(f_b), g_a(f_a)], [B, A]) \text{ where } f = \phi(f_a, f_b) \\
&= [\hat{f}_b(g_b(f_b), [B, X]), X] \text{ where } X = \hat{f}_a(g_a(f_a), A) \\
&= [f_b(B, X), X] \text{ where } X = f_a(A) \\
&= f([B, A])
\end{aligned}
$$

which shows that $O_a \times O_b$ is a class of bounded operators and hence the combined loop is a bounded recurrence.

References

[1] J. R. Allen, D. Callahan, and K. Kennedy. Automatic decomposition of scientific programs for parallel execution. In *Conference Record of the Fourteenth ACM Symposium on the Principles of Programming Languages*, Munich, West Germany, January 1987.

[2] J. R. Allen and K. Kennedy. Automatic translation of FORTRAN programs to vector form. *ACM Transactions on Programming Languages and Systems*, 9(4):491–542, October 1987.

[3] J. R. Allen, K. Kennedy, C. Porterfield, and J. Warren. Conversion of control dependence to data dependence. In *Conference Record of the Tenth ACM Symposium on the Principles of Programming Languages*, Austin, Tx., January 1983.

[4] R. Alverson, D. Callahan, D. Cummings, B. Koblenz, A. Porterfield, and B. Smith. The Tera computer system. In *Proceedings of the International Conference on Supercomputing*, Amsterdam, 1990.

[5] U. Banerjee, S. C. Chen, D. Kuck, and R. Towle. Time and parallel processor bounds for Fortran-like loops. *IEEE Transactions on Computers*, C-28(9):660–670, September 1979.

[6] J. Ferrante, K. J. Ottenstein, and J. D. Warren. The program dependence graph and its use in optimization. *ACM Transactions on Programming Languages and Systems*, 9(3):319–349, July 1987.

[7] D. Heller. Some aspects of cyclic reduction algorithm for block tridiagonal systems. *SIAM Journal of Numerical Analysis*, 13(4):484–496, 1976.

[8] P. M. Kogge and H. S. Stone. A parallel algorithm for the efficient solution of a general class of recurrence equations. *IEEE Transactions on Computers*, C-22(8):786–792, August 1973.

[9] C. Kruskal, L. Rudolph, and M. Snir. The power of parallel prefix. In *Proceedings of the 1985 International Conference on Parallel Processing*, pages 180–183, August 1985.

[10] D. J. Kuck, R. H. Kuhn, B. Leasure, D. A. Padua, and M. Wolfe. Compiler transformation of dependence graphs. In *Conference Record of the Tenth ACM Symposium on the Principles of Programming Languages*, Williamsburg, Va, January 1983.

[11] R. E. Ladner and M. J. Fisher. Parallel prefix computation. *Journal of the ACM*, 27(4):831–839, October 1980.

[12] F. H. McMahon. The Livermore Fortran kernels: A computer test of the numerical performance range. Technical Report UCRL-53745, Lawrence Livermore National Laboratory, December 1986.

[13] A. Nicolau and H. Wang. Optimal schedules for parallel prefix computation with bounded resources. In *Third ACM SIGPLAN Symposium on Principles and Practice of Parallel Programming*, April 1991.

[14] S. S. Pinter and R. Y. Pinter. Program optimization and parallelization using idioms. In *Conference Record of the Eighteenth ACM Symposium on the Principles of Programming Languages*, January 1991.

[15] G. Rodrigue, editor. *Parallel Computations*. Academic Press, !982.

[16] A. Sameh and R. Brent. Solving triangular systems of equations. *SIAM Journal of Numerical Analysis*, 14(6):1101–1113, 1977.

[17] M. Snir. Depth-size trade-offs for parallel prefix computation. *Journal of Algorithms*, 7:185–201, 1986.

[18] Y. Tanaka, K. Iwasawa, Y. Umetani, and S. Gotou. Compiling techniques for first-order linear recurrences on a vector computer. *The Journal of Supercomputing*, 4(1):63–82, March 1990.

12 Communication-Free Hyperplane Partitioning of Nested Loops

C.-H. Huang and P. Sadayappan
The Ohio State University

Abstract

This paper addresses the problem of partitioning the iterations of nested loops, and data arrays accessed by the loops. Hyperplane partitions of disjoint subsets of data arrays and loop iterations that result in the elimination of communication are sought. A characterization of necessary and sufficient conditions for communication-free hyperplane partitioning is provided.

1 Introduction

The high cost of data communication in distributed-memory machines and the tedium of explicit user-specification of data partitioning and message-passing has prompted much recent interest into automatic or semi-automatic approaches to the derivation of parallel programs for such machines. Several groups have developed systems that accept shared-address-space parallel programs along with user specified data partitions and synthesize message-passing parallel programs to execute on distributed-memory parallel computers [1, 2, 3, 7, 11]. Less attention has been directed towards automatic derivation of data partitions [4, 6, 8, 9, 10]. The benefits of compiler generated data partitions include greater portability, reduced programming effort and potentially better performance of parallel programs.

Li and Chen [8] have formulated the data mapping problem as an *alignment* problem of optimally matching each dimension of each data array with some dimension of one of the arrays (of maximal dimension). They show that this formulation of the data mapping problem is NP-complete, and propose effective heuristics to align arrays. Gupta and Banerjee [4] consider a class of block/cyclic partitions of arrays among processor arrays and propose measures of goodness to characterize mappings. Ramanujam [9, 10] considers the problem of communication-free partitioning of arrays along hyperplanes in the data space of the arrays.

In this paper, we consider again the issue of communication-free hyperplane partitioning. By explicitly modeling the iteration and data spaces and the relation that maps one to the other, we provide a precise characterization of necessary and sufficient conditions for the feasibility of communication-free partitioning along hyperplanes. Section 2 defines the notions of iteration and data spaces and hyperplanes in these spaces. Section 3 describes communication-free partitions. Section 4 discusses communication-free partitions with each partition element containing a single hyperplane from an iteration space or a data space. Communication-free partitions whose elements may contain multiple hyperplanes are treated in Section 5. Necessary and sufficient conditions for communication-free single-hyperplane and multiple-hyperplane partitioning and procedures for deriving these partitions are given in these two sections. Concluding remarks are provided in Section 6. Due to space limitations, all results are stated without proofs; the reader is referred to [5] for details.

2   Iteration Space and Data Space

We consider programs consisting of sequences of nested loops. The iteration space of an r-nested loop, denoted by IS, is a subset of the r-dimensional integer space, Z^r. The iteration of a nested loop with loop indices $(i_1, \ldots, i_r)$ can be specified as a point of the iteration space. We also use an r-component column vector $I = [i_1, \ldots, i_r]^T$ to denote iteration $(i_1, \ldots, i_r)$, where the superscript T denotes the transposition operation.

An iteration may access elements of several data arrays. We characterize the elements of a data array using its index set DS, called a data space, which is a subset of the s-dimensional integer space Z^s. A data index $(d_1, \ldots, d_s)$ is also denoted as a column vector $D = [d_1, \ldots, d_s]^T$.

Array elements are accessed by an iteration via array references. An array reference is defined as an access function from the iteration space to the data space of that array. For example, if i and j are the indices of a two-level nested loop and $A[i + 1, j + 1]$ is a reference to array A in iteration (i, j), the corresponding access function is defined as $access(i, j) = (i + 1, j + 1)$. Frequently, an array reference contains linear combinations of loop indices, i.e.,

$$access(i_1, \ldots, i_r) = (a_{1,1}i_1 + \cdots + a_{1,r}i_r + a_{1,0}, \ldots, a_{s,1}i_1 + \cdots + a_{s,r}i_r + a_{s,0})$$

where $i_1, \ldots,$ and i_r are loop indices and $a_{m,n}$ are integer constants. This linear access function can also be written as a transformation from IS to DS

$$access(I) = AI + a = D$$

where

$$I \in IS, \quad D \in DS, \quad A = \begin{bmatrix} a_{1,1} & \cdots & a_{1,r} \\ \vdots & \ddots & \vdots \\ a_{s,1} & \cdots & a_{s,r} \end{bmatrix}, \quad \text{and} \quad a = \begin{bmatrix} a_{1,0} \\ \vdots \\ a_{s,0} \end{bmatrix}.$$

We will limit our discussion to linear access functions.

In this paper, we will discuss partitioning of iterations and data arrays along hyperplanes of the iteration and data spaces. An *iteration hyperplane* is a set of iterations $\{(i_1, \ldots, i_r) | h_1 i_1 +$

$\cdots + h_r i_r = c_i\}$ where h_1, ..., and $h_r \in Q$ (rational numbers) are hyperplane coefficients and $c_i \in Q$ is the constant term of the hyperplane. Similarly, a *data hyperplane* is a set of data indices $\{(d_1, \ldots, d_s)|g_1 d_1 + \cdots + g_s d_s = c_j\}$, where g_1, ..., and $g_s \in Q$ are hyperplane coefficients and $c_j \in Q$ is the constant term of the hyperplane. Note that the coefficients of a hyperplane cannot be all zeros. Moreover, only those hyperplanes containing at least one integer-valued point are considered. We will often express an iteration hyperplane and a data hyperplane in terms of dot products $\{I|HI = c_i\}$ and $\{D|GD = c_j\}$, where H and G are row vectors containing the hyperplane coefficients.

3 Communication-Free Iteration and Data Partition

The iterations of an iteration space may be executed by different processors in distributed-memory multiprocessors and the elements of data arrays are typically distributed among processors. If an iteration accesses a data element which is not allocated to the processor executing that iteration, data communication is required to fetch (or store) a read (or written) data element. Usually, the cost of data communication is much higher than that of a primitive computation. Therefore, a major issue in the design of compilers for distributed-memory multiprocessors is to reduce data communication and to completely eliminate data communication, if possible.

In this paper, we will focus on partitions of iterations and data arrays that eliminate data communications. In a computation, all iterations in an element of an iteration partition must be executed by the same processor and all data elements in an element of a data partition must be distributed to the same processor. An iteration partition and a data partition must satisfy the following conditions if the computation is to be free of communication:

1. no two data elements in an element of the data partition are accessed by two iterations belonging to different elements of the iteration partition,

2. no two data elements belonging to different elements of the data partition are accessed by any iterations from the same element of the iteration partition.

A communication-free iteration partition and data partition always exists. Obviously, a single iteration set containing all iterations and a single data set containing all elements of a data array is communication-free. However, this trivial partition implies a single processor computation that contradicts the goal of parallel computing. We will deal with non-trivial partitions.

We consider partitions of the iteration space and the data space along their hyperplanes. For a hyperplane partition of an iteration space (or a data space), a partition element is the union of a finite number of iteration (or data) hyperplanes. Moreover, we require that any two hyperplanes from an iteration (data) space be parallel to each other. A partition element P_I (or P_D) of an iteration (or a data) hyperplane partition is given as

$$P_I = \bigcup_{i=1}^{k} \{I|H_i I = c_i\} \quad (\text{or} \quad P_D = \bigcup_{i=1}^{k} \{D|G_i D = c_i\})$$

where k is a positive integer. We reiterate the communication-free hyperplane partitioning requirement in the following definition.

Definition 3.1 An iteration hyperplane partition $\{P_{I_1}, P_{I_2}, \ldots\}$ and a data hyperplane partition $\{P_{D_1}, P_{D_2}, \ldots\}$ are said to be *communication-free*, if

$$\forall I, I' \in IS, \forall D, D' \in DS, access_1(I) = D \wedge access_2(I') = D' :$$
$$(\exists P_{I_j} : I \in P_{I_j} \wedge I' \in P_{I_j} \iff \exists P_{D_k} : D \in P_{D_k} \wedge D' \in P_{D_k})$$

where $access_1$ and $access_2$ are any two access functions.

Note that, in the case of multiple arrays, DS is the discriminating union of the data spaces from all data arrays and an element of the data partition contains hyperplanes from all data arrays. Also, in the case of multiple nested loops, IS is the discriminating union of the iteration spaces from all nested loops and an element of the iteration partition contains hyperplanes from all nested loops.

In the remainder of the paper, we will lift the boundaries of iteration spaces and data spaces to unbounded spaces. This lifting abstraction allows us to reason about the partitioning problem more effectively. Given any access function, we will also assume that, for every data element, there exists at least one iteration in the unbounded space accessing that data element. With these restrictions, some necessary conditions obtained may not hold in a bounded space for all access functions. However, sufficient conditions will remain true. More importantly, hyperplane partitions obtained from the procedures discussed in this paper are still communication-free when restricted to bounded spaces. In the following section, we consider communication-free partitions where each element of a partition contains a single hyperplane.

4 Single-Hyperplane Partitioning

We first consider a data hyperplane $\{D | GD = c_j\}$ of a given array and an access function $access(I) = AI + a$ referencing this array. If an iteration I references a data element using $access$ and the index of the data element is on the data hyperplane $\{D | GD = c_j\}$, we must have $GD = G(AI + a) = c_j$ or $(GA)I = c_j - Ga$, i.e., I is on the iteration hyperplane $\{I | (GA)I = c_j - Ga\}$.

Conversely, consider an iteration hyperplane $\{I | HI = c_i\}$ such that $H = GA$ for some G. The index of the data element accessed by iteration I in this hyperplane via $access$ is given as $D = AI + a$. Therefore,

$$GD = G(AI + a) = (GA)I + Ga = c_i + Ga$$

because $(GA)I = HI = c$. Thus, data element D accessed by an iteration I on the iteration hyperplane $\{I | HI = c_i\}$ lies on the data hyperplane $\{D | GD = c_i + Ga\}$. This one-to-one relation between data hyperplanes and iteration hyperplanes is stated in the following lemma.

Lemma 4.1 *Given an access function $access(I) = AI + a$, all iterations accessing data elements on a data hyperplane $\{D | GD = c_j\}$ via the access function lie on the iteration hyperplane $\{I | (GA)I = c_j - Ga\}$; all data elements accessed by iterations on an iteration hyperplane $\{I | (GA)I = c_i\}$ via the access function lie on the data hyperplane $\{D | GD = c_i + Ga\}$.*

Given an arbitrary coefficient vector G for a data hyperplane, a corresponding coefficient vector H for an iteration hyperplane can always be found. The converse is not true. Only those iteration hyperplanes whose coefficient vector is expressible as a product GA for some G have corresponding data hyperplanes. However, if A is invertible, i.e., a data element is accessed by only one iteration via *access*, the one-to-one correspondence always exits. Given any arbitrary coefficient vector H for an iteration hyperplane, we can choose $G = HA^{-1}$.

In the following subsection, we will discuss single-hyperplane partitioning, starting with the simple case where an iteration contains only one access function, i.e., an iteration accesses only a single array with a single reference. Then, we proceed to characterize the case of a single array with multiple references, multiple arrays with a single reference to each array, and finally multiple arrays with multiple references to each array in multiple nested loops.

4.1 Single Array, Single Reference

Recall that we require all hyperplanes in an iteration partition or a data partition to be parallel to each other. Therefore, each partition element of a single-hyperplane iteration partition P_{I_i} contains hyperplane $\{I|HI = c_i\}$ for some H, and each partition element of a single-hyperplane iteration partition P_{D_j} contains hyperplane $\{D|GD = c_j\}$, for some G. In the following, we will often denote a partition by its elements. Communication-free partitioning is always possible for the case of a single array with a single reference.

Theorem 4.1 *Given a nested loop that references a single array with a single array access function $access(I) = AI + a$, the iteration hyperplane partition $\{I|HI = c_i\}$ and the data hyperplane partition $\{D|GD = c_j\}$ are communication-free if and only if $H = \alpha GA$, for some $\alpha, \alpha \neq 0$.*

To compute a communication-free iteration and data partition for a single array with a single reference, it is easier to choose a data hyperplane partition first and then compute its corresponding iteration hyperplane partition, if the coefficient matrix of the access function is not invertible; otherwise, we can choose either an iteration hyperplane partition or a data hyperplane partition first.

Example 1

> **do** $i_1 = 1, n$
> > **do** $i_2 = 1, n$
> > > $A[i_1 - i_2 + 2, 3 * i_1 - 2 * i_2 + 1] = A[i_1 - i_2 + 2, 3 * i_1 - 2 * i_2 + 1] + 1$
> **enddo enddo**

Since the coefficient matrix of the access function is invertible,

$$A = \begin{bmatrix} 1 & -1 \\ 3 & -2 \end{bmatrix}, \quad A^{-1} = \begin{bmatrix} -2 & 1 \\ -3 & 1 \end{bmatrix}, \quad \text{and} \quad a = \begin{bmatrix} 2 \\ 1 \end{bmatrix}$$

we may first choose an iteration hyperplane partition, e.g., each partition element contains all iterations on the hyperplane $\{(i_1, i_2)|i_1 - i_2 = c_i\}$, for $H = [1 \; -1]$. The corresponding partition element of the communication-free data hyperplane partition will contain all data elements with their indices in $\{(d_1, d_2)|d_1 = c_i + 2\}$, for $G = HA^{-1} = [1\ 0]$ and $Ga = 2$. □

Example 2

$$\mathbf{do}\ i_1 = 1, n$$
$$\mathbf{do}\ i_2 = 1, n$$
$$B[i_1 + i_2] = 2 * B[i_1 + i_2]$$
$$\mathbf{enddo}\ \mathbf{enddo}$$

Since the coefficient matrix of the access function is not invertible, we will first choose a data hyperplane partition, e.g., $\{(d_1)|d_1 = c_j\}$, for $G = [1]$. The corresponding communication-free iteration hyperplane partition is $\{(i_1, i_2)|i_1 + i_2 = c_j\}$, for $GB = [1\ 1]$ and $Gb = [0]$. □

4.2 Single Array, Multiple References

We consider next the possibility of communication-free hyperplane partitioning when multiple distinct references to a single array occur in a nested loop. We state the following necessary and sufficient condition for communication-free partitioning.

Theorem 4.2 *Given a nested loop referencing a single array A with k distinct access functions $access_i(I) = A_i I + a_i$, $1 \le i \le k$, the iteration hyperplane partition $\{I|HI = c_i\}$ and the data hyperplane partition $\{D|GD = c_j\}$ are communication-free if and only if*

$$\frac{1}{\alpha}H = GA_1 = GA_2 = \ldots = GA_k \quad and \quad Ga_1 = Ga_2 = \ldots = Ga_k$$

The existence of such a data hyperplane coefficient vector G depends on the access matrices A_i and a_i, for $1 \le i \le k$. In fact, G can be obtained by solving the following system of homogeneous equations:

$$G \begin{bmatrix} A_1 - A_2 & A_1 - A_3 & \cdots & A_1 - A_k & a_1 - a_2 & a_1 - a_3 & \cdots & a_1 - a_k \end{bmatrix} = \begin{bmatrix} 0 & \cdots & 0 \end{bmatrix} \quad (1)$$

To guarantee the existence of a corresponding iteration hyperplane coefficient vector H, we also require G is not an element of thè null space of A_i. We state this condition as Corollary 4.1.

Corollary 4.1 *Given a nested loop referencing a single array A with k distinct access functions $access_i(I) = A_i I + a_i$, $1 \le i \le k$, a communication-free single-hyperplane partition exists if and only if the system of equations Eq. (1) has a solution G such that $G \notin NS(A_i)$.*

A necessary condition of Corollary 4.1 is that G have a non-zero solution, i.e., the rank of the following matrix is less than the dimensionality of array A:

$$rank \begin{bmatrix} A_1 - A_2 & A_1 - A_3 & \cdots & A_1 - A_k & a_1 - a_2 & a_1 - a_3 & \cdots & a_1 - a_k \end{bmatrix} < dim(DS_A) \quad (2)$$

Example 3

$$
\begin{aligned}
&\textbf{do } i_1 = 1, n \\
&\quad \textbf{do } i_2 = 1, n \\
&\qquad A[i_1 + 1, i_2] = A[i_2, i_1 + 1] - 1 \\
&\quad \textbf{enddo enddo}
\end{aligned}
$$

$$
A_1 = \begin{bmatrix} 1 & 0 \\ 0 & 1 \end{bmatrix}, \quad a_1 = \begin{bmatrix} 1 \\ 0 \end{bmatrix}, \quad A_2 = \begin{bmatrix} 0 & 1 \\ 1 & 0 \end{bmatrix}, \quad a_2 = \begin{bmatrix} 0 \\ 1 \end{bmatrix},
$$

$$
rank \begin{bmatrix} A_1 - A_2 & a_1 - a_2 \end{bmatrix} = rank \begin{bmatrix} 1 & -1 & 1 \\ -1 & 1 & -1 \end{bmatrix} = 1 < 2
$$

Solving G in the following system of equations

$$
G \begin{bmatrix} 1 & -1 & 1 \\ -1 & 1 & -1 \end{bmatrix} = [g_1 g_2] \begin{bmatrix} 1 & -1 & 1 \\ -1 & 1 & -1 \end{bmatrix} = \begin{bmatrix} 0 & 0 & 0 \end{bmatrix},
$$

we obtain $G = [1 \; 1]$. $GA_1 = GA_2 = [1 \; 1]$ and $Ga_1 = Ga_2 = 1$. The communication-free partition is given by data hyperplanes $\{(d_1, d_2)|d_1 + d_2 = c_j\}$ and the corresponding iteration hyperplanes $\{(i_1, i_2)|i_1 + i_2 = c_j - 1\}$. $\quad \square$

Example 4

$$
\begin{aligned}
&\textbf{do } i_1 = 1, n \\
&\quad \textbf{do } i_2 = 1, n \\
&\qquad A[i_2, i_1 - 1] = A[i_1 + 1, i_2] \\
&\quad \textbf{enddo enddo}
\end{aligned}
$$

$$
A_1 = \begin{bmatrix} 0 & 1 \\ 1 & 0 \end{bmatrix}, \quad a_1 = \begin{bmatrix} 0 \\ -1 \end{bmatrix}, \quad A_2 = \begin{bmatrix} 1 & 0 \\ 0 & 1 \end{bmatrix}, \quad a_2 = \begin{bmatrix} 1 \\ 0 \end{bmatrix}
$$

$$
rank \begin{bmatrix} A_1 - A_2 & a_1 - a_2 \end{bmatrix} = rank \begin{bmatrix} -1 & 1 & -1 \\ 1 & -1 & -1 \end{bmatrix} = 2 \not< 2
$$

By Corollary 4.1 and the rank test in Eq. (2), a communication-free single-hyperplane partition does not exist. As shown later in Section 5, this example is amenable to a communication-free multiple-hyperplane partitioning. $\quad \square$

4.3 Multiple Arrays, Single Reference

We now consider nested loops that reference multiple arrays. We first treat the simpler case of a single access to each of the arrays. By Theorem 4.1, for any given family of parallel hyperplanes in the data space of a singly accessed array, a corresponding family of hyperplanes can be found in the iteration space to yield a communication-free partition. When multiple arrays are involved, communication-free single-hyperplane partitioning is possible if hyperplanes can be chosen in each of the array spaces so that the corresponding iteration hyperplanes are all defined by the same direction.

Theorem 4.3 *Given a nested loop with a single reference to each of the arrays A_1, ..., A_m with access functions $access_j = A_j I + a_j$, for $1 \leq j \leq m$, the single-hyperplane partition $\{I | HI = c_i\}$ of the iteration space and $\{D | G_j D = c_j\}$ of the data spaces DS_{A_j} are communication-free, if and only if $H = \alpha_j G_j A_j$, for some $\alpha_j \neq 0$, $1 \leq j \leq m$.*

By Theorem 4.3, a communication-free single-hyperplane partition for multiple arrays with single reference to each array exists, if and only if there are data hyperplane coefficient vectors G_1, G_2, $\cdots$, and G_m such that $G_1 A_1 = G_2 A_2 = \cdots = G_m A_m$. These coefficient vectors can be obtained by solving the following system of homogeneous equations:

$$G_1 A_1 - G_2 A_2 = \begin{bmatrix} 0 & \cdots & 0 \end{bmatrix}$$
$$\cdots \tag{3}$$
$$G_1 A_1 - G_m A_m = \begin{bmatrix} 0 & \cdots & 0 \end{bmatrix}$$

Furthermore, G_j must not be in the null space of A_j to ensure the existence of a non-zero iteration hyperplane coefficient vector. We state this result in the following corollary.

Corollary 4.2 *Given a nested loop with a single reference to each of the arrays A_1, ..., A_m with access functions $access_j = A_j I + a_j$, for $1 \leq j \leq m$, a communication-free single-hyperplane partition exists if and only if the system of equations Eq. (3) has a solution $G_1, \ldots, G_m$ such that $G_j \notin NS(A_j)$.*

A necessary condition of Corollary 4.2 is $G_j \neq (0, \ldots, 0)$. The necessary condition holds if and only if the rank of the following matrix is less than the number of unknowns in the system, i.e., the sum of dimensionalities of arrays A_j, for $1 \leq j \leq m$

$$rank \begin{bmatrix} A_1 & \cdots & A_1 \\ -A_2 & \cdots & 0 \\ \vdots & \ddots & \vdots \\ 0 & \cdots & -A_m \end{bmatrix} < \sum_{j=1}^{m} dim(DS_{A_j}) \tag{4}$$

Example 5

$$\mathbf{do}\ i_1 = 1, m$$
$$\mathbf{do}\ i_2 = 1, n$$
$$A[i_1 - 1, i_2 + 1] = B[i_1 + i_2, i_1 - i_2 + 2] + C[i_2 + 2, i_1 - 1]$$
$$\mathbf{enddo}\ \mathbf{enddo}$$

$$A = \begin{bmatrix} 1 & 0 \\ 0 & 1 \end{bmatrix}, \quad a = \begin{bmatrix} -1 \\ 1 \end{bmatrix}, \quad B = \begin{bmatrix} 1 & 1 \\ 1 & -1 \end{bmatrix}, \quad b = \begin{bmatrix} 0 \\ 2 \end{bmatrix}, \quad C = \begin{bmatrix} 0 & 1 \\ 1 & 0 \end{bmatrix}, \quad c = \begin{bmatrix} 2 \\ -1 \end{bmatrix}$$

The following matrix has rank 4

$$rank \begin{bmatrix} A & A \\ -B & 0 \\ 0 & -C \end{bmatrix} = rank \begin{bmatrix} 1 & 0 & 1 & 0 \\ 0 & 1 & 0 & 1 \\ -1 & -1 & 0 & 0 \\ -1 & 1 & 0 & 0 \\ 0 & 0 & 0 & -1 \\ 0 & 0 & -1 & 0 \end{bmatrix} = 4$$

which is less than the sum of dimensionalities of arrays A, B, and C. Therefore, there may exist a communication-free single-hyperplane partition. Solving the following system of equations

$$
\begin{bmatrix} g_{A_1} & g_{A_2} & g_{B_1} & g_{B_2} & g_{C_1} & g_{C_2} \end{bmatrix}
\begin{bmatrix}
1 & 0 & 1 & 0 \\
0 & 1 & 0 & 1 \\
-1 & -1 & 0 & 0 \\
-1 & 1 & 0 & 0 \\
0 & 0 & 0 & -1 \\
0 & 0 & -1 & 0
\end{bmatrix}
= \begin{bmatrix} 0 & 0 & 0 & 0 \end{bmatrix}
$$

we obtain the solution

$$
g_{A_1} = s_1, \quad g_{A_2} = s_2, \quad g_{B_1} = \tfrac{s_1 + s_2}{2}, \quad g_{B_2} = \tfrac{s_1 - s_2}{2}, \quad g_{C_1} = s_2, \quad g_{C_2} = s_1.
$$

Choosing $s_1 = 1$ and $s_2 = -1$, the three hyperplane coefficient vectors are $G_A = [1 \;\; -1]$, $G_B = [0\;1]$, $G_C = [-1\;1]$, and $H = G_A A = G_B B = G_C C = [1 \;\; -1]$. The hyperplanes of the iteration space partition are $\{(i_1, i_2) | i_1 - i_2 = t\}$, and the hyperplanes of the data space partition are $\{(d_{A_1}, d_{A_2}) | d_{A_1} - d_{A_2} = t_A\}$, $\{(d_{B_1}, d_{B_2}) | d_{B_2} = t_B\}$, and $\{(d_{C_1}, d_{C_2}) | -d_{C_1} + d_{c_2} = t_C\}$. The iteration and data hyperplanes with $t_A = t - G_A a = t - 2$, $t_B = t - G_B b = t + 2$ and $t_C = t - G_C c = t - 3$ are grouped in the same partition element. $\quad\square$

4.4 Multiple Arrays, Multiple References, Multiple Loops

The results from Sections 4.2 and 4.3 can be combined for the case of multiple arrays, multiple references, and a sequence of nested loops. We summarize the necessary and sufficient condition for communication-free single-hyperplane partitioning in this section.

Let $access_{j,k}^i(I) = A_{j,k}^i(I) + a_{j,k}^i$ be the k-th reference of the j-th data array in the i-th nested loop. Considering separately each possible pair of a nested loop and a data array, by Theorem 4.2 and Theorem 4.3, the following conditions must hold

$$
G_j A_{j,k_1}^i = G_j A_{j,k_2}^i \tag{5}
$$

$$
G_j a_{j,k_1}^i = G_j a_{j,k_2}^i \tag{6}
$$

$$
H_i = \alpha_j^i G_j A_{j,1}^i \tag{7}
$$

for some hyperplane coefficient vectors H_i and G_j.

In addition, we must ensure consistency when grouping hyperplanes in multiple nested loops and data arrays. Consider two data hyperplanes $\{D|G_{j_1} D = c_{j_1}\}$ and $\{D|G_{j_2} D = c_{j_2}\}$ in data spaces DS_{j_1} and DS_{j_2}, respectively. If the i-th nested loop references arrays A_{j_1} and A_{j_2}, the iteration hyperplanes corresponding to these two data hyperplanes are given as $\{I|H_i I = \alpha_{j_1}^i(c_{j_1} - G_{j_1} a_{j_1,1}^i)\}$ and $\{I|H_i I = \alpha_{j_2}^i(c_{j_2} - G_{j_2} a_{j_2,1}^i)\}$. To construct a communication-free single-hyperplane partition, we can only group two data hyperplanes $\{D|G_{j_1} D = c_{j_1}\}$ and $\{D|G_{j_2} D = c_{j_2}\}$ in the same partition element if their corresponding hyperplanes are identical. Hence, we have

$$
\alpha_{j_1}^i(c_{j_1} - G_{j_1} a_{j_1,1}^i) = \alpha_{j_2}^i(c_{j_2} - G_{j_2} a_{j_2,1}^i).
$$

If both arrays A_{j_1} and A_{j_2} are referenced in iteration spaces IS_{i_1} and IS_{i_2}, data hyperplanes in data spaces DS_{j_1} and DS_{j_2} are grouped in the same partition element when

$$\alpha_{j_1}^{i_1}(c_{j_1} - G_{j_1}a_{j_1,1}^{i_1}) = \alpha_{j_2}^{i_1}(c_{j_2} - G_{j_2}a_{j_2,1}^{i_1}) \text{ and } \alpha_{j_1}^{i_2}(c_{j_1} - G_{j_1}a_{j_1,1}^{i_2}) = \alpha_{j_2}^{i_2}(c_{j_2} - G_{j_2}a_{j_2,1}^{i_2})$$

$$\equiv \quad c_{j_1} = \frac{\alpha_{j_2}^{i_1}}{\alpha_{j_1}^{i_1}}(c_{j_2} - G_{j_2}a_{j_2,1}^{i_1}) + G_{j_1}a_{j_1,1}^{i_1} = \frac{\alpha_{j_2}^{i_2}}{\alpha_{j_2}^{i_2}}(c_{j_2} - G_{j_2}a_{j_2,1}^{i_2}) + G_{j_2}a_{j_1,1}^{i_1}$$

$$\equiv \quad \alpha_{j_1}^{i_1}\alpha_{j_2}^{i_2} = \alpha_{j_2}^{i_1}\alpha_{j_1}^{i_2} \wedge \frac{\alpha_{j_2}^{i_1}}{\alpha_{j_1}^{i_1}}G_{j_2}a_{j_2,1}^{i_1} - G_{j_1}a_{j_1,1}^{i_1} = \frac{\alpha_{j_2}^{i_2}}{\alpha_{j_2}^{i_2}}G_{j_2}a_{j_2,1}^{i_2} - G_{j_2}a_{j_1,1}^{i_1}$$

(The previous equation needs to hold for all c_{j_2})

$$\equiv \quad \alpha_{j_1}^{i_1}\alpha_{j_2}^{i_2} = \alpha_{j_2}^{i_1}\alpha_{j_1}^{i_2} \wedge \alpha_{j_1}^{i_1}G_{j_1}(a_{j_1,1}^{i_1} - a_{j_1,1}^{i_2}) = \alpha_{j_2}^{i_1}G_{j_2}(a_{j_2,1}^{i_1} - a_{j_2,1}^{i_2}) \tag{8}$$

We add the condition in Eq. (8) to the necessary and sufficient conditions for communication-free single-hyperplane partitioning.

Theorem 4.4 *Consider a sequence of nested loops with multiple references to multiple data arrays. Let $access_{j,k}^i(I) = A_{j,k}^i(I) + a_{j,k}^i$ be the access function of the k-th reference to the j-th data array in the i-th nested loop. The single-hyperplane partition $\{I|H_iI = c_i\}$ in the iteration spaces and $\{D|G_jD = c_j\}$ in data spaces are communication-free if and only if the following conditions hold*

1. $G_j A_{j,k_1}^i = G_j A_{j,k_2}^i$

2. $G_j a_{j,k_1}^i = G_j a_{j,k_2}^i$

3. $H_i = \alpha_j^i G_j A_{j,1}^i$

4. $\alpha_{j_1}^{i_1}\alpha_{j_2}^{i_2} = \alpha_{j_2}^{i_1}\alpha_{j_1}^{i_2} \wedge \alpha_{j_1}^{i_1}G_{j_1}(a_{j_1,1}^{i_1} - a_{j_1,1}^{i_2}) = \alpha_{j_2}^{i_1}G_{j_2}(a_{j_2,1}^{i_1} - a_{j_2,1}^{i_2})$

We choose all α_j^i to be 1 when computing H_i and G_j. For a program containing m nested loops and referencing n data arrays, the coefficient vectors G_j can be obtained by solving the systems of Equations Eq. (1), Eq. (3) and

$$G_{j_1}(a_{j_1,1}^{i_1} - a_{j_1,1}^{i_2}) + G_{j_2}(a_{j_2,1}^{i_2} - a_{j_2,1}^{i_1}) = 0$$

for $1 \le i_1, i_2 \le m$ and $1 \le j_1, j_2 \le n$.

Example 6

```
do i₁ = 1, m
    do i₂ = 1, n
        do i₃ = 1, p
            A[i₁, i₂, i₃] = B[i₁ + i₂ + 1, i₁ - i₂ - 1] + B[i₁ + i₃ - 1, i₁ - i₃ + 1]
enddo enddo enddo;
do i₁ = 1, r
    do i₂ = 1, s
        B[i₁ + i₂ - 1, i₁ - i₂ + 1] = A[i₁, i₂, i₁ + i₂ - 1] + A[i₁, i₂, i₁ - i₂ + 1]
enddo enddo
```

$$A_1^1 = \begin{bmatrix} 1 & 0 & 0 \\ 0 & 1 & 0 \\ 0 & 0 & 1 \end{bmatrix}, \quad a_1^1 = \begin{bmatrix} 0 \\ 0 \\ 0 \end{bmatrix}, \quad B_1^1 = \begin{bmatrix} 1 & 1 & 0 \\ 1 & -1 & 0 \end{bmatrix}, \quad b_1^1 = \begin{bmatrix} 1 \\ -1 \end{bmatrix},$$

$$B_2^1 = \begin{bmatrix} 1 & 0 & 1 \\ 1 & 0 & -1 \end{bmatrix}, \quad b_2^1 = \begin{bmatrix} -1 \\ 1 \end{bmatrix}, \quad A_1^2 = \begin{bmatrix} 1 & 0 \\ 0 & 1 \\ 1 & 1 \end{bmatrix}, \quad a_1^2 = \begin{bmatrix} 0 \\ 0 \\ -1 \end{bmatrix},$$

$$A_2^2 = \begin{bmatrix} 1 & 0 \\ 0 & 1 \\ 1 & -1 \end{bmatrix}, \quad a_2^2 = \begin{bmatrix} 0 \\ 0 \\ 1 \end{bmatrix}, \quad B_1^2 = \begin{bmatrix} 1 & 1 \\ 1 & -1 \end{bmatrix}, \quad b_1^2 = \begin{bmatrix} -1 \\ 1 \end{bmatrix}$$

Solving the following systems of equations:

$$G_B \begin{bmatrix} B_1^1 - B_2^1 & b_1^1 - b_2^1 \end{bmatrix} = \begin{bmatrix} g_{B_1} & g_{B_2} \end{bmatrix} \begin{bmatrix} 0 & 1 & -1 & 2 \\ 0 & -1 & 1 & -2 \end{bmatrix} = \begin{bmatrix} 0 & 0 & 0 & 0 \end{bmatrix}$$

$$\begin{bmatrix} G_A & G_B \end{bmatrix} \begin{bmatrix} A_1^1 \\ -B_1^1 \end{bmatrix} = \begin{bmatrix} g_{A_1} & g_{A_2} & g_{A_3} & g_{B_1} & g_{B_2} \end{bmatrix} \begin{bmatrix} 1 & 0 & 0 \\ 0 & 1 & 0 \\ 0 & 0 & 1 \\ -1 & -1 & 0 \\ -1 & 1 & 0 \end{bmatrix} = \begin{bmatrix} 0 & 0 & 0 \end{bmatrix}$$

$$G_A \begin{bmatrix} A_1^2 - A_2^2 & a_1^2 - a_2^2 \end{bmatrix} = \begin{bmatrix} g_{A_1} & g_{A_2} & g_{A_3} \end{bmatrix} \begin{bmatrix} 0 & 0 & 0 \\ 0 & 0 & 0 \\ 0 & 2 & -2 \end{bmatrix} = \begin{bmatrix} 0 & 0 & 0 \end{bmatrix}$$

$$\begin{bmatrix} G_A & G_B \end{bmatrix} \begin{bmatrix} A_1^2 \\ -B_1^2 \end{bmatrix} = \begin{bmatrix} g_{A_1} & g_{A_2} & g_{A_3} & g_{B_1} & g_{B_2} \end{bmatrix} \begin{bmatrix} 1 & 0 \\ 0 & 1 \\ 1 & 1 \\ -1 & -1 \\ -1 & 1 \end{bmatrix} = \begin{bmatrix} 0 & 0 \end{bmatrix}$$

$$\begin{bmatrix} G_A & G_B \end{bmatrix} \begin{bmatrix} a_1^1 - a_1^2 \\ -(b_1^1 - b_1^2) \end{bmatrix} = \begin{bmatrix} g_{A_1} & g_{A_2} & g_{A_3} & g_{B_1} & g_{B_2} \end{bmatrix} \begin{bmatrix} 0 \\ 0 \\ 1 \\ -2 \\ 2 \end{bmatrix} = \begin{bmatrix} 0 \end{bmatrix}$$

we obtain the solution

$$g_{A_1} = 2s, \quad g_{A_2} = 0, \quad g_{A_3} = 0, \quad g_{B_1} = s, \quad g_{B_2} = s$$

The solution allows us to choose coefficient vectors of the hyperplanes over the data spaces DS_A and DS_B:

$$G_A = \begin{bmatrix} 1 & 0 & 0 \end{bmatrix} \quad \text{and} \quad G_B = \begin{bmatrix} 1 & 1 \end{bmatrix}.$$

We also choose $\alpha_A^1 = \alpha_A^2 = 1$ and $\alpha_B^1 = \alpha_B^2 = \frac{1}{2}$, and derive the coefficient vectors of the hyperplanes over the iteration spaces IS_1 and IS_2:

$$H_1 = \begin{bmatrix} 1 & 0 & 0 \end{bmatrix} \quad \text{and} \quad H_2 = \begin{bmatrix} 1 & 0 \end{bmatrix}$$

The communication-free single-hyperplane partition is given as $\{(i_1, i_2, i_3)|i_1 = c_1\}$ over iteration space IS_1, $\{(i_1, i_2)|i_1 = c_2\}$ over iteration space IS_2, $\{(d_1, d_2, d_3)|d_1 = c_A\}$ over data space DS_A, and $\{(d_1, d_2)|d_1 + d_2 = c_B\}$ over data space DS_B. These hyperplanes are grouped in the same partition element if $c_A = \frac{c_1}{\alpha_A} - G_A a_1^1$, $c_A = \frac{c_2}{\alpha_A} - G_A a_1^2$, $c_B = \frac{c_1}{\alpha_B} - G_B b_1^1$, and $c_B = \frac{c_2}{\alpha_B} - G_B b_1^2$, i.e., when $c_1 = c_2 = c_A = \frac{1}{2} c_B$. □

5 Multiple-Hyperplane Partitioning

We presented communication-free single-hyperplane partitioning of the iteration and data spaces in the previous section. We now consider the more general case of groups of parallel hyperplanes for communication-free partitioning.

5.1 Single Array, Multiple References

We first deal with communication-free multiple-hyperplane partitioning for a single nested loop with multiple references to a single array. We state the following necessary condition for the case of single-array references.

Theorem 5.1 *Given a nested loop with access functions $access_k(I) = A_k I + a_k$, $k = 1, 2$, to a single array A, a finite-hyperplane communication-free partition of the iteration and data spaces exists, only if there exists a data hyperplane coefficient vector G such that $G A_1 = \beta G A_2 \neq 0$, $\beta = \pm 1$.*

The first solution $\beta = 1$ corresponds to the case of single-hyperplane partitioning discussed in Section 4. The other solution $\beta = -1$ corresponds to double hyperplane partitioning, where each partition element of the data space contains a pair of data hyperplanes and they are mapped to a pair of hyperplanes in the iteration space. In the case of double-hyperplane partitioning, the necessary condition in Theorem 5.1 is also a sufficient condition.

We re-examine Example 4 where the sufficient condition for a communication-free single-hyperplane partitioning fails.

Example 7

$$\textbf{do } i_1 = 1, n$$
$$\textbf{do } i_2 = 1, n$$
$$A[i_2, i_1 - 1] = A[i_1 + 1, i_2]$$
$$\textbf{enddo enddo}$$

$$A_1 = \begin{bmatrix} 0 & 1 \\ 1 & 0 \end{bmatrix}, \quad a_1 = \begin{bmatrix} 0 \\ -1 \end{bmatrix}, \quad A_2 = \begin{bmatrix} 1 & 0 \\ 0 & 1 \end{bmatrix}, \quad a_2 = \begin{bmatrix} 1 \\ 0 \end{bmatrix}$$

$$(A_1 + A_2)^T = \begin{bmatrix} 1 & 1 \\ 1 & 1 \end{bmatrix}$$

Since the null space $NS((A_1 + A_2)^T)$ is not empty, there exists a G such that $GA_1 = -GA_2$, i.e., a communication-free double-hyperplane partition exists. Choosing $G = [1\ -1]$ such that G^T is a vector in $NS((A_1 + A_2)^T)$, we calculate $GA_1 = [-1\ 1]$, $Ga_1 = 1$, $GA_2 = [1\ -1]$, and $Ga_2 = 1$. Given any hyperplane $\{D | GD = c_j\}$, the paired hyperplane is $\{D | GD = -c_j + G(a_1 + a_2)\} = \{D | GD = -c_j + 2\}$. The corresponding pair of iteration hyperplanes are $\{I | GA_1 I = c_j - Ga_1\}$ and $\{I | GA_2 I = c_j - Ga_2\}$, i.e., $\{(i_1, i_2) | i_1 - i_2 = c_j - 1\}$ and $\{(i_1, i_2) | -i_1 + i_2 = c_j - 1\}$. $\quad\square$

5.2 Multiple Arrays, Multiple References, Multiple Loops

In the case of multiple arrays referenced in multiple loops, we must ensure consistency when grouping their hyperplanes. We present the necessary and sufficient conditions in the theorem below. The reader is referred to [5] for details.

Theorem 5.2 *Given a sequence of nested loops and access functions $access_{j,k}^i(I) = A_{j,k}^i(I) + a_{j,k}^i$ for the k-th reference of the j-th data array in the i-th nested loop, a communication-free finite-hyperplane partition exists if and only if there exist the iteration hyperplane coefficient vector H_i for the i-th loop and the data hyperplane coefficient vector G_j for the j-th array, such that the following conditions hold*

1. $G_j A_{j,1}^i = \beta_{j,k}^i G_j A_{j,k}^i \wedge \beta_{j,k}^i = \pm 1$

2. $\beta_{j,k_1}^i \beta_{j,k_2}^i = 1 \Longrightarrow G_j a_{j,k_1}^i = G_j a_{j,k_2}^i$

3. $H_i = \alpha_i^i G_j A_{j,1}^i \neq (0, \ldots, 0)$

4. $\beta_{j_1,k_1}^i = \beta_{j_2,k_2}^i = -1 \Longrightarrow \alpha_{j_1}^i G_{j_1}(a_{j_1,1}^i - a_{j_1,k_1}^i) = \alpha_{j_2}^i G_{j_2}(a_{j_2,1}^i - a_{j_2,k_2}^i)$

5. $\beta_{j,k_1}^{i_1} = \beta_{j,k_2}^{i_2} = -1 \Longrightarrow G_j(a_{j,1}^{i_1} + a_{j,k_1}^{i_1}) = G_j(a_{j,1}^{i_2} + a_{j,k_2}^{i_2})$

6. $\forall i, j, k : \beta_{j,k}^i = 1 \Longrightarrow (\alpha_{j_1}^{i_1} \alpha_{j_2}^{i_2} = \alpha_{j_1}^{i_2} \alpha_{j_2}^{i_1} \wedge \alpha_{j_1}^{i_1} G_{j_1}(a_{j_1,1}^{i_1} - a_{j_1,1}^{i_2}) = \alpha_{j_2}^{i_2} G_{j_2}(a_{j_2,1}^{i_1} - a_{j_2,1}^{i_2}))$

7. $\forall i, k : \beta_{j_1,k}^i = 1 \wedge \exists i', j', k' : \beta_{j',k'}^{i'} = -1 \Longrightarrow$
   $(\alpha_{j_1}^{i_1} \alpha_{j_2}^{i_2} = \alpha_{j_2}^{i_1} \alpha_{j_1}^{i_2} \wedge \alpha_{j_1}^{i_1} G_{j_1}(a_{j_1,1}^{i_1} - a_{j_1,1}^{i_2}) = \alpha_{j_2}^{i_2} G_{j_2}(a_{j_2,1}^{i_1} - a_{j_2,1}^{i_2})) \vee$
   $(\alpha_{j_1}^{i_1} \alpha_{j_2}^{i_2} = \alpha_{j_2}^{i_1} \alpha_{j_1}^{i_2} \wedge \alpha_{j_1}^{i_1} G_{j_1}(a_{j_1,1}^{i_1} - a_{j_1,1}^{i_2}) = \alpha_{j_2}^{i_2} G_{j_2}(a_{j_2,1}^{i_1} - a_{j_2,1}^{i_2}) + \frac{\alpha_{j'}^{i'}}{\alpha_{j_1}^{i'}} G_{j'}(a_{j',1}^{i'} - a_{j',k'}^{i'}))$

8. $\exists i', k' : \beta_{j_1,k'}^{i'} = -1 \Longrightarrow$
   $(\alpha_{j_1}^{i_1} \alpha_{j_2}^{i_2} = \alpha_{j_2}^{i_1} \alpha_{j_1}^{i_2} \wedge \alpha_{j_1}^{i_1} G_{j_1}(a_{j_1,1}^{i_1} - a_{j_1,1}^{i_2}) = \alpha_{j_2}^{i_2} G_{j_2}(a_{j_2,1}^{i_1} - a_{j_2,1}^{i_2})) \vee$
   $(\alpha_{j_1}^{i_1} \alpha_{j_2}^{i_2} = -\alpha_{j_2}^{i_1} \alpha_{j_1}^{i_2} \wedge \alpha_{j_1}^{i_1} G_{j_1}(a_{j_1,1}^{i_1} - a_{j_1,1}^{i_2}) = \alpha_{j_2}^{i_1} G_{j_2}(a_{j_2,1}^{i_1} - a_{j_2,1}^{i_2}) + G_{j_1}(a_{j_1,1}^{i_1} - a_{j_1,k'}^{i'})).$

The derivation of hyperplane coefficient vectors H_i and G_j includes the determination of $\beta_{j,k}^i$ which is exponential in the numbers of access functions. We use a heuristic to reduce the time for determining $\beta_{j,k}^i$:

For each access functions $access_{j,k}^i(I) = A_{j,k}^i I + a_{j,k}^i$, if the system of equations

$$G(A_{j,1}^i - A_{j,k}^i) = \begin{bmatrix} 0 & \cdots & 0 \end{bmatrix} \quad \text{and} \quad G(a_{j,1}^i - a_{j,k}^i) = \begin{bmatrix} 0 \end{bmatrix}$$

has its solution space contained in $NS(A_{j,1}^i)$, set $\beta_{j,k}^i = -1$; otherwise, set $\beta_{j,k}^i = 1$.

This heuristic assigns $\beta_{j,k}^i = -1$ for those access functions $access_{j,k}^i$ that must form double-hyperplane with $access_{j,1}^i$. For the other access functions whose $\beta_{j,k}^i$ could be 1 or -1, we heuristically choose $\beta_{j,k}^i = 1$. This assignment does not guarantee a feasible communication-free finite-hyperplane partitioning even when one exists. However, it gives a reasonable approximation of choosing $\beta_{j,k}^i$. If an exhaustive search of all possible $\beta_{j,k}^i$ is to be implemented, this heuristic cuts down the search space by limiting it to those assigned to 1. After determining the values of $\beta_{j,k}^i$, we can solve the systems of equations described in Theorem 5.2 by choosing all $\alpha_j^i = 1$. A communication-free finite-hyperplane partitioning exists, if a non-zero solution of H_i and G_j is obtained.

Example 8

```
do i₁ = 1, m
    do i₂ = 1, n
        A[i₁ + 1, i₂] = A[i₂, i₁ + 1] + B[i₁ + i₂ + 2, 1] * B[1, i₁ + i₂ - 1]
    enddo enddo;
do i₁ = 1, m
    do i₂ = 1, n
        B[i₁ + i₂, -i₁ + i₂ - 2] = B[-i₁ - i₂ + 1, i₁ - i₂] +
                        A[2 * i₁ - i₂ + 3, i₂ - 1] - A[-i₁ - 1, -i₁ + 2]
    enddo enddo
```

$$A_1^1 = \begin{bmatrix} 1 & 0 \\ 0 & 1 \end{bmatrix}, \quad a_1^1 = \begin{bmatrix} 1 \\ 0 \end{bmatrix}, \quad A_2^1 = \begin{bmatrix} 0 & 1 \\ 1 & 0 \end{bmatrix}, \quad a_2^1 = \begin{bmatrix} 0 \\ 1 \end{bmatrix},$$

$$B_1^1 = \begin{bmatrix} 1 & 1 \\ 0 & 0 \end{bmatrix}, \quad b_1^1 = \begin{bmatrix} 2 \\ 1 \end{bmatrix}, \quad B_2^1 = \begin{bmatrix} 0 & 0 \\ 1 & 1 \end{bmatrix}, \quad b_2^1 = \begin{bmatrix} 1 \\ -1 \end{bmatrix},$$

$$A_1^2 = \begin{bmatrix} 2 & -1 \\ 0 & 1 \end{bmatrix}, \quad a_1^2 = \begin{bmatrix} 3 \\ -1 \end{bmatrix}, \quad A_2^2 = \begin{bmatrix} -1 & 0 \\ -1 & 0 \end{bmatrix}, \quad a_2^2 = \begin{bmatrix} -1 \\ 2 \end{bmatrix},$$

$$B_1^2 = \begin{bmatrix} 1 & 1 \\ -1 & 1 \end{bmatrix}, \quad b_1^2 = \begin{bmatrix} 0 \\ -2 \end{bmatrix}, \quad B_2^2 = \begin{bmatrix} -1 & -1 \\ 1 & -1 \end{bmatrix}, \quad b_2^2 = \begin{bmatrix} 1 \\ 0 \end{bmatrix}.$$

Solving the systems of equations

$$G_1(A_1^1 - A_2^1) = 0 \quad \text{and} \quad G_1(a_1^1 - a_2^1) = 0$$
$$G_2(A_1^2 - A_2^2) = 0 \quad \text{and} \quad G_2(a_1^2 - a_2^2) = 0$$
$$G_3(B_1^1 - B_2^1) = 0 \quad \text{and} \quad G_3(b_1^1 - b_2^1) = 0$$
$$G_4(B_1^2 - B_2^2) = 0 \quad \text{and} \quad G_4(b_1^2 - b_2^2) = 0$$

we have $G_1 = (s, -s)$ and $G_2 = G_3 = G_4 = (0,0)$. Therefore, we set $\beta_{A,1}^1 = 1$ and $\beta_{A,2}^2 = \beta_{B,1}^1 = \beta_{B,2}^2 = -1$. Formulating and solving the systems of equations according to the conditions in Theorem 5.2, we obtain the following solutions:

$$G_A = \begin{bmatrix} 1 & 1 \end{bmatrix}, \quad G_B = \begin{bmatrix} 1 & -1 \end{bmatrix}, \quad H_1 = \begin{bmatrix} 1 & 1 \end{bmatrix}, \quad \text{and} \quad H_2 = \begin{bmatrix} 2 & 0 \end{bmatrix}.$$

The partition element of communication-free finite-hyperplane partition contains a pair of hyperplanes in each data space and iteration space:

$$DS_A \ :: \ \{(d_1, d_2)|d_1 + d_2 = c_A\} \ \text{and} \ \{(d_1, d_2)|d_1 + d_2 = -c_A + 3\}\}$$
$$DS_B \ :: \ \{(d_1, d_2)|d_1 - d_2 = c_B\} \ \text{and} \ \{(d_1, d_2)|d_1 - d_2 = -c_B + 3\}\}$$
$$IS_1 \ :: \ \{(i_1, i_2)|i_1 + i_2 = c_1\} \ \text{and} \ \{(i_1, i_2)|i_1 + i_2 = -c_1 + 1\}$$
$$IS_2 \ :: \ \{(i_1, i_2)|2i_1 = c_2\} \ \text{and} \ \{(i_1, i_2)|2i_1 = -c_2 - 1\}$$

for $c_A = c_B = c_1 + 1 = c_2 + 2$. □

6 Conclusions

This paper has addressed the issue of communication-free hyperplane partitioning of nested loops. This has previously been addressed as an array distribution/alignment problem. By explicitly modeling the iteration and data spaces and the relation between them, a more precise and more extensive treatment has been provided. Work is in progress in extending this work to develop strategies for effectively partitioning loops that are not amenable to communication-free partitions.

References

[1] D. Callahan and K. Kennedy. Compiling programs for distributed-memory multiprocessors. *The Journal of Supercomputing*, 2:151–169, Oct. 1988.

[2] M. Chen, Y. Choo, and J. Li. Compiling parallel programs by optimizing performance. *The Journal of Supercomputing*, 2:171–207, Oct. 1988.

[3] H. M. Gerndt. Array distribution in SUPERB. In *Proceedings 1989 ACM International Conference on Supercomputing*, pages 164–174, Athens, Greece, June 1989.

[4] M. Gupta and P. Banerjee. Automatic data partitioning on distributed memory multiprocessors. Technical Report UILU-ENG-90-2248, Coordinated Science Laboratory, College of Engineering, University of Illinois at Urbana-Champaign, Oct. 1990.

[5] C.-H. Huang and P. Sadayappan. Communication-free hyperplane partitioning of nested loops. Technical Report OSU-CISRC-7/91-TR18, Dept. of Comp/Info Sci., Ohio State Univ., July 1991.

[6] K. Knobe, J. D. Lukas, and G. L. Steele Jr. Data optimization: Allocation of arrays to reduce communication on SIMD machines. *J. Par. Dist. Comp.*, 8(2):102–118, Feb. 1990.

[7] C. Koelbel, P. Mehrotra, and J. van Rosendale. Supporting shared data structures on distributed memory machines. In *Proc. Principles and Practice of Parallel Programming*, pages 177–186, 1990.

[8] J. Li and M. Chen. Index domain alignment: Minimizing cost of cross-referencing between distributed arrays. Technical Report YALEU/DCS/TR-275, Dept. of Comp. Sc., Yale Univ, 1989.

[9] J. Ramanujam. *Compile-time Techniques for Parallel Execution of Loops on Distributed Memory Multiprocessors*. PhD thesis, Dept. of Comp/Info. Sc., Ohio State Univ., 1990.

[10] J. Ramanujam and P. Sadayappan. Compile-time techniques for data distribution for distributed-memory machines. *IEEE Transactions on Parallel and Distributed Systems*, 1991. To appear.

[11] A. Rogers and K. Pingali. Process decomposition through locality of reference. In *Proc. ACM SIGPLAN 89 Conf. Programming Language Design and Implementation*, pages 69–80, 1989.

13 Parallelizing Loops with Indirect Array References or Pointers

L.-C. Lu and M. Chen
Yale University

Abstract

This paper presents a hybrid compiler/run-time approach for parallelizing loops with indirections and pointers. A *scheduler* is generated by the compiler based on information deduced from dependence analysis and program slicing. At run-time, the scheduler records dynamic dependences and allocates work to processors based on the run-time reference patterns. The central point is that compiler analysis can help to make the overhead incurred by the run-time scheduler insignificantly low. Two new techniques are developed: (1) *scheduler generation* using program slicing and *dependence recording procedures*, and (2) *redundant reference elimination* for reducing both the space and time required to record the dynamic references. The effectiveness of this approach is demonstrated by parallelizing a waveform-relaxation-based circuit simulator, which is a 12,000-line C program.

1 Introduction

Automatic parallelization has so far been unsuccessful in dealing with many real-world programs where extensive indirect array references or pointers are used. Though programs using pointers can be analyzed to some extent [7, 12, 13, 14, 16, 19, 20], those containing input-dependent or dynamic-changing structures are not amenable to compile-time analysis. For such programs, many run-time scheduling techniques have been proposed [10, 31, 25, 27, 26, 29, 30, 32, 35].

In this paper, we present a hybrid compile-time and run-time approach where a *scheduler* is generated by the compiler based on information deduced from static analysis. At run-time, the scheduler records dynamic data references and allocates work to processors based on the run-time reference patterns. The central point is that compiler analysis can help to make the overhead incurred by the run-time scheduler insignificantly low, thereby lessening the major problem often faced by a run-time system.

In this context, the compiler's main task is to do *scheduler generation* in addition to *parallel program generation*. Upon seeing each read (or write) reference, the *scheduler generator* emits a call to a *recording procedure* for flow dependence (or anti- or output dependence) in conjunction with the necessary *static* program slices [33] that control the program's flow to that reference. However, care must be taken to avoid either the space or time blowing up due to the sheer number of references in any real program. Those indirect references or pointers that do not produce dependences (e.g. pointer dereferencing, induction variable, etc.), or produce only redundant dependences, must be identified and no calls to the recording procedure shall be emitted for them. The technique is called *redundant reference elimination* (RRE).

Our approach applies to both FORTRAN-style programs with indirect array references and C-style programs with pointers.

The rest of the paper is organized as follows. In Section 2, we survey various run-time parallelization approaches by classifying them according to (1) how and when work is assigned to processors, (2) how the work is scheduled within each processor. We also compare our work with related work, in both run-time scheduling and redundant dependence elimination. In Section 3, we first give an overview of our system, and then present the main technique of scheduler generation with algorithms for the recording procedures. In Section 4, we describe several redundant reference elimination techniques. In Section 5, preliminary experimental results are presented.

2 A Survey of Run-time Loop Parallelization Approaches

2.1 Characterizing Loop-Parallelization Techniques

Various run-time loop parallelization (automatic or manual) approaches can be broadly characterized by two orthogonal factors: (1) *assignment strategy* specifying how and when work is assigned to processors and (2) *scheduling method* dictating how the work is scheduled within each processor. We consider three assignment strategies and two scheduling methods as follows:

Assignment Strategies

compile-time: The work is assigned at compile-time, independent of any input data or dynamic behavior of the program.

run-time invariant: The work is assigned at run-time but before entering the loop, and stays invariant throughout the entire loop execution.

run-time dynamic: The work is assigned to processors during the loop execution, and the behavior of the computation may affect the assignment.

Scheduling Methods To describe scheduling methods for loop iterations, we represent each iteration as a node of a directed graph, which will be formally defined as the *iteration dependence graph* (IDG) in Section 3.3. Any loop-carried dependence from iteration I to iteration J is represented by a directed edge from node I to node J. An IDG is always acyclic because the directed arcs represent loop-carried dependences, and, for any two dependent iterations, one must be lexically prior to the other.

Since any IDG is acyclic, we can define the notion of the *wavefront number* of a node: the maximum path length leading into the node from some source node, where a source node is one that does not have any incoming edge. A *wavefront* is just the set of all nodes with the same wavefront number. Clearly, those iterations of the same wavefront can execute in parallel. Thus if the set of wavefronts of a loop is known either at compile-time or at run-time before entering the loop, it can be used to determine the execution sequence of the iterations beforehand. One technical detail is that a global synchronization between the processors is required to control the progress from one wavefront to the next.

Another way of scheduling the iterations is *data-driven*, which allows each iteration to start execution as soon as all its required data become available. In this case, the synchronization among the processors is done locally in a distributed fashion.

	Compile-time	run-time Invariant	run-time Dynamic
Wavefront	CW	IW	DW
Data-driven	CD	ID	DD

Figure 1: Loop-parallelization techniques characterized by assignment strategies and scheduling methods

The choice of the two methods depends on the nature of the computation and the tradeoffs in the implementation cost. The wavefront method is most suitable for programs with regular data structures, where the schedule can be obtained at compile-time. The advantage is that there will be no overhead to support data-driven execution. For programs with irregular data structures, where the computation load of different iterations in the same wavefront can vary a great deal, the data-driven method usually works better because the wavefront method will incur unnecessary delay due to the global synchronization.

Characterization Using these two orthogonal factors, we can now characterize various compile-time and run-time loop-parallelization techniques. For each of the entries on compile-time techniques in the table below, an example is given. The run-time techniques are described in greater detail since they relate closely to our work.

CW Performing loop skewing followed by iteration space tiling is an example of compiler-time assignment and wavefront scheduling.

CD Assigns iterations to processors randomly. Data-driven scheduling is the natural choice to combine with random assignment.

IW Saltz, Mirchandaney, et al. [26, 29, 30] describe a technique where an *inspector* collects data references of a code block or a DoConsider loop at run-time, constructs a DAG representing the dependences, and assigns work to processors by partitioning the DAG. An *executor* then computes the code block or the loop on either shared-memory or distributed-memory machines.

ID Johnson, Zukowski and Shea [31] at IBM have developed a parallel circuit simulator running on the Victor multiprocessor systems consisting of an array of transputers. A hand-coded run-time module reads input data structures, analyzes dependences, partitions the loop iteration space and the data structures associated with it, and assigns each portion to a processor. The processors run in a data-driven fashion, sending required circuit information between one another. The module is written with the knowledge of the specific application program as well as properties of input streams.

DW Computing wavefront at the last minute when tasks are dynamically assigned seems hardly worthwhile; using data-driven execution will be much easier and more efficient.

DD Fang, Tang, Yew and Zhu [10] describe a method in which each iteration of the loop as a *task*. It uses data-driven scheduling in the sense that all active tasks, defined to be those whose predecessors have been completed, are placed in a *task pool*. Whenever a processor becomes free, it goes to the task pool and picks up an executable task. The *guided self-scheduling* method from Polychronopoulos and Kuck [27] and the *shortest-delay self-scheduling* method from Tang, Yew and Zhu [32] also fall into this class.

In addition to the above, Zhu and Yew [35] and Midkiff and Padua [25] have developed techniques to insert the synchronization primitives into loops with loop-carried dependence to ensure proper parallel execution. These methods should be combinable with all three assignment strategies.

Our Work The dynamic scheduling approach we are going to describe falls into the class of run-time invariant assignment using either wavefront or data-driven schedule, each requiring different code for house-keeping. We choose to investigate run-time invariant assignment because (1) many important applications such as circuit simulators [31], computational fluid dynamic computation and sparse matrix solvers [26, 29, 30] can be dealt with effectively with this strategy, and (2) the techniques to be presented can be extended for run-time dynamic assignment strategy (which will be part of our future work).

2.2 Related Work

Comparison with Shared-Memory Model Experimental results [10, 27, 32] show that the overhead of systems using run-time dynamic assignment with asynchronous data-driven schedule are low on shared-memory machines. But techniques such as the task pool can incur high communication overhead on distributed-memory machines.

Comparing with Saltz et al.'s Approach The work by Saltz et al. on run-time systems [26, 29, 30] for both shared-memory and distributed-memory machines can be characterized as a pure run-time approach in the sense that all mechanisms (DAG encoding routine, inspector routines, etc.) pertaining to the scheduler are hand-written run-time library routines. Code blocks and variables of the source program are annotated for the needs of run-time support. Their work focuses on scientific applications written in FORTRAN with simple loop structures and reference patterns where the data size rather than redundant references is the main problem.

In contrast, our scheduler is generated by the scheduler generator for each application program, customized by the program slices extracted from the original program. This meta-level processing is necessary because the application at hand is a large C program with complex pointer structures rather than special forms of FORTRAN loops. In this scheduler generation framework, we can deal with nested loops where each level can be recursively scheduled over the processors, useful for problems operating over a hierarchy of more and more refined data structures. In addition, compile-time analysis such as redundant reference elimination can be used to lower the run-time overhead significantly.

Comparison with Work on Redundant Dependence Elimination Li and Abu-Sufah [22], Midkiff and Padua [25], and Krothapalli and Sadayappan [18] have studied *redundant dependence elimination* techniques in the context of parallelizing loops by inserting synchronization primitives. Such analysis reduces the number of synchronizations issued.

Our work is motivated by distributed-memory machines where communication costs must be carefully considered. We consider iteration-level parallelism, which is more coarse-grained than the shared-memory approach. Since data must be partitioned, it is more important to collect dependent iterations into the same processor to minimize communication. The focus will be on distributing the independent iterations over different processors as opposed to overlapping the execution of dependent iterations. These differences in perspective result in quite different techniques for reducing redundant references. We will discuss these in Section 4.

3 Scheduler Generator

3.1 System Overview

The hybrid system consists of a run-time component and a compile-time component as shown in Figure 2. The run-time component consists of, in addition to the target parallel program, an *IDG-constructor*, an *IDG-partitioner*, and a *data partitioner* customized for the source program.

The IDG-constructor builds the iteration dependence graph (IDG) at run time. The IDG-partitioner then assigns and schedules loop iterations by performing graph-partitioning on the IDG. By the so-called

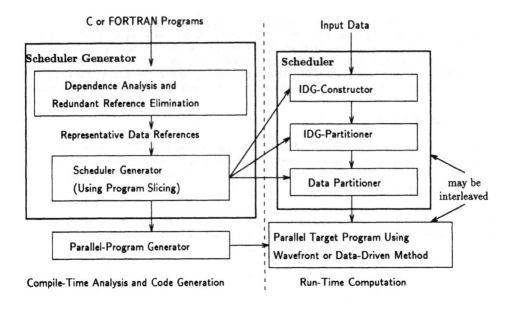

Figure 2: Structure of the Hybrid Compiler/Run-Time Parallelization System

owner-compute rule (the inverse) of SPMD style programs, the input data structure is partitioned according to the iteration partition over the IDG. Together, these three parts are referred to as the *run-time scheduler*.

The compiler consists of two main components: a *schedule generator* and a *parallel-program generator*. We do not describe the parallel-program generator in this paper, which is an extension of our previous work [21] and closely relates to the work by Saltz et al. [29]. The focus is on the scheduler generator, and in particular, the one with low run-time overhead. To construct the IDG, read and write references of the source program must be recorded at run-time. If one does this naively, the space and time may both blow up for large programs. The idea behind our approach is to examine the minimum number of references necessary to construct an IDG. Some references such as pointer dereferencing and induction variables do not create dependence. Others form equivalence classes whereby only representative ones need to be recorded.

In the following, we first describe the IDG representation, then the primitives for scheduler generation, and finally the methods and optimizations. A C programming example is also given. Some terminologies and notations first.

3.2 Terminology and Notation

Throughout this paper, programming examples with pointers are written in a C-like notation. Programming examples with indirect array references are written in a FORTRAN-like notation.

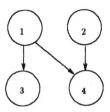

Figure 3: An Example of an Iteration Dependence Graph

Iteration Space of a Loop Nest Let $[a, b]$ be an *interval domain* of integers from a to b. An *iteration space E* [34] of an e-level *perfectly nested* loop

$$\text{DO } (i_1 = l_1, u_1) \{$$
$$\text{DO } (\ldots) \{$$
$$\text{DO } (i_e = l_e, u_e) \{$$
$$\text{body } \} \qquad \} \}$$

is the Cartesian product $[l_1, u_1] \times \ldots \times [l_e, u_e]$. Throughout the paper, we use I to denote the tuple of loop indices $(i_1, \ldots, i_e)$. Similarly for J and K. With the tuple notation, the loop nest above can be rewritten as $\text{DO } (I{:}E)\{body\}$.

Definitions of Data Dependences We now review data dependences between statements. Let S_1 and S_2 be two statements of a program. A *flow dependence* exists from S_1 to S_2 if S_1 writes data that can subsequently be read by S_2. An *anti-dependence* exists from S_1 to S_2 if S_1 reads data that S_2 can subsequently overwrite. An *output dependence* exists from S_1 to S_2 if S_1 writes data that S_2 can subsequently overwrite. We use the notation $S_1 \Rightarrow S_2$ to denote a dependence from S_1 to S_2.

If, at iteration J, S_1 computes data that is read by S_2 at iteration K, then we say S_2 at iteration K is flow dependent on S_1 at iteration J, denoted by $S_1@J \Rightarrow S_2@K$. The same notation is used for anti- and output dependences.

Loop-independent and Loop-carried Dependences We define "$\prec$" to be the lexicographic ordering: we say $I \prec J$ if there exists k, $1 \leq k \leq d$, such that $i_l = j_l$ for all l, $l < k$, and $i_k < j_k$. Similarly, we say $I \preceq J$ if $I \prec J$ or $I = J$.

Clearly, if dependence $S_1@J \Rightarrow S_2@K$ exists, then $J \preceq K$ must hold. A dependence $S_1@J \Rightarrow S_2@K$ is either *loop-independent* if $J = K$, or *loop-carried* if $J \prec K$.

Dependence Analysis Dependence analysis techniques presented in [3, 4, 5, 6, 23, 24, 34] can analyze array subscripts which are linear in terms of loop indices. Dependence analysis of pointers has been studied in [7, 12, 13, 14, 16, 19, 20]. We rely on these techniques to perform redundant reference elimination, which is described in Section 4.

From data references, we can detect dependences among iterations. The dependence information among iterations is captured by the *iteration dependence graph* defined below.

3.3 The Iteration Dependence Graph (IDG)

We define the *iteration dependence graph* (IDG for short) of a loop L to be a directed graph with one vertex for each iteration of L. There is an edge from node J to node K, denoted by $J \Rightarrow K$, in the IDG if and only if for some statements S_1 and S_2 in the loop a loop-carried dependence $S_1@J \Rightarrow S_2@K$ exists in L. Since only loop-carried dependences are presented in the IDG, $J \prec K$ must hold for an edge $J \Rightarrow K$ in the IDG. Therefore, any IDG is acyclic.

Let "$\overset{*}{\Rightarrow}$" be the reflexive and transitive closure of the dependence relation "$\Rightarrow$" over iterations. If $J \overset{*}{\Rightarrow} K$ holds, then iterations J and K are dependent. If neither $J \overset{*}{\Rightarrow} K$ nor $K \overset{*}{\Rightarrow} J$ holds, then iterations J and K are independent.

An example of an IDG is shown in Figure 3. Iterations are assigned to processors by partitioning the IDG. In order to reduce communication overhead for distributed-memory machines, dependent iterations, e.g. iterations 1 and 3, should be aggregated to the same processor. Additionally, in order to maximize parallelism, independent iterations, e.g. iterations 1 and 2, should be distributed to different processors.

This representation is similar to the DAG representation in [8, 28, 26], except that an IDG is defined with respect to a loop nest while the others are defined with respect to a set of recursive definitions or an annotated code block.

As discussed above, the IDG is built at run-time by the IDG-constructor, which is generated by the compiler. The IDG-constructor records read and write references to build the IDG. We now define the notion of *read set* and *last write* to capture the relationship between data references and loop iterations.

3.4 Read Set and Last Write

Let X be a *memory location* being referenced. We define $\mathcal{R}(X)$, called the *read set* for X, to be a set containing the iterations I in the iteration space at which X is read after X is last written.

Similarly, we define $\mathcal{W}(X)$, called the *last write* for X, to be the iteration at which X is last written, or null if X is not yet written.

Note that, for FORTRAN, "memory location" is replaced by "array name" applied to an "array index".

3.5 Recording Procedures

For each reference in the source program, the compiler generates a call to a procedure which updates the read set and the last write, deduces dependences and constructs edges in the IDG. Since a reference can be either a read or a write, we need two procedures for constructing the IDG. Procedure record_f_dep is for recording possible flow dependence caused by a read reference. Procedure record_o_a_dep is for recording possible output and anti-dependences caused by a write reference. We now discuss these two procedures in detail.

Procedure record_f_dep We first discuss the procedure record_f_dep for recording possible flow dependence caused by a read reference. Let X be the memory location of a read reference, and let I be the current iteration. Clearly, I should be added to the read set $\mathcal{R}(X)$. If the last write $\mathcal{W}(X)$ is not null, i.e. $J = \mathcal{W}(X)$, then location X is last written at iteration J and the flow dependence $J \Rightarrow I$ exists, which implies an edge in the IDG. On the other hand, if $\mathcal{W}(X)$ is null, then X has not yet been written and there is no flow dependence.

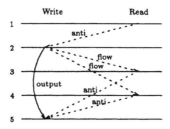

Figure 4: An Example of Dependences

Procedure record_o_a_dep We now discuss the procedure record_o_a_dep for recording possible flow and anti-dependences caused by a write reference. Let X be the memory location of a write reference, and let I be the current iteration. If the last write $\mathcal{W}(X)$ is not null, i.e. $J = \mathcal{W}(X)$, then X is also written at iteration J and the output dependence $J \Rightarrow I$ exists. Now I is the last iteration which writes X; therefore, the last write $\mathcal{W}(X)$ should be assigned a new value I. On the other hand, if the last write $\mathcal{W}(X)$ is null, then there is no output dependence and we only need to assign I to $\mathcal{W}(X)$.

Similar discussion holds for anti-dependences as follows. If the read set $\mathcal{R}(X)$ is not empty, then for all J in $\mathcal{R}(X)$, the anti-dependence $J \Rightarrow I$ exists. In addition, the read set $\mathcal{R}(X)$ should be reset to the empty set because there is no new read after the latest write at iteration I. To summarize, procedures record_f_dep and record_o_a_dep are defined as:

record_f_dep (X, I)
X:a reference location
I: an iteration
   $\mathcal{R}(X) = \mathcal{R}(X) \cup \{I\}$
   if $(\mathcal{W}(X) \neq null)$
   then $J = \mathcal{W}(X)$
        there is a flow dependence $J \Rightarrow I$
        (an edge from J to I in the IDG)

record_o_a_dep (X, I)
R:a reference location
I: an iteration
   if $(\mathcal{W}(X) \neq null)$
   then $J = \mathcal{W}(X)$
        the output dependence $J \Rightarrow I$ exists
   $\mathcal{W}(X) = I$
   for all $J \in \mathcal{R}(X)$
        the anti-dependence $J \Rightarrow I$ exists
   $\mathcal{R}(X) = \{\}$

An Example for Dependences Consider the following example: Let a location X be read at iterations 1, 3 and 4, and be written at iterations 2 and 5 as shown in Figure 4. The results from calling record_f_dep or record_o_a_dep at these iterations are:

After iteration 1, no dependence is found, $\mathcal{R}(X) = \{1\}$ and $\mathcal{W}(X) = null$.
After iteration 2, anti-dependence $1 \Rightarrow 2$ is found, $\mathcal{R}(X) = \{\}$ and $\mathcal{W}(X) = 2$.
After iteration 3, flow dependence $2 \Rightarrow 3$ is found, $\mathcal{R}(X) = \{3\}$ and $\mathcal{W}(X) = 2$.
After iteration 4, flow dependence $2 \Rightarrow 4$ is found, $\mathcal{R}(X) = \{3, 4\}$ and $\mathcal{W}(X) = 2$.
After iteration 5, output dependence $2 \Rightarrow 5$ and anti-dependences $3 \Rightarrow 5$ and $4 \Rightarrow 5$ are found, $\mathcal{R}(X) = \{\}$ and $\mathcal{W}(X) = 4$.

We now use an example to illustrate how to generate the IDG-constructor with calls to these two procedures.

3.6 Example

The example C program with pointers is in Figure 5. We want to parallelize the while loop from line 12 to line 17.

Functionality of the Program The relationships among structures and pointers are shown in Figure 6. Instances of structure **A** form a linked list, and similarly for instances of structure **B**. Each instance of **A** has two pointers **rB** and **wB** pointing to some instances of **B**, which can be different. (We use **r** for labeling a read access, **w** for labeling a write access, and **wr** for labeling an access which can be either read or write.) These two pointers take on values returned by the function **lookup**, which finds a particular instance of **B** that matches the identifier given as the first argument of **lookup** as shown in lines 9 and 10 of the code. The identifiers **id1** and **id2** are read from the input stream in line 8. Each instance of **B** has a pointer **rwC** pointing to an instance of structure **C** created by the **malloc** function.

The **while** loop goes through every instance of structure **A** where the current one is pointed by **topA**. Lines 14, 15 and 16 in the loop body read three integers to compute three other integers contained in the instances of **A**, **B** and **C** respectively.

Note that, since the pointers from instances of **B** to instances of **C** are input dependent, and dependences are determined by those pointers, this while loop cannot be parallelized by static compile-time analysis.

3.7 Algorithm for Generating A Naive IDG-Constructor

We now focus on the while loop (line 12-17) which is repeated on top of Figure 7 for easy reference.

Nodes of the IDG For each instance of the iteration space of the loop, a call to procedure create_node is generated which creates a node corresponding to the current iteration instance in the IDG. For identifying these nodes, we need an explicit loop iteration counter. In this example, variable i is used as the iteration counter. Clearly, i should be incremented for each iteration, and i is used as a parameter for the procedure calls create_node, record_f_dep and record_o_a_dep.

Edges of the IDG For each read reference, a call to procedure record_f_dep is generated which creates edges between the nodes of the IDG. For example, a read reference to location $\&(topA \rightarrow wB)$ in line 12 implies a call to record_f_dep($\&(topA \rightarrow wB), i$).

Similarly, for each write reference, a call to procedure record_o_a_dep is generated. For example, a write reference to location $\&bar$ in line 12 implies a call to record_o_a_dep($\&bar, i$).

Program Slices In addition to generating those procedure calls, we also need to copy some statements from the source loop to the IDG-constructor as follows. If a variable is necessary to determine the reference location, e.g. bar is used in the call to record_o_a_dep($\&(bar \rightarrow rwC \rightarrow valC), i$), then the set of statements that directly or indirectly contributed to the value of that variable needs to be copied from the source program to the IDG-constructor. Similarly for control statements like if-then-else, since they determine whether a location is referenced or not.

The technique of *static program slicing* [33], which is based on data flow analysis and execution trace, can be used to find the program slice with respect to one variable. A program slice with respect to a set of variables can be obtained by taking the union of slices with respect to individual variables in the set. In this example, the program slice we need consists of statements in lines 12, 13 and 17 of the source program which compute bar, foo and $topA$.

```
typedef struct C {
    int valC;
    other fields ...} *pointerC;
typedef struct B {
    int idB, valB;
    pointerC rwC;
    struct B *next; } *pointerB;
typedef struct A {
    int valA;
    pointerB rB, wB;
    struct A *next; } *pointerA;

main()
{    int id1, id2;
     pointerA nodeA, topA;
     pointerB nodeB, topB, foo, bar;
     pointerC nodeC;
     int nA, nB, i;

     scanf("%d %d",&nB,&nA);
     for(i=0; i<nB; i++) {    /* initialize B and C */
1      nodeB = (pointerB) malloc(sizeof *nodeB);
2      scanf("%d %d",&(nodeB->idB),&(nodeB->valB));
3      nodeC = (pointerC) malloc(sizeof *nodeC);
4      scanf("%d",&(nodeC->valC));
5      nodeB->rwC = nodeC; nodeB->next = topB; topB = nodeB;} /* build list */

     for(i=0; i<nA; i++) {    /* initialize A */
6      nodeA = (pointerA) malloc(sizeof *nodeA);
7      scanf("%d",&(nodeA->valA));
8      scanf("%d %d",&id1,&id2); /* read input id */
9      nodeA->rB = (pointerB) lookup(id1,topB); /* find two B instances */
10     nodeA->wB = (pointerB) lookup(id2,topB); /* that match the id */
11     nodeA->next = topA; topA = nodeA; } /* build list */

     while(topA != NULL) {
12     bar = topA->wB;
13     foo = topA->rB;
14     bar->rwC->valC = foo->rwC->valC+1;
15     bar->valB = foo->valB+2;
16     topA->valA = topA->valA+3;
17     topA = topA->next; } }

int lookup(id,topB)
int id; pointerB topB;
{    pointerB nodeB;
     nodeB = topB;
     while(nodeB != NULL) {
        if(nodeB->idB == id) return(nodeB);
        nodeB = nodeB->next; }}
```

Figure 5: An example

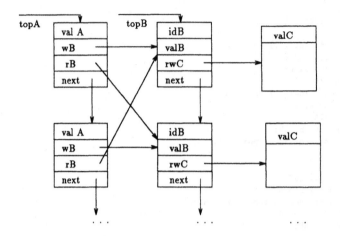

Figure 6: Relationship among structures and pointers of the example

The Source Loop from Figure 5:

```
     while(topA != NULL) {
12       bar = topA->wB;
13       foo = topA->rB;
14       bar->rwC->valC = foo->rwC->valC+1;
15       bar->valB = foo->valB+2;
16       topA->valA = topA->valA+3;
17       topA = topA->next; }
```

A Naive IDG-Constructor:

```
  i = 0;
  while  (topA ≠ NULL){
      i++; /*explicit iteration counter*/
      create_node(i); /*create a node of the IDG*/
      bar = topA → wB;                                                    /*12 slicing*/
      foo = topA → rB;                                                    /*13 slicing*/
      record_f_dep(&(topA → wB), i); record_o_a_dep(&bar, i);            /*12 recording*/
      record_f_dep(&(topA → rB), i); record_o_a_dep(&foo, i);            /*13 recording*/
      record_f_dep(&(foo → rwC → valC), i);                             /*14 recording*/
      record_o_a_dep(&(bar → rwC → valC), i);
      record_f_dep(&(foo → valB), i); record_o_a_dep(&(bar → valB), i);  /*15 recording*/
      record_f_dep(&(topA → valA), i); record_o_a_dep(&(topA → valA), i); /*16 recording*/
      record_f_dep(&(topA → next), i); record_o_a_dep(&topA, i);         /*17 recording*/
      topA = topA → next;                                                /*17 slicing*/}
```

Figure 7: IDG-constructor Consists of Program Slices and Calls to Dependence Recording Procedures

```
    i = 0;
    while  (topA ≠ NULL){
            i + +;   create_node(i);
            bar = topA → wB;                                    /* 12 slicing */
            foo = topA → rB;                                    /* 13 slicing */
            record_f_dep(&(foo → valB), i); record_o_a_dep(&(bar → valB), i); /* 15 recording */
            topA = topA → next;                                 /* 17 slicing */}
```

Figure 8: An Optimized IDG-constructor

For program slicing including control statement, let us look at the following example. The source code is on the left-hand side, and the corresponding IDG-constructor is on the right-hand side, which includes both conditional expressions as shown below:

```
while (...) {                    i = 0;
    if(a > 0)  b → c = ...       while (...) {
    else  b → d = ...      }         i + +;
                                     if(a > 0)  record_o_a_dep(&(b → c), i)
                                     else  record_o_a_dep(&(b → d), i)
                                     ...                                    }
```

Another point to mention is that we need *static* program slicing [33] instead of *dynamic* program slicing [1, 17]. The difference between the two is that the static slice is the set of all statements that might affect the value of a given variable for *any* program input, while the dynamic slice consists of all statements that actually affect the value of a variable for a *given* program input. We need static slicing because the scheduler should work for any program input. For loops with procedure calls, we need *interprocedural program slicing* [15].

3.8   Optimizing IDG-Constructor

The naive IDG-constructor constructs the IDG by recording all data references. In fact, some references do not contribute to edges in the IDG and some other references contribute to redundant edges in the IDG. All those references are called *redundant references* and should not be made into the IDG-constructor.

For this example, dependence analysis on pointers tells us that

- Instances of structure A do not cause loop-carried dependence.

- *foo* and *bar* are used for pointer dereferencing; they do not cause true dependences.

- *topA* is an "induction" variable for navigating through the linked list.

In addition, RRE says that instances of structures B and C cause identical dependences, and therefore, only the references to instances of either B or C need to be recorded. After removing those recording procedure calls for redundant references, the optimized IDG-constructor is as shown in Figure 8. The optimized IDG-constructor is much smaller and uses much less space for the read sets and the last writes.

3.9 IDG-Partitioner and Data Partitioner

Once the IDG is constructed, an IDG-partitioner partitions the nodes of the IDG into disjoint sets such that dependent iterations are aggregated into the same processor as much as possible and independent iterations are distributed to different processors. This is as hard as the *minimum cut* problem which is NP-complete [11]. Therefore, we use a heuristic to do the partition. How to choose a good heuristic algorithm is beyond the scope of this paper.

Partition on IDG induces a partition on the data using the inverse of the so-called owner-compute rule: $A(X(I))$ will be written by processor P which is assigned iteration I.

3.10 Summary of Scheduler Generating Steps

To summarize, the compiler generates the run-time scheduler in the following steps:

1. Use dependence analysis and redundant reference elimination techniques to obtain representative references in the source loop.

2. For each representative reference, generate a call to the recording procedure record_f_dep or record_o_a_dep in the IDG-constructor.

3. Find the program slice which computes the values of the variables necessary to determine the reference locations.

4. Generate a code based on a chosen heuristic for partitioning the IDG into p disjoint subsets, where p is the number of processors of the target distributed-memory machine.

5. Generate a code for data partitioning using the inverse of the owner-compute rule.

4 Redundant Reference Elimination (RRE)

We now discuss how to eliminate redundant references to reduce the run-time overhead of the scheduler. We consider both array and pointer references.

Common References to Arrays and Fields   If an array is read more than once in the loop body with common subscript expressions, then we say these reads are *common references*. Similarly for multiple writes. Clearly, all except one common reference is redundant. Therefore, the IDG-constructor only needs to record one reference from a set of common references.

Similarly, if a field of an instance of a structure is read (written) several times in the loop body, all except one reference is redundant.

Common References to Multiple Arrays and Fields   Common references to a single array or a single field can be generalized to multiple arrays and multiple fields of the same instance of a structure due to the underlying assumptions that (1) if arrays have common references, then they will be aligned and assigned to processors in the same way, and (2) an entire instance of a structure will be assigned to the same processor. For example, arrays A and B and fields x and y have common references in the following loops:

```
DO (I:E) {                      while (...) {
    A(X(I)) = ...                   a = ...
    ... = A(Y(I))                   a → x = ...
    B(X(I)) = ...                   a → y = ... }
    ... = B(Y(I)) }
```

Partial Reference If some components of subscripts are ignored in dependence analysis, then we call it *partial dependence analysis*. An array reference with some components of subscripts being ignored is called a *partial reference*. The components used in partial reference and partial dependence analysis are called *critical components*.

It is easy to see that partial dependence analysis is always conservative [34]. This is because considering more components will further differentiate the reference locations and make dependence less possible. Consider the following loops:

Loop 1   **Loop 2**

$$DO\ (i = 1, n)\ \{$$ $$DO\ (i = 1, n)\ \{$$
$$A(i, B(i)) = ...$$ $$A(i) = ...$$
$$... = A(i, C(i))\ \}$$ $$... = A(i)\ \}$$

Let the first component of the subscripts of array A be the critical component. After ignoring the second component, Loop 1 becomes Loop 2 above. No loop-carried dependence in Loop 2 implies no loop-carried dependence in Loop 1, and loop-independent dependence in Loop 2 implies that loop-independent dependence may exist in Loop 1. In fact, there is loop-independent dependence in Loop 1 only when i exists in $[1, n]$ such that $B(i) = C(i)$.

Subsumed Partial Reference

Theorem 1 *(Subsumed partial reference)*
If the partial references at critical components to array A are subsumed by complete references of the same symbolic forms to array B, then references to array A are redundant.

This is because references to B will cause more conservative dependences than references to A. Consider the following loop:

$$DO\ (I{:}E)\ \{$$
$$B(X(I)) = ...$$
$$... = B(Y(I))$$
$$A(X(I), U(I)) = ...$$
$$... = A(Y(I), V(I))\ \}$$

By choosing the first component as the critical component of subscripts of array A, Theorem 1 says that references to A are redundant.

Subsumed Pointer Reference To obtain a pointer version of Theorem 1, we need to review some definitions.

A *structure* is an object composed of a collection of *fields*. A collection of structures can be modeled by a directed graph $G = (V, E)$, which is called a *structure graph* in [19, 20]. Each vertex a in V corresponds to an instance of a structure. We use a to denote both the vertex and the structure instance represented by a. Each edge in E from vertex a to vertex b indicates that the structure instance a contains a pointer in a field to the structure instance b.

A directed graph is *rooted* at vertex r if there is a path from r to every vertex in the graph [2]. We assume that the structure graph is rooted. (Otherwise, we just add a root and some edges to make it rooted.) Vertex a is a *dominator* of vertex b if every path from the root to b contains a [2].

Theorem 2 *(Pointer version of Theorem 1)*
Let vertex a be a dominator of vertex b in the structure graph. Let x be a field of a. If the fields of b are read only when x is read and the fields of b are written only when x is written, then the references to all fields of b are redundant.

In the following example, if a is a dominator of b in the structure graph, then Theorem 2 says that write references to field y of b is redundant:

$$\text{while } (\ldots) \{$$
$$a = \ldots$$
$$a \rightarrow x = \ldots$$
$$a \rightarrow b \rightarrow y = \ldots \}$$

This theorem can be used to detect that references to foo→rwC→valC and bar→rwC→valC are redundant in the code in Figure 5.

Common References under Simultaneous Permutation of Components

Theorem 3 *(Simultaneous permutation of components)*
Common references under simultaneous permutation of components are redundant.

Consider the following loop:

$$\text{DO } (I{:}E) \{$$
$$A(X(I), Y(I)) = \ldots$$
$$\ldots = A(U(I), V(I))$$
$$B(Y(I), X(I)) = \ldots$$
$$\ldots = B(V(I), U(I)) \}$$

This theorem says that the references to either A or B, but not both, are redundant.

5 Preliminary Experimental Results

The application we use to demonstrate the effectiveness of our techniques is a waveform-relaxation circuit simulator [9] developed at IBM by Shea, Johnson and Zukowski [31]. The simulator is a 12,000-line C program. At the moment, dependence analysis, redundant reference elimination, and code generation are all hand-compiled. The experimental timing of executing the circuit simulation loop for a specific circuit is collected as follows:

- The sequential loop takes 6000 seconds on a Sun Sparcstation 1.

- The run-time scheduler takes 37.65 seconds on a Sun Sparcstation 1.

- The parallel loop takes 99.45 seconds on a 256-transputer Victor, the 256-node transputer array developed at IBM.

The scheduling time is 0.63% (37.65/6000) of the sequential execution time. Experimental results from Saltz et al. [30] show that the overhead of their run-time scheduler ranges from 20% to 60% of the sequential execution time of the source code. The overhead of their scheduler is much higher because their programming examples do not contain redundant references, while the circuit simulator we use contains many redundant references. However, if we apply Saltz et al.'s scheduler, which records all references, to the circuit simulator, the overhead will still be more or less in the range of 20% to 60%.

Therefore, our run-time scheduling system with redundant reference elimination reduces the scheduling overhead by one to two orders of magnitude for large programs with many redundant references.

The scheduling time is 27.5% of the parallel execution time:

$$37.65/(37.65 + 99.45) = 27.5\%.$$

Note that the overhead is significantly amplified by parallelization. This is another reason why using compile-time analysis to reduce the run-time overhead is critical.

Acknowledgment

We are grateful to Dennis Shea, Tom Johnson, and Deborra Zukowski for spending many hours telling us about the sequential as well as the parallel versions of the circuit simulator. Their work provided us with insights into the systematic approach to parallelizing programs with pointers. Our thanks also go to Joel Saltz for helpful discussions on the inspector/executor approach.

The generous supports provided by an IBM student research associate fund 1990-91, Office of Naval Research Contract N00014-91-J-1559, and National Science Foundation contract CCR-8908285 are greatly appreciated.

References

[1] H. Agrawal and J.R. Horgan. Dynamic program slicing. In *Proc. SIGPLAN '90 Conf. Program. Lang. Design and Implement.*, pages 246–256, 1990.

[2] A.V. Aho, J.E. Hopcroft, and J.D. Ullman. *The Design and Analysis of Computer Algorithms.* Addison-Wesley Publishing Company, 1974.

[3] J.R. Allen and K. Kennedy. Automatic translation of fortran programs to vector form. *ACM Trans. on Programming Languages and Systems*, 9(4):491–542, October 1987.

[4] U. Banerjee. Data dependence in ordinary programs. Master's thesis, University of Illinois at Urbana-Champaign, November 1976.

[5] U. Banerjee. *Dependence Analysis for Supercomputing.* Kluwer Academic Publishers, 1988.

[6] M. Burke and R. Cytron. Interprocedural dependence analysis and parallelization. In *Proceedings of the SIGPLAN'86 Symposium on Compiler Construction*, pages 162–175. ACM, 1986.

[7] D.R. Chase, M. Wegman, and F.K. Zadeck. Analysis of pointers and structures. In *Proc. SIGPLAN '90 Conf. Program. Lang. Design and Implement.*, pages 296–310, 1990.

[8] Marina C. Chen. A design methodology for synthesizing parallel algorithms and architectures. *Journal of Parallel and Distributed Computing*, December 1986.

[9] P. Debefve, F. Odeh, and A.E. Ruehli. *Waveform Techniques*, pages 41–127. Elsevier Science Publishers B.V., 1987.

[10] Z. Fang, P. Tang, P.C. Yew, and C.Q. Zhu. Dynamic processor self-scheduling for general parallel nested loops. *IEEE Trans. on Computers*, 39(7):919–929, July 1990.

[11] M.R. Garey and D.S. Johnson. *Computers and Intracrability A Guide to the Theory of NP-Completeness.* 1979.

[12] W.L. Harrison. Compiling Lisp for evaluation on a tightly coupled multiprocessor. Technical Report 565, University of Illinois at Urbana-Champaign, March 1986.

[13] L.J. Hendren and A. Nicolau. Parallelizing programs with recursive data structures. *IEEE Trans. on Parallel and Distributed Systems*, 1(1):35–47, January 1990.

[14] S. Horwitz, P. Pfeiffer, and T. Reps. Dependence analysis for pointer variables. In *Proc. SIGPLAN '89 Conf. Program. Lang. Design and Implement.*, pages 28–40, 1988.

[15] S. Horwitz, T. Reps, and D. Binkley. Interprocedural slicing using dependence graph. *ACM Trans. on Programming Languages and Systems*, 12(1):26–60, Jan. 1990.

[16] N.D. Jones and S. Muchnick. A flexible approach to interprocedural data flow analysis and programs with recursive data structures. In *9th ACM Symp. Principles Program. Lang.*, pages 66–74, 1982.

[17] B. Korel and J. Laski. Dynamic program slicing. *Information Processing Letters*, 29:155–163, October 1988.

[18] V.P. Krothapalli and P. Sadayappan. Removal of redundant dependences in DOACROSS loops with constant dependences. In *Proc. of the Third ACM SIGPLAN Symposium on Principles & Practice of Parallel Programming*, pages 51–60, 1991.

[19] J.R. Larus and P.N. Hilfinger. Detecting conflicts between structure accesses. In *Proc. SIGPLAN '88 Conf. Program. Lang. Design and Implement.*, pages 21–34, 1988.

[20] J.R. Larus and P.N. Hilfinger. Restructuring Lisp programs for concurrent execution. In *ACM/SIGPLAN PPEALS Parallel Program.: Exp. Appl. Lang. Syst.*, pages 100–110, 1988.

[21] J. Li and M.C. Chen. Generating explicit communication from shared-memory program references. In *Proc. Supercomputing '90*, pages 865–876, 1990.

[22] Z. Li and W. Abu-Sufah. On reducing data synchronization in multiprocessed loops. *IEEE Trans. on Computer*, C-36(1):105–109, January 1987.

[23] Z. Li, P.C. Yew, and C.Q. Zhu. An efficient data dependence analysis for parallelizing compilers. *IEEE Trans. on Parallel and Distributed Systems*, 1(1):26–34, January 1990.

[24] L.C. Lu and M.C. Chen. Subdomain dependence test for massive parallelism. In *Proc. Supercomputing '90*, pages 962–972, 1990.

[25] S.P. Midkiff and D.A. Padua. Compiler algorithms for synchronization. *IEEE Trans. on Computer*, C-36(12):1485–1495, December 1987.

[26] R. Mirchandaney, J.H. Saltz, R.M. Smith, D.M. Nicol, and K. Crowley. Principles of runtime support for parallel processors. In *Proc. 1988 ACM Int'l. Conf. Supercomput.*, pages 140–152, July 1988.

[27] C.D. Polychronopoulos and D.J. Kuck. Guided self-scheduling: A pratical scheduling scheme for parallel supercomputers. *IEEE Trans. on Computers*, C-36(12):1425–1439, Dec. 1987.

[28] J.H. Saltz and M.C. Chen. Automated problem mapping: the crystal run-time system. In *The Proceedings of the Conference on Hypercube Microprocessors, Knoxville, TN*, September 1986.

[29] J.H. Saltz, K. Crowley, R. Mirchandaney, and H. Berryman. Run-time scheduling and execution of loops on message passing machines. *J. Parallel Distributed Comput.*, 8:303–312, April 1990.

[30] J.H. Saltz, R. Mirchandaney, and K. Crowley. Run-time parallelization and scheduling of loops. *IEEE Trans. on Computers*, 40(5):603–612, May 1991.

[31] D.G. Shea, T.A. Johnson, and D.J. Zukowski. Joint study. *IBM T.J. Watson Research Center*, 1990-1991.

[32] P. Tang, P.C. Yew, and C.Q. Zhu. Impact of self-scheduling order on performance of multiprocessor systems. In *Proc. 1988 ACM Int'l. Conf. Supercomput.*, pages 593–603, July 1988.

[33] M. Weiser. Program slicing. *IEEE Trans. on Software Engineering*, 10(4):352–357, July 1984.

[34] M. Wolfe. *Optimizing Supercompilers for Supercomputers*. The MIT Press, 1989.

[35] C.Q. Zhu and P.C. Yew. A scheme to enforce data dependence on large multiprocessor systems. *IEEE Trans. on Computer*, C-36(6):726–739, June 1987.

14 Register Allocation, Renaming and Their Impact on Fine-Grain Parallelism

A. Nicolau, R. Potasman, and H. Wang
University of California at Irvine

Abstract

It is well known that renaming is an important tool for enhancing parallelization. However, at the fine-grain level renaming involves the addition of extra registers which may affect register allocation. Thus a tradeoff between register allocation and parallelism has to be made to optimize the code performance for fine-grain parallel machines (i.e. pipelined, VLIW's, superscalars). Because of the complexity involved, previous compilers have avoided making this tradeoff by separating register allocation from code reorganization (scheduling). Unfortunately, this separation can lead to severe performance problems. We propose in this paper a new approach which circumvents these traditional problems while yielding an efficient implementation. Some benchmarks are used to illustrate the effect of our technique.

1 Introduction

Registers have been considered for years as one of the most precious resources in any architecture design. Integration (space) and timing (address decoding) limitations restrict the total number of registers on chip. Accordingly, a good style of programming and/or a good policy of register allocation for a compiler has been one that makes efficient use of registers. This has been accomplished by compiling source programs into machine language using minimal number of registers,

*This work was supported in part by ONR grant N00014-91-J-1406 and NSF grant CCR8996124.

assigning the same registers to variables whose runtime life-spans do not overlap. Such use of registers is beneficial for sequential machines. However, the re-use of registers in high-performance, pipelined, fine-grain parallel architectures may severely decrease performance since it limits the ability of fine-grain parallelizing compilers to compact programs [10, 6].

In parallel architectures, ideally, only true data dependency (and resources availability) should limit the parallelism. Re-use of registers limits the achievable parallelism since it introduces a false ordering (dependency) between operations.[1] This could cause a substantial degradation in performance. Consider, for example, the following program segment:

```
1:    a := b + c;
2:    d := a * e;
3:    a := f + g;
4:    h := a + k;
```

Here, $d := a * e$ has to be executed *after* $a := b + c$. That is a strict data-dependency. On the other hand, $a := f + g$ is prevented from being scheduled in parallel with $a := b + c$, *only because* it re-uses register a which is read by $d := a * e$. This dependency is called an *anti-dependency* [6]. But this dependency need not limit the parallelism. Renaming register a to a' would yield the following:

```
1:    a := b + c;        a' := f + g;
2:    d := a * e;        h := a' + k;
```

which is two cycles shorter. Thus by using an additional register (a') we have increased the parallelism of the program. Another source of false dependency is called *output dependency* which occurs when two operations write to the same output register. In the example above, operations $a := f + g$ and $a := b + c$ modify the same registers. Without renaming, $a := f + g$ cannot move above $a := b + c$. As will be shown in Section 2, the effect of renaming becomes even more important while performing loop pipelining [16, 12, 7, 2] when operations are allowed to move out of their original iteration in order to achieve parallelization both across and within loop iterations.

Thus fine-grain parallelizing compilers face two mutually contradictory constraints: on the one hand registers should be aggressively re-used to avoid spilling and its ensuing inefficiency, while

---

[1]While in uni-cycle operations this artificial dependency prevents an operation from moving up one step, for multi-cycle operations it blocks a move of several cycles (equal to the latency of the operation which causes this anti-dependency).

on the other hand anti/output dependencies should be eliminated to increase parallelism. In this context the time (before/during/after compaction) when register allocation is done becomes critical to the quality of the code produced. This has long presented a serious problem for such compilers.

If register allocation is carried out before compaction, the best strategy to avoid undully limiting parallelism is to use as many registers as necessary (essentially equivalent to transforming the code into quasi static-single-assignment (SSA) form [5]). Unfortunately, the total number of registers needed is usually greater than the number physically available. Hence, some registers have to be re-used. Ideally, we would like to refrain from re-use in places where it actually inhibits the compaction, and allow re-use where it is insignificant. However, if register allocation precedes the compaction phase, this information is unavailable and we may end up with re-use of registers in the wrong places.

A second approach is to perform register allocation after compaction has been completed. This means that during compaction unlimited (virtual) registers are allowed.[2] In a post compaction pass, the virtual registers are mapped to the actual architecture's registers. Of course, if the number of registers needed exceeds the number of actual registers—spilling to memory is required. Performing spilling after compaction may severely damage the carefully parallelized ("packed") code, yielding much less efficient schedules. In fact, the performance obtained by this approach on its own can be so poor that compilers using it (e.g., Cydrome, Fujitsu) resort to repeated compaction of the new program whenever a spill occurs. While after such iterative compaction the code quality is very good, this repeated computation can be very inefficient in cases where many spills occur.

Ideally, we would do register allocation during compaction making meaningful trade-offs possible. However, this implies dealing with two NP-hard problems (functional units allocation and register allocation) *during* compaction, making this approach exceedingly complex. Because of the difficulty involved, this approach has been avoided by existing compilers who chose one of the simpler approaches above.

In this paper we propose a simple alternative that allows the flexibility of renaming during compaction while avoiding spilling and the complexity of performing full register allocation during the parallelization process. We start by performing conventional register allocation before compaction. However, during compaction we allow renaming to remove false dependencies *that prevent*

---

[2]That is, a new virtual register is used for each computed operand and its associated use(s). This may be achieved simply during translation of the input into intermediate code, for non-loop code. However, for maximizing parallelism in loops (in the context of loop pipelining), renaming is still necessary as will be discussed in Section 2.

otherwise desirable/feasible code transformations—provided a register is available at that point. So, extra registers are used only when actually needed to enhance parallelism, and only if the benefits are not offset by spilling cost.

2 Renaming in fine-grain parallelizing compilers

The price paid for register renaming is not only the increase in number of registers. If renaming is to be done during fine-grain compaction, it needs to be very efficient. In particular, we simply cannot afford global searches for uses of the registers being renamed, and potentially complex code transformations to allow semantically correct renaming. Consider again the previous example. Register a in $a := f + g$ has been renamed to $a' := f + g$. Consequently, in all following operations using a, we substituted a'. In general there might be multiple, distant, uses of register a requiring a global search throughout the program. Furthermore, even if all uses are located, renaming may not be immediately feasible, as shown in the example in Section 2.3. To avoid these problems during compaction, renaming can be carried out by leaving a copy operation in place of the renamed operation, to reassign the value computed to the original register. Thus, by adding an extra copy to the code, renaming is converted into a local, efficient transformation and the need for search and issues of semantic preservation are eliminated:

1:	$a := b + c;$	$a' := f + g;$
2:	$d := a * e;$	$a := a';$
3:	$h := a + k;$	

However, the copies introduced may create their own set of problems. The effect of introducing extra copies is especially critical when loop pipelining is performed and a considerable number of operations (from multiple iterations of the loop) are exposed to renaming. This may cause significant code-explosion. Furthermore, if these copies are left in the code, their execution results in a waste of functional units. So, when considering renaming as a parallelization aid in fine-grain compilers, special care must be taken to maintain a good schedule taking into account all the resources available (functional units and registers)—otherwise renaming may not be beneficial.

2.1 Percolation Scheduling and Machine model

For the purpose of this paper we illustrate the application of our technique in the context of our parallelizing transformations (called Percolation Scheduling) and our loop pipelining technique.

However, the problem and the solution apply to virtually all fine-grain parallelizing techniques (e.g., Trace Scheduling [11]) as well as all loop pipelining techniques.

Percolation Scheduling (PS) is a system of semantic-preserving transformations that convert an original *program control-flow graph* into a more parallel one. PS globally rearranges code in an attempt to exploit parallelism. Its core consists of four primitive program transformations. The transformations are atomic and thus can be combined with a variety of guidance rules to direct the parallelization process. Above this core level, guidance rules and transformations which extend the applicability of the core transformations to exploit coarser parallelism, and/or introduce resource constraints are applied. For further detail refer to [14, 9].

The machine model can be thought of as directly executing a *program graph*, one node at a time. Each node in the graph contains one or more RISC-like operations, all of which can be executed in parallel. In addition the node may contain one or more conditional branches. In general, these jumps form a decision-tree and serve to select the next node to execute.[3] Originally, each node contains a single operation. Making a program more parallel involves compaction of several operations into one node. The model used is a realistic one, and actually matches VLIW machines (e.g., the IBM VLIW machine [8]). The transformations and the model have also been extended to allow for pipelined operations, extending the applicability of the approach to superscalars and hybrid VLIW architectures such as Motorola's 88000, Intel's i860, IBM's R6000 etc.) as well as conventional deep pipelined machines.

2.2 Local copy bypassing

The renaming process, using copy operations in the code, does not (by itself) significantly increase parallelism. Another local substitution is required to tap the full potential of renaming. Refer again to the previous example. Here, $h := a + k$ cannot move up into cycle 2 since it depends on $a := a'$. However, since this data dependency is generated by a copy operation, we can always substitute a' in $h := a + k$ and rewrite the schedule as:

1:   $a := b + c$; $a' := f + g$;
2:   $d := a * e$; $a := a'$; $h := a' + k$;

which is one cycle shorter. This optimization is *local* (applied during one of the local PS transformations) and therefore simple and efficient. Obviously, if all operations using a move above the copy during PS, $a := a'$ becomes dead and can be removed *locally* from the code.

---

[3]Obviously, for machines that do not support multiway branching mechanism, no more than one conditional jump per node is allowed.

2.3 Renaming during loop pipelining

Since ordinary programs tend to spend most of their time executing loops, the ability to parallelize loops has a major impact on the overall parallelization of the program. Loop pipelining is a class of techniques for extracting parallelism within and across iterations, by overlapping execution of operations from multiple iterations of the same loop. This causes a pipelining effect similar to the one found in hardware pipelining.

Loop pipelining involves unwinding of the loop body and compacting the resulting code. This incremental process repeats until data dependencies force the emergence of a repeating pattern which then becomes the compacted loop body. In general, the amount of unwinding cannot be precisely predetermined, particularly in the presence of conditional jumps. Thus, static renaming (e.g., on the loop body or on some small and fixed number of unrolled iterations) is not satisfactory. Dynamic renaming is needed.

The overlapping effect is achieved in our technique by allowing operations from the next iteration to percolate up into nodes containing operations from the current iteration. To illustrate the process of loop pipelining and the application of renaming, consider the following example:

$$for(i = 1; i < 20; i + +)$$
$$A[i] = 4 * (A[i] + 8) + A[i];$$

This loop translates into the following three-address-code (all operations listed in the same node number are executed in parallel)[4]:

PROG_BEGIN:
    node 1: $i := 0;$
LABEL LOOP:
    node 2: $a := M[i + 4];$
    node 3: $b := a + 8;$
    node 4: $c := b * 4;$
    node 5: $d := a + c;$
    node 6: $i := i + 4;$
    node 7: $M[i + 0] := d;$

---

[4]For simplicity, we do not draw the program graph but use labels to denote nodes. We use a RISC-like instruction set with explicit load/store operations. All arithmetic operations are register to register. $M[i + 4]$ means the value in memory location $i + 4$.

| node 8: | $cc0 := i < 80;$ |
| node 9: | IF $cc0$ GOTO LABEL LOOP; |

LABEL EXIT:

| node 10: | RETURN; |

PROG_END

Also, in order to simplify the explanation we ignore the exit test operations (nodes 8 and 9). Omitting these two operations and compacting the loop body yields the (partially) compacted code:

PROG_BEGIN:

| node 1: | $i := 0;$ |

LABEL LOOP:

node 2:	$a := M[i + 4];$	$i := i + 4;$
node 3:	$b := a + 8;$
node 4:	$c := b * 4;$
node 5:	$d := a + c;$
node 6:	$M[i + 0] := d;$	GOTO LOOP

LABEL EXIT:

| node 7: | RETURN; |

PROG_END

The next step is to unfold the next iteration of the loop and try to percolate its operations upwards. For example, after operations from the first node of the second iteration have percolated the code would be:

PROG_BEGIN:

| node 1: | $i := 0;$ |
| node 2: | $a := M[i + 4];$ | $i := i + 4;$ |

LABEL LOOP:

node 3:	$b := a + 8;$
node 4:	$c := b * 4;$
node 5:	$d := a + c;$	$a := M[i + 4];$
node 6:	$M[i + 0] := d;$	$i := i + 4;$	GOTO LOOP

LABEL EXIT:

| node 7: | RETURN; |

PROG_END

Without renaming, neither $a := M[i + 4]$ nor $i := i + 4$ can move any further. Both a and i are used by other operations in their corresponding nodes. This sort of dependency is common in loops since the index (as well as other variables) are often used repeatedly in successive iterations, greatly restricting parallelism. However, with renaming further motion is allowed. This process continues and further iterations are unfolded and percolated until a repeating pattern emerges in the schedule. For our example the final schedule (after pipelining of the next iterations) results in:

PROG_BEGIN:

node 1:	$i := 0$;			
node 2:	$a := M[i + 4]$;	$i := i + 4$;		
node 3:	$b := a + 8$;	$a' := M[i + 4]$;	$i' := i + 4$;	
node 4:	$c := b * 4$;	$b := a' + 8$;	$a'' := M[i + 4]$;	
	$i'' := i' + 4$;			
node 5:	$d := a + c$;	$a := a'$;	$a' := a''$;	$c := b * 4$;
	$b := a'' + 8$;	$a'' := M[i'' + 4]$;	$i''' := i'' + 4$;	

LABEL LOOP:

node 6:	$M[i + 0] := d$;	$i := i'$;	$i' := i''$;	$i'' := i'''$;
	$d := a + c$;	$a := a'$;	$a' := a''$;	$c := b * 4$;
	$b := a'' + 8$;	$a'' := M[i''' + 4]$;	$i''' := i''' + 4$;	GOTO LOOP

LABEL EXIT:

node 7:	RETURN;

PROG_END

The final schedule shows that the whole loop (6 cycles in sequential form) is compacted into one cycle (speed-up of 6) *given enough resources.*[5] If renaming were not performed, on the other hand, the overlap of iterations would have been minimal, yielding a speed-up of 2 only. However, renaming resulted in numerous copy operations. If only two functional units were available, no speed-up would be obtained without eliminating these copies. Since 5 extra copies are added to the original 6 operations in the loop, 6 cycles are required to issue the 11 operation in the new loop body.

Conventional copy propagation techniques will fail to remove the copies generated in this example. In node 6, i is both defined and used and two different definitions of i are reaching the node. Consequently, conventional copy propagation (and/or induction variable elimination) techniques will not work (cannot substitute for i).

---

[5]The speed-up achieved when considering the exit test operation would be 8.

3 Previous work

The effect of storage allocation on parallelism and storage requirements for Fortran programs is discussed in [13]. It is shown that 'anti-dependency' inhibits the parallelism exhibited in scientific programs therefore renaming (or storage reallocation) is needed.

In IBM's VLIW machine [8], whose compiler performs register renaming during the parallelization process, an intermediate approach similar in spirit to the one proposed here is taken. Instead of rewriting the whole program in a single-assignment-form to allow maximal compaction— loops are unrolled several times (the amount of unrolling is determined empirically) so that each iteration uses a new set of registers. Consequently, renaming is de-facto achieved for registers which are defined and used inside the loop body. Besides the fact that the amount of unrolling is determined heuristically in an extra (preliminary) phase—by unrolling the source program, the running time of the compiler is considerably increased as the code size explodes. Furthermore, this is wasteful in terms of registers required.

In order to alleviate this problem [3] suggests a refinement on this idea. Instead of unrolling the loop at the source level, the loop is unrolled in its pipelined form (renaming using copies is done during loop pipelining). The amount of unrolling can be determined from the length of the longest chain of copy operations *on each path through the loop*. In this way there is no need for an extra run of compaction, but code duplication is still problematic.

4 Our approach to copy elimination

Copies created by renaming during the parallelization process may become dead and be removed locally (see Section 2.2) and thus only the remaining copies need to be considered for elimination after compaction. Furthermore, another reason for delaying the application of copy elimination is that sometimes these copies do not affect the resource-constrained schedule (if there are enough functional units)—and thus removal may be unnecessary.

It is convenient to differentiate between two types of renaming candidates during loop pipelining: loop induction variables (IVs) and non-induction variable operations which are eliminated by loop unwinding. Furthermore, we were looking for an algorithm that, while removing copies generated by renaming of IVs, will remove redundant IVs as well. The approach described here includes two parts, each corresponding to a different source of renaming. Since the technique for removal of IVs-generated copies does not involve code duplication it is applied first. In this way less code duplication is required.

4.1 Elimination of copies generated by induction variables renaming

In this Section, we describe our technique to remove redundant induction variables and copy operations generated during renaming of IVs. For details of our algorithm refer to [15].

4.1.1 Definitions

- A variable i is defined using (defined by) j iff $i = j + a$ or $i = j$.

- Variables $i_1, \ldots, i_k$ ($k >= 1$) are *induction variables* (IVs) in loop L iff i_1 is defined exactly once by i_2, $\ldots, i_{k-1}$ is defined exactly once by i_k and i_k is defined exactly once by i_1. i_1, $\ldots, i_k$ are said to be circularly defined.

- A variable i is an *induction variable (IV)* in loop L iff i is defined only once in L by one of the operations $i = i + a, i = j, i = j + a$, where j is an IV and a is a loop invariant or a constant. An operation that assigns a value to an iv is also called a definition of that IV.

- An IV whose definition in L is of the form $i = i + a$ is called a *basic IV*, otherwise it is called a *non-basic IV*.

- Two IVs i and j are in the same *IV family* iff:

  1. there exist IVs $i_1, \ldots, i_k$ ($k >= 0$) such that i is defined by i_1, i_l is defined by i_{l+1} for for $l = 1, \ldots, k - 1$, and i_k is defined by j, or,

  2. there exist IVs $i_1, \ldots, i_k$ ($k >= 0$) and $j_1, \ldots, j_m$ ($m >= 0$) and i_0 such that i is defined by i_1, i_l is defined by i_{l+1} for $l = 1, \ldots, k - 1$, and i_k is defined by i_0, and j is defined by j_1, j_n is defined by j_{n+1} for $n = 1, \ldots, m - 1$, and j_m is defined by i_0.

- An IV is said to be an *effective IV* iff it is used as the memory address register in some memory access operation (load or store). It is called an *ineffective IV* otherwise.

4.1.2 The technique

The goal of the technique is to remove as many redundant IVs as possible and all copy operations generated by renaming of IVs (during loop pipelining) for each IV family in a given loop L. Naturally, this has to be done while preserving the semantics of loop L. Application of conventional copy propagation techniques with loop unrolling is neither efficient nor practical for removing redundant IVs created by renaming. Furthermore, the conventional IV elimination algorithm described in [17] cannot remove redundant IVs from IV families that have no basic IV since that algorithm assumes the existence of a basic IV for each IV family. The following examples illustrates this:

$$i := 5;$$
$$i' := i + 4;$$
$$i'' := i' + 4;$$
$$i''' := i'' + 4;$$

LABEL LOOP: LABEL LOOP1:

$$r := M[i + 0];$$ $$\ldots;$$
$$r := r + 1;$$ $$l = k + 1;$$
$$M[i''' + 0] := r;$$ $$k = j + 2;$$
$$i := i';$$ $$j = i + 3;$$
$$i' := i'';$$ $$i = l + 4;$$
$$i'' := i''';$$ GOTO LOOP1
$$i''' := i'' + 4;$$
GOTO LOOP;

In example LOOP, there is no basic IV but i, i', i'' and i''' form an IV family. The IV elimination algorithm in [17] would fail. In addition, the IV detection algorithm in [17] cannot detect this IV family. Suppose we want to remove i, i', i'' and to keep i'''. Since i is going to be removed, but is an effective IV, we need to know the expression that calculates i''' and the expression of i in terms of i'''. In other words, we need an algorithm that can derive the expression for each IV in terms of an iteration count[6]. Using iteration count will facilitate the expression of an IV in terms of any other IV. LOOP1 above illustrates that it is non-trivial in general to express an IV in terms of the iteration count (see below). We outline our algorithm and then the new technique involved in step 3.

procedure Redundant_IV_and_Copies_Elimination(L)

    detect IV families in L;

    for each IV family **do**

        1. detect effective and ineffective IVs in the family;

        2. determine in the IV family which IVs to keep and which to remove;

        3. derive all IVs in terms of initial values and loop iteration count L_c;

        4. select a base IV among the IVs to be kept and express all other
           IVs as the sum of the base IV and a constant;

---

[6]The iteration count of a loop counts the number of iterations executed. It can be thought of as a canonical IV.

5. remove copies generated by ineffective IVs;

6. for all memory accesses using removed, effective IV replace uses
   with the base IV and adjust the offset accordingly;

7. for all the removed IVs that are live at the loop exit add a
   copy operation that assigns it the same value as in original L;

end

end (Redundant_IV_and_Copies_Elimination)

Before giving our IV derivation algorithm used in step 3, we state the problem of IV derivation as follows: Given a loop L and IV set $\{i_1, \cdots, i_n\}$, where each IV is defined only once in L by $i_k = i_l + a$, $k = 1, \ldots, n$, $l = 1, \ldots, n$, $a \in Z$, and let I be the iteration count of loop L, we want to express all IVs in the form $i = \delta_i I + i_0$, where δ_i is the *progression* of i in each iteration and i_0 is the initial value of i upon entering the loop. We denote the derivation of i in iteration I to be $der(i, I)$. The iteration count I starts from one. $der(i_{k_0}, I)$ gives the value of i_{k_0} immediately after its assignment in an iteration of loop L. The value of i_{k_0} immediately before the assignment to i_{k_0} is determined by decrementing the iteration count I in the derivation of i_{k_0}.

Our derivation algorithm computes the progression that a given IV makes in each iteration. The minimum number of iterations in which a fixed progression on the IV is repeatedly made gives the *progression pattern* and is thus referred to as the *progression period*. The period is represented by η in the derivation algorithm. In the LOOP example above, the progression pattern of i indicates that i increases by a progression of 4 in a period of 1 iteration. In general, the progression will not be so obvious as shown in example LOOP. In LOOP1 the progression is more complex to derive. For example, i spans 2 iterations and has a progression of 10 with period of 2. For iteration I with $(I-1) \bmod \eta = r$ where $r = 0$, or, 1, ..., or $\eta - 1$, i starts with different initial values and increases by progression 10 in every $\eta = 2$ iterations. The derivation algorithm uses five derivation rules. Rule 1 to rule 3 of the algorithm are used to track backwards the iterations until the progression pattern emerges. The condition part of rule 4 states the progression pattern in its general form: the first term on the right hand side of the derivation indicates the emergence of the progression pattern and thus the period, while the second term represents the total progression made in the period. The action part of rule 4 gives the formula to determine the values for the IV for all iterations. It is read this way: for a period of η iterations, the top expression on the right hand side of the formula gives the value for the IV for the first iteration, the second top expression on the right hand side gives the value for the IV for the second iteration, and so on. The first term on the right hand side of the formula represents the initial values upon entering the loop body for all iterations in the period, and the second term represents the total progression for all iterations in the period. The following algorithm computes the derivations of all IVs in a given IV family.

Algorithm: for each IV in IV family execute the following rules:

Rule 1: If i references i, then $der(i, I) = der(i, I-1) + \delta_i$.

Rule 2: If i references j, and the definition of i is a successor of the definition of j in L through forward edge (not a backedge), **then** $der(i, I) = der(j, I) + \delta_i$.

Rule 3: If i references j, and the definition of i is a predecessor of the definition of j in L through forward edge (not a backedge), **then** $der(i, I) = der(j, I-1) + \delta_i$.

Rule 4: If i_{k_0} references i_{k_0} indirectly, i.e.,

$$der(i_{k_0}, I) = der(i_{k_0}, I_p) + \sum_{m \in \{0, \cdots, p-1\}} \delta_{i_{k_m}},$$

where in $L, der(i_{k_0}, I) = der(i_{k_1}, I_1) + \delta_{i_{k_0}}, \cdots, der(i_{k_{p-1}}, I_{p-1}) = der(i_{k_0}, I_p) + \delta_{i_{k_{p-1}}}$, **then**

$$der(i_{k_0}, I) = \begin{cases} der(i_{k_0}, 1) + \lfloor \frac{I-1}{\eta} \rfloor \sum_{m \in \{0, \cdots, p-1\}} \delta_{i_{k_m}} & (I-1) \bmod \eta = 0 \\ der(i_{k_0}, 2) + \lfloor \frac{I-1}{\eta} \rfloor \sum_{m \in \{0, \cdots, p-1\}} \delta_{i_{k_m}} & (I-1) \bmod \eta = 1 \\ \cdots & \cdots \\ der(i_{k_0}, \eta) + \lfloor \frac{I-1}{\eta} \rfloor \sum_{m \in \{0, \cdots, p-1\}} \delta_{i_{k_m}} & (I-1) \bmod \eta = \eta - 1 \end{cases}$$

where $\eta = I - I_p$ and $\eta \geq 1$.

Rule 5: If a definition of i outside L reaches this use of i in iteration 1 of loop L, **then** $der(i, 0) = i_0$ and terminate the derivation.

Let us apply the algorithm on the example described in Section 2. First, we detect the IV family in loop L. Step 1 found that IV i and i''' are effective IVs and that i' and i'' are ineffective IVs. Step 2 decides to keep i''' and remove others. In step 3, the derivations for all IVs are obtained by applying the derivation rules to the IV family as shown:

$der(i, I)$ (use rule 3)

$\quad = der(i', I-1) + 0$ (use rule 3)

$\quad = der(i'', I-2) + 0$ (use rule 3)

$\quad = der(i''', I-3) + 0$ (use rule 1)

$\quad = der(i''', I-4) + 4$ (use rule 4)

$\quad = der(i''', 1) + 4(I-3-1)/(I-3-(I-4))$ (use rule 1)

$\quad = der(i''', 0) + 4 + 4(I-4)$ (use rule 5)

$\quad = i_0''' + 4(I-3).$

Similarly, we have

$der(i', I) \quad = i_0''' + 4(I-2).$

$der(i'', I) \quad = i_0''' + 4(I-1).$

$der(i''', I) \quad = i_0''' + 4I.$

Note that the derivation is correct for $I >= 0$ because the results of the derivation give the difference between each pair of IVs in an IV family. Moving on to step 4, i''' is selected as the base IV because it is the only IV that step 2 decided to keep. An IV can always be expressed as the sum of another IV in the same IV family and a constant provided that such IV family is generated by the loop pipelining transformation. In general, as indicated by derivation rule 4, IVs in the same family may have different progression and there are trade-offs between the number of IVs to be removed and the number of replacement-operations. Step 5 removes three copy operations $i = i', i' := i''$ and $i'' := i'''$. Note that i was effectively used in the memory store operation in loop L and thus its use should be replaced by i'''. In step 6 we first calculate the difference $i - i''' = -12$. Then we figure out how much to adjust the offset of the store operation using i''' to replace i as the memory address register. In this example, the adjusted offset is -12. Note that the offset adjustment depends also on the order in which the operations involved appear in loop L.

4.2 Copy elimination through unwinding

Previous section presented a technique to remove copies generated by renaming of IVs. However, some copies cannot be eliminated without loop unwinding. Copies generated during renaming do *not* produce new values but rather serve to 'shift' (already computed) value for future uses. In other words, multiple values produced by a single operation are used in several iterations. Loop unwinding introduces distinct versions of this single operation for each value produced, thus enabling copy elimination.

A *loop* is a set of nodes in the program graph such that there is a path from each node in the loop to another node in the loop. The loop may be irreducible. *Loop unwinding* means duplicating the whole loop and directing the backedges of the previous iteration to the appropriate nodes of the unrolled iteration. See example in Figure 1.

The main goal of this technique is to unwind the loop sufficiently to eliminate copies. The unwinding process is performed incrementally where at each step we chase use-def chains eliminating all intermediate copies (and substituting corresponding registers). Since this process may require different number of unwindings on different paths and since we want to refrain from introducing new copies which are needed to preserve correctness *on all paths*—careful matching of backedges to appropriate loop headers has to be done.

Since the number of copies is finite and so is the number of different paths in the loop—the number of possible permutations of operations vs. registers is also finite (we do *not* add new

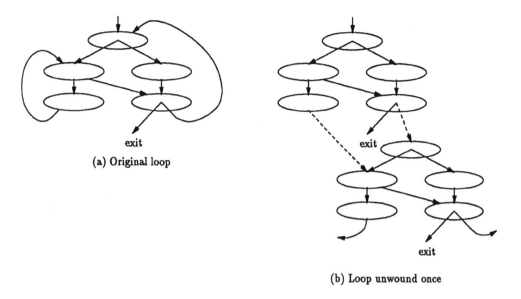

(a) Original loop

(b) Loop unwound once

Figure 1: loop unwinding

registers during the substitution process). In practice, we found that the number of unwindings required is small.

5 Results

In order to gauge the effect of renaming on the overall performance and to compare the obtained speed-up with and without copy operations, we carried out a series of experiments on the first 14 Livermore loops kernels. The initial sequential code, as well as the register allocation we start with, is produced by the GNU compiler. Column A represents the unlimited-resources *static* speed-up, measured by the ratio between the number of cycles in the innermost serial loop and the number of cycles in the compacted loop. Column B represents the unlimited-resources *dynamic* speed-up achieved by running the compacted program on a simulator. This represents the actual speed-up extracted by the compiler should we have enough functional units available. Column C describes the unlimited-resources *dynamic* speed-up achieved *without* register renaming. Column D represents the *dynamic* speed-up when resources limit us to issue no more than two operations at a time and at most one is a memory load/conditional branch (copies are not removed). Column E details the speed-up achieved with our identical schedule (and resource constraints) as in D except that copies are eliminated.

As seen from the results the speed-up decreases considerably (from 7.39 to 3.25—over a factor of 2 loss on average) when renaming is not performed (i.e., when the initial GNU register allocation is not modified during parallelization by the approach proposed in this paper. When performing renaming without copy elimination and the resources are limited as described above, the speed-up is drastically affected by the overhead of executing copy operations. While the performance is still reasonable (71.5% of peak on average, given the machine specifications), we can do much better after application of redundant copy-elimination. The speed-up improves significantly and approaches the theoretical peak for the given resources (95.5% of peak, on average). Note, for example, the dramatic effect that removal of redundant copy operations has on loops 1, 7, 10 and 14. The speed-up obtained for loop 9 is comparably low since this example includes a considerable number of load operations that prevent better performance under the resource constraints imposed.

It is worth pointing out that the speed-up exceeds 2.00 in two cases since during the parallelization we apply some other optimizations that are able to eliminate operations which become redundant in the process. While it is not difficult to switch off these optimizations in order to get the 'pure' parallelization, they are part of our compiler and occur as a by product of the compaction process, so that we believe they are fairly representing the capabilities of our compiler. In any case, these optimizations are common to all columns and consequently do not change significantly the ratio between the speed-ups.

References

[1] A. S. Aiken. Compaction-Based Parallelization. PhD thesis, Cornell University, 1988.

[2] A. Aiken and A. Nicolau. Perfect Pipelining: A new loop parallelization technique. In *Proceedings of the 1988 European Symposium on Programming.* Springer Verlag Lecture Notes in Computer Science no. 300, March 1988.

[3] M. Breternitz Jr. Architecture Synthesis of High-Performance Application-Specific Processors. PhD thesis, Carnegie Mellon University, April 1991.

[4] R. Cytron and J. Ferrante. What's in a name? or The value of renaming for parallelism detection and storage allocation. Proceedings of the 1987 International Conference on Parallel Processing, 1987.

Table 1: Benchmark results

Benchmark	Static speed-up	Dynamic speed-up			
	A unlimited resources	B unlimited resources	C unlimited resources w/o rename	D limited resources with copies	E limited resources w/o copies
Livermore L1	14.0	13.69	2.00	1.27	2.00
Livermore L2	3.66	3.01	2.52	1.51	1.87
Livermore L3	9.0	8.94	8.94	1.80	1.80
Livermore L4	3.0	2.99	2.99	1.72	2.00
Livermore L5	5.5	5.49	2.75	1.22	2.20
Livermore L6	3.75	3.64	3.64	1.61	1.81
Livermore L7	31.0	27.86	1.72	1.08	1.83
Livermore L8	3.94	3.98	2.83	1.50	1.78
Livermore L9	3.56	3.56	3.01	1.50	1.51
Livermore L10	4.3	4.29	3.58	0.50	1.95
Livermore L11	9.0	8.93	3.00	1.80	2.25
Livermore L12	9.0	8.94	3.00	1.50	1.80
Livermore L13	3.0	2.97	2.62	1.74	1.93
Livermore L14	8.0	5.20	2.87	1.23	1.97
Average	7.91	7.39	3.25	1.43	1.91

[5] R. Cytron, J. Ferrante, B. K. Rosen, M.N. Wegman and F.K. Zadeck. An efficient method of computing static single assignment form. 16th Annual ACM Symposium on Principles of Programming Languages, Austin, TX, January 1989.

[6] R. Cytron, D.J. Kuck and A.V. Veidenbaum. The effect of restructuring compilers on program performance for high-speed computers. Computer Physics Communications, 37:37-48, 1985.

[7] K.Ebcioglu. A Compilation Technique for Software Pipelining of Loops with Conditional Jumps. Proceedings of MICRO20, pp. 69-79, ACM Press, 1987.

[8] K.Ebcioglu. Some Design Ideas for a VLIW Architecture for Sequential-Natured Software. Proceedings IFIP, 1988.

[9] K.Ebcioglu, and A.Nicolau. A *global* resource-constrained parallelization technique. In Proc. ACM SIGARCH ICS-89: International Conference on Supercomputing, Greece, June 1989.

[10] J. R. Ellis. Bulldog- A Compiler for VLIW Architectures. MIT Press, 1986.

[11] J. A. Fisher. Trace Scheduling: A technique for global microcode compaction. IEEE Transactions on Computers, No. 7,pp. 478-490, 1981.

[12] T. Gross, M. S. Lam. Compilation for high-performance systolic array. Proceedings of the 1986 SIGPLAN Symposium on Compiler Construction, July 1986.

[13] M. Kumar. Effect of Storage Allocation/Reclamation Methods on Parallelism and Storage Requirements. Proceedings of the 14th Annual International Symposium on Computer Architecture, Pittsburgh, PA, June 1987.

[14] A. Nicolau. Uniform Parallelism Exploitation in Ordinary Programs. Proceedings of the 1985 International Conference on Parallel Processing, 1985.

[15] A. Nicolau, R. Potasman and H. Wang. Register allocation, renaming and their impact on parallelism. Technical Report, University of California, Irvine, April 1991.

[16] B. R Rau, C. D. Glaeser. Efficient Code Generation for Horizontal Architectures: Compiler Techniques and Architectural Support. Proceedings of the 9th Symposium on Computer Architecture, April 1982.

[17] R. Sethi, A. Aho, J.D. Ullman. Compilers: Principles, Techniques and Tools. Addison-Wesley, Reading, Mass., 1986.

15 Data Flow and Dependence Analysis for Instruction Level Parallelism

B.R. Rau

Hewlett-Packard Laboratories

Abstract

Instruction-level parallel architectures present their own set of opportunities and needs, requiring the development of a new class of compiler optimization techniques. Dynamic single assignment is presented as a parallel program representation that permits programs, with cyclic control flow graphs, to be expressed in their maximally parallel form (i.e., with a minimal number of dependence arcs). Also, a data flow analysis technique is outlined that extends to subscripted references the full power of conventional techniques that normally only work with scalar variables. The focus is on the representation and analysis of programs containing subscripted references with an emphasis on innermost loops whose bodies contain arbitrary, acyclic control flow.

1 Introduction and Motivation

The objective of this paper is twofold: first, to note that instruction-level parallel architectures have their unique set of opportunities and needs that require the development of a new class of optimization techniques and, secondly, to present a new parallel intermediate representation and data flow analysis methodology to support instruction-level parallelism. These have particular merit when exploiting instruction-level parallelism, but also have value when compiling for conventional scalar processors. The focus is on the representation and analysis of programs containing subscripted references with an emphasis on cyclic control flow graphs. This paper also describes some compiler contributions, made at Cydrome from 1984 through 1988, which have not been previously published.

An **instruction-level parallel (ILP)** processor is a parallel processor in which the unit of computation, for which decisions such as scheduling and synchronization are made, is the individual operation, e.g., an add, multiply, load or store. It is not necessary that any or all of these decisions be made during the execution of the program; they could be made at compile time. For instance, with VLIW processors [5,14], all of these decisions are made during compilation. Even though superscalar processors [11] are capable of making such decisions at run time, they, too, benefit from the compiler making these decisions.

For the purposes of this paper, we shall restrict the term ILP to refer to processors whose *only* form of parallelism is ILP and which, in particular, cannot execute multiple loci of control simultaneously. Thus, although dataflow processors [2,8] utilize instruction-level parallelism, we shall not refer to them as ILP processors because they can execute massively many loci of control simultaneously. This distinction is not arbitrary; as we shall see, the fact that there is a single locus of control has a significant effect on the compiler's objectives and implementation.

1.1 An Assessment of Existing Compiler Technologies

The types of computation on which a particular architecture can perform well, determine the set of challenges that are extended to the compiler writer. These challenges, in turn, motivate the development of the requisite code generation technology. Traditional scalar processors present little or no opportunity for parallelism. Thus, the main stream of compiler theory, as typified by [1], has not concerned itself very much with this issue. In keeping with its general-purpose orientation, one of the strengths of this school of compiler theory has been its emphasis on the ability to analyze and optimize programs with arbitrary control flow, and a very rich theory of program analysis and optimization has been developed over the past forty years. However, it has two shortcomings from our point of view. Firstly, the intermediate representation (IR) used by a conventional compiler is unable to fully express instruction-level parallelism. Recently, progress has been made in the form of static single assignment [6] but (as we shall see) this is still unable to express the full parallelism that is present in loops. The second shortcoming of conventional compiler theory has been its relative neglect of subscripted variables, and its consequent inability to bring the same power to bear on the analysis and optimization of programs containing references to arrays.

It is in the dataflow literature [8,2,16] that most thought has been given to the issue of representing instruction-level parallelism. It could be argued that the most important contribution that the dataflow school has made is in its powerful and extremely elegant model of computation, which also has merit as an ILP compiler's intermediate representation [13]. However, when used as an IR, the dataflow model needs to be extended to cope with the requirements of traditional, imperative languages which include:

- arbitrary, unstructured control flow graphs,
- the unconstrained use of load and store operations upon an updateable memory, and
- the ability to express representations in which the implicit copy operations associated with switch and merge nodes have been optimized away[1].

Vector processors (e.g., [4]) exploit parallelism of a particular, stylized form. Since vector instructions are equivalent to loops with a single operation in the loop body and a limited number of iterations, the primary task of vector code generation is loop distribution and strip mining. Vectorizing compiler technology has concentrated on these loop transformations and other ones that enable vectorization. The analysis of array subscripts, to determine whether two references could be to the same memory location, is key to such loop transformations and has been the focus of vectorizing compiler research (as summarized in [17]).

---

[1] Dataflow's stylized program schemas imply a large and unnecessary number of hidden copy operations due to switches and merges. A literal implementation of switches and merges can be quite non-optimal.

These techniques can be important in ILP compilers but, by themselves, are insufficient. From the viewpoint of ILP compilation, vectorizing technology suffers from a couple of shortcomings. Firstly, little attention has been paid to anything other than simple, nested DO-loops. Specifically, WHILE-loops, loops with conditional branching in their body, and arbitrary cyclic control flow graphs have been largely ignored. Such computations are of little interest in the context of vector processors since the hardware is unable to accelerate them. In contrast, ILP processors, with the ability to exploit parallelism even in such constructs, motivate the development of more powerful dependence analysis techniques that work in such cases.

```
            DO 10 I = 2,50                      T = B(1)
              A(I) = B(I) + B(I-1)              DO 10 I = 2,50
10    CONTINUE                                    S = B(I)
                                                  A(I) = S + T
                                                  T = S
                                          10    CONTINUE

                    (a)                                      (b)
```

Figure 1. (a) A loop with a redundant load of B(I-1). (b) The corresponding code after the redundant load has been eliminated.

From the viewpoint of scalar or ILP processors, compiler techniques can be classified as either **optimizations**, which eliminate redundant operations and otherwise reduce the total amount of computation, or as **transformations**, which rearrange the computation to have better properties such as outer loop parallelism or improved locality of data reference. From this perspective, a second shortcoming of the vectorizing literature is that it has focused almost entirely on program transformations which re-order the computation (e.g., loop interchange, fusion and distribution) and very little on program optimizations which reduce the computation (e.g., redundant subscripted reference elimination). For instance, in Figure 1a, the load of B(I-1) is unnecessary from the second iteration onward because it was loaded in the previous iteration as B(I). This is of little interest when one is generating code for a vector machine, unable as it is to exploit the fact that the two vector loads are skewed by one element. On the other hand, a scalar or ILP processor benefits from the compiler putting the code into the form in Figure 1b with one less load per iteration.

The Cydrome compiler performs such optimizations of array references. Table 1 demonstrates the improvements realized on the Cydra 5 by optimizing away subscripted references in the Livermore Fortran Kernels [12]. Optimization and elimination of loads and stores is of major importance for an ILP processor for a couple of reasons [7]. If the request ports to memory happen to be the performance bottleneck, reducing the number of memory operations can yield a proportionate increase in performance. This is the case with kernels 2, 4, 6, 12 and 13. In certain cases, a load operation may be part of the recurrence circuit of dependence arcs that is limiting performance as with kernels 5 and 11. Eliminating the load, especially if the memory latency is relatively long, can increase performance by factors of as much as 5 and 8. When these speedups are compared to the data reported in [3] for a similar experiment on a scalar processor, one finds that the Cydra 5 consistently benefits more from these optimizations than does the scalar processor except when the bottleneck was not memory to begin with. Due to the absence of a data cache in the Cydra 5, these optimizations are especially valuable on kernels 5 and 11 which would otherwise have a recurrence circuit involving a main memory load latency.

LFK Kernel	Without Optimization[1]		With Optimization		Speedup	Comments
	# Mem. Ops.	MFLOPS	# Mem. Ops.	MFLOPS		
1	4	20.42	3	20.42	1.00	FLP multiplier bottleneck
2	6	6.93	5	7.45	1.07	
3	2	23.42	2	23.42	1.00	No optimization possible
4	4	10.79	2	18.95	1.76	
5	4	1.22	3	6.14	5.05	Load was on recurrence path
6	4	6.76	2	9.32	1.38	
7	10	24.73	4	24.73	1.00	FLP adder bottleneck
8	30	20.52	12	20.52	1.00	FLP adder bottleneck
9	11	22.12	11	22.12	1.00	FLP adder bottleneck
10	20	10.39	20	10.39	1.00	No optimization possible
11	3	0.76	2	6.10	8.08	Load was on recurrence path
12	3	8.07	2	11.91	1.48	
13	26	3.01	18	3.64	1.21	
14	35	3.93	21	3.93	1.01	Unexplained lack of speedup

Table 1. Effect of subscripted reference optimization on the Cydra 5 for the Livermore Fortran Kernels. The second and third columns list the number of memory operations per iteration and the achieved performance without optimization, respectively. The next two columns list the same data, but with optimization on.

1.2 Compiler Requirements for ILP

As far as ILP is concerned, there is a vacuum that needs to be filled. With respect to program analysis and optimization, it is necessary to combine the power of the vectorizing compiler's subscript analysis with conventional compiler theory's ability to perform data flow analysis and optimization in the presence of arbitrary control flow. Scheduling and code generation require an IR that can accurately and precisely specify the dependences that exist between operations and which permits the program to be specified in its most parallel form. In every case, subscripted references must be first-class citizens.

It is important to distinguish between capabilities required to support optimization and code generation and those required to effect program transformations of the kind described in the vectorizing and parallelizing literature. When performing program transformations, the need is to understand the space of all possible execution orders of a series of loops or of a nest of loops so that the computation can be re-arranged to reflect the best execution order with respect to some criteria (e.g., vectorizability, parallelism or data locality). ILP processors, too, can benefit from such program transformations and, in this context, an ILP compiler is no different from a vectorizing compiler. What can be different is the desired outcome of the transformation. For instance, in a vector machine, the objective is to perform loop interchange so that the innermost loop does not have a recurrence (as is the case in Figure 2a). On an ILP processor, it will often be preferable to move the recurrence into the innermost loop (as has

---

[1] The performance without optimization involves a small amount of estimation and extrapolation since it was difficult to turn all of the optimization off.

been done in Figure 2b). The load and store of C(I,J) can be moved out of the loop resulting in fewer memory operations per floating point operation. On ILP processors, such as the Cydra 5, the latter code performs better.

From the viewpoint of optimization and code generation, ILP offers some simplifications that relax the requirements on the intermediate representation and dependence analysis. Specifically, it is important to understand the nature of the dependence between two memory operations only if either

- there is the danger of the dependence being violated, or
- if there is the opportunity for eliminating a load or store by promoting the variable, which is common to both operations, to a register.

In every case, we are interested in understanding the dependences between only those operations that are temporally close enough to interact with one another. This principle has significant implications with respect to the options available to us for data flow analysis, optimization and code generation.

``` DO 10 I = 1,N DO 10 K = 1,N DO 10 J = 1,N 10 C(I,J) = C(I,J) + A(K,J)*B(I,K) ```	``` DO 10 I = 1,N DO 10 J = 1,N DO 10 K = 1,N 10 C(I,J) = C(I,J) + A(K,J)*B(I,K) ```
(a)	(b)
``` DO 10 I = 1,N X(I+K) = ... 10 CONTINUE : : DO 20 I = 1,N ... = X(I+L) 20 CONTINUE ```	``` DO 30 I = 1,N 10 ... = X(I-K) : : 20 X(I) = ... 30 CONTINUE ```
(c)	(d)

Figure 2. Code examples that illustrate the differences in the imperatives for vectorizing and ILP compilers.

For instance, while scheduling or optimizing the two loops that are at the same nesting level in Figure 2c, it will rarely be important to know whether a dependence exists between the store in the first loop and the load in the second. Firstly, there is no danger of the two being scheduled to execute in the reverse order. Secondly, it will generally not be possible to hold in registers all the values that were stored by the first loop in order to eliminate the load operation in the second loop. So, whether or not a dependence exists is irrelevant. What we really might need is to know what dependences, if any, exist between the last few iterations of the first loop and the first few iterations of the second loop. These computations are close enough temporally to have the potential for interaction.. For similar reasons, even within the same loop, as in Figure 2d, it will generally be irrelevant whether the load and store from iterations that are, say, 100 apart are dependent on one another.

Unlike a vectorizing or parallelizing compiler, an ILP compiler can benefit even from partial dependence information. In the case of a loop with a recurrence, its performance after performing software pipelining increases with the number of iterations that are on the recurrence circuit [7] since this is proportional to the number of iterations that are executing in parallel. It can often be worth a factor of two in performance merely to prove that operations in consecutive iterations are independent, even if nothing can be said about operations that are separated by a greater number of iterations. Assume that, in Figure 2d, the store in statement 20 is dependent upon the load in statement 10 via the computation in between. If K is zero or negative, there can be no recurrence. If K is greater than zero, the load in a given iteration is dependent upon the store that is K iterations earlier. If K is unknown, the worst must be assumed (that K=1) and there will be essentially no overlap of successive iterations. If it can be proved that K>1, the conservative assumption now is that K=2. This permits successive iterations to be started about twice as frequently and approximately twice the performance can be achieved.

2 Intermediate Representations For ILP

An intermediate representation for ILP must provide the ability
- to explicitly and precisely represent the dependences between operations (including those between subscripted memory references) in the presence of arbitrary control flow graphs, especially cyclic ones, and
- to express the program in a maximally parallel form (i.e., a minimum of anti-dependences and output dependences), whether or not the parallelism is explicit, while controlling the number of copy operations that are introduced as a result of eliminating the anti- and output dependences.

Achieving a maximally parallel program representation requires the elimination of all dependence arcs that are not essential for ensuring correct semantics. Using standard terminology [17], data dependences can be classified as true (or flow) dependences, anti-dependences and output dependences. Of the three, only true dependences are essential for semantic correctness. The other two are artifacts of assigning results of multiple operations to the same variable. In principle, these two types of dependences can be eliminated in the IR by never assigning a result to a virtual register more than once, using the well understood concept of single assignment [15]. Thus, the storage model employed, i.e., single or multiple assignment, affects the amount of parallelism that is present either implicitly or explicitly.

Explicit dependences and single assignment are independent properties of an IR. Either one, both or neither may be present in a particular representation. Explicit dependences are essential to the scheduling task but are optional, though highly desirable [13], for program analysis and optimization. Single assignment is generally desirable during scheduling since the number of precedence arcs is minimized. However, it is essential for dependence analysis and, therefore, for optimization. This is because precise dependence analysis needs, as a prerequisite, the ability to uniquely specify each definition of a variable. Single assignment provides this ability.

2.1 Explicit representation of dependences

The single assignment principle is straightforward to implement within a single basic block using the procedure known as value numbering [1]. In effect, value numbering constructs the textual equivalent of the dataflow graph corresponding to the original sequential basic block. In the dataflow world, the dataflow graphs corresponding to individual basic blocks are connected by switch and merge nodes [2]. The boolean switching input to the switch node is identical to the branch condition used by the branch that would have been at the end of that basic block. Since dataflow semantics are such that an operation executes only when all its inputs have arrived, the switch node, in addition to specifying the live-in/live-out hookups, in effect also specifies the predicate under which the operations in a particular basic block execute.

The processor architecture [14] and compiler [7] for the Cydra 5 (developed at Cydrome from 1984 through 1988), draw heavily on these dataflow concepts. The IR for a basic block represents the computation as a single assignment graph with the ability to express all three types of dependences if needed. Larger graphs are constructed out of the graphs for individual basic blocks by using equivalents of switch and merge nodes. The hardware views the normal dyadic operation as having three inputs, one of which is the predicate. The operation is executed normally if the predicate is true and is completely suppressed if the predicate is false. Each operation is predicated on the boolean condition under which flow of control arrives at the basic block containing that operation. This makes switch nodes unnecessary. The predicate for all the operations in a basic block is computed as the union over all predecessor blocks of the predecessor's predicate AND-ed with the branch condition in that predecessor. The two-way merge node is directly supported in hardware by the Select operation. Multi-way merges are implemented using a tree of select operations. Unlike traditional dataflow graphs, Cydrome's IR can represent arbitrary control flow graphs. Loads and stores are treated just like any other operations. (For a store operation, the address is viewed as a source operand and there is no result operand).

The parallelism of Cydrome's IR could have been increased by incorporating the notion of control dependence that is an aspect of program dependence graphs (PDG) [10]. Control dependence defines the earliest point at which the predicate for the operations in a basic block can be computed. The sooner the predicate is computed, the sooner can the dependent operations be executed, thereby yielding more parallelism. Although not included in the Cydrome compiler, this would have been of value.

The importance of incorporating dataflow concepts into a compiler's IR is gaining increasing acceptance. Apollo's language system is based on an IR that has much in common with the SSA representation. The ongoing compiler research at Cornell [13] is predicated on the belief that dataflow graphs constitute the best vehicle for efficient, powerful analyses and optimizations.

2.2 Dynamic Single Assignment (DSA)

The conventional sequential IR for the Fortran example in Figure 3a is shown in Figure 3b and the static single assignment (SSA) form [6] is shown in Figure 3c. The variables K, J and I are live into the body of the loop. The definitions for these variables come either from the code prior to the loop (for the first iteration) or from the previous iteration. Accordingly, the ø-functions [6] in statements s10 through s12 are present to select the appropriate definitions of K, J and I, respectively. As required by SSA, each virtual register, t04 through t15, appears exactly once on the left-hand side of an assignment. Nevertheless, dynamically, multiple assignments are made to each of the virtual registers (t07, t08 and t10 through t15), once each for each iteration of the loop. This results in anti-dependences between the operations in the loop. Also, it is impossible to distinguish between the multiple definitions of a particular virtual register, thereby making it impossible to specify dependences precisely. What is needed is a representation that permits single assignment in the dynamic sense.

(a)	(b)	(c)
	`% t00 = 0, t01 = 1` `% t02 = 5, t03 = 50`	`% t00 = 0, t01 = 1` `% t02 = 5, t03 = 50`
`K = 0`	`s00  t04 = copy(t00)`	`s00  t04 = copy(t00)`
`J = 1`	`s01  t05 = copy(t01)`	`s01  t05 = copy(t01)`
`DO 10 I = 1,50`	`s02  t06 = copy(t01)`	`s02  t06 = copy(t01)`
		`s10  t10 = ø(t04,t14)`
		`s11  t11 = ø(t05,t13)`
		`s12  t12 = ø(t06,t15)`
`L = J`	`s03  t07 = copy(t05)`	`s03  t07 = copy(t11)`
`J = J+K`	`s04  t05 = iadd(t05,t04)`	`s04  t13 = iadd(t11,t10)`
`K = L`	`s05  t04 = copy(t07)`	`s05  t14 = copy(t07)`
`10    CONTINUE`	`s06  t06 = iadd(t06,t01)`	`s06  t15 = iadd(t12,t01)`
	`s07  t08 = ile(t06,t03)`	`s07  t08 = ile(t15,t03)`
	`s08       brt(t08,s03)`	`s08       brt(t08,s10)`
`K = J+5`	`s09  t09 = iadd(t05,t02)`	`s09  t09 = iadd(t13,t02)`

Figure 3. (a) A Fortran loop example containing a recurrence. (b) A sequential intermediate representation. (c) The static single assignment representation.

Definition: A program representation is said to be in the **dynamic single assignment (DSA)** form if the same virtual register is never assigned to more than once on any dynamic execution path (even though the static code may have multiple statements with the same virtual register on the left hand side).

The situation is exactly the opposite with static single assignment; a virtual register is never found more than once on the left hand side of a statement but, within a cyclic flow graph, that virtual register must necessarily be assigned to multiple times. DSA addresses this problem by doing for virtual registers what scalar expansion does for scalar variables. We shall define here a slightly more primitive but more general capability than that employed in the Cydrome compiler.

Definition: An **expanded virtual register (EVR)** is an infinite[1], linearly ordered set of virtual registers with a special operation, **remap()**, defined upon it. The elements of an EVR, t, can be addressed, read, and written as t[n], where n is any integer. For convenience, t[0] may be referred to as merely t. The effect of remap(t) is that whatever element was accessible as t[n] prior to the remap operation will be accessible as t[n+1] after the remap operation.

If remap(t) is executed prior to each assignment of a result to t, the previous value assigned to t will be in t[1] and the current assignment will be to a different element t[0]. Although

---

[1] In fact, only a finite, contiguous set of the elements of an EVR may be expected to be live at any point in time, and only these need to be allocated physical registers. The Cydra 5 provides a circular register file for this purpose [14]. The remapping capability is implemented by providing a pointer into the circular register file that can be decremented each time a new iteration is started. Addressing into the register file is relative to this pointer. In the absence of such hardware support, remapping can be adequately implemented by code replication.

textually it appears that t[0] is being assigned results repeatedly, dynamically it is still single assignment; a different element is assigned to on each occasion, and the DSA property is retained. The result of this formal transformation to the SSA representation yields the canonical DSA representation of Figure 4a. The insertion of the remap operation for t5 prior to the use of t5 in statement s04 requires that the reference to t5 on the right-hand side of s04 be changed to t5[1]. Likewise, statement s06 is altered to use t6[1]. However, note that although the program is in DSA form it is not in SSA form; t4, t5 and t6 appear twice each on the left-hand side of a statement.

The next formal transformation, that of moving all the remap operations to the beginning of the loop body, results in the IR of Figure 4b. By moving the remaps for t4 and t5, respectively, ahead of the statements s04 and s03 that use them, the right-hand side references change to t4[1] and t5[1].

```
    % t0=0, t1=1              % t0=0, t1=1              % t0=0, t1=1
    % t2=5, t3=50             % t2=5, t3=50             % t2=5, t3=50

s00  t4=copy(t0)        s00  t4=copy(t0)        s00  t5[1]=copy(t0)
s01  t5=copy(t1)        s01  t5=copy(t1)        s01  t5=copy(t1)
s02  t6=copy(t1)        s02  t6=copy(t1)        s02  t6=copy(t1)

s10      remap(t7)      s10      remap(t7)
s03  t7=copy(t5)        s11      remap(t5)      s11      remap(t5)
s11      remap(t5)      s12      remap(t4)
s04  t5=iadd(t5[1],t4)  s13      remap(t6)      s13      remap(t6)
s12      remap(t4)      s14      remap(t8)      s14      remap(t8)
s05  t4=copy(t7)        s03  t7=copy(t5[1])
s13      remap(t6)      s04  t5=iadd(t5[1],t4[1])  s04  t5=iadd(t5[1],t5[2])
s06  t6=iadd(t6[1],t1)  s05  t4=copy(t7)
s14      remap(t8)      s06  t6=iadd(t6[1],t1)  s06  t6=iadd(t6[1],t1)
s07  t8=ile(t6,t3)      s07  t8=ile(t6,t3)      s07  t8=ile(t6,t3)
s08      brt(t8,s10)    s08      brt(t8,s10)    s08      brt(t8,s11)

s09  t9=iadd(t5,t2)     s09  t9=iadd(t5,t2)     s09  t9=iadd(t5,t2)
         (a)                    (b)                    (c)
```

Figure 4. (a) The canonical dynamic single assignment representation for the sequential IR of Figure 3b obtained by inserting a remap operation before each assignment in the loop body. (b) The DSA form after moving all the remap operations to the beginning of the loop. (c) The DSA form after performing copy optimization.

The final step is to optimize away unnecessary copy operations by noting that t7 always has the same value as t5[1] and t4[1] always has the same value as t7[1] which, in turn, has the same value as t5[2]. After substituting t5[1], t5[1] and t5[2] for t7, t4 and t4[1], respectively, statements s03 and s05 are dead code and may be removed. This, in turn, makes statements s10 and s12 unnecessary. The resulting IR is shown in Figure 4c[1]. Note that, in effect, statement s04 says that the result of the addition on this iteration is the sum of the results of the same statement on the previous two iterations. This notation is considerably less opaque than

---

[1] This closely resembles the code that would be generated for the Cydra 5. The difference is that the remap operations and the branch operation are replaced by a single instruction, brtop, which, in addition to combining the function of a conventional branch with the remapping of all EVRs that are assigned to within the loop, also performs certain other loop control functions [7].

the clumsy way in which one must express the same computation in Fortran. More importantly, when in the DSA form, the computation possesses no anti-dependences and there is an unambiguous means by which each definition in the computation can be specified.

3 Analysis of Subscripted Variables

In this section we introduce a somewhat novel way of analyzing array references. It is predicated on the premise that if we wish array reference analysis to be as powerful as conventional scalar variable analysis, then we should treat an array reference just like a scalar reference. After all, an element of an array, such as $X(I,J)$, is no different from a scalar variable except in one way. The difference is that, unlike a scalar variable, the same array element can be referenced in many different ways, for instance, as $X(I,J)$, $X(I+1,J-1)$ or $X(L,M)$. At different points in time, and for appropriate values of I, J, L and M, all three references can correspond to the same memory location. So, merely recognizing that two references refer to the same memory location is quite a bit more challenging. We depart from conventional compiler theory by making the following rather simple observation. If, for instance, we know that $X(I)$ is available at a given point in a program, just prior to a statement of the form $I = I+1$, then $X(I-1)$ is available immediately after that statement. Instead of "killing" the value corresponding to $X(I)$, the statement "re-incarnates" it with the new name $X(I-1)$.

When analyzing subscripted variables, it is not important that dependences be explicit. So, we shall describe the analysis procedure in the context of sequential code. However, as we shall see, it is important that the code be in the DSA form. To simplify the exposition, we shall restrict our discussion in two ways that, strictly speaking, may not be necessary. The two restrictions are that:

- we assume that the subscripts of all references to the same array have been normalized so that they are in the form $a*J+b$, where a and b are loop invariant expressions and J is some scalar integer valued variable that is repeatedly modified within the loop. We shall refer to J as the subscript variable for a subscript of the form $a*J+b$. The subscripts of all references to the same array should be in terms of the *same* subscript variable J for the analysis to be successful[1], and
- within the loop, all definitions of subscript variables, such as J, are of the form $J = J+k_i$, where the various k_i are loop-invariant integer valued quantities. Dynamically, there may be multiple such definitions of a subscript variable within the loop.

3.1 Dependence analysis of subscripted references

All references which either definitely are, or may be, to the same array are considered at the same time. We shall only attempt to compare two subscripted references which are at the same point in the program and which have the same subscript variable J. The significance of the former clause is that the value of J is the same for both subscripts. For two subscripts, a_1*J+b_1 and a_2*J+b_2, that are at the same point in the program to be equal, $(a_1-a_2)*J+(b_1-b_2)$ must be 0

---

[1] In general, this might be quite difficult to do and might involve the use of symbolic algebra as described in [9].

for some integer value of J. If we consider two subscripted references[1], $X(a_1*J+b_1)$ and $X(a_2*J+b_2)$, at the same point in the program and inquire whether the two can be to the same memory location, there are five different answers we can get.

1. <u>Never equal</u>. There are a number of possibilities here. First, $(a_1-a_2) = 0$ but $(b_1-b_2) \neq 0$. Second, $(a_1-a_2) \neq 0$ but (a_1-a_2) does not divide (b_1-b_2). Third, $(a_1-a_2) \neq 0$ and (a_1-a_2) divides (b_1-b_2) but $(b_1-b_2)/(a_1-a_2)$ can be proven to be outside of the range of values that J assumes.

2. <u>Always equal</u>. Regardless of the value of J, the two references are to the same location if $(a_1-a_2) = 0$ and $(b_1-b_2) = 0$. In other words, the two references are textually identical.

3. <u>Recurrently equal</u>. There is one value of J for which the two references are to the same memory location if $(a_1-a_2) \neq 0$, (a_1-a_2) divides (b_1-b_2) and $(b_1-b_2)/(a_1-a_2)$ can be proven to be within the range of values that J assumes. Furthermore, J repeatedly takes on this value but, perhaps, in some irregular or unpredictable fashion.

4. <u>Transiently equal</u>. As in the previous case, there is one value of J for which the two references are to the same memory location. However, J assumes this value only once. This is what one might expect if the value of J changes monotonically (as it will if it is the loop index).

5. <u>Inconclusive</u>. It is not possible to prove that the references fall into any of the above four categories. This will be the outcome if the two references are to arrays that are possible aliases, if the two references are to the same array but with different subscript variables which cannot be related to each other, or when the difference of the two subscripts is not in the normalized, linear form.

We shall say that the two memory locations are **different** in the first case (never equal); that they are **identical** in the second case (always equal); and that they are **possibly-identical** in the remaining three cases. References to different locations are independent, which yields parallelism. References to identical locations are always dependent. This often provides opportunities for optimizing away loads and stores. For the purposes of this paper, we shall treat the remaining three cases as having little redeeming value[2] and shall classify the two references as being **possibly-dependent**.

3.2 Data flow analysis of subscripted references

The mapping, at any point in the program, between memory locations and expanded virtual registers is provided in the form of a set of **map tuples**, each one being of the form $<X(f(I))$, $t[n]>$. We shall term the two elements of the pair the **M-name** and the **R-name**, respectively. The assertion made by such a tuple is that the memory location that is addressable by the textual name, $X(f(I))$, *at that particular point in the program*, is associated with the element of the

---

[1] Although our discussion considers only singly-dimensioned arrays, it is equally applicable to multi-dimensional arrays either by considering the subscript for each dimension separately or by considering the single subscript for the linearized array.

[2] In fact, a transient dependence does offer some interesting possibilities. With such a dependence, the span of the dependence decreases to zero at some point and then increases once again. Except for a small number of iterations around this point, the dependence span is large enough that it imposes no constraint on the parallelism achievable by software pipelining. To exploit this, the loop must be split into three loops. The second one executes the set of iterations around the point of zero span and is performed sequentially. The other two execute the iterations where the dependence span is large. These are software pipelined. Recurrent dependences can be dealt with by using a slight generalization of this scheme.

expanded virtual register whose current name is t[n] *at that same point in the program*. Let S be a set of map tuples such that all the tuples in the set possess the same property. For the purposes of this discussion, the property is that "the contents of the memory location $X(f(I))$ are currently available in the corresponding EVR element t[n]". Such a set may be manipulated in much the same way that, for instance, the set of available expressions is manipulated by conventional data flow algorithms.

1. Insertion and deletion of map tuples. The map tuple $<X(f(J)), t[n]>$ is deleted from S at each point in the program where there is a store to a memory location that is identical or possibly-identical to $X(f(J))$. The map tuple $<X(f(J)), t[n]>$ is inserted into the set S at each point in the program where a load operation loads $X(f(J))$ into t[n] or a store operation stores t[n] into $X(f(J))$.

2. Remapping of memory locations. Whenever the set S is propagated in the forward direction past a statement of the form $J = g(J)$, all tuples, $<X(f(J)), t[n]>$, whose M-name is a function of J, are deleted. If the function $g(\cdot)$ is admissible[1], then the tuple $<X(f(g^{-1}(J))), t[n]>$ is added to the set. For instance, if $X(J+5)$ is available before the statement $J = J+2$, then $X(J+3)$ is available after it. Likewise, whenever the set S is propagated in the backward direction over a statement of the form $J = g(J)$, all tuples, $<X(f(J)), t[n]>$, whose M-name is a function of J, are deleted and, if the function $g(\cdot)$ is admissible, the tuple $<X(f(g(J))), t[n]>$ is added to the set.

3. Remapping of expanded virtual registers. Whenever the set S is propagated in the forward direction past a statement of the form remap(t), all tuples, $<X(f(J)), t[n]>$, whose R-name is an element of t, are replaced by the tuple $<X(f(J)), t[n+1]>$. Likewise, whenever the set S is propagated in the backward direction over a statement of the form remap(t), all tuples, $<X(f(J)), t[n]>$, whose R-name is an element of t, are replaced by the tuple $<X(f(J)), t[n-1]>$.

4. The meet operation. Consider a point in the program where n control flow paths meet. Let S_i, $i = 1,..,n$, be the sets that are propagating along these paths. The set S, just beyond the confluence of the paths, is constructed as follows. If the meet operation is conjunctive, a tuple with the M-name, $X(f(J))$, is placed in S if and only if on every incoming path i there is a tuple of the form $<X(f(J)), t_i>$ in the set S_i. In other words, we must have identical M-names[2] coming in on each path for it to propagate past the conjunctive meet. Furthermore, when this is so, if the R-names, t_i, for all the matching incoming tuples are identical both in their EVR name and their index, the same R-name is placed in the outgoing tuple. Otherwise, a new EVR, r, is allocated and r[0] is used as the M-name for the outgoing tuple. With forward propagation, a merge node (or ϕ-function in SSA parlance) is inserted immediately after the meet point. With backward propagation a switch node is inserted immediately before the meet point. If the meet operation is disjunctive, every incoming tuple on any incoming path is placed in the outgoing set S.

In this way, map tuples from one point in a program are correctly propagated to another point in the program so that the comparison of two array subscripts can be performed at the same point in the program. Monotone data flow analysis may be performed as usual, by iteratively

---

[1] In this discussion, we have already restricted ourselves to the view that $g(\cdot)$ is admissible only if it corresponds to incrementing or decrementing by some loop-invariant quantity.

[2] Note that we only compare M-names that are at the same point in the program.

computing the values of the sets S_i at all points of interest, until a stable solution is arrived at. Once the equations have been solved, the set S at any point in the program specifies exactly which M-names are accessible in EVRs and in which specific EVR elements the contents of those memory locations are to be found.

In general, the set S could grow indefinitely as it is repeatedly propagated around a loop and the M-names are repeatedly remapped by statements that redefine the subscript variables. If the subscript variables change monotonically, i.e., they are either only incremented or only decremented, this runaway growth of S can be contained by imposing a window on the subscripts that are of interest. Whenever an M-name, after remapping, falls outside of this window, that tuple is discarded from the set of map tuples. No useful information is lost if the window can be defined such that it contains all the textual references in the region of code that is being analyzed. Once an M-name has moved outside the window, further propagation round the loop will only move it further outside the window, and it can never again be equal to any reference in the program region. Hence, it is of no value and can be discarded. With this "truncation" of the map tuple sets, the iterative process converges to a solution.

If, for whatever reason, the window cannot be defined as described above, a fall back position is to iterate the map tuple sets around the loop some fixed number of times, D. This gives accurate information about the dependences between iterations that are up to D apart. Beyond that, no information is available and one would need to conservatively assume that every reference in one iteration is possibly-dependent upon every reference more than D iterations away. As noted earlier, good software pipelining performance can be achieved even under such circumstances.

3.3 Optimization of Subscripted References

Space does not permit a complete and meaningful discussion, here, of any of the applications of this data flow analysis technique. Instead, we shall merely sketch out one of these applications. The input is naively generated code, where each operation loads its source operands from memory and stores the result back in memory. The procedure consists of optimizing away scalar and subscripted memory loads that are fully redundant. Data flow analysis is performed as described in the previous sub-section. While so doing, any load operation that specifies an M-name, V, that has a corresponding tuple, $<V, v>$, in the map tuple set S at that point in the program, can be eliminated since the contents of that memory location are in a known EVR element. The operations that would have used the result of the load operation, are changed to reference the EVR element v. An equivalent backward flow analysis procedure can eliminate redundant subscripted store operations. Using various different criteria for membership in the map tuple sets, it is possible to perform fairly comprehensive optimizations of subscripted references such that partially redundant as well as fully redundant loads and stores are eliminated. A simple example of such optimization is shown in Figure 5. The ad hoc optimization of subscripted references performed in the Cydra 5 compiler (Table 1) is systematized and rendered more powerful by the use of map tuple flow analysis.

```
                                        T1[1] = A(5)
                                        T2[1] = A(3)
                                        T2[2] = A(2)
                                        T2[3] = A(1)
        DO 10 I = 6,50                  DO 10 I = 6,50
          A(I-2) = B(I)                   T2 = B(I)
                                          A(I-2) = T2
          IF ... THEN                     IF ... THEN
            A(I) = A(I-1) + 5               T1 = T1[1] + 5
          ELSE                            ELSE
            A(I-1) = A(I-5) * 4             T1[1] = T2[3] * 4
                                           T1 = A(I)
          ENDIF                           ENDIF
          C(I) = A(I-3)                   C(I) = T2[1]
10      CONTINUE                   10   CONTINUE
                                        A(I) = T1
                                        A(I-1) = T1[1]

             (a)                                  (b)
```

Figure 5. A simple example of subscripted reference optimization that one would like to achieve. (a) The original code with four references to array A per iteration. (b) A source code level representation of the code after subscripted references optimization. There are now at most two references to array A per iteration.

4 Conclusions

Compilers for instruction-level parallel processors face a different set of challenges. Given the greater flexibility of such processors, there is the need as well as the opportunity for developing at least as rich a repertoire of compiler techniques for instruction-level parallelism as has been developed for vectorization. Dynamic single assignment and the data flow and dependence analysis methodology outlined in this paper may provide some of the capabilities needed by ILP compilers. However, this paper opens up more possibilities and issues than it puts to rest. Various restrictions were imposed upon the applicability of the data flow methodology. Although they simplified the discussion, some of them may be unnecessary. A better understanding is needed of the true extent of the generality of this approach. The benefit of having of multi-dimensional EVRs needs to be investigated. The conceptual description of the data flow technique is clearly not the best way to actually implement it. More efficient algorithms need to be developed.

5 Acknowledgements

The Cydra 5 Fortran compiler incorporates a number of novel concepts and techniques which were unique at the time that the compiler was built and, three years later, are still ahead of the state of the art. The Cydrome compiler team deserves credit for making these contributions under the pressure of product schedules in a start-up. In particular, the dependence analysis, loop optimizations and transformations in the Cydrome compiler are mainly due to Ross Towle and Jim Dehnert. The concepts in this paper were sharpened and improved by constant discussions with and comments from Mike Schlansker, Vinod Kathail, Rajiv Gupta and Meng Lee. Meng Lee and P. Tirumalai developed the data regarding the effect of subscripted reference optimization on the Livermore Fortran Kernels.

References

1. Aho, A. V., Sethi, R. and Ullman, J. D. *Compilers: Principles, Techniques, and Tools.* Addison-Wesley, Reading, Mass. 1985.
2. Arvind and Gostelow, K. The U-interpreter. *Computer,* 15, 2, February 1982.
3. Callahan, D., Carr, S. and Kennedy, K. Improving Register Allocation for Subscripted Variables. *Proc. ACM SIGPLAN'90 Conf. on Prog. Lang. Design and Implem.,* 53-65, White Plains, New York, June 1990.
4. Chen, S. S. Large-Scale and High-Speed Multiprocessor System for Scientific Applications: CRAY-X-MP Series. In *High-Speed Computation,* J. S. Kowalik, Ed., NATO ASI Series F: Computer and System Sciences, Vol. 7, Springer, Berlin, 1984.
5. Colwell, R. P., et al. A VLIW Architecture for a Trace Scheduling Compiler. *Proc. 2nd Intl. Conf. on Arch. Support for Prog. Lang. and Oper. Syst.,* Palo Alto, California, October 1987.
6. Cytron, R., Ferrante, J., Rosen, B. K., Wegman, M. N., Zadek, K. An efficient method of computing static single assignment. *Proc. 16th Ann. Symp. on Principles of Prog, Lang.,* 25-35, Austin, Texas, January 1989.
7. Dehnert, J. C., Hsu, P. Y.-T. and Bratt, J. P. Overlapped Loop Support in the Cydra 5. *Proc. 3rd Intl. Conf. on Arch. Support for Prog. Lang. and Oper. Syst.,* Boston, Mass., 26-38, April 1989.
8. Dennis, J. B. First Version of a Data Flow Procedure Language. *Proc. of Programming Symp., Paris 1974,* Lecture Notes in Computer Science 19, Springer Verlag, Berlin, 1974.
9. Ellis, J. R. *Bulldog: A Compiler for VLIW Architectures.* The MIT Press, Cambridge, Mass. 1985.
10. Ferrante, J., Ottenstein, K. J. and Warren, J. D. The Program Dependence Graph and its Use in Optimization. *ACM Trans. on Prog, Lang. and Systems,* 9, 3, 319-349, July 1987.
11. Johnson, M. *Superscalar Microprocessor Design.* Prentice-Hall, Englewood Cliffs, New Jersey. 1991.
12. McMahon, F. H. The Livermore Fortran Kernels: A Computer Test of the Numerical Performance Range. Technical Report UCRL-53745, Lawrence Livermore National Laboratory, December 1986.
13. Pingali, K., Beck, M., Johnson, R., Moudgill, M. and Stodghill, P. Dependence flow graphs: an algebraic approach to program dependencies. *Conf. Record of the 18th Ann. ACM Symp. on Principles of Programming Languages,* 67-78, Orlando, Florida, January 1991.
14. Rau, B. R., Yen, D. W. L., Yen, W. and Towle, R. A. The Cydra 5 Departmental Supercomputer: Design Philosophies, Decisions and Trade-offs. *Computer,* 22, 1, January 1989.
15. Tesler, L. G. and Enea, H. J. A Language Design for Concurrent Processes. *Proc. AFIPS Spring Joint Computer Conference,* 403-408, 1968.
16. Traub, K. R. A Compiler for the MIT Tagged-Token Dataflow Architecture. Technical Report MIT/LCS/TR-370, MIT Laboratory for Computer Science, Cambridge, Mass., August 1986.
17. Zima, H. and Chapman, B. *Supercompilers for Parallel and Vector Computers.* ACM Press, New York. 1990.

16 Extending Conventional Flow Analysis to Deal with Array References

A. Kallis and D. Klappholz
Stevens Institute of Technology

Abstract

Traditional optimization-oriented flow analysis provides methods for solving a wide assortment of problems (e.g., forward and backward problems; problems with confluence operators of union, intersection, etc.). Traditional methods deal extremely well with *scalar variables* because it is easy to determine whether or not two *scalar variable* references refer to the same memory location(s). Traditional methods, on the other hand, deal with references to *array variables* by ignoring the fact that they are *array variables*, i.e., by treating them as though they were references to *scalar variables*; the reason is, of course, that it is more difficult to determine whether two references to the same *array variable* refer to the same memory location(s). Using methods derived from the field of *array subscript analysis*, we have developed methods for the enhancement of the flow analysis of code containing array references. In the present paper we present some elementary results which are useful in solving flow problems which require *must kill* information, problems such as *ud-chaining*, *du-chaining*, and *live variable analysis*. In a later paper we will show how the principles underlying these results may be extended to the solution of problems requiring *must not kill* information, problems such as *global common subexpressions*.

1 Introduction

Traditional optimization-oriented flow analysis [15] performs far better with references to scalar variables than with references to array variables. If A is the identifier of a scalar variable, then all occurrences of A within a single scope cause exactly the same memory location(s) to be accessed. This makes it easy to determine whether a block of code *definitely* accesses the location(s) referred to by a particular variable. This, in turn, makes it easy to obtain certain types of *must information* used in code optimization, e.g., the *must kill* information used in computing *ud chains*.

Suppose, on the other hand, that we are dealing with two references, with lexically identical subscript expressions, to the same array, e.g., two references of the form $A(exp)$. Suppose, further, that $x_1, x_2, ... , x_k$ are *all* the variables which occur in exp. If none of $x_1, x_2, ... , x_k$ is defined on any control path between the two references to $A(exp)$, then the two refer to the same memory location. If not, then it is difficult to determine whether or not they do.

If exp_1 and exp_2 are non-identical integer-valued expressions, then the relation between the referents of occurrences of $A(exp_1)$ and $A(exp_2)$ are even harder to determine. This makes it difficult to obtain *must kill* information.

The present paper addresses the question of computing *must kill information* in the face of

- •array references with lexically identical subscript expressions which do not satisfy the condition described above

- •array references with non-identical subscript expressions

In Section 2 we present a number of preliminaries, culminating with a definition of *killing* appropriate to the case of array references. In Section 3 we develop a formal result which enables us to compute *killing* information. Space limitations prevent us from including proofs of theorems. Later papers will fill this gap.

2 Preliminaries

Array references are most useful when they occur in loops. The techniques presented below, originating, as they do, in the field of *subscript analysis* [1]-[14], are most effective in the context of *Fortran-like loops*.

Definition 1

A *Fortran-like loop* is a loop (the natural loop corresponding to a back edge[15]) which has an induction variable [15] whose initial and final values, and whose per-iteration increment are determined before entry.

■

Fortran *DO* loops are, of course, Fortran-like loops in the sense of Definition 1. In addition, it is often possible to detect Fortran-like loops in code written in languages other than Fortran, e.g. C [18]. In what follows, we will assume that all detected Fortran-like loops have been converted into *DO*-loop syntax; such loops will be referred to simply as *DO loops*. For the sake of simplifying the presentation, we will restrict our attention to nests of *DO* loops. The analysis presented below is easily extended to nests of loops consisting of both *DO* loops and non-*DO* loops, although, as indicated above, non-*DO* loops reduce its effectiveness.

Since we are interested in the question of whether one reference to an array variable kills another reference to that array variable, we will have to be concerned with

> •the set of *all* loops in which a particular reference to
> (definition or use of) a variable is enclosed

> •the set of *all* loops which enclose one reference to a
> variable, but do not enclose a second reference to
> that variable

The following notation provides for the compact discussion of such sets of loops.

Definition 2

For $n > 0$, the notation $DO\ I^{(n)} = M^{(n)}, N^{(n)} \dots END\ I^{(n)}$ will be used to denote the nest of n loops shown in Figure 1, where

> •For $1 \le i \le n\text{-}1$, the code block A_i contains a *DO* statement
> only if the corresponding *END* statement is also in A_i.

> •For $1 \le i \le n\text{-}1$, the code block C_i contains a *DO* statement
> only if the corresponding *END* statement is also in C_i.

•The code block B may contain entire DO loops.

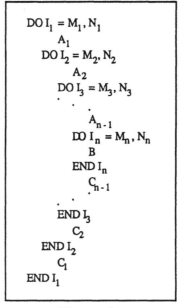

Figure 1

In order to define an appropriate notion of *killing* in the context of array references, we first review some standard notion.

Definition 3

Let P be a program. For integers a and b, $a \leq b$, let $[a, b]$ denote the set of integers i such that $a \leq i \leq b$.

If $L = DO\ I^{(n)} = M^{(n)}, N^{(n)} \ldots END\ I^{(n)}$ is a nest of loops in P, where $n > 0$, then $ITERSET(L)$ is defined as $[M_1, N_1] \times [M_2, N_2] \times \ldots \times [M_n, N_n]$.

If A is a variable declared in P, and γ is a reference to A in P, and $L = DO\ I^{(n)} = M^{(n)}, N^{(n)} \ldots END\ I^{(n)}$ is the nest of all loops in which γ is enclosed (in P), where $n > 0$, then $ITERSET(\gamma)$ is defined as $ITERSET(L)$.

For every $i = (i_1, i_2, \ldots, i_n) \in ITERSET(\gamma)$ there is a potential execution of γ, *potential* because γ may be embedded in conditionals. This potential execution will be denoted by $\gamma(i)$ or $\gamma(i_1, i_2, \ldots, i_n)$. Because we are interested in the (must) notion of *killing*, we will not make the assumption, made in the conservative (may) computation of data dependences, that every potential reference is an actual reference.

■

One last bit of notation is necessary before we define *killing*.

Definition 4

Let P be a program, and let A be an array variable declared in P. Let γ_1 and γ_2 be two references to A in P where

$$\bullet L_1 = DO \ I_1^{(n_1)} \ = \ M_1^{(n_1)}, \ N_1^{(n_1)} \ \ldots \ END_1^{(n_1)}$$

is the nest of all *DO* loops in P which enclose γ_1 but not γ_2

$$\bullet L_2 = DO \ I_2^{(n_2)} \ = \ M_2^{(n_2)}, \ N_2^{(n_2)} \ \ldots \ END_2^{(n_2)}$$

is the nest of all *DO* loops in P which enclose γ_2 but not γ_1

$$\bullet L_3 = DO \ I_3^{(n_3)} \ = \ M_3^{(n_3)}, \ N_3^{(n_3)} \ \ldots \ END_3^{(n_3)}$$

is the nest of all *DO* loops in P which enclose both γ_1 and γ_2

and *DO* $I^{(0)} = M^{(0)}, N^{(0)} \ldots END \ I^{(0)}$ denotes the null nest. (I.e., P contains the complex loop nest of the form shown in Figure 2, where any of the three nests may be the null nest.)

Let $i = (i_{31}, i_{32}, \ldots, i_{3n_3}, i_{11}, i_{12}, \ldots, i_{1n_1}) \in ITERSET(L_3) \times ITERSET(L_1)$,

and let $i' = (i'_{31}, i'_{32}, \ldots, i'_{3n_3}, i'_{21}, i'_{22}, \ldots, i'_{2n_2}) \in ITERSET(L_3) \times ITERSET(L_2)$

$\gamma_1(i)$ is said to *precede* $\gamma_2(i')$, denoted $\gamma_1(i) < \gamma_2(i')$ if

$\bullet n_3 = 0$ and γ_1 precedes γ_2 in P

$\bullet$ or $n_3 > 0$, and γ_1 precedes γ_2 in P and

$$(i_{31}, i_{32}, \ldots, i_{3n_3}) = (i'_{31}, i'_{32}, \ldots, i'_{3n_3})$$

- or $n_3 > 0$, and $(i_{31}, i_{32}, \dots, i_{3n_3})$ precedes $(i'_{31}, i'_{32}, \dots, i'_{3n_3})$

  lexicographically

We are now in a position to define the notion of *killing*.

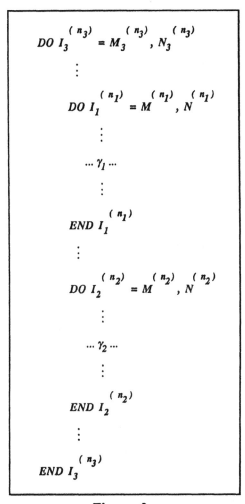

Figure 2

Definition 5

Let P be a program. Let α and α' be two definitions of an array A in P, and let β be a use of A in P.

Let

$$\bullet DO \quad I_\alpha^{(n_\alpha)} = M_\alpha^{(n_\alpha)}, \quad N_\alpha^{(n_\alpha)} \quad \ldots \quad END_\alpha^{(n_\alpha)} \quad be$$

the nest of all DO loops in P in which α is embedded

$$\bullet DO \quad I_{\alpha'}^{(n_{\alpha'})} = M_{\alpha'}^{(n_{\alpha'})}, \quad N_{\alpha'}^{(n_{\alpha'})} \quad \ldots \quad END_{\alpha'}^{(n_{\alpha'})} \quad be$$

the nest of all DO loops in P in which α' is embedded

$$\bullet DO \quad I_\beta^{(n_\beta)} = M_\beta^{(n_\beta)}, \quad N_\beta^{(n_\beta)} \quad \ldots \quad END_\beta^{(n_\beta)}$$

be the nest of all DO loops in P in which β is embedded

Note that no a priori assumption is being made about the degree of overlap of the three loops. They may overlap *completely*, *partially*, or *not at all*.

The definition α' will be said to *kill the definition α with respect to the use β* if the following is true for every $i_\alpha \in ITERSET(\alpha)$:

> if $\alpha(i_\alpha)$ defines some element of A, say $A(c)$, and there
> exists an $i_\beta \in ITERSET(\beta)$ such that $i_\alpha < i_\beta$ and $\beta(i_\beta)$
> uses $A(c)$, then there exists an $i_{\alpha'} \in ITERSET(\alpha')$ such
> that $i_\alpha < i_{\alpha'} < i_\beta$ and $\alpha'(i_{\alpha'})$ also defines $A(c)$

■

The reason for defining the notion of α' *killing α with respect to β* rather than α' *killing α* is, of course, that the latter would lead to less precise approximations of the desired flow information than does the former.

3 Computing Killing Information

As is usual in the field of subscript analysis, our most powerful results will hold when the subscript expression of an array reference γ embedded in a nest of DO loops $DO \ I^{(n)} = M^{(n)}, N^{(n)} \ \ldots \ END \ I^{(n)}$ is a linear expression, with integer coefficients, in the variables $I_1, I_2, \ldots, I_n$. The following theorem, which deals with such expressions, and which begins our discussion of the computation of *killing information* is proved in [2]-[3].

Theorem 1

Let $c = (c_0, c_1, \ldots, c_n)$ be an $(n+1)$-tuple of integers, and let $m = ((M_1, N_1), (M_2, N_2), \ldots, (M_n, N_n))$ be an n-tuple of pairs of integers such that $M_k < N_k$ for each $k, 1 \leq k \leq n$.

If I_k is restricted to vary between M_k and N_k for $1 \leq k \leq n$, then the values assumed by the expression $c_0 + c_1 I_1 + c_2 I_2 + \ldots + c_n I_n$ lie between

$$minspan(c, m) = c_0 + \sum_{k=1}^{n} (c_k^+ M_k - c_k^- N_k)$$

and

$$maxspan(c, m) = c_0 + \sum_{k=1}^{n} (c_k^+ N_k - c_k^- M_k)$$

∎

Corollary 2 uses Theorem 1 to enable us to determine upper and lower bounds on the subscripts of the elements of an array which are accessed by a reference to that array.

Corollary 2

Let P be a program, and let $\gamma \equiv A(c_0 + c_1 I_1 + c_2 I_2 + \ldots + c_n I_n)$ be a reference to an array A in P, where $DO\ I^{(n)} = M^{(n)}, N^{(n)} \ldots END\ I^{(n)}$ is the set of all loops in which γ is enclosed, and $c = (c_0, c_1, \ldots, c_n)$ is an $(n+1)$-tuple of integers.

The subscripts of the elements of array A which are referenced by the up to $(N_1 - M_1 + 1) \times (N_2 - M_2 + 1) \times \ldots \times (N_n - M_n + 1)$ executions of γ lie between $minspan(c, ((M_1, N_1), (M_2, N_2), \ldots, (M_n, N_n)))$ and $maxspan(c, ((M_1, N_1), (M_2, N_2), \ldots, (M_n, N_n)))$.

∎

Proof

Immediate from Theorem 1.

■

But, knowing upper and lower bounds is typically not enough. The question of *which particular elements* of A between A(minspan) and A(maxspan) are accessed by γ is, however, a more complicated matter. This is precisely the reason that it is difficult to determine whether one array definition is killed by another definition of the same array. Theorem 4 (see [17] for a proof) provides a first step in a method for approximating kill sets.

Theorem 4

Let $c_1 < c_2 < ... < c_n$ be non-zero integers. For each k, $1 \leq k \leq n$, let M_k and N_k be integers, $M_k < N_k$.

For every integer x in the interval

$$\left[\sum_{k=1}^{n} (c_k^+ M_k - c_k^- N_k) \quad , \quad \sum_{k=1}^{n} (c_k^+ N_k - c_k^- M_k) \right]$$

there exist integers $j_1, j_2, ... , j_n$ such that

$$\bullet c_1 j_1 + c_2 j_2 + ... + c_n j_n = x.$$

$$\bullet \text{for each } i, \ 1 \leq i \leq n, M_i \leq j_i \leq N_i$$

if

$$|c_1| = 1$$

and

for each j, $2 \leq j \leq n$,

$$|c_j| \leq 1 + \sum_{k=1}^{j-1} |c_k| (N_k - M_k)$$

■

The following definition serves to name the condition discussed in Theorem 4.

Definition 6

Let $c_0, c_1, c_2, \ldots, c_n$ be integers, none of which is necessarily non-zero. For each k, $1 \leq k \leq n$, let M_k and N_k be integers, $M_k < N_k$. Let $c'_1, c'_2, \ldots, c'_n$ be $c_1, c_2, \ldots, c_n$ in ascending order of magnitude. Let r be the smallest integer greater than zero such that $c'_r > 0$.

If $|c'_r| = 1$ and for each j, $r+1 \leq j \leq n$,

$$|c'_j| \leq 1 + \sum_{k=1}^{j-1} |c'_k| (N_k - M_k)$$

then the $(n+1)$-tuple of integers $(c_0, c_1, c_2, \ldots, c_n)$ will be said to *span its range with respect to* the n-tuple of pairs $((M_1, N_1), (M_2, N_2), \ldots, (M_n, N_n))$.

■

If the coefficients of a subscript expression span their range with respect to the appropriate pairs of loop limits, a situation which empirical results [16] suggest happens quite frequently in actual code, then Corollary 5, an immediate consequence of Theorem 4, enables us to determine precisely which array elements are accessed by the reference -- so long as the reference is executed on every iteration of the relevant loops.

Corollary 5

Let P be a program, and let $\gamma \equiv A(c_0 + c_1 I_1 + c_2 I_2 + \ldots + c_n I_n)$ be a reference to an array A in P, where $DO\ I^{(n)} = M^{(n)},\ N^{(n)} \ldots END\ I^{(n)}$ is the set of all loops in which γ is enclosed, and $c = (c_0, c_1, \ldots, c_n)$ is an $(n+1)$-tuple of integers.

If c spans its range with respect to $((M_1, N_1), (M_2, N_2), \ldots, (M_n, N_n))$, and γ is executed unconditionally, then the executions of γ access *all elements of A* between $minspan(c, ((M_1, N_1), (M_2, N_2), \ldots, (M_n, N_n)))$ and $maxspan(c, ((M_1, N_1), (M_2, N_2), \ldots, (M_n, N_n)))$

■

Proof
Immediate from Theorem 4 and Definition 6.

■

Before stating our major result, we first review the notion of the *direction* of a data dependence between two array references, both for the case in which there are common loops which enclose the two, and for the case in which there are no such common loops.

Definition 7
Let $P, \gamma_1, \gamma_2, L_1, L_2, L_3, n_1, n_2$, and n_3 be as in definition 4, where

$$\bullet \gamma_1 = A(c_{10} + c_{11} I_{11} + c_{12} I_{12} + \ldots + c_{1n_1} I_{1n_1} + c_{31} I_{31} + c_{32} I_{32} + \ldots + c_{3n_3} I_{3n_3})$$

$$\bullet \gamma_2 = A(c_{20} + c_{21} I_{21} + c_{22} I_{22} + \ldots + c_{2n_2} I_{2n_2} + c'_{31} I_{31} + c'_{32} I_{32} + \ldots + c'_{3n_3} I_{3n_3}).$$

There is said to be a data dependence *from γ_1 to γ_2* if

$\bullet$ either $n_3 = 0$ and there exist

$$i = (i_{11}, i_{12}, \ldots, i_{1n_1}) \in ITERSET(L_1)$$

$$i' = (i'_{21}, i'_{22}, \ldots, i'_{2n_2}) \in ITERSET(L_2)$$

such that

$\bullet \gamma_1(i) < \gamma_2(i')$

$\bullet$ and

$$c_{10} + c_{11}i_{11} + c_{12}i_{12} + \cdots + c_{1n_1}i_{1n_1} = c_{20} + c_{21}i'_{21} + c_{22}i'_{22} + \cdots$$
$$+ c_{2n_2}i'_{2n_2}$$

$\bullet$ or $n_3 > 0$, and there exist

$$i = (i_{31}, i_{32}, \cdots, i_{3n_3}, i_{11}, i_{12}, \cdots, i_{1n_1}) \in ITERSET(L_3) \times ITERSET(L_1)$$

$$i' = (i'_{31}, i'_{32}, \cdots, i'_{3n_3}, i'_{21}, i'_{22}, \cdots, i'_{2n_2}) \in ITERSET(L_3) \times$$
$$ITERSET(L_2)$$

such that

$\bullet \gamma_1(i) < \gamma_2(i')$

$\bullet$ and

$$c_{10} + c_{11}I_{11} + c_{12}I_{12} + \cdots + c_{1n_1}I_{1n_1} + c_{31}I_{31} + c_{32}I_{32} + \cdots + c_{3n_3}I_{3n_3}$$
$$= c_{20} + c_{21}I_{21} + c_{22}I_{22} + \cdots + c_{2n_2}I_{2n_2} + c'_{31}I_{31} + c'_{32}I_{32} + \cdots$$
$$+ c'_{3n_3}I_{3n_3}$$

■

The following theorem, which is the formal result referred to in Section 1, enables us to compute an approximation to *kill* sets which will, in fact, be exact in some of the most frequently-occurring cases.

Theorem 6

Let P be a program. Let

$$\bullet \alpha = A(c_{\alpha 1}I_{\alpha 1} + c_{\alpha 2}I_{\alpha 2} + \cdots + c_{\alpha n_\alpha}I_{\alpha n_\alpha}) \text{ be a definition of}$$

A in P, where

$$DO\ I_\alpha^{(n_\alpha)} = M_\alpha^{(n_\alpha)}, \quad N_\alpha^{(n_\alpha)} \quad \cdots \quad END_\alpha^{(n_\alpha)}$$

is the nest of all *DO* loops in P in which α is embedded

• $\alpha' = A(c_{\alpha'1}I_{\alpha'1} + c_{\alpha'2}I_{\alpha'2} + \ldots + c_{\alpha'n_{\alpha'}}I_{\alpha'n_{\alpha'}})$ be a

definition of A in P, where

$$DO \quad I_{\alpha'}^{(n_{\alpha'})} = M_{\alpha'}^{(n_{\alpha'})}, \quad N_{\alpha'}^{(n_{\alpha'})} \quad \ldots \quad END_{\alpha'}^{(n_{\alpha'})}$$

is the nest of all *DO* loops in P in which α' is embedded

• $\beta = A(c_{\beta1}I_{\beta1} + c_{\beta2}I_{\beta2} + \ldots + c_{\beta n_{\beta}}I_{\beta n_{\beta}})$ be a use of A in P,

where

$$DO \quad I_{\beta}^{(n_{\beta})} = M_{\beta}^{(n_{\beta})}, \quad N_{\beta}^{(n_{\beta})} \quad \ldots \quad END_{\beta}^{(n_{\beta})}$$

is the nest of all *DO* loops in P in which β is embedded

• $\mu_{\alpha} = ((M_{\alpha1}, N_{\alpha1}), (M_{\alpha2}, N_{\alpha2}), \ldots, (M_{\alpha n_{\alpha}}, N_{\alpha n_{\alpha}}))$,

• $\mu_{\alpha'} = ((M_{\alpha'1}, N_{\alpha'1}), (M_{\alpha'2}, N_{\alpha'2}), \ldots, (M_{\alpha'n_{\alpha'}}, N_{\alpha'n_{\alpha'}}))$

• $\mu_{\beta} = ((M_{\beta1}, N_{\beta1}), (M_{\beta2}, N_{\beta2}), \ldots, (M_{\beta n_{\beta}}, N_{\beta n_{\beta}}))$,

(Note that we are making no assumption about the relative order of occurrence of α, α' and β in P, nor are we making any assumption about the amount of overlap, if any, among the three loop nests. Each pair of nests may overlap *not at all*, *partially*, or *completely*. The overlap of all three may be *empty*, *partial*, or *total*.)

If

•the execution of α' is unconditional on every iteration of

$$DO \quad I_{\alpha'}^{(n_{\alpha'})} = M_{\alpha'}^{(n_{\alpha'})}, \quad N_{\alpha'}^{(n_{\alpha'})} \quad \ldots \quad END_{\alpha'}^{(n_{\alpha'})}$$

•and α' spans its range with respect to $\mu_{\alpha'}$

•and the set of elements of A referenced by α' is a superset of the intersection of the sets of elements referenced by α and β, i.e.,

$$[max(minspan(\alpha, \mu_\alpha), minspan(\beta, \mu_\beta)),$$

$$min(maxspan(\alpha, \mu_\alpha), maxspan(\beta, \mu_\beta))]$$

$$\subseteq [minspan(\alpha', \mu_{\alpha'}), maxspan(\alpha', \mu_{\alpha'})]$$

•and there is no data dependence *from β to α'*.

•and there is no data dependence from α' to α.

then

α' kills α with respect to β

■

The method for computing *killing* information embodied in Theorem 6 can be incorporated into an iterative approximation algorithm [15] for computing *ud chains*, *du chains* or *live variable information* in a number of fairly straightforward ways. The full-length version of the present paper discusses all of these issues; it will also show how the methods discussed here may be extended to the solution of flow analysis problems requiring *must not kill* information such as as global common subexpressions.

References

[1] Lamport, L. "The Parallel Execution of DO Loops," *Communications of the ACM*, Vol. 17, No. 2, February, 1974.
[2] Banerjee, U., "Data Dependence in Ordinary Programs," M.S. thesis, Univ. of Ill at Urbana-Champaign, Nov., 1976.
[3] Banerjee, U., "Speedup of Ordinary Programs," Ph.D. thesis, Univ. of Ill at Urbana-Champaign, 1979.
[4] Banerjee, U., *Dependence Analysis for Supercomputing*, Kluwer Academic Publishers, Norwell, Mass., 1988.
[5] Towle, R.A., "Control and Data Dependence for Program Transformations," Ph.D. thesis, University of Illinois at Urbana-Champaign, 1976.

[6] Kuck, D.J., R.H. Kuhn, D. Padua, B.R. Leisure, and M.J. Wolfe, "Dependence Graphs and Compiler Optimizations," Proceedings of 8th ACM Symposium on Principles of Programming Languages, January, 1981.

[7] Wolfe, Michael, "Optimizing Supercompilers for Supercomputers," Ph.D. Thesis, Univ. of Ill. at Urbana-Champaign, Oct., 1982.

[8] Wolfe, Michael, *Optimizing Supercompilers for Supercomputers*, Pitman Publishing Co., London, and MIT Press, Cambridge, Mass, 1989.

[9] Allen, J.R., "Dependence Analysis for Subscripted Variables and its Application to Program Transformations", Ph.D. Thesis, Rice University, April, 1983

[10] Allen, J.R., and K. Kennedy, "Automatic Loop Interchange," Sigplan '84 Symposium on Compiler Construction, Montreal, June, 1984.

[11] Allen, J.R., and K. Kennedy, "Automatic Translation of Fortran Programs to Vector Form," *ACM Transactions on Programming Languages and Systems*, Vol. 9, No. 4, October, 1987.

[12] Burke, M., and R. Cytron, "Interprocedural Dependence Analysis and Parallelization," Proceedings of SIGPLAN '86 Symposium on Compiler Construction, Palo Alto, CA, June, 1986.

[13] Rosene, Carl M., "Incremental Dependence Analysis," Ph.D. thesis, Rice University, March, 1990; Rice COMP TR90-112.

[14] Goff, Gina, Ken Kennedy, and Chau-Wen Tseng, "Practical Dependence testing," Proceedings of SIGPLAN '91, June, 1991

[15] Aho, A., Sethi, R., and Ullman, J., *Compilers: Principles, Techniques and Tools*, Addison-Wesley, 1986

[16] Shen, Z., Z. Li, and P. Yew, "An Empirical Study on Array Subscripts and Data Dependences," Proceedings of 1989 International Conference on Parallel Processing, August, 1989.

[17] Klappholz, D., K. Psarris, and X. Kong, "On the Perfect Accuracy of an Approximte Subscript Analysis Test," Proceedings of the International Conference on Supercomputing, Amsterdam, June 1990.

[18] Allen, Randy, and Steve Johnson, "Compiling C for Vectorization, Parallelization, and Inline Expansion," Proceedings of the Sigplan '88 Conference on Programming Language design and Implementation, Atlanta, June, 1988.

17 Run-Time Management of Lisp Parallelism and the Hierarchical Task Graph Program Representation

M. Furnari
Istituto de Cibernetica
C. Polychronopoulos
University of Illinois at Urbana-Champaign

Abstract

This paper suggests how to extend the *Hierarchical Task Graph* program representation, and its execution model to address the LISP code parallelization problems. The advantages of this approach lie in the fact of on avoiding to annotate LISP programs, and in accounting for run-time scheduling policies all into a unified environment. We start by reviewing the problem of run-time parallelism management, first in the imperative languages setting, and next in LISP setting. Before describing the *Hierarchical Task Graph* (*HTG*) program representation [7], we review the basic notions of control and data dependence analysis. Finally we describe how to modify the *HTG* and its execution model to take into account for the *Lazy Task Creation* model [19], and the *Sponsor Model* for exploiting speculative computations in LISP[20].

1 Introduction

The general applicability and use of parallel processing depends critically on the effective and efficient exploitation of parallelism at all granularity levels. However, when a parallel algorithm is manually coded, the resulting program often produces tasks of a finer grain than that which the implementation can exploit efficiently. To overcome these difficulties the parallelization task has been splitted into two problems, the first one involve the discovering of parallel opportunities in a program, the second deals with the efficient management of the execution of the parallelized code.

To cope with the problem of discovering the parallel opportunities in a program, two approaches have been pursued, either using parallelizing compiler (*restructuring systems*), or using parallel language extensions (*annotating systems*).

To improve the execution of parallelized code, tools for building task of acceptable granularity have been developed. They are essentially based on a cheap way to create processes. But fine-tuning may be necessary in some cases to maximize performance, with possible drawbacks such as the cost in programming effort and the program clarity. Furthermore, this often involves calibration of program parameters through experimentation, and this work may be repeated for a different target machine or data set. Or, worst yet, it may become impractical when the program runs in a multiprogramming/multiprocessing environment. The complexity of parallel programming makes fine performance-tuning impossible at the programmer level, and in a general-purpose environment.

The key to solve this problem is the ability of the compiler to:

- compile the program once and package parallel threads at all granularity levels, and

- adjust the granularity of parallel threads created at run-time, and based on the size and type of the rest of the workload present in the system.

In fact, to be really usable the parallelization must enable the user to run simultaneously several parallel programs on the same machine without a significant drop on parallel program performance.

For the imperative languages there are many efforts addressing this problem, for example, Polychronopoulos [22] suggests moving the scheduling policy inside the program, by introducing the notion of autoscheduling. For the LISP-like languages Mohr proposed in [19] the *Lazy Task Creation* strategy; Osborne in [20] proposed the *sponsor* model to cope with symbolic speculative computations, and Pehoushek in [21] proposed to split the global ready processes queue on each processors to reduce contention on accessing it.

In this paper we describe the use of an extension of the *autoscheduling* technique, the *Hierarchical Task Graph* program representation[7], and its corresponding computational model, in the LISP realm. Starting from the algorithm described in [22], we show step by step how to modify it to accommodate the lazy tasks creation computation model [19] and the touching sponsor for the speculative computations [20]. The main advantage of this approach lies in avoiding to annotate the LISP programs.

In Section 2 we report on the current status of the parallel LISP extensions, and the strategies used to manage task granularity at run-time. Attention is focussed on the *lazy task creation* proposed in [19], and the *sponsor model* for *speculative computations* proposed in [20].

In Section 3 we review and summarize the most important notions of *control* and *data dependence analysis*. Next, in Section 4 we describe the efforts in using this framework to parallelize imperative languages. Special attention will be payed to the problem of automatically discovering and managing at run-time different parallel constructs, with a dynamic and varying granularity. In this context we review the *HTG*, and the task allocation algorithm proposed in [22]. Finally, in Section 5, we extend the previous proposal to LISP, showing how the *HTG* is a good candidate for synthesizing both the *lazy task creation*, and the *sponsor model* avoiding the use of *ad hoc* techniques such as described in [19,20].

2   Parallelism and Lisp-Like languages

In order to cope with parallelism in LISP two approaches have been pursued:

- the first one, extends LISP with *parallel* constructs to help the compiler to parallelize a LISP program. In other words, the parallelism is annotated by the added language constructs (*annotating systems*) [9,10,3,4,5].

- the second one relies on using the existing code and smart compiling methods to parallelize the source code [12,14,6] (*restructuring systems*).

The former approach places a significant burden on the programmer (which depend directly on the level and complexity of constructs). Furthermore, the definition of a complete and orthogonal parallel constructs-set, satisfying simplicity and expressiveness, have yet to be solved.

By contrast, the latter approach is attractive for it allows the use of already existing code without modifications, and it relieves the programmer from significant conceptual effort needed for manual parallelization. Unfortunately, LISP restructuring is a difficult problem, and many related problems has been proved to be *NP-complete* [17].

2.1 Annotation systems

Widespreaded multiprocessing LISP dialects include the QLISP [3,4,5], and the MULTILISP [10].

The QLISP design goals include the following: 1) targeting multiprocessors with shared memory organization; 2) the ability to limit the degree of multiprocessing at run-time; 3) minimal extensions with respect to ordinary LISP to cope with parallelism; and 4) all constructs should work also in a uni-processing setting. All the LISP processes are activated and maintained in a global process queue.

The parallel constructs are qlet and qlambda. The evaluation of (qlet pred ((x_1 arg_1) (x_n arg_n)) . body) creates a process for the evaluation of each expression arg_i. When these processes terminate, the values of arg_i are respectively bound to each of x_i, and body is then evaluated. The value of qlet is the value of body. If pred, called *propositional parameter*, evaluates to :eager, then the evaluation of body is overlapped with the evaluation of the arg_i's.

The form (qlambda pred (lambda (lambda-list) . body) is used to create *process closures*. A process closure may be activated as a new process when it is applied. Applying a *process closure* causes the associated process to be started, and the arguments are evaluated by the spawning processes.

MULTILISP is an extension of *Scheme*, developed by Halstead [10], which retains the *Scheme* possibility of side effects. It may be characterized as a LISP dialect with the following features: 1) lexical scoped binding discipline; 2) shared memory computer organization; 3) sequential default computation mechanism; 4) a small set of constructs to cope with parallelism.

A programmer may use the constructs future, pcall, and delay to introduce parallelism in a MULTILISP program.

The (future exp) evaluation will result in a concurrent computation for a value and the disposition or use of that value. That is, the form (future exp) immediately returns a *future-cell* for the value of the expression exp, and it concurrently begins its evaluation.

When the evaluation of exp yields a value, it replaces *future-cell*. Initially the future is said to be in an undetermined state; it becomes determined when its value is computed. The programmer can trigger this state transition, by requesting the value of a future object; this action is called *touching* a future. Touching a future will put the touching process into the wait state just until the process computing the future value is completed.

The MULTILISP expression (pcall form arg_1 ... arg_n) will result in the concurrent evaluation of the expressions form, arg_1, arg_2, ..., arg_n, after which the value of form is applied to the values of arg_1, arg_2, ..., arg_n returning the value of its application. Thus, pcall embodies an implicit *fork-join* followed by a procedure call.

MULTILISP provides the construct delay, whose value it is not computed by the associated process until it is explicitly required. In other words, a process is associated with the form (delay exp), but it does not start until an explicit or implicit touch to exp is carried out.

2.2 Restructuring systems

Gray at MIT investigated inserting futures into side-effect-free LISP programs [6]. He sought concurrency in two places. The first, was concurrent execution of syntactically parallel tasks, such as the evaluation of actual arguments in a function call. The second, involved overlapped execution of a subexpression and its containing expression. For example, executing a function concurrently with the computation of its arguments. Since side-effects-free programs contain only simple flow dependence, data dependence analysis was unnecessary and futures provided all the required synchronization. In this context the major difficulty is avoiding spawning too many processes.

Katz proposed a general approach for concurrently executing LISP programs with side-effects [16]. His system, *ParaTran*, relies on a combination of program transformations and run-time error checking to implement *optimistic* concurrency. Under this scheme (borrowed from databases) a transaction is assumed to have few conflicts with other transactions. Transactions execute without regarding possible conflicts. A monitor examines the read and write traces for each transaction to detect conflicts and restart transactions that violate the serializability constraints. A transaction commits its results when it can no longer conflict with any other transactions.

Harrison [12] proposed techniques for concurrently executing non-*pure* LISP. His transformation system, PARCEL, contains a new representation for lists that allows the use of parallel algorithms normally associated with numeric programs. This list representation stores the car pointers of a list segment contiguously, without the *cdr* pointers. The representations also contain the number of elements remaining in the list. Its main advantage is that the ith element of a list can be obtained faster by treating blocks of pointers as a vector. PARCEL also carry out an extensive dependence analysis based on abstract interpretation to discover variable conflicting accesses

CURARE is another restructuring system, developed by Larus [17,18] which automatically transforms sequential LISP programs into semantically equivalent concurrent programs. CURARE treats recursive functions, because they offer several advantages over loops and provide a convenient framework for inserting locks and handling the dynamic behaviour of symbolic programs. Loops, or their recursive counterparts (*tail-recursive functions*), which are suitable for concurrent execution are changed to execute on a set of concurrent server processes. These servers execute single loop iterations and therefore they need to be extremely inexpensive to invoke.

3 Managing Parallelism in the current parallel LISP dialects

One of the major drawbacks of all LISP parallel systems described above is their static nature: they determine the number of parallel tasks at *compile-time*. This is a very limiting factor in spreading their use in practical applications of symbolic computation, such as expert systems, natural language recognizers, and so on.

QLISP [3,4] provides the *propositional parameters* as tools for building tasks of acceptable granularity at run-time. Such fine-tuning may be necessary in some cases to maximize performance, but it involves programming effort and may compromise program clarity. Also, certain program parameters need to be calibrated through experimentations, and this work may need to be repeated for a different target machine or data set. Or, worst yet for each job submission, when the program runs in a parallel multiprogramming.

A system is described in [19] in which the programmer decides on what can be computed safely in parallel, leaving the decision on how task-splitting will done to the run-time system. This system relies on the freedom to interpret the future operational semantics.

In the operational interpretation of a future form, there is a symmetric relationship between the parent and child tasks, when they coexist as parallel activities. In such a case either the parent or the child process may resolve the future.

For example, let (C (future expr)) be a future expression. This may be interpreted such as:

- the computation of expr may be performed by the child process, and it can proceed in parallel with its parent continuation C;

- reversing the task roles, the parent task can compute expr while the child task computes C;

- the parent task computes first expr then C, ignoring the future. This process is called inlining.

The run-time task spawning strategy adopted in [19] consists of inlining every task at compile-time, saving sufficient information in such a way as to be selectively un-inlined as processing resources become available at run-time. The main advantages of this approach with respect to the QLISP *propositional parameters* consist of more clear code, and the elimination of the *calibration process*.

3.1 Speculative computation and the sponsor model in parallel LISP

Models of speculative parallelism classify computations in three groups: (1) computations known to be required, *relevant* (or *mandatory*) computations; (2) computations known not to be required, or *irrelevant* computations; and (3) computation not known to be required or not required, or *speculative computations*.

Thus a speculative computation may become mandatory during the course of a computation, as more information becomes available.

An eager computation is a computation that is started early before it is required, but with certainty that it will be required. A speculative computation is a computation that is started before it is required, like eager, but without any assurance that it will be required later, unlike eager computation.

Since a large number of speculative computations may swamp the machine resources, it is necessary to control it. The main issues in controlling speculative computation are:

1. *ordering* - we need some way to allocate resources to computations according to the relative promise of necessity.

2. *demand transitivity* - to avoiding the changing of the desired ordering among the computations, it is necessary to impose some sort of transitivity. In other words, the priority of a computation C must be at least as high as that of all the computations which are blocked awaiting C's result.

3. *modularity* - a way to preserve the functionality of a group of related speculative computation wherever the group appears. In other words we may be able to embed any group of speculative computations as a subcomputation in any other speculative computation and retain the local ordering within the group.

4. *reclaim* - to make an efficient and effective use of the machine resources we need a means for reclaiming irrelevant computations.

We must also take into account side effects, which cause two types of problems with speculative computation. First, the pursuit of multiple approaches and the temporary relaxation of synchronization constraints can lead to interference. Second, computations performing relevant side-effects may be aborted.

The *sponsor model* allows the allocation of the resources to tasks in a controlled way, where the controlling parameters are the *attributes* that the task possesses. Sponsors supply these attributes, for examples priorities. Each task may have zero or more sponsors which contribute to its attributes. In other words, the sponsors of a task collectively determine the computation resources allocated to that task. A task without a sponsor does not run. The attributes contributed by a tasks's sponsors are combined according to a combining rule to yield the effective attributes of a task.

The sponsor types may be one of the following:

1. *External sponsors* - this type of sponsors supply the absolute attributes.

2. *Toucher sponsors* - when one task touches another, in the sense of a *future-touching* operation, the toucher sponsor sponsors the touched task with the effective attributes of the touching task.

3. *Task sponsors* - a task may sponsor any other task. The sponsor attributes in this case are the effective attributes of the sponsoring task.

4. *Controller sponsors* - the three previous types of sponsors are all passive; they merely act as fixed attribute sources or pass on attributes from other sources. Controller sponsors receive sponsorship and actively distribute it among the tasks in their control domain according to some built-in control strategy.

In [20] only the *touching model* implementation is described, together with some applications. He reports a significant performance improvement for the eight-puzzle problem, where it is necessary to search for a solution in very large state space.

4 Basic notions of flow & dependence analysis

An essential tool for program optimization techniques is *Program Flow Analysis*. It consists of collecting informations along all possible execution paths, and it can be split in *Control Flow* and *Data Flow Analysis*. Control flow, takes into account instructions dependence generated by the language control operators. Data flow, takes into account instruction dependence arising from different memory usage.

Many interesting techniques has been developed to solve in an efficient way the flow analysis problems for most imperative programming languages, such as FORTRAN, C, PASCAL, etc., see for example [1]. Some of them have been developed to cope with parallelization problems, both vectorization and concurrentization, see for example [7,8,2].

Although in the last decade much attention has been devoted to *data dependence analysis*, and later to *control dependence analysis*, to parallelize a program, only recently attempts have been carried out to develop unique framework which can be used to carry out both kinds of analysis.

Flow analysis is carried out on the *control flow graph* (*CFG*), *CFG = (V_F,E_F)* with unique nodes $START$, $STOP \in V_F$ such that there exists a path from $START$ to every node in V_F, and a path from every node to $STOP$. $START$ has no incoming edges, and $STOP$ has no outgoing edges. In a *CFG* vertices represent *Basic Blocks* (sequences of assignment statements, possibly terminated by a conditional or unconditional branch to the first statement of a basic block), and edges between vertices represent possible transfers of control between basic blocks.

A node x *dominates* node y, denoted by $x \Delta_d y$, iff every path from $START$ to y contains x. We use the notation $x \not\Delta_d y$ to denote that x does not dominate y.

A node y *post-dominates* node x, denoted by $y \Delta_p x$, iff every path from x to $STOP$ contains y. The notation $x \not\Delta_p y$ will denote x does not post-dominate y.

In [2,7] has been proved that the set of post-dominators of a node x form a *chain*. Therefore, there exists a least element called the *immediate post-dominator* of x. The graph obtained by joining each node x with its *immediate post-dominator* y is called *post-dominator tree*, and it is rooted at $STOP$.

4.1 The Data Dependences Graph

To each *basic block* we can associate the information about its memory usage. For example we can associate the sets of the *input variables*, and the set of the *output variables*, within a basic block. There are three types of *Data Dependences* [15]:

- a *flow dependence*, in which one statement writes a value read by a later statement, and will be denoted by δ;

- an *anti-dependence*, in which one statement reads a location subsequently written by another statement, and will be denoted by $\bar{\delta}$;

- an *output dependence*, in which two statements write the same location, and will be denoted by δ^o.

These dependence may be *loop independent* or *loop carried*, depending on whether the conflicting statements execute in the same or different loop iterations. The *distance* of a loop-carried dependence is the number of loop iterations separating the conflicting statements.

Let x and y be two distinct nodes, then exactly one of the following conditions is true:

1. y is reachable from x;

2. x is reachable from y;

3. x is not reachable from y, and y is not reachable from x.

In case 1 and 2 we may have a *data dependence* relation, denoted respectively $x \, \delta_d y$ and $y \, \delta_d x$. In case 3 the conflict does not matter as x and y will not execute together in any execution instance of the *CFG*, and hence can be ignored.

The *Data Dependence Graph DDG* $= (\, V_d, \, E_d)$ is defined as the directed graph with labeled arcs such that:

- $V_d = V_F$ and

- $(x,y) \in E_d$ if $x \, \delta_d y$.

Since $x \, \delta_d y$ implies a path from x to y in *CFG*, the graph containing the arcs of both *CFG* and *DDG* is also acyclic if the *CFG* is acyclic.

4.2 The Control Dependence Graph

Let y, and (x,a) be respectively a node and an arc of a *CFG*. Then we say that y is *control dependent* on node x with label x-a, and will be denoted by $x \, \delta_c y$, iff:

1. $y \not\Delta_p x$ and

2. $\exists$ a non null path $P = \langle \, x,a,\ldots,y \, \rangle$, such that for any $z \in P$ (excluding x and y) $y \, \Delta_p \, z$.

The control dependence graph *CDG*, of a control flow graph *CFG*, is defined as the directed graph with labeled arcs such that:

1. $V_C = V_F$

2. $(x, y) \in E_C$ with label x-a iff $x \, \delta_c y$ with label x-a.

In [7] a procedure to build and optimize the *CDG*, based on the *CFG* and the loop hierarchy, is described.

Since $x \, \delta_c y$ implies a path from x to y in *CFG*, the graph containing the arcs of both *DDG* and *CDG* is also acyclic if the *CDG* is acyclic.

5 The Hierarchical Task Graph

Both *Control Dependence* and *Data Dependence* relations can be framed together in the *Hierarchical Task Graph (HTG)* [7].

The hierarchical task graph is a directed acyclic graph $HTG = (V_H \, E_H)$ with unique nodes *START* and *STOP* belonging to V_H such that there exists a path from *START* to every node in V_H and a path from every node to *STOP*. *START* has no incoming arcs and *STOP* has no outgoing arcs. Each node in V_H can be one of the following types:

1. *simple* node, representing a task that has no subtasks,

2. *compound* node, representing a task that consists of other tasks in an *HTG*, or

3. *Loop* node, representing a task that is a loop whose iteration body is an *HTG*.

At each level, the corresponding *Task Graph* is constructed by merging the corresponding *CDG*, and *DDG* graphs. Since both the *CDG* and *DDG* are acyclic, the resulting graph is acyclic. The *Task Graph* can be viewed as a maximal graph of computational nodes for which a subset is executed in a given execution of the program, and for a given set of input data.

5.1   The *HTG* and the *condition tags*

In absence of data dependence, the parallel execution of *CFG* is based on *CDG* where identically control dependent nodes are executed in parallel:

- Initially, only nodes that do not have any incoming arcs in the *CDG* may begin execution in parallel;

- After executing a node, say x, if the label x-a is true (i.e., the branch x-a would have been taken in a sequential execution of *CFG*), then all nodes y such that x $\delta_c y$ with label x-a start execution in parallel.

- The execution terminates when all nodes finish their execution.

With the addition of data dependencies, when a node is to be executed, it must be verified whether the nodes on which it is data dependent have completed the execution or are not going to be executed. In other words we have that a node x will be ready to execute when:

- the control conditions which force the execution of x are true.

- if x $\delta_d y$ then either y has finished execution or it is known that y will not be executed.

For each node $x \in HTG$ we associate the *execution tag* $\varepsilon(x) = \varepsilon_d(x) \wedge \varepsilon_c(x)$, where $\varepsilon_c(x)$ denotes the *control condition tag* and $\varepsilon_d(x)$ denotes the *data condition tag*. The *execution tags* will be used at run-time to determine when task nodes become ready for execution. Nodes with *execution conditions* evaluated to true are activated and queued for actual execution.

Control Dependence Condition Tag: Let node x of the *TG* be control dependent on nodes $a_1, a_2, \ldots, a_k$ with labels $(a_1 - b_1)$, $(a_2 - b_2)$, $\ldots$, $(a_k - b_k)$, respectively. Then in any execution of the *TG*, node x will execute under the following control dependence condition:

$$\varepsilon_c(x) = (a_1 - b_1) \vee (a_2 - b_2) \vee \ldots \vee (a_k - b_k) = \bigvee_{i=1}^{n} (a_i - b_i)$$

Data Dependence Condition Tag: Let node x of the *TG* be data dependent on nodes $x_1, x_2, \ldots, x_l$. Then in any execution of the TG, node x will become ready to execute when the conjunction of all data dependence conditions evaluate to true:

$$\varepsilon_d(x) = (x_1 \vee \neg \varepsilon_c(x_1)) \wedge \ldots \wedge (x_n \vee \neg \varepsilon_c(x_n)) = \bigwedge_{i=1}^{l} (x_i \vee \neg \varepsilon_c(x_i))$$

where $\neg \varepsilon_c(x_i)$ is the disjunction of control flow paths that result in x_i, not being executed, and then the dependence need not be enforced in that execution of the program.

ENTRY *Blocks*:
Task-independent module [optional]:

- allocate private variable/stack
- copy parent stack (optional)

Task-dependent module [optional]:

- execute initialization code (if any)
- loops scheduling policy

EXIT *Blocks*:
Task-dependent module [optional]:

- barrier synchronization
- select processor to queue next

Task-independent module [optional]:

- update control and data dependences
- queue ready tasks/threads

Figure 1: General ENTRY and EXIT block formats

5.2 The *Auto-Scheduling* environment and the *HTG*

Here we review how the HTG abstract program representation is used in [22] together the auto-scheduling environment. Remember that at each level the *HTG* is derived merging the *CDG* and the *DDG*, and annotating the nodes with the control conditions. The idea behind the *HTG* may be easily captured looking at it as a graph clusterization. Where each cluster represents a node in the *task graph* of the previous level. The subgraph clustering criteria may be based either on its complexity, or its cyclicity. If we use as clustering criteria the partition on cyclic subgraph we get the *Loop Hierarchy*.

To delay the decision to split the program in different tasks at run-time, we need to envelope each node with special code, located at the entrance and at the exit of each node candidate to be parallelized. These blocks of code are respectively called the ENTRY and EXIT blocks. Each *HTG* node is enveloped in the ENTRY and EXIT blocks, whose general formats are shown in Figure 1.

In the Polychronopoulos execution model, the ENTRY blocks play a secondary role, because the compiler initialization take into account all the fork point actually inserted in the *HTG* program representation.

In the rest of our discussion we assume a multi-user environment, and that it is possible to get an approximate workload estimate at every instance.

Let us recall here also the drive *code generation* algorithm and *HTG execution model*.

We assume that in the *HTG execution environment* we have: a *ready-task* Q, which is managed by the user program; an indivisible *fetch-and-decrement* instruction F&D(X) on memory location X; an efficient primitive to queue the task # at the end of the queue Q_f, queue(Q_f,#); a system call C_RT, which returns the approximate value of the *current workload* L_w.

The *drive code generation* algorithm
The *drive code* is generated, for each level of an *HTG*, in such a way that the evaluation of the condition tag for a task x is *distributed* to the exit blocks of the task nodes that control the execution of x. The algorithm generates:

- for each task node x with a *execution tag* $\varepsilon(x) = \varepsilon_d(x) \wedge \varepsilon_c(x)$ an EXIT block:
  - for all the nodes a such that $x \, \delta_c a$ specified by $\varepsilon_c(x)$, and
  - for all node y such that $x \, \delta_d a$, specified by $\varepsilon_d(x)$.

- for each node x associates:

- a boolean variable C_CON(x), that will be true if the control condition of x evaluate to true, and
- a counter COUNT$_x$ that will be initialized to the total number of task nodes that x depends on.

The compiler initializes C_CON(x)=true for all tasks z with no control dependences; all other nodes x have C_CON(x)=false. Similarly the compiler initializes the static dependence counters COUNT$_x$ appropriately.

Now we need to summarize also the run-time *HTG* model behaviour.

The *HTG run-time* behaviour
It is so characterized:

- If the task x is control dependent on node a with label a-b, then as soon as a completes execution, and the path a-b is taken, the control condition for task x becomes true; and
- in the absence of pending data dependences for a, the EXIT block of task a will proceed to queue x in the ready-queue Q.
- Otherwise the processor involved in the execution of a proceeds with a new thread, or goes back to Q for another dispatch.
- If task x is also data dependent on another task y, then x must wait (before queued): for y to complete execution, or for a control path that avoids y to be taken.
- The EXIT block of task y will read and decrement the corresponding counter COUNT$_x$, checks to see if it is the last pending dependence, and test the control condition. The condition C_CON(x)=true and COUNT$_x$=0 implies that node y is the last that caused the condition to evaluate to true, and hence the last node that can queue x.

To correctly manage the many concurrent threads on executing the *HTG* the correct *termination conditions* for a program must be considered. In particular it is necessary to determine the task graph termination condition to signal the completion of the corresponding composite node at the next lower level in the *HTG*. To this end, a special thread called *stop* is inserted, and made artificially data dependent on all the leaf nodes of the task graph.

Control passes from one hierarchy level G_i to a deeper level G_{i+1}, by making the unique task node to which G_{i+1} exits at level, i, artificially dependent on the unique *stop* node of G_i.

It may be interesting to point out here that this *run time behaviour* does not have any provision to dynamically expand the *HTG* hierarchy in depth, past its static depth. This capability is useful in accommodating recursion.

6 The *HTG* and parallel task management in LISP

To extend *HTG* [22], we need first of all to accommodate for recursive call. Recursion provides the most important control structuring LISP construct. Next, we are faced with the large number of function calls present in a LISP program. Also iterative constructs are written using tail-recursion in LISP. That, necessitates efficient interprocedural analysis to gather useful information used to limit the explosion of fine grain parallelism. There are many approaches that allow us to control useless fine grain parallelism. The most widely used are *quickness* and *strictness* analysis.

A function is considered quick if it can be sequentially evaluated in less time than it would take for the new evaluating process to return a value for it. A function is considered immediately strict with respect to an argument if its body will be expected to block quickly if attempting to evaluate it before the value of its argument has been returned.

In the rest of the paper we assume that we have gathered sufficient control and data dependence information, using one of the tools described in [13,23], and that have also been strictness and quickness analysis carried out to take into account for sources of not useful parallelism.

Let us briefly recall the future insertion strategy. The rules are such that the futures are inserted in following cases:

1. the parallel evaluation of expressions that can completely evaluate without using each other's values, for example in a code such as:

   `(+ (future expr₁) (future expr₂) (future expr₃))`

2. the concurrent evaluation of a sub-expression and a portion of its enclosing expression, such as:

   `(f (future expr₁) (future expr₂))`

and are not inserted in following cases:

1. when the arguments are quick, as in the following code fragment:

   `(f (+ 3 10) (cons 'a '(b c)))`

2. when the arguments are not-quick, but the function body is immediately strict with respect to all of its arguments:

   `(+ (f expr₁) (g expr₂))`

In our *HTG* extension we consider only these kinds of nodes:

1. *simple node*, representing either small fragments of straight-line code, or function calls that are quick and/or strict on some of their arguments.

2. *compound node*, representing all other types of function calls; in other words the functions that are not quick and strict.

Beside the *data dependences* described in Section 4.1, and represented by *DDG*, we introduce another kind of data dependence, strictly related to Lisp program parellelization, and arising from the insertion of the artificial *stop* node in the *HTG*. We call this kind of data dependence *parallel data dependence*, and denote it by $\delta_{\parallel}$.

We envelope with ENTRY and EXIT blocks only complex node. We will use the ENTRY block to cross the *HTG* hierarchy levels, and we use the EXIT block to propagate the *parallel data dependency* to the next node in the *HTG* staying always at the same level. The ENTRY must also take care to unroll at run-time recursive calls without forbidding parallelism.

We assume that we have already clustered the *HTG*, i.e. we have already available the static hierarchy, where G_i denote an *HTG* at level i, G_{i+1} an *HTG* at level i+1, and $stop_{i+1}$ the artificially exiting node of G_{i+1}.

6.1 The *lazy task creation* and the *HTG*

Consider the function psum-tree (Figure 2), which computes the sum of all the leaves of a binary tree, and its parallel version. Where the future has been inserted in only the first argument of the + (strict) operator.

```
(defun psum-tree (tree)                    (defun psum-tree (tree)
   (if (leaf? tree)                           (if (leaf? tree)
      (leaf-value tree)                          (leaf-value tree)
      (+ (psum-tree (left tree))                 (+ (future (psum-tree (left tree)))
         (psum-tree (right tree)))))))              (psum-tree (right tree)))))))
```

Figure 2: The function psum-tree, which computes the sum of all the leaves of a binary tree, and its *parallel* version.

The *lazy tasks creation* execution model is:

- envelope each future call with sufficient code to capture its continuation;
- inline each future call, i.e. inhibits the spawning part of future code.

The *run-time behaviour* is:

- if there are free processors, then un-inline the future call, otherwise
- run it in a sequential way.

This scheduling strategy is called *oldest-first stealing policy* [19], i.e., when an idle processor steals a task, the oldest fork point is chosen[1] to un-inlining the futures.

Only a small change in the *execution run-time* behaviour is sufficient to take into account the *oldest-first stealing policy* in the *HTG* framework.

For each node x in the *HTG* at level i we have that the *run-time behaviour* will be:

- If the task x is control dependent on node a with label a-b, then as soon as a completes execution, and the path a-b is taken, the control condition for task x becomes true.
- In the absence of pending data dependences[2] for a, the EXIT block of task a will proceeds to queue x in the ready-queue Q, and to propagate the *parallel data dependence* ($\delta_{\parallel}$) to the next node.
- Otherwise the processor involved in the execution of a proceeds with a new thread, or goes back to Q for another dispatch.
- If task x is also data dependent on another task y, then x must wait (before queued) for y to complete execution, or for a control path that avoids y to be taken.
- The EXIT block of task y will read and decrement the corresponding counter $COUNT_x$, check to see if it is the last pending dependence, and test the control condition. The condition C_CON(x)=true and $COUNT_x$=0 implies that node y is the last that caused the condition to evaluate to true, and hence the last node that can queue x.

Figure 3 shows the flat *HTG* of the psum-tree LISP program shown above. Task 1 represents the conditional, task 2 represents the leaf-value and tasks 3 and 4 represent the recursive calls to the left and right subtrees. Task 5 represents the summation of the partial results and start and stop function as defined in [22,7]. The solid edges represent data and control dependences, and the shaded edge represents data parallel dependence. Notice that during execution, the dynamic unfolding of the *HTG* will cause task 5 at level i to block until control returns from the completion of psum-tree at level i+1.

---

[1]The *fork point* are made explicit by the programmer using the MultiLisp parallel annotations construct future

[2]Here we include also the $\delta_{\parallel}$, not only the data dependences included in $e_d(x)$.

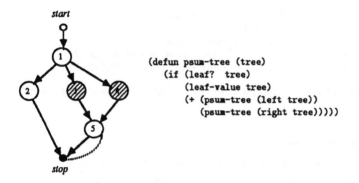

```
(defun psum-tree (tree)
  (if (leaf?  tree)
      (leaf-value tree)
      (+ (psum-tree (left tree))
         (psum-tree (right tree)))))
```

Figure 3: The flat HTG for psum-tree

6.2   The *sponsor model* for the *speculative computation* and the *HTG*

To accommodate the *sponsor model* for the *speculative computation* in the *HTG* environment we need to put in the ENTRY blocks also the code to save the data dependent structures to be able to have a consistent computation on evaluating in parallel *complex nodes* that may killed.

For the *touching sponsorship* model the *run-time behaviour* will be:

For each node x in the *HTG* at level i:

- If task x controls a set of nodes a_i with labels $a_i - b_i$, $i = 1, ..., k$ then the ENTRY DRIVE code proceeds to queue each a_i in the ready-queue Q. If there are also true *data dependences* then it saves the values of the conflicting variables, to do a roll-back when one of this *speculative process* is killed. Finally, propagate the *parallel data dependence* to x, and make true the control condition for x.

- In the absence of pending data dependences for a, the EXIT block of task a will proceed to queue x in the ready-queue Q, and to propagate the *parallel data dependence* ($\delta_{\parallel}$) to the next node.

- Otherwise the processor involved in the execution of the a_i will proceed with a new thread, or goes back to Q for another dispatch.

- If task x is also data dependent on another task y, then x must wait (before queued) for y to complete execution, or for a control path that avoids y to be taken.

- The EXIT block of task y will read and decrement the corresponding counter COUNT$_x$, check to see if it is the last pending dependence, and test the control condition. The condition C_CON(x)=true and COUNT$_x$=0 implies that node y is the last that caused the condition to evaluate to true, and hence the last node that can queue x.

Once again a simple modification allowed us to take into account for the *touching sponsorship* scheduling strategy.

7 Related work

Tasks creation, synchronization, and scheduling account for the additional cost on executing a parallelized version of a program. The balancing between this increased complexity and the benefit of the parallelism has been investigated both for the annotating and restructuring parallelizing systems.

Since the time of its definition QLISP offered to the users the *propositional parameters* to the fine-tuning of the run-time parallelism. Pehoushek in [21] describes the use of dynamic processes partition and scheduling methods to improve the run-time performance of parallel LISP code. The dynamic processes partition allows to delay the decision to split a task at fixed points (the process partition points) according to emptiness of the processor private queue.

This techniques was extended in defining the *lazy task creation* [19], by means of the inlining method. The main difference among the *dynamic processes partition* and the *lazy task creation* resides into the inlining process, for it allows to selectively un-inline the task as processing resources become available.

For the restructuring systems we have that PARCEL uses multiple procedure versions to improve run-time performance, where the switching criteria between the sequential and the parallel procedure version is based on the load balancing strategy. The CURARE systems relies heavily on the assumption that the *servers*, on which single loop iterations are executed, are inexpensive to call.

8 Conclusion

Since the first development of annotating and restructuring systems no unifying framework is yet emerged in which all the problems involved on program parallelization process may be considered.

It appears that the *Hierarchical Task Graph* can be efficiently used to describe different execution models, scheduling strategies, and parallel discovering strategies in an unique environment. The most interesting aspect is that it gives us the means to move, at least in some aspects, the program scheduling from the operating system to user's program, without using parallel annotating language constructs. Furthermore, some incompatibility between sequential and parallel constructs, like the future and the *Scheme call/cc*, may be solved in a natural way.

We are now implementing these *HTG* extensions to get some quantitative results, and comparing them with the original scheduling policy. We hypothesize that one of the possible sources of inefficiency may come from the operating system service to get the workload approximations, and from the fact the processes enqueueing take places inside the user's code.

References

[1] V. Aho, R. Sethi, J.D. Ullman *Compilers: Principles, Techniques, and Tools* Addison Wesley, Reading, Mass. U.S.A., 1986

[2] J. Ferrante, K.J. Ottenstein, J.D.Warren The Program Dependence Graph and Its Use in Optimization *ACM-TOPLAS*, 9, 1987, pp. 319-343

[3] Gabriel R. P., and McCarthy J., Queue-based MultiProcessing LISP *Conference Record of the 1984 ACM Symposium on LISP and Functional Programming*, 1984, pages 25 - 43.

[4] Goldman R. and Gabriel R. P.,QLISP: Experience and New Directions *Symposium on Parallel Programming: Experience with Applications, Language and Systems. ACM*, pages. 111-123, July 1988

[5] Goldman R. and Gabriel R. P., QLISP: Parallel Processing in Lisp *IEEE Software* 6, pages. 5159, 1989

[6] Gray S. L. Using Future to Exploit Parallelism in Lisp *M.S. Thesis, Dept. Electrical Engineering and Computer Science, M.I.T.* 1986

[7] M. Girkar, C.D. Polychronopoulos The HTG: An Intermediate Representation for Programs Based on Control and Data Dependences *CSRD TR1046, University of Illinois at Urbana-Champaign, Illinois, U.S.A.*, 1990

[8] M. Girkar, C.D. Polychronopoulos Automatic Detection and Generation of Unstructured Parallelism in Ordinary Programs to appear in *IEEE Transaction on Parallel & Distributed Processing*, and *CSRD TR, University of Illinois at Urbana-Champaign, Illinois, U.S.A.*, 1990

[9] Halstead R.H. Jr., Implementation of Multilisp: LISP on a multiprocessor *Conference Record of the 1984 ACM Symposium on LISP and Functional Programming*, 1984, pages. 9 - 17.

[10] R.H. Halstead Multilisp: a language for concurrent symbolic computations *ACM TOPLAS*, vol 7, 1985 pp 501-538

[11] C.T. Haynes, D.P. Friedman, M. Wand Obtaining Coroutines with continuation *Computer Languages*, 11, 1986, pp. 143-153

[12] W.L. Harrison Compiling Lisp for Evaluation on a Tightly Coupled Multiprocessor *CSRD TR-565 University of Illinois at Urbana-Champaign, Illinois, U.S.A.*, 1986

[13] W.L. Harrison The interprocedural Analysis and Automatic Parallelization of Scheme Programs *Int. Journal of Lisp and Symbolic Computation*, 2, 1989, pp. 179-396

[14] Harrison W.L., Padua D. A. PARCEL: Project for the Automatic Restructuring and Concurrent Evaluation of LISP *TR. 653, Dept. Computer Science, University of Illinois*, 1987

[15] D. Kuck *The Structure of Computers & Computations* John Wiley & Sons, Boston, Ma, 1978

[16] M. Katz ParaTran: A Transparent, Transaction-Based Runtime Mechanism for Parallel Execution of Scheme *Master Thesis, Dept. Electrical Engineering and Computer Science, M.I.T.*, 1986

[17] Larus J.R, Hilfinger P.N., Restructuring LISP Programs for concurrent executions *Symposium on Parallel Programming: Experience with Applications, Language and Systems. ACM*, pages. 100 - 110, 1988

[18] J.L. Larus Compiling Lisp Programs for Parallel Execution *Int. Journal of Lisp and Symbolic Computation*, 4, (1991), pp. 29-99

[19] E. Mohr, D.A. Kranz, R.H. Halstead Lazy Task Creation: A Technique for Increasing the Granularity of Parallel Programs *ACM Lisp Conf. On Lisp and Functional Languages*, Nice, 1990, pp. 185-197

[20] R.B. Osborne Speculative Computation in Multilisp: An Overview *ACM Lisp Conf. On Lisp and Functional Languages, Nice*, 1990, pp. 198-208

[21] J.D. Pehoushek, J.S. Weening Low-cost process Creation and Dynamic Partiotion in QLISP, I *Parallel Lisp: Languages and Systems* Y.Ito, R.H. Halstead ed, Springer Verlag, Berlin, 1990, pp 182-199

[22] C.D. Polychronopoulos Autoscheduling: Control and Data Flow Come Together *CSRD TR-1058 University of Illinois at Urbana-Champaign, Illinois, U.S.A.*, 1990

[23] O. Shivers Control Flow Analysis in Scheme *SIGPLAN Conf on Language Design and Implementation, Atlanta, Georgia*, 1988, pp 164-174

18   A Multi-Grain Parallelizing Compilation Scheme for OSCAR (Optimally Scheduled Advanced Multiprocessor)

H. Kasahara, H. Honda, A. Mogi, A. Ogura,
K. Fujiwara, and S. Narita
Waseda University

Abstract

This paper proposes a multi-grain parallelizing compilation scheme for Fortran programs. The scheme hierarchically exploits parallelism among coarse grain tasks, such as, loops, subroutines or basic blocks, among medium grain tasks like loop iterations and among near fine grain tasks like statements. Parallelism among the coarse grain tasks called the macrotasks is exploited by carefully analyzing control dependences and data dependences. The macrotasks are dynamically assigned to processor clusters to cope with run-time uncertainties, such as, conditional branches among the macrotasks and variation of execution time of each macrotask. The parallel processing of macrotasks is called the macro-dataflow computation. A macrotask composed of a Do-all loop, which is assigned onto a processor cluster, is processed in the medium grain in parallel by processors inside the processor cluster. A macrotask composed of a sequential loop or a basic block is processed on a processor cluster in the near fine grain by using static scheduling. A macrotask composed of subroutine or a large sequential loop is processed by hierarchically applying macro-dataflow computation inside a processor cluster. Performance of the proposed scheme is evaluated on a multiprocessor system named OSCAR. The evaluation shows that the multi-grain parallel processing effectively exploits parallelism from Fortran programs.

1 INTRODUCTION

In parallel processing of Fortran programs on multiprocessor systems, the loop concurrentization[4][8][10], such as, the Do-all and the Do-across, has so far been used widely. Currently, many types of Do-loops can be concurrentized with support of strong data dependency analysis[2][3][4] and program restructuring[4][9]. There still exist, however, sequential loops which can not be concurrentized efficiently because of complex data dependences among iterations and conditional branches to the outside of the loops.

Also, parallelism outside Do-loops, namely, parallelism inside a basic block and parallelism among loops, subroutines and basic blocks, has not effectively been exploited on multiprocessor systems.

Therefore, in order to further improve the effective performance of multiprocessor systems, it is important to exploit the coarse grain parallelism among loops, subroutines, and basic blocks and the fine grain parallelism inside a sequential loop and a basic block as well as the medium grain parallelism among iterations in a Do-all or Do-across loop.

A basic concept of the coarse grain parallel processing on a hierarchical multiprocessor system, namely, the macro-dataflow computation, has been proposed for Cedar[5]-[7]. In order to realize the macro-dataflow computation of a Fortran program, a definition of a coarse grain task, or a macrotask, and a scheme to automatically extract parallelism among the macrotasks should be made clear.

As to fine grain parallelism, VLIW processors[12]-[16] and superscalar processors[17] can efficiently process instructions in parallel. Generally, they need the help of compilation techniques like trace scheduling[12]-[14] and percolation scheduling[16] to globally exploit fine grain parallelism over conditional branches. However, static scheduling at compile-time used in VLIW sometimes has difficulties to deal with conditional branches, of which branch probabilities are unknown at compile-time.

In the fine grain parallel processing on multiprocessor systems[30][33], an instruction level grain seems too fine compared with the data transfer overhead among processors. Therefore, parallelism among near fine grain tasks, namely, parallelism among statements, has been exploited with the supports of a static scheduling algorithm considering data transfer overhead[30] and architectures which allow us efficient synchronizations[29] and efficient data transfers[30]. However, the parallel processing of near fine grain tasks using the static scheduling on multiprocessor systems also has problems to handle run-time uncertainties.

In light of the above facts, this paper proposes a multi-grain parallel processing scheme on a multiprocessor system which effectively combines the macro-dataflow computation, the loop concurrentization and the near fine grain processing. In the scheme, macrotasks are dynamically scheduled onto processor clusters to cope with the runtime uncertainties caused by conditional branches. The application of dynamic scheduling to the coarse grain tasks allows us to keep dynamic scheduling overhead relatively small. A macrotask assigned to a processor cluster is processed among processors inside the processor cluster by the use of the loop concurrentization or the near fine grain parallel processing.

Section 2 in this paper proposes the multi-grain parallelizing compilation scheme for a multiprocessor system. Section 3 describes a shared memory multiprocessor system named OSCAR on which the multi-grain parallel processing scheme has been implemented. Section 4 evaluates the performance of the multi- grain parallel processing on OSCAR.

2 MULTI-GRAIN PARALLEL PROCESSING SCHEME

The proposed multi-grain parallelizing compilation scheme includes three key issues related with the macro-dataflow computation, the loop concurrentization and the fine grain parallel processing. This section mainly describes, however, compilation schemes for the macro-dataflow and the near fine grain parallel processing because the well-known compilation schemes[4][8]-[10][20][34] can be used for the loop concurrentization.

2.1 Macro-dataflow computation[33]

This section describes a compilation scheme for macro-dataflow computation of Fortran programs.

2.1.1 Generation of macrotasks

In the macro-dataflow computation, a Fortran program is decomposed into macrotasks having relatively large processing time compared with dynamic scheduling overhead and data transfer overhead among macrotasks. The macrotasks are classified into three types, namely, a Block of Pseudo Assignment statements (BPA), a Repetition Block (RB) and a Subroutine Block (SB).

A BPA is composed of a basic block (BB)[1] or multiple basic blocks. The BPA composed of multiple basic blocks is defined by fusing small basic blocks. BPA is also defined by decomposing a BB into independent blocks. More concretely, when a BB has disjoint data dependence graphs, the BB is decomposed into blocks each of which consists of one of the dependence graphs. By this decomposition, we can exploit more parallelism among macrotasks. For example, in Fig. 1(a), BB2 includes two disjoint parts, such as, a post-processing part for a preceding Do-loop, or RB1, and a pre-processing part for succeeding Do-loops, namely RB3 and RB4. Since the two parts are disjoint, BB2 can be decomposed into BB2A and BB2B as shown in Fig.1(b). By this decomposition, a group composed of RB1 and BB2A and another group composed of BB2B, RB3 and RB4 can be processed in parallel.

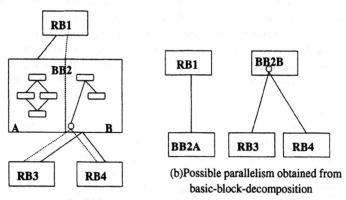

(a)An example of a basic block
having disjoint task graphs

(b)Possible parallelism obtained from
basic-block-decomposition

Fig.1 Generation of BPAs by basic block decomposition.

A RB is a Do loop or a loop generated by a backward branch, namely, an outermost natural loop[1]. This decomposition can be easily applied to reducible flow graphs[6] and also to irreducible flow graphs by using node splitting[6].

The RB can be hierarchically decomposed into sub-macrotasks when the loop concurrentization and the near fine grain parallel processing can not be applied efficiently to the RB. The sub-macrotasks are dynamically scheduled onto processors inside a processor cluster at run-time. In the decomposition of RB to sub-macrotasks, structuring overlapped loops by copying codes[27] is useful to exploit more parallelism among sub-macrotasks.

As to subroutines, the in-line expansion is applied as much as possible taking code length into account. Subroutines for which the in-line expansion technique can not efficiently be applied are defined as SBs. In order to fully exploit parallelism among SBs and the other macrotasks in a flow graph, strong inter-procedural analysis techniques are required[28] though the inter-procedural analysis itself is beyond the scope of this paper. SBs can also be hierarchically decomposed into sub-macrotasks as well as RBs.

2.1.2 Generation of macroflow graph (MFG)

A macroflow graph is a kind of flow graph which explicitly represents both control flow and data dependences among macrotasks. Fig. 2 shows an example of a macroflow graph. In this macroflow graph MFG(N,E,C), a set of nodes N represents macrotasks like BPAs, RBs and SBs. A set of edges E consists of two kinds of edges, namely, E_{CF} representing control flow edges, which are shown by dotted edges, and E_D representing data dependence edges, which are shown by solid edges. C is a set of conditional branches inside macrotasks, which are shown by small circles inside nodes. In this graph, directions of the edges are assumed to be downward though arrows are omitted. MTG is generally a directed acyclic graph since RBs contain all back edges inside them.

2.1.3 Generation of a macrotask graph (MTG)

The MFG explicitly represents the control flow and data dependences among macrotasks though it does not show any parallelism among macrotasks. Generally, the control dependence graph, or the program dependence graph[26], represents maximum parallelism if there are not data dependences among macrotasks[25]. In practice, there exist, however,

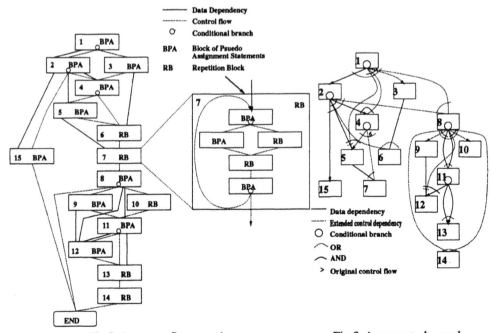

Fig.2 A macro-flow graph.　　　　Fig.3 A macrotask graph.

data dependences among macrotasks. Therefore, in order to effectively extract parallelism among macrotasks from a macroflow graph, the control dependences and the data dependences should be analyzed together.

In this paper, an earliest executable condition of each macrotask[31][36] is used to show the maximum parallelism among macrotasks considering control dependences and data dependences. The earliest executable condition of a macrotask i, MT_i, is an condition on which MT_i may begin its execution earliest. In other words, satisfying the earliest executable condition of MT_i means that precedence constraints caused by control dependences and data dependences of MT_i are satisfied.

For example, an earliest executable condition of MT_8 in Fig. 2, which is control-dependent on conditional branch statements inside MT_1 and MT_2, is the following:

MT_1 branches to MT_3 **OR** MT_2 branches to MT_4.

An earliest executable condition of MT_6, which is control-dependent on MT_1 and on MT_2 and is data-dependent on MT_3, is:

MT_3 completes execution **OR** MT_2 branches to MT_4.

Here, "MT_3 completes execution" means to satisfy the data dependence of MT_6 on MT_3 because the following conditions for macro-dataflow execution are assumed in this paper:

1) If macrotask i (MT_i) is data-dependent on macrotask j (MT_j), MT_i can not begin execution before MT_j finishes execution.

2) A conditional branch statement inside a BPA may be executed as soon as data dependences of the branch statement are satisfied because statements inside a BPA including the conditional branch statement are processed in parallel by processors inside a processor cluster. In other words, MT_i, which is control-dependent on MT_j, can begin execution as soon as the branch direction is determined even if MT_j has not completed execution.

The above earliest executable condition of MT_6 represents the simplest form of the condition[31][33]. An original form of the condition of MT_i[31][33] can be represented in the following;

(MT_j, on which MT_i is control dependent, branches to MT_i)
AND
(Every macrotask on which MT_i is data dependent, MT_k: $0 \le k < |N|$, completes execution **OR** it is determined that MT_k is not be executed).

For example, the original form of the earliest executable condition of MT_6 is:

(MT_1 branches to MT_3 **OR** MT_2 branches to MT_4)
AND
(MT_3 completes execution **OR** MT_1, on which MT_3 is control-dependent, branches to MT_2).

The first partial condition before **AND** represents an earliest executable condition determined by the control dependences. The second partial condition after **AND** represents an earliest executable condition to satisfy the data dependence. The second partial condition means that MT_6 may begin execution after MT_3 completes execution or after it is determined that MT_3 is not executed. In the condition, the execution of MT_3 means that MT_1 has branched to MT_3 and also the execution of MT_2 means that MT_1 has branched to MT_2. Therefore, this condition is redundant and its simplest form is:

MT_3 completes execution **OR** MT_2 branches to MT_4.

Similarly, an earliest executable condition of MT_4 is;

MT_1 branches to MT_3 **OR** [MT_2 branches to MT_4 **AND** completes its execution].
The simplest earliest executable conditions of macrotasks on Fig.2, which are given by OSCAR compiler automatically[31], are shown in Table 1. The simplest condition is important to reduce dynamic scheduling overhead when macrotasks are assigned to processor clusters at run-time. In OSCAR Fortran compiler, simplest conditions are obtained automatically[31].

TABLE 1 Logical Expression of Earliest Executable Conditions

Macrotask No.	Earliest Executable Condition
1	
2	1_2
3	$(1)_3$
4	2_4 **OR** $(1)_3$
5	$(4)_5$ **AND** { 2_4 **OR** $(1)_3$ }
6	3 **OR** $(2)_4$
7	5 **OR** $(4)_6$
8	$(2)_4$ **OR** $(1)_3$
9	$(8)_9$
10	$(8)_{10}$
11	8_9 **OR** 8_{10}
12	11_{12} **AND** { 9 **OR** $(8)_{10}$ }
13	11_{13} **OR** 11_{12}

Girkar and Polychronopoulos[35] proposed another algorithm to obtain the earliest executable conditions based on the original research[31]. They solved a simplified problem to obtain the earliest executable conditions by assuming a conditional branch inside a macrotask is executed in the end of the macrotask.

The earliest executable conditions of MTs are represented by a directed acyclic graph named the macrotask graph[31][33][36], or MTG, as shown in Fig. 3. In MTG(N,E,ARC,C), N is a set of nodes representing macrotasks. E is a set of edges consisting of two kinds of edges, such as extended control-dependence edges(E_{ECD}) represented by dotted edges and data-dependence   edges(E_D) by solid edges.

The extended control dependence edges, or dotted edges, are classified into two types of edges, namely ordinary control dependence edges and co-control dependence edge representing conditions on which data dependence predecessor of MT_i, namely MT_k mentioned before on which MT_i is data dependent, is not be executed[31].

Also, a data dependence edge, or a solid edge, originating from a small circle has two meanings, namely, an extended control- dependence edge and a data-dependence edge.

ARC is a set of arcs connecting edges at their tails or heads of the edges. The ARC consists of two kinds of arcs, such as, solid arcs and dotted arcs. A solid arc (ARC$_{AND}$) represents that the edges connected by the arc are in AND relationship. A dotted arc (ARC$_{OR}$) represents that edges connected by the arc are in OR relationship. C is a set of small circles which represent conditional branches.

In the MTG, the directions of the edges are also assumed to be downward though most arrows are omitted. The arrows at heads of some edges in the MTG usually show that the edges are the original conditional flow edges which originate from the small circles in the MFG.

For instance, in Fig.3, a dotted edge from the circle inside MT_1 to MT_8 is connected to another dotted edge having the arrow from the circle of MT1 to MT_3 by the solid arc (AND arc). In this case, the dotted edge to MT_8 means that the MT_8 may begin its execution anytime after MT_1 branches to MT_3. Also the dotted edge from MT_2 to MT_8 connected with the solid edge from MT_2 to MT_4 by the solid arc means that the MT_8 may begin execution after MT_2 branches to MT_4. Furthermore, the dotted edges from MT_1 and MT_2 to MT_8 are connected by a dotted arc at their heads. This dotted arc means that MT_8 may begin execution after MT_1 branches to MT_3 **or** after MT_2 branches to MT_4.

This MTG also shows that MT_3, MT_4 and MT_8 can be processed in parallel if MT_1 branches to MT_3.

2.1.4 Generation of dynamic scheduling routine

In the macro-dataflow computation, the macrotasks are dynamically scheduled to processor clusters (PCs) at run-time in order to cope with runtime uncertainties, such as, conditional branches among macrotasks and a variation of macrotask execution time. The use of dynamic scheduling[20][22] for coarse grain tasks keeps the relative scheduling overhead small. Furthermore, the dynamic scheduling in this scheme is performed not by OS calls like in popular multiprocessor systems but by a special scheduling routine generated by the compiler in order to minimize the dynamic scheduling overhead. In other words, the compiler generates an efficient dynamic scheduling routine exclusively for each Fortran program based on the earliest executable conditions, or the macrotask graph. The scheduling routine is executed by a processor element which serves as a dynamic scheduler.

As a dynamic scheduling algorithm, Dynamic-CP algorithm, which is an extended version of the static scheduling algorithm called CP[18], is employed taking into consideration the scheduling overhead and quality of the generated schedule. In the Dynamic-CP algorithm, the scheduling routine assigns an executable macrotask to a PC based on a priority determined at compile-time, namely, the estimated longest path length from each macrotask to the exit node in MTG.

2.2 Medium Grain Parallel Processing

Macrotasks are assigned to PCs dynamically as mentioned in the previous section. If a macrotask assigned to a PC is composed of a Do-all loop, the macrotask is processed in the medium grain, or iteration level grain, by PEs inside the PC. For the Do-all, several dynamic scheduling schemes, such as the self scheduling, the chunk scheduling and the guided self scheduling, have been proposed[10][20]. On OSCAR described in the next section, however, a simple static scheduling scheme, in which the compiler assigned the same number of iterations to each processors, is mainly used because OSCAR does not have a hardware support for the dynamic iteration scheduling.

If a macrotask assigned to a PC is a loop, in which there exist data dependences among iterations, the compiler first tries to apply the Do-across with restructuring to minimize the synchronization overhead[8][9]. Next, the compiler compares an estimated processing time by the Do-across and an estimated processing time by the near fine grain parallel processing of the loop body mentioned in section 2.3. If the processing time by the Do-across is shorter than the one by the near fine grain processing, the compiler generates a machine code for the Do- across.

2.3 Near Fine Grain Parallel Processing[31][33]

If a macrotask assigned to a PC is a BPA, the macrotask is decomposed into the near fine grain tasks[31], each of which consists of a statement, and processed by PEs inside the PC.

2.3.1 Generation of tasks and task graph

In order to efficiently process a BPA in parallel, computation in the BPA must be decomposed into tasks in such a way that parallelism is fully exploited and overhead related with data transfer and synchronization is minimized.

In the proposed scheme, the statement level granularity is chosen as the finest granularity for OSCAR, which is detailed in the next section, taking into account OSCAR's processing capability and data transfer capability.

Fig. 4 shows an example of statement level tasks, or near fine grain tasks, generated for a basic block which solves a sparse matrix by using the Crout algorithm. A large basic block having computational pattern like Fig.4 is generated by the symbolic generation technique[32] which has been proposed for solving sparse linear systems in the electronic circuit simulation.

Among the generated tasks, there exist data dependencies[2]-[4]. The data dependences, or precedence constraints, can be represented by arcs in a directed acyclic graph called a "task graph"[18][23] as shown in Fig.5, in which each task corresponds to a node. In Fig. 5, figures inside a node circle represents task number, i, and those beside it for a task processing time on a PE, t_i. An edge directed from node N_i toward N_j represents partially ordered constraint that task T_i precedes task T_j. When we also consider a data transfer time between tasks, each edge generally has a variable weight. Its weight, t_{ij}, will be a data transfer time between

<< LU Decomposition >>

1) $u_{12} = a_{12} / l_{11}$
2) $u_{24} = a_{24} / l_{22}$
3) $u_{34} = a_{34} / l_{33}$
4) $l_{54} = -l_{52} * u_{24}$
5) $u_{45} = a_{45} / l_{44}$
6) $l_{55} = a_{55} - l_{54} * u_{45}$

<< Forward Substitution >>

7) $y_1 = b_1 / l_{11}$
8) $y_2 = b_2 / l_{22}$
9) $b_5 = b_5 - l_{52} * y_2$
10) $y_3 = b_3 / l_{33}$
11) $y_4 = b_4 / l_{44}$
12) $b_5 = b_5 - l_{54} * y_4$
13) $y_5 = b_5 / l_{55}$

<< Backward Substitution >>

14) $x_4 = y_4 - u_{45} * y_5$
15) $x_3 = y_3 - u_{34} * x_4$
16) $x_2 = y_2 - u_{24} * x_4$
17) $x_1 = y_1 - u_{12} * x_2$

Fig.4 An example of near fine grain

Fig.5 A task graph for near fine grain tasks.

task T_i and T_j if T_i and T_j are assigned to different PEs. It will be zero or a time to access registers or local data memories if the tasks are assigned to the same PE.

A task processing time on an ordinary processor, however, is not always a fixed value, because the time required for a floating-point operation varies with the value of operand. It has been confirmed on an actual multiprocessor system that this problem can be resolved by using the average processing time of each operation [24]. However, in OSCAR, the task processing time can be exactly estimated at compile-time because OSCAR's RISC processor executes an instruction in one clock as mentioned in Section 3.

2.3.2 Static multiprocessor scheduling algorithm

In order to process a set of tasks on a multiprocessor system efficiently, an assignment of tasks onto PEs and an execution order among the tasks assigned to the same PE must be determined optimally. The problem which determines the optimal assignment and the optimal execution order can be treated as a traditional minimum execution time multiprocessor scheduling problem[18][23]. To state formally, the scheduling problem is to determine such a nonpreemptive schedule in which execution time or schedule length be minimum, given a set of n computational tasks, precedence relations among them, and m processors with the same processing capability. This scheduling problem, however, has been known as a "strong" NP-hard problem[19].

In light of this fact, a variety of heuristic algorithms and a practical optimization algorithm have been proposed[18][20][23]. In OSCAR compiler, a heuristic scheduling algorithm CP/DT/MISF (Critical Path/ Data Transfer/ Most Immediate Successors First) considering data transfer[31] has been adopted taking into account a compilation time and quality of generated schedules.

CP/DT/MISF is a kind of list scheduling algorithms, namely, data-driven-type scheduling algorithms using a priority for task assignment. It consists of the following steps:

Step.1 Determine the level l_i for each task. The l_i is the longest path from N_i to the exit node on a task graph.

Step.2 Execute a kind of list scheduling considering data transfers.

> Step 2.1 Set a scheduling time instant, $t_{current}$, to zero. Find ready tasks and idle processors at $t_{current}$.
>
> Step 2.2 Calculate data transfer time required for every possible assignment of ready tasks having the highest level to idle processors at $t_{current}$ by taking into consideration a partial schedule generated before $t_{current}$.
>
> Step 2.3 Choose an assignment of a ready task to an idle processor which gives the minimum data transfer time. If there are more than one assignment which give the minimum data transfer time, give priority to a task with the most immediate successors. If there is no idle processor, go to Step 2.4. Otherwise, repeat Step 2.3.
>
> Step 2.4 Find next scheduling time instant, $t_{current}$, which is the earliest time instant when at least one processor finishes executing the assigned task and becomes idle. Find ready tasks and idle processors at new $t_{current}$. If there are one or more ready tasks, go to Step2.2. Otherwise, repeat Step 2.4 until all processors complete execution. If all the processors complete their execution, Stop.

Though time complexity of CP/DT/MISF is $O(n^3 m)$, it only takes several seconds on a workstation to solve a problem with about several hundreds tasks.

2.3.3 Machine code generation

For efficient execution on an actual multiprocessor system, the optimal machine codes must be generated by using the scheduled results. A scheduled result gives us the following information:

1) which tasks are executed on each PE,
2) in which order the tasks assignedtothe same PE are executed,
3) when and where data transfers and synchronization among PEs are required,

and so on. Therefore, we can generate the machine codes for each PE by putting together instructions for tasks assigned to the PE and inserting instructions for data transfer and synchronization into the required places. The "version number" method[30] is used for synchronization among tasks.

At the end of a BPA, instructions for the barrier synchronization, which is supported by OSCAR's hardware, are inserted into a program code on each PE.

The compiler can also optimize the codes by making full use of all information obtained from the static scheduling. For example, when a task should pass shared data to other tasks assigned to the same PE, the data can be passed through registers on the PE. The optimal use of registers reduces the processing time markedly. In addition, the compiler can minimize the synchronization overhead by carefully considering the information about the tasks to be synchronized, the task assignment and the execution order[31].

3 OSCAR'S ARCHITECTURE

This section describes the architecture of OSCAR (Optimally Scheduled Advanced Multiprocesso r), on which the proposed multi- grain compilation scheme has been implemented. Fig.6 shows the architecture of OSCAR. As shown in Fig.6, OSCAR is a shared memory multiprocessor system in which up to sixteen processor elements (PEs) and a Control & I/O processor are uniformly connected to three centralized common memories(CMs) and to distributed shared memories on the PEs through three buses.

Each PE is a custom-made RISC processor with throughput of 5 MFLOPS. It consists of a main processing unit with sixty-four 32- bit general purpose registers, an integer processing unit and a floating point processing unit, a data memory, two banks of program memories, a dual-port memory used as a distributed shared memory, a 4-kw stack memory(SM) and a DMA controller. The main processing unit executes every instruction including a floating point addition and a multiplication in one clock. The distributed shared memory on each PE can be accessed simultaneously by the PE itself and another PE.

Also, OSCAR provides the following three types of data transfer modes by using the DPMs and the CMs:

1) One PE to one PE direct data transfers using DPMs,
2) One PE to all PEs data broadcasting using the DPM,
3) One PE to several PEs indirect data transfers via CMs.

Each CM is a simultaneously readable memory on which the same address or different addresses can be read by three PEs in the same clock.

3.1 Architectural Supports for the Macro-dataflow

By using the three buses, OSCAR can be used as a multiple-PC system by partitioning the PEs into a two or three PCs and by assigning one bus to each PC. A number of PCs and a number of PEs inside PC can be changed even at run-time according to parallelism of the target program, or the macrotask graph, since partitioning of PEs into PCs is made by a change of software. Furthermore, each bus has a control line for the barrier synchronization. Therefore, each PC can take barrier synchronization efficiently.

For macro-dataflow execution on OSCAR, the one PE to one PE direct data transfer mode and the data broadcast transfer mode are mainly used for dynamic scheduling. The ordinary data transfer mode using CMs is used for exchanging shared data among PCs because all shared data are assigned to CMs in this macro-dataflow computation scheme on OSCAR.

3.2 Architectural Supports for the Fine Grain Parallel Processing

For the near fine grain parallel processing on OSCAR, the one PE to one PE direct data transfer and the data broadcasting using the DPM are used for minimizing data transfer overhead. The direct data transfer using the DPM needs only one "data-write" onto a DPM, namely one data-transfer, for passing one data from one PE to another PE though the conventional indirect data transfer using a CM requires one "data-write" to a CM and one "data-read" from the CM, namely two data-transfers. Also, the data broadcasting reduces the data transfer time remarkably compared with the indirect data transfer via CM. Therefore, the optimal use of the three data transfer modes using static scheduling allows

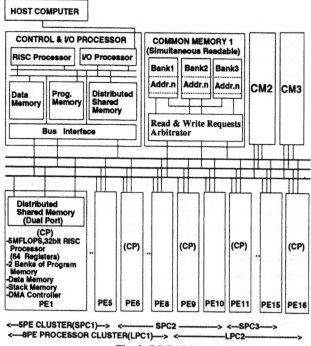

Fig.6 OSCAR's architecture.

us to reduce data transfer overhead. Also, synchronization using DPMs reduces synchronization overhead because assigning synchronization-flags onto the DPMs prevents degradation of bus band width which is caused by the busy wait to check synchronization-flags on CMs.

4 PERFORMANCE OF THE MULTI-GRAIN PARALLEL PROCESSING ON OSCAR

This section describes the performance of the multi-grain parallel processing on OSCAR. Fig.7(a) is a macroflow graph of a Fortran program composed of 17 macrotasks including RBs, SBs and BPAs. In the figure, BPAs are denoted by BASs. Fig.7(b) represents a macrotask graph for the macroflow graph. This macrotask graph shows that the parallelism among the macrotasks in Fig. 7(a) is well extracted.

Fig.8 shows actual execution traces of the program in Fig.7 on OSCAR. The Gantt chart in Fig 8(a) shows an execution trace in a case where the program is sequentially executed by 1 PC having 1 PE, namely, by 1 PE. In this case, the processing time was 9.63s. Fig.8(b) is an execution trace for 3 PCs, each of which has 1 PE. The processing time for the 3 PCs, namely the processing time for the macro-dataflow computation using 3 PEs, was 3.32s. Also, Fig.8(c) shows a trace for 3 PCs, each of which has 2 PEs. The processing time for the multi-grain computation using 3 PCs, namely, 6 PEs, was 1.83s. On the trace, it is observed that the dynamic scheduling overhead, which should be appeared between macrotasks, is negligibly small.

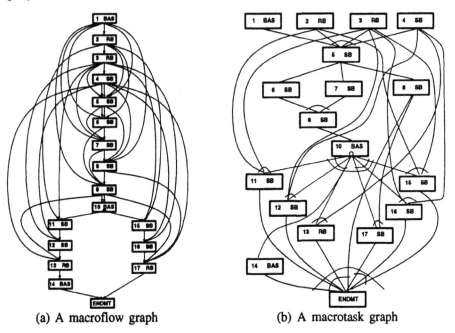

(a) A macroflow graph   (b) A macrotask graph

Fig.7 Macroflow and macrotask graphs for a Fortran program having 17 macrotasks.

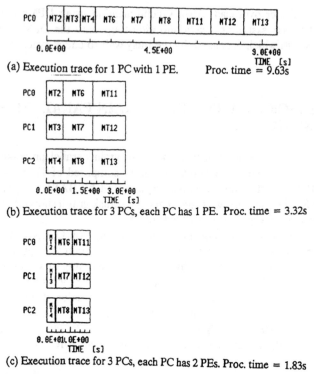

(a) Execution trace for 1 PC with 1 PE.   Proc. time = 9.63s

(b) Execution trace for 3 PCs, each PC has 1 PE. Proc. time = 3.32s

(c) Execution trace for 3 PCs, each PC has 2 PEs. Proc. time = 1.83s

Fig.8 Performance of multi-grain computation of Fig.7 on OSCAR.

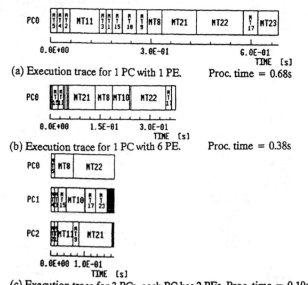

(a) Execution trace for 1 PC with 1 PE.   Proc. time = 0.68s

(b) Execution trace for 1 PC with 6 PE.   Proc. time = 0.38s

(c) Execution trace for 3 PCs, each PC has 2 PEs. Proc. time = 0.19s

Fig.9 Performance of multi-grain computation for a Fortran program in which loop con-currentization and the near fine grain processing are not effective.

From these execution traces, it is confirmed that the proposed multi-grain parallel processing allows us to effectively exploit both the parallelism among macrotasks and the parallelism inside a macrotask.

Fig. 9 shows execution traces on OSCAR for another Fortran program in which the loop concurrentization and the near fine grain parallel processing are not effective. Fig. 9(a) shows a trace for 1 PC with 1PE, namely 1 PE. Its processing time was 0.68s. Fig.9(b) shows a trace for 1 PC having 6 PEs. The processing time using the Do-all and the fine grain parallel processing was 0.38s. Fig. 9(c) shows the trace for 3 PCs, each of which has 2 PEs. The processing time using the multi-grain parallel processing was 0.19s. In other words, the speed-up by the multi-grain parallel processing using 6 PEs (3 PCs * 2PEs) was nearly 4 though the processing time by the loop concurrentization using 6 PEs (1 PC * 6 PEs) was less than 2.

5 CONCLUSIONS

This paper has proposed a multi-grain parallelizing compilation scheme for Fortran programs on OSCAR. It allows us to automatically process coarse grain tasks, such as, loops, subroutine and basic blocks, in parallel by using multiple processor clusters. It also realizes hierarchical parallel processing of medium grain tasks like loop-iterations and near fine grain tasks like statements by using processors inside a processor cluster.

A Fortran compiler using the proposed multi-grain parallelization scheme has been implemented for OSCAR. Its performance has been evaluated on OSCAR. The evaluation has shown that the multi- grain parallel processing allows us to efficiently process even programs, to which the loop concurrentization can not be applied effectively, by exploiting the parallelism among coarse and fine grain tasks.

Another advantage of the multi-grain parallel processing is that it allows us to effectively use much more processors compared with the single level loop concurrentization.

ACKNOWLEDGMENT
The authors express their thanks to Messrs. Yoshida, Tomizawa, Hashimoto, Ohhigashi and Yamamoto of Fuji-Facom Corp. in Tokyo who implemented the hardware of OSCAR.

REFERENCES
[1] A.V.Aho, R.Sethi and J.D.Ullman, Compilers: Principles, Techniques, and Tools, Addison Wesley, 1988.

[2] U.Banerjee, Dependence Analysis for Supercomputing, Kluwer Pub., 1988

[3] D.A.Padua, D.J.Kuck and D.H.Lawrie, "High-speed multiprocessor and compilation techniques," IEEE Trans. Comput., Vol. C-29, No.9,pp.763-776, Sep. 1980.

[4] D.A.Padua, and M.J.Wolfe,"Advanced Compiler Optimizations for Supercomputers," C.ACM, Vol.29, No.12, pp.1184-1201,Dec.1986.

[5] D.Gajski, D.Kuck, D.Lawrie and A.Sameh,"CEDAR,"Report UIUCDCS-R-83- 1123, Dept. of Computer Sci., Univ. Illinois at Urbana-Champaign, Feb. 1983.

[6] D.D.Gajski, D.J.Kuck, D.A.Padua, "Dependence Driven Computation," Proc. of COMPCON 81 Spring Computer Conf., pp.168-172, Feb. 1981.

[7] H.E.Husmann, D.J.Kuck and D.A.Padua,"Automatic Compound Function Definition for Multiprocessors," Proc. 1988 Int"l. Conf. on Parallel Processing,Aug.1988.

[8] M.Wolfe, "Multiprocessor synchronization for concurrent loops," IEEE software, Vol. pp. 34-42, Jan. 1988.

[9] M.Wolfe,Optimizing Supercompilers for Supercomputers,MIT Press, 1989.

[10] C.D.Polychronopoulos and D.J.Kuck, "Guided self-scheduling : A practical scheduling scheme for parallel supercomputers," IEEE Trans. Comput., Vol.c-36,12, pp.1425-1439,Dec. 1987.

[11] D.J.Kuck, E.S.Davidson, D.H.Lawrie and A.H.Sameh, "Parallel Supercomputing Today and Cedar Approach," Science, Vol.231, pp.967- 974, Feb. 1986.

[12] J.A.Fisher, "The VLIW Machine: A Multiprocessor for Compiling Scientific Code," IEEE Computer, Vol. 17, No.7, pp.45-53, Jul.1984.

[13] R.P.Colwell, et.al.,"A VLIW Architecture for a Trace Scheduling Compiler," IEEE Trans. Comp., Vol.C-37, No.8, pp.967-979, Aug.1989.

[14] J.R.Ellis, "Bulldog: A Compiler for VLIW Architectures," MIT Press,1985.

[15] A.Nicolau and J.A.Fisher, "Measuring the Parallelism Available for Very Long Instruction Word Architectures," IEEE Trans. on Computers, Vol. C-33, No. 11, pp.968-976, Nov.1984.

[16] A.Nicolau, "Uniform Parallelism Exploitation in Ordinary Programs," Proc. 1985 Int. Conf. Parallel Processing, Aug.1985.

[17] N.P.Jouppi, "The Nonuniform Distribution of Instrction-Level and Machine Paralellism and Its Effect on Performance," IEEE Trans. on Comput., vol. C-38, No.12, pp.1645-1657, Dec.1989.

[18] E.G.Coffman Jr.(ed.), Computer and Job-shop Scheduling Theory. New York : Wiley, 1976.

[19] M.R.Garey and D.S.Johnson, Computers and Intractability : A Guide to the Theory of NP-Completeness. San Francisco : Freeman, 1979.

[20] C.D.Polychronopoulos, Parallel Programming and Compilers, Kluwer Academic Pub., 1988.

[21] V.Sarkar, "Determining Average Program Execution Times and Their Variance'", Proc. Sigplan'89, June 1989.

[22] V.Sarkar, Partitioning and Scheduling Parallel Programs for Multiprocessors, MIT Press,1989.

[23] H.Kasahara and S.Narita, "Practical Multiprocessor Scheduling Algorithms for Efficient Parallel Processing," IEEE Trans. Comput., Vol.c-33, No.11,pp. 1023-1029,Nov.1984.

[24] H.Kasahara and S.Narita, "An approach to supercomputing using multiprocessor scheduling algorithms, " in Proc. IEEE 1st Int'l Conf. on Supercomputing, pp.139-148,Dec. 1985.

[25] F.Allen, M.Burke,R.Cytron,J.Ferrante,W.Hsieh and V.Sarkar, "A Framework for Determining Useful Parallelism," Proc. 2nd ACM Int'l. Conf. on Supercomputing, 1988.

[26] J.Ferrante,K.J.Ottenstein,J.D.Warren,"The Program Dependence Graph and Its Use in Optimization," ACM Trans. on Prog. Lang. and Syst, Vol.9,No,3.pp.319-349, July 1987.

[27] B.S.Baker,"An Algorithm for Structuring Flowgraphs," J. ACM, Vol.24, No.1, pp.98-120, Jan.1977.

[28] M.Burke and R.Cytron, "Interprocedural Dependence Analysis and Parallelization," Proc. ACM SIGPLAN'86 Symposium on Compiler Construction, 1986.

[29] M.O'Keefe and H. Dietz, "Hardware Barrier Synchronization: Static Barrier MIMD," Proc. 1990 Int'l Conf. on Parallel Processing, pp. I35-42, Aug. 1990.

[30] H.Kasahara, H.Honda, S.Narita, "Parallel Processing of Near Fine Grain Tasks Using Static Scheduling on OSCAR," in Proc. IEEE ACM Supercomputing'90, Nov. 1990.

[31] H.Honda, M.Iwata, H.Kasahara, "Coarse Grain Parallelism Detection Scheme of Fortran programs," Trans. IEICE, Vol.J73-D-I, No,12, Dec.1990 (in Japanese).

[32] F.G.Gustavson, W.Liniger and R.A.Willoughby, "Symbolic Generation of an Optimal Crout Algorithm for Sparse Systems of Linear Equations," J.ACM, vol.17, pp.87-109, Jan. 1970.

[33] H.Kasahara, Parallel Processing Technology, Corona Publishing, Tokyo, (in Japanese), Jun. 1991.

[34] S.S.Munshi and B.Simons, "Scheduling Sequential Loops on Parallel Processors," SIAM J. Comput., Vol. 19, No.4, pp.728-741, Aug., 1990.

[35] M.Girkar and C.D.Polychronopoulos, "Optimization of Data/Control Conditions in Task Graphs," Proc. 4th Workshop on Languages and Compilers for Parallel Computing, Aug. 1991.

[36] H.Kasahara, H.Honda, M.Iwata and M.Hirota, "A Macro-dataflow Compilation Scheme for Hierarchical Multiprocessor Systems," Proc. Int'l. Conf. on Parallel Processing, Aug. 1990.

19 Balanced Loop Partitioning Using GTS

J. Labarta, E. Ayguade, J. Torres, M. Valero, and J.M. Llaberia
Universitat Politècnica de Catalunya

Abstract

Graph Traverse Scheduling is a loop partitioning method for shared memory multiprocessors that achieves minimum execution time of the parallel code generated assuming that a sufficient number of processors are available and synchronization cost is negligible. The method considers the set of statements in the loop body in the partitioning process.

In this paper we study how static schedules can be generated analyzing the compromise between number of processors, load balance and execution time. The method is presented in a descriptive way based on synthetic examples.

1 Introduction

Many methods have been presented in the literature for partitioning DO loops into computations that can be executed in parallel. It is possible to obtain parallel independent computations when there are not cyclic dependence chains in the dependence graph. Problems arise when recurrences or cycles appear. In this case, some loop parallelizing methods try to obtain fully independent partitions [6], [7], [8]. Other methods try to obtain more parallelism by synchronizing dependent computations assigned to different processors [4], [9]. **Graph Traverse Scheduling** (GTS) falls into the latter group of loop partitioning methods.

GTS is a static partitioning method conceived for parallelizing loops with tight recurrences and constant distance dependences known at compile-time. The method is based on a Hamiltonian dependence cycle that is used for scheduling purposes. This recurrence is called Scheduling Recurrence Rsch. The basic idea of the method is to obtain a schedule in which dependences imposed by the original sequential execution are preserved either by internalizing them in the computations assigned to each processor (dependences included in Rsch) or by synchronizing them using some inter-task synchronization mechanism.

The method was presented in [1] for single-nested loops and extended in [2], [3] for multiple-nested loops. The scheduling method goes together with a static evaluation of some loop characteristics which in fact are used as a guidance in the process of determining the efficiency of the parallelization process.

Table 1 introduces terminology used along this paper. The most important concept from the point of view of GTS is the concept of thread. A thread is considered to be a set of computations among which an execution order is imposed by the Rsch. In the single-nested loop case, the parallelism of the loop is constant leading to equally sized threads. However, in the multiple-nested loop case, the instantaneous parallelism varies along the execution of the loop. As a result, some of the threads determine the execution time of the whole parallel set of threads whereas others take less time to complete their execution.

A static scheduling is obtained by assigning the execution of threads to processors, avoiding run-time scheduling overheads. A multiprogrammed execution of those threads is also possible when fewer processors than the number of threads generated are allocated. In the general case of loops with other dependences apart from those in Rsch, a preemptive run-time scheduling would be necessary in order to avoid deadlocks.

GTS, as presented in [3], determines from the Rsch and the limits of the iteration space the number of processors that can be used to execute the loop in minimum time. In this paper we describe how to reduce the number of processors by statically grouping the execution of several threads in a task. We present a grouping strategy and study the compromise between number of processors, load balance and execution time.

Basic Concepts and Definitions

- Normalized Loop **L**: its a perfect nested-loop structure that iterates in each loop dimension k from 0 to some upper bound $N^k - 1$ in steps of 1.
- Iteration Space **IS**: the IS of a d-nested loop is a d-dimensional discrete Cartesian space in which each point represents the execution of all the statements in one iteration of the loop. Each point is identified by the values of the loop control variables.
- Statement per Iteration Space **SIS**: it is a (d+1) dimensional discrete space defined by the Cartesian product **IS x V**, being V the set of statements in the body of the innermost loop. Each point represents an instance of a given statement.
- Free-Point set **FP**: given a set of dependence relations **E**, the FP set is defined as the set of points in SIS which do not depend on any previous execution.
- Thread: it is a set of points in SIS among which an execution order is implied by a dependence chain of the dependence graph.
- Thread Set **TS**: subset of points of the unbounded SIS from which the whole set of threads generated by a dependence chain can be obtained.
- Task: collection of threads statically assigned for being executed on a given processor.
- TAsk Set **TAS**: subset of points of the TS from which the whole set of tasks generated by a dependence chain and a grouping arc can be obtained.

Table 1: Basic Concepts and Definitions

Although the number of processors needed is dependent on the size of the iteration space, the process of grouping that we describe gives the hint on how to achieve a scheduling for a desired number of processors.

An important feature of the method is that it considers the set of statements in the loop body and loop bounds in the scheduling process. In other words, the loop partitioning process is done in what is named the Statement per Iteration Space. Other methods partition loop computations analyzing unbounded spaces or just iteration spaces. Alignment and loop limits computation, which are considered as preconditioning or final steps in other methods, are considered as a whole in GTS. In this way, a clearer control of what can or should be done in the scheduling process is achieved.

In the scope of this paper we only consider the double-nested loop case, although we give some hints on how it extends to more deeply nested loops. Concepts and problems related with the grouping process are presented in a descriptive way based on some examples and synthetic loops.

The paper is structured as follows. In section 2 we consider the case of loops with one statement and a single recurrence. The basic ideas of how threads are grouped are presented in this section. In section 3 we consider the presence of several recurrences and the problems that appear in the synchronized execution of grouped threads. We analyze how grouping should be done without increasing the execution time, or from another point of view, to what extent a reduction of the parallelism is accepted as a result of a reduction in the number of processors required. Section 4 briefly considers the existence of several statements in the loop body and additional problems that appear. In section 5 we outline the general structure of the parallel code generated. Finally, section 6 concludes the paper and presents future work.

2   SINGLE STATEMENT, SINGLE RECURRENCE LOOPS

In this section we consider loops including one statement in their body and a single recurrence Rsch that generates the set of threads that are statically assigned to processors. Figure 1.a shows the dependence graph of a normalized loop that is used as reference in this section. We draw pictures as the one shown in figure 1.b in which the completely unrolled Iteration Space IS of the loop is represented. Each point or cell represents the execution of a given iteration of the loop body. Arrows represent execution order imposed by the recurrence. The weight of the recurrence is denoted by w(Rsch). In the example of figure 1, the weight is a two component vector w(Rsch) = <2, 1>.

2.1   Set of threads

When dealing with this kind of loops, the set of threads generated by Rsch are independent and wholly cover the iteration space IS. In order to generate parallel code, a one-to-one relationship between threads and an index set has to be found [3]. A set of parallel DOALL loops generates the values that identify the set of threads generated, as outlined in section 5. A rectangular characterization of such index set can be found making easier the generation of parallel code.

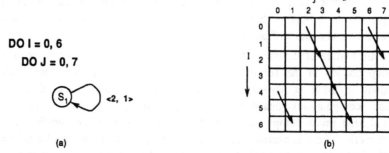

Figure 1: Single statement, single recurrence loop considered in section 2. (a) Dependence Graph and (b) graphical representation of the bounded Iteration Space on which some dependences have been drawn.

Any thread can be characterized by an initial point from which the whole thread can be executed by traversing Rsch. The initial point can belong or not to the bounded IS. In the first case, points of the Free-Point set **FP** characterize the set of threads generated. Figure 2.a shows the **FP** set for the example of figure 1. Points outside the bounded IS can also be used to characterize the set of threads generated. These points can be obtained by traversing the Rsch backwards. In fact, the **FP** set consists of a row and a column of free-points of width w^i (Rsch) and w^j (Rsch), respectively. One of the two parts of the **FP** set can be projected traversing backwards Rsch into a rectangle. The set of points in the rectangle is named Thread Set **TS** and is used to identify the set of threads in the parallel code generated.

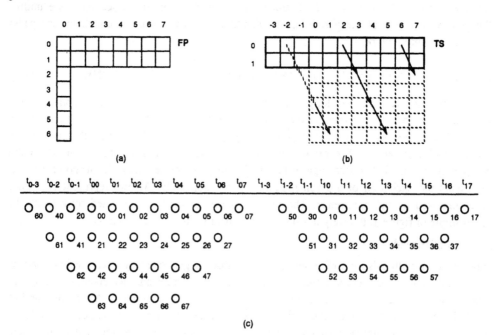

Figure 2: (a) FP set, (b) TS and (c) Thread composition for the example of figure 1.

Figure 2.b shows one of the two possible thread sets, (TS = (0..1 • -3..7)). In this case, the part of the FP set with less points has been projected. Figure 2.c shows the composition of each thread in terms of points of the bounded IS. Subindexes represent the values of the iteration variables associated to each statement instance. This approach to thread composition leads to an unbalanced load partition.

2.2 Execution time and Utilization

In general, the minimum execution time of a single-statement loop with a single recurrence Rsch is

$$t(R_{sch}) = \min \; (\lfloor \; (N^i - 1) / \; |w^i(R_{sch})| \; \rfloor, \; \lfloor \; (N^j - 1) / \; |w^j(R_{sch})| \; \rfloor) + 1 \qquad (1)$$

The loop dimension that minimizes this expression is called the parallelism determining dimension.

When a single thread is allocated to each processor, the degree of unbalance can be measured by the Utilization U defined by

$$U = \#operations \; / \; (\#threads \cdot t) \qquad (2)$$

In the example of figure 2, the execution time is $t = t(Rsch) = 4$ and the utilization is $U = 0.63$.

2.3 Grouping threads in tasks

In order to increase the utilization U and improve the degree of balance, we look for schedules that achieve the same execution time but require a smaller number of processors. The basic idea is to statically group the execution of several threads in a single task. An ordered and sequential execution of threads assigned to a task is considered in the scope of this paper to generate parallel code. Interleaving the execution of such threads would also be possible.

The grouping strategy proposed in this paper executes in the same task those threads of the original TS whose k^{th} coordinate differs by N^k, the size of the iteration space in the dimension on which the FP set has been projected. Figure 3.a shows the schedule obtained for the loop considered in figure 1. Observe that now 16 tasks are generated and can be identified with a rectangular TAS = (0..1 • 0..7). Solid and dashed shapes are used to differentiate the threads that are grouped in the same task.

As a further step, information about the order in which threads belonging to a task are executed can be included in the TAS space. We consider that the task identifier corresponds to the identifier of the thread that is first executed in the task. In this way, a TAS = (0..1 • -3..4) would represent the same set of threads grouped within each task, but executed in the opposite order. This schedule in terms of points of the iteration space is shown in figure 3.b.

As before, a one-to-one relationship between tasks generated and an index set has to be found in order to allow parallel code generation. The process of grouping threads can be formulated as a mapping between points (t^i, t^j) in TS and (ta^i, ta^j) in TAS, given by

$$ta^i = t^i \qquad and \qquad ta^j = ((t^j + order) \; mod \; M) - order \qquad (3)$$

where $M = N^j$, assuming in this case that dimension i^{th} determines the parallelism of the loop, i.e. the vertical part of FP has been projected. Order is a positive integer value that determines the order in which the threads belonging to a task are executed. If order = 0, threads within a task are executed lexicographically. If order equals the absolute value of the minimum j coordinate in TS, threads grouped in the same task will not be executed in lexicographic order. For intermediate values, some of the tasks execute their threads in lexicographic order whereas others do not. Although all values of order give a valid schedule, we are interested just in these two extreme solutions because it is easier to generate parallel code for them.

t_{00} t_{01} t_{02} t_{03} t_{04} t_{05} t_{06} t_{07} t_{10} t_{11} t_{12} t_{13} t_{14} t_{15} t_{16} t_{17}

O_{00} O_{01} O_{02} O_{03} O_{04} O_{05} O_{06} O_{07} O_{10} O_{11} O_{12} O_{13} O_{14} O_{15} O_{16} O_{17}

O_{21} O_{22} O_{23} O_{24} O_{25} O_{26} O_{27} $\bigcirc_{20}$ O_{31} O_{32} O_{33} O_{34} O_{35} O_{36} O_{37} $\bigcirc_{30}$

O_{42} O_{43} O_{44} O_{45} O_{46} O_{47} $\bigcirc_{40}$ $\bigcirc_{41}$ O_{52} O_{53} O_{54} O_{55} O_{56} O_{57} $\bigcirc_{50}$ $\bigcirc_{51}$

O_{63} O_{64} O_{65} O_{66} O_{67} $\bigcirc_{60}$ $\bigcirc_{61}$ $\bigcirc_{62}$

(a)

t_{0-3} t_{0-2} t_{0-1} t_{00} t_{01} t_{02} t_{03} t_{04} t_{1-3} t_{1-2} t_{1-1} t_{10} t_{11} t_{12} t_{13} t_{14}

$\bigcirc_{60}$ $\bigcirc_{40}$ $\bigcirc_{20}$ O_{00} O_{01} O_{02} O_{03} O_{04} O_{15} $\bigcirc_{50}$ $\bigcirc_{30}$ O_{10} O_{11} O_{12} O_{13} O_{14}

O_{05} $\bigcirc_{61}$ $\bigcirc_{41}$ O_{21} O_{22} O_{23} O_{24} O_{25} O_{36} O_{16} $\bigcirc_{51}$ O_{31} O_{32} O_{33} O_{34} O_{35}

O_{26} O_{06} $\bigcirc_{62}$ O_{42} O_{43} O_{44} O_{45} O_{46} O_{57} O_{37} O_{17} O_{52} O_{53} O_{54} O_{55} O_{56}

O_{47} O_{27} O_{07} O_{63} O_{64} O_{65} O_{66} O_{67}

(b)

Figure 3: Balanced schedules with (a) order = 0 and (b) order = 3.

The projection of FP could also have been done into a vertical TS (in our example a TS = (-14..6 • 0) would have been obtained) and the grouping implemented by applying a modulo operation in the ith dimension.

In our example, the grouping mechanism we have presented uses $p = N^j \cdot w^i$ (Rsch) = 16 processors and achieves an optimal execution time of 4. The utilization is only U = 0.875 because of the small size of the iteration space, but it tends to 1 as the loop bounds grow.

2.4 Grouping arc

From the point of view of code generation, grouping can be seen as a continuation of the original idea in GTS. The goal is to schedule within a single thread all loop operations directly dependent on each other through the Rsch. After grouping, two threads are joined in a single task. The jump from the last operation of one thread to the first of the other grouped thread corresponds to introduce a dummy dependence which is used for scheduling purposes once the first thread gets out of the iteration space. Figure 4 shows this idea when both grouping solutions are taken into consideration in the example of figure 1. If order = 0, as shown in figure 4.a, the weight of the grouping arc is <2, -7>. If order = 3, as shown in figure 4.b, the grouping arc has an associated weight of <-6, 5>.

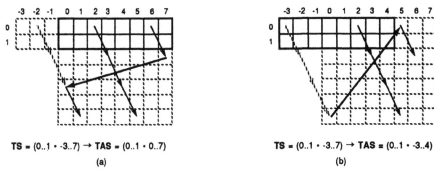

TS = (0..1 · -3..7) → TAS = (0..1 · 0..7)

(a)

TS = (0..1 · -3..7) → TAS = (0..1 · -3..4)

(b)

Figure 4: Grouping arc for the two characterizations of the TAS: (a) order = 0 and (b) order = 3.

To conclude this section, some comments to the n-dimensional case are given. The process to identify the **FP** set and **TS** is identical leading to a characterization of the threads that will be an n-dimensional prism. After grouping, each task may contain between one and n threads. Instead of a single grouping arc, n-1 dummy arcs are introduced even if the **TAS** corresponds to one of the corners of the **TS**.

In general, the grouping of threads in tasks presented is done by applying a modulo N^k operation stated in expression (3) on all loop dimensions k^{th} except for the one that determines the parallelism of the loop. The number of processors required to execute the loop in its minimum time is

$$p = w^i (R_{sch}) \cdot \prod_{k \neq i} N^k \qquad (4)$$

being i the dimension that determines the parallelism (i.e. minimizes expression (1)).

3   SINGLE STATEMENT, MULTIPLE RECURRENCE LOOPS

In this section we consider the case of loops including one statement to introduce the problematic of grouping in the presence of several recurrences. We will discuss the trade-off between execution time, number of processors required to achieve this execution time and processor utilization.

When several recurrences appear in the dependence graph, one of them should be chosen as Rsch and the others have to be explicitly synchronized, as described in [3]. In general, the most restrictive recurrence, taking into consideration the loop bounds, is selected as Rsch. The most restrictive is the recurrence for which expression (1) is maximized.

As a reference, in this section we consider the double-nested loop including four recurrences (<3, 2>, <0, 5>, <1, 4> and <4, 1>) shown in figure 5.a. The length of the critical path is in this case 6, as shown in the sample critical paths of figure 5.b. In this case, recurrence <3, 2> is chosen as Rsch. Figures 5.c and 5.d show two **TAS** characterizations. As discussed in section 2.4, the grouping arcs would be in our example <3, -13> if **TAS** = (0..2 · 0..14) and <-12, 7> if **TAS** = (0..2 · -8..6).

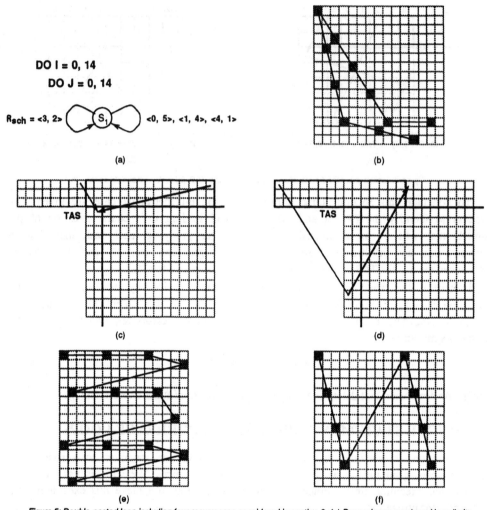

Figure 5: Double-nested loop including four recurrences considered in section 3. (a) Dependence graph and loop limits, (b) two critical dependence chains before grouping, (c) TAS when order = 0 and (d) TAS when order = 8. (e) and (f) show the critical paths that appear when TAS characterizations (c) and (d) are chosen.

3.1 Grouping arc, execution time and number of processors

When several recurrences are present in the dependence graph, the introduction of a dummy grouping arc can increase the length of the critical dependence chain.

Figure 5.e shows the longest path when a grouping arc of weight <3, -13> is introduced. In this case, the length is 15. Figure 5.f shows the longest path when a grouping arc of weight <-12, 7> is introduced. In this case, the length is 8. Without grouping, GTS would use $p = 69$ threads, with a utilization of $U = 0.54$. When order = 0, $p = 45$ tasks are generated. A utilization of $U = 0.33$ and slowdown of 2.5 with respect to its maximum speed are obtained. The second schedule (order = 8) would use also $p = 45$ tasks but the utilization would be $U = 0.625$ with a slowdown factor of 1.33.

Observe in this example that there is one order of grouping that generates a better schedule from the point of view of speed and load balance. It is also possible that the schedule obtained when grouping in a given direction be worse than the original schedule, in terms of speed and utilization.

In the same way that the grouping arc arises artificially from the modulo transformation from TS to TAS, we could consider other grouping arcs that may introduce less delay in the critical path of the loop. Alternatively we might be interested in grouping arcs that introduce more delay but reduce the number of tasks. This could be used to improve the load balance or to generate a scheduling for a given number of processors on a given architecture.

As stated in expression (3), the parameters that can be modified in order to tune the characteristics of the scheduling obtained are order and M. Initially, we equal M to the size of the iteration space IS in the non determining dimension. A smaller value would reduce the number of processors used while a larger one would increase it. From the point of view of execution time, increasing the value of M would reduce the length of the critical chain due to the influence of M on the grouping arc.

Table 2.a shows different choices of grouping arcs for the example considered in figure 5 when grouping arcs ranging from <-12, 0> to <-12, 10> are analyzed. In schedules using less than 45 tasks, more that two threads are assigned to some tasks. Although in the example of figure 5 we have concluded that grouping with order=0 is worse than grouping with order=8, we show in table 2.b how the execution and utilization evolves when grouping arcs between <3, -13> and <12, -13> are introduced. All these considerations rise the possibility of generating many different schedules controlling the actual performance and utilization we want to achieve.

grouping arc	time	processors	U	slowdown
<-12,0>	19	24	.47	3.33
<-12,1>	15	27	.56	2.50
<-12,2>	12	30	.62	2.00
<-12,3>	11	33	.62	1.83
<-12,4>	9	36	.69	1.50
<-12,5>	8	39	.64	1.50
<-12,6>	8	42	.67	1.33
<-12,7>	8	45	.62	1.33
<-12,8>	8	48	.59	1.33
<-12,9>	7	51	.63	1.16
<-12,10>	6	54	.69	1.00

(a)

grouping arc	time	processors	U	slowdown
<3,-13>	15	45	.33	2.50
<6,-13>	9	51	.49	1.50
<9,-13>	8	57	.49	1.33
<12,-13>	7	63	.51	1.16

(b)

Table 2: Influence of different grouping arcs in the execution time, number of processors and utilization.

3.2 Lexicographic order and deadlock

Adding a dummy grouping arc with the first component negative causes that certain orders of executing threads in a task may not be valid. In this case, the operations executed within some tasks are not lexicographically ordered. It is possible for a dependence chain of the original loop to connect two statements assigned to the same task in a way that the sink of the dependence is scheduled first. This situation would lead to deadlock.

A necessary condition for deadlock is that a closed chain with weight equal to zero is formed traversing the dependences of the graph and the grouping arc introduced. This can be formulated as an integer programming problem in terms of the recurrences and the grouping arc g. In the example of figure 5, the system of equations

$$\alpha \cdot <0, 5> + \beta \cdot <1, 4> + \gamma \cdot <4, 1> + \delta \cdot <3, 2> + \phi \cdot g = 0 \qquad (5)$$

should have a non trivial solution with non-negative integer coefficients. The value of ϕ has to be between one and the number of threads that can be grouped in a task minus one. Changing the order of the threads in the task would be enough in the case that the necessary condition is satisfied for a given grouping arc. Of course this may increase significantly the execution time, and in such case, other grouping arcs that do not satisfy the condition should be tried.

4   MULTIPLE STATEMENT LOOPS

In this section we consider the existence of several statements in the loop body. In this case, GTS takes into consideration the new dimension introduced by the set of statements of the loop in the scheduling process. GTS is an alignment-based partitioning algorithm that tries to reduce the number of cross-iteration dependences in order to maximize the number of tasks generated. The basic goal is to internalize all the dependences of a Hamiltonian recurrence, i.e. a recurrence going through all the statements in the loop body, in the sequential execution of each task. Other dependences not included in are preserved by explicit synchronization.

4.1   ACS: Aligned SIS

The Statement per Iteration Space SIS can be considered as a set of planes, each one representing the iteration space of a statement of the loop. When dealing with loops including several statements, the previously described mechanism to obtain TS and TAS is preceded by an alignment process in which the planes are shifted in such a way that all the dependences in the Hamiltonian recurrence except one are reduced to zero. If all the planes are collapsed in the statement dimension, the Aligned and Collapsed Space (ACS) is obtained, on which the ideas presented in sections 2 and 3 can be applied.

Figure 6.a shows a normalized loop with two statements and 6.b its associated ACS. The planes associated to each statement are shaded with different texture. Observe that there is a part in the ACS in which one instance of each statement is executed. This part is called the core part. The rest (ACS - core part), for which only some statements have to be executed, is called peel part. The Hamiltonian recurrence is represented in the ACS as a single arc that accounts for all the weight of the recurrence.

The previously summarized process to obtain a characterization of TS and TAS can be applied to the ACS. In figure 6.c we show the FP set and in 6.d the TS obtained after an appropriate projection of the FP points. Observe that these sets are numerated with respect to the thread that executes the first iteration of the first statement in the body of the loop. This influences the process of code generation that is briefly outlined in the next section.

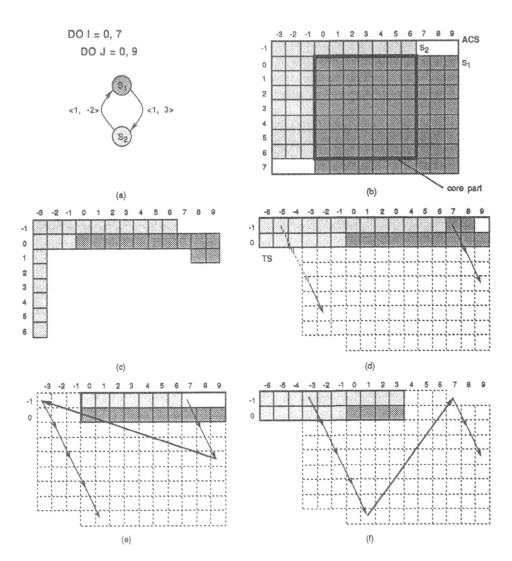

Figure 6: (a) Sample loop including two statements and a Hamiltonian recurrence. (b) Obtaining of the ACS, (c) FP set and (d) characterization of the TS set. Two possible characterizations for the TAS: (e) order = 0 and (f) order = 6.

By applying the modulo transformation in the jth dimension to TS, the characterizations of TAS shown in figures 6.e and 6.f are obtained. Figure 7.a shows the scheduling before grouping and figure 7.b the balanced scheduling after grouping when the TAS shown in figure 6.e is considered. Observe that a utilization U=1 is obtained in this case.

4.2 Grouping arc

Figures 6.e and 6.f show how one task is formed by connecting two threads by the grouping arc. In the former, which corresponds to a characterization of TAS using order = 0, a grouping arc in the ACS of weight <-4, -12> is introduced. In the latter, which corresponds to a characterization of **TAS** using order = 6, a grouping arc of weight <-8, 6> links the two threads that compose the task. Observe that these arcs have a negative component in their first dimension when represented in the original iteration space (<-3, -9> and <-7, 9>, respectively). This implies that the scheduling generated does not preserve the lexicographic order between the operations assigned to a task.

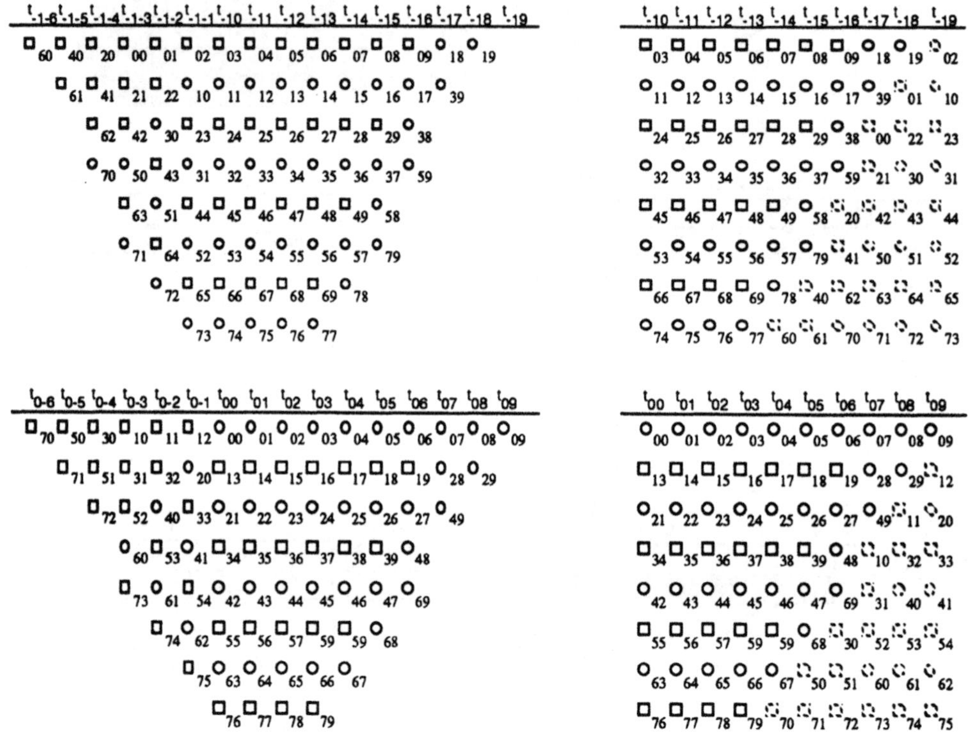

Figure 7: (a) Thread composition in terms of points of the statement per iteration space. Statements are drawn with different shapes. (b) Task composition when order = 0.

The lexicographic order of the operations assigned to a task is preserved if the peels of the two threads that are grouped in a task are correctly interleaved. The interleaving corresponds to introduce several grouping arcs, one from each border of the **ACS** to the other, as shown in figure 8. The existence of several grouping arcs makes difficult the generation of parallel code and it is not considered in this paper.

4.3 Deadlock

The existence of a grouping arc with its first component negative is not important in the single recurrence case because all dependences are embedded in the sequential execution of the threads generated and synchronization is not needed. However, a deadlocking execution of such threads can appear when synchronization is needed.

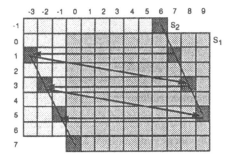

Figure 8: Grouping arcs when threads are executed in a interleaved manner.

grouping arcs (in the original space):

$$g_{12} = <1, -7>$$

$$g_{21} = <1, 8>$$

For example, Figure 9.a shows the same loop of figure 5 to which a new dependence between S_2 and S_1 of weight <1, 8> and a self dependence of S_2 of weight <2, -4> have been added. In the **ACS** of this loop, the new arcs would have after the alignment process weights of <2, 11> and <2, -4> respectively. In figure 9.b we have represented two threads that would be grouped in a first approach. Unfortunately there is a chain from each thread to the other. None of them can be executed first in its totality.

One possible solution to this problem would be to appropriately interleave the peels of the two threads. Several problems must be taken into consideration when this approach is used. First, the appropriate interleaving is not necessarily the one obtained by just applying the modulo N^j transformation, being very dependent on the chains that cause deadlock. Interleaving has also the problem of making more difficult the generation of code and synchronization. The fact that it corresponds to introducing more than one grouping arc in the **ACS** makes it unattractive for other computations on this space such as parallelism.

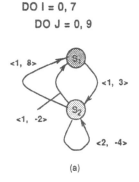

DO I = 0, 7

DO J = 0, 9

(a)

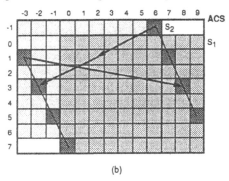

(b)

Figure 9: (a) Yet Another dependence graph and (b) deadlock between two grouped threads.

The second solution is to modify the grouping arc so that the threads that are grouped are different. It this example, the ith component of the grouping arc can always be increased by a value less than the weight of the scheduling recurrence, eliminating the deadlock.

In the multiple statement case, the necessary condition for deadlock is that the equation (5) be satisfied for both grouping arcs, i.e. no relative execution order among threads in a task can be established. An exact decision of the existence or not of deadlock is harder than in the single statement case.

5 PARALLEL CODE GENERATION

Parallel code must be generated so that each processor of the system executes the set of threads assigned and perform the appropriate synchronization operations. The general structure of the parallel code corresponding to the schedule presented in this section is shown in figure 10. Synchronization generation is not considered in this paper [2].

An n-dimensional DOALL defines the set of parallel tasks generated. Each task first executes an *intersect_ACS* in order to locate the beginning of the ACS. Loop peeling is used in order to peel off boundary iterations of the ACS in which some of the statements are missing. In the execution of a thread we distinguish two different parts: core and peel part. The core includes those iterations that executes the whole aligned loop body. In general, each task will first traverse the peel, then proceed through the core and finally traverse the peel again before leaving the ACS.

```
DOALL t̄ ∈ TAS
    v̄ = intersect_ACS(t̄)
    WHILE (v̄ ∈ ACS)
        WHILE (v̄ ∈ peel) DO
            IF (v̄ ∈ IS)  S₁(v̄) ENDIF
            IF ((v̄ + w̄₁₂) ∈ IS)  S₂(v̄ + w̄₁₂)
                ...                                                    peel part
            IF ((v̄ + w̄₁ₛ) ∈ IS)  Sₛ(v̄ + w̄₁ₛ)
            v̄ = v̄ + w̄_R
        ENDWHILE
        IF (v̄ ∉ ACS)  v̄ = intersect_ACS (v̄ + ḡ - w̄_R)

        WHILE (v̄ ∈ core) DO
            S₁(v̄)
            S₂(v̄ + w̄₁₂)
                ...                                                    core part
            Sₛ(v̄ + w̄₁ₛ)
            v̄ = v̄ + w̄_R
        ENDWHILE
        IF (v̄ ∉ ACS)  v̄ = intersect ACS (v̄ + ḡ - w̄_R)
    ENDWHILE
ENDDOALL
```

Figure 10: General structure of the parallel code generated. IS accounts for the original loop bounds.

A grouping arc of weight g is used when a thread goes out of the ACS. The function *intersect_ACS* returns the first point inside the ACS that can be reached after traversing the grouping arc g. If the ACS is not reachable from a given point, the function returns a point below the bottom end of the ACS.

6   CONCLUSIONS AND FUTURE WORK

In this paper we have studied the degree of load balancing achieved by GTS, a loop parallelizing method that achieves minimum execution time of the parallel code generated assuming that a sufficient number of processors are available and synchronization cost is negligible. [3]. In this paper we analyze the compromise between number of processors, load balance and execution time.

The evaluation of the critical path is a hard problem. Simple heuristics for what could be the situation in real programs (recurrence weights much smaller than loop bounds and a single grouping arc of weight comparable to the loop bounds) are being examined and the results are very promising.

Sometimes the method proposed for grouping threads in tasks leads to a deadlocking execution. Control on the dummy arc introduced by grouping allows the compiler to avoid the existence of deadlock, although at the expense of obtaining worse schedules. Correctness and deadlock avoidance when optimizing parallel loops is also discussed in [5].

The method requires a Hamiltonian recurrence to generate a scheduling. In the same way we have introduced a dummy dependence in order to group threads, other dependences could be added in order to obtain a Rsch. Many alternatives arise on how to generate it. Similar considerations to those done in the paper can be used in the process of selection.

REFERENCES

1. Ayguadé E., Labarta J., Torres J. and Borensztejn P. (1989), "GTS: Parallelization and Vectorization of Tight Recurrences", Supercomputing'89, Reno-Nevada, pp.531-539.
2. Ayguadé E., Labarta J., Torres J., Llabería J.M. and Valero M. (1990), "Nested-Loop Partitioning for Shared-Memory Multiprocessor Systems", Workshop on Compilers for Parallel Computers, Paris-France, pp. 377-385.
3. Ayguadé E., Labarta J., Torres J., Llabería J.M. and Valero M. (1991), "Parallelism Evaluation and Partitioning of Nested Loops for Shared Memory Multiprocessors", Advances in Languages and Compilers for Parallel Processing, Research Monographs in Parallel and Distributed Computing, Pitman/MIT, pp.220-242.
4. Cytron R.G. (1986), "Doacross: Beyond Vectorization for Multiprocessors", 1986 Int'l Conf. on Parallel Processing, St. Charles IL, pp. 836-844.
5. Midkiff S. and Padua D. (1990), "Issues in the Compile-time Optimization of Parallel Programs", 1990 Int'l. Conf. on Parallel Processing, St. Charles IL, vol. II, pp. 105-113.
6. Padua D.A. (1979), "Multiprocessors: Discussions of Some Theoretical and Practical Problems", Ph.D. Thesis, Univ. of Illinois at Urbana-Champaign, DCS Report No. UIUCDCS-R-79-990.
7. Peir J. and Cytron R. (1989), "Minimum Distance: A Method for Partitioning Recurrences for Multiprocessors", IEEE Trans. on Computers, vol. 38, no. 8, pp. 1203-1211.
8. Shang W. and Fortes J.A.B. (1988), "Independent Partitioning of Algorithms with Uniform Dependencies", Technical report School of Electrical Engineering, Purdue University.
9. Polychronopoulos C.D. (1988), "Parallel Programming and Compilers", Kluwer Academic Pub., London.

Please, address all correspondence regarding the paper to :
Eduard Ayguadé.
Departament d'Arquitectura de Computadors. Universitat Politècnica de Catalunya.
c/ Gran Capità s/n, Mòdul D-4, 08034 - Barcelona, SPAIN.
eduard@ac.upc.es
This work has been supported by the Ministry of Education of Spain (CICYT) in programs TIC 299/89 and 392/89.

20 An Iteration Partition Approach for Cache or Local Memory Thrashing on Parallel Processing

J. Fang
Hewlett-Packard Laboratories
M. Lu
Texas A&M University

Abstract
Parallel processing systems with cache or local memory in the memory hierarchies have become very common. These systems have large-size cache or local memory in each processor and usually employ copy-back protocol for the cache coherence. In such systems, a problem called "cache or local memory thrashing" may arise in executions of parallel programs, when the data unnecessarily moves back and forth between the caches or local memories in different processors. The techniques associated with parallel compilers to solve the problem are not completely developed.

In this paper we present an approach to eliminate unnecessary data moving between the caches or local memories for nested parallel loops. This approach is based on relations between array element accesses and enclosed loop indexes in the nested parallel loops. The relations can be used to assign processors to execute the appropriate iterations for parallel loops in the loop nests with respect to the data in their caches or local memories. An algorithm to calculate the correct iteration of the parallel loop in terms of loop indexes of the previous iterations executed in the processor is presented in the paper, even though there is more than one subscript expression of the same array variable in the loop.

This method benefits parallel code with nested loop constructs in a wide range of applications, in which the array elements are repeatedly referenced in the parallel loops. The experimental results show that the technique is extremely effective – capable of achieving double speedups over application programs such as Linpack benchmarks.

1. Introduction

In recent years, shared memory parallel processing systems with complicated memory hierarchies have become very common. For instance, cache is usually introduced as a means to bridge the gap between fast processor cycles and slow main memory access time in hardware design. Most parallel processing systems have local cache in each processor in the memory hierarchies, and some of them use more than one level of cache to enhance the cache bandwidth. In general, a copy-back cache protocol is employed to maintain cache coherence in these parallel processing systems, and the size of the cache memory becomes larger and larger. Another example in

[1]Supported by the National Science Foundation under grant no. MIP 8809328.

some supercomputing systems is local memory (or programmable cache), which stores copies of frequently used data and local variables. In order to avoid hot spot contention in the interconnection network, some supercomputer systems include secondary local memory in the memory hierarchy for a small cluster of processors. In such multiprocessor systems, the memory access time from a processor to its own cache or local memory is much faster than the time either to the global memory or to the caches or local memories in other processors. When executing parallel code, the frequently used data may be shared by multiple processors, which may run the multiple threads for a parallel program at the same time. The local cache may result in severe inefficiencies when a parallel code requires data moving back and forth between processors. This phenomena is called "cache or local memory thrashing" in shared memory parallel processing systems. The cache or local memory thrashing degrades the system performance.

Although great efforts have been devoted to developing compilers to take advantage of parallel processing systems, the techniques associated with parallel compiler to solve the "cache or local memory thrashing" problem are not completely developed yet. The parallel compiler concepts underlying Illinois PARAFRASE compiler [11] and Rice Parallel Fortran Converter [2] are based on the shared memory multiprocessor architecture, in which a large memory block is assumed to be directly addressable by all processors, and the memory access time from different processors is assumed to be the same [13].

Most of research work, which attempts to enhance the cache hit ratios, focuses on improving of the data localities by restructuring the original program at compiler time. These research results can be used for uniprocessor and multiprocessor systems. Early researchers in this area studied similar phenomena in virtual memory systems. In [1] W. Abu-Sufah, D. Kuck, and D. Lawrie presented a few source program transformation techniques that improve the paging behavior of programs. These transformations, called "loop-blocking", consist of breaking iterative loops into smaller loops (strip-mining) and then recombining and reindexing these smaller loops (loop-fusing and loop-interchange). Following the spirit of [1], a lot of different loop-blocking algorithms have been developed for different computer architectures. These modified blocking algorithms, such as "loop-tiling" [14] and "loop-jam" [6], are able to take advantage of cache or local memory, because there is a high degree of data reuse during computing within a block. But for most of the application code with complicated program constructs, the benefit of the blocking algorithms is very limited.

In this paper we present an approach to eliminate, at least to reduce, the "cache or local memory thrashing" problem. The technique benefits parallel programs with complicated parallel constructs in a wide range of applications, in which parallel loops are enclosed by a serial loop and the array elements are frequently reused in the parallel loops in different iterations of the enclosed serial loop. The technique calculates the appropriate parallel loop indexes for each processor in terms of the data stored in its cache or local memory, then reduces unnecessary data moving between caches or local memories in the systems.

To compute the appropriate loop index, a mathematical concept is introduced in this paper to define the relations between the array element accesses and the enclosed loop indexes in nested parallel constructs. The relations determined by the array subscript expressions can be used to partition an iteration space into equivalence classes. All vectors of the iteration space in an equivalence class may access some common array elements. The concept helps to develop a method to find the next vector in an equivalence class in terms of the previous vectors in the same equivalence class.

The rest of the paper is organized as follows. In section 2, the cache or local memory thrashing problem on our simple machine model is introduced. In section 3, the programming model that we focus on in the paper is discussed. In section 4, the results in a simple case, which has only single array subscript expression, are described first. Then these results are extended to the more complicated case with multiple subscript expressions. In section 5, the application of the results to parallel compiler is presented. The experimental results are shown that this technique is extremely effective for some application programs in section 6. In section 7, we conclude our discussion.

2. Background

2.1 Machine Model

A simple shared memory parallel processing system model is comprised of a number of processors and a global memory, which are connected by data-bus, crossbar or interconnection network. The system provides a set of synchronization primitives to support concurrent execution of multiple threads in parallel program constructs. These synchronization primitives can be fetch/increment or semaphore instructions.

To match fast processor speed, the system has caches or local memories incorporated in its memory hierarchy. To simplify our presentation, we ignore other complicated considerations in hardware cache design[3]. The cache design in the simple shared memory parallel processing system model has the following characteristics:

(1) It is local to a processor.
(2) Its size is large enough.
(3) It uses copy-back coherence strategy.
(4) Its line size is one word.
(5) It has only one level.

A more complicated machine model can be viewed as an extension of the simple model with more levels of local memories in the memory hierarchy, such as the CEDAR supercomputer[10]. The approach presented in this paper can be extended to the complicated machine model by analyzing multi-level parallel loops in nested parallel constructs.

2.2 Cache or Local Memory Thrashing Problem

In a parallel program, the execution of a piece of code specified by parallel constructs is called a **thread** [12]. A thread can be viewed as a unit of work that is programmer-defined or parallel-compiler-specified in parallel program constructs. Parallel-loop is the most common parallel construct, which can be viewed as a straightforward parallel version of the conventional DO-loop: a thread is the execution of an iteration (or a chunk of iterations if we use strip-mining or other techniques) of the loop, and the threads spawned on entering the parallel-loop merge at the end of the loop. The order in which the iterations of the loop are performed is arbitrary. For example, consider the following program:

```
       DIMENSION B(200), A(1000, 1000)
       DO I = 1, 100
             B(I) = A(I,I) − B(I−1)
             X = 1.0
             PDO J = 1, 100
                  X =  A(I,J) * B(I)
                  DO K = 1, 100

                  .....
S:                A(I+2*J+5*K, I+J+3*K) = A(I+2*J+5*K, I+J+3*K) − X
```

```
     .....
     END DO
     A(J,J) = A(J,J) + X
   END PDO
END DO
```

There are one hundred threads spawned by the parallel loop in the example if each iteration of the loop is a thread. In general, each thread in a parallel loop is determined by the body of the loop and the indexes of its enclosed loops, which can be either serial or parallel.

When programs with nested parallel loops are executed on multiprocessor systems, some frequently used data may be repeatedly used and modified by different threads for the nested loops. If the threads, which may access the same data, are not assigned to the same processor, the data may be unnecessarily moved back and forth between the caches in the systems. This phenomena is called **cache** or **local memory thrashing** in shared memory parallel processing systems.

In the above example the statement S doesn't have data dependence in the DO J loop by increment-Banerjee test [4]. If there is not other loop-carried dependence between statements of the loop body, the J loop can be parallelized. There are a total of 10,000 threads $T_{I,J}$ in the execution of the parallel loop. Each thread requests 100 elements of array A. Many of the array elements are repeatedly referenced in these threads.

For instance, thread $T_{1,1}$ requests data

A(8,5), A(13,8), A(18,11), A(23,14), ..., A(498,299), A(503,302)

for the innermost serial loop index K from 1, ..., 100 respectively.

Meanwhile, thread $T_{2,3}$ requests data

A(13,8), A(18,11), A(23,14), ..., A(498,299), A(503,302), A(508,305)

and thread $T_{3,5}$ requests data

A(18,11), A(23,14), ..., A(503,302), A(508,305), A(513,308).

It can be observed that there exists a set of threads: $T_{1,1}$, $T_{2,3}$, $T_{3,5}$, $T_{4,7}$, ..., $T_{49,99}$, which reuse most of the array elements referenced in the previous thread. If the threads of the set are assigned to different processors, the data of array A are unnecessarily moved back and forth between caches or local memories in the system.

3. Programming Model For Cache or Local Memory Thrashing Solution

3.1 Preliminaries

In this section, the preliminary concepts relevant to the iteration space and data dependence analysis are reviewed and the notations used in this paper are introduced. Standard definitions are used to analyze the array accesses [2, 13, 6]. Considering a nested parallel construct of k loops with an array **A** of dimension d, the **iteration space** denoted as **C** is defined by the product $\prod_{j=1}^{k} N_j$, where N_j is the range of the index in loop j, [L_j : U_j], where L_j and U_j are the low bound and up bound in the loop j respectively. The **domain space** denoted as **D** is defined by the product $\prod_{i=1}^{d} M_i$, where M_i is the size of array A in the i-th dimension. Any array subscript expressions in statements of a parallel nested loop can be more precisely defined by h, g: **C** $\rightarrow$ **D**.

There exists a total order in the iteration space **C** that is defined by the point in time at which the element is executed. We say that a vector **t** is greater than a vector **s**, where

$\mathbf{t} = (t_1, t_2, ..., t_k)$ and

$\mathbf{s} = (s_1, s_2, ..., s_k)$,

if there is a point m, which is from 1 to k, such that $t_i = s_i$ for $i < m$ and $t_m > s_m$.

The standard data dependence definition in [11, 13, 5] is given as follows. If two statements access the same memory location, we say that there is a data dependence between them. A **flow dependence** from a statement S_1 to a statement S_2 exists if a variable is computed in S_1 and is later referenced and used in S_2. An **antidependence** from S_1 to S_2 exists if a variable is referenced by S_1 before it is rewritten by S_2. An **output dependence** or **input dependence** from S_1 to S_2 exists if both statements write or read the same memory location respectively.

3.2 Study of Program Structures in Applications

We have studied a broad range of application programs including well-known Linpack and Perfect benchmarks. A profile software tool, which is able to obtain statistic information at execution time such as the percentage of runtime for each subroutine and the percentage of each loop in a subroutine for a benchmark, was very helpful in our study. A parallel compiler with inter-procedural analysis helps us also to explore program constructs containing subroutine calls. In the study, we assume that only one-level loops are parallel or there are multi-level parallel loops but only one-level loops are parallelized in the parallel loop nests. It is reasonable to match our simple machine model in section 2, which doesn't introduce the hardware processor cluster concept.

In our study, the nested loop constructs may contain subroutine calls in the loop body. The subroutine may have loop nests containing other subroutine calls. Since both Linpack and Perfect benchmarks are written in standard Fortran, there are no recursive calls in our benchmarks. Table 1 lists the number of loop nests and the most time-consuming loop nests in 11 perfect benchmarks.

Benchmark	Number of Loop Nests		Time-Consuming Loop Nests		
	Total	Parallel	Total	Percentage	Parallel
ADM (APS.f)	186	146	2	26%	2
ARC2d (SRS.f)	156	141	8	44%	8
BDNA (NAS.f)	183	103	3	56%	3
DYFESM (SDS.f)	156	91	4	65%	4
FLO52 (TFS.f)	115	96	8	53%	8
MDG (LWS.f)	36	30	1	85%	0
OCEAN (OCS.f)	89	65	2	33%	0
QCD (LGS.f)	124	88	1	22%	0
SPICE (CSS.f)	341	41	2	49%	0
TRACKER (MTS.f)	65	47	2	41%	0
TRFD (TIS.f)	32	29	3	88%	3

Table 1: Nested Loops in Perfect Benchmarks

In the study, we focus on the most time-consuming nested loops, each of which requires at least 3% of the execution time. By using parallel/vectorized compiler with interprocedural analysis, the parallel loops are interchanged to the outer levels even cross the subroutine call boundary, if it is possible. The serial loop, which immediately encloses the parallel loop after loop-interchange, is called **wrap loop**. The serial loop, which is immediately enclosed by the interchanged parallel loop, is called **encl loop**. Table 2 illustrates the loop structure of the time-consuming parallel loop nests in Perfect benchmarks. It shows the number of time-consuming parallel loops, the wrap loop, the number of loop levels, the level of parallel loops, the encl serial loops and the percentage of execution time required by the parallel loops.

Benchmark	Total	WrapLp	Lvls	ParLp	ParLvl	EnclLp	Percentage
Linpack	1	#134	3	#161	2	#325	49%
ADM (APS.f)	2	#4320	6	#4453	5	#4454	16%
		#4729	6	#4858	5	#4859	11%
ARC2d (SRS.f)	8	#2155	4	#2165	3	#2165	7%
			4	#2215	3	#2218	7%
			4	#3144	3	#3145	5%
		#2310	4	#2348	3	#2350	5%
			4	#2366	3	#2367	5%
			4	#3722	3	#3723	4%
		#313	3	#2723	2	#2724	5%
			3	#2783	2	#2784	4%
BDNA (NAS.f)	3	#238	3	#3546	2	#3548	36%
			3	#3061	3	-	10%
			3	#3088	3	-	10%
DYFESM (SDS.f)	4	#6845	5	#875	4	#877	10%
			5	#891	4	#893	10%
		#698	7	#4358	5	#4362 #4265	35%
		#796	7	#4513	5	#4514 #4518	11%
FLO52 (TFS.f)	8	#874	4	#880	3	#879	5%
			4	#904	3	#903	5%
			4	#1014	3	#1013	10%
			5	#1027	4	#1025	4%
			4	#1040	3	#1039	10%
			5	#1053	4	#1051	5%
			5	#1269	4	#1264	7%
			5	#1278	4	#1265	7%
QCD (LGS.f)	1	#1138	14	#1144	14	-	22%
TRFD (TIS.f)	3	#279	6	#285	5	#289	35%
			6	#300	5	#303	30%
		#338	7	#346	6	#350	23%

Table 2: Parallel Loops in Nested Constructs in Perfect Benchmarks

From the table, it can be seen that most of the time-consuming parallel loops in the benchmarks are in the middle level of the loop nests (or can be interchanged to the middle level). They enclose at least one level serial loop. The serial wrap loop usually encloses more than one parallel loop. For instance. in FLO52 a serial loop #874 encloses all time-consuming parallel loops of the benchmark. In our study, we noticed that most of the non-time-consuming parallel loops have such constructs also, which are contained by some serial wrap loop and may enclose other serial loops. The array access patterns in the parallel loops are studied for such nested parallel nested constructs. We concentrated on the major array variables with largest sizes, which have to be bigger than the size of cache memory.

In the study, we noticed that most of the major arrays are two-dimensional. Some of them have three dimensions, but one dimension is always a constant in the time-consuming loop nests. These three-dimension arrays can be considered to be two-dimension arrays also.

A loop-alignment technique [5] in parallel/vectorized compiler was used to transform the array expressions into the same form for the different parallel loops enclosed by the same wrap loop in the same format. Especially, we pay attentions on a phenomena called **inherent thrashing** in our study, which is similar to the alignment conflict condition in [5]. The inherent thrashing phenomena may happen in the parallel loop nests with multiple major arrays. Let's check a parallel loop nest with arrays A and B. Suppose that A is assigned and B is used in the first parallel loop, B is assigned and A is used in the second parallel loop, and these parallel loops are enclosed by the same wrap loop. If the expressions of A and B are different or they cannot be aligned due to the alignment conflict, then there always exists cache or local memory thrashing for array A or array B at the execution of the common serial wrap loop. Actually, it is easy for parallel compilers to detect the inherent thrashing condition between two major arrays by checking the dependence graph. Fortunately, we did not find any inherent thrashing loop in the time-consuming parallel nests in the Perfect benchmarks.

Lemma 1. For a pair of array variables with loop-independent flow dependence in two parallel loops, which are enclosed by the same wrap loop, if there exists a cycle of flow dependence edges carried by the wrap loop between the variables in dependence graph, and the array subscript expressions are not the same or cannot be aligned to the same, then the array variables is called **inherent thrashing**.

3.3 Programming Model

In this section, we define a programming model, which represents certain types of parallel loop nests that are encountered very often in a wide range of applications and easy to be identified by parallel/vectorized compilers.

Based on the results of study shown in the previous section, if the cache or local memory thrashing is eliminated at the execution of the wrap loop, the speed up of the benchmarks will be significantly enhanced. In this paper, we present a solution to eliminate, or at least to reduce the cache or local memory thrashing on a common program construct in benchmark analysis: a serial wrap loop encloses parallel loops and each of the parallel loops may contain one or more serial loops. The loop constructs are not necessary to be perfect nested. Scalar code can be contained in the wrap loop or in the parallel loop. To simplify our presentation, we assume that there exists only one major array variable A. The results in the paper can be easily extended to the same program model with multiple major arrays, if they do not satisfy the inherent thrashing condition.

The programming model for the solution of the cache or local memory thrashing has the following characteristics:

1. It has a serial wrap-loop in the outermost level, denoted as **DO Loop i** , which cannot be distributed in that level.

2. There are only one level loops parallel (or parallelized) denoted as **PDO Loop j** in the loop nest, which are immediately enclosed by the wrap-loop.

3. The parallel loops may contain serial loops after loop-interchange. The immediately enclosed

serial·loop, named encl-loop, is denoted as **DO Loop k**. The encl-loop k may be an empty loop.

4. It may be a non-perfectly nested loop construct and have arbitrary IF-THEN-ELSE structure. Loop bounds are not necessary to be constants.

5. Only one two-dimensional major array variable **A** is in the loop nest, which has linear subscript expressions in terms of the indexes of wrap-loop, parallel loop and encl-loop after induction variable replacement.

6. The array **A** may have more than one expression in a parallel loop, but it has to have the same expressions in the different parallel loops after loop-alignment.

We assume that there are **r** different subscript expressions on the two dimension array $A[1..D_1, 1..D_2]$. These expressions are linear functions f_m and g_m respectively in column and row:

$$f_m(i,j,k) = a_{m,1}i + b_{m,1}j + c_{m,1}k + d_{m,1} \text{ and}$$

$$g_m(i,j,k) = a_{m,2}i + b_{m,2}j + c_{m,2}k + d_{m,2}.$$

These linear functions **f, g**: $Z^3 \rightarrow Z^2$ are mapping from $N \times M \times L$ to $D_1 \times D_2$, where $N = U_{wrap} - L_{wrap}$ is the loop bound of the serial wrap loop, $M = \max(U_{par1} - L_{par1}, U_{par2} - L_{par2})$ is the maximal number of the parallel loop bounds if there are **t** parallel loops contained by the wrap loop, and $L = \max(U_{encl1} - L_{encl1}, U_{encl2} - L_{encl2}, U_{enc2} - L_{enc2})$ is the maximal number of the serial enclosed loops if there are **s** enclosed loops contained by the parallel loops.

We studied lots of scientific computation benchmarks such as mechanical CAE, structural analysis, fluid dynamics, heat transfer, computational chemistry, petroleum, and geographic applications. Most of the time-consuming parallel loop nests in the benchmarks have very similar characteristics with the programming model.

To compare with other approaches to eliminate or reduce the cache or local memory thrashing problem, we must mention blocking algorithms. Several research groups demonstrated the effectiveness of blocking algorithms for shared memory multiprocessors with memory hierarchies [7]. In general, a blocking algorithm needs to partition the array variables and broadcast the blocks to several processors if they reference data in the blocks for different iterations. In our program model, the wrap loop in the model is serial and cannot be distributed. The entire array is referenced in each iteration of the outermost serial loop. We have to rewrite the programs to use blocking algorithms. The approach presented in this paper can be applied in automatic parallel compilers and runtime library support. It doesn't require programs to rewrite application programs like most of the blocking algorithms.

The nature of the cache or local memory thrashing can be described in the following way. When a serial outermost wrap-loop encloses several parallel loops, the dependences carried by the serial loop may cause the data moving back and forth between threads that execute the iterations of the parallel loops in the different iterations of the outer serial loops. Some array elements may be reused in the different iterations of the serial loop due to the loop-carried dependences in the loop. Meanwhile, these array elements need to be moved in the caches or local memories between processors in each iteration of the serial loops due to the parallel loops.

4. Main Results

4.1 An Important Lemma

In the program model described in Section 3.3, the linear array subscript expressions can be used to partition the set of the pairs of wrap-loop index and the parallel loop index. The linear functions f_m and g_m, where m is from 1 to r, specify a map from the **reduced iteration space**, $N \times M$, to the set of subsets of the **domain space**.

$$\textbf{f, g: } N \times M \rightarrow 2^{D_1 \times D_2}.$$

In section 4.1 and 4.2, we discuss the simple case, where only one array subscript expression exists in the parallel construct. The subscript m for functions and coefficients can be omitted in the simple case. Then the results will be extended to the multiple expressions in section 4.3.

In the program model shown in section 3.3 with only one expression in the parallel construct, we define a set of elements of array A, which are accessed within thread T_{i_0,j_0} as follows.

Definition 1. For a given pair i_0 and j_0, the set of elements $A(f(i_0, j_0, k), g(i_0, j_0, k))$ of array A, which are accessed within thread T_{i_0,j_0}, is denoted by A_{i_0,j_0}, where $1 \leq k \leq L$.

$$A_{i_0,j_0} = \{A(f(i_0, j_0, k), g(i_0, j_0, k)) \mid \text{for given } i_0 \text{ and } j_0, \text{ where } k \in [1, L]\}.$$

Since both f and g are linear in terms of i, j, and k, the following lemma is obvious and useful in the rest of this section.

Lemma 2.: In a loop construct in the programming model described above, if there exist two points in iteration space, (i, j, k) and (i', j', k'), such that

$$f(i, j, k) = f(i', j', k')$$

and

$$g(i, j, k) = g(i', j', k'),$$

then for any constant n_0, we have a series of points in the space, (i, j, k + n_0) and (i', j', k' + n_0) satisfying the following equations:

$$f(i, j, k+n_0) = f(i', j', k'+n_0)$$

and

$$g(i, j, k+n_0) = g(i', j', k'+n_0)$$

where $1 \leq k' + n_0 \leq L$ and $1 \leq k + n_0 \leq L$.

It is clear from Lemma 2 that if

$$A^{(m)}_{i_1,j_1} \cap A^{(m)}_{i_2,j_2} \neq \Phi,$$

then threads S_{i_1,j_1} and S_{i_2,j_2} should be assigned to the same processor, because they may access some common elements of array A.

4.2 Result in Single Expression

Lemma 2 in the previous section can be used to collect a set of loop index pairs (i,j), whose corresponding threads may reuse some elements of array variable A. The following theorem provides an efficient method to compute the parallel loop index from the current outer serial loop index and the previous parallel loop index in such a way that the thread to execute the current parallel loop iteration may access some array elements that were accessed in the thread of the previous parallel loop iteration within the previous serial loop iterations.

Theorem 1. In the program model described in Section 3.3, we have two points (i,j,k) and (i',j',k') in iteration space such that

$$f(i,j,k) = f(i',j',k') \text{ and}$$
$$g(i,j,k) = g(i',j',k'),$$

if they satisfy the following condition:

$$i' - i = b_1 c_2 - b_2 c_1$$
$$j - j' = a_1 c_2 - a_2 c_1$$
$$k - k' = a_2 b_1 - a_1 b_2.$$

Let us denote: $\alpha = b_1 c_2 - b_2 c_1$
$$\beta = a_1 c_2 - a_2 c_1$$
$$\gamma = a_2 b_1 - a_1 b_2.$$

From α, β, γ, we can compute a set of points in the reduced iteration space for a given pair (i_0, j_0). The threads corresponding to these points may access some common array elements at execution time. By α, β, γ and the loop low bounds, it is easy to calculate the initial points for each set from which the following points can be computed from Theorem 1.

To prove that the sets of points in the reduced iteration space specified by Theorem 1 can partition the space, we give the following definition.

Definition 2. In the programming model described in Section 3.3, for a given pair i_0 and j_0, S_{i_0,j_0} denotes a set of points (i, j) in the reduced iteration space of size $N \times M$, which satisfy the following condition:

$$S_{i_0,j_0} = \{(i,j) \mid A_{i_0,j_0} \cap A_{i,j} \neq \Phi\}.$$

By Lemma 1 given in the previous section, the definition can be described as:

$$S_{i_0,j_0} = \{(i,j) \mid \text{there is } k_0 \text{ and } k \text{ such that } f(i_0,j_0,k_0) = f(i,j,k) \text{ and } g(i_0,j_0,k_0) = g(i,j,k)\}.$$

Theorem 2. In the programming model in Section 3.3, $S_{i,j}$ is an equivalence class in the reduced iteration space $N \times M$. Therefore the relation defined in Theorem 1 partitions the reduced iteration space.

By Theorem 2, the thread corresponding to a point of an equivalence class never accesses the element of array A, which is accessed in the threads corresponding to the points of the different equivalence classes. This means that if the threads corresponding to the points of an equivalence class are not assigned to the other processor, there is no unnecessary data moving between processors for array A. Of course, additional execution time is required to compute the current parallel loop index in terms of the current serial wrap-loop index, the previous wrap-loop and parallel loop indexes.

4.3 Results in Multiple Expression Case

In this section we discuss complicated case in which there are multiple expressions in the parallel loops of the programming model described in Section 3.3. As shown in Section 4.2, each linear function gives a particular value of α, β, and γ by Theorem 1.

Section 4.2 gave the definition of a set of points (i,j) in the reduced iteration space, S_{i_0,j_0}, in which each point may access some elements of array A that are referenced in thread T_{i_0,j_0} for given (i_0, j_0).

This definition can be rewritten below, where the superscript (1) indicates that only one linear subscript expression is in the parallel loops.

$$S_{i_0,j_0}^{(1)} = \{(i,j) \mid i = i_0 + p \times \alpha \text{ and } j = j_0 + p \times \beta \text{ for } p \in Z\}.$$

Now we extend the definition from one linear expression to multiple linear expressions in the parallel loop. As shown in the program model in Section 3.3, there is more than one subscript expression for a major array variable in the parallel loops. Assume the number of the different array subscript expressions is r. By Theorem 1, we have a list of m triples: $(\alpha_1, \beta_1, \gamma_1)$, $(\alpha_2, \beta_2, \gamma_2)$, ..., $(\alpha_r, \beta_r, \gamma_r)$.

The set of points in the reduced iteration space defined as follows can be viewed as an extension of the equivalence class defined in section 4.2. If the relationship defined by Definition 3 can partition the reduced iteration space, then the corresponding threads may access some common elements of the array or arrays that are stored in the local cache by thread T_{i_0, j_0} for given i_0, j_0.

Definition 3. In reduced iteration space of wrap-loop i and parallel loop j, there are r different subscript expression for a major array variable. The set of the pairs of i and j, whose corresponding threads may access some common elements of the array or arrays that are stored in the local cache by thread T_{i_0, j_0}, is defined as $S^{(r)}_{i_0, j_0}$.

$$S^{(r)}_{i_0, j_0} = \left\{ (i,j) \mid i = i_0 + \sum p_m \times \alpha_m \text{ and } j = j_0 + \sum p_m \times \beta_m \text{ for } p_1, ..., p_r \, \epsilon \, Z \right\}.$$

The following Theorem shows that the relation defined in the above definition can partition the reduced iteration space. If all threads corresponding to the points $S_{i,j}$ are assigned into the same processor, the processor never accesses any data in the caches or local memories of the other processors. Therefore, we can reduce the unnecessary data moving between processors and improve the system performance.

Theorem 3. $S^{(r)}_{i_0, j_0}$ is an equivalence class in the reduced iteration space of loop i and loop j.

By Theorem 1 and Definition 3, it is obvious that there is no memory access from one processor to cache or local memory of other processor, if all threads in the same equivalence class are assigned to one processor.

Theorem 4: Every thread $T_{i,j} \epsilon S^{(r)}_{i_0, j_0}$ may reuse some data in the other threads belonging to the other equivalence classes $S^{(r)}_{i_0, j_0}$, but never access the data referenced by the threads belonging to the other equivalence classes.

A similar but more complicated calculation for the current parallel loop index in terms of the current serial wrap-loop index and the previous wrap-loop and parallel loop indexes as one in Section 4.2 can be developed from Theorem 1 and Theorem 3 in [8].

5. Application of the Results in Parallel Compilers

In this section, we briefly describe a way to apply the above results in parallel compilers to eliminate the cache or local memory thrashing. Here we only show the essential idea of the approach, and leave the detailed implementation to readers.

In general, parallel/vectorized compilers hold the information of nested loop structure. After dependence analysis and loop transformation, the serial wrap-loop that immediately encloses parallel loops is easy to be determined, assuming only one level loops are parallel or parallelized. A heuristic algorithm may be required to estimate the execution time for the loop nest. If the loop nest might be time-consuming, the results in this paper are applied.

The algorithm to determine whether the time-consuming loop nest satisfies the programming model in section 3.3 can be described as follows:

1. An heuristic algorithm is required to choose the major array variables by estimating the amount of elements referenced in the loop nest and checking the linear expressions.

2. Check the expression in each dimension for these major arrays. If an array has more than two dimensions and more than two subscript expressions using the wrap-loop and parallel loop indexes, move the array from the major array set.

3. If an array appears in more than one parallel loops in the loop nest and the loop-alignment cannot make its expression in the same form for the parallel loops, move the array from the major array set.

4. Appling the approach presented in **Lemma 1** for each pair of arrays, if there is *inherent thrashing condition* between them, move one of them from the major array set.

5. If the major array set is not empty, calculate the initial points for each equivalence class by using the approach in this paper, and save all information in a shared data structure.

6. Create run-time library for the parallel loops in the loop nest, which will compute the current parallel loop index in terms of the previous wrap-loop and parallel loop indexes and the current wrap loop index as shown in Theorem 1, 2 and 3. The information in the shared data structure can be used to schedule processor dynamically at the execution time.

We want to emphasize here that the approach presented in the paper may eliminate some unnecessary data moving then reduce the cache or local memory thrashing. In worst case, the approach cannot predicate the right major arrays, but it never increases cache missing and degrade the system performance.

If the parallel nested constructs are found in the time-consuming loops satisfying our program model, the implementation will be straightforward. In general, sequential optimizers create template control variables such as "loop-increment", "loop-bound" and "control counter" to perform loop control. The loop index variable is recomputed in the beginning of the loop body at the execution time. The same idea can be employed in parallel loops to compute the right iteration to be executed for the processor.

In static scheduling, all the equivalence classes can be computed and assigned to the processors at the compiler time. The initial points of each equivalence class can be determined by calculating the loop lower bounds and the α, β, γ in Theorem 1. Each processor requires some local memory locations to keep the α, β, γ, and other information.

In self-scheduling [9], the initial points of the equivalence classes are prepared at compile time, and are stored in a shared data structure. In the first iteration of the outermost serial loop, the processors get the initial points from the shared data structure and execute the corresponding equivalence classes. After that, each processor can calculate the current vectors from the previous vectors which are stored in the local memory in the processor. If all iterations in an equivalence class have completed, the processor can check the shared data structure to find whether any other equivalence classes are available.

The approach presented in the paper may be against the idea of load balancing in self-scheduling, because restricting each processor to specific set of array elements to minimize cache or local memory thrashing may interfere with the load balancing mechanism. Some hueristic needs to be developed for a processor, which have completed all iterations in the equivalence classes with data in its own cache or local memory, to move data in other equivalence class from the other processors if these processors have heavy working load. The heuristic development will depend on results of experiment and is beyond the scope of the paper.

6. Experimental Results

We have implemented the results of this paper in a parallel compiler prototype, which performs the dependence analysis and parallel transformations for FORTRAN programs. The prototype computes the α, β, γ in Theorem 1, and the initial points at compiler time, then uses the information for dynamic scheduling as in [9] at execution time. The parallel code generated by the prototype is running on a shared memory multiprocessor simulator bas MIPS-based system simulator. The system can simulate 4 to 16 processors, sizes of cache memories, cache coherence protocols, cache line sizes and memory bandwidth of data bus, crossbar or interconnection network. The processor and the cache in the simulation system are based on MIPS R3000 and R4000. The prototype, simulates different scheduling strategies also. They include static scheduling, self-scheduling, and guided-self-scheduling. The experimental results show that these scheduling approaches are slightly different on the execution performance. But the technique presented in this paper to reduce the cache thrashing problem made a significant improvement for the execution performance, no matter which scheduling approach was used in the experiments.

In examining the experimental results, the reader should be aware that some of the improvements cited may have been achieved because the huge cost of the cache is missing in RISC architecture. We compared the parallel code execution with or without the compiler strategy presented in this paper for the cache thrashing problem and found significant enhancement by eliminating the unnecessary data moving back and forth between processors. In the experiment, we assume that the memory and crossbar bandwidth is proportionally improved when the number of processors gets increased.

Gaussian Elimination. Gaussian Elimination is a basic matrix operation that is used in many application programs. We use a 1K by 1K array in the experimental benchmark.

Number Processor	Original Serial Code	Parallel Code with Cache Thrashing	Parallel Code without Cache Thrashing	Speed Up
4	285.0s	163.5s	102.2s	1.6
8	285.3s	109.8s	59.9s	1.7
16	286.2s	83.6s	39.8s	2.1

Linpack Benchmark. Linpack benchmark is vectorized/parallelized code. We chose the loops containing SAXPY and SMXPY subroutine calls, and inlined these routines in the loops, most of which have three level loops: Serial, parallel, serial. As the table below shows, our approach achieved better performance from the original parallel code that doesn't have any consideration for the cache thrashing problem. To make this measurement, we use 1K by 1K Linpack benchmark.

Number processor	Original Serial Code	Parallel Code with Cache Thrashing	Parallel Code without Cache Thrashing	Speed Up
4	514.7s	327.5s	234.0s	1.4
8	514.3s	226.9s	151.3s	1.5
16	515.2s	161.0s	94.7s	1.7

A Complete Application. We also performed the test on a complete application program benchmark, a computational chemistry application program. The kernel of the most frequently used routine has the following form:

```
      K = 0
100   K = K + 1
      ................
      PARALLEL DO I = 1, M
         ................
         DO 200 J = 1, M
            X(I+K,J+I+K) = .......
            ................
            .... = X(I+K, J+I+K) * .......
200      CONTINUE
         ................
      END_PARALLEL_DO
      ................
      IF (K .LT. MAX_BOUND) GO TO 100
```

The dimension of the array X is 3K by 1K. The approach presented in the paper works perfectly for the program. The table below shows the results when our approach was applied to eliminate cache thrashing.

Number Processor	Original Serial Code	Parallel Code with Cache Thrashing	Parallel Code without Cache Thrashing	Speed Up
4	1732.0s	1415.6s	832.7s	1.7
8	1734.1s	843.2s	481.8s	1.75
16	1735.7s	557.8s	309.9s	1.8

The compilation time was measured also on our experience. Since the loops and array subscript expressions in the loops are well represented in vectorized/parallel compiler, the implementation of the approach presented in the paper only costs less than 7000 line C code. The compilation time only increases less than 5% for all benchmarks with thousands line FORTRAN code. In dynamic scheduling, the approach presented in the paper requires more complicated shared data structure than one described [9]. It usually takes couple thousands bytes for a 1K × 1K array variable to save the initial points for the equivalence classes.

7. Conclusions

Most of the compiler techniques used to enhance the cache hit ratio focus on data locality by blocking the original programs. This paper describes another phenomena called "cache or local memory thrashing", which degrades the cache hit ratio and increases unnecessary data-bus, crossbar or interconnection network traffic. A mathematical concept is presented in this paper, which partitions the iteration space so that the threads in the same equivalence class never access the caches or local memories in other processors if they are assigned to the same processor. The approach in this paper is good for some program constructs that are very common in application programs. For these application programs, our approach can significantly reduce the cache or local memory thrashing phenomena.

We only discuss a simple machine model and a simple program model in this paper. Even with that, the multiple linear expression case complicates the algorithm to compute the appropriate parallel loop index at the execution time. Future research work on this topic includes mathematical concepts for more complicated machine models and more complex program models, and simpler algorithms for the multiple linear expression cases. Studying new algorithms for the other features of cache hardware design, such as different cache coherence strategies, multiple word cache lines, or multiple level cache memory, is also important in developing parallel compilers.

Reference

[1] Abu-Sufah, W., Kuck, D., and Lawrie, D., On the Performance Enhancement of Paging Systems Through Program Analysis and Transformations, *IEEE Transactions on Computers*, C-30, 5, May 1981.

[2] Allen, J.R., and Kennedy, K., PFC: A Program to Convert Fortran to Parallel Form, *Report MASC-TR82-6*, Rice University, Mar. 1982.

[3] Baer, J., and Wang, W., Multilevel Cache Hierarchies: Organizations, Protocols, and Performance, *Journal of Parallel and Distributed Computing*, Vol. 6, 451-476.

[4] Burke, M., and Cytron, R., Interprocedural Dependence Analysis and Parallelization, *Proceedings of SIGPLAN 1986 Symposium on Compiler Construction*, July 1986.

[5] Calahan, D., A Global Approach to Detection of Parallelism, Feb. 1987, *Ph.D. Thesis*, Computer Science Department, Rice University, Houston, TX.

[6] Callahan, D., Carr, S., and Kennedy, K., Improving Register Allocation for Subscripted Variables, *Proceedings of the ACM SIGPLAN'90 Conference on Programming Language Design and Implementation*, White Plains, NY, June 20-22, 1990.

[7] Dongarra, J., Sorensen, D., and Brewer, O., Tools and Methodology for Programming Parallel Processors, *Aspects of Computation on Asynchronous Parallel Processors*, IFIP 1989, pp. 125-137.

[8] Fang, Z., and Lu, M., A Solution of Cache Ping-Pong Problem in RISC Based Parallel Processing Systems, *Proceedings of International Conference on Parallel Processing 1991*, St. Chalse, pp. I-238 - 245.

[9] Fang, Z., Yew, C., Tang, T., and Zhu, C., Dynamic Processor Self-scheduling for General Parallel Nested Loops, *IEEE Transactions on Computer*, Vol. 39, No. 7, (July 1990), 919-929.

[10] Kuck, D., et. al., Parallel Supercomputing Today and Cedar Approach, *Science*, (Feb. 1986), 967-974.

[11] Kuck, D.J., Kuhn, R.H., Leasure, B., and Wolfe, M.,The Structure of an Advanced Vectorizer for Pipeline Processor, *Proceedings of IEEE Computer Society Fourth International Computer Software and Applications Conference*, Oct. 1980.

[12] Leasure, B., et. al., PCF Fortran: Language Definition by the Parallel Computing Forum, *Proceedings of International Conferences on Parallel Processing*, Aug. 1988.

[13] Padua, D.A., and Wolfe, M., Advanced Compiler Optimizations for Supercomputers, *Communications ACM*, (Dec. 1986), 1184-1201.

[14] Wolfe, M., Iteration Space Tiling for Memory Hierarchies, *Proceedings of the Third SIAM Conference on Parallel Processing*, Los Angeles, CA, Dec. 1-4, 1987.

21 On Estimating and Enhancing Cache Effectiveness

J. Ferrante
IBM T.J. Watson Research Center
V. Sarkar
IBM Palo Alto Scientific Center
W. Thrash
University of Washington

Abstract

In this paper, we consider automatic analysis of a program's cache usage to achieve greater cache effectiveness. We show how to estimate efficiently the number of distinct cache lines used by a given loop in a nest of loops. Given this estimate of the number of cache lines needed, we can estimate the number of cache misses for a nest of loops. Our estimates can be used to guide program transformations such as loop interchange to achieve greater cache effectiveness. We present simulation results that show our estimates are reasonable for simple cases such as matrix multiply. We analyze the array sizes for which our estimates differ from our simulation results, and provide recommendations on how to handle such arrays in practice.

1   Introduction

High performance sequential and parallel computing requires efficient use of the memory hierarchy. The best performance for a given program may require careful hand coding, but automatic compiler analysis providing good use of the memory hierarchy would be acceptable in most cases. In this paper, we consider automatic analysis of a program's cache usage to achieve greater cache effectiveness. We use the IBM RS/6000 [4] cache parameters in our examples, but the analysis techniques are applicable to other cache architectures as well.

To show how cache effectiveness could be achieved by automatic analysis of cache usage, consider the standard Fortran matrix multiply example with loop order i,j,k in Figure 1. We consider all possible loop interchanges [17] to determine which loop would be the best

---

*IBM Research Division, T. J. Watson Research Center, P.O. Box 704, Yorktown Heights, NY 10598.
†IBM Palo Alto Scientific Center, 1530 Page Mill Road, Palo Alto, CA 94304.
‡Department of Computer Science and Engineering, FR-35, University of Washington, Seattle, WA 98195. This work was partly supported by IBM and an NSF Graduate Fellowship.

choice for the innermost position. Suppose bounds on the number of cache lines needed for the arrays a, b and c are supplied for each choice of i, j and k as *innermost* loop, as in the table in Figure 1 (based on a line size of 16 words). For a cache with 512 lines, such as the RS/6000, only the choice of i as innermost loop will fit in cache. Given these bounds, an automatic system could determine that to enhance cache utilization, i as innermost loop is the right choice. In this paper, we will show how such cache line bounds can be efficiently computed for array variables in a given nest of loops.

```
DO i = 1,500
  DO j = 1,500
    DO k = 1,500
      c(i,j) = c(i,j) + a(i,k) * b(k,j)
    ENDDO
  ENDDO
ENDDO
```

Cache Line Bounds for Different Innermost Loops

Innermost	c	a	b	a+b+c
i	32	32	1	65
j	500	1	500	1001
k	1	500	32	533

Figure 1. Matrix Multiply Example

Computing at compile time the exact number of cache lines used by a given variable is difficult, and undecidable in general. Our philosophy in attacking this problem is to seek easily computed bounds that also provide reasonable estimates in practice, and can therefore be used by a compiler to guide tranformations to improve cache usage.

In general, to determine the number of cache misses for a given loop ordering, we start by determining an upper bound on the total number of distinct lines (DL) accessed by only the innermost loop, then the inner two loops, and so on. The innermost loop that causes the cache to overflow is called the *overflow loop* (following [18]). An upper bound for the total number of misses is obtained by multiplying the DL value for all loops contained within the overflow loop, by the product of the number of iterations of the overflow loop and all its containing loops. If the cache is not fully associative, then the bound may need to be adjusted to take into account the possibility of set conflicts. Our estimates are obtained in terms of either constant or symbolic values. For example, if we consider loop order j, k, i for the loop order in Figure 1, then loop k will be the overflow loop, and the total number of misses will be estimated as $500 \times 500 \times 65$.

We now discuss related work. The problem of estimating the amount of local memory needed by array references contained within a nest of loops was considered by Gallivan, Gannon and Jalby in [12, 11]. They introduced the notion of uniformly generated data dependences and based their analysis for this class of dependences. Since many data dependences are not uniformly generated, it limits the applicability of their technique in practice. As evidence of this, in [21], in a sample of Fortran programs (including library packages such as Linpack and Eispack and numeric programs such as SPICE) 86% of dependences found had non-constant distance vectors. The main causes as reported imply the dependences are *non*-uniformly generated. Our techniques can be applied more generally to linear subscript expressions, including those with coefficients not known at compile time. Further, the work in [12, 11] focussed on optimizing for a software-controlled local memory (as in a distributed-memory multiprocessor), rather than for a hardware-controlled cache memory.

The problem of estimating the number of cache lines for uniprocessor machines was considered by Porterfield in [18]. However, Porterfield's technique assumes a cache line size of one element; in our work, no such assumption is made. Further, the analysis in [18] only applies to the special case of data dependences with constant direction vectors, which is not the usual case in practice [21]. The approach in [18] is based on computing all the "cache dependences" of the program (similar to data dependences). Instead, we use multiple applications of the GCD test, the simplest test for data dependence, and compute the bounds from Banerjee's inequality once per array reference. For examples in which the loop body has complicated control flow, [18] may be more exact due to the flow-sensitive nature of data dependence information; however, in other cases, we either obtain the same answer as [18] with considerably less work or provide an answer where [18] would not. For these reasons, our work will be more efficient and more generally applicable than [18].

In [22], Wolf and Lam developed another cost model based on the number of loops carrying reuse. As in our analysis, such reuse can either be temporal (relating to the same data item) or spatial (relating to data items in the same cache line) and is given for both single and multiple references. Our cost estimates should be more accurate than theirs in counting reuse since ours take into account more factors than just the number of loops carrying reuse, e.g., the periodicity of data items generated by reference expressions. Their work considers overlap of only uniformly generated references, whereas ours is more generally applicable. They also develop an algorithm to improve locality based on their cost estimates. Our cost estimates could also be used in conjunction with their algorithm to better improve locality.

Related work in summarizing array dependence information for interprocedural analysis can be found in [5] and the references contained therein. While less costly than full dependence analysis, such summaries are usually more costly and precise than needed for our cache analysis, since they need to provide a summary of the accesses while we only need to count them. Summary techniques such as the data access descriptors of [5] may extend the precision we obtain at not too great a cost. We plan to examine this in future work. Cache miss estimates have also been used in estimating execution times for different machines [19].

The rest of the paper is organized as follows: In Section 2, we make clear our assumptions about the input program and the architectural model. Section 3 shows how to bound the number of distinct element accesses (DA) and the number of distinct cache lines (DL), for a single array reference in a given nest of loops. Section 4 extends the results of Section 3 for multiple references to the same array variable. In Section 5, we present simulation results for matrix multiply, and analyze the impact of different array sizes on set conflicts and cache miss ratios. Finally, in Section 6, we present our conclusions and comment on future work.

2 Program and Architecture Models

In this section, we make clear the assumptions and limitations of our program and architecture models. We first consider the input program. Henceforth, any read or write occurrence of a variable in the program is referred to as a *reference* of the variable.

We assume for our analysis a set of normalized, perfectly nested loops. Loop normalization [23] guarantees that both the lower limit and the increment of each loop index variable will equal one. Perfect nesting guarantees that all array references are contained within the innermost loop. The analysis presented in this paper can also be performed on a reference contained within imperfectly nested loops, by identifying the loops that contain the reference. However, imperfectly nested loops are less interesting from the viewpoint of our work because they do not allow for loop interchange. Instead, our recommendation is to use loop distribution [23] to transform imperfectly nested loops into perfectly nested loops as far as possible. The loop nest is assumed to consist entirely of DO loops; induction variable analysis [2] can be used to convert non-DO loops into DO loops, when possible.

Our analysis is applicable to array references with subscripts that are linear functions of the loop indices. Array references with non-linear subscript expressions will be assumed to incur one miss per access (the worst-case assumption).

Our work ignores conditionals within loops; that is, we conservatively assume that all array references in the loop body are executed in every iteration. This may lead to an over-estimation of the number of misses. To take conditionals partly into account, data flow analysis [1] could be used to determine if there is a possible execution path between references of a given array. The lack of such a path allows us to treat the references separately. In addition, execution profiling [20] can be used to determine the probability of execution of each reference, and our estimates can be weighted by such probabilities. Future work will consider the use of execution profiling information with our techniques.

We now turn to our architectural model. For now, we assume a uniprocessor model with a memory hierarchy. In future work, we plan to extend our results to parallel machines. As defined in [14], a *cache* is the first level of the memory hierarchy between the CPU and main memory (registers are assumed to be part of the CPU). We consider only the data cache. A *block* is the unit of transfer from a cache; the *block size*, B, is the number of bytes in a block. In this paper, we often use the term *cache line* instead of cache block. A cache line is viewed as a sequence of array elements, rather than as a sequence of bytes. The *line size*, L, is the number of elements in a cache line. Whereas the block size, B, is a fixed parameter of the cache hardware, the line size $L = B/ES$ also depends on ES, the array element size in bytes. If a line can be placed anywhere in cache, then the cache is *fully associative*. If only k possible places exist, they are referred to as a *set* of size k, and we say the cache is *k-way set associative*. If $k = 1$, then the cache is called *direct-mapped*. Real cache systems usually have a small value of k.

Since we use the RS/6000 as our machine example throughout the paper, we list here its cache parameters [3]. The RS/6000 cache has 512 blocks with block size, $B = 128$ bytes. It is 4-way set associative with 128 sets, each containing 4 blocks. For the examples in this paper, we assume an element size of $ES = 8$ bytes (double precision), and a line size of $L = 16$ elements.

3 Bounding the Number of Cache Lines for a Single Reference

We now consider the problem of bounding the number of distinct array elements and the number of distinct cache lines accessed by a given array reference in a given nest of loops. In this section we provide bounds for a single array reference; in Section 4 we show how to combine bounds for multiple references. A single reference includes all occurrences of the array variable that always have the same subscript values in the same iteration (*i.e.*, all occurrences that can be determined to be the same by common subexpression elimination).

3.1 Counting and Bounding Distinct Accesses

In this subsection we consider DA—the number of distinct accesses of a single array reference in a nest of loops. We shall give the exact value of DA for some simple cases, and give bounds for loops with more complex single references.

Consider a simple example with a single array reference, a(i):

```
DO i = 1,100
    a(i) = a(i) + 5
ENDDO
```

We can easily compute DA in this example; since the subscript expression $f(i) = i$ takes on distinct values as i ranges from 1 to 100, DA is just 100. More generally, any nonconstant linear susbscript expression of exactly one loop variable will have DA equal to the iteration count for that variable.

Unfortunately, things are not always so simple. Consider the slightly more complicated single array reference in the following example:

```
DO i = 1,8
  DO j = 1,5
      a(6i+9j-7) = a(6i+9j-7) + 5
  ENDDO
ENDDO
```

Here there are 40 accesses to a in the loop nest, as can easily be seen from the loop bounds, but only 25 distinct accesses. We have determined the following exact formula for $DA(f)$ [10], when $f(i_1, i_2) = a_0 + a_1 i_1 + a_2 i_2$:

$$DA(f) = (UB_1 \times UB_2) - (UB_1 - |a_2| / \gcd(a_1, a_2))^+ (UB_2 - |a_1| / \gcd(a_1, a_2))^+ \quad (1)$$

where $(exp)^+$ represents the positive part of (exp), that is, $\max(exp, 0)$, and UB_j is the upper bound of the iteration of the i_j loop (also equal to the number of iterations in the i_j loop, since all loops are assumed to be normalized). It remains an open problem to determine an exact formula for DA in the general case, when f is a linear function of more than two variables.

How can we bound DA when $f(i_1, \ldots, i_d) = a_0 + \sum_{k=1}^d a_k i_k$ is too complicated for our exact methods? First, we use Banerjee's inequality [6, 7] to determine f^{lo} and f^{hi}, the lower and upper bounds of function f. Next, we compute $g = \gcd(a_1, \ldots, a_d)$, the greatest common divisor of the coefficients $a_1, \ldots, a_d$. The key observation is that all values of f must belong to the set $\{f^{lo}, f^{lo} + g, f^{lo} + 2 \times g, \ldots, f^{hi}\}$, because $f^{lo} \leq f \leq f^{hi}$, and all values of f belong to the same congruence class modulo g. If $a_i = 0$ for all $i = 1, \ldots, d$, then $DA(f) = 1$. Otherwise, we bound $DA(f)$ by the number of elements in this set, namely

$$DA(f) \leq \frac{(f^{hi} - f^{lo})}{g} + 1 \quad (2)$$

Since $(f^{hi} - f^{lo})$ is divisible by g, this will yield an integer bound.

The values of f^{lo} and f^{hi} are computed as follows, based on Banerjee's inequality: If the iteration space is a d-dimensional *rectangle* defined by $LB_k \leq i_k \leq UB_k$, then the lower and upper bounds of function f are given by

$$
\begin{aligned}
f^{lo} &= \sum_{k=1}^d (a_k^+ LB_k - a_k^- UB_k) + a_0 \\
f^{hi} &= \sum_{k=1}^d (a_k^+ UB_k - a_k^- LB_k) + a_0
\end{aligned}
$$

where $a_k^+ = \max(a_k, 0)$ and $a_k^- = \max(-a_k, 0)$ are the positive and negative parts of a_k. If UB_k and LB_k are not known at compile-time, we can use execution profile information or some default value for the number of iterations [20], or leave UB_k as an unknown variable and compute the mathematical formulae in this paper symbolically. If the loop bounds define a trapezoidal iteration space (i.e., for each k, UB_k is a linear function of the index variables of the loops that enclose loop k), then f^{lo} and f^{hi} can be determined by using a simple elimination algorithm [7].

The upper bound in Equation (2) may be a gross over-estimate in pathological cases characterized by coefficient values that are much larger than the number of iterations. In practice, however, most coefficient values have small absolute values prior to linearization [21]. Note also that Equation (2) is guaranteed to be an equality if f has at most one non-zero coefficient in the set, $\{a_1, \ldots, a_d\}$, a case that occurs frequently in practice.

The upper bound for $DA(f)$ in Equation (2) can be extended to handle multi-dimensional array references by taking the cross-product of the number of accesses in each dimension.

Here, the subscript functions are $f_1, \ldots, f_m$ for dimensions $1 \ldots m$, and g_j is the gcd of the coefficients of non-constant terms, as before:

$$DA(f_1, \ldots, f_m) \leq \prod_{j=1}^{m} DA(f_j) \leq \prod_{j=1}^{m} \left(\frac{(f_j^{hi} - f_j^{lo})}{g_j} + 1 \right) \tag{3}$$

This upper bound may be a gross over-estimate when the subscript expressions are *coupled*, *i.e.*, when some index variable appears in at least two dimensions. Consider the array reference a(i,i) for $1 \leq i \leq 100$. Using our method directly, we would obtain $DA \leq 10000$, whereas clearly $DA = 100$. A more accurate bound for the case of coupled subscripts can be obtained by first *linearizing* [8, 7] the subscript expressions into a single subscript expression, then treating the reference as one-dimensional. In general, we can perform *partial linearization* on each set of coupled, contiguous dimensions. Linearizing the example above yields the single subscript expression $f(i) = 101i + addr(a(0,0))$. Applying our method to this single function, we get $DA \leq 100$.

The following table shows the DA values obtained for the matrix multiply program from Figure 1, for loop i in the innermost position:

	Array c	Array a	Array b
Dimension 1	500	500	1
Dimension 2	1	1	1
$DA(f_1, f_2)$	500	500	1

3.2 Upper Bound on the Number of Distinct Lines

In this subsection, we extend the results from subsection 3.1 to bound DL, the number of distinct cache lines accessed by a single array reference.

Consider the function $f(i) = 100i$. If the cache line size, L, is 16, then there is at most 1 access per cache line, since each pair of values of the function is spaced at least distance 100 apart. In this case of sparsely-distributed array elements, we have $DL(f) = DA(f)$. On the other hand, consider $f(i) = 2i$, where $1 \leq i \leq 8$, and $L = 16$. Then all accesses could fit in a single cache line. Because overlap could occur between two cache lines, we have $DL(f) \leq 2$. In this case of densely distributed array elements in a cache line, we can bound DL by counting the values between f^{hi} and f^{lo} as follows:

$$DL(f) \leq \left\lceil \frac{(f^{hi} - f^{lo})}{L} \right\rceil + 1$$

The ceiling function ($\lceil \ \rceil$) guarantees that the first term will be integer-valued; adding one is necessary to ensure an upper bound, due to overlap.

For a one-dimensional array reference, our bound on $DL(f)$, shown below in equation (4), is a minimum of two arguments. Since it is always the case that $DL(f) \leq DA(f)$, the first argument is either our exact formula for $DA(f)$ or its upper bound. This first argument gives a good bound for a sparsely-referenced array, i.e. when $g \geq L$. The second argument of the min function bounds the number of cache lines spanned by the accesses when the array is densely referenced. This second argument comes into play when $g < L$, in which case the number of distinct lines is independent of g, and depends only on the range of cache lines spanned by the accesses (i.e. on the values of f^{lo}, f^{hi}, and L). Equation (4) gives an integer-valued upper bound for $DL(f)$, since both arguments of the min function are integer-valued.

$$DL(f) \leq \min\left(DA(f), \left\lceil \frac{(f^{hi} - f^{lo})}{L} \right\rceil + 1\right) \leq \min\left(\frac{(f^{hi} - f^{lo})}{g} + 1, \left\lceil \frac{(f^{hi} - f^{lo})}{L} \right\rceil + 1\right) \quad (4)$$

Consider the example of $f(i) = 2i$, where $1 \leq i \leq 8$. We have $f^{lo} = 2$, $f^{hi} = 16$, and $DA(f) = 8$. Using the bound for $DL(f)$ in equation (4) and assuming $L = 16$, we get $DL(f) \leq 2$. It is possible that this reference will access only a single cache line; this depends on the offset of the array in the cache. In [10] we show how to adjust the DL estimates to account for cache line offsets.

To extend equation (4) to the multi-dimensional case, we assume as in [22] that accesses can be densely distributed only in the first (least significant) dimension, and are sparsely distributed in higher dimensions. Then the number of unique lines accessed can be bounded in a manner similar to equation (3) from subsection 3.1:

$$DL(f_1, \ldots, f_m) \leq DL(f_1) \times \prod_{j=2}^{m} DA(f_j) \quad (5)$$

The above bound provides a reasonable estimate for DL, in practice. It may become a noticeable over-estimate if the size of the first (least significant) dimension is less than the line size, leading to the possibility of cache line sharing in higher dimensions. This possibility is taken into account in a more refined version of Equation (5) included in [10]. Equation (5) also assumes that the dimensions are uncoupled, as in equation (3); linearization can be used as before to obtain a better bound in the presence of coupled dimensions.

The following table shows the DL values obtained using equation (5) for the matrix multiply program from Figure 1, for loop i in the innermost position:

	Array c	Array a	Array b
$DL(f_1)$	$\lceil 500/16 \rceil = 32$	$\lceil 500/16 \rceil = 32$	1
$DA(f_2)$	1	1	1
$DL(f_1, f_2) = DL(f_1) \times DA(f_2)$	32	32	1

A similar analysis can be used to obtain the other DL estimates in the table in Figure 1.

4 Combining Accesses from Multiple References

In this section, we extend the functions DA and DL, which provide bounds on the number of distinct array elements and number of distinct cache lines, to consider the effect of multiple references to the same array within a given loop nest.

4.1 Upper Bound on the Number of Distinct Accesses

We shall simplify the presentation in this section by first considering the case of two one-dimensional array references, $f1$ and $f2$.

We start by analyzing the functions $f1$ and $f2$ separately, as in Section 3, to obtain their lower and upper bounds, $f1^{lo} \leq f1 \leq f1^{hi}$ and $f2^{lo} \leq f2 \leq f2^{hi}$, and the gcds $g1$ and $g2$ of their respective coefficients. As we saw in Section 3, the values of function fi must belong to the set $\{fi^{lo}, fi^{lo} + gi, fi^{lo} + 2 \times gi, \ldots, fi^{hi}\}$, for $i = 1, 2$.

The number of distinct array elements accessed by functions $f1$ and $f2$ is given by $DA(\{f_1, f_2\}) = DA(f1) + DA(f2) - OVERLAP(f1, f2)$, where $OVERLAP(f1, f2)$ is the number of array elements accessed by both $f1$ and $f2$. All elements in $OVERLAP(f1, f2)$ must belong to the set $LO(f_1, f_2), LO(f_1, f_2) + l, LO(f_1, f_2) + 2 \times l, \ldots, HI(f_1, f_2)$, where $LO(f_1, f_2) \geq \max(f1^{lo}, f2^{lo})$ is the smallest value of $f1$ and $f2$ for which $f1 = f2$, $HI(f_1, f_2) \leq \min(f1^{hi}, f2^{hi})$ is the largest value for which $f1 = f2$, and $l = LCM(g1, g2)$ is the *least common multiple* of $g1$ and $g2$. Thus an upper bound on the number of common accesses is given by $OVERLAP(f1, f2) \leq (HI(f_1, f_2) - LO(f_1, f_2))/l + 1$.

For example, consider $f1(i) = 2i$, and $f2(i) = 6i$ for $1 \leq i \leq 8$. Then, $DA(f_1)$, $DA(f_2)$, $OVERLAP(f_1, f_2)$ can all be computed exactly, yielding

$$DA(\{f1, f2\}) = (\frac{16 - 2}{2} + 1) + (\frac{48 - 6}{6} + 1) - (\frac{12 - 6}{6} + 1) = 8 + 8 - 2 = 14$$

This is exact, since each subscript expression has 8 accesses in the given range, and there is an overlap of 2 accesses (namely at 6 and 12).

Of course, $OVERLAP(f1, f2)$ may be empty; for example, let $f1(i) = 2i$, and $f2(i) = 2i + 1$ for $1 \leq i \leq 8$. There is no overlap, since the accesses are to even and odd elements respectively. We can use the gcd test of data dependence [23] to see whether the equation $f1 = f2$ has any integer solutions. Let $f1 = a1_0 + \sum_{j=1}^{d} a1_j i_j$ and $f2 = a2_0 + \sum_{j=1}^{d} a2_j i_j$. If $\gcd(g1, g2)|(a1_0 - a2_0)$, then we set $TEST(f1, f2) = 1$ to indicate that the equation $f1 = f2$ has integer solutions; otherwise, we set $TEST(f1, f2) = 0$ (which also implies that $OVERLAP(f1, f2) = 0$). In this example, $\gcd(g1, g2) = 2$, which does not evenly divide $(a1_0 - a2_0) = 1$. We therefore correctly conclude that there is no overlap, and $DA(f1, f2) = DA(f1) + DA(f2) = 8 + 8 = 16$. If $OVERLAP(f1, f2)$ is not empty, then $LO(f_1, f_2)$ and $HI(f_1, f_2)$ can be computed using the elimination technique described in [15, pages 326-327].

Putting it all together, the number of unique array elements accessed by functions $f1$

and $f2$ is bounded by

$$
\begin{aligned}
DA(\{f1, f2\}) &= DA(f1) + DA(f2) - OVERLAP(f1, f2) \\
&\leq \frac{(f1^{hi} - f1^{lo})}{g1} + 1 + \frac{(f2^{hi} - f2^{lo})}{g2} + 1 \\
&\quad - TEST(f1, f2) \times \left(\frac{(HI(f1, f2) - LO(f1, f2))}{LCM(g1, g2)} + 1 \right)
\end{aligned} \tag{6}
$$

Note that we used an upper bound for $OVERLAP(f1, f2)$ even though it has a negative contribution to $DA(\{f1, f2\})$. This holds because the upper bound for $OVERLAP(f1, f2)$ is counted twice in the corresponding upper bounds for $DA(f1)$ and $DA(f2)$.

As in Section 3, this bound for DA may be a gross over-estimate if the array coefficient values are greater than the number of iterations. Consider, for example, $f1(i_1, i_2) = -20i_1 + 53i_2 + 10402$ and $f2(i_1, i_2) = -29i_1 + 23i_2 + 10447$ for $1 \leq i_1 \leq 361$ and $1 \leq i_2 \leq 5$. The exact number of distinct accesses by these functions is 3300; the bound for DA above gives $7413 + 10533 - 7192 = 10754$.

The bound for $DA(f1, f2)$ can be improved substantially in such cases by applying the following correction, described in [10]: If $UB_2 < |a1_1|$ (as in the example above) divide the bounds of $DA(f1)$ and of $OVERLAP(f1, f2)$ by $|a1_1| / (UB_2 * g1)$; then if $UB_2 < |a2_1| / g2$ (as above) divide the bounds of $DA(f2)$ and of $OVERLAP(f1, f2)$ by $|a2_1| / (UB_2 * g2)$. Similar corrections apply when UB_1 is small. Applying these corrections to the bound above gives $1853 + 1816 - 310 = 3359$, a much closer bound.

To consider how Equation (6) generalizes to more than two references, consider three functions, $f1$, $f2$, $f3$. Here $DA(f1, f2, f3)$ is given by

$$
\begin{aligned}
DA(\{f1, f2, f3\}) &= DA(f1) + DA(f2) + DA(f3) \\
&\quad - OVERLAP(f1, f2) - OVERLAP(f2, f3) \\
&\quad - OVERLAP(f1, f3) + OVERLAP(f1, f2, f3)
\end{aligned} \tag{7}
$$

Intuitively, we need to subtract out the $OVERLAP$ for every pair of functions, but, in doing so, we subtract out the $OVERLAP$ of all 3 functions once for each pair. The $OVERLAP$ of all 3 functions is included in each $DA(fi)$, and so has been added in three times. Thus we need to include the final term, $OVERLAP(f1, f2, f3)$ to obtain the correct quantity. A general formula for k references is given in [10]; in the worst case, it can involve 2^{k-1} terms.

Consider the Successive Over-Relaxation (SOR) example in Figure 2 to see how multiple references would be handled (since no array variable has multiple references in the matrix multiply example). For the first dimension, there are three subscript expression functions: $f1(i) = i$, $f2(i) = i - 1$, and $f3(i) = i + 1$. The table in Figure 2 gives the values of $\frac{(HI(fx_1, ..., fx_j) - LO(fx_1, ..., fx_j))}{LCM(gx_1, ..., gx_j)} + 1$ for each subset of $\{1, 2, 3\}$, where HI and LO are generalized for multiple functions. Here, $TEST = 1$ for all such subsets. Using equation (7), we determine the number of unique accesses in the first dimension,

$$
DA(\{f1, f2, f3\}) = (N-2) + (N-2) + (N-2) - (N-3) - (N-4) - (N-3) + (N-4) = N.
$$

```
DO i = 2,N-1
  DO j = 2,N-1
    a(i,j) = 2 * a(i,j) + a(i-1,j) + a(i+1,j) + a(i,j-1) + a(i,j+1)
  ENDDO
ENDDO
```

Subsets	{1}, {2}, {3}	{1,2}	{2,3}	{1,3}	{1,2,3}
$(HI - LO)/LCM + 1$	N - 2	N - 3	N - 4	N - 3	N - 4

Figure 2. SOR Example

The second dimension also has three subscript expressions: $f1(j) = j$, $f2(j) = j - 1$, and $f3(i) = j + 1$. Since the j loop has the same bounds as the i loop, the number of unique accesses in the second dimension will also be $DA(\{f1, f2, f3\}) = N$. Multiplying the two dimensions, gives $N \times N = N^2$ unique accesses for array a, due to both i and j loops.

4.2   Bound on the Number of Distinct Lines

Extending the above formulae bounding the number of distinct accesses (DA) to the number of distinct lines (DL), is trickier than for a single reference because two access functions may yield elements that fall in the same cache line, even if the functions have no elements in common. For example, consider the functions $f1(i) = 2i$ and $f2(i) = 2i + 1$ for $1 \leq i \leq 100$.

We start with the case of two one-dimensional references, $f1$ and $f2$. Note that the range of function values can be split up into three subranges: the first containing only the function with the smaller minimum value; the second containing both functions; and the third containing only the function with the larger maximum value. The three subranges of interest are as follows:

S_1: $\min(f1^{lo}, f2^{lo}) \leq f1, f2 < \max(f1^{lo}, f2^{lo})$
  All accesses in this subrange must either come from function $f1$ or from function $f2$, depending on which of $f1^{lo}$ or $f2^{lo}$ is smaller. Therefore, the number of lines accessed in this subrange can be bounded by the formulae for the single reference case (subsection 3.2).

S_2: $\max(f1^{lo}, f2^{lo}) \leq f1, f2 \leq \min(f1^{hi}, f2^{hi})$
  Let $f^{lo} = \max(f1^{lo}, f2^{lo})$ and $f^{hi} = \min(f1^{hi}, f2^{hi})$. Since both $f1$ and $f2$ have accesses in this subrange, we bound the number of unique lines as follows:

$$DL(\{f1, f2\}) \leq \min\left(DA(\{f1, f2\}), \left\lceil \frac{(f^{hi} - f^{lo})}{L} \right\rceil + 1\right) \qquad (8)$$

where $DA(\{f1, f2\})$ is bounded as in equation (6).

S_3: $\min(f1^{hi}, f2^{hi}) < f1, f2 \leq \max(f1^{hi}, f2^{hi})$

Like subrange S_1, all accesses in this subrange must either come from function $f1$ or from function $f2$, depending on which of $f1^{hi}$ or $f2^{hi}$ is larger. Therefore, the number of lines accessed in this subrange can be bounded by the formulae for the single reference case (subsection 3.2).

An upper bound on the number of distinct lines accessed by functions $f1$ and $f2$ is obtained by summing up the DL values for the three subranges, $DL \leq DL(S_1) + DL(S_2) + DL(S_3)$.

We show how this technique can generalize by presenting an example with three references; the general solution is presented in [10], where the effect of cache line offsets are also considered. To determine the number of distinct lines for the SOR example from Figure 2, assuming $N = 500$, consider the three subscript expressions for dimension 1, $f1_1(i) = i$, $f2_1(i) = i - 1$, and $f3_1(i) = i + 1$. These lead to 5 subranges of interest for dimension 1:

Subrange	Functions	DA	(HI - LO)/LCM + 1	$DL_1(S_i)$
$1 \ldots 1$	$f2_1$	1	1	1
$2 \ldots 2$	$f1_1, f2_1$	1	1	1
$3 \ldots n - 2$	$f1_1, f2_1, f3_1$	$n - 4$	$n - 4$	$\lceil (n-4)/L \rceil = 31$
$n - 1 \ldots n - 1$	$f1_1, f3_1$	1	1	1
$n \ldots n$	$f3_1$	1	1	1

Therefore, we have $DL_1 \leq DL_1(S_1) + DL_1(S_2) + DL_1(S_3) + DL_1(S_4) + DL_1(S_5)$, which implies that $DL_1 \leq 35$, and $DL_2 \leq 35 \times 500 = 17500$ is the total bound on the number of lines accessed. The more exact bound in [10] would yield $DL_1 \leq \min(35, \lceil 500/16 \rceil) = 32$. and $DL_2 \leq 32 \times 500 = 16000$.

5 Simulation Results and Implications

We performed several simulation studies and found good agreement between our theoretical results and our simulations in many cases. However, some of the simulations revealed potential problems for any simple methods of estimation. In this section we shall discuss some of our results and propose ways of dealing with some of the problems revealed by the simulations.

We concentrated our simulation studies on matrix multiply, making simplifying assumptions that allowed us to simulate tens of millions of accesses in a reasonable amount of time. We counted only array references, assuming that instruction and data caches were separate and that scalars had been successfully allocated to registers. We did not assume that array references would be register-allocated; rather, we simulated a naive matrix multiply with all its array references in the innermost loop. The simulations discussed in this paper assumed a four-way associative cache with least-recently-used (LRU) replacement and 128 bytes (16 double-precision matrix elements) per block.

We first simulated the multiplication of 500 × 500 matrices, assuming a cache with 128 sets (as in the RS/6000). Simulating the multiply with the loops in the i, j, k order produced an overall miss ratio of 7.67%, while the miss ratios for the j, k, i and k, j, i orders were 1.57% and 1.62%, respectively. Our decision in Section 1 to make i the innermost loop was clearly a good one.

Our second study showed that cache behavior can sometimes elude prediction by simple formulas. In this study we simulated $N \times N$ matrix multiplication for N from 96 to 160. We reduced the number of sets in our simulated cache from 128 to 32 and ran the loops in the i, j, k order, to produce an interestingly large number of misses without using hundreds of hours of simulation time. If any simple formula is to be a good predictor of cache misses, then values for the miss ratio must be tightly clustered along some line or curve. In this study, misses for the a matrix were not well-behaved; its miss ratio was 1.0 for $N = 96$, 128, and 160, and also unusually high for $N = 102$, 103, 114, 118, 122, 146 and 159.

These high miss ratios are an artifact of LRU replacement and set conflicts, that cause problems for certain array sizes. Similar phenomena have been reported in [9] and [16]. Using the method illustrated below, we can predict such behavior and take steps to compensate for these anomalies or to avoid them.

In our example, when the loops are executed in i, j, k order, the array reference a(i,k) repeatedly steps across the ith row of a as j goes from 1 to N, and then moves on to the $i+1^{st}$ row. It seems that 32 cache sets with 4 blocks per set have room to hold one row of a in cache, at least for $N \leq 128$, but that is not the case. With 32 cache sets, and a line size of 16 array elements, the cache set number corresponding to an array reference a(i,k) is $\lfloor (kN + i + C)/16 \rfloor$ mod 32, where C is an address constant. If there are positive integers, k_1 and k_2, such that $1 \leq k_2 < k_1 \leq N$ and $(k_1 - k_2)N = 512m$ for some m, then a(i,k_1) and a(i,k_2) will map to the same cache set. If $(k_1 - k_2)$ is small, then on average $N/(k_1 - k_2)$ values in a row of a will map to the same set.

Large numbers of misses occur when the number of elements in a row of a that map to the same set is greater than the set size. Consider $N = 96$. Since $16*96 = 3*512$, every sixteenth element in a row of a, *i.e.*, six elements per row, will map to the same set. Since our cache is only four-way associative, some replacement is necessary. LRU replacement actually leads to a miss ratio of 100% in this case; see [18] for a detailed discussion of a similar example. Note that increasing the degree of associativity (while maintaining a constant cache size) may lead to a larger number of cache misses due to LRU replacement. For example, $N=129$ incurs a miss ratio of 1.0 on a fully associative cache with 128 lines, but incurs a miss ratio of 0.34 on a 4-way associative cache with 32 sets.

Because a cache line can contain more than one element, we need not have $(k_1 - k_2)N$ precisely equal to $512m$ to have trouble; there will be some overlap, and some occurrence of the LRU artifact, whenever there exists $k = k_1 - k_2$, such that kN mod 512 is close to zero. For N between 96 and 160, the cases in which kN mod 512 is between -3 (i.e. 509) and 3 for some positive integer $k \leq N/5$ are $N = 96$, 102, 103, 114, 118, 122, 128, 146, 159 and 160. (Note that choosing $k \leq N/5$ guarantees that $\lfloor N/k \rfloor \geq 5$ values will map to the same set, thus causing set overflow.) This accounts for all our troublesome cases.

Thus, we can recognize the cases in which our predictions may mislead us. What can we do about those cases? We can reduce the cache parameter for the number of lines to account for the effective shrinking of the cache in those cases, we can pad the arrays to a larger size (if this is allowed by the language semantics), or we can use copying as in [16]. Further work remains in this area.

6 Summary and Future Work

In this paper, we have provided simple formulae to approximate the number of distinct accesses (DA) and distinct lines (DL) for a single array reference in a given nest of loops, and have shown how to combine such estimates where there are multiple references. Our approximations entail polynomial evaluations when cache line offsets are ignored; the more exact formulaes that take cache line offsets into account [10] may require more computational effort. Given these estimates of DA and DL, we have shown how to estimate the number of cache misses for a given set of loops, and how these estimates can be used to guide loop interchange. [18] shows how other tranformations can be guided by such estimates. The formulae from this paper can also provide the basis for automatic selection of block sizes e.g. when using the approach in [13]. Our simulation results show good general agreement between the predicted values and actual values for number of misses. More work is needed on realistic examples to determine how well our ideas work in practice. We also plan to investigate the extension of our work to parallel machines.

Acknowledgements

We would like to thank Fran Allen, Michael Burke, Larry Carter, Ron Cytron, Susan Eggers, Kourosh Gharachorloo, and Alexander Klaiber for helpful discussions. We would like to thank Vasanth Balasundaram, Larry Carter, Rafael Saavedra-Barrera, and Edith Schonberg for comments on an initial draft.

References

[1] A.V. Aho, R. Sethi, and J.D. Ullman. *Compilers: Principles, Techniques, and Tools.* Addison-Wesley, 1986.

[2] Frances Allen, Michael Burke, Philippe Charles, Ron Cytron, and Jeanne Ferrante. An overview of the ptran analysis system for multiprocessing. *Proceedings of the ACM 1987 International Conference on Supercomputing*, 1987. Also published in The Journal of Parallel and Distributed Computing, Oct., 1988, Vol. 5, No. 5, pp. 617-640.

[3] H. B. Bakoglu, G. F. Grohoski, and R. K. Montoye. The ibm risc system/6000 processor: Hardware overview. *IBM Journal of Research and Development*, 34(1):12–23, January 1990.

[4] H. B. Bakoglu and T. Whiteside. Risc system/6000 hardware overview. *IBM RISC System/6000 Technology*, pages 8–15, 1990. IBM Corporation SA23-2619.

[5] Vasanth Balasundaram. A mechanism for keeping useful internal information in parallel programming tools: The data access descriptor. *Journal of Parallel and Distributed Computing*, 9:154–170, 1990.

[6] Utpal Banerjee. Data dependence in ordinary programs. Technical report, University of Illinois at Urbana-Champaign, 1976. M.S. Thesis.

[7] Utpal Banerjee. *Dependence Analysis for Supercomputing*. Kluwer Academic Publishers, Norwell, Massachusetts, 1988.

[8] Michael Burke and Ron Cytron. Interprocedural dependence analysis and parallelization. *Proceedings of the Sigplan '86 Symposium on Compiler Construction*, 21(7):162–175, July 1986.

[9] David Callahan and Allan Porterfield. Data cache performance of supercomputer applications. *Proceedings of Supercomputing '90*, pages 564–572, November 1990. New York, New York.

[10] Larry Carter, Jeanne Ferrante, Vivek Sarkar, and Wendy Thrash. On estimating and enhancing cache effectivness, 1991. Full paper corresponding to this extended abstract.

[11] Kyle Gallivan, William Jalby, and Dennis Gannon. On the problem of optimizing data transfers for complex memory systems. Technical report, U. of IL-Center for Supercomputing Research and Development, July Also in Proc. of ACM 1988 Int'l. Conf. on Supercomputing, St. Malo, France, July 4-8, 1988, pp.238-253. 1988.

[12] Dennis Gannon, William Jalby, and Kyle Gallivan. Strategies for cache and local memory management by global program transformations. *Proceedings of the First ACM International Conference on Supercomputing*, June 1987.

[13] Kourosh Gharachorloo and Vivek Sarkar. Loop partitioning and blocking to reduce communication and cache miss traffic. Foils documenting work done at the IBM T.J. Watson Research Center during the summer of 1989., August 1989.

[14] John L. Hennessy and David A. Patterson. *Computer Architecture: A Quantitative Approach*. Morgan Kaufmann Publishers, 1990.

[15] Donald E. Knuth. *Seminumerical Algorithms, Volume 2, The Art of Computer Programming, Second Edition*. Addison-Wesley, 1981.

[16] Monica S. Lam, Edward E. Rothberg, and Michael E. Wolf. The cache performance and optimization of blocked algorithms. *Proceedings of the Fourth International Conference on Architectural Support for Programming Languages and Operating Systems*, April 1991.

[17] David A. Padua and Michael J. Wolfe. Advanced compiler optimizations for supercomputers. *Communications of the ACM*, 29(12):1184–1201, December 1986.

[18] Allan K. Porterfield. *Software Methods for Improvement of Cache Performance on Supercomputer Applications.* PhD thesis, Rice University, May 1989. Rice COMP TR89-93.

[19] Rafael Saavedra-Barrera. Private communication, March 1991.

[20] Vivek Sarkar. Determining average program execution times and their variance. *Proceedings of the 1989 SIGPLAN Conference on Programming Language Design and Implementation,* 24(7):298–312, July 1989.

[21] Zhiyu Shen, Zhiyuan Li, and Pen-Chung Yew. An empirical study on array subscripts and data dependences. Technical report, University of Illinois-CSRD, May 1989. CSRD Rpt. No. 840 Appeared in the Proceedings of the 1989 Int'l Conf. on Parallel Processing.

[22] Michael E. Wolf and Monica S. Lam. A data locality optimization algorithm. *Proceedings of the ACM SIGPLAN Symposium on Programming Language Design and Implementation,* June 1991.

[23] Michael J. Wolfe. *Optimizing Supercompilers for Supercomputers.* Pitman, London and The MIT Press, Cambridge, Massachusetts, 1989. In the series, Research Monographs in Parallel and Distributed Computing This monograph is a revised version of the author's Ph.D. dissertation published as Technical Report UIUCDCS-R-82-1105, U. Illinois at Urbana-Champaign, 1982.

22 Reduction of Cache Coherence Overhead by Compiler Data Layout and Loop Transformation

Y.-J. Ju and H. Dietz
Purdue University

Abstract

This paper presents a systematic approach that integrates compiler optimization of data layout and traditional loop transformations to reduce cache coherence overhead. A formal model based on an interference graph, overview of the optimization algorithms, and an example are given. Excerpts from an empirical evaluation of the complexity of the compiler analysis, and the simulation study of the resulting reductions in bus traffic and execution time, are also presented. Additional details appear in [7].

1 Introduction

It has long been known that caches can greatly reduce the impact of the mismatch between reference rate and memory bandwidth [6]. In a multiprocessor system with multiple caches in it, however, the cache coherence must be preserved. This overhead is largely determined not only by its coherency protocol but also by the programmed access patterns of cache blocks [4] [5] [10] [13]. Rather than seeking to improve the protocol, we try to *improve the access patterns* so that less coherency overhead is required.

Memory access patterns are the result of combining the access patterns of variables with their data layout (the mapping between symbolic data structures and runtime memory locations). Traditional optimizations focus on changing the variable access patterns; however, it is also possible to alter the data layout [1] [3] [9] [12].

We attempt to optimize data layout by first constructing an interference graph that expresses the interactions between different potential data layouts and the code structures (loops) which reference them. After some additional processing, this graph is used to drive a pruned search for the best possible data layout.

2 The Model

The greatest potential benefits of an improved data layout scheme arise in layout of arrays which are referenced in loops. Hence, we can think of performing an exhaustive search based on:

[1]   The set of legal structures for each loop or set of nested loops. Here, we define legal to mean that the functionality of the loops is equivalent to that of the original loops [14].

[2]   The set of possible data layouts for each array. For practical reasons, only a small set of index transformations is generally considered.

[3]   External constraints on loop structure and data layout. For example, the data layout for a particular array may be constrained to a particular layout because it is accessed by other code (e.g., an operating system function) which assumes that layout.

[4]   Internal constraints on loop structure and data layout. For example, if an array has one layout in a particular loop, it cannot easily have a different layout in another loop; hence, optimizing for one loop might not optimize the total performance.

However, as [4] suggests, both loop restructuring and data layout optimizations can change access patterns in a program, so the best results are obtained by considering interactions between these two types of transformations on a global level. For this purpose, we propose an analytic model of the interactions — an interference graph model.

2.1 Constructing the Interference Graph

The proposed interference graphs are constructed as:

- An interference graph, G, is an ordered triple $(V(G), E(G), \psi)$ consisting of a nonempty set $V(G)$ of vertices, a set $E(G)$ of edges, and an incidence function ψ that associates with each edge of G an unordered pair of vertices of G.

- In the program being analyzed, each array corresponds to a vertex, called array vertex, in the graph. Similarly, each loop nest in the program corresponds to a vertex, call loop vertex, within this graph.

- Let A and L represent the set of all array vertices and loop vertices, respectively. And an edge exists between a loop vertex l_i and an array vertex a_j if and only if array A_j is accessed in loop nest L_i. Clearly, G is a bipartite graph [2] with a partition (A, L) where each edge has one end in A and one end in L.

As defined above, the graph provides a useful formal framework for a pruned search. However, the graph may be very complex, hence transformations to reduce the graph complexity would be desirable. Some simplifications can be made without sacrifice, e.g., vertex cuts (as per Theorem 3). However, some simplifications are those which can eliminate edges by recognizing that the penalty for not considering those edges is likely to be low. For this reason, each edge is labeled with a cost:

- Each edge is labeled with its cost, the *maximum* possible coherence overhead provided that an optimal solution for the pair of vertices is not found.

It is significant that the costs suggested are not the average costs, but rather reflect the expected worst-case overheads. These costs are used as an indication of where optimizations are likely to be least productive; they are not used to predict actual cache coherence overhead.

In actuality, each edge is annotated with a cost table, of the general form shown in Table 1, which records the expected cost for each possible combination of loop nest structure and data layout for that edge. These tables are highly machine-dependent and are derived by applying a detailed model of cache coherence cost. For example, the "write-run" model given in [4] can be applied to compute these costs; further details appear in [7]. The expected worst case cost, which is used to label each edge, is simply the largest cost value in that edge's table.

Opt.		Loop restructuring			
		TYPE 1	TYPE 2	TYPE 3	TYPE 4
Data	TYPE 1	$c_{(1,1)}$	$c_{(1,2)}$	$c_{(1,3)}$	$c_{(1,4)}$
	TYPE 2	$c_{(2,1)}$	$c_{(2,2)}$	$c_{(2,3)}$	$c_{(2,4)}$
Layout	TYPE 3	$c_{(3,1)}$	$c_{(3,2)}$	$c_{(3,3)}$	$c_{(3,4)}$

Table 1: The cost table of an edge

For an example of a complete interference graph, suppose that a source program contains 7 loop nests, each of which makes the array references listed in Table 2.

Loop	1	2	3	4	5	6	7
Arrays Accessed	1, 2, 3	1, 4	4	3	5	7, 5	6

Table 2: Arrays referenced by each loop nest

The corresponding interference graph is shown in Figure 1.

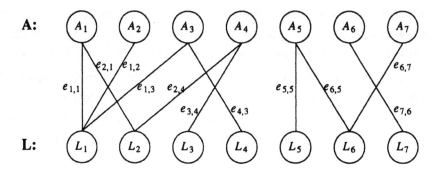

Figure 1: An example of interference graph G

2.2 Optimizing the Interference Graph

To optimize an interference graph is to minimize the sum of costs of its edges; this is accomplished by chosing data layout and loop restructuring which reduce the expected worst case costs for some edges.

Suppose there are d_i different types of data layout for array a_i, and r_j different (legal) structures for loop l_j, the complexity to find an optimal solution by exhaustive search is:

$$O(|E| \times (\prod_{l_j \in V} r_j) \times (\prod_{a_i \in V} d_i))$$

Where V is the set of all vertices and $|E|$ is the number of edges in G. Clearly, if there are many vertices, it becomes impractical to search the entire solution space. However, the search space usually can be greatly reduced without severely degrading the quality of the results. One helpful observation is:

Theorem 1. Optimizing two vertices are independent *if* these two vertices are not in the same (connected) component of the interference graph.

By applying this theorem, the search space given a complete interference graph is the sum, not the product, of the search spaces for the graph's components. Further, because each component is treated separately, it is also sufficient to discuss an algorithm for the search over a single component.

While it is a simple matter to detect the components naturally occurring in a graph, it is also possible to artificially cut a graph into components by temporarily ignoring or deferring particular edges in the graph. Theorems 2, 3, 4, and 5 discuss principles by which graphs can be artificially simplified.

Theorem 2. Given two arrays A and B, v_A and v_B *must* be in the same component *iff* A is in $R^*(B)$ (R-closure of B), where $R \triangleq (U, \text{or } D)$[1].

This implies that if two arrays are in the same R^*, they cannot be separated into two components by loop fission and/or array renaming [14]. However, if the arrays are not in the same $R*$, they need not be maintained in the same component; further, even if the arrays are in the same $R*$, it is possible to separate them by the following technique:

Theorem 3. Even in the presence of groups as described in theorem 2, and vertex cuts can be made and an optimal solution found by the following algorithm:

[1] Choose a vertex cut, VC, of G, where $VC \subset V$.

[2] Assign a possible solution to this vertex cut.

    [a] Find the optimal solution *independently* for each of the new components resulting from the partitioning as per [1].

    [b] Compute the solution for entire component for this particular assignment

[3] Repeat step [2] until all possible solutions of VC have been assigned.

[4] Find the solution providing the minimum cost among those in step 3.

Given an interference graph segmented into components as above, the optimal solution always can be found. However, it is also possible to artificially introduce cuts such that optimality is not guaranteed:

Theorem 4. If the set of edges removed is an edge cut, EC, of G, then an *approximate* solution can be found with complexity

$$\sum_{i=1}^{m} (p_i \times |E_i|)$$

---

[1] Informally, $R*(B)$ is simply the set of all arrays whose values are involved, directly or indirectly, in an expression which references or is stored into B. Unfortunately, the precise definition of $R*$ is too large to include in this paper; it is hoped that the reader will be able to understand the principle from the example in section 2.2.

where p_i is the number of possible solutions for the i-th newly separated component, and $|E_i|$ is the number of edges incident to any vertex in that component. Compared to the overhead for the optimal solution, the approximate solution will have no more than $\sum_{e \in EC} c(e)$ additional overhead.

Finally, there is a special situation which sometimes occurs relative to dangling vertices. A vertex is said to be dangling if its degree equals 1, $degree(v)=1$. A dangling edge is an edge which has at least one end is a dangling vertex.

Theorem 5. Let e be a dangling edge with two ends v_1 and v_2, and v_1 be the dangling vertex. If e is a dangling edge and satisfies

$$\max_{v_2}(\min_{v_1}(c(e)\,|\,{}_{given\ soln\ v_2})) - \min_{v_2}(\min_{v_1}(c(e)\,|\,{}_{given\ soln\ v_2})) = 0$$

then an optimal solution can be found by optimizing G' first and determining the optimal solution for the edge e afterwards, where G' is constructed by removing e and v_1 from G.

Hence, the combined effect of above five theorems is that the search space can be substantially reduced without severely complicating the search algorithm, yet high-quality solutions can be found.

3 The Search Procedure

In the previous sections, we have discussed the model and the principles by which the search is guided. In this section, we briefly overview the actual search algorithm and give an example of its application.

3.1 The Algorithm

First, an interference graph is constructed using data dependencies and parallelization information derived from the source program. Then, the following algorithm[2] is applied to optimize the graph and conduct the search:

INPUT: The source program, data dependencies, and parallelization information.

OUTPUT: Data layouts and loop restructurings.

METHOD:

[1] Find R-closures and perform array renaming and loop fission.

[2] Construct cost tables for this interference graph (see [7] for details) and label each edge with the maximum value in its cost table.

---

[2] A more detailed version appears in [7].

[3] Remove edges with insignificant cost

[4] For each component, remove all dangling edges which satisfy the equation in Theorem 5.

[5] For each component, if the component is simple enough then apply the heuristics given in [7]; otherwise find a vertex cut and for newly separated components recursively repeat step 5.

[6] Use the obvious solution for each removed dangling edge, as determined by examining the cost tables.

[7] Restore the edges which had been removed in step 3 and update the edge cost tables to reflect that some solutions are no longer possible. (This tends to reduce the expected worst-case cost for the edges.) Apply step 5 to solve for these edges.

3.2 An Example

The example program given in listing 1 is used to demonstrate the algorithm described in the previous section. Following the guidelines given in Section 1, this program generates the initial interference graph shown in Figure 2.

```
   DO 10 I = 1, 250
10 Z(1,I) = 1.0
   DO 20 I = 1, 250
        t = s(I)
        DO 30 J = 2, 250
             Z(I,J) = Z(I,J) * t
             Y(I,J) = Y(I,J-1) + X(I,J)
30       CONTINUE
20 CONTINUE
   DO 40 I = 2, 249
        DO 50 J = 1, 250
             Z(I,J) = Z(I-1,J) + Z(I+1,J)
50       CONTINUE
40 CONTINUE
```

Listing 1: The original program

In order to compute the edge cache coherence cost tables, a number of machine parameters are needed. Here, we assume the program is parallelized for a bus-based shared memory multiprocessor with 4 processors and a write-invalidate ownership protocol [8] whose cost parameters appear in Table 3.

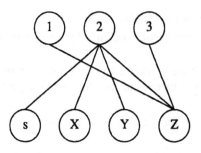

Figure 2: The interference graph of the original program

System parameters	Symbols	Values
cache access time	T_c	1
memory word access time	T_M	11
cache line size	L	8
memory block access time from memory	T_B	18
invalidate time	T_{inv}	$\approx T_M$
block read from owner	T_{cr}	$\approx T_B$
no. of processor	P	4

Table 3: The table of machine cost parameters

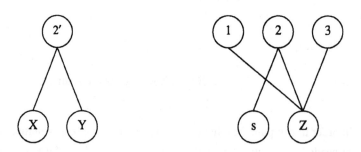

Figure 3: The interference graph after R^* processing

In applying step 1 of the algorithm, $R^*(\cdot)$ is used to find independent groups. This suggests that the second loop nest should be distributed resulting in the interference graph of Figure 3.

Step 2 then computes the edge cost tables, one of which appears in Table 4. In that table, <J, I> denotes the outermost index is J, and the second outermost is I.

$e_{2',X}$	<I,J>	<J,I>
row	0	> 60000
column	> 60000	0

Table 4: Edge cost table for $e_{2',X}$

Edge cuts are applied in step 3. The cost of $e_{1,Z}$ is relatively insignificant, hence it is temporarily removed.

At step 4, we determine which optimizations can be deferred (as determined by Theorem 5). Clearly, data layout of array X can be ignored until the rest part of that component is determined. Thus, the interference graph after step 4 is shown in Figure 4 (a dotted line denotes a removed dangling edge; a dashed line denotes an edge in an edge cut).

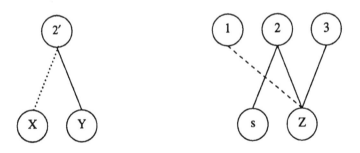

Figure 4: The simplified interference graph

Next, step 5 uses Theorem 3 to determine the optimal solution for the graph of Figure 4. Since both loop 1 and array s, under our assumption, have only option, v_s and v_1 are constrained vertices. The resulting interference graph appears in Figure 5 and the partial solution is given in Table 5.

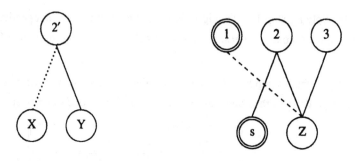

Figure 5: Graph after step 5

Array s	constrained	Loop 1	constrained
Array X	deferred	Loop 2	< J, I >
Array Y	row major	Loop 2′	< I, J >
Array Z	column major	Loop 3	< J, I >

Table 5: The partial solution

Step 6 considers the dangling edges that were removed in step 4. By checking the cost table (Table 4), the row-major data layout is selected. The final solution is given in Table 6 and the restructured program appears in Listing 2.

Finally, in step 7, the edge that was removed in step 4 is restored. Since the solutions for both ends already have been found, no more optimizations are required for this (constrained) edge.

Array s	sequential	Loop 1	< I >
Array X	row major	Loop 2	< J, I >
Array Y	row major	Loop 2′	< I, J >
Array Z	column major	Loop 3	< J, I >

Table 6: The final solution

It is clear that optimizing data layout in general is very difficult for a programmer, however, the model and algorithm proposed provide a simple treatment which is well-suited to implementation within an optimizing compiler. Unless X and Y are stored row major (as our algorithm selected), false sharing and contention seem unavoidable. Notice that the final transformed program may be further improved by using tiling [11] to tailor the reference pattern to the exact size of the cache.

```
C          LOOP 1
           DOALL 10 I = 1, 250
        10 Z(1,I) = 1.0
C          LOOP 2'
           DOALL 20 I = 1, 250
              DO 30 J = 2, 250
                  Y(I,J) = Y(I,J-1) + X(I,J)
        30    CONTINUE
        20 CONTINUE
C          LOOP 2
           DOALL 21 J = 2, 250
              DO 31 I = 1, 250
                  Z(I,J) = Z(I,J) * s(I)
        31    CONTINUE
        21 CONTINUE
C          LOOP 3
           DOALL 50 J = 1, 250
              DO 40 I = 2, 249
                  Z(I,J) = Z(I-1,J) + Z(I+1,J)
        40    CONTINUE
        50 CONTINUE
```

Listing 2: The restructured program

4 Empirical Performance

There are two key performance issues for the proposed technique: showing that the compile-time overhead is reasonable and showing that significant reduction in cache coherence overhead is obtained.

The complexity of the proposed compiler algorithm (number of lookup operations performed on the cost tables) was measured for each of the 72 routines which constitute EISPACK. Figure 6 represents the search time for each routines with a vertical line drawn between the complexity using exhaustive search (the top point) and the complexity obtained by the proposed algorithm (the bottom point). Although exhaustive search could be prohibitively expensive, the proposed algorithm always yielded complexity less than 10,000.

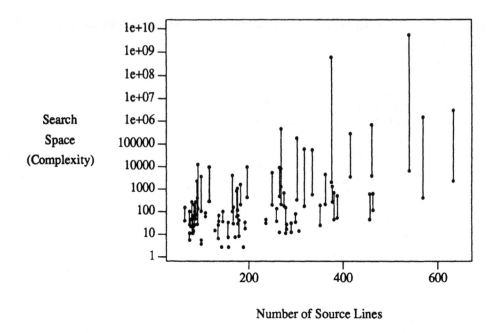

Figure 6. Complexity reduction by applying heuristics

To determine the reduction in cache coherence overhead achieved by applying the proposed technique, a number of trace-driven simulations were performed. These simulations were highly detailed, and directly measured execution time, system bus traffic, etc. The target machine was a shared-memory multiprocessor in which a single bus interconnects a number of DLX RISC processors with floating-point hardware [6]. Each processor has a unified cache, with coherence managed using the Berkeley Ownership protocol [8]. Although a number of SPMD (single program, multiple data) parallel programs were simulated over a wide range of parameters, space permits inclusion of results for only a single program — the example used throughout this paper. Additional results appear in [7].

The execution time and bus traffic (the number of cycles that the bus is busy) are plotted versus block size in Figure 7. As shown in Figure 7, the bus traffic for the traditionally-optimized version initially decreases and then increases due to a high degree of false sharing for large block sizes. Bus traffic for our improved version (with both traditional and proposed optimizations), however, decreases as the block size increases. This reflects a major reduction in false sharing and the coherence overhead it implies. Execution time showed a similar improvement.

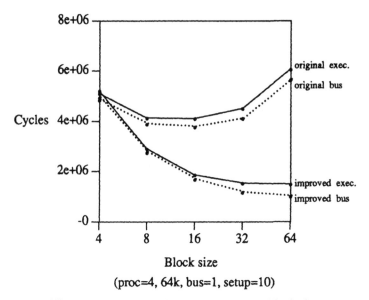

Figure 7: Execution time and bus use vs. block size
for original EXAMPLE and improved EXAMPLE

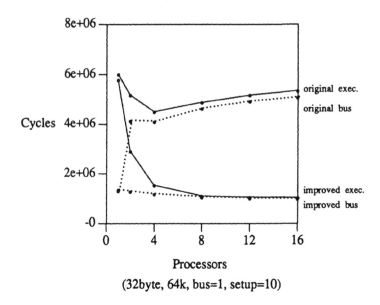

Figure 8: Execution time and bus use vs. number of processors
for original EXAMPLE and improved EXAMPLE

In Figure 8, the bus traffic and execution time are plotted versus the number of processors. For the original version, employing more processors does not speedup the program substantially — additional synchronization overhead actually slows program execution for more than 4 processors. For the improved version, very little false sharing occurs and hence the coherence overhead remains small despite the use of additional processors. However, no additional speedup was obtained for more than 8 processors because the bus becomes saturated at that point.

Of course, here we have presented results for only one program; improvements in bus traffic and execution time vary widely depending on the program. The effectiveness of the proposed technique depends on the fraction of bus traffic that is due to coherence operations; it also depends on how good the original program's data reference pattern was.

5 Conclusions

In this paper, we have presented a systematic approach to the integration of data layout and code transformations to reduce cache coherence overhead. This approach is based on the construction and manipulation of an interference graph, and easily incorporates a detailed model of the machine-specific cost characteristics of the cache coherence mechanism used by the target architecture.

The performance of the proposed technique was empirically evaluated. First, we demonstrated that the complexity of the compiler analysis was reasonable for real codes by measuring the complexity for analyzing the entire EISPACK library. Second, we undertook detailed simulation studies to determine how effective the improvements were in reducing both bus use and execution time. Due to space limitations, only a small fraction of the empirical results were presented.

Future work considers data layout for scalar variables, trade-offs between "aggressive" data layouts and the additional address computation overhead they imply, and the interaction between data layout and compiler-assisted cache coherence policies.

References

1. Chang, L.Y., and Dietz, H.G., *Data Layout and Loop Restructuring for Paged Memory Systems,* Purdue University, 1990, TR-EE 90-43, Purdue university.
2. Deo, M., *Graph Theory with Applications to Engineering and Computer Science,* Prentice-Hall, 1974, pp. 314.
3. Fang, Z., *Cache or Local Memory Thrashing and Compiler Strategy in Parallel Processing System,* ICPP, 1990, vol. II, pp 271-275.

4. Eggers, S.J., and Katz, R.H., *A Characterization of Sharing in Parallel Programs and its Application to Coherency Protocol Evaluation,* Proceedings of the 15th Annual International Symposium on Computer Architecture, Honolulu HA (May 1988), pp. 373-383.

5. Eggers, S.J., and Katz, R.H., *The Effect of Sharing on the Cache and Bus Performance of Parallel Programs,* Proceedings of the 3rd International Conference on Architectural Support for Programming Languages and Operating Systems, Boston, MA (April 1989).

6. Hennessy, J.L., and Patterson, D.A., *Computer Architecture: A Quantitative Approach,* Morgan Kaufmann Publishers, Inc. 1990.

7. Ju, Y.J., *Compiler Data Layout and Code Transformation for Redcuing Cache Coherence Overhead,* Ph.D. dissertation, School of Electrical Engineering, Purdue University, 1991.

8. Katz, R.H., Eggers, S.J., Wood, D., Perkins, C.L., and Sheldon, R., *Implementing a Cache Consistency Protocol,* Proceedings of the 12th Annual International Symposium on Computer Architecture, 13, 3 (June 1985), pp. 276-283.

9. Mace, M.E., *Memory Storage Patterns in Parallel Processing,* Klumer Academic Publishers, 1987.

10. Owicki, S., and Agarwal, A., *Evaluating the Performance of Software Cache Coherency,* ASPLOS III, April 1989.

11. Padua, D.A., and Wolfe, M., *More Iteration Space Tiling,* International Conference on Supercomputing, Reno, Nevada, November 1989, 655-664.

12. Torrellas, J., Lam, M.S., and Hennessy, J.L., *Shared Data Placement Optimization to Reduce Multiprocessor Cache Miss Rates,* ICPP, 1990, vol. II, pp 266-270.

13. Weber, W., and Gupta, A., *Analysis of Cache Invalidation Patterns in multiprocessors,* 3rd International Conference on Architectural Support for Programming Languages and Operating Systems (ASPLOS-III), April 1989, pp. 243-256.

14. Wolfe, M.J., *Optimizing Supercomputer for Supercomputers,* Ph.D. Thesis, Univ. of Illinois, October 1982.

23 Loop Storage Optimization for Dataflow Machines

G. Gao and Q. Ning

McGill University

Abstract

In scientific computation, loops are frequently used to compute large quantities of data organized in arrays. On a dataflow machine, the main challenge is how to maximally exploit fine-grain parallelism to speed up loop execution while not incurring excessive storage space overhead than what is necessary.

The main contributions of this paper include:

- The minimum storage requirement to support the maximum computation rate is analyzed and a storage minimization scheme called *limited balancing* is introduced. The basic intuition is that, since maximum computation rate is dominated by critical cycles in the loop, we should not allocate extra storage beyond a certain limit bounded by the ratios of the critical cycles. In other words, all cycles should be *balanced* to have the same balancing ratio.

- The limited balancing problem is formulated as a integer linear programming problem. An efficient solution of the problem is presented. It reduces the problem to a network flow problem called "minimum circulation flow" problem. Therefore, a polynomial time algorithm is established for the solution of the linear relaxation of the limited balancing problem.

Our formal framework is developed under a *FIFO* dataflow model where each arc in the dataflow graph is a FIFO queue of certain size. we establish the maximum computation rate of a loop under *earliest firing schedule*, and show that the maximum computation rate is dominated by the *critical cycles* of the dataflow graph. We discuss how our results may be applied to both the static dataflow model and the dynamic dataflow model.

1   Introduction

Efficient execution of loops is among one of the most important challenges for high-performance computer architectures. This is true for both conventional computers and dataflow computers [4, 2, 10, 15, 28].

Under the dataflow model, a computation is described by a dataflow graph—a directed graph with nodes representing actors and arcs transmitting tokens which carry the values to be processed by the actors. Actors become activated for execution when tokens are present at their input arcs. Unlike von Neumann computers, dataflow computers have no program counter or other form of centralized sequential control mechanism. Consequently, the order of instruction execution is restricted only by data dependencies within the dataflow programs.

In recent years much research has been conducted on dataflow architectures [1, 11, 14, 13, 32]. Two major approaches to the architectures of dataflow computers have been proposed: the static dataflow model [15] and the tagged-token model [5, 35]. The dynamic model has evolved into the development of the "modern" dynamic dataflow machines such as the Monsoon dataflow machine at MIT and the SIGMA-I/EM-4 dataflow machines in Japan [32, 34, 36]. Meanwhile some "modern" static dataflow architecture proposals can be found in [22, 12].

One of the long standing issues in loop execution on dataflow machines is how to manage the fine-grain parallelism and the storage requirement supporting such parallelism. Under static dataflow model, the storage for a loop is completely determined at compile-time — simply the storage required for one instance of the loop body. A main restriction of this approach is that it may not be able to fully exploit the parallelism in the loop, although *dataflow software pipelining* has been proposed to organized the code such that several iterations may be proceeding simultaneously [19, 20]. The number of concurrent iterations is bounded by the amount of storage allowed for one copy of the loop body. Under pure dynamic dataflow model, such restriction has been eliminated. Instead, the loop is "unraveled" dynamically at runtime, and the execution can initiate as many iterations as possible, limited only by data dependencies [3]. Although the model provides opportunity to fully exploit fine-grain parallelism in the loop, managing the amount of storage it needs to do so has been a challenge.

In the present paper, we have developed a framework to determine, at compile-time, the minimum storage requirement enough to fully exploit the fine-grain parallelism in a loop. Our formal framework is developed under a *FIFO* dataflow model where each arc in the dataflow graph is a FIFO queue of certain size. We study the storage allocation problem for a class of loops called *dataflow software pipeline* (DFSP). The maximum computation rate of a DFSP is bounded by the *critical cycles* in the dataflow graph [23].

2   Loop Storage Minimization: An Example

In this section, we give an example to show the challenge of minimizing storage requirement while keeping maximum computation rate of loop execution on dataflow machines. Let's consider the *for* loop with *loop-carried dependencies* as shown in Figure 1 (a).

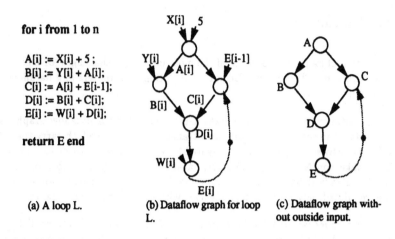

for i from 1 to n

A[i] := X[i] + 5 ;
B[i] := Y[i] + A[i];
C[i] := A[i] + E[i-1];
D[i] := B[i] + C[i];
E[i] := W[i] + D[i];

return E end

(a) A loop L.

(b) Dataflow graph for loop L.

(c) Dataflow graph without outside input.

Figure 1: Dataflow graph for loop L

Figure 1 (b) shows the dataflow graph with external input arcs which is omitted from Figure 1 (c). Note that a complete translation of L also contains loop control actors, such as switch and merge actors [11]. For simplicity, we omit them from Figure 1. [1]

The solid arcs in the dataflow graph represent the data dependencies within one iteration, and the dotted arcs represent loop carried data dependencies across the iterations. There are some initial tokens on the dotted arcs. The number of the initial tokens on a dotted arc corresponds to the *dependence distance* [6].

Dataflow software pipelining was originally proposed to exploit fine-grain parallelism in loops on static dataflow computers [20, 19]. A main limitation of static dataflow model is that it may not be able to fully exploit the parallelism in the loop. Under dynamic dataflow model, such limitation is eliminated via *loop unraveling* [1]. As pointed out in [9], however, exploiting more parallelism will invariably increase the resource requirement of a program. The challenge is not to allow the loop to consume more storage than necessary to fully exploit the parallelism in a loop.

Let us ask the following question: what is the minimum amount of storage that the loop (L) needs to run at the *maximum computation rate*? Let's illustrate this by the example loop L. Note that, the cycle C^* in L, $CDEC$, contains the loop carried data dependence arc. The maximum computation rate of L is dominated by C^*, which is the so-called *critical cycle* of L [23]. Thus the maximum computation rate of L is 1/3, where we assumed that the execution time for each actor is 1 unit of time. In the static dataflow computation model, each solid arc in the graph need one memory location. Therefore, **five** memory locations are allocated for the loop L. However, **three** memory locations are enough to achieve the maximum computation rate, thus reducing the memory requirement by 40%. The rest of this paper will develop a procedure to achieve the minimization of the storage requirement.

---

[1]We assume that the loop is executed a very large number of iterations. Therefore, it is reasonable to assume that the switch and merge actors for loop control will always take a fixed branch path except the start and termination of the loop.

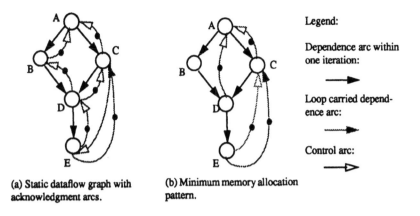

(a) Static dataflow graph with acknowledgment arcs.

(b) Minimum memory allocation pattern.

Legend:

Dependence arc within one iteration:

Loop carried dependence arc:

Control arc:

Figure 2: Minimize Storage Allocation

Before we proceed, let us give an intuitive explanation of the method to be developed in the rest of this paper. Recall that the one-token-per-arc memory requirement for static dataflow graph is implemented by adding an acknowledgment arc for each pair of successor and predecessor nodes. There will be an initial token on such an acknowledgment arc, if it is the acknowledgment arc of an arc in D, denoting the fact that one storage cell is required by this arc. If the acknowledgment arc is for a loop carried dependency arc, then there is no initial tokens on this acknowledgment arc. The result graph is shown in Figure 2 (a). We can see from Figure 2 (a) that there are more cycles in the graph which are newly formed by the addition of the acknowledgment arcs. A key observation is that we can reduce the memory allocated to other (non-critical) cycles without decreasing the maximum computation rate dominated by the critical cycle ($CDEC$). For example, the cycles C_1 (ABA), and C_2 (BDB) are not critical cycles, we can reduce their storage allocation as shown in Figure 2 (b). The optimal computation rate remains unchanged, but the total memory allocation of the loop is reduced by 40%!

3   The Framework

In this section, we develop the FIFO dataflow model and state a maximum computation rate result without proof (proof can be found in [23] or [33]).

3.1   The FIFO dataflow model

We consider an arc in the dataflow graph as a pool of memory locations which can hold data tokens. In particular, if the loop does not contain recursive function calls, we may assume that the pool is a FIFO queue. In our present paper, we don't handle loops that contain function calls, so the FIFO model is enough for us.

The firing rule of an actor in the FIFO model is:

- The actor is enabled if each input FIFO of the actor contains at least one token.

- An enabled actor can be fired and the firing of an actor will remove one token from the head of each input FIFO and put one token at the tail of each of the output FIFOs.

When an actor is fired, it removes the input token and starts the current activation. Meanwhile, the actor is ready to begin the next activation after certain number k of time steps. For simplicity, we assume that $k = 1$ in this paper. However, the results can be generalized straightforwardly to the cases where k is greater than 1. As long as the input queues are not empty, an actor can continue to be fired more than once, thus allow multiple activations in concurrent execution. This essentially has the effect of *loop unraveling* in dynamic dataflow model, but the unraveling is done in a "fine-grain" manner — i.e. the synchronization between activations of different iterations is performed at each individual actor, instead of at the boundary of individual iterations.

3.2 Dataflow Software Pipeline (DFSP)

In this section, we will define the class of loops known as the *dataflow software pipelines* (DFSP). The class of loops which are of interest are non-nested loops. The loops may contain both loop-independent and loop-carried dependencies.

Definition 3.1

1. *A DFSP is a directed graph* $(N, D, LC; M, L)$, *where N is the set of the nodes representing the actors, D the set of arcs representing data dependencies within one iteration (which will be represented by solid arcs in the diagrams), and LC the set of arcs representing the loop carried dependencies (which will be represented by dotted arcs in the diagrams). For convenience, we will use E^+ to denote the union of D and LC, that is $E^+ = D \cup LC$.*

2. *M is a function $M : LC \cup D \to Z$, where Z is the integer set. We will also use m_e to denote $M(e)$. For each arc $e \in LC \cup D$, m_e is the number of initial tokens on arc e.*

3. *L is a length function on the arcs. If an arc e comes out of a node n, the L_e is the execution time of node n.*

Thus, an arc in a DFSP can hold multiple tokens and there is no *a priori* bounds on the number of tokens that arc can hold. This implies that appropriate amount of storage must be allocated to each arc to accommodate the tokens which may present.

We assume that a DFSP G is operating under the following initial conditions: (1) the input/output environment for G is *maximally loaded*, i.e., it can produce input values for G and consume the output values from G without any delay (this will allow us to use a simple representation of the dataflow graph for loops in which the select actors and loop bound test actor can be omitted); and (2) the loop will run through a sufficient large number of iterations, thus the start-up and termination time can be ignored.

Finally, in a dataflow graph, a conditional expression is represented by the so-called *well-formed conditional dataflow graph* [20]. Switch and merge nodes are used in the implementation. These nodes have special firing rules which depend on run time decisions. To overcome these problems, the firing rules of the switch nodes and the merge nodes are altered to produce and consume *dummy tokens* on their unselected branches. A detailed discussion can be found in [23]. Under this treatment, the switch and the merge nodes have the same firing rule as the other regular nodes. Hence, a conditional dataflow graph can be handled as an ordinary DFSP.

3.3 Maximum Computation Rate

Given a DFSP representing a loop, the computation rate of an actor in this loop under some scheduling scheme is the average number of firings of the actor over a long period of time. Assuming that we have an *idealized dataflow machine*, i.e., the resources of the machine are unlimited, we can achieve the maximum computation rate by adopting *the earliest firing rule* for the scheduling. The earliest firing rule of a DFSP is to fire an actor as soon as all its operands have arrived (all of its input FIFO's are not empty). Obviously, under the earliest firing rule of the idealized machine model, a DFSP will achieve its maximum computation rate.

An important observation is that: the maximum computation rate of the entire DFSP is determined by the maximum possible computation rate of the nodes on "slowest cycles" (known as *critical cycles*). To formally state this result, let us first introduce the following definition.

Definition 3.2 *Given a DFSP graph $G = (N, D, LC; M, L)$. Let $C(G)$ be the set of all directed cycles in G. For any directed cycle $C \in C(G)$,*

1. *$P(C) = \sum_{e \in C} m_e$.*

2. *$K(C) = \sum_{e \in C} L_e$.*

3. *$\frac{P(C)}{K(C)}$ is called the B(alance)-ratio of C.*

4. *Cycles with minimum B-ratio are called critical cycles.*

We state the following theorem about the computation rate. The reader can find its proof in [23] or [33].

Theorem 3.1 *Given a DFSP graph $G = (N, D, LC; M, L)$ which represents a loop. The maximum computation rate (after an initial transient period) of every node in the graph is $\frac{P(C^*)}{K(C^*)}$, where C^* is a critical cycle in the DFSP.*

In our example loop L in Figure 1 (c), there is only one cycle $CDEC$, therefore it is also a critical cycle. The number of tokens on it is 1. Its length is 3. Therefore the B-ratio is $\frac{1}{3}$. This cycle will dominate the computation rate of the whole graph so that every node will be fired once at a maximum rate of every 3 time steps. Although node A is not on the cycle, it can not be fired every time step.

4 The Limited Balancing Problem

From Theorem 3.1 in the last section we know that the maximum computation rate of a loop is dominated by its critical cycles. Therefore, there is no need to allocate more storage to other non-critical cycles beyond what is bounded by the B-ratio of the critical cycles (the critical B-ratio). In this paper, we propose that a compiler should be able to determine the storage allocation such that all cycles have the same balancing ratio as that of the critical cycle. For historical reasons, we call this procedure *limited balancing* [21].

In this section we will show how to formulate the limited balancing problem into a linear programming problem. There are two steps in the formulation process. The first step is called *chain replacement*, i.e. replace each chain in the DFSP with a single arc. The second step is to derive a linear programming formulation which will optimize the memory requirements. The solution of the linear programming problem will be the subject of Section 5.

4.1 Simplify a DFSP with Chain Replacement

Let's first state what is a chain.

Definition 4.1 *Given a DFSP, if a node n has only one input arc and only one output arc, then it is called simple. A path is called a chain if all the nodes lying internally in the path (i.e. not including the two end nodes) are simple.*

Our method will allocate storage to a DFSP on a chain by chain bases. For instance, consider a chain CH of length m. Our algorithm may assign a total of n storage cells to the chain CH. Conceptually, the n storage cells will be shared by the tokens traveled along CH and operated on by all operations along the chain. This is very important, as the minimum value n may be less than m. As shown by our example in Figure 2 (b), the chain ABD has length $m = 2$, and is assigned $n = 1$ storage cell.

For simplicity in later formulation, we can replace each chain by an arc.

Definition 4.2 *Given a DFSP, and a chain Q in it. Let n_i be the starting node of chain Q, and n_j the end node of Q. A chain replacement of Q is to replace Q by a new arc joining n_i and n_j. The weight of the new arc is the sum of the weights of arcs along the chain Q. This procedure is called the chain replacement.*

After the chain replacement, we get a new DFSP in which no node is simple. We will call this new DFSP, denoted by S-DFSP, the *skeleton* of the old DFSP.

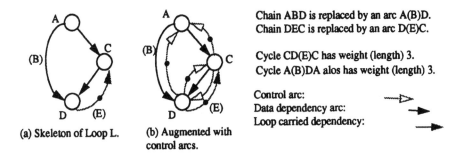

Chain ABD is replaced by an arc A(B)D.
Chain DEC is replaced by an arc D(E)C.

Cycle CD(E)C has weight (length) 3.
Cycle A(B)DA alos has weight (length) 3.

Control arc:
Data dependency arc:
Loop carried dependency:

(a) Skeleton of Loop L.

(b) Augmented with control arcs.

Figure 3: A example of DFSP and its augmented S-DFSP-C

4.2   Linear Programming Formulation

After we do the chain replacement for a given DFSP we get the skeleton. In the following we will use S-DFSP to denote the skeleton.

To limit the number of memory spaces allocated on the arcs in the S-DFSP, we introduce a new storage "control arc" for each old arc in the DFSP. A control arc will have the effect to limit the number of tokens that can reside on an arc at any moment. But control arcs are only used for the purpose of calculating the amount of memory that should be allocated to each individual arc in the original DFSP. In actual execution of the DFSP, control arcs do not exist.

For an arc $e_{ij} = (n_i, n_j) \in E^+$, add a control arc $e'_{ji} = (n_j, n_i)$ with x_{ji} initial tokens (which is a variable to be determined later). The set of control arcs will be denoted by E^- as they are in the opposite direction of their corresponding dependence arcs. Each arc in E^- has a length of 1 which reflect the timing assumption we made in Section 3 that each node will use one time step to take a token from its input arc and is ready to take the next token after this step. The augmented (by control arcs) graph is called S-DFSP-C. See Figure 3 for an example.

DFSPs have the property that during their execution the sum of tokens on any cycle does not change [23]. Each arc we just added in, together with its original dependence arc, forms a cycle with a sum of $x_{ji} + m_{ij}$ tokens on it, where m_{ij} is the number of original tokens on the arc e_{ij}. Therefore the number of tokens arc e_{ij} can hold in the S-DFSP-C is at most $x_{ji} + m_{ij}$. From here we can see that the total memory required for the execution of the DFSP is

$$\sum_{e=(n_i,n_j)\in E^-} x_{ij} + \sum_{e=(n_i,n_j)\in E^+} m_{ij}.$$

where the second sum in the above formula is a constant.

The introduction of the additional arcs also introduces many more new cycles in the S-DFSP-C that do not appear in the original DFSP. The B-ratio of the new cycles might be smaller than that of the original critical cycles if the x_{ij}'s are not properly chosen. In order to maintain the maximum computation rate we must keep enough tokens (or equivalently allocate enough memory spaces) in all cycles such that the B-ratio of the new cycles is not smaller than that of the original critical cycles. The following is the mathematical formulation of the minimum memory allocation problem to maintain the maximum computation rate.

$$\min \sum_{e=(n_i,n_j)\in E^-} x_{ij}$$

subject to

$$\frac{\sum_{e\in C^-} x_e + \sum_{e\in C^+} m_e}{K(C)} \geq \frac{P(C^*)}{K(C^*)}, \forall C \in \mathcal{C}$$

$$x_e \geq 0, \quad x_e \text{ integer}, \forall e \in E^-$$

where $\mathcal{C}$ is the set of all cycles in S-DFSP-C, $C^- = C \cap E^-$, $C^+ = C \cap E^+$, and C^* is a critical cycle in the original DFSP (a critical cycle can be found in $O(|N|^3 \log|N|)$ time [31]).

The problem can be reformulated into the following form:

Problem (Main)
Original problem:

$$\min \sum_{e=(n_i,n_j)\in E^-} x_{ij}$$

subject to

$$\sum_{e\in C^-} x_e \geq b_c, \forall C \in \mathcal{C}$$

$$x_e \geq 0, \forall e \in E^-$$

$$x_e \text{ integer}, \forall e \in E^-$$

Problem (I)
Its linear relaxation:

$$\min \sum_{e=(n_i,n_j)\in E^-} x_{ij}$$

subject to

$$\sum_{e\in C^-} x_e \geq b_c, \forall C \in \mathcal{C}$$

$$x_e \geq 0, \forall e \in E^-$$

Problem (II)
Its linear dual:

$$\max \sum_{C\in\mathcal{C}} b_c z_c$$

subject to

$$\sum_{C\ni e} z_c \leq 1, \forall e \in E^-$$

$$z_c \geq 0, \forall C \in \mathcal{C}$$

where $b_c = K(C)\frac{P(C^*)}{K(C^*)} - \sum_{e\in C} m_e$.

We should notice that there could be an exponential number of cycles in the S-DFSP-C (or in other words, an exponential number of constraints in the primal problem). Therefore the dual problem could have an exponential number of variables. The consequence is that the methods for solving the linear programming are expensive and may not directly applicable to solve **Problem I** or **Problem II**.

5 A Polynomial Time Solution

In this section, we show that the primal problem of the linear program **Problem I** can be solved in polynomial time. We will show that the dual problem **Problem II** is equivalent to the so-called *circulation flow problem* [17]. Since circulation flow problem can be solved in polynomial time [16, 31] we need to show that the optimal solution of the circulation flow problem can be translated into an optimal solution of the dual problem *in polynomial time*.

The general circulation flow problem is very similar to the minimum cost flow problem. The distinction is that in minimum cost flow problem, it has a source node and it has a sink node. And the objective is to send a fixed amount of flow from the source to the sink so that certain objective function is minimized. Where as in circulation flow problem, it has no source node and sink node. So flow will just circulate in the graph. Now let us consider the circulation flow problem formulation that fits our need. The problem is that given a graph, find a (circular) flow so that certain objective function is optimized (maximized or minimized). The formulation of the circulation flow problem is:

Problem (III)

$$\max \sum_{e \in E} p_e f_e$$

subject to

$$\sum_{e \in \delta^+(n)} f_e - \sum_{e \in \delta^-(n)} f_e = 0, \forall n \in N$$

$$f_e \leq 1, \forall e \in E^-$$

$$f_e \geq 0, \forall e \in E$$

where p_e is the cost coefficients which is defined as $p_e = L_e \frac{P(C^*)}{K(C^*)} - m_e$, $\delta^+(n)$ is the set of arcs going out from n, $\delta^-(n)$ is the set of arcs going into n, f_e is a variable which indicates the amount of flow along the arc e, and $E = E^+ \cup E^-$.

Lemma 5.1 *Given a (feasible) optimal solution of (III), we can construct a (feasible) optimal solution of (II), and vice versa.*

Proof of Lemma: Let $f^1 = \{f_e^1\}$ be a feasible solution of (III). Let $S(f^1)$ be the support set of f^1, that is, the subset of arcs $\{e\}$ such that $f_e^1 > 0$. Choose any directed cycle C_1 in $S(f^1)$. Define

$$z_{C_1} = min\{f_e^1; e \in C_1\},$$

and

$$f_e^2 = \begin{cases} f_e^1 - z_{C_1}, & \text{if } e \in C_1, \\ f_e^1, & \text{if } e \notin C_1. \end{cases}$$

It is easy to check that $f^2 = \{f_e^2\}$ is another feasible circulation flow of (III). But the number of arcs in $S(f^2)$ is strictly less than that in $S(f^1)$. We can repeat the above procedure to define another z_{C_2} and $\{f^3\}$ etc, until the support set of the circulation flow is empty.

By that time, we have defined $z_c > 0$ for several cycles. We define $z_c = 0$ for all the other directed cycles in E. We show next that such defined $\{z_c\}$ is a feasible solution of (II).

First let us notice that for such defined $\{z_c\}$, the following property holds:

$$\sum_{C \ni e} z_c = f_e, \forall e \in E.$$

For any arc $e \in E^-$, the constraint for e in problem (II) demands that the sum of the z_c's for the cycles C containing e is bounded above by 1. This is true by the property stated in the above equation since $f_e \leq 1$ for $e \in E^-$.

Now the objective value of such defined feasible $\{z_c\}$ is

$$\sum_{C \in C} b_c z_c = \sum_{C \in C} \left\{ K(C) \frac{P(C^*)}{K(C^*)} - \sum_{e \in C} m_e \right\} z_c = \sum_{C \in C} \left\{ \sum_{e \in C} L_e \frac{P(C^*)}{K(C^*)} - \sum_{e \in C} m_e \right\} z_c$$

$$= \sum_{C \in C} \sum_{e \in C} p_e z_c = \sum_{e \in E} \sum_{C \ni e} p_e z_c = \sum_{e \in E} p_e \sum_{C \ni e} z_c = \sum_{e \in E} p_e f_e$$

So the objective value of problem (II) is the same as that of problem (III).

On the other hand, if $\{z_c\}$ is a feasible solution of (II), then it is easy to check that the flow defined by the following formula is a feasible solution to (III):

$$f_e = \sum_{C \ni e} z_c, \forall e \in E.$$

Of course, if one of the feasible solution is optimal, the other is also optimal since they will produce the same objective value. $\square$

Therefore (II) and (III) are equivalent in the sense that the solution of one problem also gives the solution of the other. We can see from our formulation that (III) has $2|N|$ constraints and $|E|$ variables. Both of these two numbers are in polynomial to the original size of the graph. As a matter of fact, the circulation flow problem (III) can be solved by a polynomial time algorithm [18, 16, 31] much better than the general methods of simplex algorithm, ellipsoid algorithm [29] or the Karmarkar's algorithm [27].

Lemma 5.2 *Circulation flow* **Problem (III)** *can be solved in $O(|E|^2 \log |N|)$ time [31], where $|E|$ is the number of arcs of the graph and $|N|$ number of nodes in the graph.*

The final step is to solve problem (I). Since the dual of (I) is (II), and (II) has a polynomial time algorithm which will return an optimal solution for (II), the optimal solution for (I) can be read off from the tableau constructed using the simplex method in polynomial time [8]. Hence we have proved the following theorem.

Theorem 5.1 *The linear relaxation* **Problem I** *of the minimum memory requirement* **Problem Main** *can be solved in polynomial time $O(|E|^2 \log |N|)$.*

The solution for problem (I) can be round-up to give an integer solution for the **Problem Main**. In our example of Figure 3, the optimal solution of the circulation flow problem will be that the amount of flow on each arc of the graph is 1. Therefore problem (II) will get an optimal solution:

$$z_{C_{A(B)DA}} = z_{C_{ACA}} = z_{C_{CD(E)C}} = 1.$$

This solution can be transformed to a solution of problem (I) as

$$x_{DA} = 1, x_{DC} = 1, \text{and } x_{CA} = \tfrac{2}{3}.$$

When round-up to an integer solution, it is

$$x_{DA} = 1, x_{DC} = 1, \text{and } x_{CA} = 1,$$

which is optimal.

Although we have shown that **Problem I** can be solved in polynomial time, the integer version of it **Problem Main** remains open to be solved in polynomial time.

6 Related Work

In this section, we briefly compare our method with other related work.

The method developed in this paper has addressed the limitations of the loop storage management of both static and dynamic dataflow models, and see Section 2 for more information.

The limited balancing method developed in this paper provides a framework where the loop scheduling and storage allocation are studied under a unified framework.

In real life compilers, register allocation is treated as a separate phase from the code scheduling itself. For example, two approaches have been suggested to treat the register allocation problems in conjunction with code scheduling for pipelined machine architectures. In the first approach, it is assumed that a large number of registers are available, hence the code scheduling can be handled independently of the register constraints. After the scheduling is done, the global register allocation can be performed using graph coloring methods, assuming there will be enough registers [30]. In the second approach, register allocation is done before the scheduling phase. This may introduce new constraints which may limit possible reordering of the instructions, as reported in [24, 26]. As pointed in [25], the two phases often have conflicting goals [25]. There has been no clear criteria on how the two parts can be integrated under a unified compiling framework to achieve the desired of both time and space efficiency [7].

We believe that the limited balancing method is a promising first step toward a solution to such problems in the context of loop scheduling. A compiler may use the procedure developed here to estimate the minimum amount of register space required for a loop. The loop can be scheduled when there is enough register reserved during the compilation. We expect that the number of registers on a processor chip will increase continuously in the future, and such a techniques may well be feasible.

7 Conclusions

In this paper, we have outlined a new scheme for determining the minimum loop storage allocation to support maximum computation rate under dataflow software pipelining. A limited balancing scheme has been presented to perform the storage allocation for a class of loops. We demonstrated that the algorithm of limited balancing can be performed in polynomial time. We argue that our method provides a new basis to handle loop storage allocation for both static and dynamic dataflow models. A comparison with other related work in loop scheduling and storage allocation is presented.

References

[1] Arvind and D. E. Culler. Dataflow architectures. *Annual Reviews in Computer Science*, 1:225–253, 1986.

[2] Arvind and et al. The tagged token dataflow architecture (preliminary version). Technical report, Laboratory for Computer Science, MIT, Cambridge, MA., August 1983.

[3] Arvind and K. P. Gostelow. The U-Interpreter. *IEEE Computer*, 15(2):42–49, February 1982.

[4] Arvind, K. P. Gostelow, and W. Plouffe. *An Asynchronous Programming Language and Computing Machine*. Department of Information and Computer Science, University of California, Irvine, December 1978.

[5] Arvind and R. A. Iannucci. A critique of multiprocessing von Neumann style. In *Proceedings of the Tenth Annual International Symposium on Computer Architecture*, pages 426–436, 1983.

[6] U. Banerjee. *Dependence Analysis for Supercomputing*. Kluwer Academic Publishers, Boston, MA, 1988.

[7] D. Bernstein and I. Gertner. Scheduling expressions on a pipelined processor with a maximal delay of one cycle. *ACM Transactions on Programming Languages and Systems*, 11(1):57–66, January 1989.

[8] V. Chvatal. *Linear Porgramming*. W.H. Freeman and Company., 1983.

[9] D. E. Culler. Managing parallelism and resources in scientific dataflow programs, Ph.D thesis. Technical Report TR-446, Laboratory for Computer Science, MIT, 1989.

[10] J. B. Dennis. First version of a data flow procedure language. Technical Report MIT/LCS/TM-61, Laboratory for Computer Science, MIT, 1975.

[11] J. B. Dennis. Data flow for supercomputers. In *Proceedings of the 1984 CompCon*, March 1984.

[12] J. B. Dennis. Evolution of the static dataflow architecture. In *Advanced Topics in Dataflow Computing*. Prentice-Hall, 1991.

[13] J. B. Dennis and G. R. Gao. An efficient pipelined dataflow processor architecture. In *Proceedings of the Supercomputing '88 Conference*, pages 368–373, Florida, November 1988. IEEE Computer Society and ACM SIGARCH.

[14] J. B. Dennis, G. R. Gao, and K. W. Todd. Modeling the weather with a data flow super-computer. *IEEE Transactions on Computers*, C-33(7):592–603, 1984.

[15] J. B. Dennis and D. P. Misunas. A preliminary architecture for a basic data-flow processor. In *The Second Annual Symposium on Computer Architecture*, pages 126–132, January 1975.

[16] J. Edmonds and R.M. Karp. Theoretical improvements in algorithmic efficiency for network flow problems. *J. ACM*, 1972.

[17] L. R. Ford and D. R. Fulkerson. *Flow in Networks*. Princeton University Press, Princeton, NJ, 1962.

[18] D.R. Fulkerson. An out-of-kilter method for minimal cost flow problems. *J. SIAM*, 1961.

[19] G. R. Gao. A pipelined code mapping scheme for static dataflow computers. Technical Report TR-371, Laboratory for Computer Science, MIT, 1986.

[20] G. R. Gao. *A Code Mapping Scheme for Dataflow Software Pipelining*. Kluwer Academic Publishers, Boston, December 1990.

[21] G. R. Gao, H. H. J. Hum, and Y. B. Wong. An efficient scheme for fine-grain software pipelining. In *Proceedings of the CONPAR '90-VAPP IV Conference*, Zurich, Switzerland, September 1990.

[22] G.R. Gao. A flexible architecture model for hybrid data-flow and control-flow evaluation. In *Advanced Topics in Dataflow Computing*. Prentice-Hall, 1991.

[23] G.R. Gao, Y.B. Wong, and Q. Ning. A petri net model for loop scheduling. In *the Proceedings of ACM SIGPLAN'91, Toronto, Canada*. June 1991.

[24] P. B. Gibbons and S. S. Muchnik. Efficient instruction scheduling for a pipelined architecture. In *Proceedings of the ACM Symposium on Compiler Construction*, pages 11–16, Palo Alto, CA, June 1986.

[25] T.R. Gross. *Code Optimization of Pipeline Constraints*. PhD thesis, Computing System Lab., Stanford University, 1983.

[26] J. Hennessy and T. Gross. Postpass code optimization of pipelined constraints. *ACM Transactions on Programming Languages and Systems*, 5(3):422–448, July 1983.

[27] N. Karmarkar. A new polynomial-time algorithm for linear programming. *Combinatorica*, 1984.

[28] R. M. Keller, G. Lindstrom, and S. Patil. A loosely-coupled applicative multi-processing system. In *AFIPS Conference Proceedings, vol. 48*, pages 613–622, 1979.

[29] L. G. Khachian. A polynomial algorithm in linear programming. *Soviet Math. Doklady*, 20:191–194, 1979.

[30] J. R. Larus and P. N. Hilfinger. Register allocation in the SPUR Lisp compiler. In *Proceedings of the ACM Symposium on Compiler Construction*, pages 255–263, Palo Alto, CA, June 1986.

[31] E. Lawler. *Combinatorial Optimization Networks and Matroids.* Holt, Rinehart, and Winston, 1976.

[32] G. M. Papadopoulos and D. E. Culler. Monsoon: An explicit token-store architecture. In *Proceedings of the Seventeenth Annual International Symposium of Computer Architecture, Seattle, WA*, pages 82–91, 1990.

[33] C. V. Ramamoorthy and G. S. Ho. Performance evaluation of asynchronous concurrent systems using Petri Nets. *IEEE Transactions on Computers*, pages 440–448, September 1980.

[34] S Sakai and et al. An architecture of a dataflow single chip processor. In *Proceedings of the 16th International Symposium on Computer Architecture*, pages 46–53, Israel, 1989.

[35] I. Watson and J. Gurd. A practical data flow computer. *IEEE Computer*, 15(2):51–57, February 1982.

[36] T. Yuba and et al. Sigma-1: A dataflow computer for scientific computations. *Computer Physics Communications*, 37:141–148, 1985.

24 Optimal Partitioning of Programs for Data Flow Machines

R. Hardon and S. Pinter
Technion - Israel Institute of Technology

Abstract

Data flow computers execute programs by dividing a data flow graph into instruction templates which are scheduled as early as possible. Implementing this scheme involves communication overheads which affect the running time of the program. In this paper we present a model for data flow machines which includes both communication and execution times. With this model we derive lower and upper bounds on the execution time of programs represented as trees and DAGs. We provide algorithms for optimally partitioning a program into sets of instruction templates, for both tree and DAG like programs, when there are enough execution units. The algorithms are of time complexity $O(|V|^2)$ and $O(|V|^5)$, respectively. For the case with limited number of execution units, we show that the algorithm presented for trees, approximates the best solution with a ratio of 4.

1 Introduction

Data Flow programs are represented as directed graphs. A node in the graph represents an operation, an edge in the graph represents a data dependency between two operations. Data Flow computers schedule such programs at run time. Graph nodes (operations) are scheduled as soon as their arguments arrive, and executed as soon as there is a free execution unit to handle them. In this work we consider scheduling *grains* instead of single instructions. A grain is a cluster of instructions, that will be scheduled together, to be executed on a single execution unit, as soon as the arguments for all it's nodes arrive. When using grains, some of the intermediate results would not consume "communication" time and therefore execution time might be reduced.

We provide a model for Data Flow computers capturing both communication and computation times, and consider programs which can be represented as Directed Acyclic Graphs (DAGs). Considering DAG programs, could be used for a whole program on a "static" data flow machine, or a basic block of a "dynamic" machine. With this model we look for grains, such that scheduling them yields the shortest execution time on a given machine.

The problem of optimally scheduling a DAG on our data flow machine model is a generalization of the precedence constrained scheduling problem which is NP-complete [4, 11]. There is a polynomial time algorithm for solving the precedence constrained scheduling problem when the precedence graph is a tree [8]. We consider the case with an unlimited number of processors and provide a lower bound for the generalized problem of scheduling computation trees in our model, and algorithms for optimally dividing a program with n nodes into grains for both trees (time complexity $O(n^2)$) and DAGs (time complexity $O(n^5)$). In addition we can show (to appear in a later version) that the grains chosen for trees for an unlimited number of processors approximate the best solution, for the case with a limited number of processors, with a ratio of 4.

Similar scheduling problems in different computation models, with an unlimited number of processors, have been investigated [1, 9]. We show that algorithms for these machine models do not provide an optimal solution for our data flow model even for the simple case where the computation graph is a tree. In addition, we show that the obvious solution of one-instruction per packet (*minimal grain size*) is not optimal due to communication (and matching) time overhead.

In Section 2 we present our model of data flow machines and formally define the problem of optimally computing their programs. Then, in Section 3, we review other relevant work on similar models. Section 4 includes our results as stated above. We conclude with questions for further research.

2 The Model

Our model of a data flow computer consists of one control unit, several execution units, and three data structures (see Figure 1). The instruction templates are waiting for their

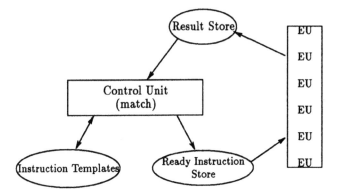

Figure 1: data flow machine model

arguments to arrive in order to be passed to the *ready instructions store*. There the instructions get fetched and executed. The results are passed to the *result store* and afterwards moved into their destination (matched).

A classification of data flow machines with respect to communication networks is given in [12]. Our model fits two stage machines such as in [3] as well as two level machines. A slight modification in parameters makes it possible to apply some of our results to one level machines [12] such as the EM-4 [10].

A program for a data flow machine is represented as a DAG. A node in the graph represents an operation, an edge in the graph represents a data dependency between two operations. An instruction template is composed of an operation and its arguments. A *grain* is a set of (one or more) instructions (a subgraph of the graph). The arguments of the grain are the arguments for the contained instructions whose dependency edges are not in the grain. The machine schedules grains to the execution units. Each grain is executed on a single execution unit. We assume the existence of enough registers (or memory) and some control mechanism on the execution units that will enable execution of grains instead of instructions. Scheduling grains saves some of the run-time communication overhead and reduces program execution time.

Model assumptions and parameters:

- The execution time of a single instruction v is $ex(v)$.

- The size of each grain is linear in the number of the arguments to the grain.

- Passing one argument from the instruction ready store to the execution units takes t_f time units.

- Writing the result plus the match operation and moving a grain to the ready instruction store takes t_m time units.

- The program's output (which is the output of some node(s)) is delivered through the network and takes t_m time units as well.

Let t_0 be the time in which the last argument of a k argument grain, P, arrives at the ready instruction store. Then the execution of P can start at $t_1 = t_0 + k \times t_f$ and end at $t_2 = t_1 + \sum_{v \in P} ex(v)$. The computed result will arrive (for use in the next grain) at time $t_3 = t_2 + t_m$.

Denoting the time t_0, the execution starting time of the grain, by WS($grain$), $t_2 - t_0$ by $t(grain)$, and t_3 by $T(grain)$ we get: $T(P) = \text{WS}(P) + t(P) + t_m$.

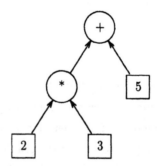

Figure 2: expression tree example

Consider the expression tree in Figure 2. We can partition it either into one grain including both operations or into two grains each containing one of the operations.

Assuming $ex(v) = 1$ for all nodes, in the first case we have[1]:

$$t(\text{root grain}) = 2 + 3 \times t_f$$
$$WS(\text{root grain}) = 0$$
$$T(\text{root grain}) = 2 + 3 \times t_f + t_m$$

In the second case we have:

$$t(\text{root grain}) = 1 + 2 \times t_f$$
$$WS(\text{root grain}) = 1 + 2 \times t_f + t_m$$
$$T(\text{root grain}) = 2 + 4 \times t_f + 2 \times t_m$$

It is clear that for this example the larger grain yields faster execution.

In the rest of the paper we use the following notations. Let $G = (V, E)$ be a program graph and let $u, v \in V$. Node v is a *predecessor* of node u if there is a directed path from v to u in G, and v is a direct *son* of u if there is an edge (v, u) (directed from v to u) in G. Let $D \subset G$ be a connected DAG, then

$$\text{SONS}(D) \equiv \{u \,|\, u \notin D \text{ is a direct son of a node in } D\}$$

2.1 Formalization

The scheduling problem is defined as follows: Given a DAG $G = (V, E)$, numbers t_f, t_m, a number of execution units p, and a mapping $ex : V \to N$, find a set of connected sub-DAGs (i.e. their underlying graphs are each connected) $G_i = (V_i, E_i)$ covering all internal nodes (not leaves) of G (each sub-DAG represents a grain), such that the number of active grains at time t, which is the number of grains G_i satisfying $WS(G_i) \leq t < WS(G_i) + t(G_i)$, is less than or equal to p, and such that $T(\text{DAG}) \equiv \max_i\{T(G_i)\}$ is minimized. (Note that the V_i's are not required to be disjoint.)

The following notation is used in the above definition:

- $V_i \subseteq V$; $\cup_i\{V_i\} = V \setminus \{v \,|\, v \text{ is a leaf}\}$

---

[1]The root grain is the grain containing the root of the expression tree; this grain's output is the tree's result.

- $E_i \equiv \{(u, v) \in E \mid u, v \in V_i\}$

- $d_{in}(G_i) \equiv | \{u \mid (u, v) \in E , u \notin V_i , v \in V_i\} |$

- $WS(G_i) \equiv \max_U \left\{ T(U) \,\middle|\, \begin{array}{l} U \in \{V_j\}, \text{ or } U = \{y\} \text{ where } y \text{ is a leaf, } U \neq V_i \text{ and} \\ \text{there is an edge in } E \text{ from } u \in U, u \notin V_i, \text{ to } v \in V_i \end{array} \right\}$

- $t(G_i) \equiv t_f \times d_{in}(G_i) + \sum_{v \in V_i} ex(v)$

- $T(\{y\}) \equiv 0$, where y is a leaf

- $T(G_i) \equiv WS(G_i) + t(G_i) + t_m$

In one level machines there is a match unit dedicated to each execution unit. This enables the pipelining of the fetch and execute phases. The effect of such an implementation on the model is the change of the parameter $t(grain)$. For these machines (assuming that execution phase time equals fetch phase time, denoted t_f)

$$t(grain) = t_f \times \max\{\text{number of operands} + 1, \text{number of operations} + 2\}$$

In this paper we present the results for the two stage machines, however the algorithm for trees from section 4.2 (slightly modified) will yield the optimal grains for one level machines too.

3 Previous work

Our formalized problem is a generalization of the *precedence constrained scheduling* problem [4] which was proved to be NP-complete in [11]. In [5] a study of the optimal resolution of actors (similar to grain sizes) for data flow programs is performed analytically and an optimal mean resolution size is found. However no algorithm for dividing the program is given. In [2] iterative instructions are used as a tool for reducing communication overhead for a data flow machine. Sakai *et al.* designed the EM-4 [10], a dataflow machine allowing the scheduling and execution of *grains*. Some of our results are applicable for this machine. Similar scheduling problems in different computation models, with an unlimited number of processors, were investigated in [1, 9].

Aggarwal *et al.* [1] considered a model of a PRAM in which, in addition to the shared memory, each execution unit has a local memory access to which takes no time. They gave an algorithm to find a schedule within a factor of two from the optimal schedule for tree like programs. The main difference between the two models is that in their model an execution unit can start executing its grain (fetching the arguments) before all arguments arrive. As a result optimal solutions of one model cannot be used for the other. As an example consider a binary chain program graph. The optimal solution of [1] is composed of $\sqrt{n}$ grains in sizes increasing from 1 to $\sqrt{n}$. This schedule requires $\sqrt{n}$ computation steps. For our model the optimal solution is composed of one grain. Thus, making use of one algorithm is a bad choice.

Papadimitriou and Yannakakis [9] considered a model where a broadcast operation can characterize communication overhead in a multiprocessor system. In that model too the execution of a grain can be started before all the arguments arrive. In addition, due to the broadcast mechanism, an execution unit does not have to fetch the arguments before starting. In this model, they gave two algorithms to find a schedule within a factor of two from the optimal schedule, for DAGs. Again as this model has only one parameter, which resembles t_m in our model, the application of this algorithm to our model does not yield optimal solutions. A simple example is a full binary tree program graph. In [9] the optimal solution is composed of subtrees with height log(communication time) and in our model the optimal size of a grain changes according to the relations between t_f, t_m, and ex. However, our algorithm for trees seems somewhat similar in concept to the "generalization" algorithm of [9].

4   Results

We consider the case with an unlimited number of execution units. A lower bound for the execution time of trees is derived and algorithms which produce optimal instruction scheduling for trees and DAGs are presented. The minimal grain size solution is shown to be non optimal.

4.1 Bounds

We first prove a simple lemma on the computation times of subtrees.

Lemma 1 *Consider two binary program trees $G_1 = (V_1, E_1)$ and $G_2 = (V_2, E_2)$ such that $G_1 \subset G_2$. Then $t(G_1) < t(G_2)$.*

Proof : The execution time of a tree grain $G = (V, E)$ is

$$t(G) = \sum_{v \in V} ex(v) + d_{in}(G) \times t_f$$

Now $G_1 \subset G_2$ implies that $d_{in}(G_1) \leq d_{in}(G_2)$ (as every node we add to G_1 in order to create G_2 has at least one new son). In addition $|V_1| < |V_2|$ concluding the proof. $\blacksquare$

To get the lower bound for trees let h be the height of the tree, and consider the "heaviest" chain to be the set of nodes G_* composed of all nodes on a directed path from a leaf to the root for which $t_f \times d_{in}(G_*) + \sum_{v \in G_*} ex(v)$ is maximal. Consider the chain G_* as one grain and denote the grain cover using G_* by S_1. The completion time of S_1, which is $T(G_*)$ is at least $t(G_*) + t_m$. In the following we show that $t(G_*) + t_m$ is a lower bound for the completion time of the tree.

Consider any other grain cover for the tree, S_2. The cover S_2 separates G_* to j parts $(j \leq h)$. Every part of G_* belongs to a grain in S_2. Denote these parts of G_* by $Y_1, \ldots, Y_j$ and the corresponding grains of S_2 by $Z_1, \ldots, Z_j$, and let Z_j be the grain containing the root. For all i, $Y_i \subseteq Z_i$. Using Lemma 1 we have:

$$
\begin{aligned}
T_{S_2}(Z_j) &\geq \sum_{i=1}^{j}(t(Z_i) + t_m) \\
&\geq \sum_{i=1}^{j}(t(Y_i) + t_m) \\
&= \sum_{i=1}^{j}\left(d_{in}(Y_i) \times t_f + t_m + \sum_{v \in Y_i} ex(v)\right) \\
&\geq d_{in}(G_*) \times t_f + t_m + \sum_{v \in G_*} ex(v)
\end{aligned}
$$

This provides a lower bound in terms of the graph and the model parameters alone. Since Lemma 1 is not true for DAGs, this lower bound is applicable only to trees.

An obvious upper bound for the completion time is the case when every node is a grain. In this case if the depth of the DAG is h and $ex(v) = 1$ for all nodes then the DAG can be completed in $h \times (2 \times t_f + t_m + 1)$ time units. However this solution is not optimal. As an example, in the case of scheduling a binary chain (a path in a binary tree), our algorithm finds a solution (which is the lower bound) with a completion time at least half that of the upper bound.

4.2 Algorithm for binary trees

Assuming an unlimited number of processors, all we have to do is to calculate the best possible completion time $T(grain)$ for the grain containing the root of the tree. The algorithm traverses the tree from leaves to root (in postorder), calculating for every node v its best completion time $T(v)$ associated with an optimal grain $ST(v)$. For an internal node v this is done by sorting all the nodes in the grains of the direct predecessors according to their best completion times and computing a grain for v assuming each time a different node v_i is the last one computed before the grain of v can be started. The final grain of v is chosen to be the one which provides the best completion time. We prove, later on, that whenever a node v_i (of the subtree) is selected to be the last one to be executed before the grain of v can be started, the grain for v, denoted by $ST_i(v)$ in this case, must include all the nodes in the subtree with completion time larger than that of v_i.

Given a tree $G = (V, E)$, numbers t_f, t_m, and a mapping $ex : V \rightarrow N$, traverse the tree from leaves to root (in postorder), computing for each node as follows:

ST(v) — a subtree rooted at v which is the grain calculating v and delivering its result at the best possible time.

WS(v) — the start time of $ST(v)$. (The completion time of the worst son of $ST(v)$.)

$t(v)$ — the number of time units needed to execute the grain $ST(v)$.

$T(v)$ — the completion time of $ST(v)$.

1. For all leaves v define $ST(v) \equiv \phi$, $T(v) \equiv 0$, $WS(v) \equiv 0$, $t(v) \equiv \infty$.

2. For a node v having two sons x, y (x and y have been evaluated due to postorder):

   (a) Define

      - $\tilde{S}_*(v) = \{v\} \cup ST(x) \cup ST(y)$
      - $S_*(v) = \tilde{S}_*(v) \setminus \{z \,|\, T(z) \leq \max\{WS(x), WS(y)\}\}$

   (b) Let $|S_*(v)| = k + 1$. Sort the $(k+1)$ nodes of $S_*(v)$ in decreasing order of their completion times to get[2]:

   $$T(v_0 = v) > T(v_1) \geq T(v_2) \geq \cdots \geq T(v_k)$$

   (c) For all $i = 1, \ldots, k$ calculate:

      - $ST_i(v) = \{z \,|\, z \in S_*(v), T(z) > T(v_i)\}$
        $ST_{k+1}(v) = S_*(v)$
      - $WS_i(v) = T(v_i)$
        $WS_{k+1}(v) = \max\{WS(x), WS(y)\}$

      For all $i = 1, \ldots, (k+1)$ calculate :

      - $t_i(v) = t_f \times d_{in}(ST_i(v)) + \sum_{s \in ST_i(v)} ex(s)$
      - $T_i(v) = WS_i(v) + t_i(v) + t_m$

   (d) Choose of the $k+1$ possible grains for v the best one (denoted by index i^*)

      - $T(v) = T_{i^*}(v) = \min_{i=1}^{k+1}\{T_i(v)\}$
      - $WS(v) = WS_{i^*}(v)$
      - $t(v) = t_{i^*}(v)$
      - $ST(v) = ST_{i^*}(v)$

Now we have a grain associated with each node. However, grains might not be disjoint. For trees it is sufficient for each node to be calculated only in one grain. This induces a grain cover comprising only *required* grains which are defined as follows: (a) The root's grain is required. (b) For every direct son x of a required grain, the grain rooted at x is required.

---

[2] We prove that $T(v) > T(v_1)$ and that each $ST_i(v)$ of step (2c) is a connected subtree.

Lemma 2 *Consider a DAG program graph $G = (V, E)$ and two distinct nodes $u, v \in V$. If there is a path from u to v then $T_{optimal}(u) < T_{optimal}(v)$*

Proof : Consider G_v, the best grain calculating v. If G_v does not include u then it is clear that $T(v) > WS(v) \geq T(u)$. Otherwise consider the grain G_{uv} containing all the nodes in G_v except for v. Clearly v is not in G_{uv}, thus G_{uv} is finished executing $ex(v)$ time units before G_v, therefore $T(u) < T(v)$. ∎

Theorem 1 *Let $G=(V,E)$ be a program graph which is a binary tree. For every node v, $T(v)$ — the completion time of the grain rooted at v calculated by the algorithm — is the smallest over all possible grain covers having a grain rooted at v.*

The proof is ommitted for lack of space and can be found in [7].

Considering a tree $G = (V, E)$ where $|V| = n$, the time complexity of the algorithm is $O(n^2)$. For every node the grains of its sons are already sorted, so merging the sets is enough and can be done in time $O(n)$. Finding d_{in} can be done (incrementally) in constant time. In addition, at most n subtrees are considered, so that for every node the time complexity is $O(n)$, getting a total of $O(n^2)$.

4.3   Algorithm for DAGs

Similar to the tree algorithm we traverse the DAG, $G = (V, E)$, from the leaves calculating for every node v its best completion time $T(v)$ associated with an optimal grain ST(v). For an internal node v this is done by sorting all the predecessors of v, according to their best completion time and computing a grain for v assuming each time a different node v_i is the last one to be computed before the grain of v can be started. The final grain of v is chosen to be the one which provides the best completion time. Computing the grain of v whenever a node v_i is considered the last one to be executed before the grain of v can be started, is more complicated than in a tree graph. In this case, in order to compute the grain for v denoted by ST$_i(v)$, we construct a flow-graph and look for the maximum flow and minimum cut in it. The minimum cut generated defines the grain ST$_i(v)$.

1. For all leaves v define $\mathrm{ST}(v) \equiv \phi$, $T(v) \equiv 0$.

2. For a non leaf node v (all predecessors have been evaluated due to postorder):

   (a) Sort all predecessors of v in decreasing order of their completion times to get:

   $$T(v_1) \geq T(v_2) \geq \cdots \geq T(v_k)$$

   (b) For all $i = 1, \ldots, k$ do:

   - Define[3] :
     - $\mathrm{ST}_i^U(v) \equiv \{u \mid u \text{ is a predecessor of } v \text{ and } T(u) > T(v_i)\} \cup \{v\}$
     - $\mathrm{SL}_i(v) \equiv \left\{ u \left| \begin{array}{l} u \text{ is a predecessor of } v_i \text{ and every path from } u \text{ to } v \\ \text{passes through } v_i \text{ (including } v_i) \end{array} \right. \right\}$
     - $\mathrm{ST}_i^D(v) \equiv \{u \mid u \text{ is a predecessor of } v \text{ and } u \notin \mathrm{ST}_i^U(v) \cup \mathrm{SL}_i(v)\}$

   - Construct the following max-flow problem : $F_i = (V_{iF}, E_{iF})$.

     The flow graph F_i is constructed from $\mathrm{ST}_i^D(v)$. Every node u of $\mathrm{ST}_i^D(v)$ is split into two nodes u^1, u^2 connected by an edge (u^1, u^2), and all original edges of $\mathrm{ST}_i^D(v)$ change direction. In addition source and target nodes and some more edges are added as formally described bellow.

     $$\begin{aligned}
     V_{iF} &= V^1 \cup V^2 \cup \{s, t\} \\
     V^1 &= \{u^1 \mid u \in \mathrm{ST}_i^D(v)\} \\
     V^2 &= \{u^2 \mid u \in \mathrm{ST}_i^D(v)\} \\
     E_{iF} &= E^1 \cup E^2 \cup E^3 \cup E^4 \cup E^5 \\
     E^1 &= \{(u^1, u^2) \mid u \in \mathrm{ST}_i^D(v)\} \\
     E^2 &= \{(u^2, w^1) \mid u, w \in \mathrm{ST}_i^D(v) \text{ and } (w, u) \in E\} \\
     E^3 &= \{(s, u^1) \mid u \in \mathrm{ST}_i^D(v) \text{ and } u \in \mathrm{SONS}(\mathrm{ST}_i^U(v))\} \\
     E^4 &= \{(u^2, t) \mid u \in \mathrm{ST}_i^D(v) \text{ is a leaf }\} \\
     E^5 &= \{(u^2, t) \mid u \in \mathrm{ST}_i^D(v) \text{ is not a leaf }\}
     \end{aligned}$$

   Where the capacity of edges from E^2, E^3, E^4 is unlimited, the capacity of edges from E^1 is t_f and the capacity of edges from E^5 is $ex(u)$ where u is the original split node.

   - Solve the max-flow problem in F_i, let the maximum flow value found be MaxFlow, find a saturated cut, and define :

     $$\begin{aligned}
     \mathrm{ST}_i^L(v) &= \left\{ u \left| \begin{array}{l} \text{the node } u^2 \text{ is between the source node } s \\ \text{and the saturated cut} \end{array} \right. \right\} \\
     \mathrm{ST}_i(v) &= \mathrm{ST}_i^U(v) \cup \mathrm{ST}_i^L(v)
     \end{aligned}$$

---

[3]Lemma 2 implies that each $\mathrm{ST}_i^U(v)$ of step (2b) is a connected subdag.

- Calculate

$$T_i(v) \;=\; T(v_i) + d_{in}(ST_i(v)) \times t_f + t_m + \sum_{u \in ST_i(v)} ex(u)$$

(c) Choose

- $T(v) = T_{i^\bullet}(v) = \min_{i=1}^k \{T_i(v)\}$
- $ST(v) = ST_{i^\bullet}(v)$

Now we have a grain associated with each node. However some grains might be useless. To get the required grains, traverse the DAG from the root to the leaves collecting the required grains. The root's grain is required. For every direct son x of a required grain, the grain rooted at x is required.

Lemma 3

$$
\begin{aligned}
T_i(v) \;&=\; T(v_i) + d_{in}(ST_i(v)) \times t_f + t_m + \sum_{u \in ST_i(v)} ex(u) \\
&=\; T(v_i) + t_f + \text{MaxFlow} + t_m + \sum_{u \in ST_i^U(v)} ex(u)
\end{aligned}
$$

Proof : Consider the saturated cut. The edges on this cut are from the sets E^1 and E^5 only. In addition knowing the edges from set E^1 defines the other edges in the following way: All edges of the form (u^2, t) such that u^2 is between s and the cut are in the cut. All edges of the form (u^2, t) such that u^2 is between t and the cut are not in the cut. Therefore for every node $u \in ST_i^L(v)$ there is exactly one edge with capacity $ex(u)$ in the cut. Now the value of the saturated minimum cut is:

$$\text{MinCut} = t_f \times \big|\{e \mid e \text{ is an edge of type } E^1 \text{ in the minimum cut }\}\big| + \sum_{u \in ST_i^L(v)} ex(u)$$

Looking at $ST_i(v)$ we get:

$$
\begin{aligned}
d_{in}(ST_i(v)) \;&=\; 1 + d_{in}(ST_i^L(v)) + \big|\text{SONS}(ST_i^U(v)) \setminus ST_i^L(v) \setminus \{v_i\}\big| \\
&=\; 1 + \big|\{e \mid e \text{ is an edge of type } E^1 \text{ in the minimum cut }\}\big|
\end{aligned}
$$

Now using the max-flow min-cut theorem the rest follows. ∎

Theorem 2 *Let $G=(V,E)$ be a DAG program graph. For every node v, $T(v)$ — the completion time of the grain rooted at v calculated by the algorithm — is the smallest over all possible grain covers having a grain rooted at v.*

The proof is ommitted for lack of space and can be found in [7].

To get the time complexity, observe that for every node v we consider k max-flow problems, and that $k \leq |V|$. So we have at most $|V|^2$ max-flow problems. In addition, in Step 2b the max-flow problem can be constructed in time $O(|V| + |E|)$ since $|V_{iF}| \leq 2 \times |V| + 2$ and $|E_{iF}| \leq 3 \times |V| + |E|$. All other parts of Step 2 of the algorithm can be completed in $O(|V| \log(|V|))$ time units. Thus the complexity of the algorithm is

$$O(|V|^2 \times \max\{(|V| + |E|), (|V| \log(|V|), \text{max-flow algorithm's complexity}\})$$

The max-flow problem can be solved in time $O(|V_{iF}|^3) = O(|V^3|)$ (for an overview of flow problems and their solution techniques see [6]) therefore the total running time of the algorithm is bounded by $O(|V|^5)$.

When the number of execution units is limited and the program graph is a tree, we have the following strategy:

1. Choose the grains assuming the number of execution units is unlimited (using the algorithm from section 4.2)

2. Schedule the grains in any order that preserves the precedence constrains.

We can show [7] that regardless of the scheduling order, chosen in step 2, the completion time, of scheduling these grains, is not worse than 4 times the shortest schedule for any set of grains.

Open problems: Considering a finite number of processors is a harder problem. In fact for DAGs it is NP-complete. Resolving the complexity of this problem for trees and finding an approximation algorithm for DAGs are interesting problems for future work.

Acknowledgment. We would like to thank Efim Dinic for a fruitful discussion resolving the flow problem.

References

[1] A. Aggarwal, A.K.Chandra, and M.Snir. Communication complexity of PRAMs. In *Proc. of the 15th International Coll. on Automata, Languages and Programming, Springer Verlag Lecture Notes in Computer Science*, number 317, pages 1–18, July 1988.

[2] A.P. Böhm and J.R.Gurd. Iterative instructions in the Manchester dataflow computer. *IEEE Trans. on Parallel and Distributed Systems*, 1(2), April 1990.

[3] J.B. Dennis and D.P.Misunas. A preliminary architecture for a basic data flow processor. In 2nd annual *Symposium on Computer Architecture*, pages 126–132, 1974.

[4] M.R. Garey and D.S.Johnson. *Computers and Intractability: a Guide to the Theory of NP-completeness*. w.h.freeman and company, 1979.

[5] J.L. Gaudiot and M.D.Ercegovac. Performance evaluation of a simulated data flow computer with low resolution actors. *Journal of Parallel and Distributed Computing*, 2(4):321–351, 1985.

[6] A.V. Goldberg and D.Gusfield. Book review: Flow algorithms by E.A.Dinic and A.V.Karzanov. *Tech.Rep.STAN-CS-90-1313*, June 1990.

[7] R. Hardon and S. S. Pinter. Optimal partitioning of programs for data flow machines. Technical Report EE-PUB to appear, Dept. of Electrical Engineering, Technion — Israel Institute of Technology, 1991.

[8] T.C. Hu. Parallel sequencing and assembly line problems. *Operations Res.*, 9:841–848, 1961.

[9] C.H. Papadimitriou and M.Yannakakis. Towards an architecture independent analysis of parallel algorithms. *SIAM J.Computing*, 19(2):322–328, April 1990.

[10] S. Sakai, Y. Yamaguchi, k. Hiraki, Y. Kodama, and T. Yuba. An architecture of a dataflow single chip processor. In *International Symposium on Computer Architecture*, pages 46–53, 1989.

[11] J.D. Ullman. NP-complete scheduling problems. *Journal of Computer and System Sciences*, 10(3):384–393, 1975.

[12] A.H. Veen. Dataflow machine architecture. *ACM Computing Surveys*, 18(4):365–396, December 1986.

25 A Foundation for Advanced Compile-time Analysis of Linda Programs

N. Carriero and D. Gelernter
Yale University

Abstract

Efficient implementations of Linda must address two potentially expensive properties of tuple space: associative access and uncoupled communications. Current compile-time analyses have significantly reduced the cost of associative access to tuple space. We propose a set of new analyses that help tackle uncoupling, as well as establish a more general framework for optimizations. We relate these analyses to new optimization strategies and give example applications of the latter.

1 Introduction

We present a collection of analysis techniques for Linda[1] programs, along with related optimization strategies. Our goal is to improve the efficiency of program execution by reducing the impact of Linda's *uncoupled* style of coordination: in general a producer of a tuple (collection of values) is unconcerned with the position in space or time of the consumer(s) of the tuple. This property is good for the programmer—he does not have to choreograph multiple execution threads to ensure correct and efficient communications. Combined with the associative character of Tuple Space it means the programmer can design distributed data structures[7] that reflect the structure of the problem, not the topology of the machine. This leads to easier and more portable coding. But the associative and uncoupled nature of communication presents challenges for efficient implementations: rendezvous, searching, buffering, and copying are some of the issues that must be addressed.

Linda already makes use of compile-time analyses to structure tuple space and characterize reference patterns. This makes it possible to map high-level, associative operations to fairly

---

*This research is supported by National Science Foundation grant CCR-8657615 and by the Air Force Office of Scientific Research under grant number AFOSR-91-0098

[1] Linda is a registered trademark of Scientific Computing Associates

cheap data structure manipulations at runtime. Large areas, however, remain untouched. Additional analyses could help support optimization strategies such as idiom recognition and mapping, tuple aggregation, tuple coupling, prefetching, and others. We define and discuss these below.

Linda systems have been used on a variety of platforms to implement a variety of applications. This experience has been largely positive, convincing us (as if we needed convincing) and others (they did) that the concept of a coordination language and its embodiment in Linda were important for parallelism. The experience has also been, in part, negative—we've confronted codes that have ultimately found reasonably efficient expression in Linda, but only after bending; as well as codes that have refused to bend. The additional analysis techniques that we will explore support optimization strategies that can reduce or eliminate some of this friendly persuasion. These should combine to improve efficiency and the ease of attaining acceptably efficient codes.

We want, in addition, to broaden the domain of applicability by bringing previously elusive codes into the fold. Working codes have tended to be medium to coarse grain. Linda can be used to express fine grain programs. Current systems, however, simply don't cater to fine grain codes—we believe they can by using more advanced analyses and by borrowing technology that is successful for fine grain MIMD (and possibly SIMD) parallelism.

Success will give us a hat trick—a workable, usable tool for fine, medium and coarse grain codes enjoying the general benefits of the Linda approach. (Among the more important: simplicity; continuity of language environment and experience; portability.)

Finally, we hope also to improve the attractiveness of Linda as an "intermediate" language for parallelizers. The marriage of a parallelizer and Linda creates a potentially powerful environment for code development. Current parallelizers excel at handling highly stylized, fine-grained computations.[2] These tend to be embedded in larger codes with more complex structure then current parallelizers can comfortably handle. If the user could work with an automatically Lindafied version of his code, he would enjoy the benefits of a parallelizer handling numerous small-scale details while being provided a simple mechanism for expressing a high-level organizational understanding that avoids missing the forest for the trees.

2 Current Approach

Current Linda implementations use compile-time analysis to streamline associative memory lookup and to provide some structural information that can be exploited to improve the concurrent management of tuple space.[6]

We need to introduce a few terms before presenting a brief sketch of the current analyses. We may use *tuple* to describe either an actual tuple (i.e. a runtime data object) or a "proto" tuple, the argument list of an out or **eval**. We use *template* in a similar way with respect to ins and rds. We will often use out to mean either out or **eval** and in to mean either in or rd—when the context requires a finer distinction, we will be more specific. The fields of a tuple or a template may be either *actuals* (data values) or *formals* (place holders—much more frequently used with ins than outs).

The simplest possible approach to the implementation of a content addressable tuple "memory" in software is to maintain a single collection of all tuples. A match would exhaustively search the collection. Starting from this point, things can only get better. First, observe that Linda's matching rules preclude any match between a tuple and a template that differ in their

---

[2] By this we mean the analyses targets tend to be fine-grain operation sequences, typically embedded in loops. One of the strengths of these systems is their ability to generate coarse grain tasks from these slim pickings.

basic structure. A three element tuple will never match a four element template, just as a tuple whose type structure is `<int, char *, float>` will never match a template whose type structure is `<char *, float, double>`. The current system's first step is to exploit this observation. All tuple space operations[3] are partitioned into disjoint sets using a filter based on type structure.

The analyzer further refines this partitioning by applying to each partition in turn a slightly weaker version of the full set of matching rules. Each template and tuple in a partition is matched "weakly"—field comparisons that require data available at runtime (both fields are non-constant actuals) are assumed to match—against every object of the opposite sense (templates against tuples and vice versa). When a successful match occurs, the partner is added to a list of matchables for that object. When the cross matching is complete, the analyzer recursively collapses these lists of matchability to form chains of matchability. Each chain becomes a new set in the partitioning.

Each new set is then scanned to determine patterns of field usage. Based on information discovered during this scan, a paradigm is selected for managing each set. The original Linda operations in the user source are then replaced by calls to subroutines in the run-time library that implement the appropriate paradigm.

As an example, consider some common distributed data structures: a queue and a table. Assume the type structure pass has produced the following partition (`task_info` must be encoded as an integer):

```
S1   out("task", ++j, task_info);/*Add to ordered task list.*/

S2   out("squares'', i, i*i);     /*Extend table of squares.*/

S3   rd("squares", i, ? i2);      /*Consult table.*/

S4   in("task", t, ?ti);          /*Grab task.*/
```

The weak-match partitioning will generate two sets of operations: {S1, S4} and {S2, S3}. The field usage analysis will notice that for each set: the first field can be suppressed at runtime (it is subsumed by the set identifier); the last field requires data copying but no runtime matching; the middle field must be matched, but is always available as actual data so it may be used as input to a hash function. Based on these observations, the analyzer will choose the *hash* paradigm for managing these sets. It is up to the run-time system to implement such a paradigm efficiently.

Other set management paradigms include counting semaphore, queue, private hash (a variation on hash), and list (exhaustive search). The last, in fact, is rarely needed.

The analyzer described here is shared by all current Yale/SCA systems for shared memory, disjoint memory, and LAN environments. It attacks the associative lookup problem by mapping associative lookups to a collection of cheap and simple data structure manipulations. Bjornson[3] reports one measure of its success: measurements from his hypercube kernel on a wide range of applications indicate that satisfying an `in` requires touching, on average, less than two tuples. The analyzer also provides structural information that can be used to aid in synchronizing access to, or the distribution of, tuple space.

---

[3]These analyses take place at link time. Object files derived from Linda modules contain an additional data section that describes the Linda operations within the module. The Linda systems's link phase extracts these data from each module enabling the analyses to span multiple modules.

3 New Foundations

It should already be clear from this brief description of current techniques that analyses appropriate to Linda differ in character from those found in many other parallel support systems[12, 8, 2, 9, 15]. There are several fundamental reasons why this is so. Linda is explicitly parallel, so analyses in Linda systems are not charged with the responsibility of *discovering* parallelism—the user has already expressed it using eval. Linda programs are factory-equipped with a clear distinction between local and global data. And the notion of *generative communication*[10] implies that we have two perspectives from which to gather information: that of the *producer* and of the *consumer* of a tuple. Nonetheless there are important ways in which Linda is related to implicit parallelizers: there is an intimate connection between coordination constructs (Linda operations) and the computation language (i.e. not a simple library interface, which would shut the door on many analyses), both want to make the best of existing computation languages, and there is a shared concern for understanding an index space. It follows that we may be able to borrow some ideas from existing parallelizing systems, but probably not without significant alteration.

Abstractly, we begin with a graph representation of a Linda program. We add links corresponding to traditional analyses—callgraph, U/D, basic blocks, etc.. We augment this foundation with links to relate potential out/in matches (so-called *weak matches* previously discussed), links to relate nodes that participate in the evaluation of a match field value, and a time/iteration dimension sensitive not only to loops but evals as well. Finally we add data that characterizes evaled tasks. The new links should permit information to flow forward (in the natural direction: from the surrounding program context to an out; from an out to the in it satisfies; from an in to the surrounding program context). They also should permit information to flow *backward* (e.g., from an in to an instance of a potentially satisfying out).

Whether this abstract data structure is realized whole or as a collection of separate structures is not important here. We want to explore some general techniques for comprehending the information in this augmented structure. In support of this, we will concentrate on projections of this abstract data structure onto a few different points of view. These projections will highlight data that inform a few new analysis techniques which will, in turn, support more specific optimization strategies, some of which we will enumerate as examples of the overall approach and applications of the new analyses.

Four such projections seem particularly central; we describe them now. When describing them, we will mention in passing certain optimization strategies which will be more fully discussed in section 4.

3.1 eval context

We create an eval context for each Linda operation by determining if the operation can occur in a thread of control spawned by an eval, and if so under what conditions. An out operation not in an eval context that has a weak-match link to an in operation that is in an eval context implies a potentially distributed communication event. It can be handled a number of ways— which way is best may be determined by examining the results of the other analyses. If we reverse the direction, we may need to funnel tuples from many sources back to one. Note that if neither of a pair of potentially matching operations occurs in an eval context, the process may be talking to itself (which is not unreasonable—and useful to know).

We may also augment this basic structure with additional multiplicity data to achieve finer resolution (unlike a traditional callgraph, an eval graph could potentially have many "live" invocations with the same source node). This multiplicity data may be definite (statically deducible, e.g. via standard loop analysis) or indefinite (but possibly determined at runtime). Certain optimizations can exploit the finer resolution. In the example above, multiplicity data would distinguish between truly distributed (any one of a number of recipients) vs. a particular recipient (whose compile time location is unknown). Another example: eval context, multiplicity, and a rd class operator may add up to distributing localized read-only copies of a tuple data structure (see below).

So in general, given this, we can support communications optimizations that exploit differences in underlying support facilities for one-one, one-many, many-one, and many-many communications. In addition, this information can help classify patterns of usage, supporting idiom recognition to refine variable-like or message-like distinctions. Information here may also allow us to replace "degenerate" tuple space usage with process private variables.

3.2 Generalized tuples

Generalized tuples captures the notion of a collection of tuples in which a statement group has a "common" interest—given that one of the tuples is produced or consumed, all will be. This notion embraces both spatial and temporal dimensions. For example, a generalized tuple might include the multiset of tuples that may be produced or consumed (we are usually interested in the latter) by a given operation instance that occurs in a loop, as well as straight-line sequence of operations. In support of this concept we need to appeal to traditional analyses (including, again, loop analyses).

The existence of a generalized spatial tuple for a statement group suggest the possibility of aggregation, while a generalized temporal tuple suggests possibilities for both prefetching and aggregation in the presence of clumping. A finer study of the underlying operations in a generalized tuple supports idiom recognition—distinguishing between message-like and variable-like tuple use. This in turn can lead to further optimization refinements via field sub-context and eval context.

3.3 The field sub-context

A field sub-context is the collection of program statements and expressions (including other Linda operations) that are tied together by collectively defining the value of a particular match field. Clearly this too will borrow heavily from existing technology. In particular, field sub-context is a cousin of traditional index-based analyses.

Field sub-context can lead to "coupling" optimizations if other Linda operations are in the context. By gathering together all of the context involved in the collective manipulation of a group of otherwise distinct tuples, it lays the foundation for general multi-operation idiom recognition. If the field context is amenable to analysis we can derive information that may place constraints on match values, flesh out generalized tuples, or help task characterization (task information, after all, is often passed through tuple space).

We can also use field sub-context to improve existing analysis. More detailed information about the space of values a field can take can aid in several ways. Two examples: if a field is always match and actual, but is completely defined by some small enumeration set, we can treat the field as a variation on an always constant field, and reclassify based on the remaining fields. If we can constrain the field (something like range bounds for an index variable), we may be able to develop a better distribution for tuples based on the value of the field.

3.4 Task characterization

Task characterization includes "traditional" items such as closure and run time estimates, as well as new data such as personalization information. The latter is the collection of data that distinguish one **eval** of **foo** from another. Such task personalization is sometimes nothing more than an id value passed to or ined by the process. This and other "simple" values like the number of workers can often be used to help parameterize the space of match field values of concern to field sub-context. We may use this parameterization to characterize the set of tuples this task will/may/won't consume. Given Linda semantics this information should come either from the invocation arguments or will be properly subsumed by field sub-context (will be passed via tuple space).

Note that while clearly related to interprocedural analysis, this analysis has a much different spin. Linda says each **eval**ed process starts in its own clean image and the evaluation of an **eval**ed process cannot alter the state of any other **eval**ed process except for the shared state of tuple space.

3.5 Relationship between these techniques

It should be clear that there are no rigid walls dividing these—and in particular there are close relationships between **eval** context and task characterization as well as between generalized tuples and field sub-context. Because of these similarities, it helps to keep in mind the way they differ. **eval** context focuses on characterizing the *multiplicity* of an object of interest—how many instances of a given operation could possible execute concurrently? Task characterization attempts to quantify the nature of a process that is to be **eval**ed: what local and global data does it reference? Can we guess how long it will run? How can we distinguish between multiple instances (the determination of multiplicity is part of determining the **eval** context) of an **eval**ed process?

Generalized tuples concentrate on tuples that are related either by a common consumption or production site (where "site" is left vague—but is roughly an attempt to capture the notion of operations that are chained together by a common execution thread). Field sub-context also attempts to relate multiple Linda operations, and normal codes as well. Here the common link is a contribution to the computation of a value that appears in a match field.

We cannot claim that this is a minimal (or even sufficient) set from which to build a general Linda optimizer. But it is a start—the combination of the field sub-context with **eval** context and task characterization can yield a mapping of tuples to **eval**ed processes which in combination with a compile- or run-time derived **eval**ed-process-to-processor map "solves" uncoupling. In support of this (admittedly weak) claim we will relate in the next section these analysis techniques to new (to Linda) optimization strategies and to the refinement of existing ones. We also comment on the relationship of the analyses to more "traditional" ones for sequential and parallel systems.

4 Optimization Strategies

As with the analyses, the optimizations we will describe are by no means disjoint. Nor is there a one-to-one mapping between the strategies and the techniques. The general goal of these optimizations is to reduce the impact of Linda's "uncoupling" property and to reduce communication costs. We will also briefly discuss the possibility of other optimizations that wrestle with improving the efficiency of **eval**ed tasks.

We will see emerge from this discussion a few common themes: tuple coupling, tuple aggregation, operation movement (code motion), and idiom recognition and mapping. *Tuple coupling* is the merging of the contents of two or more tuples from different partitions. Merging the contents of multiple tuples from within the same partition is an instance of *tuple aggregation*. *Operation movement* is the repositioning of Linda operations.

Detecting patterns of usage that involve multiple operations and then replacing these with operations based on a more efficient internal representation is the goal of *idiom recognition and mapping*. This is similar to, but more sophisticated than, the current analysis. We will see instances of message, shared variable and stream idioms. The latter come in a variety of flavors; see [5] for a full discussion. [5] also discusses techniques for improving efficiency which, in that context, are applied by the user. We will revisit some of them here in the context of their automatic application. In particular, we will occasionally appeal in our examples to the technique of *clumping*: the aggregation of many small tasks into one larger one. This is strongly related to techniques already in use by parallelizers to coarsen granularity.

The distinctions realized by idiom recognition can be particularly important. An "active" shared variable is a potentially dangerous thing—its existence in an "important" bit of code may argue strongly for attempting optimizations to work around it, or perhaps even warning the user of the performance implications.

These can be combined in various ways to improve the efficiency of Linda programs. We present some examples of their application. The examples will be loosely organized by focusing on whether the content of tuples, the timing of operations or larger, task-level, effects are at issue.

4.1 Tuple Content Optimizations

We begin with tuples and their contents. Consider the following:

```
MASTER:
S1   out("task index", 0);

S2   while(gen_task(&td)) out("task", i++, td);


WORKER:
     while (1) {
S3     in("task index", ?t);
S4     out("task index", t+1);
S5     in("task", t, ?td);
       /* compute ... */
     }
```

MASTER and WORKER distinguish two execution contexts that occur in a frequently used framework for parallelism (variously known as "task farm", "hungry puppies", "master/slave", etc.). The master generates the initial distributed data structures and tasks, the workers cooperatively consume tasks and transform the initial distributed data structure into a result structure that is then consumed by the master.

So this example is common enough—it's used by the members of a pool of workers to consume a queue of tasks dynamically. We can use field sub-context to couple S3, S4, S5:

given S3 completes (if we consume, say, ("task index", 5)) we are guaranteed to consume ("task", 5, ...) (or block).

Given this fragment and the ensuing analysis, we can "recognize" this coupling pattern as one member of the class of stream distributed data structures. In this case, a one-outer, many-inner stream. If additional analysis, e.g. **eval** context (or barring that, a runtime operation), can fix the size of the pool of workers at size N, we may be able to replace the above with, for example, a collection of operations similar to:

```
MASTER:
count = i = phase = 0;
while (gen_task(&td)) {
  out("task", phase, i++, td);
  if (++count == N) {
    ++phase;
    count = 0;
  }
}


WORKER:
phase = 0;
while (1) {
  in("task", phase++, ?t, ?td);
  /* compute ... */
}
```

(This implements a multi-phase ticket-based task assignment.)

This transformation does have an impact on the execution order—we must make sure any order resulting from the transformed code is a "plausible" one.[4] We have ensured that every task is executable as it is created—and the phasing ensures that no worker gets 'too far' ahead while allowing the master to build up a buffer pool of tasks. There are some issues here that bear close examination, the most important revolving around dynamic load balancing—the above makes sense only if we can assume all workers make progress at roughly the same rate. But it is clear the potential for powerful optimizations exists.

The most important payoff is that we have eliminated a hotspot (the task index tuple).[5] A worker also needs fewer Linda operations per iteration. Note that while the solution is realizable by the user, it's the kind of complex technology (especially when done up with extra control for better buffering and so on) that you would like to hide—if you do hide it, you have significantly simplified the programmer's job. Other optimizations will have this character (an interesting property of Linda?), but many will be premised on underlying support facilities that are not user visible (e.g. prefetch). We should also note that even for this example there are transformations other than the one presented, and indeed one way to tackle load balancing concerns could involve lower level functionality that is not visible to the user. In practice, we would expect to combine

---

[4]By "plausible" we mean that we can detect no operational difference with the original. For example, imagine we added a synchronizing token that must be passed from worker to worker in task order. Clearly the original code would never suffer deadlock pushing this token along. Similarly, a "plausible" execution must not assign tasks in such a way that the smallest index of all currently assigned tasks is greater than an outstanding task—if such were to happen, the synchronizing token would get stuck at the unassigned index.

[5]We conjecture, for that matter, that phases can probably be executed by multiple phase masters.

this with other optimizations, e.g. those base on the `eval` context could be used to pre-send one task instance to each worker (see the discussion of LU).

This example is an instance of a particular type of stream (one-outer many-inner, many-outer one-inner, etc.). In general, once a stream has been detected, the above or other techniques may be used to optimize the implementation. It is important to note, however, that we have swept some significant machinery under the rug—even the conventional analyses we need to support this are non-trivial. But even if we cannot succeed in producing a general technique for recognizing these usage patterns directly, we may be able to use others tools to aid in the characterization. Perhaps the most important is the Linda Program Builder (LPB)[1]. LPB is an environment for building Linda programs. Among its features is a collection of commonly used combinations of Linda operations (e.g. the skeleton of a master/worker code; some of the streams we have mentioned). The user's selection of such combinations can be recorded by LPB and relayed to the compiler—eliminating the need to deduce the user's intent.

Another instance of tuple content manipulation can be illustrated with an example of generalized tuples. Suppose in the previous example we had just the increment operation:

```
in("counter", ?i);
out("counter", i+1);
```

This pattern of paired `in` and `out` operations suggest `counter` should be treated like a shared variable—another instance of idiom recognition. Instead of carrying out two separate tuple operations we could generate support to implement them as a function that effectively did an update in place—a state change of the shared variable. Effectively we have collapsed the multiset in the time dimension of `counter` tuples into one single tuple that is repeatedly updated.

This observation was one of the early motivations for more advanced compiling techniques and a prototype implementation of it exists. More sophisticated analysis is needed to allow generalization of the above to handle the transformation of

```
in("variable", ?val);
out("variable", f(val));
```

into

```
val = update_f("variable")
```

We need to know how much state `f` accesses and how much it changes as well as a sense of how complex `f` is. In order to obtain the maximum benefit from this optimization we may want (in a disjoint memory system, for example) `f` to execute on the node responsible for managing the underlying tuple—if `f` is compute intensive it may be a bad idea to move it to another node (this touches on the related topic of task characterization to be discussed below).

The recognition process for shared variables is more complex than these examples would indicate—in particular we have to filter out message-like usage (the operations do *not* occur in matched pairs) that occurs at initialization and cleanup. The latter are both indicated by a single-instance `eval` context (i.e. either not in a statement group that is accessible via `eval`, or in the latter but qualified by task characterization information that admits a "disjoint" execution test—for example the comparison of a worker index with 0).

We make a similar use of `eval` context to enable the optimization of "read only" tuples. It is often the case that some effectively-read only data structure is set up during an initialization phase, consulted throughout a computation phase and then torn down during the cleanup phase of execution. (Note: a read only tuple enjoys the distinction of being a degenerate case of both shared variables and message passing idioms). Taken together, the operations that access this data structure will include not only rd but out (startup) and in (cleanup). Like shared-variables (and indeed, this should be properly understood as a subtopic of shared variables), recognizing the middle read-only section requires context information about the ins and outs in the startup and cleanup phases. If a successful characterization is possible, a couple of optimizations follow. If we can statically characterize size and if the size is modest, the most efficient and simplest approach is to localize the read only data. A secondary optimization to this is to reformat the data, if possible, as the underlying data structure, and modify the access operations accordingly. If the size isn't known, we may still be able to use dynamically available data to make a runtime decision about localizing (or possibly caching) when the read-only phase is entered. Note that tricky startup and cleanup phases may be managed via explicitly synchronized read-only phases—but unbridled use could be a pessimisation.

If, on the other hand, the tuple exchange amounts to message passing, that argues for a completely different set of techniques—we have seen examples of some of these.

We saw that a shared variable, viewed as a multiset in time, can be collapsed into a single "real" tuple. A multiset of tuples in the space dimension (i.e. many simultaneous instances of a given class of tuple) may also be aggregated to form a single, large tuple. Content aggregation (in many ways a specialized case of coupling) is a technique that may apply to either variable or message style usage—although the latter is the more likely to occur (in the former scenario, aggregation is naturally done by the coder; while in the latter it is less natural—the latter situation is also more likely to arise from other optimizations such as clumping).

As an example, consider this fragment from an LU code:

```
MASTER:
for (i=0; i < N; ++i) out("worker info", i, N);
for (i=0; i < dim; ++i) out("col", i, col_vecs[i]);


WORKER:
in("worker info", ? id, ? N); /* Who am I? */

for (i=id; i < dim; i+=N)     /* Collect my columns. */
    in("col", i, ? local_vecs[local_index++]);
```

Using the field sub-context, loop analysis and generalized tuples, we can trace the influence of id and N, we see that we have an opportunity to coalesce many ins into one that contains the sub-collection of column vectors bound for a particular worker. Doing so eliminates much of the Linda overhead. (By the way, if this were the only use of id, we would also have an opportunity for coupling.) Pulling this off requires analysis closely related to traditional work on indexing.

4.2 Some Comments on Content Optimizations

We have seen that a general framework for advanced compiling techniques involves both tuple coupling and tuple aggregation. One common thread to coupling and aggregation is a generalization of the index problem—we want to characterize the contents of those fields used in tuple selection much like parallelizers characterize the relation of array indices. For some fine grain codes these may merge into the same problem, but for most others, our perspective is different. We have seen examples of both coupling and aggregation in existing codes. We turn briefly to codes that wouldn't be practical now but might be made practical by exploiting these techniques.

Fine grain computations (such as arise from recurrence relations or array manipulations) are an example for which aggregation would be an important optimization when combined with computational clumping. See, for example, [4]. Here we can use "off-the-shelf" technology to unravel the matching (index) field references. Further we borrow virtual processor ideas to coarsen somewhat the actual work done by any processor. Given these two we can aggregate the input tuples into one tuple and perhaps use additional techniques relating the **eval** context to the execution topology to map the communication requirements for the coarsened processes to the underlying hardware. A related example is discussed in task-level optimizations.

A more exotic example of coupling can be found in codes that want to build dynamic data structures. For example, imagine a linked tuple list:

```
next_cell = start_id;
do {
  cell = next_cell;
  rd("cell", cell, ? val, ? next_cell);
} while(next_cell);
```

If we can use idiom recognition to identify this as a list data structure, then clearly a huge array of options exists for optimizing the manipulation of these tuples. But we admit that, except for certain very stylized usages, it's unlikely that idiom recognition will succeed. Cases like these may be much more easily handled via LPB.

Note that in these examples, our claim to be exploring content optimizations has already begun to fray at the edges—while we have concentrated on the content aspect, we have also re-arranged the timing of Linda operations, which leads into the optimizations of the next section.

4.3 Optimizing the timing of tuple exchanges

In the larger framework, understanding when a tuple may be generated and when it is likely to be consumed can lead to a greatly streamlined exchange process.

As an example, generalized tuples can also be applied to the problem of work distribution—in this instance the less synchronized case of a pure "task bag". This is a single-source, multiple-sink message-style non-stream usage (we can determine this from the **eval** context combined with the generalized tuple and field sub-context). From the body of a worker process:

```
while (1) {
  in("task", ? t);

  if (poison_p(t)) break;
  out("result", execute_task(t));
}
```

The generalized tuple for this block contains, in the time dimension, both the task and result tuples. Assuming "traditional" analysis can tell us something about **execute_task**, passing the conditional means we can prefetch the next task. One important issue that would have to be addressed is the tradeoff between accurately assessing the safety of the prefetch (which would include understanding the flow of control in `execute_task()` and its use of `t`) and relaxing the analysis by allowing for the possibility of a less than safe prefetch with a recovery mechanism.[6]

In addition we can use a variation of the ticket approach to balance the creation and consumption of tasks, reducing tuple space storage requirements. Or we can go to a more general scheduling framework to develop a lower-level, load-balancing policy.

If the result collection is a funnel (multiple-source, single-sink message-style non-stream) and the generalized tuple for the sink process is simple enough, we can partially collate results at the workers, permitting us to amortize message overhead over many "virtual" tuples.

We can look to LU for another example with `rd` rather than `in`:

```
for () {
  rd("pivot col multipliers", ...);
  for () {
    ...
  }
}
```

First, using standard techniques it should be possible to predict the range of the outer loop and to know that, barring abnormal termination, all iterations will complete. Given this, it should be possible while computing the inner loop to do a prefetch of the next pivot vector. Where to put the new vector is a little problematic—we may not be able to reuse the old vector (it could be busy in the `saxpy` computation). Non-copying double buffering may be possible but pushes up the analysis costs and is potentially expensive in space. Copying double buffering has, obviously, move overhead but simpler analysis requirements and can allow for optimistic prefetch (we can throw it back if we don't want it after all). In either case there can be additional runtime support that disables the prefetch if the data is too big to buffer. But compile-time analysis can help here too—it may often be possible to characterize either the actual or maximum size of the data at compile time. One issue we have glossed over is that here, as with the read-only discussion, we do have to filter out startup and cleanup phases.

This fragment also presents an opportunity for broadcast-based optimizations. By studying the `eval` context, we can detect that the vector has a single source and multiple sinks, suggesting that it be multicast over the collection of nodes executing the worker process.[7]

The repositioning in time of Linda operations has, in general, a number of applications. At least two other instances are of interest: rearranging `eval`s and `out`s and moving `out`s to the earliest possible moment (although the latter is probably of limited value unless combined with generalized tuples leading to improved aggregation). Data is often placed into tuple space during an initialization phase; processes are then `eval`ed to crunch on it. If we reverse this order, and assuming some of the other techniques discussed apply, it may be possible to exploit task personalization to direct the `out`ed data to the one task that will want it. We cannot do this, though, until the task has been created and bound to some location. Note that we can move either the `out`s *or* the `eval`s—we suspect the latter will often be easier than the former. In addition we have another degree of freedom—we may be able to add additional Linda operations to the mix to handle more complex synchronization situations and still realize a net improvement.

---

[6] If we could somehow propagate backwards the check to the (single) source out statement, we could internalize the whole shutdown procedure.

[7] Task-level optimizations can involve "tagging" an `eval`ed process with information about what the process `in`s (possibly parameterized by personalization information). In this example, such information would make possible the construction at run time of such a multicast group.

4.4 Task-level Optimizations

Task-level optimizations have already cropped up. We have mentioned, for example, the possible aggregation and coupling of tuples that will be consumed by a given **evaled** process (see, for example, the first LU example). We also touched on the possibility of tagging **evaled** processes with data about their tuple consumption, with the aim of using this information to form runtime communication subgroups.

Beyond this, using field sub-context and task personalization information, we may be able to deduce a communication graph that connects a group of tasks. Consider an example from a genetic sequence analysis code:

```
    WORKER:
    int subblock[n][n];

S1  in("worker id", ? id);   /* Who am I? */

    for (j = 0; j < num_subblocks; ++j) {
      if (id)
S2      in("top edge", id, j, ? subblock[0]);
      compute(subblock, edge);
      if (id < (num_subblocks-1))
S3      out("top edge", id+1, j, subblock[n-1]);
    }
```

Loop analysis and task personalization data (`id`) can be used to discover that a given process, `id`, will consume (S2) an ordered stream of tuples from `id-1` and generate (S3) an ordered stream of tuples for `id+1`. Thus the communication graph is a pipeline; knowing this, tasks can be distributed at runtime onto the underlying network to exploit locality.

The next step is to find some parameterization that will characterize a task's size, run time and data usage (local, global and tuples). This information will inform compile and runtime decisions as to the effective size (many virtual tasks may be mapped onto one real one, perhaps leading to tuple aggregation), the representation of tasks (lightweight threads or heavy processes), and the placement of tasks and data.

Perhaps the most ambitious (outrageous?) optimizations are those based on inferring more complex "eval graphs". Consider a skeleton divide and conquer (assume no external data, say `uid()` is intrinsic, and `compute()` is well behaved.):

```
  dc_func(r)
  {
    l = r.h - r.l;
    if (l > LIM) {
      t.l = r.l; t.h = r.l + l/2;
      eval((id0 = uid()), dc_func(t));
      t.l = t.h + 1; t.h = r.h;
      eval((id1 = uid()), dc_func(t));
      in(id0, ? v0); in(id1, ? v1);
      return merge(v0, v1);
    }
    compute(r);
    }
```

If we could infer the implied partitioning, we could separate this code into an auxiliary function that did the partitioning (very small—no computational code or data) and a function for the computation (no split/merge code or data) (Note that while code size is not usually a big issue, it could well be for massively parallel machines with small memories per node.) In addition, field sub-context and task personalization may yield enough data to build a communication structure that reflects the tree of results.

While certainly the most speculative of a speculative bunch of optimization strategies, task-level optimizations strike closest to the heart of the uncoupling problem. And they underscore an important freedom accorded the implementor of Linda—the lack of commitment to a topology is a curse and a blessing: the processes have to go somewhere, but the decision is up to the system. If we know nothing, we punt.[8] But if we *can* infer something about an evaled process's communication patterns, data needs and cycle consumption, we are free to act on this information via judicious placement of the evaled task.

5   The Old and the New

To a large degree, much of the new material extends, more than complements, existing analyses and optimizations. But there are some interesting interactions with and relationships to existing efforts.

It has been known for some time that a relatively simple extension of the hashing system could be useful in a number of cases. Segall [13] and Krishnaswamy [11] have both discussed the need for multi-field hash keys: the current system chooses the leftmost field that can be used as a hash field, but using all such fields will generally result in a better hash value. Tuples representing pieces of multi-dimensional arrays are a common example. Multi-field keys would be one result of the general treatment afforded by field sub-contexts.

Ning-Yang Wang [14] has done a preliminary investigation of a limited form of idiom recognition. The results of his system were used by a specially modified version of Bjornson's kernel[3] to implement a simple version of update-in-place.

Bjornson has also explored a dynamic (runtime) technique for optimizing tuple mapping. Bjornson's kernel uses a rendezvous mechanism for connecting templates with tuples. Initially, rendezvous locations are scattered arbitrarily throughout the nodes of a hypercube. This implies that most match resolution usually involves a third party in addition to the producer and consumer. However, runtime statistics are kept that can be used to detect stable consumption patterns (a given tuple type consistently consumed by one process). When such a pattern is detected, the kernel dynamically remaps the rendezvous location to the consuming node—eliminating the middle man. This dynamic optimization can be subsumed, in some cases, by applications of task personalization, field sub-context and generalized tuples. See, for example, the discussion of the column distribution in the LU example and the discussion of the genetic sequence code in task-level optimizations.

Does such an optimization's existence obviate the need for Bjornson's approach? After all, there is some overhead and there are some limitations to doing this at runtime, including a training period—if the patterns are such that the training period happens to be about the duration of one phase, there are no benefits (and quite possibly pessimisation). On the other

---

[8] Actually, it is possible for a user to effect a process mapping in many cases by simply including topology in tuples.

hand, here as throughout, we presume the existence of rather sophisticated analysis technology—we may be presumptuous. Where the technology doesn't exist, or fails, the dynamic system is a good back up (it works, for example, in non-compiled domains).

6 Conclusions

We have identified a core group of analyses (or perhaps more accurately analytic results) whose existence would support a variety of strategies for optimizing Linda programs. The focus has been on going beyond the current mechanisms for streamlining associative lookup to the more general performance implications of Linda's uncoupled nature. We have also touched on ways in which we can characterize and manage explicitly specified parallel tasks.

What we have not said is also significant. We have not presented algorithms for the proposed analysis—indeed we haven't even proved that efficient algorithms exist. We propose to investigate these *in vitro* prior to *in vivo* use. This will allow us to control for "undesirable" aspects of the real world, enabling initial explorations of analyses that, in fact, might not be possible in general; or rendering efficient "seriously" inefficient analysis algorithms. We will then work to eliminate or relax imposed constraints. It's interesting to note the role LPB can play here. It provides a convenient framework for user specification of semantic relationships that could not otherwise be (efficiently) deduced. Even if in some cases we are not successful in producing a workable solution for a reasonably broad class of codes, exploration of these techniques nonetheless helps in discovering a manual methodology for the refinement of Linda codes. If, in the final analysis, the application of some of these techniques is too complex either automatically or manually, the ultimate impact is merely the reduction of the domain of applicability of those techniques. Linda is demonstrably viable now, and will only improve with time.

References

[1] S. Ahmed, N. Carriero, and D. Gelernter. The Linda Program Builder. In *Proc. Third Workshop on Languages and Compilers for Parallelism*, Irvine, 1990.

[2] M. Burke and R. Cytron. Interprocedural depenedence analysis and parallelization. In *Proc. of ACM SIGPLAN Symposium on Compiler Construction*, pages 162–175. ACM, July 1986.

[3] R. Bjornson. *Linda on Distributed-Memory Multiprocessors*. PhD thesis, Yale University Department of Computer Science, New Haven, Connecticut, 1991. Department of Computer Science.

[4] N. Carriero and D. Gelernter. Linda in context. *Commun. ACM*, 32(4):444–458, Apr. 1989.

[5] N. Carriero and D. Gelernter. *How to Write Parallel Programs: A first course*. MIT Press, Cambridge, 1990.

[6] N. Carriero and D. Gelernter. Tuple analysis and partial evaluation strategies in the Linda pre-compiler. In D. Gelernter, A. Nicolau, and D. Padua, editors, *Languages and Compilers for Parallel Computing*, pages 114–125. MIT Press, Cambridge, 1990.

[7] N. Carriero, D. Gelernter, and J. Leichter. Distributed data structures in Linda. In *Thirteenth ACM Symposium on Principles of Programming Languages Conf.*, pages 236–242, St. Petersburg, Florida, Jan. 1986. Association for Computing Machinery.

[8] M. C. Chen. A parallel language and its compilation to multiprocessor machines or VLSI. In *Thirteenth Annual ACM Symposium on Principles of Programming Languages*, pages 131–139. Association for Computing Machinery, Jan. 1986.

[9] D. Callahan and K. Kennedy. Compiling programs for distributed-memory multiprocessors. *The Journal of Supercomputing*, 2:151–169, 1988.

[10] D. Gelernter. Generative communication in Linda. *ACM Trans. Prog. Lang. Syst.*, 7(1):80–112, Jan. 1985.

[11] V. Krishnaswamy. *The Linda Machine*. PhD thesis, Yale University Department of Computer Science, New Haven, Connecticut, 1991. Department of Computer Science (in preparation).

[12] D. Padua and M. J. Wolfe. Advanced Compiler Optimizations for Supercomputers. *Commun. ACM*, 29(12):1184–1201, Dec. 1986.

[13] E. Segall. *In preparation*. PhD thesis, Rutgers University, New Brunswick, New Jesey, 1991. CAIP.

[14] N. Yang Wang. 690 project report. Report on preliminary thesis research., 1990.

[15] H. Zima, H.-J. Bast, and M. Gerndt. SUPERB: A tool for semi-automatic MIMD/SIMD parallelization. *Parallel Computing*, 6:1–18, 1988.

26 Analyzing Programs with Explicit Parallelism

H. Srinivasan and M. Wolfe
Oregon Graduate Institute

Abstract

When analyzing programs with parallel imperative constructs (*e.g.,* cobegin/coend), standard computer intermediate representations (Control Flow Graphs) are inadequate. This paper discusses semantics for parallel constructs, and introduces new intermediate forms, called the *Parallel Control Flow Graph* and the *Parallel Precedence Graph*. These data structures have certain advantages for compiler analysis and optimization. As an example of the advantages, the analysis requirements of converting an explicitly parallel program into Static Single Assignment form are given. To do this, the dominance relation and dominance frontiers for explicitly parallel programs must be defined.

1 Introduction

Given the failure of automatic parallelizing compilers, many users want to explore writing explicitly parallel programs. Some language and compiler researchers believe that explicit parallelism should be avoided, and functional or applicative implicitly parallel languages should be used. Nonetheless, a significant user community desires and demands language constructs for expressing explicit parallelism in programs. The Parallel Computing Forum was formed to generate portable syntax and semantics for parallel extensions to Fortran-77 [12]; this consortium of industry and academic parties has now spawned an ANSI standards committee to complete the project. In order to deliver the very best performance, compilers will soon be required to perform aggressive optimization in the presence of explicit parallelism.

The standard intermediate form for compilers is the Control Flow Graph, or CFG. To help with compiler optimizations, other information is generally collected about the program; this information is sometimes represented explicitly in an auxiliary data structure, or replaces the CFG as the primary data structure, *e.g.*, the *data dependence graph, program dependence graph, program dependence web, dependence flow graph*, and so on. Many optimizations have been designed around the Static Single Assignment (SSA) form of the program [7]. This paper focuses on how to convert an explicitly parallel program to SSA form.

The standard algorithms for converting a program to SSA form use the information in the CFG; focusing on the **Parallel Sections** construct of PCF Fortran, we show here that adding parallelism to a CFG is non-trivial. Instead we propose a new model for control flow in parallel programs, imaginatively named the Parallel Control Flow Graph (PCFG). Explicit ordering between different sections is represented by a Parallel Precedence Graph (PPG).

Two important concepts used in deriving the SSA form of a program are the dominance relation defined between nodes in a Control Flow Graph, and the dominance frontiers of nodes in a CFG. Extending these definitions to nodes in a PCFG is not straightforward; a PCFG has two types of nodes, those representing parallel constructs and those representing basic blocks. This paper defines the dominance relation and dominance frontiers for PCFGs; efficient algorithms to compute these are described in the references [14, 15].

Of critical importance for creating the SSA form of a parallel program is the definition of what are the reaching definitions for a variable in an explicitly parallel program. The concept of reaching definitions comes from the semantics of the language; we explore *copy-in/copy-out* semantics for parallel constructs, both for clarity in writing parallel programs, and to simplify and improve compiler analysis.

2 Parallel Section Semantics

The **Parallel Sections** construct [12] is similar to a **cobegin/coend** [5] or the **Parallel Cases** statement introduced by Allen et al [1]. It is a block structured construct used to specify parallel execution of identified sections of code. The parallel sections may also be nested. The sections of code must be data independent, except where an appropriate synchronization mechanism is used. Here we consider only structured synchronization

```
1: v = 1                      1: v₁ = 1
2: w = 2                      2: w₁ = 2
   Parallel Sections             Parallel Sections
   Section A                     Section A
3:    w = 3                   3:    w₂ = 3
4:    v = 4                   4:    v₂ = 4
5:    t = v                   5:    t₁ = v₂
   Section B                     Section B
6:    v = w                   6:    v₃ = w₁
7:    w = 7                   7:    w₃ = 7
8:    u = w                   8:    u₁ = w₃
   End Parallel Sections         End Parallel Sections
                                 v₄ = ψ(v₂, v₃)
                                 w₄ = ψ(w₂, w₃)
   Print 't=',t,', u=', u        Print 't=',t₁,', u=', u₁

        (a)                          (b)
```

Figure 1: Parallel Sections Construct and its SSA Form

expressed as Wait clauses, *i.e.*, DAG parallelism. Transfer of control into or out of a parallel section is not supported.

Some definition must be made when two sections of code that can execute in parallel both modify the same variable, or when one section modifies a variable that is used by the other. Consider the program in Figure 1(a) as an example. What values should be printed for t and u? What values for w can reach statement 6? What assignments to v can reach statement 5? Can statements 3 and 4 be interchanged? Can the compiler forward substitute statement 4 into statement 5? These are all questions that the compiler should be able to answer via analysis of the program.

Under some models of parallelism, such as a model allowing any *sequentially consistent* execution [10], there is more than one legal output for this program; we might consider the following possibilities (to save space, only a few orderings are shown):

statement ordering	output
3,4,5,6,7,8	t=4, u=7
3,4,6,7,5,8	t=3, u=7
3,6,4,5,7,8	t=4, u=7
3,6,4,7,5,8	t=4, u=7
6,3,4,5,7,8	t=4, u=7
6,7,3,4,5,8	t=4, u=3

Note that optimization within a parallel section is restricted; even though statements 3 and 4 are completely data independent, interchanging these two statement would allow the statement order: 4,6,7,3,5,8, which would give the unexpected output t=2,u=3. The legal outputs for this program depend on how the anomalous parallel updates to the variables are resolved, and this depends on the rules for the language. Several different rules can be (and have been) proposed for such syntax:

Error: The language might define anomalous updates to variables as a programmer error. In this case no output is a legal output, since this is an illegal program. With the Ada view of a language, such errors should be detected and reported, either at compile time (if possible) or at run time. While detection of potential anomalous updates at compile time is possible, precise compile time analysis would in general be intractible. The user may want to know about potential anomalies in explicitly parallel code, since it may indicate a programming error, even when it is legal. Thus, compiler analysis for potential anomalies may be a very useful option [6, 3, 8, 2].

Undefined: This is the Fortran view of languages: anything not required is optional, and there are no illegal options. Thus, compiler implementers are free to do whatever they want; any output is a legal output (from the compiler point of view). Often the implementers define some meaning, either actively or passively ("the definition is what the compiler does"), and then are forced into compatibility for the rest of eternity.

Sequential: Here the only legal output is one that could have arisen by a sequential execution of the statements in lexical order. This view is sometimes expressed for anomalous parallel loops. In any case, with this definition there is only one unambiguous legal output, t=4,u=7.

Immediate Update: This view is often taken due to hardware support for coherent multiprocessor caches. Here, any update to a variable must be visible to all other processors (or processes). This is closely related to the problem of multiprocessor memory coherence, where a sequentially consistent implementation is considered indistinguishable from a strict conflict-free shared memory multiprocessor [10]; sometimes a *weak consistency* model is used to overcome long latency operations for shared variable updates [9]. Under this model, any of the statement orderings in the table above would be legal, with three different possible outputs. The problems for the compiler are to detect what statement orderings are required, and what optimizations are illegal in the presence of other code that might execute in parallel with this code [11]. The statement reordering question mentioned above is one such example. This problem is even more insidious than it seems; if the language allows subroutines to be called in parallel (as does PCF Fortran) with potentially anomalous updates to global variables, the compiler can't even know the scope of the parallelism nor the variables that might be volatile, much less the interaction between multiple variables. Such a definition would essentially invalidate all compiler optimizations involving global variables.

Copy-in/Copy-out: This is similar to the value/result style of parameter passing. The values of shared variables in a parallel section are defined to be initialized to the values they had when the parallel block was entered; any updates are made (conceptually) to *local copies* of the variable. When the parallel block is complete, the global state is updated with any modifications made within any section. This completely defines the values to be used for shared variables that are defined and used in different sections. If any shared variable is updated by more than one parallel section, some definition must still be made, corresponding to one of the previous choices. With this definition, the compiler can know that statement 4 can always be forward substituted into statement 5, since no anomalous updates are allowed to any variable while the section is executing. The only legal output is the same (for this program) as for sequential semantics, t=4, u=7.

Of these possible definitions, sequential semantics is the most well-defined, and also the most restrictive. Many current coherent memory parallel computers support immediate update semantics; however preserving immediate update semantics may be too restrictive in terms of the optimizations allowed. We advocate using copy-in/copy-out semantics. This gives a well-defined program without volatile variables, and allows optimization within a parallel section independent of code in other sections. The model has several potential problems, such as the overhead of making local copies of variables, and atomic merging of updated variables. There is more opportunity for compiler optimization here; the compiler can try to distinguish variables which are read-only in the parallel block (so no local copies need be made), those that are read and written in different parallel sections (so local copies must be made), and those that are read and written, but for which updates can be made in place. The analysis for update-in-place will be similar to that for functional languages, such as SISAL. For read-write variables which must be merged, the compiler must generate code to merge the updated values efficiently, without causing a bottleneck in the executing program. The Myrias SPS-1 control mechanism supported copy-in/copy-out semantics by clever use of the virtual paging translation hardware and operating system primitives [4]; in that system, multiple updates to a shared variable by parallel tasks gave an undefined result after the parallel block.

3 Static Single Assignment Form

After converting a program into SSA form, it has the following two properties [7]:

- Each use of a variable is reached by exactly one assignment to that variable.

- The program contains merge functions, called ϕ-functions to distinguish values of variables transmitted from *distinct* incoming control flow edges.

Cytron et al [7] present a fast algorithm to convert a program into SSA form in which the number of ϕ-functions inserted is minimal. The algorithm uses the dominance relation and dominance frontiers as reviewed briefly here.

A CFG is a directed graph with a distinguished unique *Entry* vertex. We say a vertex v *dominates* another vertex w, written $v \gg w$, if v appears on every path from *Entry* to w. By this definition, every vertex dominates itself, and *Entry* dominates every other vertex. The *dominance frontier* of a node v, DF(v), is the set of all CFG nodes z such that v dominates a predecessor of z but does not strictly dominate z. Note that v may itself be a member of DF(v).

The SSA algorithm uses dominance frontiers to determine where to place ϕ-functions. ϕ-functions for a variable X are required at all the nodes in the iterated dominance frontier of S, where the set S is the union of all the nodes where X is assigned. The dominance frontier sets are constructed in a single bottom-up traversal of the dominator tree. Thus, both the dominance relation and the dominance frontiers are crucial to the conversion of a program to SSA form. We need to be able to extend these concepts to explicitly parallel code, and we want to have a meaningful SSA form of a parallel program.

4 Flow Graphs for Parallel Constructs

In the case of sequential programs, CFGs accurately model potential control flow. We might be tempted to model **Parallel Sections** in a CFG by treating the fork point as a

```
X = 1              X = 1
Y = 1              Y = 1
if P then          Parallel sections
                   Section
    X = 2              X = 2
else               Section
    Y = 5              Y = 5
endif              end parallel sections
Z = X+Y            Z = X+Y
```

Figure 2: Conditional and Parallel programs

```
X₁ = 1             X₁ = 1
Y₁ = 1             Y₁ = 1
if P then          Parallel sections
                   Section
    X₂ = 2             X₂ = 2
else               Section
    Y₂ = 5             Y₂ = 5
endif              end parallel sections
X₃ = φ(X₂,X₁)
Y₃ = φ(Y₁,Y₂)
Z₁ = X₃+Y₃         Z₁ = X₂+Y₂
```

Figure 3: SSA Forms of Conditional and Parallel programs

branch node and the join as a merge node. The CFGs for the two programs in Figure 2 will then look the same. However, the execution semantics of the two programs are very different. In the sequential program, only one of the two assignments $X = 2$ or $Y = 5$ will be executed; the value of Z will be 3 or 6, depending on the branch taken. In the parallel program, however, both assignments will be executed, and the value of Z will always be 7; in fact, the two initial assignments to X and Y are dead code. The proper SSA forms of these two programs are shown in Figure 3. No ϕ-functions are needed in the parallel program, since only the X_2 and Y_2 assignments reach the Z_1 assignment. Clearly, trying to model this parallel program with a simple CFG is incorrect; the simple CFG would model the parallel construct just like it models conditionals, and would then add unnecessary ϕ-functions at the join point.

What we would like to have is a representation where the X_2 assignment *dominates* the Z_1 assignment, Y_2 assignment *dominates* the Z_1 assignment, but there is no dominance relation between the X_2 and Y_2 assignments at all. No Control Flow Graph will give us this kind of relationship. To handle this, we introduce Parallel Control Flow Graphs.

5 Parallel Control Flow Graphs

This section presents the *Parallel Control Flow Graph* (PCFG) that models control flow in parallel programs accurately and the *Parallel Precedence Graph* (PPG) that models concurrent execution within a parallel construct. A set of PCFGs and PPGs make up the Extended Flow Graph set (EFG) that model an entire program unit.

A *Parallel Control Flow Graph* (PCFG) is a CFG which may have a special type of node called a *supernode*. A supernode essentially represents an entire Parallel Sections construct. Parallel execution of the sections within a parallel block is represented by a *Parallel Precedence Graph* (PPG). Wait clauses in a parallel block impose *wait-dependence* between the waiting section and the sections specified in the Wait clause. Nodes in the PPG represent the sections in the parallel block with two additional nodes, cobegin and coend. The edges in the PPG (also called *wait-dependence arcs*) represent the wait dependences. To conserve space, we do not discuss wait dependence arcs in detail here.

Formally a PCFG is defined as the graph $G = \langle V_G, E_G, Entry_G, Exit_G \rangle$ where

- V_G is a set of vertices, each representing a basic block (basic block node) or an entire parallel block (supernode).

- E_G is a set of edges $\{a \rightarrow b \mid a, b \in V_G\}$, representing potential flow of control in the program.

- $Entry_G \in V_G$ is the unique start node (or entry node) of the PCFG, with all vertices reachable from $Entry_G$.

- $Exit_G \in V_G$ is the exit node of the PCFG, where $Exit_G$ is reachable from all vertices in V_G.

Parallel execution within a parallel block is represented by a PPG which is formally defined as a graph $P = \langle V_P, E_P, Entry_P, Exit_P \rangle$ where

- V_P is a set of vertices, each representing a section in a parallel block (section node).

- E_P is a set of edges or wait-dependence arcs in the PPG.

- $Entry_P \in V_P$ is the cobegin node.

- $Exit_P \in V_P$ is the coend node.

By definition of the language, the PPG graph must be a DAG.

Each section S is again represented by a PCFG $S = \langle V_S, E_S, Entry_S, Exit_S \rangle$ where $Entry_S$ marks the entry into that section and $Exit_S$ marks the exit from that section.

The Extended Flow Graph set (EFG) is the set of PCFG's and PPG's representing control flow and parallelism for a single program unit. The distinguished PCFG corresponding to the program unit is called G_{main}. When we talk about the nodes in an EFG, we mean the union of all the nodes in all the PCFG's and PPG's in the EFG. The nodes may be *Entry* or *Exit* nodes, basic block nodes, supernodes, cobegin or coend nodes, or section nodes.

The EFG of the parallel program in Figure 1(a) is shown in Figure 4. G_{main} has 5 vertices: *Entry*, m (an assignment basic block), $P1$ (a parallel block), n (a print basic block), and *Exit*. The parallel block is represented by PPG_{P1} with four vertices: the cobegin, A and B (one for each of the two sections), and coend. The two parallel sections are then again represented by PCFGs, each (in this case) with three vertices, one of which represents the basic block of assignments.

6 Dominance Relation Between Vertices of an EFG

Given a parallel program and its EFG, we want to compute the SSA form of the program. As mentioned before, the SSA algorithm depends on the dominance relation in the program. However, the vertices of the EFG are now spread over several graphs. While we have an intuitive feel for how the graphs are "nested," there is little formal basis for this. For instance, in Figure 4, by the semantics of the language, we want to have the relationships $m \gg q$ and $q \gg n$, but not to have $q \gg r$. Since m and q do not appear in the same directed graph, the canonical dominance relation between them is not defined. Here we address this problem.

One way to define the execution relationships of vertices from different PCFGs is to consider all possible combinations of paths through all the parallel blocks in the program. We use a method to derive a set of sequential CFGs from an EFG, referred to as **factoring** [14]. Since there are only two paths through the only parallel block in Figure 4, there are only two factors, shown in Figure 5.

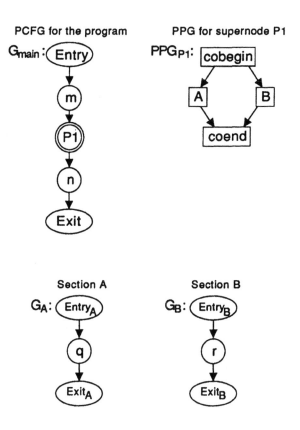

Figure 4: Extended Flow Graph set

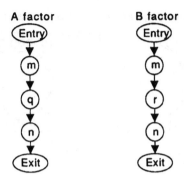

Figure 5: Factors of an EFG

Computing the dominance relation between nodes in the sequential CFGs obtained by *factoring* the EFG can be done easily using the standard definition of dominance. We define the *parallel dominance relation* to be the dominance relation for a basic block node in an EFG, computed as the *union* of the sequential dominators of in each of the sequential CFGs obtained by factoring the EFG.

In the sequential factors in Figure 5, the dominance relations $m \gg q$ and $q \gg n$ hold in the first factor, and $m \gg r$ and $r \gg n$ in the second factor. We thus define this to be the set of parallel dominance relations for the program. Note that the parallel dominance relation can not be represented by a tree.

Similarly, we define the *parallel dominance frontier* of a basic block node to be the dominance frontier in the EFG, computed as the union of the sequential dominance frontiers in each of the sequential CFGs derived by factoring the EFG.

7   SSA with Copy-in/Copy-out Semantics

The advantage of using the copy-in/copy-out semantics is that the SSA form of the program can be easily constructed from the parallel dominance frontier. In fact, the same algorithms used to construct the SSA form in [7] can be easily modified to construct the SSA form of a parallel program. The key property of copy-in/copy-out semantics that makes this possible is that the only definitions for a variable that can reach a use within a parallel block must reach that use by some path from the cobegin vertex. We took advantage of this when defining the parallel dominance relation. Some examples will show the advantages; our first example program can be simply converted to SSA form as shown in Figure 1(b). Note for instance that the only definition of w that reaches statement 6 is from statement 2. No ϕ-functions are needed here since there is no conditional code. The ψ-functions will be explained shortly.

A second example shows conditional code within and surrounding the parallel block, in Figure 7. In every case, the only ϕ-functions needed in the program are those that are needed in some factor of the graph.

8 Anomalous Updates

When only one section updates a shared variable, the value of that variable after the parallel block is complete is well defined. Even if other sections use that variable, they will always get the "old" value of the variable (in the absence of any synchronization or wait clauses); for example, see variable a in Figure 7. Section A increments a, but Section B still sees the old value of a, namely a_1, which is equal to 1. In fact, constant propagation could be used to forward substitute the constant value 1 into all uses of a_1; this would then allow a_2 to be computed as the value 2, and so on.

However, when two parallel sections update the same variable, the value of the variable after the parallel block is indeterminate. In Figure 1(b), variables v and w were updated in both sections; within the sections, the values to be used for each variable is well defined. A use of v outside the parallel block, however, might be reached by either v_2 or v_3; to keep the Static Single Assignment rules, where each use is reached by only a single assignment, we must somehow merge these two updates at the End Parallel Sections statement. This is the reason for the ψ-functions in the parallel SSA programs.

The presence of a ψ-function may indicate to the compiler that the program contains an actual or potential anomaly. A useful compiler option would be to flag all potential anomalies such as this. Note that such anomalies may only be potential; in Figure 7, the variable e is only potentially updated in the two sections. If the two conditions are mutually exclusive, then in fact only one update will be done, and the semantics of the language should preserve whichever update is performed. Nonetheless, the ψ-function is needed to preserve the SSA properties.

```
a = 1                           a₁ = 1
b = 2                           b₁ = 2
if a = c then                   if a₁ = c₀ then
   b = b + 1                       b₂ = b₁ + 1
else                            else
   Parallel Sections              Parallel Sections
   Section A                      Section A
      a = a + 1                      a₂ = a₁ + 1
      if e > 0 then                  if e₀ > 0 then
         e = 99                         e₁ = 99
      endif                          endif
                                     e₂ = φ(e₁, e₀)
   Section B                      Section B
      c = a                          c₁ = a₁
      if b = c then                  if b₁ = c₁ then
         e = 1                          e₃ = 1
      endif                          endif
                                     e₄ = φ(e₃, e₀)
      d = e + 1                      d₁ = e₄ + 1
   End Parallel Sections          End Parallel Sections
                                  e₅ = ψ(e₂, e₄)
endif                           endif
                                a₃ = φ(a₁, a₂)
                                b₃ = φ(b₂, b₁)
                                c₂ = φ(c₀, c₁)
                                d₂ = φ(d₀, d₁)
                                e₆ = φ(e₀, e₅)
print a,b,c,d,e                 print a₂, b₃, c₂, d₂, e₆
```

Figure 6: Original and SSA Form of Extended Example

9 Conclusion

Previous work has shown that the Static Single Assignment intermediate representation forms a practical basis for optimizing sequential programs. We have shown how to extend Control Flow Graphs, dominance relation and dominance frontiers used in computing SSA to include parallel constructs. SSA is discussed in detail in [7]. By extending SSA to include parallel constructs, the resulting intermediate language will form a powerful platform for many classical code optimization algorithms that can be run on parallel programs.

Our current work has found an efficient and simple algorithm for finding the parallel dominators and parallel dominance frontiers [15]. We are implementing this algorithm as well as the algorithm to find anomalous updates in parallel programs in our prototype compiler, Nascent.

References

[1] Frances Allen, Michael Burke, Philippe Charles, Ron Cytron, and Jeanne Ferrante. An overview of the PTRAN analysis system for multiprocessing. *J. Parallel and Distributed Computing*, 5(5):617–640, October 1988.

[2] Todd R. Allen and David A. Padua. Debugging Fortran on a shared memory machine. In Sartaj K. Sahni, editor, *Proc. 1987 International Conf. on Parallel Processing*, pages 721–727, St. Charles, IL, August 1987.

[3] Vasanth Balasundaram and Ken Kennedy. Compile-time detection of race conditions in a parallel program. In *Proc. 3rd International Conference on Supercomputing*, pages 175–185, June 1989.

[4] Monica Beltrametti, Kenneth Bobey, and John R. Zorbas. The control mechanism for the Myrias parallel computer system. *Computer Architecture News*, 16(4):21–30, September 1988.

[5] Per Brinch Hansen. *Operating Systems Principles*. Automatic Computation. Prentice-Hall, 1973.

[6] David Callahan, Ken Kennedy, and Jaspal Subhlok. Analysis of event synchronization in a parallel programming tool. In *Second ACM SIGPLAN Symposium on Principles and Practice of Parallel Programming* [13], pages 21–30.

[7] Ron Cytron, Jeanne Ferrante, Barry K. Rosen, Mark N. Wegman, and Kenneth Zadeck. An efficient method of computing static single assignment form. In *Conf. Record 16th Annual ACM Symp. on Principles of Programming Languages*, pages 25–35, Austin, TX, January 1989.

[8] Anne Dinning and Edith Schonberg. An empirical comparison of monitoring algorithms for access anomaly detection. In *Second ACM SIGPLAN Symposium on Principles and Practice of Parallel Programming* [13], pages 1–10.

[9] Michel Dubois, Christoph Scheurich, and Faye Briggs. Memory access buffering in multiprocessors. In *Conf. Proc. 13th Annual International Symp. on Computer Architecture*, pages 434–442, Tokyo, June 1986.

[10] Leslie Lamport. How to make a multiprocessor computer that correctly executes multiprocess programs. *IEEE Trans. on Computers*, C-28(9):690–691, September 1979.

[11] Samuel P. Midkiff, David A. Padua, and Ron Cytron. Compiling programs with user parallelism. In David Gelernter, Alexandru Nicolau, and David A. Padua, editors, *Languages and Compilers for Parallel Computing*, Research Monographs in Parallel and Distributed Computing, pages 402–422. MIT Press, Boston, 1990.

[12] Parallel Computing Forum. *PCF Fortran*, April 1990.

[13] *Second ACM SIGPLAN Symposium on Principles and Practice of Parallel Programming*, Seattle, Washington, March 1990. ACM Press.

[14] Harini Srinivasan. Analyzing programs with explicit parallelism. M.S. thesis 91-TH-006, Oregon Graduate Institute, Dept. of Computer Science and Engineering, July 1991.

[15] Michael Wolfe and Harini Srinivasan. Data structures for optimizing programs with explicit parallelism. In *Proc. First International Conference of the Austrian Center for Parallel Computation*, Salzburg, September 1991. to appear.

This work was supported by NSF Grant CCR-8906909 and DARPA Grant MDA972-88-J-1004.

Lecture Notes in Computer Science

For information about Vols. 1–504
please contact your bookseller or Springer-Verlag

Vol. 505: E. H. L. Aarts, J. van Leeuwen, M. Rem (Eds.), PARLE '91. Parallel Architectures and Languages Europe, Volume I. Proceedings, 1991. XV, 423 pages. 1991.

Vol. 506: E. H. L. Aarts, J. van Leeuwen, M. Rem (Eds.), PARLE '91. Parallel Architectures and Languages Europe, Volume II. Proceedings, 1991. XV, 489 pages. 1991.

Vol. 507: N. A. Sherwani, E. de Doncker, J. A. Kapenga (Eds.), Computing in the 90's. Proceedings, 1989. XIII, 441 pages. 1991.

Vol. 508: S. Sakata (Ed.), Applied Algebra, Algebraic Algorithms and Error-Correcting Codes. Proceedings, 1990. IX, 390 pages. 1991.

Vol. 509: A. Endres, H. Weber (Eds.), Software Development Environments and CASE Technology. Proceedings, 1991. VIII, 286 pages. 1991.

Vol. 510: J. Leach Albert, B. Monien, M. Rodríguez (Eds.), Automata, Languages and Programming. Proceedings, 1991. XII, 763 pages. 1991.

Vol. 511: A. C. F. Colchester, D.J. Hawkes (Eds.), Information Processing in Medical Imaging. Proceedings, 1991. XI, 512

Vol. 512: P. America (Ed.), ECOOP '91. European Conference on Object-Oriented Programming. Proceedings, 1991. X, 396 pages. 1991.

Vol. 513: N. M. Mattos, An Approach to Knowledge Base Management. IX, 247 pages. 1991. (Subseries LNAI).

Vol. 514: G. Cohen, P. Charpin (Eds.), EUROCODE '90. Proceedings, 1990. XI, 392 pages. 1991.

Vol. 515: J. P. Martins, M. Reinfrank (Eds.), Truth Maintenance Systems. Proceedings, 1990. VII, 177 pages. 1991. (Subseries LNAI).

Vol. 516: S. Kaplan, M. Okada (Eds.), Conditional and Typed Rewriting Systems. Proceedings, 1990. IX, 461 pages. 1991.

Vol. 517: K. Nökel, Temporally Distributed Symptoms in Technical Diagnosis. IX, 164 pages. 1991. (Subseries LNAI).

Vol. 518: J. G. Williams, Instantiation Theory. VIII, 133 pages. 1991. (Subseries LNAI).

Vol. 519: F. Dehne, J.-R. Sack, N. Santoro (Eds.), Algorithms and Data Structures. Proceedings, 1991. X, 496 pages. 1991.

Vol. 520: A. Tarlecki (Ed.), Mathematical Foundations of Computer Science 1991. Proceedings, 1991. XI, 435 pages. 1991.

Vol. 521: B. Bouchon-Meunier, R. R. Yager, L. A. Zadek (Eds.), Uncertainty in Knowledge-Bases. Proceedings, 1990. X, 609 pages. 1991.

Vol. 522: J. Hertzberg (Ed.), European Workshop on Planning. Proceedings, 1991. VII, 121 pages. 1991. (Subseries LNAI).

Vol. 523: J. Hughes (Ed.), Functional Programming Languages and Computer Architecture. Proceedings, 1991. VIII, 666 pages. 1991.

Vol. 524: G. Rozenberg (Ed.), Advances in Petri Nets 1991. VIII, 572 pages. 1991.
pages. 1991.

Vol. 525: O. Günther, H.-J. Schek (Eds.), Advances in Spatial Databases. Proceedings, 1991. XI, 471 pages. 1991.

Vol. 526: T. Ito, A. R. Meyer (Eds.), Theoretical Aspects of Computer Software. Proceedings, 1991. X, 772 pages. 1991.

Vol. 527: J.C.M. Baeten, J. F. Groote (Eds.), CONCUR '91. Proceedings, 1991. VIII, 541 pages. 1991.

Vol. 528: J. Maluszynski, M. Wirsing (Eds.), Programming Language Implementation and Logic Programming. Proceedings, 1991. XI, 433 pages. 1991.

Vol. 529: L. Budach (Ed.), Fundamentals of Computation Theory. Proceedings, 1991. XII, 426 pages. 1991.

Vol. 530: D. H. Pitt, P.-L. Curien, S. Abramsky, A. M. Pitts, A. Poigné, D. E. Rydeheard (Eds.), Category Theory and Computer Science. Proceedings, 1991. VII, 301 pages. 1991.

Vol. 531: E. M. Clarke, R. P. Kurshan (Eds.), Computer-Aided Verification. Proceedings, 1990. XIII, 372 pages. 1991.

Vol. 532: H. Ehrig, H.-J. Kreowski, G. Rozenberg (Eds.), Graph Grammars and Their Application to Computer Science. Proceedings, 1990. X, 703 pages. 1991.

Vol. 533: E. Börger, H. Kleine Büning, M. M. Richter, W. Schönfeld (Eds.), Computer Science Logic. Proceedings, 1990. VIII, 399 pages. 1991.

Vol. 534: H. Ehrig, K. P. Jantke, F. Orejas, H. Reichel (Eds.), Recent Trends in Data Type Specification. Proceedings, 1990. VIII, 379 pages. 1991.

Vol. 535: P. Jorrand, J. Kelemen (Eds.), Fundamentals of Artificial Intelligence Research. Proceedings, 1991. VIII, 255 pages. 1991. (Subseries LNAI).

Vol. 536: J. E. Tomayko, Software Engineering Education. Proceedings, 1991. VIII, 296 pages. 1991.

Vol. 537: A. J. Menezes, S. A. Vanstone (Eds.), Advances in Cryptology – CRYPTO '90. Proceedings. XIII, 644 pages. 1991.

Vol. 538: M. Kojima, N. Megiddo, T. Noma, A. Yoshise, A Unified Approach to Interior Point Algorithms for Linear Complementarity Problems. VIII, 108 pages. 1991.

Vol. 539: H. F. Mattson, T. Mora, T. R. N. Rao (Eds.), Applied Algebra, Algebraic Algorithms and Error-Correcting Codes. Proceedings, 1991. XI, 489 pages. 1991.

Vol. 540: A. Prieto (Ed.), Artificial Neural Networks. Proceedings, 1991. XIII, 476 pages. 1991.

Vol. 541: P. Barahona, L. Moniz Pereira, A. Porto (Eds.), EPIA '91. Proceedings, 1991. VIII, 292 pages. 1991. (Subseries LNAI).

Vol. 542: Z. W. Ras, M. Zemankova (Eds.), Methodologies for Intelligent Systems. Proceedings, 1991. X, 644 pages. 1991. (Subseries LNAI).

Vol. 543: J. Dix, K. P. Jantke, P. H. Schmitt (Eds.), Nonmonotonic and Inductive Logic. Proceedings, 1990. X, 243 pages. 1991. (Subseries LNAI).

Vol. 544: M. Broy, M. Wirsing (Eds.), Methods of Programming. XII, 268 pages. 1991.

Vol. 545: H. Alblas, B. Melichar (Eds.), Attribute Grammars, Applications and Systems. Proceedings, 1991. IX, 513 pages. 1991.

Vol. 546: O. Herzog, C.-R. Rollinger (Eds.), Text Understanding in LILOG. XI, 738 pages. 1991. (Subseries LNAI).

Vol. 547: D. W. Davies (Ed.), Advances in Cryptology – EUROCRYPT '91. Proceedings, 1991. XII, 556 pages. 1991.

Vol. 548: R. Kruse, P. Siegel (Eds.), Symbolic and Quantitative Approaches to Uncertainty. Proceedings, 1991. XI, 362 pages. 1991.

Vol. 549: E. Ardizzone, S. Gaglio, F. Sorbello (Eds.), Trends in Artificial Intelligence. Proceedings, 1991. XIV, 479 pages. 1991. (Subseries LNAI).

Vol. 550: A. vån Lamsweerde, A. Fugetta (Eds.), ESEC '91. Proceedings, 1991. XII, 515 pages. 1991.

Vol. 551:S. Prehn, W. J. Toetenel (Eds.), VDM '91. Formal Software Development Methods. Volume 1. Proceedings, 1991. XIII, 699 pages. 1991.

Vol. 552: S. Prehn, W. J. Toetenel (Eds.), VDM '91. Formal Software Development Methods. Volume 2. Proceedings, 1991. XIV, 430 pages. 1991.

Vol. 553: H. Bieri, H. Noltemeier (Eds.), Computational Geometry - Methods, Algorithms and Applications '91. Proceedings, 1991. VIII, 320 pages. 1991.

Vol. 554: G. Grahne, The Problem of Incomplete Information in Relational Databases. VIII, 156 pages. 1991.

Vol. 555: H. Maurer (Ed.), New Results and New Trends in Computer Science. Proceedings, 1991. VIII, 403 pages. 1991.

Vol. 556: J.-M. Jacquet, Conclog: A Methodological Approach to Concurrent Logic Programming. XII, 781 pages. 1991.

Vol. 557: W. L. Hsu, R. C. T. Lee (Eds.), ISA '91 Algorithms. Proceedings, 1991. X, 396 pages. 1991.

Vol. 558: J. Hooman, Specification and Compositional Verification of Real-Time Systems. VIII, 235 pages. 1991.

Vol. 559: G. Butler, Fundamental Algorithms for Permutation Groups. XII, 238 pages. 1991.

Vol. 560: S. Biswas, K. V. Nori (Eds.), Foundations of Software Technology and Theoretical Computer Science. Proceedings, 1991. X, 420 pages. 1991.

Vol. 561: C. Ding, G. Xiao, W. Shan, The Stability Theory of Stream Ciphers. IX, 187 pages. 1991.

Vol. 562: R. Breu, Algebraic Specification Techniques in Object Oriented Programming Environments. XI, 228 pages. 1991.

Vol. 563: A. Karshmer, J. Nehmer (Eds.), Operating Systems of the 90s and Beyond. Proceedings, 1991. X, 285 pages. 1991.

Vol. 564: I. Herman, The Use of Projective Geometry in Computer Graphics. VIII, 146 pages. 1992.

Vol. 565: J. D. Becker, I. Eisele, F. W. Mündemann (Eds.), Parallelism, Learning, Evolution. Proceedings, 1989. VIII, 525 pages. 1991. (Subseries LNAI).

Vol. 566: C. Delobel, M. Kifer, Y. Masunaga (Eds.), Deductive and Object-Oriented Databases. Proceedings, 1991. XV, 581 pages. 1991.

Vol. 567: H. Boley, M. M. Richter (Eds.), Processing Declarative Kowledge. Proceedings, 1991. XII, 427 pages. 1991. (Subseries LNAI).

Vol. 568: H.-J. Bürckert, A Resolution Principle for a Logic with Restricted Quantifiers. X, 116 pages. 1991. (Subseries LNAI).

Vol. 569: A. Beaumont, G. Gupta (Eds.), Parallel Execution of Logic Programs. Proceedings, 1991. VII, 195 pages. 1991.

Vol. 570: R. Berghammer, G. Schmidt (Eds.), Graph-Theoretic Concepts in Computer Science. Proceedings, 1991. VIII, 253 pages. 1992.

Vol. 571: J. Vytopil (Ed.), Formal Techniques in Real-Time and Fault-Tolerant Systems. Proceedings, 1992. IX, 620 pages. 1991.

Vol. 572: K. U. Schulz (Ed.), Word Equations and Related Topics. Proceedings, 1990. VII, 256 pages. 1992.

Vol. 573: G. Cohen, S. N. Litsyn, A. Lobstein, G. Zémor (Eds.), Algebraic Coding. Proceedings, 1991. X, 158 pages. 1992.

Vol. 574: J. P. Banâtre, D. Le Métayer (Eds.), Research Directions in High-Level Parallel Programming Languages. Proceedings, 1991. VIII, 387 pages. 1992.

Vol. 575: K. G. Larsen, A. Skou (Eds.), Computer Aided Verification. Proceedings, 1991. X, 487 pages. 1992.

Vol. 576: J. Feigenbaum (Ed.), Advances in Cryptology - CRYPTO '91. Proceedings, X, 485 pages. 1992.

Vol. 577: A. Finkel, M. Jantzen (Eds.), STACS 92. Proceedings, 1992. XIV, 621 pages. 1992.

Vol. 578: Th. Beth, M. Frisch, G. J. Simmons (Eds.), Public-Key Cryptography: State of the Art and Future Directions. XI, 97 pages. 1992.

Vol. 579: S. Toueg, P. G. Spirakis, L. Kirousis (Eds.), Distributed Algorithms. Proceedings, 1991. X, 319 pages. 1992.

Vol. 580: A. Pirotte, C. Delobel, G. Gottlob (Eds.), Advances in Database Technology – EDBT '92. Proceedings. XII, 551 pages. 1992.

Vol. 581: J.-C. Raoült (Ed.), CAAP '92. Proceedings. VIII, 361 pages. 1992.

Vol. 582: B. Krieg-Brückner (Ed.), ESOP '92. Proceedings. VIII, 491 pages. 1992.

Vol. 583: I. Simon (Ed.), LATIN '92. Proceedings. IX, 545 pages. 1992.

Vol. 584: R. E. Zippel (Ed.), Computer Algebra and Parallelism. Proceedings, 1990. IX, 114 pages. 1992.

Vol. 585: F. Pichler, R. Moreno Díaz (Eds.), Computer Aided System Theory – EUROCAST '91. Proceedings. X, 761 pages. 1992.

Vol. 587: R. Dale, E. Hovy, D. Rösner, O. Stock (Eds.), Aspects of Automated Natural Language Generation. Proceedings, 1992. VIII, 311 pages. 1992. (Subseries LNAI).

Vol. 588: G. Sandini (Ed.), Computer Vision – ECCV '92. Proceedings. XV, 909 pages. 1992.

Vol. 589: U. Banerjee, D. Gelernter, A. Nicolau, D. Padua (Eds.), Languages and Compilers for Parallel Computing. Proceedings, 1991. IX, 419 pages. 1992.